# WEBSTER'S NEW WORLD™

# POCKET FRENCH DICTIONARY

***English-French***

***French-English***


Series Editor:
Michael W. Keathley
Editor:
Michael Janes
Consulting Editors:
Lillian Clem
Al


MAC

MACMILLAN
A Simon & Schuster Macmillan Company
15 Columbus Circle
New York, NY 10023

First published in the United States in 1998.

First published in Great Britain 1995
by Chambers Harrap Publishers Ltd.
7 Hopetoun Crescent, Edinburgh EH7 4AY

Consultant Editors
Fabrice Antoine
Stuart Fortey

© Chambers Harrap Publishers Ltd. 1995
All rights reserved. No part of this
publication may be reproduced in any
form or by any means without the prior
permission of Chambers Harrap Publishers Ltd.

MACMILLAN is a registered trademark of Macmillan, Inc.

ISBN 0-02-860572-1

Manufactured in the United States of America

2 3 4 5 6 7 8 9 10    98 99 00 01 02

**TRADEMARKS**

Words considered to be trademarks have been designated in this dictionary by the symbol ®. However, no judgment is implied concerning the legal status of any trademark by virtue of the presence or absence of such a symbol.

# Contents

# Preface

Based on the text of *Harrap's Micro French Dictionary,* this handy dictionary provides a concise, up-to-date, reliable guide to the language that is particularly helpful for beginning and occasional learners. It offers a practical vocabulary of over 25,000 of the most useful English and French words and expressions, with a focus on American English. The dictionary is designed to be easily read and used, with bold headwords and a compact, time-saving format.

The dictionary's clear text gives maximum guidance in pinpointing exact language equivalents. All headwords are arranged in strict alphabetical order. Different translations of the same headword or phrase are clearly identified by context words in parentheses. English phrasal verbs (e.g., bring down) and normally French pronominal verbs (e.g., se battre), as well as many English compounds (e.g., birth certificate) are given as separate entries. Context words or explanations are also given when considered helpful for the understanding of single translations—***article*** (*object, in newspaper, in grammar*) article *m.* or ***putty*** mastic *m.* In addition, labels are used to indicate the level of style (e.g., *Fam* for 'familiar' or colloquial). Finally, these context indicators and labels are presented in French in the French section and in English in the English section. All labeling has been kept to a minimum so as not to distract the reader.

A headword is represented with its first letter when it appears as an example in the same form (e.g., at **h.** stands for at **home** at the entry home). Likewise, the different grammatical divisions of a headword are easily identified by means of Arabic numerals in bold print (e.g., **1, 2, 3, 4**) and important sense divisions within longer entries are clearly marked by the use of a block ▪. Finally, a slash within an entry is a space-saving device to separate non-interchangeable parts of a phrase or expression matched exactly in French and English (e.g., **to be able to swim/drive** savoir nager/conduire is to be understood as: **to be able to swim** savoir nager and **to be able to drive** savoir conduire).

# Grammar notes

In French, the feminine of an adjective is formed, when regular, by adding **e** to the masculine form (eg grand, grande; carré, carrée: fin, fine). If the masculine already ends in **e,** the feminine is the same as the masculine (eg utile). Both regular and irregular feminine forms of adjectives (eg généreux, généreuse; léger, légère; doux, douce) are given on the French-English side of the dictionary. On the English-French side, French adjectives are shown in the masculine, but highly irregular feminine forms (eg frais, fraîche; faux, fausse) have also been included to help the user.

To form the plural of a French noun or adjective **s** is usually added to the singular (eg arbre, arbres; taxi, taxis; petit, petits). The plural form of a noun ending in **s, x** or **z** (eg pois, croix, nez) is the same as that of the singular. Plurals of nouns and adjectives which do not follow these general rules (eg where **x** or **aux** is added in the plural, or where there is a highly irregular plural such as œil, yeux) are listed in the French section. Also included are the plurals of French compounds where the formation of the plural involves a change other than the addition of final **s** (eg chou-fleur, choux-fleurs; arc-en-ciel, arcs-en-ciel). The irregular plurals of French nouns (and irregular masculine plurals of French adjectives) ending in **al, eau, eu, au, ail** and **ou** are listed on the French-English side (eg cerveau, -x; général, -aux). Included on the English-French side, to help the user, are the plurals of French nouns (and adjectives) ending in **al, eu** and **au** where **s,** and not the usual **x,** forms the plural (eg pneu, pneus; naval, navals) and of those nouns in **ail** and **ou** where the plural is formed with **x,** and not the usual **s** (eg travail, travaux; chou, choux).

In English also, **s** is added to form the plural of a noun (eg cat, cats; taxi, taxis) but a noun ending in **ch, s, sh, x** or **z** forms its plural by the addition of **es,** pronounced [-ɪz] (eg glass, glasses; match, matches). When a noun ends in **y** preceded by a consonant, **y** is changed to **ies** to form the plural (eg army, armies). Irregular English plurals (eg hero, heroes; leaf, leaves) are given on the English-French side, including the plurals of English compounds where the formation of the plural involves a change other than the addition of final **s** (eg brother-in-law, brothers-in-law). Common English irregular plurals involving a change of vowel (eg tooth, teeth) are given at both singular and plural headword positions.

Most French verbs have regular conjugations though some display spelling anomalies (see French verb conjugations on p (i)). In the French section an asterisk is used to mark an irregular French verb, and refers the user to the table of irregular verbs on p (v).

Most English verbs form their past tense and past participle by adding **ed** to the infinitive (eg look, looked) or **d** to an infinitive already ending in **e** (eg love, loved). When a verb ends in **y** preceded by a consonant, **y** becomes **ied** (eg satisfy, satisfied). To form the third person singular of a verb in the present tense **s** is added to the infinitive (eg know, knows) but an infinitive in **ch, s, sh, x** or **z** forms its third person singular by the addition of **es,** pronounced [-ɪz] (eg dash, dashes). When an infinitive ends in **y** preceded by a consonant, **y** is changed to **ies** to form the third person singular (eg satisfy, satisfies).

The English present participle is formed by the addition of **ing** to the infinitive (eg look, looking) but final **e** is omitted when an infinitive ends in **e** (eg love, loving). When the infinitive ends in a single consonant preceded by a vowel (eg tug), the final consonant is often doubled in the past tense, past and present participles (eg tug, tugged, tugging, but traveled, traveling).

An asterisk is used, in the English section as on the French side, to show an irregular English verb.

# Pronunciation of French

## Table of phonetic symbols

### Vowels

| | | | |
|---|---|---|---|
| [i] | vite, cygne, sort**ie** | [y] | cr**u**, s**û**r, r**ue** |
| [e] | **été**, donn**er**, l**é**gal | [ø] | f**eu**, m**eu**le, n**œu**d |
| [ɛ] | **e**lle, m**ai**s, p**è**re, pr**ê**t | [œ] | **œu**f, j**eu**ne, c**ue**illir [kœjir] |
| [a] | ch**a**t, f**a**meux, toit [twa] | [ə] | l**e**, r**e**faire, entr**e** |
| [ɑ] | p**a**s, **â**ge, t**â**che | [ɛ̃] | v**in**, pl**ein**, f**aim**, s**ain**t |
| [ɔ] | d**o**nne, f**o**rt, alb**um** | [ɑ̃] | **en**f**an**t, t**em**ps, p**aon** |
| [o] | d**o**s, ch**au**d, p**eau**, d**ô**me | [ɔ̃] | m**on**, n**om**bre, h**on**te |
| [u] | t**ou**t, c**ou**r, r**oue**, g**oû**t | [œ̃] | l**un**di, h**um**ble, **un** |

### Consonants

| | | | |
|---|---|---|---|
| [p] | **p**ain, a**b**solu, ta**p**er, fra**pp**er | [r] | **r**a**r**e, **rh**ume, sorti**r**, ba**rr**eau |
| [b] | **b**eau, a**bb**é, ro**b**e | [m] | **m**on, fla**mm**e, ai**m**er |
| [t] | **t**able, ne**tt**e, vi**t**e | [n] | **n**é, ca**nn**e, a**n**imal |
| [d] | **d**onner, su**d**, rai**d**e | [ɲ] | campa**gn**e, a**gn**eau |
| [k] | **c**amp, **k**épi, **qu**i, taxe [taks], accès [aksɛ] | [ŋ] | joggi**ng** |
| [g] | **g**arde, **gu**erre, se**c**ond, exister [ɛgziste] | ['] | This symbol is placed before words beginning with **h** in the headword list to show that the preceding word must not be abbreviated (e.g. la hache and |
| [f] | **f**eu, si**ff**ler, **ph**rase | | |
| [v] | **v**oir, trou**v**er, **w**agon | | |
| [s] | **s**on, **c**ire, **ç**a, cha**ss**e, na**t**ion | | |
| [z] | cou**s**in, **z**éro, ro**s**e | | |

[ʃ] **ch**ose, ha**ch**e, **sch**éma
[ʒ] **g**ilet, **j**eter, â**ge**
[l] **l**ait, faci**l**e, e**ll**e

not l'hache), and that the final consonant of the previous word must not be pronounced (e.g. les haches [leaʃ] and not [lezaʃ]).

## Semi-consonants

[j] p**i**ano, vo**y**age, fi**lle**, **y**eux
[w] **ou**est, noir [nwar], tram**w**ay
[ɥ] m**u**et, l**u**i, h**u**ile

| **Abbreviations** | | **Abréviations** |
|---|---|---|
| adjective | *a* | adjectif |
| abbreviation | *abbr, abrév* | abréviation |
| adverb | *adv* | adverbe |
| article | *art* | article |
| auxiliary | *aux* | auxiliaire |
| Canadian | *Can* | canadien |
| conjunction | *conj* | conjonction |
| definite | *def, déf* | défini |
| demonstrative | *dem, dém* | démonstratif |
| et cetera | *etc* | et cetera |
| feminine | *f* | féminin |
| familiar | *Fam* | familier |
| feminine plural | *fpl* | féminin pluriel |
| French | *Fr* | français |
| indefinite | *indef, indéf* | indéfini |
| interjection | *int* | interjection |
| invariable | *inv* | invariable |
| masculine | *m* | masculin |
| masculine and feminine | *mf* | masculin et féminin |
| masculine plural | *mpl* | masculin pluriel |
| noun | *n* | nom |
| plural | *pl* | pluriel |
| possessive | *poss* | possessif |
| past participle | *pp* | participe passé |
| preposition | *prep, prép* | préposition |
| present participle | *pres p* | participe présent |
| pronoun | *pron* | pronom |
| | *qch* | quelque chose |
| | *qn* | quelqu'un |
| registered trademark | ® | marque déposée |
| relative | *rel* | relatif |
| singular | *sing* | singulier |
| someone | *s.o.* | |

| | | |
|---|---|---|
| something | *sth* | |
| United States | *US* | États-Unis |
| auxiliary verb | *v aux* | verbe auxiliaire |
| intransitive verb | *vi* | verbe intransitif |
| pronominal verb | *vpr* | verbe pronominal |
| transitive verb | *vt* | verbe transitif |
| transitive and intransitive verb | *vti* | verbe transitif et intransitif |

# A

**a** (*before vowel or mute h* **an**) *indef art* un, une; **a man** un homme; **an apple** une pomme; **two dollars a pound** deux dollars la livre; **30 miles an hour** 50 km à l'heure; **he's a doctor** il est médecin; **twice a month** deux fois par mois.

**abandon** *vt* abandonner.

**abbey** abbaye *f.*

**abbreviation** abréviation *f.*

**ability** capacité *f* (**to do** pour faire); **to the best of my a.** de mon mieux.

**able** *a* capable; **to be a. to do** être capable de faire, pouvoir faire; **to be a. to swim/drive** savoir nager/conduire.

**abnormal** *a* anormal.

**aboard 1** *adv* (*on ship*) à bord; **all a.** (*on train*) en voiture. **2** *prep* **a. the ship** à bord du navire; **a. the train** dans le train.

**abolish** *vt* supprimer.

**abortion** avortement *m*; **to have an a.** se faire avorter.

**about 1** *adv* (*approximately*) à peu près, environ; **(at) a. two o'clock** vers deux heures; **out and a.** (*after illness*) sur pied; **up and a.** (*out of bed*) levé, debout. **2** *prep* (*concerning*) au sujet de; **to talk a.** parler de; **a book a.** un livre sur; **what's it (all) a.?** de quoi s'agit-il?; **what** *or* **how a. me?** et moi?; **what** *or* **how a. a drink?** que dirais-tu de prendre un verre? ▪ (+ *infinitive*) **a. to do** sur le point de faire.

**above 1** *adv* au-dessus; **from a.** d'en haut; **floor a.** étage *m* supérieur. **2** *prep* au-dessus de; **a. all** par-dessus tout; **he's a. me** (*in rank*) c'est mon supérieur.

**above-mentioned** *a* susmentionné.

**abreast** *adv* **four a.** par rangs de quatre; **to keep a. of** se tenir au courant de.

**abroad** *adv* à l'étranger; **from a.** de l'étranger.

**abrupt** *a* (*sudden, rude*) brusque.

**abscess** abcès *m.*

**absence** absence *f.*

**absent** *a* absent (**from** de).

**absent-minded** *a* distrait.

**absolute** *a* absolu; (*coward etc*) parfait.

**absolutely** *adv* absolument.

**absorb** *vt* (*liquid*) absorber; **absorbed in one's work** absorbé dans *ou* par son travail.

**absurd** *a* absurde.

**abuse 1** *n* abus *m* (**of** de); (*of child etc*) mauvais traitements *mpl*; (*insults*) injures *fpl*. **2** *vt* (*use badly or wrongly*) abuser de; (*ill-treat*) maltraiter; (*insult*) injurier.

**abusive** *a* grossier.

**academic 1** *a* (*year, diploma etc*) universitaire. **2** *n* (*teacher*) universitaire *mf.*

**accelerate** *vi* (*in vehicle*) accélérer.

**accelerator** accélérateur *m.*

**accent** accent *m.*

**accept** *vt* accepter.

**acceptable** *a* acceptable.

**access** accès *m* (**to sth** à qch, **to s.o.** auprès de qn).

**accessible** *a* accessible.

**accessories** *npl* (*objects*) accessoires *mpl.*

**accident** accident *m*; **by a.** (*without meaning to*) accidentellement.

**accidental** *a* accidentel.

**accidentally** *adv* accidentellement.

**accommodation** logement *m*; **accommodations** (*in hotel*) chambre(s) *f*(*pl*).

**accompany** *vt* accompagner.

**accomplish** *vt* accomplir; (*aim*) réaliser.

**accord of my own a.** volontairement.

**accordance in a. with** conformément à.

**according to** *prep* selon.

**accordion** accordéon *m.*

**account** (*with bank or firm*) compte *m*; (*report*) compte re[illegible] *m*; **accounts** (*of firm*) compta[illegible]

*f*; **to take into a.** tenir compte de; **on a. of** à cause de.
**accountant** comptable *mf*.
**account for** (*explain*) expliquer; (*represent*) représenter.
**accumulate 1** *vt* accumuler. **2** *vi* s'accumuler.
**accurate** *a* exact, précis.
**accurately** *adv* avec précision.
**accusation** accusation *f*.
**accuse** *vt* accuser (**of** de).
**accustomed** *a* habitué (**to sth** à qch, **to doing** à faire); **to get a. to** s'habituer à.
**ace** (*card, person*) as *m*.
**ache 1** *n* douleur *f*; **to have an a. in one's arm** avoir mal au bras. **2** *vi* faire mal; **my head aches** ma tête me fait mal; **I'm aching all over** j'ai mal partout.
**achieve** *vt* réaliser; (*success, result*) obtenir; (*victory*) remporter.
**achievement** (*success*) réussite *f*.
**aching** *a* douloureux.
**acid** *a* & *n* acide (*m*).
**acknowledge** *vt* reconnaître (**as** pour); **to a. (receipt of)** accuser réception de.
**acne** acné *f*.
**acorn** gland *m*.
**acquaint** *vt* **to be acquainted with s.o.** connaître qn; **we are acquainted** on se connaît.
**acquaintance** connaissance *f*.
**acquire** *vt* acquérir.
**acre** acre *f* (= *0,4 hectare*).
**acrobat** acrobate *mf*.
**acrobatic** *a* acrobatique.
**across** *adv* & *prep* (*from side to side* (*of*)) d'un côté à l'autre (de); (*on the other side* (*of*)) de l'autre côté (de); (*so as to cross, diagonally*) en travers (de); **to be half a mile a.** (*wide*) avoir un kilomètre de large; **to walk** *or* **go a.** (*street*) traverser.
**acrylic** *n* acrylique *m*; **a. socks**/*etc* chaussettes *fpl*/*etc* en acrylique.
**act 1** *n* (*deed, part of play*) acte *m*; (*in circus*) numéro *m*; **caught in the a.** pris sur le fait. **2** *vt* (*role in play or film*) jouer. **3** *vi* (*do sth, behave*) agir; (*in play or film*) jouer; **to a. as** (*secretary etc*) faire office de; (*of object*) servir de.
**act for s.o.** représenter qn.
**action** action *f*; (*military*) combat *m*; **to take a.** prendre des mesures; **to put into a.** (*plan*) exécuter; **out of a.** hors d'usage; (*person*) hors (de) combat.
**active 1** *a* actif; (*interest, dislike*) vif. **2** *n Grammar* actif *m*.
**activity** activité *f*; (*in street*) animation *f*.
**act (up)on** (*affect*) agir sur; (*advice*) suivre.
**actor** acteur *m*.
**actress** actrice *f*.
**actual** *a* réel; **the a. book** le livre même.
**actually** *adv* (*truly*) réellement; (*in fact*) en réalité.
**acute** *a* aigu; (*emotion*) vif; (*shortage*) grave.
**AD** *abbr* (*anno Domini*) après Jésus-Christ.
**ad** *Fam* pub *f*; (*private, in newspaper*) annonce *f*; **want ad** petite annonce.
**adapt** *vt* adapter (**to** à); **to a. (oneself)** s'adapter.
**adaptable** *a* (*person*) souple.
**adaptor** (*plug*) prise *f* multiple.
**add** *vt* ajouter (**to** à, **that** que); (*total*) additionner.
**addict jazz/sport a.** fanatique *mf* du jazz/du sport; **drug a.** drogué, -ée *mf*.
**addicted** *a* **to be a. to** (*music, sport*) se passionner pour; **a. to alcohol** alcoolique; **to be a. to cocaine** avoir une dépendance à la cocaïne, être cocaïnomane.
**addiction drug a.** toxicomanie *f*.
**add in** (*include*) inclure.
**addition** addition *f*; **in a.** de plus; **in a. to** en plus de.
**additional** *a* supplémentaire.
**additive** additif *m*.
**address 1** *n* (*on letter etc*) adresse *f*; (*speech*) allocution *f*. **2** *vt* (*person*)

s'adresser à; (*audience*) parler devant; (*letter*) mettre l'adresse sur.

**add to** (*increase*) augmenter.

**add together** (*numbers*) additionner.

**add up 1** *vt* (*numbers*) additionner. **2** *vi* **to a. up to** (*total*) s'élever à; (*mean*) signifier; (*represent*) constituer.

**adenoids** *npl* végétations *fpl* (adénoïdes).

**adequate** *a* (*quantity etc*) suffisant; (*acceptable*) convenable; (*person*) compétent.

**adequately** *adv* suffisamment; convenablement.

**adhesive** *a* & *n* adhésif (*m*).

**adjective** adjectif *m*.

**adjust** *vt* (*machine*) régler; (*salaries*) ajuster; **to a. (oneself) to** s'adapter à.

**adjustable** *a* (*seat*) réglable.

**adjustment** réglage *m*; (*of person*) adaptation *f*.

**administer** *vt* administrer.

**administration** administration *f*; gouvernement *m*.

**administrative** *a* administratif.

**admiral** amiral *m*.

**admiration** admiration *f*.

**admire** *vt* admirer (**for** pour, **for doing** de faire).

**admission** (*to movies etc*) entrée *f*; **a. charge** prix *m* d'entrée.

**admit** *vt* (*let in*) laisser entrer, admettre; (*acknowledge*) reconnaître, admettre (**that** que).

**admittance 'no a.'** 'entrée interdite'.

**admit to sth** (*confess*) avouer qch.

**adolescent** adolescent, -ente *mf*.

**adopt** *vt* (*child, attitude etc*) adopter.

**adopted** *a* (*child*) adoptif.

**adoption** adoption *f*.

**adorable** *a* adorable.

**adore** *vt* adorer (**doing** faire).

**adult 1** *n* adulte *mf*. **2** *a* (*animal etc*) adulte; **a. class/film/***etc* classe *f*/film *m*/*etc* pour adultes.

**advance 1** *n* (*movement, money*) avance *f*; **advances** (*of love*) avances *fpl*; **in a.** à l'avance, d'avance. **2** *a* (*payment*) anticipé; **a. reservation** réservation *f*. **3** *vt* (*put forward, lend*) avancer. **4** *vi* (*go forward, progress*) avancer.

**advanced** *a* avancé; (*studies, level*) supérieur; (*course*) de niveau supérieur.

**advantage** avantage *m* (**over** sur); **to take a. of** profiter de; (*person*) exploiter.

**adventure** aventure *f*.

**adventurous** *a* aventureux.

**adverb** adverbe *m*.

**advertise 1** *vt* (*commercially*) faire de la publicité pour; (*privately*) passer une annonce pour vendre; (*make known*) annoncer. **2** *vi* faire de la publicité; (*privately*) passer une annonce (**for** pour trouver).

**advertisement** publicité *f*; (*private, in newspaper*) annonce *f*; (*poster*) affiche *f*; **classified a.** petite annonce.

**advice** conseil(s) *m*(*pl*); **a piece of a.** un conseil.

**advisable** *a* (*wise*) prudent (**to do** de faire).

**advise** *vt* conseiller; (*recommend*) recommander; **to a. s.o. to do** conseiller à qn de faire.

**advise against** déconseiller.

**adviser** conseiller, -ère *mf*.

**aerial** antenne *f*.

**aerobics** *npl* aérobic *m*.

**aerosol** aérosol *m*.

**affair** affaire *f*; **(love) a.** liaison *f*.

**affect** *vt* (*concern, move*) toucher, affecter; (*harm*) nuire à.

**affection** affection *f* (**for** pour).

**affectionate** *a* affectueux.

**affluent** *a* riche.

**afford** *vt* (*pay for*) avoir les moyens d'acheter; (*time*) pouvoir trouver.

**affordable** *a* (*price etc*) abordable.

**afloat** *adv* (*ship, swimmer, business*) à flot.

**afraid** *a* **to be a.** avoir peur (**of, to** de); **he's a. (that) she may be sick**

il a peur qu'elle (ne) soit malade; **I'm a. he's out** (*I regret to say*) je regrette, il est sorti.

**African** *a* & *n* africain, -aine (*mf*).

**after 1** *adv* après; **the month a.** le mois suivant. **2** *prep* après; **a. all** après tout; **a. eating** après avoir mangé; **a. you!** je vous en prie!; **ten a. four** quatre heures dix; **to be a. sth/s.o.** (*seek*) chercher qch/qn. **3** *conj* après que.

**aftereffects** *npl* suites *fpl*.

**afternoon** après-midi *m or f inv*; **in the a.** l'après-midi; **good a.!** (*hello*) bonjour!

**afternoons** *adv* l'après-midi.

**aftershave (lotion)** lotion *f* après-rasage.

**afterward(s)** *adv* après, plus tard.

**again** *adv* de nouveau, encore une fois; **never a.** plus jamais; **a. and a., time and (time) a.** bien des fois, maintes fois.

**against** *prep* contre; **a. the law** illégal.

**age 1** *n* âge *m*; **(old) a.** vieillesse *f*; **the Middle Ages** le moyen âge; **five years of a.** âgé de cinq ans; **under a.** trop jeune. **2** *vti* vieillir.

**aged** *a* **a. ten** âgé de dix ans.

**agency** (*office*) agence *f*.

**agenda** ordre *m* du jour.

**agent** agent *m*; (*dealer*) concessionnaire *mf*.

**aggravate** *vt* (*make worse*) aggraver; **to a. s.o.** exaspérer qn.

**aggravation** (*annoyance*) ennui(s) *m*(*pl*).

**aggression** agression *f*.

**aggressive** *a* agressif.

**agile** *a* agile.

**agitated** *a* agité.

**ago** *adv* **a year a.** il y a un an; **how long a.?** il y a combien de temps (de cela)?

**agony** **to be in a.** souffrir horriblement.

**agree 1** *vi* (*come to an agreement*) se mettre d'accord; (*be in agreement*) être d'accord (**with** avec); (*of facts, dates*) concorder; *Grammar* s'accorder; **to a. to sth/to doing** consentir à qch/à faire; **it doesn't a. with me** (*food, climate*) ça ne me réussit pas. **2** *vt* **to a. to do** accepter de faire; **to a. that** admettre que.

**agreeable** *a* (*pleasant*) agréable.

**agreed** *a* (*time, place*) convenu; **we are a.** nous sommes d'accord; **a.!** entendu!

**agreement** accord *m*; **in a. with** d'accord avec; **to reach an a.** tomber d'accord.

**agree (up)on** (*decide*) convenir de.

**agricultural** *a* agricole.

**agriculture** agriculture *f*.

**ahead** *adv* (*in space*) en avant; (*leading*) en tête; (*in the future*) dans l'avenir; **a. (of time)** en avance (sur l'horaire); **to be one hour a.** avoir une heure d'avance (**of** sur); **a. of** (*space*) devant; (*time*) en avance sur; **straight a.** (*to walk*) tout droit; (*to look*) droit devant soi.

**aid** aide *f*; (*device*) accessoire *m*, support *m*; **with the a. of** (*a stick etc*) à l'aide de; **in a. of** (*charity*) au profit de.

**AIDS** SIDA *m*.

**aim 1** *n* but *m*; **with the a. of** dans le but de. **2** *vt* (*gun*) braquer (**at** sur); **aimed at children**/*etc* (*product*) destiné aux enfants/*etc*. **3** *vi* viser; **to a. at s.o.** viser qn; **to a. to do** *or* **at doing** avoir l'intention de faire.

**air 1** *n* air *m*; **in the open a.** en plein air; **by a.** (*to travel, send*) par avion; **(up) in(to) the a.** en l'air. **2** *a* (*raid, base*) aérien. **3** *vt* (*room*) aérer.

**air-conditioned** *a* climatisé.

**aircraft** *n inv* avion(s) *m*(*pl*).

**aircraft carrier** porte-avions *m inv*.

**air fare** prix *m* du billet d'avion.

**air force** armée *f* de l'air.

**airline** ligne *f* aérienne.

**airline ticket** billet *m* d'avion.

**airmail** poste *f* aérienne; **by a.** par avion.

**airplane** avion *m*.

**airport** aéroport *m*.

**airsickness** mal *m* de l'air.

**air terminal** aérogare *f*.

**airtight** *a* hermétique.
**air traffic controller** aiguilleur *m* du ciel.
**aisle** (*walkway in plane, theater*), allée *f*; (*in church*) nef *f* latérale; (*row of seats*) rangée *f*; (*section of supermarket*) rayon *m*.
**ajar** *a* (*door*) entrouvert.
**alarm 1** *n* (*warning, device in house or car*) alarme *f*; (*mechanism*) sonnerie *f* (d'alarme); **a. (clock)** réveil *m*. **2** *vt* alarmer.
**album** (*book, record*) album *m*.
**alcohol** alcool *m*.
**alcoholic 1** *a* (*drink*) alcoolisé. **2** *n* (*person*) alcoolique *mf*.
**alert** *a* (*watching carefully*) vigilant.
**algebra** algèbre *f*.
**alibi** alibi *m*.
**alien** étranger, -ère *mf*.
**alight** *a* (*fire*) allumé; **to set a.** mettre le feu à.
**alike 1** *a* (*people, things*) semblables; **to look** *or* **be a.** se ressembler. **2** *adv* de la même manière.
**alive** *a* vivant, en vie.
**all 1** *a* tout, toute, *pl* tous, toutes; **a. day** toute la journée; **a. (the) men** tous les hommes. **2** *pron* tous *mpl*, toutes *fpl*; (*everything*) tout; **my sisters are a. here** toutes mes sœurs sont ici; **he ate it a., he ate a. of it** il a tout mangé; **a. (that) he has** tout ce qu'il a; **a. of us** nous tous; **in a., a. told** en tout; **a. but** (*almost*) presque; **if there's any wind at a.** s'il y a le moindre vent; **not at a.** pas du tout; (*after 'thank you'*) pas de quoi. **3** *adv* tout; **a. alone** tout seul; **six a.** *Soccer* six buts partout.
**allergic** *a* allergique (**to** à).
**alley** ruelle *f*; (*in park*) allée *f*.
**alleyway** ruelle *f*.
**alliance** alliance *f*.
**alligator** alligator *m*.
**allocate** *vt* allouer (**to** à); (*distribute*) répartir.
**allotment** (*land*) lopin *m* de terre (*loué pour la culture*).
**all-out** *a* (*effort*) énergique.
**allow** *vt* permettre; (*give*) accorder; (*as discount*) déduire; **to a. s.o. to do** permettre à qn de faire; **you're not allowed to go** on vous interdit de partir.
**allowance** allocation *f*; (*for travel, housing, food*) indemnité *f*; (*for duty-free goods*) tolérance *f*; (*for children*) argent *m* de poche; **to make allowances for s.o.** être indulgent envers qn.
**allow for sth** tenir compte de qch.
**all-purpose** *a* (*tool*) universel.
**all right 1** *a* (*satisfactory*) bien *inv*; (*unharmed*) sain et sauf; (*undamaged*) intact; (*without worries*) tranquille; **it's all r.** ça va; **I'm all r.** (*healthy*) je vais bien. **2** *adv* (*well*) bien; **all r.!** (*agreement*) d'accord!; **I got your letter all r.** (*emphatic*) j'ai bien reçu votre lettre.
**all-round** *a* complet.
**ally** allié, -ée *mf*.
**almond** amande *f*.
**almost** *adv* presque; **he a. fell**/*etc* il a failli tomber/*etc*.
**alone** *a* & *adv* seul; **to leave a.** (*person*) laisser tranquille; (*thing*) ne pas toucher à.
**along 1** *prep* **(all) a.** (tout) le long de; **to go** *or* **walk a.** (*street*) passer par; **a. with** avec. **2** *adv* **all a.** (*time*) dès le début.
**alongside** *prep* & *adv* à côté (de).
**aloud** *adv* à haute voix.
**alphabet** alphabet *m*.
**alphabetical** *a* alphabétique.
**Alps** *npl* **the A.** les Alpes *fpl*.
**already** *adv* déjà.
**alright** *adv Fam* = **all right**.
**also** *adv* aussi.
**altar** autel *m*.
**alter 1** *vt* changer; (*clothing*) retoucher. **2** *vi* changer.
**alteration** changement *m*; (*of clothing*) retouche *f*.
**alternate 1** *a* alterné; **on a. days** tous les deux jours. **2** *vi* alterner (**with** avec).
**alternative 1** *a* (*other*) autre. **2** *n* alternative *f*.
**alternatively** *adv* comme alternative.

**although** *adv* bien que (+ *subjunctive*).
**altogether** *adv* (*completely*) tout à fait; (*on the whole*) somme toute; **how much a.?** combien en tout?
**aluminum** aluminium *m*.
**always** *adv* toujours.
**am** *see* **be.**
**a.m.** *adv* du matin.
**amateur 1** *n* amateur *m*. **2** *a* **a. painter/***etc* peintre/*etc* amateur.
**amaze** *vt* étonner.
**amazed** *a* stupéfait (**at sth** de qch, **at seeing** de voir); (*filled with wonder*) émerveillé.
**amazing** *a* stupéfiant; (*incredible*) extraordinaire.
**ambassador** ambassadeur *m*; (*woman*) ambassadrice *f*.
**amber a. (light)** (*of traffic signal*) (feu *m*) orange *m*.
**ambition** ambition *f*.
**ambitious** *a* ambitieux.
**ambulance** ambulance *f*.
**ambulance driver** ambulancier *m*.
**American** *a* & *n* américain, -aine (*mf*).
**ammunition** munitions *fpl*.
**among(st)** *prep* parmi, entre; **a. the crowd/books** parmi la foule/les livres; **a. themselves/friends** entre eux/amis.
**amount** quantité *f*; (*sum of money*) somme *f*; (*total of bill etc*) montant *m*.
**amount to** s'élever à; (*mean*) signifier; (*represent*) représenter.
**ample** *a* (*enough*) largement assez de; **you have a. time** tu as largement le temps.
**amplifier** amplificateur *m*.
**amputate** *vt* amputer.
**amuse** *vt* amuser.
**amusement** amusement *m*.
**amusing** *a* amusant.
**an** *see* **a.**
**analyse** *vt* analyser.
**analysis,** *pl* **-yses** analyse *f*.
**anarchy** anarchie *f*.
**anatomy** anatomie *f*.
**ancestor** ancêtre *m*.
**anchor** ancre *f*.
**anchored** *a* ancré.
**anchovy** anchois *m*.
**ancient** *a* ancien; (*pre-medieval*) antique.
**and** *conj* et; **two hundred a. two** deux cent deux; **better a. better** de mieux en mieux; **go a. see** va voir.
**anesthetic** anesthésie *f*; (*substance*) anesthésique *m*; **general a.** anesthésie générale.
**angel** ange *m*.
**anger** colère *f*.
**angle** angle *m*; **at an a.** en biais.
**angler** pêcheur, -euse *mf* à la ligne.
**angling** pêche *f* à la ligne.
**angrily** *adv* (*to speak etc*) avec colère.
**angry** *a* fâché; (*letter*) indigné; **to get a.** se fâcher (**with** contre).
**animal** *n* & *a* animal (*m*).
**ankle** cheville *f*.
**ankle sock** socquette *f*.
**annex** (*building*) annexe *f*.
**anniversary** (*of event*) anniversaire *m*.
**announce** *vt* annoncer; (*birth, marriage*) faire part de.
**announcement** (*statement*) annonce *f*; (*notice*) avis.
**announcer** (*on TV*) speaker *m*, speakerine *f*.
**annoy** *vt* (*inconvenience*) ennuyer; (*irritate*) agacer.
**annoyed** *a* fâché; **to get a.** se fâcher (**with** contre).
**annoying** *a* ennuyeux.
**annual 1** *a* annuel. **2** *n* (*book*) annuaire *m*.
**annually** *adv* annuellement.
**anonymous** *a* anonyme.
**another** *a* & *pron* un(e) autre; **a. man** un autre homme; **a. month** (*additional*) encore un mois; **a. ten** encore dix; **one a.** l'un(e) l'autre, *pl* les un(e)s les autres; **they love one a.** ils s'aiment (l'un l'autre).
**answer 1** *n* réponse *f*; (*to problem*) solution (**to** de). **2** *vt* (*person, question, phone*) répondre à; (*prayer,*

*wish*) exaucer; **to a. the door** ouvrir la porte. **3** *vi* répondre.

**answer (s.o.) back** répondre (à qn).

**answer for s.o./sth** répondre de qn/qch.

**answering machine** répondeur *m*.

**ant** fourmi *f*.

**antelope** antilope *f*.

**antenna** (*aerial*) antenne *f*.

**anthem national a.** hymne *m* national.

**anthology** recueil *m*.

**anti-** *prefix* anti-.

**antibiotic** antibiotique *m*.

**antibody** anticorps *m*.

**anticipate** *vt* (*foresee*) prévoir; (*expect*) s'attendre à.

**anticipation in a. of** en prévision de.

**antics** *npl* singeries *fpl*.

**antifreeze** antigel *m*.

**antihistamine** antihistaminique *m*.

**antique 1** *a* (*furniture etc*) ancien. **2** *n* antiquité *f*.

**antique dealer** antiquaire *mf*.

**antique shop** magasin *m* d'antiquités.

**antiseptic** *a* & *n* antiseptique (*m*).

**anxiety** (*worry*) inquiétude *f*; (*fear*) anxiété *f*.

**anxious** *a* (*worried*) inquiet (**about** de, pour); (*afraid*) anxieux; (*eager*) impatient (**to do** de faire).

**anxiously** *adv* (*to wait*) impatiemment.

**any 1** *a* (*with question*) du, de la, des; **do you have a. milk/tickets?** avez-vous du lait/des billets? ▪ (*negative*) de; **he hasn't got a. milk/tickets** il n'a pas de lait/de billets. ▪ (*no matter which*) n'importe quel. ▪ (*every*) tout; **in a. case, at a. rate** de toute façon. **2** *pron* (*no matter which one*) n'importe lequel; (*somebody*) quelqu'un; **if a. of you** si l'un d'entre vous. ▪ (*quantity*) en; **do you have a.?** en as-tu? **3** *adv* **(not) a. happier**/*etc* (pas) plus heureux/*etc*; **I don't see him a. more** je ne le vois plus; **a. more tea?** encore du thé?; **a. better?** c'est mieux?

**anybody** *pron* (*somebody*) quelqu'un; **do you see a.?** vois-tu quelqu'un? ▪ (*negative*) personne; **he doesn't know a.** il ne connaît personne. ▪ (*no matter who*) n'importe qui.

**anyhow** *adv* (*at any rate*) de toute façon; (*badly*) n'importe comment.

**anyone** *pron* = **anybody.**

**anyplace** *adv* = **anywhere.**

**anything** *pron* (*something*) quelque chose. ▪ (*negative*) rien; **he doesn't do a.** il ne fait rien. ▪ (*everything*) tout; **a. you like** (tout) ce que tu veux. ▪ (*no matter what*) **a. (at all)** n'importe quoi.

**anyway** *adv* (*at any rate*) de toute façon.

**anywhere** *adv* (*no matter where*) n'importe où. ▪ (*everywhere*) partout; **a. you go** partout où vous allez; **a. you like** là où tu veux. ▪ (*somewhere*) quelque part. ▪ (*negative*) nulle part; **he doesn't go a.** il ne va nulle part.

**apart** *adv* **we kept them a.** (*separate*) on les tenait séparés; **with legs a.** les jambes écartées; **they are three feet a.** ils se trouvent à un mètre l'un de l'autre; **a. from** (*except for*) à part.

**apartment** appartement *m*.

**apartment house** *or* **building** immeuble *m* (d'habitation).

**ape** singe *m*.

**aperitif** apéritif *m*.

**apologetic** *a* **to be a. (about)** s'excuser (de).

**apologize** *vi* s'excuser (**for** de); **to a. to s.o.** faire ses excuses à qn (**for** pour).

**apology** excuses *fpl*.

**apostrophe** apostrophe *f*.

**appall** *vt* consterner.

**appalling** *a* épouvantable.

**apparatus** appareil *m*; (*in gym*) agrès *mpl*.

**apparent** *a* apparent; **it's a. that** il est évident que.

**apparently** *adv* apparemment.
**appeal**[1] (*charm*) attrait *m*; (*interest*) intérêt *m*.
**appeal**[2] **1** *n* (*in court*) appel *m*. **2** *vi* faire appel.
**appeal to s.o.** (*attract*) plaire à qn; (*interest*) intéresser qn.
**appear** *vi* (*become visible*) apparaître; (*present oneself*) se présenter; (*seem, be published*) paraître; (*in court*) comparaître; **it appears that** il semble que (+ *subjunctive or indicative*).
**appearance** *n* (*act*) apparition *f*; (*look*) apparence *f*.
**appendicitis** appendicite *f*.
**appendix,** *pl* **-ixes** *or* **-ices** (*in book, body*) appendice *m*.
**appetite** appétit *m*.
**appetizing** *a* appétissant.
**applaud** *vti* (*clap*) applaudir.
**applause** applaudissements *mpl*.
**apple** pomme *f*; **cooking a.** pomme *f* à cuire; **a. pie** tarte *f* aux pommes.
**appliance** appareil *m*.
**applicant** candidat, -ate *mf* (**for** à).
**application** (*for job*) candidature *f*; (*for membership*) demande *f* d'adhésion; **a. (form)** (*for job*) formulaire *m* de candidature.
**apply 1** *vt* appliquer; (*brake*) appuyer sur; **to a. oneself to** s'appliquer à. **2** *vi* (*be relevant*) s'appliquer (**to** à).
**apply for** (*job*) poser sa candidature à.
**appoint** *vt* (*person*) nommer (**to sth** à qch, **to do** pour faire).
**appointment** nomination *f*; (*meeting*) rendez-vous *m inv*.
**appointment book** agenda *m*.
**appreciate** *vt* (*enjoy, value*) apprécier; (*understand*) comprendre; (*be grateful for*) être reconnaissant de.
**appreciation** (*gratitude*) reconnaissance *f*.
**apprentice** apprenti, -ie *mf*.
**apprenticeship** *n* apprentissage *m*.
**approach 1** *vt* (*person, door etc*) s'approcher de; (*age, result, town*) approcher de; (*subject*) aborder. **2** *vi* (*of person, vehicle*) s'approcher; (*of date*) approcher. **3** *n* (*method*) façon *f* de s'y prendre.
**appropriate** *a* convenable.
**appropriately** *adv* convenablement.
**approval** approbation *f*; **on a.** (*goods*) à l'essai.
**approve of** (*conduct etc*) approuver; **I don't a. of him** il ne me plaît pas; **I a. of his going** je trouve bon qu'il y aille.
**approximate** *a* approximatif.
**approximately** *adv* à peu près.
**apricot** abricot *m*.
**April** avril *m*.
**apron** tablier *m*.
**apt** *a* (*remark, reply*) juste, convenable; **to be a. to** avoir tendance à.
**aptitude** aptitude *f* (**for** à, pour).
**aquarium** aquarium *m*.
**Arab** *a* & *n* arabe (*mf*).
**Arabic** *a* & *n* (*language*) arabe (*m*); **A. numerals** chiffres *mpl* arabes.
**arc** (*of circle*) arc *m*.
**arch** (*of bridge*) arche *f*; (*of building*) voûte *f*.
**archer** archer *m*.
**archery** tir *m* à l'arc.
**architect** architecte *mf*.
**architecture** architecture *f*.
**Arctic the A.** l'Arctique *m*.
**are** *see* **be**.
**area** (*in geometry*) superficie *f*; (*of country*) région *f*; (*of town*) quartier *m*; **parking a.** aire *f* de stationnement.
**area code** (*phone number*) indicatif *m*.
**argue 1** *vi* (*quarrel*) se disputer (**with** avec, **about** au sujet de); (*reason*) raisonner (**with** avec, **about** sur). **2** *vt* **to a. that** (*maintain*) soutenir que.
**argument** (*quarrel*) dispute *f*; (*reasoning*) argument *m*; **to have an a.** se disputer.
**arise*** *vi* (*of problem, opportunity*) se présenter; (*result*) résulter (**from** de).
**arithmetic** arithmétique *f*.

**arm 1** *n* bras *m*; (*weapon*) arme *f*. **2** *vt* armer (**with** de).
**armband** brassard *m*.
**armchair** fauteuil *m*.
**armor** (*of knight*) armure *f*; (*of tank etc*) blindage *m*.
**armored** *a* (*car etc*) blindé.
**armpit** aisselle *f*.
**army 1** *n* armée *f*. **2** *a* militaire.
**around 1** *prep* autour de; (*approximately*) environ. **2** *adv* autour; **a. here** par ici; **he's still a.** il est encore là; **there's a lot of flu a.** il y a pas mal de grippes dans l'air; **there's a rumor going a.** il y a un bruit qui court; **up and a.** (*after illness*) sur pied.
**arrange** *vt* arranger; (*time, meeting*) fixer; **to a. to do** s'arranger pour faire.
**arrangement** (*layout, agreement*) arrangement *m*; **arrangements** préparatifs *mpl*; (*plans*) projets *mpl*.
**arrears** *npl* **in a.** en retard dans ses paiements.
**arrest 1** *vt* arrêter. **2** *n* arrestation *f*; **under a.** en état d'arrestation.
**arrival** arrivée *f*.
**arrive** *vi* arriver.
**arrow** flèche *f*.
**art** art *m*; **work of a.** œuvre *f* d'art.
**artery** artère *f*.
**arthritis** arthrite *f*.
**article** (*object, in newspaper, in grammar*) article *m*.
**artificial** *a* artificiel.
**artist** (*actor, painter etc*) artiste *mf*.
**artistic** *a* artistique; (*person*) artiste.
**as** *adv* & *conj* (*manner etc*) comme; **as you like** comme tu veux; **as much** *or* **as hard as I can** (au)tant que je peux; **as (it) is** (*to leave sth*) comme ça, tel quel; **as if, as though** comme si. ▪ (*comparison*) **as tall as you** aussi grand que vous; **as white as a sheet** blanc comme un linge; **as much** *or* **as hard as you** autant que vous; **twice as big as** deux fois plus grand que. ▪ (*though*) **(as) smart as he is** si intelligent qu'il soit. ▪ (*capacity*) **as a teacher** comme professeur; **to act as a father** agir en père. ▪ (*reason*) puisque; **as it's late** puisqu'il est tard. ▪ (*time*) **as I was leaving** comme je partais; **as he slept** pendant qu'il dormait; **as from, as of** (*time*) à partir de. ▪ (*concerning*) **as for that** quant à cela. ▪ (+ *infinitive*) **so as to** de manière à; **so stupid as to** assez bête pour.
**asap** *abbr* (*as soon as possible*) le plus tôt possible.
**ash** cendre *f*.
**ashamed** *a* **to be a.** avoir honte (**of** de).
**ashore** *adv* **to go a.** débarquer.
**ashtray** cendrier *m*.
**Asian 1** *a* asiatique. **2** *n* Asiatique *mf*.
**aside** *adv* de côté; **a. from** en dehors de.
**ask 1** *vt* demander; (*a question*) poser; (*invite*) inviter; **to a. s.o. (for) sth** demander qch à qn; **to a. s.o. to do** demander à qn de faire. **2** *vi* demander; **to a. for sth/s.o.** demander qch/qn; **to a. about sth** se renseigner sur qch; **to a. about s.o.** demander des nouvelles de qn; **to a. s.o. about** interroger qn sur.
**asleep** *a* **to be a.** dormir; **to fall a.** s'endormir.
**asparagus** (*for cooking*) asperges *fpl*.
**aspect** aspect *m*.
**aspirin** aspirine *f*.
**assault 1** *n* (*crime*) agression *f*. **2** *vt* (*attack*) agresser.
**assemble 1** *vt* assembler; (*people*) rassembler; (*machine*) monter. **2** *vi* se rassembler.
**assembly** (*meeting*) assemblée *f*; (*in school*) rassemblement *m*.
**assess** *vt* (*estimate*) évaluer; (*decide amount of*) fixer le montant de.
**asset** (*advantage*) atout *m*; **assets** (*of business*) biens *mpl*.
**assign** *vt* (*give*) attribuer (**to** à).
**assignment** (*task*) mission *f*.
**assist** *vti* aider (**in doing, to do** à faire).

**assistance** aide *f*; **to be of a. to s.o.** aider qn.
**assistant 1** *n* assistant, -ante *mf*; (*in shop*) vendeur, -euse *mf*. **2** *a* adjoint.
**associate 1** *vt* associer; **associated with sth/s.o.** associé à qch/avec qn. **2** *n* & *a* associé, -ée (*mf*).
**association** association *f*.
**assorted** *a* variés; (*foods*) assortis.
**assortment** assortiment *m*.
**assume** *vt* (*suppose*) présumer (**that** que); (*take on*) prendre; (*responsibility, role*) assumer.
**assurance** assurance *f*.
**assure** *vt* assurer (**s.o. that** à qn que, **s.o. of** qn de).
**asterisk** astérisque *m*.
**asthma** asthme *m*.
**asthmatic** *a* & *n* asthmatique (*mf*).
**astonish** *vt* étonner; **to be astonished** s'étonner (**at sth** de qch).
**astonishing** *a* étonnant.
**astray** *adv* **to go a.** s'égarer.
**astrology** astrologie *f*.
**astronaut** astronaute *mf*.
**astronomy** astronomie *f*.
**at** *prep* à; **at work** au travail; **at six (o'clock)** à six heures. ▪ chez; **at the doctor's** chez le médecin. ▪ en; **at sea** en mer. ▪ contre; **angry at** fâché contre. ▪ sur; **to shoot at** tirer sur. ▪ de; **to laugh at** rire de. ▪ (au)près de; **at the window** (au)près de la fenêtre. ▪ par; **six at a time** six par six.
**athlete** athlète *mf*.
**athletic** *a* athlétique.
**athletics** *npl* athlétisme *m*.
**Atlantic 1** *a* atlantique. **2** *n* **the A.** l'Atlantique *m*.
**atlas** atlas *m*.
**atmosphere** atmosphère *f*.
**atom** atome *m*.
**atomic** *a* (*bomb etc*) atomique.
**attach** *vt* attacher (**to** à); (*document*) joindre (**to** à); **attached to** (*fond of*) attaché à.
**attaché case** attaché-case *m*, mallette *f*.
**attachment** (*tool*) accessoire *m*.
**attack 1** *n* attaque *f*. **2** *vti* attaquer.
**attacker** agresseur *m*.
**attempt 1** *n* tentative *f*; **to make an a. to** tenter de. **2** *vt* tenter; (*task*) entreprendre; **to a. to do** tenter de faire.
**attend 1** *vt* (*meeting etc*) assister à; (*course*) suivre; (*school, church*) aller à. **2** *vi* assister.
**attendance** présence *f* (**at** à); **(school) a.** scolarité *f*.
**attendant** employé, -ée *mf*; (*in gas station*) pompiste *mf*; (*in museum*) gardien, -ienne *mf*.
**attend to** (*take care of*) s'occuper de (*client, tâche*).
**attention** attention *f*; **to pay a.** faire attention (**to** à).
**attentive** *a* attentif (**to** à).
**attic** grenier *m*.
**attitude** attitude *f*.
**attorney** (*lawyer*) avocat *m*.
**attract** *vt* attirer.
**attraction** (*charm*) attrait *m*.
**attractive** *a* (*price, offer etc*) intéressant; (*girl*) belle; (*boy*) beau.
**auction (off)** vendre (aux enchères).
**auctioneer** commissaire-priseur *m*.
**audible** *a* perceptible.
**audience** (*of speaker, musician*) auditoire *m*; (*in theater*) spectateurs *mpl*; (*of radio broadcast*) auditeurs *mpl*; **TV a.** téléspectateurs *mpl*.
**audio** *a* audio *inv*.
**audio-visual** *a* audio-visuel.
**August** août *m*.
**aunt** tante *f*.
**auntie** *or* **aunty** *Fam* tata *f*.
**au pair 1** *adv* au pair. **2** *n* **au p. (girl)** jeune fille *f* au pair.
**Australian** *a* & *n* australien, -ienne (*mf*).
**Austrian** *a* & *n* autrichien, -ienne (*mf*).
**author** auteur *m*.
**authority** autorité *f*; (*permission*) autorisation *f* (**to do** de faire).
**authorize** *vt* autoriser (**to do** à faire).

**autobiography** autobiographie *f.*
**autograph 1** *n* autographe *m.* **2** *vt* dédicacer (**for** à).
**automatic** *a* automatique.
**automatically** *adv* automatiquement.
**automobile** auto(mobile) *f.*
**autumn** automne *m.*
**auxiliary** *a* & *n* **a. (verb)** (verbe *m*) auxiliaire *m.*
**available** *a* disponible; **a. to all** accessible à tous.
**avalanche** avalanche *f.*
**avenue** avenue *f.*
**average 1** *n* moyenne *f*; **on a.** en moyenne. **2** *a* moyen.
**aviation** aviation *f.*
**avocado** (*pl* **-os**) **a. (pear)** avocat *m.*
**avoid** *vt* éviter; **to a. doing** éviter de faire.
**awake 1** *vi** se réveiller. **2** *a* éveillé; **to keep s.o. a.** empêcher qn de dormir; **he's (still) a.** il ne dort pas (encore).
**award 1** *vt* (*money, prize*) attribuer. **2** *n* (*prize*) prix *m*; (*scholarship*) bourse *f*; **awards ceremony** distribution *f* des prix.
**aware** *a* **a. of** (*conscious*) conscient de; (*informed*) au courant de; **to become a. of** prendre conscience de.
**away** *adv* (*distant*) loin; **far a.** au loin; **3 miles a.** à 5 km (de distance); **to play a.** (*of team*) jouer à l'extérieur. ▪ (*in time*) **ten days a.** dans dix jours. ▪ (*absent*) parti. ▪ (*continuously*) **to work/talk/***etc* **a.** travailler/parler/*etc* sans relâche.
**awful** *a* affreux; (*terrifying*) épouvantable; **an a. lot of** *Fam* un nombre incroyable de.
**awfully** *adv* (*very*) *Fam* affreusement.
**awkward** *a* (*clumsy*) maladroit; (*difficult*) difficile; (*tool*) peu commode; (*time*) inopportun.
**awning** (*over shop*) store *m.*
**ax 1** *n* hache *f.* **2** *vt* (*job etc*) supprimer.
**axle** essieu *m.*

# B

**BA** *abbr* = **Bachelor of Arts**.
**baby** bébé *m*; **b. boy** petit garçon *m*; **b. girl** petite fille *f.*
**baby carriage** landau *m* (*pl* -aus).
**baby clothes** vêtements *mpl* de bébé.
**baby-sit** *vi* garder les enfants.
**baby-sitter** baby-sitter *mf.*
**bachelor** célibataire *m*; **B. of Arts/of Science** licencié, -ée *mf* ès lettres/ès sciences.
**back[1] 1** *n* dos *m*; (*of chair*) dossier *m*; (*of hand*) revers *m*; (*of house*) derrière *m*, arrière *m*; (*of room*) fond *m*; (*of vehicle*) arrière *m*; (*of page*) verso *m*; **at the b. of the book** à la fin du livre; **b. to front** devant derrière; **in b. of** derrière. **2** *a* arrière *inv*, de derrière; **b. door** porte *f* de derrière; **b. tooth** molaire *f.* **3** *adv* (*behind*) en arrière; **to come b.** revenir; **he's b.** il est de retour, il est revenu.
**back[2]** *vt* (*with money*) financer; (*horse etc*) parier sur.
**back s.o. (up)** (*support*) appuyer qn.
**backache** mal *m* de dos; **to have a b.** avoir mal au dos.
**backfire** *vi* (*of vehicle*) pétarader.
**background** fond *m*; (*events*) antécédents *mpl*; (*education*) formation *f*; (*environment*) milieu *m*; **b. music** musique *f* de fond.
**backing** (*aid*) soutien *m*; (*material*) support *m.*
**backlog** (*of work*) arriéré *m.*
**back out** (*withdraw*) se retirer.
**backside** (*buttocks*) *Fam* derrière *m.*
**backstage** *adv* dans les coulisses.
**backward** *a* (*retarded*) arriéré; (*glance*) en arrière.
**backwards** *adv* en arrière; (*to walk*) à reculons; (*to put on garment*) à l'envers.
**backyard** jardin *m.*
**bacon** lard *m.*

**bad** *a* mauvais; (*wicked*) méchant; (*accident, wound*) grave; (*arm, leg*) malade; (*pain*) violent; **to feel b.** (*ill*) se sentir mal; **things are b.** ça va mal; **not b.!** pas mal!
**badge** insigne *m*; (*of policeman etc*) plaque *f*.
**badger** blaireau *m*.
**badly** *adv* mal; (*hurt*) grièvement; **b. affected** très touché; **to want b.** avoir grande envie de.
**bad-mannered** *a* mal élevé.
**badminton** badminton *m*.
**bad-tempered** *a* grincheux.
**baffle** *vt* déconcerter.
**bag** sac *m*; **bags** (*luggage*) valises *fpl*; (*under eyes*) poches *fpl*.
**baggage** bagages *mpl*.
**baggage check** consigne *f*.
**baggy** *a* (*trousers*) faisant des poches.
**bagpipes** *npl* cornemuse *f*.
**bail** (*in court*) caution *f*; **on b.** en liberté provisoire.
**bait** amorce *f*, appât *m*.
**bake 1** *vt* (faire) cuire (au four). **2** *vi* (*of cook*) faire de la pâtisserie *or* du pain; (*of cake etc*) cuire (au four).
**baked** *a* (*potatoes*) au four.
**baked beans** haricots *mpl* blancs (à la tomate).
**baker** boulanger, -ère *mf*.
**bakery** boulangerie *f*.
**balance 1** *n* équilibre *m*; (*of account*) solde *m*; (*remainder*) reste *m*; **to lose one's b.** perdre l'équilibre. **2** *vt* tenir en équilibre (**on** sur); (*account*) équilibrer. **3** *vi* (*of person*) se tenir en équilibre; (*of accounts*) être en équilibre.
**balance sheet** bilan *m*.
**balcony** balcon *m*.
**bald** *a* chauve.
**bald-headed** *a* chauve.
**baldness** calvitie *f*.
**ball**[1] *n* balle *f*; (*inflated*) (*for sports*) ballon *m*; (*of string, wool*) pelote *f*; (*any round shape*) boule *f*; (*of meat or fish*) boulette *f*; **on the b.** *Fam* (*alert*) éveillé; (*efficient*) au point.
**ball**[2] (*dance*) bal *m* (*pl* bals).
**ballerina** ballerine *f*.
**ballet** ballet *m*.
**balloon** ballon *m*.
**ballot** (*voting*) scrutin *m*.
**ballpoint** stylo *m* à bille, bic® *m*.
**ballroom** salle *f* de danse.
**ban 1** *n* interdiction *f*. **2** *vt* interdire (**s.o. from doing** à qn de faire); (*exclude*) exclure (**from** de).
**banana** banane *f*.
**band** (*strip*) bande *f*; (*musicians*) (petit) orchestre *m*; (*pop group*) groupe *m*; **rubber** *or* **elastic b.** élastique *m*.
**bandage** bande *f*.
**bandage (up)** (*arm, wound*) bander.
**Band-Aid**® pansement *m* adhésif.
**bang 1** *n* coup *m* (violent); (*of door*) claquement *m*. **2** *vt* cogner; (*door*) (faire) claquer. **3** *vi* cogner; (*of door*) claquer.
**bang down** (*lid*) rabattre (violemment).
**bang into sth/s.o.** heurter qch/qn.
**bangle** bracelet *m* (rigide).
**bangs** *npl* (*of hair*) frange *f*.
**banister(s)** *n*(*pl*) rampe *f* (d'escalier).
**bank** (*of river*) bord *m*; (*for money*) banque *f*.
**bank account** compte *m* en banque.
**banker** banquier *m*.
**banking** (*activity*) la banque.
**bank on s.o./sth** compter sur qn/qch.
**bankrupt** *a* **to go b.** faire faillite.
**bankruptcy** faillite *f*.
**banner** (*at rallies, on two poles*) banderole *f*.
**bar 1** *n* barre *f*; (*of gold*) lingot *m*; (*of chocolate*) tablette *f*; (*on window*) barreau *m*; (*pub, counter*) bar *m*. **2** *vt* (*way*) bloquer; (*prohibit*) interdire (**s.o. from doing** à qn de faire); (*exclude*) exclure (**from** de).
**barbecue** barbecue *m*.

**barbed** *a* **b. wire** fil *m* de fer barbelé.
**barber** coiffeur *m*.
**bare** *a* nu; (*tree*) dénudé; **with his b. hands** à mains nues.
**barefoot** *adv* nu-pieds.
**barely** *adv* (*scarcely*) à peine.
**bargain 1** *n* (*deal*) marché *m*; **a b.** (*cheap buy*) une occasion; **b. price** prix *m* exceptionnel. **2** *vi* négocier.
**bargain for sth** (*expect*) s'attendre à qch.
**barge** chaland *m*.
**barge in** (*enter a room*) faire irruption; (*interrupt s.o.*) interrompre.
**bark 1** *n* (*of tree*) écorce *f*. **2** *vi* (*of dog*) aboyer.
**barking** aboiements *mpl*.
**barley** orge *f*.
**barmaid** serveuse *f* de bar.
**barman** barman *m*.
**barn** (*for crops*) grange *f*.
**barometer** baromètre *m*.
**barracks** *npl* caserne *f*.
**barrage** (*barrier*) barrage *m*.
**barrel** (*cask*) tonneau *m*; (*of oil*) baril *m*; (*of gun*) canon *m*.
**barren** *a* stérile.
**barrette** barrette *f*.
**barricade 1** *n* barricade *f*. **2** *vt* barricader.
**barrier** barrière *f*.
**bartender** barman *m*.
**base 1** *n* base *f*; (*of tree, lamp*) pied *m*. **2** *vt* baser.
**baseball** base-ball *m*.
**baseboard** plinthe *f*.
**basement** sous-sol *m*.
**bash 1** *n* (*bang*) coup *m*. **2** *vt* (*hit*) cogner.
**bash s.o. up** tabasser qn.
**basic 1** *a* essentiel, de base; (*elementary*) élémentaire; (*pay*) de base. **2** *n* **the basics** l'essentiel *m*.
**basically** *adv* au fond.
**basin** bassin *m*; (*sink*) lavabo *m*.
**basis** (*of agreement etc*) bases *fpl*; **on the b. of** d'après; **on that b.** dans ces conditions; **on a weekly b.** chaque semaine.
**bask** *vi* se chauffer.
**basket** panier *m*; (*for bread, laundry, litter*) corbeille *f*.
**bat 1** *n* (*animal*) chauve-souris *f*; *Sports* batte *f*; **2** *vt* **she didn't b. an eye** elle n'a pas sourcillé.
**batch** (*of people*) groupe *m*; (*of letters*) paquet *m*; (*of papers*) liasse *f*.
**bath 1** *n* bain *m*; (*tub*) baignoire *f*; **to take a b.** prendre un bain. **2** *vt* baigner.
**bathe 1** *vt* baigner. **2** *vi* se baigner; prendre un bain. **3** *n* bain *m* (de mer).
**bathing suit** maillot *m* de bain.
**bathrobe** robe *f* de chambre.
**bathroom** salle *f* de bain(s); (*toilet*) toilettes *fpl*.
**bathtub** baignoire *f*.
**batter 1** *n* pâte *f* à frire. **2** *vt* (*baby*) martyriser.
**batter down** (*door*) défoncer.
**battered** *a* (*car*) cabossé.
**battery** batterie *f*; (*in radio, appliance*) pile *f*.
**battle 1** *n* bataille *f*; (*struggle*) lutte *f*. **2** *vi* se battre.
**battleship** cuirassé *m*.
**bawl (out)** *vti* beugler; **to b. s.o. out** *Slang* engueuler qn.
**bay** (*part of coastline*) baie *f*; (*for loading*) aire *f*.
**BC** *abbr* (*before Christ*) avant Jésus-Christ.
**be*** *vi* être; **she's a doctor** elle est médecin; **it's 3 (o'clock)** il est trois heures. ▪ avoir; **to be hot/right/lucky** avoir chaud /raison /de la chance; **he's 20** il a 20 ans; **to be 7 feet high** avoir 2 mètres de haut. ▪ (*health*) aller; **how are you?** comment vas-tu? ▪ (*go, come*) **I've been to see her** je suis allé *or* j'ai été la voir; **he's (already) been here** il est (déjà) venu. ▪ (*weather, calculations*) faire; **it's sunny** il fait beau; **2 and 2 are 4** 2 et 2 font 4. ▪ (*cost*) faire; **how much is it?** ça fait combien? ▪ (*auxiliary*) **I am/was doing** je fais/faisais; **he was killed** il a été tué; **I've been waiting (for) two**

hours j'attends depuis deux heures; **isn't it?, aren't you?** *etc* n'est-ce pas?, non? ▪ (+ *infinitive*) **he is to come** (*must*) il doit venir. ▪ **there is** *or* **are** il y a; (*pointing*) voilà; **here is** *or* **are** voici.

**beach** plage *f.*

**beacon** balise *f.*

**bead** perle *f*; (*of sweat*) goutte *f*; **(string of) beads** collier *m.*

**beak** bec *m.*

**beaker** (*for drinking*) gobelet *m*; (*in laboratory*) vase *m* à bec.

**beam** (*of wood*) poutre *f*; (*of light*) rayon *m*; (*of headlight*) faisceau *m.*

**beaming** *a* (*radiant*) radieux.

**bean** haricot *m*; (*of coffee*) grain *m*; **(broad) b.** fève *f.*

**beansprouts** *npl* germes *mpl* de soja.

**bear**[1] (*animal*) ours *m.*

**bear**[2]* **1** *vt* (*carry, show*) porter; (*endure*) supporter; (*responsibility*) assumer; **to b. in mind** tenir compte de. **2** *vi* **to b. left/right** tourner à gauche/droite.

**bearable** *a* supportable.

**beard** barbe *f.*

**bearded** *a* barbu.

**bearing** (*relevance*) relation *f* (**on** avec); **to get one's bearings** s'orienter.

**bear sth out** corroborer qch.

**beast** bête *f*; (*person*) brute *f.*

**beastly** *a Fam* (*bad*) vilain.

**beat 1** *n* (*of heart, drum*) battement *m*; (*of policeman*) ronde *f.* **2** *vt** battre.

**beat down 1** *vt* (*door*) défoncer. **2** *vi* (*of rain*) tomber à verse; (*of sun*) taper.

**beating** (*blows, defeat*) raclée *f.*

**beat s.o. off** repousser qn.

**beat s.o. up** tabasser qn.

**beautiful** *a* (très) beau (*f* belle).

**beauty** (*quality, woman*) beauté *f.*

**beauty mark** *or* **spot** (*on skin*) grain *m* de beauté.

**beaver** castor *m.*

**because** *conj* parce que; **b. of** à cause de.

**become*** *vi* devenir; **to b. a painter** devenir peintre; **what has b. of her?** qu'est-elle devenue?

**bed** lit *m*; **to go to b.** (aller) se coucher; **in b.** couché; **to get out of b.** se lever; **b. and breakfast** chambre *f* avec petit déjeuner.

**bedclothes** *npl* couvertures *fpl* et draps *mpl.*

**bedroom** chambre *f* à coucher.

**bedside** chevet *m*; **b. lamp/book** lampe *f*/livre *m* de chevet.

**bedtime** heure *f* du coucher.

**bee** abeille *f.*

**beech** (*tree, wood*) hêtre *m.*

**beef** bœuf *m.*

**beehive** ruche *f.*

**been** *pp de* **be**.

**beep 1** *n* bip *m; (on answering machine*) bip *m* sonore. **2** *vt* biper, appeler au Tatoo®.

**beeper** (*pager*) récepteur *m* d'appels, bip *m*, Tatoo® *m.*

**beer** bière *f*; **b. glass** chope *f.*

**beet** betterave *f* (potagère).

**beetle** scarabée *m*; (*any beetle-shaped insect*) bestiole *f.*

**before 1** *adv* avant; (*already*) déjà; (*in front*) devant; **the day b.** la veille. **2** *prep* (*time*) avant; (*place*) devant; **the year b. last** il y a deux ans. **3** *conj* avant que (+ ne + *subjunctive*), avant de (+ *infinitive*); **b. he goes** avant qu'il (ne) parte; **b. going** avant de partir.

**beg 1** *vt* **to b. (for)** solliciter; (*bread, money*) mendier; **to b. s.o. to do** supplier qn de faire. **2** *vi* mendier.

**beggar** mendiant, -ante *mf.*

**begin*** **1** *vt* commencer; (*campaign*) lancer; **to b. doing** *or* **to do** commencer *or* se mettre à faire. **2** *vi* commencer (**with** par, **by doing** par faire); **to b. with** (*first*) d'abord.

**beginner** débutant, -ante *mf.*

**beginning** commencement *m*, début *m.*

**begrudge** *vt* (*envy*) envier (**s.o. sth** qch à qn); **to b. doing sth** faire qch à contrecœur.

**behalf** *n* **on b. of** (*to act*) pour le compte de; (*to call, write*) de la part de.

**behave** *vi* se conduire; (*of machine*) fonctionner; **to b. (oneself)** se tenir bien; (*of child*) être sage.

**behavior** conduite *f*.

**behind 1** *prep* derrière; (*in making progress*) en retard sur. **2** *adv* derrière; (*late*) en retard. **3** *n* (*buttocks*) *Fam* derrière *m*.

**beige** *a* & *n* beige (*m*).

**belch 1** *vi* faire un renvoi. **2** *n* renvoi *m*.

**Belgian** *a* & *n* belge (*mf*).

**belief** croyance *f* (**in** en); (*trust*) confiance *f*, foi *f*; (*opinion*) opinion *f*.

**believable** *a* croyable.

**believe** *vti* croire (**in sth** à qch, **in God** en Dieu); **I b. so** je crois que oui; **to b. in doing** croire qu'il faut faire.

**believer** (*religious*) croyant, -ante *mf*.

**belittle** *vt* dénigrer.

**bell** cloche *f*; (*small*) clochette *f*; (*in phone*) sonnerie *f*; (*on door, bicycle*) sonnette *f*.

**bellboy** groom *m*.

**belly** ventre *m*; **b. button** *Fam* nombril *m*.

**bellyache** mal *m* au ventre.

**belong** *vi* appartenir (**to** à); **to b. to** (*club*) être membre de.

**belongings** *npl* affaires *fpl*.

**below 1** *prep* au-dessous de. **2** *adv* en dessous.

**belt** ceinture *f*; (*in machine*) courroie *f*.

**beltway** *n* périphérique *m*.

**bench** (*seat*) banc *m*; (*work table*) établi *m*.

**bend 1** *n* courbe *f*; (*in river*) coude *m*; (*in road*) virage *m*; (*of arm, knee*) pli *m*. **2** *vt** courber; (*leg, arm*) plier. **3** *vi* (*of branch*) plier; (*of road*) tourner.

**bend (down)** (*stoop*) se baisser.

**bend (over)** (*lean forward*) se pencher.

**beneath 1** *prep* au-dessous de. **2** *adv* (au-)dessous.

**beneficial** *a* bénéfique.

**benefit 1** *n* avantage *m*; (*money*) allocation *f*; **child b.** allocations familiales; **for your (own) b.** pour vous. **2** *vt* faire du bien à; (*be useful to*) profiter à. **3** *vi* **you'll b. from it** ça vous fera du bien.

**bent** *a* (*nail*) tordu; **b. on doing** résolu à faire.

**bereavement** deuil *m*.

**berry** baie *f*.

**berserk** *a* **to go b.** devenir fou.

**berth** (*in ship, train*) couchette *f*.

**beside** *prep* à côté de; **that's b. the point** ça n'a rien à voir.

**besides 1** *prep* en plus de; (*except*) excepté. **2** *adv* de plus; (*moreover*) d'ailleurs.

**best 1** *a* meilleur (**in** de); **the b. part of** (*most*) la plus grande partie de. **2** *n* **the b. (one)** le meilleur, la meilleure; **at b.** au mieux; **to do one's b.** faire de son mieux; **to make the b. of** s'accommoder de. **3** *adv* **(the) b.** (*to play, sing etc*) le mieux; **the b. loved** le plus aimé.

**best man** (*at wedding*) témoin *m*.

**best-seller** best-seller *m*.

**bet 1** *n* pari *m*. **2** *vti** parier (**on** sur, **that** que).

**betray** *vt* trahir.

**betrayal** trahison *f*.

**better 1** *a* meilleur (**than** que); **she's (much) b.** (*in health*) elle va (beaucoup) mieux; **that's b.** c'est mieux; **to get b.** (*recover*) se remettre; (*improve*) s'améliorer; **it's b. to go** il vaut mieux partir. **2** *adv* mieux; **I had b. go** il vaut mieux que je parte. **3** *vt* **to b. oneself** améliorer sa condition.

**betting** pari(s) *m*(*pl*).

**between 1** *prep* entre; **in b. sth and sth/two things** entre qch et qch/deux choses. **2** *adv* **in b.** au milieu; (*time*) dans l'intervalle.

**beware** *vi* **to b. of** se méfier de; **b.!** méfiez-vous!

**bewilder** *vt* dérouter.

**beyond 1** *prep* au-delà de; (*reach, doubt*) hors de; **b. my means** au-dessus de mes moyens; **it's b. me** ça me dépasse. **2** *adv* au-delà.
**bias** penchant *m* (**towards** pour); (*prejudice*) préjugé *m*.
**bias(s)ed** *a* partial; **to be b. against** avoir des préjugés contre.
**bib** (*baby's*) bavoir *m*.
**bible** bible *f*; **the B.** la Bible.
**bicycle** bicyclette *f*.
**bid* 1** *vt* (*money*) offrir. **2** *vi* faire une offre (**for** pour). **3** *n* (*at auction*) offre *f*; (*for doing a job*) tentative *f*.
**big** *a* grand, gros (*f* grosse); (*in age, generous*) grand; (*in bulk, amount*) gros; **b. deal!** *Fam* (bon) et alors!
**bighead** *Fam* (*conceited*) prétentieux, -euse *mf*; (*boasting*) vantard, -arde *mf*.
**bigshot** *Fam* gros bonnet *m*.
**bike** *Fam* vélo *m*.
**bike path** *Fam* piste *f* cyclable.
**bikini** deux-pièces *m inv*; **b. briefs** mini-slip *m*.
**bile** bile *f*.
**bilingual** *a* bilingue.
**bill 1** *n* (*invoice*) facture *f*, note *f*; (*in restaurant*) addition *f*; (*in hotel*) note *f*; (*money*) billet *m*; (*proposed law*) projet *m* de loi. **2** *vt* **to b. s.o.** envoyer la facture à qn.
**billboard** panneau *m* d'affichage.
**billfold** portefeuille *m*.
**billiards** *npl* (jeu *m* de) billard *m*.
**billion** milliard *m*.
**bin** boîte *f*; (*for trash*) poubelle *f*.
**bind** *vt** lier; (*book*) relier.
**binder** (*for papers*) classeur *m*.
**binding** (*of book*) reliure *f*.
**bingo** loto *m*.
**binoculars** *npl* jumelles *fpl*.
**biological** *a* biologique.
**biology** biologie *f*.
**birch (silver) b.** (*tree*) bouleau *m*.
**bird** oiseau *m*; (*fowl*) volaille *f*; **b.'s-eye view** vue *f* d'ensemble.
**birth** naissance *f*; **to give b. to** donner naissance à.
**birth certificate** acte *m* de naissance.
**birthday** anniversaire *m*; **happy b.!** bon anniversaire!
**biscuit** petit pain *m*.
**bishop** évêque *m*.
**bit** morceau *m*; **a b.** (*a little*) un peu; **quite a b.** (*very*) très; (*a lot*) beaucoup; **not a b.** pas du tout; **b. by b.** petit à petit.
**bite 1** *n* (*wound*) morsure *f*; (*from insect*) piqûre *f*; **a b. to eat** quelque chose à manger. **2** *vti** mordre; **to b. one's nails** se ronger les ongles.
**bitter 1** *a* amer; (*cold, wind*) glacial; (*conflict*) violent. **2** *n* bière *f* (pression).
**bitterness** amertume *f*; (*of conflict*) violence *f*.
**bizarre** *a* bizarre.
**black 1** *a* noir; **b. eye** œil *m* poché; **to give s.o. a b. eye** pocher l'œil à qn; **b. and blue** (*bruised*) couvert de bleus. **2** *n* (*color*) noir *m*; (*person*) Noir, -e *mf*.
**blackberry** mûre *f*.
**blackbird** merle *m*.
**blackboard** tableau *m* (noir); **on the b.** au tableau.
**blackcurrant** cassis *m*.
**blacklist 1** *n* liste *f* noire. **2** *vt* mettre sur la liste noire.
**blackmail 1** *n* chantage *m*. **2** *vt* faire chanter.
**blackmailer** maître chanteur *m*.
**black out** (*faint*) s'évanouir.
**blackout** panne *f* d'électricité; (*fainting fit*) syncope *f*.
**bladder** vessie *f*.
**blade** lame *f*; (*of grass*) brin *m*.
**blame 1** *vt* accuser; **to b. s.o. for sth** reprocher qch à qn; **you're to b.** c'est ta faute. **2** *n* faute *f*.
**blameless** *a* irréprochable.
**bland** *a* (*food*) fade.
**blank 1** *a* (*paper, page*) blanc (*f* blanche); (*check*) en blanc. **2** *a* & *n* **b. (space)** blanc *m*.
**blanket** couverture *f*.
**blare (out)** (*of radio*) beugler; (*of music*) retentir.

**blast 1** *n* explosion *f*; (*air from explosion*) souffle *m*. **2** *int Fam* zut!
**blasted** *a Fam* fichu.
**blast-off** (*of spacecraft*) mise *f* à feu.
**blaze 1** *n* (*fire*) flamme *f*; (*large*) incendie *m*. **2** *vi* (*of fire*) flamber; (*of sun*) flamboyer.
**blazer** blazer *m*.
**blazing** *a* en feu; (*sun*) brûlant.
**bleach** (*household*) eau *f* de Javel.
**bleak** *a* morne.
**bleed*** *vti* saigner.
**blemish** défaut *m*; (*on reputation*) tache *f*.
**blend 1** *n* mélange *m*. **2** *vt* mélanger. **3** *vi* se mélanger.
**blender** (*for food*) mixer *m*.
**bless** *vt* bénir; **b. you!** (*sneezing*) à vos souhaits!
**blessing** bénédiction *f*; (*benefit*) bienfait *m*.
**blew** *pt de* **blow**[1].
**blind 1** *a* aveugle; **b. person** aveugle *mf*. **2** *n* (*on window*) store *m*; **the b.** les aveugles *mpl*.
**blindfold 1** *n* bandeau *m*. **2** *vt* bander les yeux à.
**blindly** *adv* aveuglément.
**blindness** cécité *f*.
**blink 1** *vi* (*of person*) cligner des yeux; (*of eyes*) cligner. **2** *n* clignement *m*.
**bliss** félicité *f*.
**blister** (*on skin*) ampoule *f*.
**blizzard** tempête *f* de neige.
**bloat** *vt* gonfler.
**blob** goutte *f*; (*of ink*) tache *f*.
**block 1** *n* (*of stone*) bloc *m*; (*of buildings*) pâté *m* (de maisons); (*child's toy*) cube *m*. **2** *vt* (*obstruct*) bloquer.
**blockage** obstruction *f*.
**block off** (*road*) barrer.
**block up** (*pipe, hole*) bloquer.
**blond** *a* & *n* blond (*m*).
**blonde** *a* & *n* blonde (*f*).
**blood** sang *m*; **b. donor** donneur, -euse *mf* de sang; **b. group** groupe *m* sanguin; **b. pressure** tension *f* (artérielle); **to have high b. pressure** avoir de la tension.
**bloodshed** effusion *f* de sang.
**bloodshot** *a* (*eye*) injecté de sang.
**bloody** *a* sanglant.
**bloom 1** *n* fleur *f*; **in b.** en fleur(s). **2** *vi* fleurir.
**blossom 1** *n* fleur(s) *f*(*pl*). **2** *vi* fleurir.
**blot** tache *f*.
**blotchy** *a* couvert de taches.
**blotting paper** buvard *m*.
**blouse** chemisier *m*.
**blow**[1]* **1** *vt* (*of wind*) pousser (*un navire*), chasser (*la pluie*); (*of person*) (*smoke*) souffler; (*bubbles*) faire; (*trumpet*) souffler dans; **to b. one's nose** se moucher; **to b. a whistle** siffler. **2** *vi* (*of wind, person*) souffler.
**blow**[2] (*with fist, tool etc*) coup *m*.
**blow away 1** *vt* (*of wind*) emporter. **2** *vi* (*of hat etc*) s'envoler.
**blow down** *or* **over 1** *vt* (*chimney etc*) faire tomber. **2** *vi* tomber.
**blow-dry** brushing *m*.
**blow dryer** sèche-cheveux *m*.
**blow off 1** *vt* (*hat etc*) emporter. **2** *vi* s'envoler.
**blow out** (*candle*) souffler.
**blowtorch** chalumeau *m*.
**blow up 1** *vt* (*building*) faire sauter; (*pump up*) gonfler. **2** *vi* exploser.
**blue 1** *a* bleu (*mpl* bleus). **2** *n* bleu *m* (*pl* bleus).
**blueberry** myrtille *f*.
**bluff 1** *vti* bluffer. **2** *n* bluff *m*.
**blunder 1** *n* (*mistake*) bévue *f*. **2** *vi* faire une bévue.
**blunt** *a* (*edge*) émoussé; (*person, speech*) franc, brusque.
**blur 1** *n* tache *f* floue. **2** *vt* rendre flou.
**blurred** *a* flou.
**blush** *vi* rougir (**with** de).
**blustery** *a* (*weather*) de grand vent.
**board**[1] **1** *n* (*piece of wood*) planche *f*; (*for notices*) tableau *m*; (*cardboard*) carton *m*; **b. (of directors)** conseil *m* d'administration; **on b.** (*ship, aircraft*) à bord (de). **2** *vt*

monter à bord de; (*bus, train*) monter dans.

**board²** (*food*) pension *f*; **room and b.** pension *f* (complète).

**boarder** pensionnaire *mf*.

**boarding** (*of passengers*) embarquement *m*.

**boarding house** pension *f* (de famille).

**boarding school** pensionnat *m*.

**boardwalk** promenade *f* (de planches).

**boast** *vi* se vanter (**about, of** de).

**boat** bateau *m*; (*small*) barque *f*, canot *m*; (*liner*) paquebot *m*.

**bobby pin** pince *f* à cheveux.

**bodily** *a* (*need*) physique.

**body** corps *m*; (*institution*) organisme *m*.

**bodyguard** garde *m* du corps.

**bodywork** carrosserie *f*.

**bogged down** *a* **to get b. down** s'enliser.

**bogus** *a* faux (*f* fausse).

**boil¹** *n* (*pimple*) furoncle *m*.

**boil²** **1** *n* **to come to the b.** bouillir. **2** *vi* bouillir.

**boil (up)** faire bouillir.

**boiled** *a* bouilli; (*potato*) à l'eau; **b. egg** œuf *m* à la coque; **hard-b. egg** œuf *m* dur.

**boiler** chaudière *f*.

**boiling** *a* **b. (hot)** bouillant; **it's b. (hot)** (*weather*) il fait une chaleur infernale.

**boil over** (*of milk*) déborder.

**bold** *a* hardi.

**boldness** hardiesse *f*.

**bolt** **1** *n* (*on door*) verrou *m*; (*for nut*) boulon *m*. **2** *vt* (*door*) fermer au verrou. **3** *vi* (*dash*) se précipiter.

**bomb** **1** *n* bombe *f*. **2** *vt* bombarder.

**bomber** (*aircraft*) bombardier *m*.

**bombing** bombardement *m*.

**bond** (*link*) lien *m*; (*investment certificate*) bon *m*.

**bone** os *m*; (*of fish*) arête *f*.

**bonfire** (*celebration*) feu *m* de joie; (*for dead leaves*) feu *m* (de jardin).

**bonnet** (*hat*) bonnet *m*; (*of car*) capot *m*.

**bonus** prime *f*.

**bony** *a* (*thin*) osseux; (*fish*) plein d'arêtes.

**boo** **1** *vti* siffler. **2** *n* **boos** sifflets *mpl*.

**booby-trap** *vt* piéger.

**book** **1** *n* livre *m*; (*of tickets*) carnet *m*; **(exercise) b.** cahier (de brouillon) *m*; **books** (*accounts*) comptes *mpl*. **2** *vt* (*room etc*) réserver.

**book up** **booked up** (*hotel*) complet.

**bookcase** bibliothèque *f*.

**booking** réservation *f*.

**bookkeeper** comptable *mf*.

**bookkeeping** comptabilité *f*.

**booklet** (*pamphlet*) brochure *f*.

**bookmaker** bookmaker *m*.

**bookseller** libraire *mf*.

**bookshelf** rayon *m*.

**bookshop, bookstore** librairie *f*.

**boom** (*economic*) expansion *f*.

**boost** **1** *vt* (*increase*) augmenter; (*product*) faire de la réclame pour; (*economy*) stimuler. **2** *n* **to give a b. to** = **to boost.**

**boot** (*shoe*) botte *f*; **(ankle) b.** bottillon *m*; **to get the b.** *Fam* être mis à la porte; **(Denver) b.** (*on car*) sabot *m* (de Denver).

**booth** (*for phone*) cabine *f*.

**boot out** mettre à la porte.

**booze** *Fam* **1** *n* alcool *m*. **2** *vi* boire (beaucoup).

**border** (*of country*) frontière *f*; (*edge*) bord *m*.

**border (on)** (*country*) toucher à.

**borderline case** cas *m* limite.

**bore** **1** *vt* ennuyer; **to be bored** s'ennuyer. **2** *n* (*person*) raseur, -euse *mf*; (*thing*) ennui *m*.

**boredom** ennui *m*.

**boring** *a* ennuyeux.

**born** *a* né; **to be b.** naître; **he was b.** il est né.

**borrow** *vt* emprunter (**from** à).

**boss** patron, -onne *mf*, chef *m*.

**boss s.o. around** commander qn.

**bossy** *a Fam* autoritaire.

**botch (up)** (*ruin*) bâcler.

**both 1** *a* les deux. **2** *pron* tous *or* toutes (les) deux; **b. of us** nous deux. **3** *adv* (*at the same time*) à la fois; **b. you and I** vous et moi.

**bother 1** *vt* (*annoy, worry*) ennuyer; (*disturb*) déranger; (*pester*) importuner; **to b. doing** *or* **to do** se donner la peine de faire; **I can't be bothered!** je n'en ai pas envie! **2** *n* (*trouble*) ennui *m*; (*effort*) peine *f*; (*inconvenience*) dérangement *m*.

**bother about** (*worry about*) se préoccuper de.

**bottle** bouteille *f*; (*small*) flacon *m*; (*for baby*) biberon *m*; **hot-water b.** bouillotte *f*.

**bottle opener** ouvre-bouteilles *m inv*.

**bottom 1** *n* (*of sea, box*) fond *m*; (*of page, hill*) bas *m*; (*buttocks*) *Fam* derrière *m*; **to be at the b. of the class** être le dernier de la classe. **2** *a* (*part, shelf*) inférieur, du bas; **b. floor** rez-de-chaussée *m*.

**boulder** rocher *m*.

**bounce 1** *vi* (*of ball*) rebondir; (*of check*) *Fam* être sans provision. **2** *vt* faire rebondir. **3** *n* (re)bond *m*.

**bound** *a* **b. to do** (*obliged*) obligé de faire; (*certain*) sûr de faire; **it's b. to happen/snow**/*etc* ça arrivera/il neigera/*etc* sûrement; **b. for** en route pour.

**boundary** limite *f*.

**bounds** *npl* **out of b.** (*place*) interdit.

**bouquet** (*of flowers*) bouquet *m*.

**boutique** boutique *f* (de mode).

**bow**[1] (*weapon*) arc *m*; (*knot*) nœud *m*.

**bow**[2] **1** *n* révérence *f*; (*nod*) salut *m*. **2** *vi* s'incliner (**to** devant); (*nod*) incliner la tête (**to** devant).

**bowels** *npl* intestins *mpl*.

**bowl** (*for food*) bol *m*; (*for sugar*) sucrier *m*; (*for salad*) saladier *m*; (*for fruit*) coupe *f*.

**bowling (tenpin) b.** bowling *m*.

**bowling alley** bowling *m*.

**bow tie** nœud *m* papillon.

**box 1** *n* boîte *f*; (*large*) caisse *f*. **2** *vi* *Boxing* boxer.

**boxer** boxeur *m*.

**boxer shorts** caleçon *m*.

**box in** (*enclose*) enfermer.

**boxing** boxe *f*; **b. ring** ring *m*.

**box office** bureau *m* de location (*spectacles*).

**boy** garçon *m*; **American b.** jeune Américain *m*; **oh b.!** mon Dieu!

**boycott 1** *vt* boycotter. **2** *n* boycottage *m*.

**boyfriend** petit ami *m*.

**bra** soutien-gorge *m*.

**bracelet** bracelet *m*.

**bracket** (*in typography*) crochet *m*; (*for shelf etc.*) équerre *f*.

**brag** *vi* se vanter (**about, of** de).

**bragging** vantardise *f*.

**braid 1** *n* (*of hair*) tresse *f*. **2** *vt* tresser.

**brain** cerveau *m*; **to have brains** avoir de l'intelligence.

**brainwash** *vt* faire un lavage de cerveau à.

**brainy** *a Fam* intelligent.

**brake 1** *n* frein *m*. **2** *vi* freiner.

**brake light** (signal *m* de) stop *m*.

**branch** branche *f*; (*of road*) embranchement *m*; (*of store, office*) succursale *f*.

**branch off** (*of road*) bifurquer.

**branch out** (*of firm, person*) étendre ses activités (**into** à).

**brand** (*trademark*) marque *f*.

**brand-new** *a* tout neuf (*f* toute neuve).

**brandy** cognac *m*.

**brass** cuivre *m*.

**brave** *a* courageux, brave.

**bravery** courage *m*.

**brawl** bagarre *f*.

**brawny** *a* musclé.

**bread** *n inv* pain *m*; **loaf of b.** pain *m*; **(slice** *or* **piece of) b. and butter** tartine *f*.

**breadbox** coffre *m* à pain.

**breadcrumb** miette *f* (de pain); **breadcrumbs** (*in cooking*) chapelure *f*.

**breadth** largeur *f*.

**breadwinner** soutien *m* de famille.

**break 1** *vt** casser; (*into pieces*) briser; (*silence, spell*) rompre; (*strike, heart, ice*) briser; (*sports record*) battre; (*law*) violer; (*one's word, promise*) manquer à; (*journey*) interrompre; (*news*) révéler (**to** à). **2** *vi* (se) casser; se briser; se rompre; (*of news*) éclater; (*stop work*) faire la pause. **3** *n* cassure *f*; (*in bone*) fracture *f*; (*with person, group*) rupture *f*; (*in journey*) interruption *f*; (*rest*) repos *m*; (*in activity, for tea etc*) pause *f*; (*in school*) récréation *f*; **a lucky b.** une chance.

**breakable** *a* fragile.

**break away** *vi* se détacher.

**break down 1** *vt* (*door*) enfoncer. **2** *vi* (*of vehicle, machine*) tomber en panne; (*of talks*) échouer; (*collapse*) (*of person*) s'effondrer.

**breakdown** panne *f*; (*in talks*) rupture *f*; (*nervous*) dépression *f*.

**breakfast** petit déjeuner *m*.

**break in 1** *vi* (*of burglar*) entrer par effraction. **2** *vt* (*door*) enfoncer; (*vehicle*) roder.

**break-in** cambriolage *m*.

**break into** (*house*) cambrioler; (*safe*) forcer.

**break loose** s'échapper.

**break off 1** *vt* détacher; (*relations*) rompre. **2** *vi* se détacher; (*stop*) s'arrêter; **to b. off with s.o.** rompre avec qn.

**break out** (*of war, fire*) éclater; (*escape*) s'échapper.

**breakthrough** percée *f*, découverte *f*.

**break up 1** *vt* mettre en morceaux; (*fight*) mettre fin à. **2** *vi* (*of group*) se disperser; (*of marriage*) se briser.

**breakup** (*in marriage*) rupture *f*.

**breast** sein *m*; (*of chicken*) blanc *m*.

**breastfeed** *vt* allaiter.

**breaststroke** brasse *f*.

**breath** haleine *f*, souffle *m*; **out of b.** (tout) essoufflé.

**Breathalyzer**® alcootest® *m*.

**breathe** *vti* respirer; **to b. in** aspirer; **to b. out** expirer.

**breathing** respiration *f*; **b. space** moment *m* de repos.

**breathtaking** *a* époustouflant.

**breed 1** *vt** (*animals*) élever. **2** *vi* (*of animals*) se reproduire. **3** *n* race *f*.

**breeder** éleveur, -euse *mf*.

**breeze** brise *f*.

**breezy** *a* (*weather*) frais.

**brew** *vi* (*of storm*) se préparer; (*of tea*) infuser; **something is brewing** il se prépare quelque chose.

**brewery** brasserie *f*.

**bribe 1** *n* pot-de-vin *m*. **2** *vt* acheter (*qn*).

**brick** brique *f*.

**bricklayer** maçon *m*.

**bride** mariée *f*; **the b. and groom** les mariés *mpl*.

**bridegroom** marié *m*.

**bridesmaid** demoiselle *f* d'honneur.

**bridge** pont *m*.

**brief 1** *a* bref (*f* brève). **2** *vt* (*inform*) mettre au courant (**on** de). **3** *n* **briefs** (*underpants*) slip *m*.

**briefcase** serviette *f*.

**briefing** instructions *fpl*.

**briefly** *adv* (*quickly*) en vitesse.

**bright 1** *a* brillant; (*weather, room*) clair; (*clever*) intelligent; (*idea*) génial. **2** *adv* **b. and early** de bonne heure.

**brighten (up) 1** *vt* (*room*) égayer. **2** *vi* (*of weather*) s'éclaircir.

**brightly** *adv* avec éclat.

**brightness** éclat *m*.

**brilliance** éclat *m*; (*of person*) grande intelligence *f*.

**brilliant** *a* (*light*) éclatant; (*clever*) brillant.

**bring*** *vt* (*person, vehicle*) amener; (*thing*) apporter; (*to cause*) amener; **to b. to an end** mettre fin à; **to b. to mind** rappeler.

**bring about** provoquer.

**bring along** (*object*) emporter; (*person*) emmener.

**bring s.o. around** *or* **to** ranimer qn.

**bring back** (*person*) ramener; (*thing*) rapporter; (*memories*) rappeler.
**bring down** descendre (*qch*); (*overthrow*) faire tomber; (*reduce*) réduire.
**bring in** rentrer (*qch*); (*person*) faire entrer; (*introduce*) introduire.
**bring out** sortir (*qch*); (*person*) faire sortir; (*meaning*) faire ressortir; (*book*) publier; (*product*) lancer.
**bring together** (*reconcile*) réconcilier.
**bring up** monter (*qch*); (*child*) élever; (*subject*) mentionner.
**brink** bord *m*.
**brisk** *a* vif.
**briskly** *adv* (*to walk*) vite.
**bristle** poil *m*.
**British** *a* britannique; **the B.** les Britanniques *mpl*.
**British Isles** îles *fpl* Britanniques.
**Briton** Britannique *mf*.
**brittle** *a* fragile.
**broad** *a* (*wide*) large; (*outline*) général; **in b. daylight** en plein jour.
**broadcast 1** *vt** diffuser, retransmettre. **2** *n* émission *f*.
**broccoli** *n inv* brocolis *mpl*.
**brochure** brochure *f*.
**broke** (*pt de* **break**) *a* (*penniless*) fauché.
**broken** *pp de* **break**.
**broken-down** *a* (*machine*) déglingué.
**bronchitis** bronchite *f*.
**bronze** bronze *m*.
**brooch** broche *f*.
**brood 1** *n* couvée *f*. **2** *vi* méditer tristement (**over** sur).
**brook** ruisseau *m*.
**broom** balai *m*.
**broomstick** manche *m* à balai.
**brother** frère *m*.
**brother-in-law** (*pl* **brothers-in-law**) beau-frère *m*.
**brought** *pt* & *pp de* **bring**.
**brown 1** *a* brun; (*reddish*) marron; (*hair*) châtain; (*tanned*) bronzé. **2** *n* brun *m*; marron *m*.
**browse** *vi* (*in bookstore*) feuilleter des livres; (*in store*) regarder.
**bruise 1** *vt* **to b. one's knee**/*etc* se faire un bleu au genou/*etc*. **2** *n* bleu *m* (*pl* bleus), contusion *f*.
**bruised** *a* couvert de bleus.
**brunch** brunch *m*.
**brunette** brunette *f*.
**brush 1** *n* brosse *f*. **2** *vt* (*teeth, hair*) (se) brosser.
**brush aside** écarter.
**brush away** *or* **off** enlever.
**brush up (on)** (*language*) se remettre à.
**brutal** *a* brutal.
**brutality** brutalité *f*.
**brute** brute *f*.
**BS** *abbr* = **Bachelor of Science.**
**bubble 1** *n* bulle *f*. **2** *vi* bouillonner.
**bubble over** déborder.
**buck** *Fam* dollar *m*.
**bucket** seau *m*.
**buckle 1** *n* boucle *f*. **2** *vt* boucler. **3** *vti* (*warp*) voiler.
**buck up 1** *vt* remonter le moral à (*qn*). **2** *vi* (*become livelier*) reprendre du poil de la bête.
**bud 1** *n* (*of tree*) bourgeon *m*; (*of flower*) bouton *m*. **2** *vi* bourgeonner; pousser des boutons.
**Buddhist** *a* & *n* bouddhiste (*mf*).
**budge** *vi* bouger.
**budget** budget *m*.
**budget for** inscrire au budget.
**buffalo** (*pl* **-oes** *or* **-o**) buffle *m*; **(American) b.** bison *m*.
**buffet** (*table, meal*) buffet *m*.
**bug**[1] punaise *f*; (*any insect*) bestiole *f*; (*germ*) microbe *m*, virus *m*; (*in machine*) défaut *m*; (*in computer program*) erreur *f*; (*listening device*) micro *m* clandestin.
**bug**[2] *vt* (*annoy*) *Fam* embêter.
**bugle** clairon *m*.
**build 1** *n* (*of person*) carrure *f*. **2** *vt** construire; (*house*) construire, bâtir.
**builder** maçon *m*; (*contractor*) entrepreneur *m*.
**building** bâtiment *m*; (*apartments, offices*) immeuble *m*.
**build up 1** *vt* (*increase*) aug-

menter; (*collection*) constituer; (*business*) monter; (*speed*) prendre. **2** *vi* (*of tension, pressure*) augmenter.

**built-in** *a* (*closet*) encastré; (*part of machine*) incorporé.

**built-up area** agglomération *f*.

**bulb** (*of plant*) oignon *m*; (*of lamp*) ampoule *f*.

**bulge** renflement *m*.

**bulge (out)** se renfler.

**bulging** *a* renflé.

**bulk** *n inv* grosseur *f*; **the b. of** (*most*) la majeure partie de.

**bulky** *a* gros (*f* grosse).

**bull** taureau *m*.

**bulldog** bouledogue *m*.

**bulldozer** bulldozer *m*.

**bullet** balle *f* (*de revolver etc*).

**bulletin** bulletin *m*.

**bulletin board** tableau *m* d'affichage.

**bulletproof** *a* (*vest*) pare-balles *inv*; (*car*) blindé.

**bullfight** corrida *f*.

**bully 1** *n* (grosse) brute *f*. **2** *vt* brutaliser.

**bum** *Fam* (*loafer*) clochard, -arde *mf*; (*good-for-nothing*) propre *mf* à rien.

**bumblebee** bourdon *m*.

**bump 1** *vt* (*of car*) heurter; **to b. one's head/knee** se cogner la tête/le genou. **2** *n* (*impact*) choc *m*; (*jerk*) cahot *m*; (*on road, body*) bosse *f*.

**bumper** pare-chocs *m inv*.

**bump into** se cogner contre; (*of car*) rentrer dans; (*meet*) tomber sur.

**bumpy** *a* (*road, ride*) cahoteux.

**bun** (*roll*) petit pain *m* au lait.

**bunch** (*of flowers*) bouquet *m*; (*of keys*) trousseau *m*; (*of people*) bande *f*; **b. of grapes** grappe *f* de raisin.

**bundle 1** *n* paquet *m*; (*of papers*) liasse *f*. **2** *vt* (*put*) fourrer; (*push*) pousser (**into** dans).

**bundle up** (*dress warmly*) se couvrir.

**bungalow** bungalow *m*.

**bunk** couchette *f*; **b. beds** lits *mpl* superposés.

**bunny** *Fam* Jeannot *m* lapin.

**buoy** bouée *f*.

**burden 1** *n* fardeau *m*; (*of tax*) poids *m*. **2** *vt* accabler (**with** de).

**bureaucracy** bureaucratie *f*.

**bureaucrat** bureaucrate *mf*.

**burger** hamburger *m*.

**burglar** cambrioleur, -euse *mf*.

**burglar alarm** alarme *f* antivol.

**burglarize** *vt* cambrioler.

**burglary** cambriolage *m*.

**burgle** *vt* cambrioler.

**burial** enterrement *m*.

**burn 1** *n* brûlure *f*. **2** *vti** brûler; **burnt alive** brûlé vif.

**burn down 1** *vt* détruire par le feu. **2** *vi* être détruit par le feu.

**burner** (*of stove*) brûleur *m*.

**burning** *a* en feu; (*fire, light*) allumé.

**burp 1** *n* rot *m*. **2** *vi* roter.

**burst 1** *n* (*of laughter*) éclat *m*; (*of thunder*) coup *m*. **2** *vi** (*with force*) éclater; (*of bubble, balloon, boil, tyre*) crever.

**bursting** *a* (*full*) plein à craquer.

**burst into** (*room*) faire irruption dans; **to b. into tears** fondre en larmes.

**burst out to b. out laughing** éclater de rire.

**bury** *vt* enterrer; (*hide*) enfouir; (*plunge, absorb*) plonger.

**bus** (auto)bus *m*; (*long-distance*) (auto)car *m*.

**bush** buisson *m*.

**bushy** *a* broussailleux.

**business 1** *n* affaires *fpl*, commerce *m*; (*shop*) commerce *m*; (*task, concern, matter*) affaire *f*; **on b.** pour affaires; **it's your b. to . . .** c'est à vous de . . . ; **that's none of your b.!, mind your own b.!** ça ne vous regarde pas!. **2** *a* commercial; (*meeting, trip*) d'affaires; **b. hours** heures *fpl* de bureau; **b. card** carte *f* de visite.

**businessman** (*pl* **-men**) homme *m* d'affaires.

**businesswoman** (*pl* **-women**) femme *f* d'affaires.
**bus shelter** abribus *m*.
**bus station** gare *f* routière.
**bus stop** arrêt *m* d'autobus.
**bust 1** *n* (*sculpture*) buste *m*; (*woman's breasts*) poitrine *f*. **2** *a* **to go b.** (*bankrupt*) faire faillite.
**bustle 1** *vi* s'affairer. **2** *n* activité *f*.
**bustling** *a* (*street*) bruyant.
**busy** *a* occupé (**doing** à faire); (*active*) actif; (*day*) chargé; (*street*) animé; (*phone*) occupé; **to be b. doing** (*in the process of*) être en train de faire; **b. signal** sonnerie *f* 'occupé'.
**busybody to be a b.** faire la mouche du coche.
**but 1** *conj* mais. **2** *prep* (*except*) sauf; **b. for that/him** sans cela/lui. **3** *adv* (*only*) seulement.
**butcher** boucher *m*; **b.'s shop** boucherie *f*.
**butler** maître *m* d'hôtel.
**butt** (*of cigarette*) mégot *m*; (*buttocks*) *Fam* cul *m*.
**butter 1** *n* beurre *m*. **2** *vt* beurrer.
**buttercup** bouton-d'or *m*.
**butterfly** papillon *m*.
**butt in** interrompre.
**buttock** fesse *f*.
**button** bouton *m*; (*of phone*) touche *f*; (*bearing slogan*) pin's *m*.
**button (up)** (*garment*) boutonner.
**buttonhole** boutonnière *f*.
**buy 1** *vt** acheter (**from s.o.** à qn, **for s.o.** à *or* pour qn). **2** *n* **a good b.** une bonne affaire.
**buyer** acheteur, -euse *mf*.
**buzz 1** *vi* bourdonner. **2** *n* bourdonnement *m*.
**buzz off** *Fam* décamper.
**by 1** *prep* (*agent, manner*) par; **hit/***etc* **by** frappé/*etc* par; **surrounded/***etc* **by** entouré/*etc* de; **by doing** en faisant; **by sea** par mer; **by car** en voiture; **by bicycle** à bicyclette; **by day** de jour; **by oneself** tout seul. ▪ (*next to*) à côté de; (*near*) près de; **by the lake** au bord du lac. ▪ (*before in time*) avant; **by Monday** avant lundi; **by now** à cette heure-ci. ▪ (*amount*) à; **by weight** au poids; **paid by the hour** payé à l'heure. **2** *adv* **close by** tout près; **to go by, pass by** passer; **by and large** en gros.
**bye(-bye)!** *int Fam* salut!
**by-election** élection *f* partielle.
**bypass 1** *n* (*of highway*) bretelle *f* (de contournement); (*heart surgery*) pontage *m*. **2** *vt* contourner.
**bystander** spectateur, -trice *mf*.

## C

**cab** taxi *m*.
**cabbage** chou *m* (*pl* choux).
**cabin** (*on ship*) cabine *f*; (*hut*) cabane *f*.
**cabinet**[1] armoire *f*; (*for display*) vitrine *f*; **(filing) c.** classeur *m* (de bureau).
**cabinet**[2] (*in politics*) gouvernement *m*; **c. meeting** conseil *m* des ministres.
**cable** câble *m*; **c. television** la télévision par câble.
**cable car** téléphérique *m*; (*on tracks*) funiculaire *m*.
**cactus** (*pl* **-ti** *or* **-tuses**) cactus *m*.
**café** café(-restaurant) *m*.
**cafeteria** cafétéria *f*.
**caffeine** caféine *f*.
**cage** cage *f*.
**cake** gâteau *m*.
**calculate** *vti* calculer.
**calculation** calcul *m*.
**calculator** calculatrice *f*.
**calendar** calendrier *m*.
**calf** (*pl* **calves**) (*animal*) veau *m*; (*part of leg*) mollet *m*.
**call 1** *n* appel *m*; (*shout*) cri *m*; (*visit*) visite *f*; **(telephone) c.** communication *f*; **to make a c.** (*phone*) téléphoner (**to** à). **2** *vt* appeler; (*shout*) crier; (*attention*) attirer (**to** sur); **he's called David** il s'appelle David; **to c. a meeting** convoquer une assemblée; **to c. s.o. a liar**/*etc* qualifier qn de menteur/*etc*. **3** *vi*

appeler; (*cry out*) crier; (*visit*) passer.

**call back** *vti* rappeler.

**caller** visiteur, -euse *mf*; (*on phone*) correspondant, -ante *mf*.

**call for** *vt* (*require*) demander; (*summon*) appeler; (*collect*) passer prendre.

**call in** *vt* (*into room etc*) faire venir *or* entrer.

**calling card** (*for telephone*) télécarte *f*.

**call off** (*cancel*) annuler.

**call on** (*visit*) passer voir; **to c. on s.o. to do** inviter qn à faire; (*urge*) presser qn de faire.

**call out 1** *vt* (*shout*) crier; (*doctor*) appeler. **2** *vi* crier; **to c. out for** demander à haute voix.

**call up** (*phone*) appeler.

**calm 1** *a* calme; **keep c.!** du calme! **2** *n* calme *m*. **3** *vt* calmer.

**calm down 1** *vi* se calmer. **2** *vt* calmer.

**calmly** *adv* calmement.

**calorie** calorie *f*.

**camcorder** caméscope *m*.

**came** *pt de* **come**.

**camel** chameau *m*.

**camera** appareil photo *m*; (**TV** *or* **film**) **c.** caméra *f*.

**camp** camp *m*.

**camp (out)** camper.

**campaign** campagne *f*.

**camper** (*person*) campeur, -euse *mf*; (*recreational vehicle*) camping-car *m*; (*trailer*) caravane *f*.

**campfire** feu *m* de camp.

**camping** camping *m*; **c. site** camping *m*.

**campsite** camping *m*.

**can**[1] *v aux* (*pt* **could**) pouvoir; (*know how to*) savoir; **he couldn't help me** il ne pouvait pas m'aider; **she c. swim** elle sait nager; **you could be wrong** (*possibility*) tu as peut-être tort; **he can't be old** (*probability*) il ne doit pas être vieux; **c. I come in?** puis-je entrer?

**can**[2] (*for food*) boîte *f*; (*for drinks*) cannette *f*.

**Canadian** *a* & *n* canadien, -ienne (*mf*).

**canal** canal *m*.

**canary** canari *m*.

**cancel** *vt* (*flight, appointment etc*) annuler; (*goods, taxi*) décommander; (*train*) supprimer.

**cancellation** annulation *f*; (*of train*) suppression *f*.

**cancer** cancer *m*.

**candid** *a* franc (*f* franche).

**candidate** candidat, -ate *mf*.

**candle** bougie *f*; (*in church*) cierge *m*.

**candlestick** bougeoir *m*; (*tall*) chandelier *m*.

**candy** bonbon(s) *m*(*pl*).

**candystore** confiserie *f*.

**cane 1** *n* (*stick*) canne *f*; (*for punishing s.o.*) baguette *f*. **2** *vt* (*punish*) fouetter.

**cannabis** (*drug*) haschisch *m*.

**canned** *a* en boîte; **c. food** conserves *fpl*.

**cannibal** cannibale *mf*.

**canoe** canoë *m*.

**canoeing to go c.** faire du canoë.

**can-opener** ouvre-boîtes *m inv*.

**canopy** (*hood of baby carriage*) capote *f*; (*small roof*) auvent *m*.

**cantaloup(e)** (*melon*) cantaloup *m*.

**canteen** (*place*) cantine *f*; (*flask*) gourde *f*.

**canvas** toile *f*.

**canyon** canyon *m*.

**cap** (*hat*) casquette *f*; (*for shower*) bonnet *m*; (*of soldier*) képi *m*; (*of bottle, tube*) bouchon *m*; (*of milk or beer bottle*) capsule *f*; (*of pen*) capuchon *m*; (*of child's gun*) amorce *f*.

**capability** capacité *f*.

**capable** *a* (*person*) capable (**of sth** de qch, **of doing** de faire).

**capacity** (*of container*) capacité *f*; (*ability*) aptitude *f*; **in my c. as** en ma qualité de.

**cape** (*cloak*) cape *f*; (*of cyclist*) pèlerine *f*.

**capital** (*money*) capital *m*; **c. (city)** capitale *f*; **c. (letter)** majuscule *f*.
**capsize** *vti* chavirer.
**capsule** capsule *f*.
**captain** capitaine *m*.
**capture** *vt* (*person, town*) prendre.
**car** voiture *f*, auto *f*; (*of train*) wagon *m*; **c. radio** autoradio *m*.
**caramel** caramel *m*.
**caravan** caravane *f*; (*horse-drawn*) roulotte *f*.
**carbon** carbone *m*; **c. copy** double *m* (au carbone).
**carbon paper** (papier *m*) carbone *m*.
**carburetor** carburateur *m*.
**card** carte *f*; (*cardboard*) carton *m*; **(index) c.** fiche *f*; **to play cards** jouer aux cartes.
**cardboard** carton *m*.
**cardigan** gilet *m*.
**cardinal** *a* (*number, point*) cardinal.
**card index** fichier *m*.
**care 1** *vi* (*like*) aimer; **would you c. to try?** aimeriez-vous essayer?; **I don't c.** ça m'est égal; **who cares?** qu'est-ce que ça fait? **2** *n* (*attention*) soin(s) *m*(*pl*); (*protection*) garde *f*; (*anxiety*) souci *m*; **to take c. not to do** faire attention à ne pas faire; **to take c. to do** veiller à faire; **to take c. of** s'occuper de (*qch, qn*); (*keep safely*) garder (**for s.o.** pour qn); (*sick person*) prendre soin de; **to take c. of oneself** (*manage*) se débrouiller; (*keep healthy*) faire bien attention à soi.
**care about** se soucier de (*qch*); (*person*) avoir de la sympathie pour.
**career** carrière *f*.
**care for** (*a drink etc*) avoir envie de; **to c. for s.o.** s'occuper de qn; (*sick person*) soigner qn; (*like*) avoir de la sympathie pour qn; **I don't c. for it** je n'aime pas beaucoup ça.
**carefree** *a* insouciant.
**careful** *a* (*exact, thorough*) soigneux (**about** de); (*cautious*) prudent; **to be c. of** *or* **with** faire attention à.
**carefully** *adv* avec soin; (*cautiously*) prudemment.
**careless** *a* négligent; (*absent-minded*) étourdi.
**caretaker** gardien, -ienne *mf*.
**car ferry** ferry-boat *m*.
**cargo** (*pl* **-os**) cargaison *f*.
**caring** *a* (*loving*) aimant; (*understanding*) très humain.
**carnation** œillet *m*.
**carnival** carnaval *m* (*pl* -als).
**carol** chant *m* (de Noël).
**carp** (*fish*) carpe *f*.
**carpenter** charpentier *m*; (*for light woodwork*) menuisier *m*.
**carpentry** charpenterie *f*; menuiserie *f*.
**carpet** tapis *m*; (*fitted*) moquette *f*.
**carpeting (wall-to-wall) c.** moquette *f*.
**carpet sweeper** balai *m* mécanique.
**carriage** (*of train, horse-drawn*) voiture *f*.
**carrot** carotte *f*.
**carry** *vt* porter; (*goods*) transporter; (*sell*) stocker; (*in calculation*) retenir.
**carryall** fourre-tout *m inv*.
**carry away** *vt* emporter; **to get carried away** (*excited*) s'emballer.
**carry back** *vt* rapporter; (*person*) ramener.
**carry off** *vt* emporter; (*prize*) remporter; **to c. it off** réussir.
**carry on 1** *vt* continuer; (*conduct*) diriger; (*sustain*) soutenir. **2** *vi* continuer (**doing** à faire).
**carry out** *vt* (*plan, order, promise*) exécuter; (*repair, reform*) effectuer; (*duty*) accomplir; (*meal*) emporter.
**carry through** *vt* (*plan*) mener à bien.
**cart** (*horse-drawn*) charrette *f*; (*in supermarket*) caddie® *m*; **(serving) c.** table *f* roulante.
**cart (around)** *vt Fam* trimbal(l)er.
**cart away** *vt* emporter.

**carton** (*box*) carton *m*; (*of milk etc*) brique *f*; (*of cigarettes*) cartouche *f*; (*of cream*) pot *m*.
**cartoon** dessin *m* (humoristique); (*film*) dessin *m* animé; **(strip) c.** bande *f* dessinée.
**cartridge** cartouche *f*.
**carve** *vt* tailler (**out of** dans); (*initials etc*) graver.
**carve (up)** (*meat*) découper.
**car wash** (*machine*) lave-auto *m*.
**case**[1] (*instance, in hospital*) cas *m*; (*in court*) affaire *f*; **in any c.** en tout cas; **in c. it rains** pour le cas où il pleuvrait; **in c. of** en cas de; **(just) in c.** à tout hasard.
**case**[2] (*bag*) valise *f*; (*crate*) caisse *f*; (*for pen, glasses, camera, cigarettes*) étui *m*; (*for jewels*) coffret *m*.
**cash 1** *n* argent *m*; **to pay (in) c.** payer en espèces. **2** *vt* **to c. a check** encaisser un chèque; (*of bank*) payer un chèque.
**cash box** caisse *f*.
**cashier** caissier, -ière *mf*.
**cash machine** distributeur *m* de billets.
**cash price** prix *m* (au) comptant.
**cash register** caisse *f* enregistreuse.
**casino** (*pl* **-os**) casino *m*.
**casserole** cocotte *f*; (*stew*) ragoût *m* en cocotte.
**cassette** (*audio, video*) cassette *f*; (*film*) cartouche *f*.
**cassette player** lecteur *m* de cassettes.
**cassette recorder** magnétophone *m* à cassettes.
**cast**[1] (*actors*) acteurs *mpl*; (*list of actors*) distribution *f*; (*for broken bone*) plâtre *m*.
**cast**[2]* *vt* jeter; (*light, shadow*) projeter; (*doubt*) exprimer; **to c. a vote** voter.
**castle** château *m*; *Chess* tour *f*.
**castor** (*wheel*) roulette *f*.
**casual** *a* (*remark*) fait en passant; (*stroll*) sans but; (*offhand*) désinvolte; (*worker*) temporaire; (*work*) irrégulier; **c. clothes** vêtements *mpl* sport.
**casualty** (*dead*) mort *m*, morte *f*; (*wounded*) blessé, -ée *mf*.
**cat** chat *m*; (*female*) chatte *f*; **c. food** pâtée *f*.
**catalog** catalogue *m*.
**catapult** catapulte *f*.
**catastrophe** catastrophe *f*.
**catch* 1** *vt* (*ball, thief, illness, train etc*) attraper; (*grab, surprise*) prendre; (*understand*) saisir; (*attention*) attirer; (*on nail etc*) accrocher (**on** à); (*finger etc*) se prendre (**in** dans); **to c. fire** prendre feu; **to c. one's breath** (*rest*) reprendre haleine. **2** *vi* **her skirt (got) caught in the door** sa jupe s'est prise dans la porte. **3** *n* (*trick*) piège *m*; (*on door*) loquet *m*.
**catching** *a* contagieux.
**catch on** (*become popular*) prendre; (*understand*) saisir.
**catch s.o. out** prendre qn en défaut.
**catch up 1** *vt* **to c. s.o. up** rattraper qn. **2** *vi* se rattraper; **to c. up with s.o.** rattraper qn.
**category** catégorie *f*.
**cater for** *or* **to** (*need, taste*) satisfaire.
**caterpillar** chenille *f*.
**cathedral** cathédrale *f*.
**Catholic** *a* & *n* catholique (*mf*).
**cauliflower** chou-fleur *m*.
**cause 1** *n* cause *f*. **2** *vt* causer; **to c. sth to move**/*etc* faire bouger/*etc* qch.
**caution** (*care*) prudence *f*; (*warning*) avertissement *m*.
**cautious** *a* prudent.
**cautiously** *adv* prudemment.
**cave** caverne *f*.
**cave in** (*fall in*) s'effondrer.
**cavity** cavité *f*.
**CD** *abbr* (*compact disc*) CD *m*.
**cease** *vti* cesser (**doing** de faire).
**cease-fire** cessez-le-feu *m inv*.
**ceiling** plafond *m*.
**celebrate 1** *vt* fêter; (*mass*) célébrer. **2** *vi* faire la fête.

**celebration** fête *f.*
**celebrity** (*person*) célébrité *f.*
**celery** céleri *m.*
**cell** cellule *f.*
**cellar** cave *f.*
**cellophane**® cellophane® *f.*
**cement 1** *n* ciment *m.* **2** *vt* cimenter.
**cement mixer** bétonnière *f.*
**cemetery** cimetière *m.*
**cent** (*coin*) cent *m.*
**center** centre *m.*
**centigrade** *a* centigrade.
**centimeter** centimètre *m.*
**centipede** mille-pattes *m inv.*
**central** *a* central.
**century** siècle *m.*
**ceramic** *a* (*tile*) de céramique.
**cereal** céréale *f.*
**ceremony** cérémonie *f.*
**certain** *a* (*sure, particular*) certain; **she's c. to come** c'est certain qu'elle viendra; **I'm not c. what to do** je ne sais pas très bien ce qu'il faut faire; **to be c. of sth/that** être certain de qch/que; **to make c. of** (*fact*) s'assurer de; (*seat etc*) s'assurer.
**certainly** *adv* certainement; (*yes*) bien sûr.
**certainty** certitude *f.*
**certificate** certificat *m*; (*from university*) diplôme *m.*
**certified** *a* certifié, agréé, **C. Public Accountant (CPA)** expert-comptable *m.*
**certify** *vt* (*document etc*) certifier.
**chain** (*of rings, mountains*) chaîne *f.*
**chain (up)** (*dog*) mettre à l'attache; (*person*) enchaîner.
**chain saw** tronçonneuse *f.*
**chain store** magasin *m* à succursales multiples.
**chair** chaise *f*; (*armchair*) fauteuil *m.*
**chair lift** télésiège *m.*
**chairman** (*pl* **-men**) président, -ente *mf.*
**chalet** chalet *m.*
**chalk 1** *n* craie *f.* **2** *vti* écrire à la craie.
**challenge 1** *n* défi *m*; (*task*) challenge *m*, gageure *f.* **2** *vt* défier (**s.o. to do** qn de faire); (*dispute*) contester.
**challenging** *a* (*job*) exigeant.
**chamber c. of commerce** chambre *f* de commerce.
**chamois** (*leather*) peau *f* de chamois.
**champagne** champagne *m.*
**champion** champion, -onne *mf.*
**championship** championnat *m.*
**chance 1** *n* (*luck*) hasard *m*; (*possibility*) chances *fpl*; (*opportunity*) occasion *f*; **by c.** par hasard. **2** *vt* **to c. it** risquer le coup.
**chandelier** lustre *m.*
**change 1** *n* changement *m*; (*money*) monnaie *f*; **for a c.** pour changer; **it makes a c. from** ça change de; **a c. of clothes** des vêtements de rechange. **2** *vt* changer; (*exchange*) échanger (**for** contre); (*money*) changer; **to c. trains/one's skirt/***etc* changer de train/de jupe/*etc*; **to c. the subject** changer de sujet. **3** *vi* changer; (*change clothes*) se changer.
**changeable** *a* changeant.
**change over** *vi* passer (**from** de, **to** à).
**changeover** passage *m* (**from** de, **to** à).
**changing room** vestiaire *m.*
**channel** (*on television*) chaîne *f*; (*for inquiry etc*) voie *f*; **the English C.** la Manche; **to go through the normal channels** passer par la voie normale.
**chant 1** *vt* (*slogan*) scander. **2** *vi* (*of demonstrators*) scander des slogans.
**chaos** chaos *m.*
**chaotic** *a* sens dessus dessous.
**chapel** chapelle *f.*
**chapped** *a* gercé.
**chapter** chapitre *m.*
**char** *vt* carboniser; (*scorch*) brûler légèrement.
**character** caractère *m*; (*in book,*

*film*) personnage *m*; (*strange person*) numéro *m*.

**characteristic** *a* & *n* caractéristique (*f*).

**charge**[1] **1** *n* (*cost*) prix *m*; **charges** (*expenses*) frais *mpl*; **there's a c. (for it)** c'est payant; **free of c.** gratuit. **2** *vt* (*amount*) demander (**for** pour); (*person*) faire payer.

**charge**[2] **1** *n* (*in court*) accusation *f*; (*care*) garde *f*; **to take c. of** prendre en charge; **to be in c. of** (*child*) avoir la garde de; (*office*) être responsable de; **the person in c.** le *or* la responsable. **2** *vt* (*battery, soldiers*) charger; (*accuse*) accuser (**with** de). **3** *vi* (*rush*) se précipiter.

**charity** (*society*) fondation *f* charitable; **to give to c.** faire la charité.

**charm 1** *n* charme *m*; (*trinket*) amulette *f*. **2** *vt* charmer.

**charming** *a* charmant.

**chart** (*map*) carte *f*; (*graph*) graphique *m*; **(pop) charts** hit-parade *m*.

**charter flight** charter *m*.

**chase 1** *n* poursuite *f*. **2** *vt* poursuivre.

**chase after s.o./sth** courir après qn/qch, poursuivre qn/qch.

**chase s.o. away** *or* **off** chasser qn.

**chasm** *n* abîme *m*, gouffre *m*.

**chassis** (*of vehicle*) châssis *m*.

**chat 1** *n* petite conversation *f*; **to have a c.** bavarder. **2** *vi* causer.

**chatter 1** *vi* (*of person*) bavarder; **his teeth are chattering** il claque des dents. **2** *n* bavardage *m*.

**chatterbox** bavard, -arde *mf*.

**chatty** *a* bavard.

**chauffeur** chauffeur *m* (de maître).

**cheap 1** *a* bon marché *inv*; (*rate*) réduit; (*worthless*) sans valeur; **cheaper** meilleur marché. **2** *adv* (*to buy*) (à) bon marché.

**cheaply** *adv* (à) bon marché.

**cheat 1** *vt* tromper; **to c. s.o. out of sth** escroquer qch à qn. **2** *vi* (*at games etc*) tricher.

**cheater** *n* tricheur, -euse *mf*.

**check**[1] **1** *vt* (*examine*) vérifier; (*inspect*) contrôler; (*stop*) arrêter; (*baggage*) mettre à la consigne. **2** *vi* vérifier. **3** *n* vérification *f*; (*inspection*) contrôle *m*; *Chess* échec *m*; (*mark*) = croix *f*; (*receipt*) reçu *m*; (*bill in restaurant*) addition *f*; (*in banking*) chèque *m*.

**checkbook** carnet *m* de chèques.

**checked** *or* **checkered** *a* à carreaux.

**checkers** *npl* jeu *m* de dames.

**check-in** enregistrement *m* (des bagages).

**check in 1** *vt* (*luggage*) enregistrer. **2** *vi* (*at hotel*) signer le registre; (*arrive*) arriver; (*at airport*) se présenter (à l'enregistrement).

**checkmate** *Chess* échec et mat *m*.

**check off** (*names on list etc*) cocher.

**check on sth** vérifier qch.

**checkout** (*in supermarket*) caisse *f*.

**check out 1** *vt* confirmer. **2** *vi* (*at hotel*) régler sa note.

**checkup** bilan *m* de santé.

**check up** *vi* vérifier.

**cheddar** (*cheese*) cheddar *m*.

**cheek** joue *f*; (*impudence*) culot *m*.

**cheeky** *a* effronté.

**cheer 1** *n* **cheers** acclamations *fpl*; **cheers!** *Fam* à votre santé! **2** *vt* (*applaud*) acclamer. **3** *vi* applaudir.

**cheerful** *a* gai.

**cheering** acclamations *fpl*.

**cheer up 1** *vt* donner du courage à (*qn*); (*amuse*) égayer. **2** *vi* prendre courage; s'égayer; **c. up!** (du) courage!

**cheese** fromage *m*.

**cheeseburger** cheeseburger *m*.

**cheesecake** tarte *f* au fromage blanc.

**chef** (*cook*) chef *m*.

**chemical 1** *a* chimique. **2** *n* produit *m* chimique.

**chemist** chimiste *mf*.

**chemistry** chimie *f*.

**cherry** cerise *f*.

**cherry brandy** cherry *m*.
**chess** échecs *mpl*.
**chessboard** échiquier *m*.
**chest** (*part of body*) poitrine *f*; (*box*) coffre *m*; **c. of drawers** commode *f*.
**chestnut** châtaigne *f*.
**chew 1** *vt* **to c. (up)** mâcher. **2** *vi* mastiquer.
**chewing gum** chewing-gum *m*.
**chick** poussin *m*.
**chicken 1** *n* poulet *m*. **2** *a* (*cowardly*) *Fam* froussard.
**chicken out** *vi Fam* se dégonfler.
**chickenpox** varicelle *f*.
**chickpea** pois *m* chiche.
**chicory** (*for salad*) endive *f*.
**chief 1** *n* chef *m*; **in c.** en chef. **2** *a* principal.
**chiefly** *adv* principalement.
**chilblain** engelure *f*.
**child** (*pl* **children**) enfant *mf*.
**child care** (*for working parents*) crèches *fpl* et garderies *fpl*.
**childhood** enfance *f*.
**childish** *a* puéril.
**chili** (*pl* **-ies**) piment *m* (de Cayenne).
**chill 1** *n* froid *m*; (*illness*) refroidissement *m*; **to catch a c.** prendre froid. **2** *vt* (*wine, melon*) faire rafraîchir; (*meat*) réfrigérer.
**chilled** *a* (*wine*) frais.
**chilly** *a* froid; **it's c.** il fait (un peu) froid.
**chime** *vi* (*of clock*) sonner.
**chimney** cheminée *f*.
**chimneypot** tuyau *m* de cheminée.
**chimpanzee** chimpanzé *m*.
**chin** menton *m*.
**china 1** *n inv* porcelaine *f*. **2** *a* en porcelaine.
**Chinese 1** *a* & *n inv* chinois, -oise (*mf*). **2** *n* (*language*) chinois *m*.
**chip 1** *vt* (*cup etc*) ébrécher; (*paint*) écailler. **2** *n* (*break*) ébréchure *f*; (*microchip*) puce *f*; (*counter*) jeton *m*; **(potato) chips** chips *mpl*.
**chiropodist** pédicure *mf*.
**chisel** ciseau *m*.
**chives** *npl* ciboulette *f*.
**chock-a-block** *a Fam* archiplein.
**chocolate 1** *n* chocolat *m*; **milk c.** chocolat au lait; **bittersweet c.** chocolat à croquer. **2** *a* (*cake*) au chocolat.
**choice** choix *m*.
**choir** chœur *m*.
**choke 1** *vt* (*person*) étrangler; (*clog*) boucher. **2** *vi* s'étrangler (**on** avec).
**cholesterol** cholestérol *m*.
**choose* 1** *vt* choisir; **to c. to do** (*decide*) juger bon de faire. **2** *vi* choisir.
**choos(e)y** *a* difficile.
**chop 1** *n* (*of lamb, pork*) côtelette *f*. **2** *vt* couper (à la hache); (*food*) hacher.
**chop down** (*tree*) abattre.
**chop off** (*branch, finger etc*) couper.
**chopper** hachoir *m*.
**chopsticks** baguettes *fpl*.
**chop up** couper en morceaux.
**chord** (*in music*) accord *m*.
**chore** travail *m* (routinier); (*unpleasant*) corvée *f*; **chores** travaux *mpl* ménagers.
**chorus** (*of song*) refrain *m*.
**christen** *vt* baptiser.
**christening** baptême *m*.
**Christian** *a* & *n* chrétien, -ienne (*mf*).
**Christmas 1** *n* Noël *m*; **Merry C.** Joyeux Noël; **C. Eve** la veille de Noël. **2** *a* (*tree etc*) de Noël.
**chrome** chrome *m*.
**chrysanthemum** chrysanthème *m*.
**chubby** *a* potelé.
**chuck** *vt Fam* (*throw*) jeter; (*job etc*) laisser tomber.
**chuck (out)** (*old clothes etc*) *Fam* balancer.
**chum** *Fam* copain *m*, copine *f*.
**chunk** (gros) morceau *m*.
**church** église *f*.
**chute** (*for refuse*) vide-ordures *m inv*; (*in pool*) toboggan *m*.
**cider** cidre *m*.

**cigar** cigare *m*.
**cigarette** cigarette *f*.
**cigarette butt** mégot *m*.
**cigarette lighter** briquet *m*.
**cinnamon** cannelle *f*.
**circle 1** *n* cercle *m*; **circles** (*political etc*) milieux *mpl*. **2** *vt* faire le tour de; (*word*) encadrer. **3** *vi* (*of aircraft etc*) décrire des cercles.
**circuit** (*electrical path, in sports etc*) circuit *m*.
**circular 1** *a* circulaire. **2** *n* (*letter*) circulaire *f*; (*advertisement*) prospectus *m*.
**circulate 1** *vi* (*of blood etc*) circuler. **2** *vt* (*pass around*) faire circuler.
**circulation** (*of newspaper*) tirage *m*.
**circumference** circonférence *f*.
**circumstance** circonstance *f*; **in** *or* **under no circumstances** en aucun cas.
**circus** cirque *m*.
**citizen** citoyen, -enne *mf*; (*of town*) habitant, -ante *mf*.
**city** (grande) ville *f*.
**city council** conseil *m* municipal.
**city hall** hôtel *m* de ville.
**civil** *a* civil.
**civilian** *a* & *n* civil, -ile (*mf*).
**civilization** civilization *f*.
**civil servant** fonctionnaire *mf*.
**civil service** fonction *f* publique.
**claim 1** *vt* réclamer; **to c. that** prétendre que. **2** *n* (*demand*) revendication *f*; (*statement*) affirmation *f*; (*right*) droit *m* (**to** à); **(insurance) c.** demande *f* d'indemnité.
**clam** (*shellfish*) palourde *f*.
**clap** *vti* applaudir; **to c. (one's hands)** battre des mains.
**clapping** applaudissements *mpl*.
**clarinet** clarinette *f*.
**clash 1** *vi* (*of plates*) s'entrechoquer; (*of interests*) se heurter; (*of colors*) jurer (**with** avec); (*of people*) se bagarrer; (*coincide*) tomber en même temps (**with** que). **2** *n* (*noise*) choc *m*; (*of interests*) conflit *m*.
**clasp 1** *vt* serrer. **2** *n* (*fastener*) fermoir *m*; (*of belt*) boucle *f*.
**class 1** *n* classe *f*; (*lesson*) cours *m*. **2** *vt* classer.
**classic 1** *a* classique. **2** *n* (*work etc*) classique *m*.
**classical** *a* classique.
**classmate** camarade *mf* de classe.
**classroom** (salle *f* de) classe *f*.
**clause** (*in sentence*) proposition *f*.
**claw** griffe *f*; (*of lobster*) pince *f*.
**clay** argile *f*.
**clean 1** *a* (*not dirty*) propre; (*clear-cut*) net (*f* nette). **2** *adv* (*utterly*) complètement; (*to break, cut*) net. **3** *vt* nettoyer; (*wash*) laver; (*wipe*) essuyer. **4** *vi* faire le nettoyage.
**clean copy** copie *f* au propre.
**cleaner (dry) c.** teinturier, -ière *mf*.
**cleaning** nettoyage *m*; (*housework*) ménage *m*.
**cleaning woman** femme *f* de ménage.
**cleanly** *adv* (*to break, cut*) net.
**clean out** (*room etc*) nettoyer; (*empty*) vider.
**cleansing cream** crème *f* démaquillante.
**clean up 1** *vt* nettoyer. **2** *vi* faire le nettoyage.
**clear 1** *a* (*sky, outline, sound, thought etc*) clair; (*glass*) transparent; (*road*) libre; (*profit*) net; (*obvious*) évident, clair; **to be c. of** (*free of*) être libre de; **to make oneself c.** se faire comprendre. **2** *adv* **to keep** *or* **steer c. of** se tenir à l'écart de; **to get c. of** s'éloigner de. **3** *vt* (*path, table*) débarrasser; (*fence*) franchir; (*accused person*) disculper; (*check*) faire passer (sur un compte); (*through customs*) dédouaner; **to c. one's throat** s'éclaircir la gorge. **4** *vi* (*of weather*) s'éclaircir; (*of fog*) se dissiper.
**clearance** (*sale*) soldes *mpl*; (*space*) dégagement *m*.
**clear away** (*remove*) enlever.
**clear-cut** *a* net (*f* nette).
**clearly** *adv* clairement; (*obviously*) évidemment.

**clear out 1** *vt* vider; (*clean*) nettoyer; (*remove*) enlever. **2** *vi* (*go*) *Fam* décamper.
**clear up 1** *vt* (*mystery*) éclaircir. **2** *vti* (*tidy*) ranger.
**cleat** (*sports shoe*) crampon *m*.
**clementine** clémentine *f*.
**clench** *vt* (*fist*) serrer.
**clerical** *a* (*job*) d'employé; (*work*) de bureau.
**clerk** employé, -ée *mf* (de bureau); (*in store*) vendeur, -euse *mf*.
**clever** *a* intelligent; (*smart*) astucieux; (*skillful*) habile; (*machine, book etc*) ingénieux.
**click 1** *n* déclic *m*. **2** *vi* (*of machine etc*) faire un déclic.
**client** client, -ente *mf*.
**cliff** falaise *f*.
**climate** climat *m*.
**climax** point *m* culminant.
**climb (over)** (*wall*) escalader.
**climb (up) 1** *vt* (*stairs, steps*) monter; (*hill, mountain*) gravir; (*tree, ladder*) monter à. **2** *vi* monter.
**climb down 1** *vt* (*wall, tree, hill*) descendre de. **2** *vi* descendre (**from** de).
**climber** (*mountaineer*) alpiniste *mf*.
**cling*** *vi* se cramponner; (*stick*) adhérer (**to** à).
**clinic** (*private*) clinique *f*; (*public*) centre *m* médical.
**clip 1** *vt* couper; (*hedge*) tailler; (*ticket*) poinçonner; (*attach*) attacher. **2** *n* (*for paper*) trombone *m*; (*of brooch, of cyclist, for hair*) pince *f*.
**clip on** *vt* attacher (**to** à).
**clippers** *npl* (*for hair*) tondeuse *f*; (*for nails*) coupe-ongles *m inv*.
**clipping** (*newspaper article*) coupure *f*.
**cloak** (grande) cape *f*.
**cloakroom** vestiaire *m*.
**clock** horloge *f*; (*small*) pendule *f*; **around the c.** vingt-quatre heures sur vingt-quatre.
**clockwise** *adv* dans le sens des aiguilles d'une montre.
**close**[1] **1** *a* (*place, relative etc*) proche (**to** de); (*collaboration, connection*) étroit; (*friend*) intime; (*atmosphere*) lourd. **2** *adv* **c. (by)** (tout) près; **c. to** près de; **c. behind** juste derrière.
**close**[2] **1** *n* (*end*) fin *f*. **2** *vt* (*door, shop etc*) fermer; (*road*) barrer; (*deal*) conclure. **3** *vi* se fermer; (*of shop*) fermer.
**close down** *vti* (*for good*) fermer (définitivement).
**close in** *vi* approcher.
**closely** *adv* (*to follow, guard*) de près; (*to listen*) attentivement.
**closet** (*for linens, clothes etc*) placard *m*; (*for clothing only*) penderie *f*.
**close up 1** *vt* fermer. **2** *vi* (*of shopkeeper*) fermer; (*of line of people*) se rapprocher.
**closing time** heure *f* de fermeture.
**clot 1** *n* (*of blood*) caillot *m*. **2** *vi* se coaguler.
**cloth** tissu *m*; (*for dusting*) chiffon *m*; (*for dishes*) torchon *m*; (*tablecloth*) nappe *f*.
**clothes** *npl* vêtements *mpl*; **to put one's c. on** s'habiller.
**clothes brush** brosse *f* à habits.
**clothes line** corde *f* à linge.
**clothes pin** pince *f* à linge.
**clothing** vêtements *mpl*; **an article of c.** un vêtement.
**clothing store** magasin *m* d'habillement.
**cloud** nuage *m*.
**cloud over** (*of sky*) se couvrir.
**cloudy** *a* (*weather*) couvert.
**clove c. of garlic** gousse *f* d'ail.
**clown** clown *m*.
**club** (*society, stick for golf*) club *m*; **club(s)** (*at cards*) trèfle *m*.
**club soda** eau *f* gazeuse.
**clue** indice *m*; (*of crossword*) définition *f*; **I don't have a c.** *Fam* je n'en ai pas la moindre idée.
**clumsy** *a* maladroit; (*tool*) peu commode.
**clunker** (*car*) *Fam* t

**clutch 1** *vt* (*hold*) serrer; (*grasp*) saisir. **2** *n* (*in vehicle*) embrayage *m*; (*pedal*) pédale *f* d'embrayage.
**clutter up** (*room etc*) encombrer (**with** de).
**cm** *abbr* (*centimeter*) cm.
**Co** *abbr* (*company*) Cie.
**coach 1** *n* (*part of train*) voiture *f*; (*bus*) autocar *m*. **2** *vt* (*pupil*) donner des leçons (particulières) à.
**coal** charbon *m*.
**coalmine** mine *f* de charbon.
**coarse** *a* (*person, fabric*) grossier.
**coast** côte *f*.
**coat 1** *n* manteau *m*; (*jacket*) veste *f*; (*of animal*) pelage *m*; (*of paint*) couche *f*. **2** *vt* couvrir (**with** de).
**coathanger** cintre *m*.
**coating** couche *f*.
**cob corn on the c.** épi *m* de maïs.
**cobbled** *a* pavé.
**cobweb** toile *f* d'araignée.
**cocaine** cocaïne *f*.
**cock** (*fowl*) coq *m*.
**cockle** (*shellfish*) coque *f*.
**cockpit** poste *m* de pilotage.
**cockroach** (*insect*) cafard *m*.
**cocktail** cocktail *m*; **fruit c.** macédoine *f* (de fruits); **shrimp c.** crevettes *fpl* à la mayonnaise.
**cocktail party** cocktail *m*.
**cocoa** cacao *m*.
**coconut** noix *f* de coco.
**cod** morue *f*.
**code** code *m*.
**cod-liver oil** huile *f* de foie de morue.
**co-educational** *a* (*school etc*) mixte.
**coffee** café *m*; **c. with milk** café *m* au lait; (*in restaurant*) (café *m*) crème *m*.
**coffee bar** café *m*.
**coffee break** pause-café *f*.
**coffeepot** cafetière *f*.
**coffee table** table *f* basse.
**coffin** cercueil *m*.
**cognac** cognac *m*.
**coil 1** *n* (*of wire, rope etc*) rouleau *m*. **2** *vt* enrouler.
**coin** pièce *f* (de monnaie).
**coin bank** tirelire *f*.
**coincide** *vi* coïncider (**with** avec).
**coincidence** coïncidence *f*.
**coke** (*Coca-Cola*®) coca *m*.
**colander** passoire *f*.
**cold 1** *n* froid *m*; (*illness*) rhume *m*; **to catch c.** prendre froid. **2** *a* froid; **to be** *or* **feel c.** avoir froid; **my hands are c.** j'ai froid aux mains; **it's c.** (*of weather*) il fait froid; **to get c.** (*of weather*) se refroidir; (*of food*) refroidir.
**cold cuts** assiette *f* anglaise.
**coldness** froideur *f*.
**coleslaw** salade *f* de chou cru.
**collaborate** *vi* collaborer (**on** à).
**collaboration** collaboration *f*.
**collapse 1** *vi* (*of person, building*) s'effondrer. **2** *n* effondrement *m*.
**collar** col *m*; (*of dog*) collier *m*.
**collarbone** clavicule *f*.
**colleague** collègue *mf*.
**collect 1** *vt* (*pick up*) ramasser; (*gather*) rassembler; (*taxes*) percevoir; (*rent*) encaisser; (*stamps etc*) collectionner; (*fetch*) (passer) prendre; **to c. (money)** (*in street, church*) quêter. **2** *vi* (*of dust*) s'accumuler. **3** *adv* **to call c.** téléphoner en PCV.
**collection** (*group of objects*) collection *f*; (*of poems etc*) recueil *m*; (*of money in church etc*) quête *f*; (*of mail*) levée *f*.
**collector** (*of stamps etc*) collectionneur, -euse *mf*.
**college** université *f*.
**collide** *vi* entrer en collision (**with** avec).
**collision** collision *f*.
**colloquial** *a* (*word etc*) familier.
**cologne** eau *f* de Cologne.
**colon** *Grammar* deux-points *m inv*.
**colonel** colonel *m*.
**colony** colonie *f*.
**color 1** *n* couleur *f*. **2** *a* (*photo, TV set*) en couleurs. **3** *vt* colorer.
**color (in)** (*drawing*) colorier.

**colored** *a* (*pencil*) de couleur.
**colorful** *a* coloré; (*person*) pittoresque.
**coloring book** album *m* de coloriages.
**column** colonne *f*; (*newspaper feature*) chronique *f*.
**coma** coma *m*; **in a c.** dans le coma.
**comb 1** *n* peigne *m*. **2** *vt* **to c. one's hair** se peigner.
**combination** combinaison *f*.
**combine 1** *vt* joindre (**with** à); **our combined efforts achieved a result** en joignant nos efforts nous avons obtenu un résultat. **2** *vi* s'unir.
**come*** *vi* venir (**from** de, **to** à); **to c. first** (*in race*) arriver premier; (*in exam*) être le premier; **to c. close to doing** faillir faire.
**come about** (*happen*) se faire, arriver.
**come across** (*thing, person*) tomber sur.
**come along** venir (**with** avec); (*progress*) avancer; **c. along!** allons!
**come apart** (*of two objects*) se séparer.
**come around** (*visit*) venir; (*of date*) revenir; (*regain consciousness*) revenir à soi.
**come away** (*leave, come off*) partir.
**come back** revenir; (*return home*) rentrer.
**come by** obtenir; (*find*) trouver.
**comedian** (acteur *m*) comique *m*, actrice *f* comique.
**come down** descendre; (*of rain, price*) tomber.
**comedy** comédie *f*.
**come for sth/s.o.** venir chercher qch/qn.
**come forward** s'avancer; (*volunteer*) se présenter; **to c. forward with sth** offrir qch.
**come in** entrer; (*of tide*) monter; (*of train*) arriver.
**come into** (*room etc*) entrer dans; (*money*) hériter de.
**come off 1** *vi* (*of button etc*) se détacher; (*succeed*) réussir. **2** *vt* (*fall from*) tomber de; (*get down from*) descendre de.
**come on** (*progress*) avancer; **c. on!** (*reproving, encouraging*) allons!, allez!
**come out** sortir; (*of sun, book*) paraître; (*of stain*) partir.
**come over 1** *vi* (*visit*) venir. **2** *vt* (*of feeling*) saisir (*qn*).
**come through 1** *vi* (*survive*) s'en tirer. **2** *vt* (*crisis etc*) se tirer indemne de.
**come to** (*regain consciousness*) revenir à soi; (*amount to*) revenir à; (*a decision*) parvenir à.
**come under** (*heading*) être classé sous; (*s.o.'s influence*) tomber sous.
**come up** (*rise*) monter; (*of plant*) sortir; (*of question, job*) se présenter.
**come up against** (*wall, problem*) se heurter à.
**come up to** (*reach*) arriver jusqu'à.
**come up with** (*idea, money*) trouver.
**comfort 1** *n* confort *m*; (*consolation*) réconfort *m*. **2** *vt* consoler.
**comfortable** *a* (*chair etc*) confortable; (*rich*) aisé; **he's c.** (*in chair etc*) il est à l'aise; **make yourself c.** mets-toi à l'aise.
**comforter** (*quilt*) édredon *m*, couette *f*.
**comic 1** *a* comique. **2** *n* (*magazine*) bande *f* dessinée.
**comic strip** bande *f* dessinée.
**comings** *npl* **c. and goings** allées *fpl* et venues.
**comma** virgule *f*.
**command 1** *vt* (*order*) commander (**s.o. to do** à qn de faire); (*ship etc*) commander. **2** *n* (*order*) ordre *m*; (*mastery*) maîtrise *f* (**of** de); **to be in c. (of)** (*army etc*) commander; (*situation*) être maître (de).
**commemorate** *vt* commémorer.
**commence** *vti* commencer (**doing** à faire).
**comment** commentaire *m*.

**commentary** commentaire *m*; **(live) c.** reportage *m*.
**commentator** reporter *m*.
**comment on** (*event etc*) commenter.
**commerce** commerce *m*.
**commercial 1** *a* commercial. **2** *n* **commercial(s)** (*on television*) publicité *f*.
**commission** (*fee, group*) commission *f*.
**commit** *vt* (*crime*) commettre; **to c. suicide** se suicider.
**commitment** (*promise*) engagement *m*.
**committee** comité *m*.
**commodity** produit *m*.
**common** *a* (*shared, frequent etc*) commun; **in c.** (*shared*) en commun (**with** avec); **in c. with** (*like*) comme.
**commonly** *adv* (*generally*) en général.
**commonplace** *a* banal (*mpl* banals).
**common room** salle *f* commune.
**common sense** sens *m* commun.
**commotion** agitation *f*.
**communal** *a* (*bathroom etc*) commun.
**communicate** *vti* communiquer.
**communication** communication *f*.
**communion** communion *f*.
**community** communauté *f*.
**community center** centre *m* socio-culturel.
**commute** *vi* faire la navette (**to work** pour se rendre à son travail).
**commuter** banlieusard, -arde *mf*.
**commuting** trajets *mpl* journaliers.
**compact 1** *a* compact. **2** *n* (*for face powder*) poudrier *m*.
**compact disc** *or* **disk** disque *m* compact.
**companion** compagnon *m*.
**company** (*being with others, firm*) compagnie *f*; (*guests*) invités, -ées *mfpl*; **to keep s.o. c.** tenir compagnie à qn.
**comparatively** *adv* relativement.
**compare** *vt* comparer (**with, to** à); **compared to** *or* **with** en comparaison de.
**comparison** comparaison *f* (**with** avec).
**compartment** compartiment *m*.
**compass** (*for direction*) boussole *f*; (*on ship*) compas *m*; **(pair of) compasses** (*for drawing etc*) compas *m*.
**compatible** *a* compatible.
**compel** *vt* forcer, contraindre (**to do** à faire).
**compensate 1** *vt* **to c. s.o.** dédommager qn (**for** de). **2** *vi* compenser (**for sth** qch).
**compensation** dédommagement *m*.
**compete** *vi* (*take part*) concourir (**in** à, **for** pour); **to c. (with s.o.)** rivaliser (avec qn); (*in business*) faire concurrence (à qn).
**competent** *a* compétent (**to do** pour faire).
**competently** *adv* avec compétence.
**competition** (*rivalry*) compétition *f*; **a c.** (*contest*) un concours; (*in sports*) une compétition.
**competitive** *a* (*price etc*) compétitif; (*person*) aimant la compétition.
**competitor** concurrent, -ente *mf*.
**compile** *vt* (*dictionary*) rédiger; (*list*) dresser.
**complain** *vi* se plaindre (**of, about** de; **that** que).
**complaint** plainte *f*; (*in shop etc*) réclamation *f*; (*illness*) maladie *f*.
**complete 1** *a* (*total*) complet; (*finished*) achevé; **a c. idiot** un parfait imbécile. **2** *vt* compléter; (*finish*) achever; (*a form*) remplir.
**completely** *adv* complètement.
**complex 1** *a* complexe. **2** *n* (*feeling, buildings*) complexe *m*.
**complexion** (*of the face*) teint *m*.
**complicate** *vt* compliquer.
**complicated** *a* compliqué.

**complication** complication *f.*
**compliment** compliment *m.*
**comply** *vi* obéir (**with** à).
**compose** *vt* composer; **to c. oneself** se calmer.
**composed** *a* calme.
**composer** compositeur, -trice *mf.*
**composition** (*school essay*) rédaction *f.*
**compound** (*substance, word*) composé *m.*
**comprehensive** *a* complet; (*insurance*) tous risques.
**comprise** *vt* comprendre.
**compromise** compromis *m.*
**compulsive** *a* (*smoker etc*) invétéré; **c. liar** mythomane *mf.*
**compulsory** *a* obligatoire.
**computer** ordinateur *m*; **c. technician** opérateur, -trice *mf* sur ordinateur.
**computerized** *a* informatisé.
**computer science** informatique *f.*
**con** *vt* (*deceive*) *Slang* escroquer.
**conceal** *vt* dissimuler (**from s.o.** à qn); (*plan*) tenir secret.
**conceited** *a* vaniteux.
**conceivable** *a* concevable.
**concentrate 1** *vt* concentrer. **2** *vi* se concentrer (**on** sur); **to c. on doing** s'appliquer à faire.
**concentration** concentration *f.*
**concern 1** *vt* concerner; **to be concerned with/about** s'occuper de/s'inquiéter de. **2** *n* (*matter*) affaire *f*; (*anxiety*) inquiétude *f*; **his c. for** son souci de; (**business**) **c.** entreprise *f.*
**concerned** *a* (*anxious*) inquiet.
**concerning** *prep* en ce qui concerne.
**concert** concert *m.*
**concise** *a* concis.
**conclude 1** *vt* conclure; **to c. that** conclure que. **2** *vi* se terminer (**with** par); (*of speaker*) conclure.
**conclusion** conclusion *f.*
**concrete 1** *n* béton *m*. **2** *a* en béton; (*real*) concret.
**condemn** *vt* condamner (*qn*) (**to** à).
**condensation** (*mist*) buée *f.*
**condition** condition *f*; **on c. that one does** à condition de faire, à condition que l'on fasse.
**conditioner** (**hair**) **c.** après-shampooing *m.*
**condo** *abbr* (*pl* **-os**) = **condominium.**
**condom** préservatif *m.*
**condominium** (*building*) copropriété *f*; (*apartment*) appartement *m* dans une copropriété.
**conduct 1** *n* conduite *f*. **2** *vt* conduire; (*orchestra*) diriger.
**conducted tour** excursion *f* accompagnée.
**conductor** (*of orchestra*) chef *m* d'orchestre; (*on bus*) receveur, -euse *mf*; (*on train*) chef *m* de train.
**cone** cône *m*; (*of ice cream*) cornet *m.*
**conference** conférence *f*; (*scientific etc*) congrès *m.*
**confess 1** *vt* avouer (**that** que). **2** *vi* **to c. (to)** avouer.
**confession** aveu(x) *m(pl).*
**confetti** confettis *mpl.*
**confidence** (*trust*) confiance *f*; **(self-)c.** confiance *f* en soi; **in c.** en confidence.
**confident** *a* sûr; **(self-)c.** sûr de soi.
**confidential** *a* confidentiel.
**confidently** *adv* avec confiance.
**confine** *vt* limiter (**to** à); **to c. oneself to doing** se limiter à faire.
**confined** *a* (*space*) réduit; **c. to bed** cloué au lit.
**confirm** *vt* confirmer (**that** que).
**confirmation** confirmation *f.*
**confirmed** *a* (*bachelor*) endurci.
**confiscate** *vt* confisquer (**from s.o.** à qn).
**conflict 1** *n* conflit *m*. **2** *vi* être en contradiction (**with** avec).
**conflicting** *a* (*views etc*) contradictoires; (*dates*) incompatibles.
**conform** *vi* (*of person*) se conformer (**to** à).
**confront** *vt* (*problems, dang*
faire face à; **to c. s.o.** (*be face t*

*with*) se trouver en face de qn; (*oppose*) affronter qn.

**confuse** *vt* (*make unsure*) embrouiller; **to c. with** (*mistake for*) confondre avec.

**confused** *a* (*situation*) confus; **to be c.** (*of person*) s'y perdre; **to get c.** s'embrouiller.

**confusing** *a* déroutant.

**confusion** confusion *f*.

**congested** *a* (*street*) encombré.

**congestion** (*traffic*) encombrement(s) *m*(*pl*).

**congratulate** *vt* féliciter (**s.o. on sth** qn de qch).

**congratulations** *npl* félicitations *fpl* (**on** pour).

**congregate** *vi* se rassembler.

**congress** congrès *m*; **C.** (*political body*) le Congrès.

**Congressman** (*pl* **-men**) membre *m* du Congrès.

**conjugate** *vt* (*verb*) conjuguer.

**conjugation** conjugaison *f*.

**conjunction** *Grammar* conjonction *f*.

**conjurer** prestidigitateur, -trice *mf*.

**conjuring trick** tour *m* de prestidigitation.

**con man** escroc *m*.

**connect 1** *vt* relier (**with, to** à); (*telephone etc*) brancher; **to c. s.o. with s.o.** (*by phone*) mettre qn en communication avec qn. **2** *vi* **to c. with** (*of train, bus*) assurer la correspondance avec.

**connected** *a* (*facts*) liés; **to be c. with** (*have dealings with, relate to*) être lié à.

**connection** (*link*) rapport *m* (**with** avec); (*train etc*) correspondance *f*; (*phone call*) communication *f*; **connections** (*contacts*) relations *fpl*; **in c. with** à propos de.

**conquer** *vt* (*country*) conquérir; (*enemy, habit*) vaincre.

**conscience** conscience *f*.

**conscientious** *a* consciencieux.

**conscious** *a* (*awake*) conscient; **c. of sth** (*aware*) conscient de qch; **to be c. of doing** avoir conscience de faire.

**consent 1** *vi* consentir (**to** à). **2** *n* consentement *m*.

**consequence** (*result*) conséquence *f*.

**consequently** *adv* par conséquent.

**conservation** économies *fpl* d'énergie; (*of nature*) protection *f* de l'environnement.

**conservative** *a* & *n* conservateur, -trice (*mf*).

**conservatory** (*room*) véranda *f*.

**conserve** *vt* **to c. energy** faire des économies d'énergie.

**consider** *vt* considérer (**that** que); (*take into account*) tenir compte de; **to c. doing** envisager de faire.

**considerable** *a* (*large*) considérable; (*much*) beaucoup de.

**considerate** *a* plein d'égards (**to** pour).

**consideration** considération *f*; **to take into c.** prendre en considération.

**considering** *prep* compte tenu de.

**consignment** (*goods*) arrivage *m*.

**consist** *vi* consister (**of** en, **in** dans, **in doing** à faire).

**consistent** *a* (*unchanging*) constant; (*ideas*) logique; **c. with** compatible avec.

**consistently** *adv* (*always*) constamment.

**consolation** consolation *f*; **c. prize** lot *m* de consolation.

**console**[1] *vt* consoler.

**console**[2] (*control desk*) console *f*.

**consonant** consonne *f*.

**conspicuous** *a* visible; (*striking*) remarquable.

**constant** *a* (*frequent*) incessant; (*unchanging*) constant.

**constantly** *adv* constamment.

**constipated** *a* constipé.

**constitution** constitution *f*.

**construct** *vt* construire.

**construction** construction *f*; **under c.** en construction.

**consul** consul *m*.

**consulate** consulat *m*.
**consult 1** *vt* consulter. **2** *vi* **to c. with** discuter avec.
**consultant** (*doctor*) spécialiste *mf*; (*financial, legal*) expert-conseil *m*.
**consultation** consultation *f*.
**consulting firm** cabinet *m* d'experts-conseils.
**consume** *vt* (*food, supplies*) consommer.
**consumer** consommateur, -trice *mf*.
**consumption** consommation *f* (**of** de).
**contact 1** *n* contact *m*; (*person*) contact *m*, relation *f*; **in c. with** en contact avec. **2** *vt* contacter.
**contact lenses** lentilles *fpl* or verres *mpl* de contact.
**contagious** *a* contagieux.
**contain** *vt* contenir.
**container** récipient *m*; (*for goods*) conteneur *m*.
**contemporary** *a* & *n* contemporain, -aine (*mf*).
**contempt** mépris *m*.
**contend with** (*problem*) faire face à; (*person*) avoir affaire à.
**content**[1] *a* satisfait (**with** de).
**content**[2] (*of text etc*) contenu *m*; **contents** (*of container*) contenu *m*; **(table of) contents** (*of book*) table *f* des matières.
**contented** *a* satisfait.
**contest** concours *m*; (*fight*) lutte *f*.
**contestant** concurrent, -ente *mf*; (*in fight*) adversaire *mf*.
**context** contexte *m*.
**continent** continent *m*.
**continental** *a* continental; **c. breakfast** petit déjeuner *m* à la française.
**continual** *a* continuel.
**continually** *adv* continuellement.
**continue 1** *vt* continuer (**to do** *or* **doing** à *or* de faire); **to c. (with)** (*work etc*) poursuivre; (*resume*) reprendre. **2** *vi* continuer; (*resume*) reprendre.
**continuous** *a* continu.
**continuously** *adv* sans interruption.
**contraceptive** *a* & *n* contraceptif (*m*).
**contract** contrat *m*.
**contradict** *vt* contredire.
**contradiction** contradiction *f*.
**contrary 1** *adv* **c. to** contrairement à. **2** *n* **on the c.** au contraire.
**contrast** contraste *m*; **in c. to** par opposition à.
**contrasting** *a* (*colors, opinions*) opposés.
**contribute 1** *vt* donner (**to** à); (*article*) écrire (**to** pour); **to c. money to** contribuer à. **2** *vi* **to c. to** contribuer à; (*publication*) collaborer à.
**contribution** contribution *f*; (*to fund etc*) cotisation(s) *f*(*pl*).
**contrive** *vt* **to c. to do** trouver moyen de faire.
**contrived** *a* artificiel.
**control 1** *vt* (*organization*) diriger; (*traffic*) régler; (*prices, quality, situation, emotion*) contrôler; **to c. oneself** se contrôler. **2** *n* autorité *f* (**over** sur); (*over prices, quality*) contrôle *m*; **controls** (*of train etc*) commandes *fpl*; (*of TV set etc*) boutons *mpl*; **everything is under c.** tout est en ordre; **in c. of** maître de; **to lose c. of** perdre le contrôle de.
**control tower** tour *f* de contrôle.
**convalesce** *vi* être en convalescence.
**convalescence** convalescence *f*.
**convalescent home** maison *f* de convalescence.
**convenience** commodité *f*; **c. foods** plats *mpl* tout préparés; **(public) conveniences** toilettes *fpl*.
**convenient** *a* commode; (*well-situated*) bien situé (**to shopping/***etc* par rapport aux magasins/*etc*); (*moment*) convenable; **to be c. (for)** (*suit*) convenir (à).
**convent** couvent *m*.
**conversation** conversation *f*.
**converse** *vi* s'entretenir [illegible] avec).

**convert** *vt* convertir (**into** en, **to** à); (*building*) aménager (**into** en).
**convertible** (*car*) (voiture *f*) décapotable *f*.
**convey** *vt* (*goods, people*) transporter; (*sound, message*) transmettre; (*idea*) communiquer.
**conveyor belt** tapis *m* roulant.
**convict** *vt* déclarer coupable.
**conviction** (*for crime*) condamnation *f*; (*belief*) conviction *f*.
**convince** *vt* convaincre (**of** de).
**convincing** *a* convaincant.
**convoy** (*cars*) convoi *m*.
**cook 1** *vt* (*food*) (faire) cuire. **2** *vi* (*of food*) cuire; (*of person*) faire la cuisine. **3** *n* cuisinier, -ière *mf*.
**cookbook** livre *m* de cuisine.
**cookie** biscuit *m*.
**cooking** cuisine *f*.
**cooking apple** pomme *f* à cuire.
**cool 1** *a* (*weather, place, drink etc*) frais (*f* fraîche); (*manner*) calme; (*unfriendly*) froid; **to keep sth c.** tenir qch au frais. **2** *n* (*of evening*) fraîcheur *f*; **to lose one's c.** perdre son sang-froid.
**cool (down) 1** *vi* (*of angry person*) se calmer; (*of hot liquid*) refroidir. **2** *vt* refroidir.
**cooler** (*for food*) glacière *f*.
**cool-headed** *a* calme.
**coolness** fraîcheur *f*; (*unfriendliness*) froideur *f*.
**cool off** (*refresh oneself*) se rafraîchir.
**co-op** appartement *m* en copropriété.
**cooperate** *vi* coopérer (**in** à, **with** avec).
**cooperation** coopération *f*.
**coop up** (*person*) enfermer.
**cop** (*policeman*) *Fam* flic *m*.
**cope** *vi* **to c. with** s'occuper de; (*problem*) faire face à; **(to be able) to c.** (savoir) se débrouiller.
**copper** (*metal*) cuivre *m*.
**copy 1** copie *f*; (*of book, magazine etc*) exemplaire *m*. **2** *vti* copier.
**copy out** *or* **down** (*address etc*) (re)copier.
**cord** cordon *m*; (*electrical*) cordon *m* électrique.
**cordial (fruit) c.** sirop *m*.
**cordon off** (*of police etc*) interdire l'accès de.
**corduroy** velours *m* côtelé; **corduroys** pantalon *m* en velours (côtelé).
**core** (*of apple etc*) trognon *m*.
**cork** liège *m*; (*for bottle*) bouchon *m*.
**cork (up)** (*bottle*) boucher.
**corkscrew** tire-bouchon *m*.
**corn** maïs *m*; (*hard skin on foot*) cor *m*.
**corned beef** corned-beef *m*.
**corner 1** *n* coin *m*; (*bend in road*) virage *m*. **2** *vt* (*person in corridor etc*) coincer; (*market*) monopoliser.
**cornflakes** *npl* céréales *fpl*.
**corny** *a* (*joke*) rebattu.
**coronary** infarctus *m*.
**corporal** caporal(-chef) *m*.
**corpse** cadavre *m*.
**correct 1** *a* exact, correct; (*proper*) correct; **he's c.** (*right*) il a raison. **2** *vt* corriger.
**correction** correction *f*.
**correctly** *adv* correctement.
**correspond** correspondre (**to, with** à); (*by letter*) correspondre (**with** avec).
**correspondence** correspondance *f*; **c. course** cours *m* par correspondance.
**corresponding** *a* (*matching*) correspondant.
**corridor** couloir *m*.
**corrugated** *a* **c. iron** tôle *f* ondulée.
**corrupt** *a* corrompu.
**cosmetic** produit *m* de beauté.
**cosmonaut** cosmonaute *mf*.
**cost 1** *vti* coûter; **how much does it c.?** ça coûte combien? **2** *n* prix *m*; **at all costs** à tout prix.
**costly** *a* coûteux.
**costume** costume *m*.
**costume ball** bal *m* masqué.
**costume jewelry** bijoux *mpl* de fantaisie.

**crime** crime *m*; (*not serious*) délit *m*; (*criminal practice*) criminalité *f*.
**criminal** *a* & *n* criminel, -elle (*mf*).
**crisis** (*pl* **-ses**) crise *f*.
**crisp** *a* (*cookie*) croustillant; (*apple*) croquant.
**critic** critique *m*.
**critical** *a* critique.
**critically** *adv* (*ill*) gravement.
**criticism** critique *f*.
**criticize** *vti* critiquer.
**crochet 1** *vt* faire au crochet. **2** *vi* faire du crochet. **3** *n* (travail *m* au) crochet *m*.
**crocodile** crocodile *m*.
**crocus** crocus *m*.
**crook** (*thief*) escroc *m*.
**crooked** *a* (*stick*) courbé; (*path*) tortueux; (*hat, picture*) de travers.
**crop** (*harvest*) récolte *f*; (*produce*) culture *f*.
**crop up** *vi* se présenter.
**croquet** croquet *m*.
**cross**[1] **1** *n* croix *f*; **a c. between** (*animal*) un croisement entre *or* de. **2** *vt* (*street, room etc*) traverser; (*barrier*) franchir; (*legs*) croiser. **3** *vi* (*of paths*) se croiser.
**cross**[2] *a* (*angry*) fâché (**with** contre).
**cross-country race** cross(-country) *m*.
**cross-eyed** *a* qui louche.
**crossing** (*by ship*) traversée *f*; **(pedestrian) c.** passage *m* clouté.
**cross off** *or* **out** (*word, name etc*) rayer.
**cross over** *vti* traverser.
**cross-reference** renvoi *m*.
**crossroads** carrefour *m*.
**cross-section** coupe *f* transversale; (*sample*) échantillon *m*.
**crosswalk** passage *m* clouté.
**crossword (puzzle)** mots *mpl* croisés.
**crouch (down)** *vi* s'accroupir.
**crow** corbeau *m*.
**crowbar** levier *m*, pied *m* de biche.
**crowd** foule *f*; (*particular group*) bande *f*.
**crowded** *a* plein (**with** de).
**crowd into** (*of people*) s'entasser dans.
**crowd round s.o./sth** se presser autour de qn/qch.
**crown** couronne *f*.
**crucial** *a* crucial.
**crude** *a* (*manners, language*) grossier; (*work*) rudimentaire.
**cruel** *a* cruel.
**cruelty** cruauté *f*; **an act of c.** une cruauté.
**cruet** petit flacon *m*; (*for oil and vinegar*) huilier *m*.
**cruise 1** *vi* (*of ship*) croiser; (*of car*) rouler; (*of plane*) voler. **2** *n* croisière *f*; **to take a c.** faire une croisière.
**crumb** miette *f*.
**crumble 1** *vt* (*bread*) émietter. **2** *vi* (*in small pieces*) s'effriter; (*of bread*) s'émietter; (*become ruined*) tomber en ruine.
**crumbly** *a* friable.
**crummy** *a Fam* moche.
**crumple** *vt* froisser.
**crunch** *vt* (*food*) croquer.
**crunchy** *a* (*apple etc*) croquant; (*bread, cookie*) croustillant.
**crush 1** *n* (*crowd*) cohue *f*; (*rush*) bousculade *f*. **2** *vt* écraser; (*clothes*) froisser; (*cram*) entasser (**into** dans).
**crust** croûte *f*.
**crusty** *a* (*bread*) croustillant.
**crutch** (*of invalid*) béquille *f*.
**cry 1** *n* (*shout*) cri *m*; **to have a c.** *Fam* pleurer. **2** *vi* pleurer; (*shout*) pousser un cri.
**crying** (*weeping*) pleurs *mpl*.
**cry off** *vi* abandonner.
**cry out 1** *vi* pousser un cri; (*exclaim*) s'écrier. **2** *vt* crier.
**cry out for sth** demander qch (à grands cris); **to be crying out for sth** avoir grand besoin de qch.
**cry over sth/s.o.** pleurer (sur) qch/qn.
**crystal** cristal *m*.
**cub** (*scout*) louveteau *m*.

**cube** cube *m*; (*of meat etc*) dé *m*.
**cubic** *a* (*metre etc*) cube.
**cubicle** (*in office building*) box *m*.
**cuckoo** (*bird*) coucou *m*.
**cucumber** concombre *m*.
**cuddle 1** *vt* (*hug*) serrer; (*caress*) câliner. **2** *vi* se serrer. **3** *n* caresse *f*.
**cuddle up to s.o.** se serrer contre qn.
**cuddly** *a* câlin; (*toy*) doux (*f* douce).
**cue** (*in theatre*) réplique *f*; (*signal*) signal *m*.
**cuff** (*of shirt*) poignet *m*; (*of trousers*) revers *m*.
**cuff link** bouton *m* de manchette.
**cul-de-sac** impasse *f*.
**culprit** coupable *mf*.
**cultivate** *vt* cultiver.
**cultivated** *a* cultivé.
**cultural** *a* culturel.
**culture** culture *f*.
**cultured** *a* cultivé.
**cumbersome** *a* encombrant.
**cunning 1** *a* astucieux. **2** *n* astuce *f*.
**cup** tasse *f*; (*prize*) coupe *f*.
**cupboard** armoire *f*; (*built-in*) placard *m*.
**cupful** tasse *f*.
**curable** *a* guérissable.
**curb** bord *m* du trottoir.
**cure 1** *vt* guérir (*qn*) (**of** de). **2** *n* remède *m* (**for** contre); **rest c.** cure *f* de repos.
**curiosity** curiosité *f*.
**curious** *a* (*odd*) curieux; (*inquisitive*) curieux (**about** de).
**curl 1** *vti* (*hair*) boucler. **2** *n* boucle *f*.
**curler** bigoudi *m*.
**curl (oneself) up** se pelotonner.
**curly** *a* (*hair*) bouclé.
**currant** (*dried grape*) raisin *m* de Corinthe.
**currency** monnaie *f*; (*foreign*) devises *fpl* (étrangères).
**current 1** *a* actuel; (*opinion*) courant; (*year*) courant. **2** *n* (*of river, electric*) courant *m*.
**current affairs** questions *fpl* d'actualité.
**currently** *adv* actuellement.
**curriculum** programme *m* (scolaire).
**curry** curry *m*.
**curse** *vi* (*swear*) jurer.
**cursor** (*of computer*) curseur *m*.
**curtain** rideau *m*.
**curts(e)y 1** *n* révérence *f*. **2** *vi* faire une révérence.
**curve 1** *n* courbe *f*; (*in road*) virage *m*. **2** *vi* se courber; (*of road*) faire une courbe.
**cushion** coussin *m*.
**custard** crème *f* anglaise; (*when set*) crème *f* renversée.
**custom** coutume *f*; (*customers*) clientèle *f*.
**customer** client, -ente *mf*.
**customer service** service *m* après-vente.
**customs** *n*(*pl*) **c.** la douane; **c. (duties)** droits *mpl* de douane; **c. officer** douanier *m*.
**cut 1** *n* (*mark*) coupure *f*; (*stroke*) coup *m*; (*of clothes, hair*) coupe *f*; (*in salary, prices etc*) réduction *f*; (*of meat*) morceau *m*. **2** *vt** couper; (*meat*) découper; (*glass, tree*) tailler; (*salary etc*) réduire; **to c. open** ouvrir (*au couteau etc*). **3** *vi* (*of person, scissors*) couper; **to c. in line** passer avant son tour.
**cut away** (*remove*) enlever.
**cutback** réduction *f*.
**cut back (on)** *vti* réduire.
**cut down** (*tree*) abattre.
**cut down (on)** *vti* réduire.
**cute** *a Fam* (*pretty*) mignon (*f* mignonne).
**cut into** (*cake*) entamer.
**cutlery** couverts *mpl*.
**cutlet** côtelette *f*.
**cut off** *vt* couper; (*isolate*) isoler.
**cut out 1** *vi* (*of engine*) caler. **2** *vt* (*article*) découper; (*remove*) enlever; **to c. out drinking** s'arrêter de boire; **c. it out!** *Fam* ça suffit!; **c. out to be a doctor**/*etc* fait pour être médecin/*etc*.
**cutout** (*picture*) découpage *m*.
**cut up** *vt* couper (en morceaux).
**cycle 1** *n* (*bicycle*) bicyclette *f*; (*series, period*) cycle *m*. **2** *vi* aller à bicyclette (**to** à).

**cycling** cyclisme *m.*
**cyclist** cycliste *mf.*
**cylinder** cylindre *m.*
**cymbal** cymbale *f.*

# D

**dab** *vt* (*wound*) tamponner; **to d. sth on sth** appliquer qch sur qch.
**Dacron**® tergal® *m.*
**daddy** *Fam* papa *m.*
**daffodil** jonquille *f.*
**daft** *a Fam* idiot, bête.
**daily 1** *a* quotidien. **2** *adv* quotidiennement. **3** *n* **d. (paper)** quotidien *m.*
**dairy** *a* (*product*) laitier.
**daisy** pâquerette *f.*
**dam** barrage *m.*
**damage 1** *n* dégâts *mpl*; (*harm*) préjudice *m.* **2** *vt* (*spoil*) abîmer; (*harm*) nuire à.
**damn** *Fam* **1** *int* **d. (it)!** merde!; **d. him!** qu'il aille au diable! **2** *a* (*awful*) fichu. **3** *adv* (*very*) vachement.
**damp 1** *a* humide. **2** *n* humidité *f.*
**damp(en)** *vt* humecter.
**dampness** humidité *f.*
**dance 1** *n* danse *f*; (*social event*) bal *m* (*pl* bals). **2** *vti* danser.
**dance hall** salle *f* de danse.
**dancer** danseur, -euse *mf.*
**dandelion** pissenlit *m.*
**dandruff** pellicules *fpl.*
**Dane** Danois, -oise *mf.*
**danger** danger *m* (**to** pour); **in d.** en danger; **to be in d. of falling**/*etc* risquer de tomber/*etc.*
**dangerous** *a* dangereux (**to** pour).
**Danish 1** *a* danois. **2** *n* (*language*) danois *m.*
**dare** *vt* oser (**do** faire); **to d. s.o. to do** défier qn de faire.
**daring** *a* audacieux.
**dark 1** *a* obscur, noir; (*color, eyes*) foncé; (*skin, hair*) brun; **it's d.** il fait nuit *or* noir; **d. glasses** lunettes *fpl* noires. **2** *n* noir *m*, obscurité *f.*
**dark-haired** *a* aux cheveux bruns.
**darkness** obscurité *f*, noir *m.*
**dark-skinned** *a* brun.
**darling (my) d.** (mon) chéri, (ma) chérie.
**dart** fléchette *f*; **darts** (*game*) fléchettes *fpl.*
**dartboard** cible *f.*
**dash 1** *vi* se précipiter. **2** *n* (*stroke*) trait *m.*
**dash away** *or* **off** partir en vitesse.
**dashboard** (*of car*) tableau *m* de bord.
**data** *npl* données *fpl.*
**data bank** banque *f* de données.
**data processing** informatique *f.*
**date**[1] **1** *n* (*time*) date *f*; (*meeting*) *Fam* rendez-vous *m inv* (galant); (*person*) *Fam* copain, -ine *mf*; **up to d.** moderne; (*information*) à jour; (*well-informed*) au courant (**on** de); **out of d.** (*old-fashioned*) démodé; (*expired*) périmé. **2** *vt* (*letter etc*) dater; (*girl, boy*) *Fam* sortir avec.
**date**[2] (*fruit*) datte *f.*
**date stamp** (tampon *m*) dateur *m*; (*mark*) cachet *m.*
**daughter** fille *f.*
**daughter-in-law** (*pl* **daughters-in-law**) belle-fille *f.*
**dawdle** *vi* traîner.
**dawn** aube *f.*
**day** jour *m*; (*whole day long*) journée *f*; **all d. (long)** toute la journée; **the following** *or* **next d.** le lendemain; **the d. before** la veille; **the d. before yesterday** avant-hier; **the d. after tomorrow** après-demain.
**daycare** (*for ages 3 and below*) crèche *f*; (*for older children*) garderie *f.*
**daylight** (lumière *f* du) jour *m.*
**daytime** journée *f*, jour *m.*
**dead 1** *a* mort; (*battery*) à plat. **2** *adv* (*completely*) absolument; (*very*) très.
**dead end** (*street*) impasse *f.*
**deadline** date *f* limite; (*hour*) heure *f* limite.
**deaf** *a* sourd; **d. and dumb** sourd-muet.
**deafness** surdité *f.*

**deal**[1] **a good** *or* **great d.** (*a lot*) beaucoup (**of** de).

**deal**[2] **1** *n* (*in business*) marché *m*, affaire *f*; **it's a d.** d'accord. **2** *vi** (*trade*) traiter (**with s.o.** avec qn); **to d. in** faire le commerce de; **to d. with** s'occuper de; (*concern*) traiter de. **3** *vt cards* donner.

**dealer** marchand, -ande *mf* (**in** de); (*agent*) dépositaire *mf*; (*for cars*) concessionnaire *mf*.

**dealings** *npl* relations *fpl* (**with** avec); (*in business*) transactions *fpl*.

**dear 1** *a* (*loved, expensive*) cher; **D. Sir** (*in letter*) Monsieur; **oh d.!** oh là là! **2** *n* **(my) d.** (*darling*) (mon) chéri, (ma) chérie; (*friend*) mon cher, ma chère.

**death** mort *f*.

**death certificate** acte *m* de décès.

**debate 1** *vti* discuter. **2** *n* débat *m*, discussion *f*.

**debit 1** *n* débit *m*; **my account shows a d. balance of** mon compte est débiteur de. **2** *vt* débiter (**s.o. with sth** qn de qch).

**debt** dette *f*; **to be in d.** avoir des dettes.

**decade** décennie *f*.

**decaffeinated** *a* décaféiné.

**decal** décalcomanie *f*.

**decay** (*of tooth*) carie(s) *f*(*pl*).

**deceive** *vti* tromper.

**December** décembre *m*.

**decent** *a* (*respectable*) convenable, décent; (*good*) *Fam* bon; (*kind*) *Fam* gentil.

**decide 1** *vt* (*question etc*) décider; **to d. to do** décider de faire; **to d. that** décider que. **2** *vi* (*make decisions*) décider (**on** de); (*make up one's mind*) se décider (**on doing** à faire); (*choose*) se décider (**on** pour).

**decimal 1** *a* **d. point** virgule *f*. **2** *n* décimale *f*.

**decision** décision *f*.

**decisive** *a* décisif; (*victory*) net (*f* nette).

**deck** (*of ship*) pont *m*; (*of cards*) jeu *m*; (*of house*) terrasse *f*.

**deckchair** chaise *f* longue.

**declare** *vt* déclarer (**that** que); (*verdict, result*) proclamer.

**decline 1** *vi* (*become less*) (*of popularity etc*) être en baisse. **2** *vt* (*invitation*) refuser.

**decorate** *vt* (*cake, house, soldier*) décorer (**with** de); (*hat, skirt etc*) orner (**with** de); (*paint etc*) peindre (et tapisser).

**decoration** décoration *f*.

**decorative** *a* décoratif.

**decorator** peintre *m* décorateur; **(interior) d.** décorateur, -trice *mf*.

**decrease 1** *vti* diminuer. **2** *n* diminution *f* (**in** de).

**dedicated** *a* (*teacher etc*) consciencieux.

**deduct** *vt* déduire (**from** de); (*from wage, account*) prélever (**from** sur).

**deduction** déduction *f*.

**deed** action *f*, acte *m*; (*document*) acte *m* (notarié).

**deep** *a* profond; (*voice*) grave; **to be 20 feet**/*etc* **d.** avoir six mètres/*etc* de profondeur; **the d. end** (*in pool*) le grand bain.

**deep-freeze 1** *vt* surgeler. **2** *n* congélateur *m*.

**deer** *n inv* cerf *m*.

**defeat 1** *vt* battre. **2** *n* défaite *f*.

**defect** défaut *m*.

**defective** *a* défectueux.

**defend** *vt* défendre.

**defendant** (*accused*) prévenu, -ue *mf*.

**defense** défense *f*.

**defiant** *a* (*tone, attitude*) de défi; (*person*) rebelle.

**deficiency** manque *m*; (*of vitamins etc*) carence *f*.

**deficient** *a* insuffisant; **to be d. in** manquer de.

**deficit** déficit *m*.

**define** *vt* définir.

**definite** *a* (*date, plan*) précis; (*reply, improvement*) net (*f* nette); (*order, offer*) ferme; (*certain*) certain; **d. article** *Grammar* article *m* défini.

**definitely** *adv* certainement; (*considerably*) nettement; (*to say*) catégoriquement.

**definition** définition *f*.

**deformed** *a* (*body*) difforme.

**defrost** *vt* (*fridge*) dégivrer; (*food*) décongeler.

**defy** *vt* défier (*qn*); **to d. s.o. to do** défier qn de faire.

**degenerate** *vi* dégénérer (**into** en).

**degree** (*angle, temperature*) degré *m*; (*from university*) diplôme *m*; (*Bachelor's*) licence *f*; (*Master's*) maîtrise *f*; (*PhD*) doctorat *m*; **to such a d.** à tel point (**that** que).

**de-ice** *vt* (*car window etc*) dégivrer.

**de-icer** (*substance*) dégivreur *m*.

**dejected** *a* abattu.

**delay 1** *vt* retarder; (*payment*) différer. **2** *vi* (*be slow*) tarder (**doing** à faire); (*linger*) s'attarder. **3** *n* retard *m*; (*waiting period*) délai *m*; **without d.** sans tarder.

**delegate 1** *vt* déléguer (**to** à). **2** *n* délégué, -ée *mf*.

**delegation** délégation *f*.

**delete** *vt* rayer.

**deliberate** *a* (*intentional*) intentionnel.

**deliberately** *adv* (*intentionally*) exprès.

**delicacy** (*food*) mets *m* délicat.

**delicate** *a* délicat.

**delicatessen** traiteur *m*, épicerie *f* fine.

**delicious** *a* délicieux.

**delight 1** *n* délice *m*; **to take d. in sth/in doing** se délecter de qch/à faire. **2** *vt* réjouir. **3** *vi* **to d. in doing** se délecter à faire.

**delighted** *a* ravi (**with sth** de qch, **to do** de faire, **that** que).

**delightful** *a* charmant; (*meal*) délicieux.

**delinquent** délinquant, -ante *mf*.

**deliver** *vt* (*goods etc*) livrer; (*letters*) distribuer; (*hand over*) remettre (**to** à); (*speech*) prononcer; (*warning*) lancer.

**delivery** livraison *f*; (*of letters*) distribution *f*; (*handing over*) remise *f*; (*birth*) accouchement *m*.

**delude** *vt* tromper; **to d. oneself** se faire des illusions.

**deluxe** *a* de luxe.

**demand 1** *vt* exiger (**sth from s.o.** qch de qn); (*rights, more pay*) revendiquer; **to d. that** exiger que. **2** *n* exigence *f*; (*claim*) revendication *f*; (*for goods*) demande *f*; **in great d.** très demandé.

**demanding** *a* exigeant.

**democracy** démocratie *f*.

**democratic** *a* démocratique; (*person*) démocrate.

**demolish** *vt* démolir.

**demolition** démolition *f*.

**demonstrate 1** *vt* démontrer; (*machine*) faire une démonstration de. **2** *vi* manifester.

**demonstration** démonstration *f*; (*protest*) manifestation *f*.

**demonstrative** *a* & *n* *Grammar* démonstratif (*m*).

**demonstrator** (*protester*) manifestant, -ante *mf*.

**demoralize** *vt* démoraliser.

**den** tanière *f*.

**denial** (*of rumor*) démenti *m*.

**denim** (toile *f* de) coton *m*.

**denounce** *vt* (*person, injustice etc*) dénoncer (**to** à).

**dense** *a* dense; (*stupid*) *Fam* lourd, bête.

**dent 1** *n* (*in car etc*) bosse *f*. **2** *vt* cabosser.

**dental** *a* dentaire.

**dentist** dentiste *mf*.

**dentures** *npl* dentier *m*.

**deny** *vt* nier (**doing** avoir fait, **that** que); (*rumor*) démentir; **to d. s.o. sth** refuser qch à qn.

**deodorant** déodorant *m*.

**depart** *vi* partir; (*deviate*) s'écarter (**from** de).

**department** département *m*; (*in office*) service *m*; (*in shop*) rayon *m*; (*of government*) = ministère *m*;

**D. of State** Ministère des Affaires Etrangères.
**department store** grand magasin *m*.
**departure** départ *m*; **a d. from** (*rule*) un écart par rapport à.
**depend** *vi* dépendre (**on, upon** de); **to d. (up)on** (*rely on*) compter sur (**for sth** pour qch).
**dependable** *a* sûr.
**dependant** personne *f* à charge.
**depict** *vt* (*describe*) dépeindre; (*in pictures*) représenter.
**deplorable** *a* déplorable.
**deplore** *vt* déplorer.
**deposit 1** *vt* déposer; **to d.** (*check*) verser (**to one's account**) sur son compte. **2** *n* dépôt *m*; (*part payment*) acompte *m*, arrhes *fpl*; (*against damage*) caution *f*; (*on bottle*) consigne *f*.
**depot** (*railroad station*) gare *f*; **bus d.** gare *f* routière.
**depress** *vt* (*discourage*) déprimer.
**depressed** *a* déprimé; **to get d.** se décourager.
**depression** dépression *f*.
**deprive** *vt* priver (**of** de).
**deprived** *a* (*child etc*) déshérité.
**depth** profondeur *f*.
**deputy** (*replacement*) remplaçant, -ante *mf*; (*assistant*) adjoint, -ointe *mf*.
**derailment** déraillement *m*.
**derelict** *a* abandonné.
**derive** *vt* **to d. from sth** (*pleasure etc*) tirer de qch; **to be derived from** (*of word etc*) dériver de.
**descend 1** *vi* descendre (**from** de). **2** *vt* (*stairs*) descendre.
**descendant** descendant, -ante *mf*.
**descend upon** (*of tourists*) envahir.
**descent** (*of aircraft etc*) descente *f*.
**describe** *vt* décrire.
**description** description *f*; (*on passport*) signalement *m*; **of every d.** de toutes sortes.
**desert**[1] désert *m*; **d. island** île *f* déserte.
**desert**[2] *vt* abandonner.
**deserted** *a* (*place*) désert.
**deserve** *vt* mériter (**to do** de faire).
**design 1** *vt* (*car etc*) dessiner; **designed to do/for s.o.** conçu pour faire/pour qn; **well designed** bien conçu. **2** *n* (*pattern*) motif *m*; (*sketch*) plan *m*, dessin *m*; (*type of dress or car*) modèle *m*.
**designer** dessinateur, -trice *mf*.
**designer clothes** vêtements *mpl* griffés.
**desirable** *a* désirable.
**desire 1** *n* désir *m*; **I have no d. to** je n'ai aucune envie de. **2** *vt* désirer (**to do** faire).
**desk** (*in school*) pupitre *m*; (*in office*) bureau *m*; (*in shop*) caisse *f*; **(reception) d.** réception *f*.
**desk clerk** (*in hotel*) réceptionniste *mf*.
**despair 1** *n* désespoir *m*; **to be in d.** être au désespoir. **2** *vi* désespérer (**of s.o.** de qn, **of doing** de faire).
**desperate** *a* désespéré; **to be d. for** avoir désespérément besoin de; (*cigarette, baby*) mourir d'envie d'avoir.
**despicable** *a* méprisable.
**despise** *vt* mépriser.
**despite** *prep* malgré.
**dessert** dessert *m*.
**dessertspoon** cuillère *f* à dessert.
**destination** destination *f*.
**destitute** *a* indigent.
**destroy** *vt* détruire.
**destruction** destruction *f*.
**destructive** *a* destructeur.
**detach** *vt* détacher (**from** de).
**detachable** *a* (*lining*) amovible.
**detached house** maison *f* individuelle.
**detail** détail *m*; **in d.** en détail.
**detailed** *a* détaillé.
**detain** *vt* retenir; (*prisoner*) détenir.
**detect** (*find*) découvrir; (*see, hear*) distinguer.
**detective** inspecteur *m* de police; (*private*) détective *m*.

**detector** détecteur *m.*

**detention** (*school punishment*) retenue *f.*

**deter** *vt* **to d. s.o.** dissuader qn (**from doing** de faire, **from sth** de qch).

**detergent** détergent *m.*

**deteriorate** *vi* se détériorer.

**deterioration** détérioration *f.*

**determination** (*intention*) ferme intention *f.*

**determine** *vt* déterminer; (*price*) fixer.

**determined** *a* déterminé; **d. to do** *or* **on doing** décidé à faire.

**deterrent to be a d.** être dissuasif.

**detest** *vt* détester (**doing** faire).

**detour** déviation *f.*

**develop 1** *vt* développer; (*area, land*) mettre en valeur; (*habit, illness*) contracter. **2** *vi* se développer.

**develop into** devenir.

**development** développement *m*; **housing d.** lotissement *m*; (*large*) grand ensemble *m*; **a (new) d.** (*in situation*) un fait nouveau.

**deviate** *vi* dévier (**from** de).

**device** dispositif *m*; **left to one's own devices** livré à soi-même.

**devil** diable *m*; **what/where/why the d.?** que/où/pourquoi diable?

**devise** *vt* (*a plan*) combiner; (*invent*) inventer.

**devote** *vt* consacrer (**to** à).

**devoted** *a* dévoué.

**devotion** dévouement *m* (**to s.o.** à qn).

**dew** rosée *f.*

**diabetes** diabète *m.*

**diabetic** diabétique *mf.*

**diagnosis** (*pl* **-oses**) diagnostic *m.*

**diagonal 1** *a* diagonal. **2** *n* **d. (line)** diagonale *f.*

**diagonally** *adv* en diagonale.

**diagram** schéma *m.*

**dial 1** *n* cadran *m*. **2** *vt* (*phone number*) faire; (*person*) appeler.

**dialect** dialecte *m.*

**dial tone** tonalité *f.*

**dialog** dialogue *m.*

**diameter** diamètre *m.*

**diamond** diamant *m*; (*shape*) losange *m*; *Baseball* terrain *m*; **diamond(s)** (*at cards*) carreau *m*; **d. necklace** collier *m* de diamants.

**diaper** couche *f.*

**diarrhea** diarrhée *f.*

**diary** journal *m* (intime).

**dice 1** *n inv* dé *m* (à jouer). **2** *vt* (*food*) couper en dés.

**dictate** *vti* dicter (**to** à).

**dictation** dictée *f.*

**dictionary** dictionnaire *m.*

**did** *pt de* **do**[1].

**die** *vi* (*pt & pp* **died**, *pres p* **dying**) mourir (**of, from** de); **to be dying to do** mourir d'envie de faire; **to be dying for sth** avoir une envie folle de qch.

**die away** (*of noise*) mourir.

**die down** (*of storm*) se calmer.

**die out** (*of custom*) mourir.

**diesel** *a* & *n* **d. (engine)** (moteur *m*) diesel *m*; **d. (oil)** gazole *m.*

**diet 1** *n* (*to lose weight*) régime *m*; (*usual food*) alimentation *f*; **to go on a d.** faire un régime. **2** *vi* suivre un régime.

**differ** *vi* différer (**from** de); (*disagree*) ne pas être d'accord (**from** avec).

**difference** différence *f* (**in** de); **d. (of opinion)** différend *m*; **it makes no d.** ça n'a pas d'importance; **it makes no d. to me** ça m'est égal.

**different** différent (**from, to** de); (*another*) autre; (*various*) divers.

**differently** *adv* autrement (**from, to** que).

**difficult** *a* difficile (**to do** à faire); **it's d. for us to** il nous est difficile de.

**difficulty** difficulté *f*; **to have d. doing** avoir du mal à faire.

**dig* 1** *vt* (*ground*) bêcher; (*hole*) creuser. **2** *vi* creuser.

**digest** *vti* digérer.

**digestion** digestion *f.*

**digger** (*machine*) pelleteuse *f.*

**dig sth into** (*push*) enfoncer qch dans.
**digit** (*number*) chiffre *m*.
**digital** *a* numérique.
**dig out** (*from ground*) déterrer; (*accident victim*) dégager; (*find*) dénicher.
**dig up** (*from ground*) déterrer; (*weed*) arracher; (*earth*) retourner; (*street*) piocher.
**dilapidated** *a* délabré.
**dilute** *vt* diluer.
**dim 1** *a* (*light*) faible; (*room*) sombre; (*memory, outline*) vague; (*person*) stupide. **2** *vt* (*light*) baisser; **to d. one's headlights** se mettre en code.
**dime** (pièce *f* de) dix cents *mpl*; **a d. store** = un Prisunic®.
**dimension** dimension *f*.
**dimmed headlights** codes *mpl*.
**din** vacarme *m*.
**dine** *vi* dîner (**on** de).
**dine out** dîner en ville.
**diner** dîneur, -euse *mf*; (*restaurant*) petit restaurant *m*.
**dinghy** petit canot *m*; **(rubber) d.** canot *m* pneumatique.
**dingy** *a* (*room etc*) minable; (*color*) terne.
**dining car** wagon-restaurant *m*.
**dining room** salle *f* à manger.
**dinner** dîner *m*; (*lunch*) déjeuner *m*; **to have d.** dîner.
**dinner jacket** smoking *m*.
**dinner party** dîner *m* (à la maison).
**dinner service** *or* **set** service *m* de table.
**dinosaur** dinosaure *m*.
**dip 1** *vt* plonger. **2** *vi* (*of road*) plonger; **to d. into** (*pocket, savings*) puiser dans. **3** *n* (*in road*) petit creux *m*; **to go for a d.** (*swim*) faire trempette.
**diphthong** diphtongue *f*.
**diploma** diplôme *m*.
**direct 1** *a* direct. **2** *adv* directement. **3** *vt* diriger; (*remark*) adresser (**to** à); **to d. s.o. to** (*place*) indiquer à qn le chemin de.
**direction** direction *f*; **directions (for use)** mode *m* d'emploi; **in the opposite d.** en sens inverse.
**directly 1** *adv* directement; (*at once*) tout de suite. **2** *conj* aussitôt que (+ *indicative*.)
**director** directeur, -trice *mf*; (*board member in firm*) administrateur, -trice *mf*; (*of film*) metteur *m* en scène.
**directory (telephone) d.** annuaire *m* (téléphonique).
**directory assistance** renseignements *mpl*.
**dirt** saleté *f*; (*earth*) terre *f*; **d. cheap** *Fam* très bon marché.
**dirty 1** *a* sale; (*job*) salissant; (*word*) grossier; **to get d.** se salir; **to get sth d.** salir qch; **a d. joke** une histoire cochonne. **2** *vt* salir.
**dis-** *prefix* dé-, dés-.
**disability** infirmité *f*.
**disabled 1** *a* handicapé. **2** *n* **the d.** les handicapés *mpl*.
**disadvantage** désavantage *m*.
**disagree** *vi* ne pas être d'accord (**with** avec); **to d. with s.o.** (*of food etc*) ne pas réussir à qn.
**disagreeable** *a* désagréable.
**disagreement** désaccord *m*; (*quarrel*) différend *m*.
**disappear** *vi* disparaître.
**disappearance** disparition *f*.
**disappoint** *vt* décevoir; **I'm disappointed with it** ça m'a déçu.
**disappointing** *a* décevant.
**disappointment** déception *f*.
**disapproval** désapprobation *f*.
**disapprove** *vi* **to d. of s.o./sth** désapprouver qn/qch; **I d.** je suis contre.
**disarm** *vt* désarmer.
**disaster** désastre *m*.
**disastrous** *a* désastreux.
**discard** *vt* se débarrasser de.
**discharge** (*patient, employee*) renvoyer; (*soldier*) libérer.
**discipline 1** *n* discipline *f*. **2** *vt* discipliner; (*punish*) punir.
**disc jockey** disc-jockey *m*.
**disclose** *vt* révéler.

**disco** (*pl* **-os**) disco *f*.
**discomfort** douleur *f*; **I have d. in my wrist** mon poignet me gêne.
**disconnect** *vt* détacher; (*unplug*) débrancher; (*wires*) déconnecter; (*gas, telephone*) couper.
**discontented** *a* mécontent.
**discontinued** *a* (*article*) qui ne se fait plus.
**discotheque** (*club*) discothèque *f*.
**discount** (*on article*) remise *f*, réduction *f*; **at a d.** à prix réduit.
**discount store** solderie *f*.
**discourage** *vt* décourager; **to get discouraged** se décourager.
**discover** *vt* découvrir (**that** que).
**discovery** découverte *f*.
**discreet** *a* discret.
**discriminate** *vi* **to d. against** faire de la discrimination contre.
**discrimination** (*against s.o.*) discrimination *f*.
**discuss** *vt* discuter de; (*plan, question, price*) discuter.
**discussion** discussion *f*.
**disease** maladie *f*.
**disembark** *vti* débarquer.
**disfigured** *a* défiguré.
**disgrace 1** *n* (*shame*) honte *f* (**to** à). **2** *vt* déshonorer.
**disgraceful** *a* honteux.
**disguise 1** *vt* déguiser (**as** en). **2** *n* déguisement *m*; **in d.** déguisé.
**disgust 1** *n* dégoût *m* (**for, at, with** de); **in d.** dégoûté. **2** *vt* dégoûter.
**disgusted** *a* dégoûté (**at, by, with** de); **d. with s.o.** (*annoyed*) fâché contre qn.
**disgusting** *a* dégoûtant.
**dish** (*container, food*) plat *m*; **the dishes** la vaisselle; **to do the dishes** faire la vaisselle.
**dishcloth** (*for washing*) lavette *f*; (*for drying*) torchon *m*.
**disheveled** *a* hirsute.
**dishonest** *a* malhonnête.
**dish out** *or* **up** (*food*) servir.
**dish towel** torchon *m*.
**dishwasher** (*machine*) lave-vaisselle *m inv*.
**disillusioned** *a* déçu (**with** de).
**disincentive** mesure *f* dissuasive.
**disinfect** *vt* désinfecter.
**disinfectant** désinfectant *m*.
**disk** disque *m*.
**dislike 1** *vt* ne pas aimer (**doing** faire). **2** *n* aversion *f* (**for, of** pour); **to take a d. to s.o./sth** prendre qn/qch en grippe.
**dislocate** *vt* (*limb*) démettre.
**dismal** *a* morne.
**dismantle** *vt* (*machine*) démonter.
**dismay** *vt* consterner.
**dismiss** *vt* (*from job*) renvoyer (**from** de).
**dismissal** renvoi *m*.
**disobedience** désobéissance *f*.
**disobedient** *a* désobéissant.
**disobey 1** *vt* désobéir à. **2** *vi* désobéir.
**disorder** (*confusion*) désordre *m*; (*illness*) troubles *mpl*.
**disorganized** *a* désorganisé.
**dispatch** *vt* expédier; (*troops, messenger*) envoyer.
**dispel** *vt* dissiper.
**dispenser** (*device*) distributeur *m*; **cash d.** distributeur *m* de billets.
**disperse 1** *vt* disperser. **2** *vi* se disperser.
**display 1** *vt* montrer; (*notice, electronic data*) afficher; (*painting, goods*) exposer; (*courage etc*) faire preuve de. **2** *n* (*in shop*) étalage *m*; (*of data*) affichage *m*; **on d.** exposé.
**displeased** *a* mécontent (**with** de).
**disposable** *a* (*plate etc*) à jeter, jetable.
**disposal at the d. of** à la disposition de.
**dispose** *vi* **to d. of** (*get rid of*) se débarrasser de; (*sell*) vendre.
**dispute 1** *n* (*quarrel*) dispute *f*; (*industrial*) conflit *m*. **2** *vt* contester.
**disqualify** *vt* rendre inapte (**from** à); (*in sport*) disqualifier.
**disregard** *vt* ne tenir aucun compte de.
**disrupt** *vt* (*traffic, class etc*) perturber; (*plan etc*) déranger.
**disruption** perturbation *f*; (*of plan etc*) dérangement *m*.

**disruptive** *a* (*child*) turbulent.
**dissatisfaction** mécontentement *m*.
**dissatisfied** *a* mécontent (**with** de).
**dissolve 1** *vt* dissoudre. **2** *vi* se dissoudre.
**dissuade** *vt* dissuader (**from doing** de faire).
**distance** distance *f*; **in the d.** au loin; **from a d.** de loin; **it's within walking d.** on peut y aller à pied; **to keep one's d.** garder ses distances.
**distant** *a* éloigné; (*reserved*) distant.
**distaste** aversion *f* (**for** pour).
**distasteful** *a* désagréable.
**distinct** *a* (*voice, light*) distinct; (*difference, improvement*) net (*f* nette); (*different*) distinct (**from** de).
**distinction** distinction *f*; (*at graduation*) **with d.** avec mention *f*.
**distinctive** *a* distinctif.
**distinctly** *adv* distinctement; (*definitely*) sensiblement.
**distinguish** *vti* distinguer (**from** de, **between** entre).
**distinguished** *a* distingué.
**distort** *vt* déformer.
**distract** *vt* distraire (**from** de).
**distraction** distraction *f*.
**distress** (*pain*) douleur *f*; (*anguish*) détresse *f*; **in d.** (*ship*) en détresse.
**distressing** *a* affligeant.
**distribute** *vt* distribuer; (*spread evenly*) répartir.
**distribution** distribution *f*.
**distributor** (*in car*) distributeur *m*; (*of goods*) concessionnaire *mf*.
**district** région *f*; (*of town*) quartier *m*; **d. attorney** = procureur *m* (de la République).
**distrust** *vt* se méfier de.
**disturb** *vt* (*sleep*) troubler; (*papers, belongings*) déranger; **to d. s.o.** (*bother*) déranger qn; (*worry*) troubler qn.
**disturbance** (*noise*) tapage *m*; **disturbances** (*riots*) troubles *mpl*.
**disturbing** *a* (*worrying*) inquiétant.
**ditch** fossé *m*.
**ditto** *adv* idem.
**divan** divan *m*.
**dive* 1** *vi* plonger; (*rush*) se précipiter. **2** *n* (*of swimmer, goalkeeper*) plongeon *m*; (*of aircraft*) piqué *m*.
**diver** plongeur, -euse *mf*.
**diversion** (*on road*) déviation *f*; (*distraction*) diversion *f*.
**divert** *vt* (*traffic*) dévier; (*aircraft*) dérouter.
**divide** *vt* diviser (**into** en); (*share out*) partager; (*separate*) séparer (**from** de).
**divide sth off** séparer qch (**from sth** de qch).
**divide sth up** (*share out*) partager qch.
**divided highway** route *f* à quatre voies.
**diving** plongée *f* sous-marine.
**diving board** plongeoir *m*.
**division** division *f*.
**divorce 1** *n* divorce *m*. **2** *vt* (*husband, wife*) divorcer d'avec.
**divorced** *a* divorcé (**from** d'avec); **to get d.** divorcer.
**DIY** *abbr* (*do-it-yourself*) bricolage *m*.
**dizziness** vertige *m*.
**dizzy** *a* **to be** *or* **feel d.** avoir le vertige; **to make s.o. (feel) d.** donner le vertige à qn.
**DJ** *abbr* = **disc jockey.**
**do[1]* 1** *v aux* **do you know?** savez-vous?, est-ce que vous savez?; **I do not** *or* **don't see** je ne vois pas; **he *did* say so** (*emphasis*) il l'a bien dit; **do stay** reste donc; **you know him, don't you?** tu le connais, n'est-ce pas?; **neither do I** moi non plus; **so do I** moi aussi. **2** *vt* faire; **what does she do?** (*in general*), **what is she doing?** (*now*) qu'est-ce qu'elle fait?; **what have you done (with) . . .?** qu'as-tu fait (de) . . .?;

**well done** (*congratulations*) bravo!; (*steak*) bien cuit; **to do s.o. out of sth** escroquer qch à qn; **he's done for** *Fam* il est fichu. **3** *vi* (*get along*) aller; (*suit*) faire l'affaire; (*be enough*) suffire; (*finish*) finir; **how do you do?** (*introduction*) enchanté; **he did well** *or* **right to leave** il a bien fait de partir; **do as I do** fais comme moi; **to have to do with** (*relate to*) avoir à voir avec; (*concern*) concerner.

**do²** *n* (*pl* **dos** *or* **do's**) (*party*) *Fam* soirée *f*.

**do away with sth/s.o.** supprimer qch/qn.

**dock 1** *n* (*for ship*) dock *m*. **2** *vi* (*at pier*) se mettre à quai.

**docker** docker *m*.

**dockyard** chantier *m* naval.

**doctor** médecin *m*; (*academic*) docteur *m*.

**doctorate** doctorat *m*.

**document** document *m*.

**documentary** (*film*) documentaire *m*.

**dodge 1** *vt* esquiver; (*pursuer*) échapper à; (*tax*) éviter de payer. **2** *vi* **to d. through** (*crowd*) se faufiler dans.

**does** *see* **do¹**.

**dog** chien *m*; (*female*) chienne *f*; **d. food** pâtée *f*.

**doggy bag** (*in restaurant*) petit sac *m* pour emporter les restes.

**doghouse** niche *f*.

**dog tags** plaque *f* d'identité.

**doing that's your d.** c'est toi qui as fait ça.

**do-it-yourself 1** *n* bricolage *m*. **2** *a* (*store, book*) de bricolage.

**doll** poupée *f*.

**dollar** dollar *m*.

**dollhouse** maison *f* de poupée.

**dolphin** dauphin *m*.

**dome** dôme *m*.

**domestic** *a* domestique; (*trade, flight*) intérieur.

**dominant** *a* dominant; (*person*) dominateur.

**dominate** *vti* dominer.

**domino** domino *m*; **dominoes** (*game*) dominos *mpl*.

**donate 1** *vt* faire don de; (*blood*) donner. **2** *vi* donner.

**donation** don *m*.

**done** *pp de* **do¹**.

**donkey** âne *m*.

**door** porte *f*.

**doorbell** sonnette *f*.

**doorknob** poignée *f* de porte.

**doorknocker** marteau *m*.

**doorman** (*pl* **-men**) (*of hotel*) portier *m*.

**doormat** paillasson *m*.

**doorstep** seuil *m*.

**doorstop** butoir *m* (de porte).

**doorway in the d.** dans l'encadrement de la porte.

**do sth over** (*redecorate*) refaire qch.

**dope** (*drugs*) *Fam* drogue *f*.

**dormitory** dortoir *m*; résidence *f* (universitaire).

**dosage** (*amount*) dose *f*.

**dose** dose *f*.

**dot** point *m*.

**dotted line** pointillé *m*.

**double 1** *a* double; **a d. bed** un grand lit; **a d. room** une chambre pour deux personnes. **2** *adv* (*twice*) deux fois, le double; (*to fold*) en deux. **3** *n* double *m*. **4** *vti* doubler.

**double back** (*of person*) revenir en arrière.

**double-breasted** *a* (*jacket*) croisé.

**double-decker (bus)** autobus *m* à impériale.

**double-glazing** double vitrage *m*.

**double up** (*with pain, laughter*) être plié en deux.

**doubt 1** *n* doute *m*; **no d.** (*probably*) sans doute. **2** *vt* douter de; **to d. whether** *or* **that** *or* **if** douter que (+ *subjunctive*).

**doubtful** *a* **to be d. (about sth)** avoir des doutes (sur qch); **it's d. whether** *or* **that** *or* **if** ce n'est pas sûr que (+ *subjunctive*).

**dough** pâte *f*; (*money*) *Fam* fric *m*.

**doughnut** beignet *m* (rond).
**do up** (*coat, button*) boutonner; (*zipper*) fermer; (*house*) refaire, décorer; (*goods*) emballer.
**dove** colombe *f.*
**do with sth** (*want*) **I could do with that** j'aimerais bien ça.
**do without sth/s.o.** se passer de qch/qn.
**down 1** *adv* en bas; (*to the ground*) par terre; (*of curtain, temperature*) baissé; (*in writing*) inscrit; (*out of bed*) descendu; **to come** *or* **go d.** descendre; **d. there** *or* **here** en bas; **d. with flu** grippé; **to feel d.** avoir le cafard. **2** *prep* (*at bottom of*) en bas de; (*from top to bottom of*) du haut en bas de; (*along*) le long de; **to go d.** (*hill, street, stairs*) descendre.
**down-and-out** *a* **to be d.** être sur le pavé.
**downhill** *adv* **to go d.** descendre; (*of sick person, business*) aller de plus en plus mal.
**down payment** acompte *m*, arrhes *fpl.*
**downpour** averse *f.*
**downright 1** *a* (*rogue etc*) véritable; (*refusal*) catégorique. **2** *adv* (*rude etc*) franchement.
**downstairs 1** *a* (*room, neighbors*) d'en bas. **2** *adv adv* en bas; **to come** *or* **go d.** descendre l'escalier.
**downtown** *adv* au centre-ville; **d. Chicago** le centre de Chicago.
**downward(s)** *adv* vers le bas.
**doze 1** *n* petit somme *m*. **2** *vi* sommeiller.
**dozen** douzaine *f*; **a d.** (*books etc*) une douzaine de.
**doze off** s'assoupir.
**Dr** *abbr* (*Doctor*) Docteur.
**drab** *a* terne; (*weather*) gris.
**draft** courant *m* d'air.
**draft beer** bière *f* pression.
**drafty** *a* (*room*) plein de courants d'air.
**drag** *vti* traîner.
**drag s.o./sth along** (en)traîner qn/qch.
**drag s.o. away from s.o./sth** arracher qn à qn/qch.
**drag on** *or* **out** (*last a long time*) se prolonger, s'éterniser.
**dragon** dragon *m.*
**drain 1** *n* (*sewer*) égout *m*; (*outside house*) puisard *m*; (*in street*) bouche *f* d'égout. **2** *vt* (*tank*) vider; (*vegetables*) égoutter.
**drain (off) 1** *vt* (*liquid*) faire écouler. **2** *vi* (*of liquid*) s'écouler.
**drainboard** paillasse *f.*
**drainer** (*board*) paillasse *f*; (*rack, basket*) égouttoir *m.*
**drainpipe** tuyau *m* d'évacuation.
**drama** (*event*) drame *m*; (*dramatic art*) théâtre *m.*
**dramatic** *a* dramatique; (*very great, striking*) spectaculaire.
**dramatically** *adv* (*to change etc*) de façon spectaculaire.
**drapes** *npl* (*heavy curtains*) rideaux *mpl.*
**drastic** *a* radical.
**drastically** *adv* radicalement.
**draw[1] 1** *n* (*in sports, games*) match *m* nul. **2** *vt** (*pull*) tirer; (*attract*) attirer.
**draw[2]* 1** *vt* (*picture*) dessiner; (*circle*) tracer. **2** *vi* dessiner.
**drawback** inconvénient *m.*
**drawer** tiroir *m.*
**drawing** dessin *m.*
**drawing room** salon *m.*
**draw near (to)** s'approcher (de); (*of time*) approcher (de).
**draw on** (*savings*) puiser dans.
**draw up 1** *vt* (*list, plan*) dresser. **2** *vi* (*of vehicle*) s'arrêter.
**dread 1** *vt* (*exam etc*) appréhender; **to d. doing** appréhender de faire. **2** *n* crainte *f.*
**dreadful** *a* épouvantable; (*child*) insupportable; (*ill*) malade.
**dreadfully** *adv* terriblement; **to be d. sorry** regretter infiniment.
**dream 1** *vi** rêver (**of** de, **of doing** de faire). **2** *vt* rêver (**that** que). **3** *n* rêve *m*; **to have a d.** faire un rêve (**about** de); **a d. house**/*etc* une maison/*etc* de rêve.

**dream sth up** imaginer qch.
**dreary** *a* (*gloomy*) morne; (*boring*) ennuyeux.
**drench** *vt* tremper; **to get drenched** se faire tremper.
**dress 1** *n* (*woman's*) robe *f*; (*style of dressing*) tenue *f*. **2** *vt* (*person*) habiller; (*wound*) panser; **to get dressed** s'habiller. **3** *vi* s'habiller.
**dresser** (*furniture*) coiffeuse *f*.
**dressing** (*for wound*) pansement *m*; (*seasoning*) assaisonnement *m*.
**dressing table** coiffeuse *f*.
**dressmaker** couturière *f*.
**dress up** (*smartly*) bien s'habiller; (*in disguise*) se déguiser (**as** en).
**drew** *pt de* **draw**[1,2].
**dribble 1** *vi* (*of liquids*) couler lentement. **2** *vti* (*in sports*) dribbler.
**dried** *a* (*fruit*) sec (*f* sèche); (*flowers*) séché.
**drift** *vi* être emporté par le vent *or* le courant, dériver.
**drill 1** *n* (*tool*) perceuse *f*; (*bit*) mèche *f*; (*dentist's*) roulette *f*. **2** *vt* (*hole*) percer.
**drink 1** *n* boisson *f*; (*glass of sth*) verre *m*; **to give s.o. a d.** donner (quelque chose) à boire à qn. **2** *vt** boire. **3** *vi* boire (**out of** dans); **to d. to s.o.** boire à la santé de qn.
**drinkable** *a* potable; (*not unpleasant*) buvable.
**drink sth down** boire qch.
**drinking water** eau *f* potable.
**drink up 1** *vt* boire. **2** *vi* finir son verre.
**drip 1** *vi* dégouliner; (*of laundry, vegetables*) s'égoutter; (*of faucet*) fuir. **2** *vt* (*paint etc*) laisser couler. **3** *n* goutte *f*; (*fool*) *Fam* nouille *f*.
**drip-dry** *a* (*shirt etc*) sans repassage.
**dripping** *a* & *adv* **d. (wet)** dégoulinant.
**drive 1** *n* promenade *f* en voiture; (*energy*) énergie *f*; (*road to house*) allée *f*; **an hour's d.** une heure de voiture; **four-wheel d. vehicle** quatre-quatre *m*. **2** *vt** (*vehicle, train, passenger*) conduire; (*machine*) actionner; (*chase away*) chasser; **to d. s.o. to do** pousser qn à faire; **to d. s.o. mad** *or* **crazy** rendre qn fou. **3** *vi* (*drive a car*) conduire; (*go by car*) rouler.
**drive along** (*in car*) rouler.
**drive away 1** *vt* (*chase*) chasser. **2** *vi* partir (en voiture).
**drive back 1** *vt* (*enemy*) repousser; (*passenger*) ramener (en voiture). **2** *vi* revenir (en voiture).
**drive in** (*nail*) enfoncer.
**drivel** idioties *fpl*.
**drive off** *vi* partir (en voiture).
**drive on** *vi* (*in car*) continuer.
**drive s.o./sth out** (*chase away*) chasser qn/qch.
**driver** conducteur, -trice *mf*; **(train** *or* **engine) d.** mécanicien *m*; **she's a good d.** elle conduit bien.
**driver's license** permis *m* de conduire.
**drive to** aller (en voiture) à.
**drive up** *vi* arriver (en voiture).
**driving** conduite *f*.
**driving lesson** leçon *f* de conduite.
**driving school** auto-école *f*.
**driving test** examen *m* du permis de conduire.
**drizzle 1** *n* bruine *f*. **2** *vi* bruiner.
**drool** *vi* baver.
**droop** *vi* (*of flower*) se faner.
**drop 1** *n* (*of liquid*) goutte *f*; (*fall*) baisse *f* (**in** de). **2** *vt* laisser tomber; (*price, voice*) baisser; (*passenger, goods from vehicle*) déposer; (*put*) mettre; (*leave out*) omettre; **to d. a line to** écrire un mot à. **3** *vi* tomber; (*of price*) baisser.
**drop back** *or* **behind** rester en arrière.
**drop in** (*visit s.o.*) passer (chez qn).
**drop off 1** *vi* (*fall asleep*) s'endormir; (*fall off*) tomber; (*of sales*) diminuer. **2** *vt* (*passenger*) déposer.
**drop out** (*withdraw*) se retirer.
**drought** sécheresse *f*.

**drown 1** *vi* se noyer. **2** *vt* **to d. oneself, be drowned** se noyer.
**drowsy** *a* **to be** *or* **feel d.** avoir sommeil.
**drug 1** *n* médicament *m*; (*narcotic*) stupéfiant *m*; **drugs** (*narcotics in general*) la drogue; **to be on drugs, take drugs** se droguer. **2** *vt* droguer (*qn*).
**drug addict** drogué, -ée *mf*.
**drug dealer** trafiquant *m* de drogue.
**druggist** pharmacien, -ienne *mf*.
**drugstore** drugstore *m*.
**drum** tambour *m*; (*for oil*) bidon *m*; **the drums** (*of band etc*) la batterie.
**drummer** (joueur, -euse *mf* de) tambour *m*; (*in pop or jazz group*) batteur *m*.
**drumstick** baguette *f* (de tambour); (*of chicken*) pilon *m*.
**drunk** (*pp de* **drink**) **1** *a* ivre; **to get d.** s'enivrer; **d. driving** conduite *f* en état d'ivresse. **2** *n* ivrogne *mf*.
**drunkard** ivrogne *mf*.
**dry 1** *a* sec (*f* sèche); (*well, river*) à sec; (*day*) sans pluie; (*book*) aride; **to keep sth d.** tenir qch au sec; **to feel** *or* **be d.** (*thirsty*) avoir soif. **2** *vt* sécher; (*by wiping*) essuyer.
**dry-clean** *vt* nettoyer à sec.
**dry cleaner** teinturier, -ière *mf*.
**dry cleaning** nettoyage *m* à sec.
**dryer** séchoir *m*; (*helmet-style for hair*) casque *m*; (*for laundry*) sèche-linge *m*.
**dry off** *vti* sécher.
**dry up 1** *vt* sécher. **2** *vi* sécher; (*dry the dishes*) essuyer la vaisselle.
**dual** *a* double.
**dub** *vt* (*film*) doubler.
**dubious** *a* douteux; **I'm d. about going** je me demande si je dois y aller.
**duchess** duchesse *f*.
**duck 1** *n* canard *m*. **2** *vi* se baisser (vivement).
**due** *a* (*money*) dû (*f* due) (**to** à); (*rent, bill*) à payer; **to fall d.** échoir; **he's d. (to arrive)** il doit arriver; **in d. course** en temps utile; (*finally*) à la longue; **d. to** dû à; (*because of*) à cause de.
**duel** duel *m*.
**duffel** *or* **duffle coat** duffel-coat *m*.
**duke** duc *m*.
**dull** *a* (*boring*) ennuyeux; (*color*) terne; (*weather*) maussade; (*sound, ache*) sourd.
**dullness** (*of life, town*) monotonie *f*.
**dumb** *a* muet (*f* muette); (*stupid*) idiot.
**dummy** (*for clothes*) mannequin *m*; (*person*) *Fam* idiot *m*.
**dump 1** *vt* déposer (*garbage*) **2** *n* (*dull town*) *Fam* trou *m*; **(garbage) d.** tas *m* d'ordures; (*place*) dépôt *m* d'ordures; (*room*) dépotoir *m*.
**dump truck** camion *m* à benne basculante.
**dungarees** *npl* (*of child, workman*) salopette *f*; (*jeans*) jean *m*.
**duplex** (*apartment*) duplex *m*.
**duplicate** double *m*; **in d.** en deux exemplaires; **a d. copy** une copie en double.
**durable** *a* (*material*) résistant.
**duration** durée *f*.
**during** *prep* pendant.
**dusk** crépuscule *m*.
**dust 1** *n* poussière *f*. **2** *vt* (*furniture etc*) essuyer (la poussière de). **3** *vi* faire la poussière.
**dust cloth** chiffon *m* (à poussière).
**dust jacket** (*for book*) jaquette *f*.
**dusty** *a* poussiéreux.
**Dutch 1** *a* hollandais, néerlandais; **the D.** les Hollandais *mpl*, les Néerlandais *mpl*. **2** *n* (*language*) hollandais *m*, néerlandais *m*.
**Dutchman** (*pl* **-men**) Hollandais *m*, Néerlandais *m*.
**Dutchwoman** (*pl* **-women**) Hollandaise *f*, Néerlandaise *f*.
**duty** devoir *m*; (*tax*) droit *m*; **duties** (*responsibilities*) fonctions *fpl*; **on d.** (*policeman, teacher*) de service; (*doctor*) de garde; **off d.** libre.
**duty-free** *a* (*goods, shop*) hors-taxe *inv*.
**duvet** couette *f*.

**dwarf** nain *m*, naine *f*.
**dye 1** *n* teinture *f*. **2** *vt* teindre; **to d. green** teindre en vert.
**dynamic** *a* dynamique.
**dynamite** dynamite *f*.
**dynamo** (*pl* **-os**) dynamo *f*.
**dyslexic** *a* & *n* dyslexique (*mf*).

# E

**each 1** *a* chaque. **2** *pron* **e. (one)** chacun, -une; **e. other** l'un(e) l'autre, *pl* les un(e)s les autres; **e. of us** chacun, -une d'entre nous.
**eager** *a* impatient (**to do** de faire); (*enthusiastic*) plein d'enthousiasme; **to be e. to do** (*want*) tenir (beaucoup) à faire.
**eagerly** *adv* avec enthousiasme; (*to await*) avec impatience.
**eagerness** impatience *f* (**to do** de faire).
**eagle** aigle *m*.
**ear** oreille *f*.
**earache** mal *m* d'oreille; **to have an e.** avoir mal à l'oreille.
**early 1** *a* (*first*) premier; (*age*) jeune; **it's e.** (*on clock*) il est tôt; (*referring to meeting*) c'est tôt; **it's too e. to get up** il est trop tôt pour se lever; **to be e.** (*ahead of time*) être en avance; **to have an e. meal/night** manger/se coucher de bonne heure; **in e. summer** au début de l'été. **2** *adv* tôt, de bonne heure; (*ahead of time*) en avance; **as e. as possible** le plus tôt possible; **earlier (on)** plus tôt.
**earn** *vt* gagner; (*interest*) rapporter.
**earnings** *npl* (*wages*) rémunérations *fpl*.
**earphones** *npl* casque *m*.
**earplug** boule *f* Quiès®.
**earring** boucle *f* d'oreille.
**earth** (*world, ground*) terre *f*; **where/what on e.?** où/que diable?
**earthquake** tremblement *m* de terre.
**ease 1** *n* facilité *f*; **with e.** facilement; **(ill) at e.** (mal) à l'aise. **2** *vt* (*pain*) soulager; (*mind*) calmer.
**ease (off** *or* **up)** (*become less*) diminuer; (*of pain*) se calmer; (*not work so hard*) se relâcher.
**easel** chevalet *m*.
**ease sth off** enlever qch doucement.
**easily** *adv* facilement; **e. the best/***etc* de loin le meilleur/*etc*.
**east 1** *n* est *m*; **(to the) e. of** à l'est de. **2** *a* (*coast*) est *inv*; (*wind*) d'est. **3** *adv* à l'est.
**eastbound** *a* en direction de l'est.
**Easter** Pâques *m sing or fpl*; **Happy E.!** joyeuses Pâques!
**eastern** *a* (*coast*) est *inv*; **E. Europe** Europe *f* de l'Est.
**eastward(s)** *a* & *adv* vers l'est.
**easy 1** *a* facile; (*life*) tranquille; **it's e. to do** c'est facile à faire. **2** *adv* doucement; **go e. on** (*sugar etc*) vas-y doucement avec; (*person*) ne sois pas trop dur avec; **take it e.** calme-toi; (*rest*) repose-toi; (*work less*) ne te fatigue pas.
**easy chair** fauteuil *m*.
**easygoing** *a* (*carefree*) insouciant; (*easy to get along with*) facile à vivre.
**eat*1** *vt* manger; (*meal*) prendre. **2** *vi* manger.
**eater big e.** gros mangeur *m*, grosse mangeuse *f*.
**eat out** *vi* manger dehors.
**eat sth up** (*finish*) finir qch.
**eccentric** *a* & *n* excentrique (*mf*).
**echo 1** *n* (*pl* **-oes**) écho *m*. **2** *vi* **the explosion/***etc* **echoed** l'écho de l'explosion/*etc* se répercuta.
**economic** *a* économique; (*profitable*) rentable.
**economical** *a* économique.
**economize** *vti* économiser (**on** sur).
**economy** économie *f*.
**economy class** (*on aircraft*) classe *f* touriste.
**edge** bord *m*; (*of forest*) lisière *f*; (*of town*) abords *mpl*; (*of page*) marge *f*; (*of knife*) tranchant *m*; **on e.** énervé; (*nerves*) tendu.

**edge forward** avancer doucement.

**edible** *a* comestible; (*not unpleasant*) mangeable.

**edit** *vt* (*newspaper*) diriger; (*article*) mettre au point; (*film*) monter; (*text*) éditer; (*compile*) rédiger.

**edition** édition *f*.

**editor** (*of newspaper*) rédacteur *m* en chef; (*compiler*) rédacteur, -trice *mf*.

**editorial e. staff** rédaction *f*.

**educate** *vt* éduquer; (*pupil, mind*) former.

**educated** *a* **(well-)e.** instruit.

**education** éducation *f*; (*teaching, training*) formation *f*.

**educational** *a* (*establishment*) d'enseignement; (*game*) éducatif.

**eel** anguille *f*.

**effect** effet *m* (**on** sur); **to put into e.** mettre en application; **to come into e., take e.** (*of law*) entrer en vigueur; **to take e.** (*of drug*) agir; **to have an e.** (*of medicine*) faire de l'effet.

**effective** *a* (*efficient*) efficace; (*striking*) frappant.

**effectively** *adv* efficacement; (*in fact*) effectivement.

**efficiency** efficacité *f*; (*of machine*) performances *fpl*.

**efficient** *a* efficace; (*machine*) performant.

**efficiently** *adv* efficacement; **to work e.** (*of machine*) bien fonctionner.

**effort** effort *m*; **to make an e.** faire un effort (**to** pour); **it isn't worth the e.** ça ne *or* n'en vaut pas la peine.

**e.g.** *abbr* par exemple.

**egg** œuf *m*.

**eggcup** coquetier *m*.

**eggplant** aubergine *f*.

**egg timer** sablier *m*.

**Egyptian** *a* & *n* égyptien, -ienne (*mf*).

**eiderdown** édredon *m*.

**eight** *a* & *n* huit (*m*).

**eighteen** *a* & *n* dix-huit (*m*).

**eighth** *a* & *n* huitième (*mf*).

**eighty** *a* & *n* quatre-vingts (*m*); **e.-one** quatre-vingt-un.

**either 1** *a* & *pron* (*one or other*) l'un(e) ou l'autre; (*with negative*) ni l'un(e) ni l'autre; (*each*) chaque; **on e. side** de chaque côté. **2** *adv* **she can't swim e.** elle ne sait pas nager non plus; **I don't e.** (ni) moi non plus. **3** *conj* **e. . . .or** ou (bien) . . . ou (bien); (*with negative*) ni . . . ni.

**elastic** *a* & *n* élastique (*m*).

**elbow 1** *n* coude *m*. **2** *vt* **to e. one's way** se frayer un chemin (à coups de coude) (**through** à travers).

**elder** *a* & *n* (*of two people*) aîné, -ée (*mf*).

**elderly** *a* assez âgé.

**eldest** *a* & *n* aîné, -ée (*mf*); **his** *or* **her e. brother** l'aîné de ses frères.

**elect** *vt* élire (*qn*) (**to** à).

**election 1** *n* élection *f*; **general e.** élections *fpl* législatives. **2** *a* (*campaign*) électoral; (*day, results*) du scrutin.

**electric(al)** *a* électrique.

**electric blanket** couverture *f* chauffante.

**electrician** électricien *m*.

**electrician's tape** chatterton *m*.

**electricity** électricité *f*.

**electrocute** *vt* électrocuter.

**electronic** *a* électronique.

**elegance** élégance *f*.

**elegant** *a* élégant.

**elegantly** *adv* avec élégance.

**element** élément *m*; (*of heater*) résistance *f*.

**elementary** *a* élémentaire; (*school*) primaire.

**elephant** éléphant *m*.

**elevator** ascenseur *m*.

**eleven** *a* & *n* onze (*m*).

**eleventh** *a* & *n* onzième (*mf*).

**eligible** *a* (*for post*) admissible (**for** à); **to be e. for** (*entitled to*) avoir droit à.

**eliminate** *vt* supprimer; (*applicant, possibility*) éliminer.

**else** *adv* d'autre; **everybody e.** tous les autres; **somebody/nobody/nothing e.** quelqu'un/personne/rien d'autre; **something e.** autre chose; **anything e.?** encore quelque chose?; **somewhere e.** ailleurs; **how e.?** de quelle autre façon?; **or e.** ou bien.

**elsewhere** *adv* ailleurs.

**elude** *vt* (*of word, name*) échapper à (*qn*).

**e-mail 1** *n* courrier *m* electronique. **2** *vt* envoyer un courrier électronique à.

**embark** *vi* (s')embarquer.

**embark on** (*start*) commencer.

**embarrass** *vt* embarrasser.

**embarrassing** *a* embarrassant.

**embarrassment** embarras *m*.

**embassy** ambassade *f*.

**emblem** emblème *m*.

**embrace 1** *vt* (*hug*) étreindre. **2** *vi* s'étreindre. **3** *n* étreinte *f*.

**embroider** *vt* (*cloth*) broder.

**embroidery** broderie *f*.

**emerald** émeraude *f*.

**emerge** *vi* apparaître (**from** de); (*from hole*) sortir; (*of truth, from water*) émerger.

**emergency 1** *n* urgence *f*; **in an e.** en cas d'urgence. **2** *a* (*measure*) d'urgence; (*exit, brake*) de secours; **e. room** salle *f* des urgences; **e. landing** atterrissage *m* forcé.

**emigrate** *vi* émigrer.

**emotion** (*strength of feeling*) émotion *f*; (*joy, love etc*) sentiment *m*.

**emotional** *a* (*person, reaction*) émotif; (*story*) émouvant.

**emperor** empereur *m*.

**emphasis** (*in word or phrase*) accent *m*; **to lay** *or* **put e. on** mettre l'accent sur.

**emphasize** *vt* souligner (**that** que).

**empire** empire *m*.

**employ** *vt* employer.

**employee** employé, -ée *mf*.

**employer** patron, -onne *mf*.

**employment** emploi *m*; **place of e.** lieu *m* de travail.

**employment agency** bureau *m* de placement.

**empty 1** *a* vide; (*stomach*) creux; (*threat, promise*) vain; **to return e.-handed** revenir les mains vides. **2** *vi* (*of building, tank etc*) se vider.

**empty (out)** (*box, liquid etc*) vider; (*vehicle*) décharger; (*objects in box etc*) sortir (**from**, de).

**emulsion** émulsion *f*.

**enable** *vt* **to e. s.o. to do** permettre à qn de faire.

**enamel 1** *n* émail *m* (*pl* émaux). **2** *a* en émail.

**enchanting** *a* charmant, enchanteur (*f* -eresse).

**enclose** *vt* (*send with letter*) joindre (**in, with** à); (*fence off*) clôturer.

**enclosed** *a* (*space*) clos; (*receipt etc*) ci-joint.

**enclosure** (*in letter*) pièce *f* jointe; (*place*) enceinte *f*.

**encounter 1** *vt* rencontrer. **2** *n* rencontre *f*.

**encourage** *vt* encourager (**to do** à faire).

**encouragement** encouragement *m*.

**encyclop(a)edia** encyclopédie *f*.

**end 1** *n* (*of street, box etc*) bout *m*; (*of meeting, month, book etc*) fin *f*; (*purpose*) fin *f*, but *m*; **at an e.** (*discussion etc*) fini; (*patience*) à bout; **in the e.** à la fin; **to come to an e.** prendre fin; **to put an e. to, bring to an e.** mettre fin à; **no e. of** *Fam* beaucoup de; **for days on e.** pendant des jours et des jours. **2** *vt* finir (**with** par); (*rumor*) mettre fin à. **3** *vi* finir; **to e. in failure** se solder par un échec.

**endanger** *vt* mettre en danger.

**ending** fin *f*; (*of word*) terminaison *f*.

**endive** (*curly*) chicorée *f*; (*smooth*) endive *f*.

**endless** *a* interminable.

**endorse** *vt* (*check*) endosser; (*action*) approuver.

**endorsement** (*signature*) aval *m*;

(*backing*) appui *m*; (*on check*) endossement *m*.

**end up** *vi* **to e. up doing** finir par faire; **to e. up in** (*London etc*) se retrouver à; **he ended up in prison/a doctor** il a fini en prison/par devenir médecin.

**endurance** endurance *f*.

**endure** *vt* supporter (**doing** de faire).

**enemy** *n* & *a* ennemi, -ie (*mf*).

**energetic** *a* énergique.

**energy 1** *n* énergie *f*. **2** *a* (*crisis, resources etc*) énergétique.

**enforce** *vt* (*law*) faire respecter.

**engaged** *a* **e. (to be married)** fiancé; **to get e.** se fiancer.

**engagement** (*to marry*) fiançailles *fpl*; (*meeting*) rendez-vous *m inv*; **e. ring** bague *f* de fiançailles.

**engine** (*of vehicle*) moteur *m*; (*of train*) locomotive *f*; (*of jet*) réacteur *m*.

**engineer** ingénieur *m*; (*repairer*) dépanneur, -euse *mf*.

**engineering** ingénierie *f*, génie *m*.

**English 1** *a* anglais; (*teacher*) d'anglais; **the E. Channel** la Manche; **the E.** les Anglais *mpl*. **2** *n* (*language*) anglais *m*.

**Englishman** (*pl* **-men**) Anglais *m*.

**English-speaking** *a* anglophone.

**Englishwoman** (*pl* **-women**) Anglaise *f*.

**engrave** *vt* graver.

**engraving** gravure *f*.

**enjoy** *vt* aimer (**doing** faire); (*meal*) apprécier; **to e. the evening** passer une bonne soirée; **to e. oneself** s'amuser; **to e. being in Paris** se plaire à Paris.

**enjoyable** *a* agréable.

**enjoyment** plaisir *m*.

**enlarge** *vt* agrandir.

**enlighten** *vt* éclairer (**s.o. on** *or* **about sth** qn sur qch).

**enormous** *a* énorme.

**enormously** *adv* (*very much*) énormément; (*very*) extrêmement.

**enough 1** *a* & *n* assez (de); **e. time/cups**/*etc* assez de temps/de tasses/*etc*; **to have e. to live on** avoir de quoi vivre; **e. to drink** assez à boire; **to have had e. of** en avoir assez de; **that's e.** ça suffit. **2** *adv* assez; **big/good**/*etc* **e.** assez grand/bon/*etc* (**to** pour).

**enquire** *vi* = **inquire.**

**enquiry** *n* = **inquiry.**

**enroll** *vi* s'inscrire (**in, for** à).

**enrollment** inscription *f*.

**ensure** *vt* assurer; **to e. that** s'assurer que.

**entail** *vt* supposer.

**enter 1** *vt* (*room, vehicle etc*) entrer dans; (*university*) s'inscrire à; (*race, competition*) s'inscrire pour; (*write down*) inscrire (**in** dans); **to e. s.o./sth in** (*competition*) présenter qn/qch à; **it didn't e. my head** *or* **mind** ça ne m'est pas venu à l'esprit. **2** *vi* entrer.

**enter into** (*conversation*) entrer en; (*career*) entrer dans; (*agreement*) conclure.

**enterprise** (*undertaking, firm*) entreprise *f*; (*spirit*) initiative *f*.

**enterprising** *a* plein d'initiative.

**entertain 1** *vt* amuser; (*guest*) recevoir. **2** *vi* (*receive guests*) recevoir.

**entertainer** artiste *mf*.

**entertaining** *a* amusant.

**entertainment** amusement *m*; (*show*) spectacle *m*.

**enthusiasm** enthousiasme *m*.

**enthusiast** enthousiaste *mf*; **jazz/***etc* **e.** passionné, -ée *mf* de jazz/*etc*.

**enthusiastic** *a* enthousiaste; (*golfer etc*) passionné; **to be e. about** (*hobby*) être passionné de; (*gift*) être emballé par; **to get e.** s'emballer (**about** pour).

**enthusiastically** *adv* avec enthousiasme.

**entire** *a* entier.

**entirely** *adv* tout à fait.

**entitle** *vt* **to e. s.o. to do** donner à qn le droit de faire; **to e. s.o. to sth** donner à qn (le) droit à qch.

**entitled** *a* **to be e. to do** avoir le droit de faire; **to be e. to sth** avoir droit à qch.

**entrance** entrée *f* (**to** de); (*to university*) admission *f* (**to** à); **e. exam** examen *m* d'entrée.

**entrant** (*in race*) concurrent, -ente *mf*; (*for exam*) candidat, -ate *mf*.

**entry** (*way in, action*) entrée *f*; (*bookkeeping item*) écriture *f*; (*dictionary term*) entrée *f*; (*in competition*) objet *m* (*or* œuvre *f or* projet *m*) soumis au jury; **'no e.'** 'entrée interdite'; (*road sign*) 'sens interdit'.

**entry form** feuille *f* d'inscription.

**envelope** enveloppe *f*.

**envious** *a* envieux (**of sth** de qch); **e. of s.o.** jaloux de qn.

**environment** milieu *m*; (*natural*) environnement *m*.

**environmental** *a* du milieu; de l'environnement; (*group*) écologiste; (*issue*) écologique, lié ā l'environnement.

**envy 1** *n* envie *f*. **2** *vt* envier (**s.o. sth** qch à qn).

**epidemic** épidémie *f*.

**episode** épisode *m*.

**equal 1** *a* égal (**to** à); **to be e. to** (*number*) égaler; **she's e. to** (*task*) elle est à la hauteur de. **2** *n* (*person*) égal, -ale *mf*.

**equality** égalité *f*.

**equalize** *vi* (*score*) égaliser.

**equally** *adv* également; (*to divide*) en parts égales.

**equation** équation *f*.

**equator** équateur *m*.

**equip** *vt* équiper (**with** de); **(well-) equipped with** pourvu de; **(well-) equipped to do** compétent pour faire.

**equipment** équipement *m*.

**equivalent** *a* & *n* équivalent (*m*).

**erase** *vt* effacer.

**eraser** gomme *f*.

**erect 1** *a* (*upright*) (bien) droit. **2** *vt* construire; (*statue etc*) ériger; (*scaffolding, tent*) monter.

**errand** commission *f*.

**erratic** *a* (*service, machine etc*) capricieux; (*person*) lunatique.

**error** erreur *f*; **to do sth in e.** faire qch par erreur.

**escalator** escalier *m* roulant.

**escape 1** *vi* s'échapper; **to e. from** (*person*) échapper à; (*place*) s'échapper de. **2** *vt* (*death*) échapper à; (*punishment*) éviter; **her name escapes me** son nom m'échappe. **3** *n* (*of gas*) fuite *f*; (*of person*) évasion *f*.

**escort 1** *n* (*soldiers etc*) escorte *f*. **2** *vt* escorter.

**Eskimo** (*pl* **-os**) Esquimau, -aude *mf*.

**especially** *adv* (tout) spécialement; **e. as** d'autant plus que.

**espresso** (*pl* **-os**) (café *m*) express *m inv*.

**essay** (*at school*) rédaction *f*.

**essential** *a* essentiel.

**essentially** *adv* essentiellement.

**establish** *vt* établir.

**establishment** (*institution, firm*) établissement *m*.

**estate** (*land*) terre(s) *f*(*pl*); (*property after death*) succession *f*.

**estimate 1** *vt* estimer (**that** que). **2** *n* évaluation *f*; (*price for work to be done*) devis *m*.

**etiquette** bienséances *fpl*.

**Euro-** *prefix* euro-.

**European** *a* & *n* européen, -éenne (*mf*).

**European Union** Union *f* européenne.

**evacuate** *vt* évacuer.

**evade** *vt* éviter; (*pursuer, tax*) échapper à; (*law, question*) éluder.

**evaluate** *vt* évaluer (**at** à).

**evaporated milk** lait *m* concentré.

**eve on the e. of** à la veille de.

**even 1** *a* (*flat*) uni; (*equal*) égal; (*regular*) régulier; (*number*) pair; **to get e. with s.o.** se venger de qn; **we're e.** nous sommes quittes; (*in score*) nous sommes à égalité; **to break e.** (*financially*) s'y retrouver. **2** *adv* même; **e. better/more** encore mieux/plus; **e. if** *or* **though** même si; **e. so** quand même.

**evening** soir *m*; (*whole evening, event*) soirée *f*; **in the e.** le soir; **at**

**seven in the e.** à sept heures du soir; **every Tuesday e.** tous les mardis soir; **all e. (long)** toute la soirée.
**evening dress** tenue *f* de soirée.
**evening gown** robe *f* du soir.
**evenly** *adv* de manière égale; (*regularly*) régulièrement.
**even sth out** *or* **up** égaliser qch.
**event** événement *m*; (*in sport*) épreuve *f*; **in the e. of death** en cas de décès; **in any e.** en tout cas.
**eventual** *a* final.
**eventually** *adv* finalement; (*some day or other*) un jour ou l'autre.
**ever** *adv* jamais; **more than e.** plus que jamais; **nothing e.** jamais rien; **hardly e.** presque jamais; **the first e.** le tout premier; **e. since** (*that event etc*) depuis; **e. since then** depuis lors; **for e.** pour toujours; (*continually*) sans cesse; **e. so happy**/*etc* vraiment heureux/*etc*; **why e. not?** et pourquoi pas?
**every** *a* chaque; **e. one** chacun, -une; **e. single one** tous *or* toutes (sans exception); **e. other day** tous les deux jours; **e. so often, e. now and then** de temps en temps.
**everybody** *pron* tout le monde; **e. in turn** chacun *or* chacune à son tour.
**everyday** *a* (*life*) de tous les jours; (*ordinary*) banal (*mpl* banals); **in e. use** d'usage courant.
**everyone** *pron* = **everybody.**
**everyplace** *adv* = **everywhere.**
**everything** *pron* tout; **e. I have** tout ce que j'ai.
**everywhere** *adv* partout; **e. she goes** où qu'elle aille.
**evidence** *n* preuve(s) *f*(*pl*); (*given by witness etc*) témoignage *m*; **e. of** (*wear etc*) des signes *mpl* de.
**evident** *a* évident (**that** que).
**evidently** *adv* évidemment; (*apparently*) apparemment.
**evil 1** *a* (*influence, person*) malfaisant; (*deed, system*) mauvais. **2** *n* mal *m*.
**ewe** brebis *f*.
**ex-** *prefix* ex-; **ex-wife** ex-femme *f*.
**exact** *a* exact; **to be e. about sth** préciser qch.
**exactly** *adv* exactement.
**exaggerate** *vti* exagérer.
**exaggeration** exagération *f*.
**exam** examen *m*.
**examination** (*in school etc*) examen *m*.
**examine** *vt* examiner; (*accounts, luggage*) vérifier; (*passport*) contrôler; (*question*) interroger.
**examiner** examinateur, -trice *mf*.
**example** exemple *m*; **for e.** par exemple; **to set an e.** donner l'exemple (**to** à).
**exceed** *vt* dépasser.
**excel** *vi* **to e. in sth** être excellent en qch.
**excellent** *a* excellent.
**except** *prep* sauf, excepté; **e. for** à part; **e. that** sauf que.
**exception** exception *f*; **with the e. of** à l'exception de.
**exceptional** *a* exceptionnel.
**exceptionally** *adv* exceptionnellement.
**excerpt** extrait *m*.
**excess 1** *n* excès *m*; (*surplus*) excédent *m*. **2** *a* **e. fare** supplément *m* (de billet); **e. luggage** *or* **baggage** excédent *m* de bagages.
**excessive** *a* excessif.
**excessively** *adv* (*too, too much*) excessivement; (*very*) extrêmement.
**exchange 1** *vt* échanger (**for** contre). **2** *n* échange *m*; (*of foreign currencies*) change *m*; **(telephone) e.** central *m* (téléphonique); **in e.** en échange (**for** de).
**excite** *vt* (*enthuse*) passionner.
**excited** *a* (*happy*) surexcité; (*nervous*) énervé; **to get e.** (*nervous, enthusiastic*) s'exciter; **to be e. about** (*new car etc*) se réjouir de.
**excitement** agitation *f*; (*emotion*) vive émotion *f*.
**exciting** *a* (*book etc*) passionnant.
**exclaim** *vti* s'exclamer (**that** que).
**exclamation point** point *m* d'exclamation.
**exclude** *vt* exclure (**from** de).

**exclusive** *a* exclusif; (*club*) fermé; **e. of wine**/*etc* vin/*etc* non compris.
**excursion** excursion *f*.
**excuse 1** *vt* excuser (**s.o. for doing** qn d'avoir fait, qn de faire); (*exempt*) dispenser (**from** de). **2** *n* excuse *f*.
**execute** *vt* (*criminal*) exécuter.
**execution** exécution *f*.
**executive 1** *a* (*job*) de cadre; (*car, plane*) de direction. **2** *n* (*person*) cadre *m*; **senior e.** cadre *m* supérieur; **junior e.** jeune cadre *m*; **sales e.** cadre *m* commercial.
**exempt 1** *a* dispensé (**from** de). **2** *vt* dispenser (**from** de).
**exemption** dispense *f*.
**exercise 1** *n* exercice *m*. **2** *vt* (*muscles, rights*) exercer; (*dog, horse*) promener; (*tact, judgment*) faire preuve de. **3** *vi* faire de l'exercice.
**exercise book** cahier *m*.
**exert** *vt* exercer; **to e. oneself** (*physically*) se dépenser; **don't e. yourself!** ne te fatigue pas!
**exertion** effort *m*.
**exhaust 1** *vt* épuiser; **to become exhausted** s'épuiser. **2** *n* **e. (pipe)** tuyau *m* d'échappement.
**exhausting** *a* épuisant.
**exhibit 1** *vt* (*put on display*) exposer. **2** *n* objet *m* exposé.
**exhibition** exposition *f*.
**exhibitor** exposant, -ante *mf*.
**exist** *vi* exister; (*live*) vivre (**on** de).
**existence** existence *f*; **to be in e.** exister.
**existing** *a* (*situation*) actuel.
**exit** sortie *f*.
**exorbitant** *a* exorbitant.
**expand 1** *vt* (*trade, ideas*) développer; (*production*) augmenter; (*gas, metal*) dilater. **2** *vi* se développer; (*of production*) augmenter; (*of gas, metal*) se dilater.
**expanse** étendue *f*.
**expansion** (*of trade etc*) développement *m*.
**expect** *vt* s'attendre à; (*think*) penser (**that** que); (*suppose*) supposer (**that** que); (*await*) attendre; **to e. sth from s.o./sth** attendre qch de qn/qch; **to e. to do** compter faire; **to e. that** s'attendre à ce que (+ *subjunctive*); **I e. you to come** (*want*) je compte sur votre présence; **it was expected** c'était prévu; **she's expecting (a baby)** elle attend un bébé.
**expectation** attente *f*.
**expedition** expédition *f*.
**expel** *vt* (*from school*) renvoyer.
**expenditure** (*money*) dépenses *fpl*.
**expense** frais *mpl*; **business expenses** frais *mpl* généraux; **at s.o.'s e.** (*doing s.o. no good*) aux dépens de qn.
**expensive** *a* cher.
**experience 1** *n* expérience *f*; **he's had e. of driving** il a déjà conduit. **2** *vt* connaître; (*difficulty*) éprouver.
**experienced** *a* expérimenté; **to be e. in** s'y connaître en.
**experiment 1** *n* expérience *f*. **2** *vi* faire une expérience *or* des expériences.
**expert** expert *m* (**on, in** en); **e. advice** le conseil d'un expert.
**expertise** compétence *f* (**in** en).
**expiration date** date *f* d'expiration.
**expire** *vi* expirer.
**expired** *a* (*ticket, passport etc*) périmé.
**explain** *vt* expliquer (**to** à, **that** que).
**explain sth away** justifier qch.
**explanation** explication *f*.
**explode** *vi* exploser.
**exploit 1** *vt* exploiter. **2** *n* exploit *m*.
**exploration** exploration *f*.
**explore** *vt* explorer; (*causes etc*) examiner.
**explorer** explorateur, -trice *mf*.
**explosion** explosion *f*.
**explosive** explosif *m*.
**export 1** *n* exportation *f*. **2** *vt* exporter (**to** vers, **from** de).
**expose** *vt* exposer (**to** à); (*plot etc*) révéler; (*crook etc*) démasquer.
**express 1** *vt* exprimer; **to e. one-**

**self** s'exprimer. **2** *a* (*letter, delivery*) exprès *inv*; (*train*) rapide. **3** *adv* (*to send*) par exprès *or* Chronopost®. **4** *n* (*train*) rapide *m*.

**expression** (*phrase, look*) expression *f*.

**expressway** autoroute *f*.

**extend 1** *vt* (*arm, business*) étendre; (*line, visit*) prolonger (**by** de); (*house*) agrandir; (*time limit*) reculer. **2** *vi* s'étendre (**to** jusqu'à); (*in time*) se prolonger.

**extension** (*for table*) rallonge *f*; (*to building*) agrandissement(s) *m*(*pl*); (*of phone*) appareil *m* supplémentaire; (*of office phone*) poste *m*; **e. cord** rallonge *f*.

**extensive** *a* étendu; (*repairs, damage*) important.

**extensively** *adv* (*very much*) énormément, considérablement.

**extent** (*scope*) étendue *f*; (*size*) importance *f*; **to a large/certain e.** dans une large/certaine mesure; **to such an e. that** à tel point que.

**exterior** *a* & *n* extérieur (*m*).

**external** *a* extérieur; **for e. use** (*medicine*) à usage externe.

**extinguisher (fire) e.** extincteur *m*.

**extra 1** *a* supplémentaire; **one e. glass** un verre de *or* en plus; **to be e.** (*spare*) être en trop; (*cost more*) être en supplément; **e. charge** *or* **portion** supplément *m*. **2** *adv* **to pay e.** payer un supplément; **wine costs** *or* **is 3 francs e.** il y a un supplément de 3 francs pour le vin. **3** *n* (*perk*) à-côté *m*; **extras** (*expenses*) frais *mpl* supplémentaires.

**extra-** *prefix* extra-.

**extract 1** *vt* extraire (**from** de). **2** *n* extrait *m*.

**extra-curricular** *a* extrascolaire.

**extraordinary** *a* extraordinaire.

**extra-special** *a* (*occasion*) très spécial.

**extravagant** *a* (*wasteful with money*) dépensier.

**extreme 1** *a* extrême; (*danger, poverty*) très grand. **2** *n* extrême *m*.

**extremely** *adv* extrêmement.

**eye** œil *m* (*pl* yeux); **to keep an e. on** surveiller; **to lay** *or* **set eyes on** voir; **to take one's eyes off s.o./sth** quitter qn/qch des yeux.

**eyebrow** sourcil *m*.

**eyeglasses** *npl* lunettes *fpl*.

**eyelash** cil *m*.

**eyelid** paupière *f*.

**eyeliner** eye-liner *m*.

**eye shadow** fard *m* à paupières.

**eyesight** vue *f*.

# F

**fabulous** *a* (*wonderful*) *Fam* formidable.

**face 1** *n* (*of person*) visage *m*, figure *f*; (*of clock*) cadran *m*; **f. down** face contre terre; (*thing*) tourné à l'envers; **f. to f.** face à face; **to make faces** faire des grimaces. **2** *vt* (*danger, problem etc*) faire face à; (*accept*) accepter; (*look in the face*) regarder (*qn*) bien en face; (*be opposite*) être en face de; (*of window*) donner sur; **faced with** (*problem*) confronté à; **he can't f. leaving** il n'a pas le courage de partir. **3** *vi* (*of house*) être orienté (**north**/*etc* au nord/*etc*); (*be turned*) être tourné (**towards** vers).

**facecloth** gant *m* de toilette.

**face up to** (*danger, problem*) faire face à; (*fact*) accepter.

**facilities** *npl* (*for sports, cooking etc*) équipements *mpl*; (*in harbor, airport*) installations *fpl*.

**fact** fait *m*; **as a matter of f., in f.** en fait.

**factor** facteur *m*.

**factory** usine *f*.

**fade** *vi* (*of flower*) se faner; (*of light*) baisser; (*of color*) passer; (*of fabric*) se décolorer.

**fade (away)** (*of sound*) s'affaiblir.

**fail 1** *vi* échouer; (*of business*) faire faillite; (*of health, sight*) baisser; (*of brakes*) lâcher. **2** *vt* (*exam*) rater, échouer à; (*candidate*) refuser, recaler; **to f. to do** (*forget*) manquer de faire; (*not be able*) ne pas arriver à faire. **3** *n* **without f.** à coup sûr.

**failed** *a* (*attempt, poet*) manqué.

**failing 1** *n* défaut *m*. **2** *prep* **f. that** à défaut.

**failure** échec *m*; (*of business*) faillite *f*; (*person*) raté, -ée *mf*; **f. to do** incapacité *f* de faire.

**faint 1** *a* faible; (*color*) pâle; **I haven't got the faintest idea** je n'en ai pas la moindre idée; **to feel f.** se trouver mal. **2** *vi* s'évanouir.

**faintly** *adv* faiblement; (*slightly*) légèrement.

**fair**[1] (*for trade*) foire *f*; (*for entertainment*) fête *f* foraine, kermesse *f*; (*for charity*) fête *f*.

**fair**[2] *a* (*just*) juste; (*game, fight*) loyal; **f. enough!** très bien! ▪ (*rather good*) passable; (*weather*) beau; (*price*) raisonnable; **a f. amount (of)** pas mal (de).

**fair**[3] *a* (*hair, person*) blond.

**fair-haired** *a* blond.

**fairly** *adv* (*to treat*) équitablement; (*rather*) assez.

**fairness** justice *f*; (*of person*) impartialité *f*.

**fair play** fair-play *m inv*.

**fair-sized** *a* assez grand.

**fairy** fée *f*; **f. tale** *or* **story** conte *m* de fées.

**faith** foi *f*; **to have f. in s.o.** avoir confiance en qn.

**faithful** *a* fidèle (**to** à).

**fake 1** *n* faux *m*; (*person*) imposteur *m*. **2** *vt* (*document etc*) falsifier. **3** *vi* faire semblant. **4** *a* faux (*f* fausse).

**fall 1** *n* chute *f*; (*in price etc*) baisse *f* (**in** de); (*season*) automne *m*. **2** *vi** tomber; **to f. off** *or* **out of** *or* **down sth** tomber de qch; **to f. over** (*chair*) tomber en butant contre; (*balcony*) tomber de; **to f. ill** tomber malade.

**fall apart** (*of machine*) tomber en morceaux; (*of group*) se défaire.

**fall back on sth** (*as last resort*) se rabattre sur qch.

**fall behind** rester en arrière; (*in work, payments*) prendre du retard.

**fall down** *vi* tomber; (*of building*) s'effondrer.

**fall for** tomber amoureux de; (*trick*) se laisser prendre à.

**fall in** (*collapse*) s'écrouler.

**fall off** (*come off*) se détacher; (*of numbers*) diminuer.

**fall out** (*quarrel*) se brouiller (**with** avec).

**fall over** *vi* tomber; (*of table, vase*) se renverser.

**fall through** (*of plan*) tomber à l'eau.

**false** *a* faux (*f* fausse).

**fame** renommée *f*.

**familiar** *a* familier (**to** à); **f. with s.o.** (*too friendly*) familier avec qn; **to be f. with** (*know*) connaître.

**familiarity** familiarité *f* (**with** avec).

**familiarize** *vt* **to f. oneself with** se familiariser avec.

**family** famille *f*.

**famous** *a* célèbre (**for** pour).

**fan**[1] (*held in hand*) éventail *m*; (*mechanical*) ventilateur *m*.

**fan**[2] (*of person*) fan *mf*; (*of team etc*) supporter *m*; **to be a jazz/sports f.** être passionné de jazz/de sport.

**fancy 1** *n* **I took a f. to it.** j'en ai eu envie. **2** *a* (*hat, button etc*) fantaisie *inv*. **3** *int* **f. (that)!** tiens (donc)!

**fantastic** *a* fantastique.

**far 1** *adv* (*distance*) loin; **f. bigger/** *etc* beaucoup plus grand/*etc* (**than** que); **how f. is it to?** combien y a-t-il d'ici à?; **so f.** (*time*) jusqu'ici; **as f. as** (*place*) jusqu'à; **as f. as I know** autant que je sache; **as f. as I'm concerned** en ce qui me concerne; **f. from doing** loin de faire; **f. away** *or* **off** au loin; **by f.** de loin. **2** *a* (*side, end*) autre.

**faraway** *a* (*country*) lointain.

**farce** farce *f*.

**fare** (*price*) prix *m* du billet.
**farewell** *int* adieu.
**far-fetched** *a* tiré par les cheveux.
**farm 1** *n* ferme *f*. **2** *a* (*worker, produce*) agricole; **f. land** terres *fpl* cultivées. **3** *vt* cultiver.
**farmer** fermier, -ière *mf*.
**farmhouse** ferme *f*.
**farming** agriculture *f*.
**farmyard** basse-cour *f*, cour *f* de ferme.
**far-off** *a* lointain.
**farther** *adv* plus loin; **to get f. away** s'éloigner.
**farthest 1** *a* le plus éloigné. **2** *adv* le plus loin.
**fascinate** *vt* fasciner.
**fascination** fascination *f*.
**fashion** (*style in clothes*) mode *f*; (*manner*) façon *f*; **in f.** à la mode; **out of f.** démodé.
**fashionable** *a* à la mode; (*place*) chic *inv*.
**fashion show** présentation *f* de collections.
**fast 1** *a* rapide; **to be f.** (*of clock*) avancer (**by** de). **2** *adv* (*quickly*) vite; **f. asleep** profondément endormi.
**fasten** *vt* attacher (**to** à); (*door, window*) fermer (bien).
**fastener** (*clip*) attache *f*; (*of garment*) fermeture *f*; (*of bag*) fermoir *m*; (*hook*) agrafe *f*.
**fat 1** *n* graisse *f*; (*on meat*) gras *m*. **2** *a* gras (*f* grasse); (*cheek, salary*) gros (*f* grosse); **to get f.** grossir.
**fatal** *a* mortel; (*mistake etc*) fatal (*mpl* fatals).
**fate** destin *m*, sort *m*.
**father** père *m*.
**father-in-law** (*pl* **fathers-in-law**) beau-père *m*.
**fatigue** fatigue *f*.
**fattening** *a* (*food*) qui fait grossir.
**fatty** *a* (*food*) gras (*f* grasse).
**faucet** (*tap*) robinet *m*.
**fault** faute *f*; (*defect*) défaut *m*; (*mistake*) erreur *f*; **it's your f.** c'est ta faute; **to find f. (with)** critiquer.
**faulty** *a* défectueux.
**favor 1** *n* (*act of kindness*) service *m*; **to do s.o. a f.** rendre service à qn; **to be in f. of** (*support*) être pour; (*prefer*) préférer. **2** *vt* (*encourage*) favoriser; (*prefer*) préférer.
**favorable** *a* favorable (**to** à).
**favorite** *a* & *n* favori, -ite (*mf*), préféré, -ée (*mf*).
**fax 1** *n* (*machine*) télécopieur *m*, fax *m*; (*message*) télécopie *f*, fax *m*. **2** *vt* (*message*) faxer; **to f. s.o.** envoyer une télécopie *or* un fax à qn.
**fear 1** *n* crainte *f*, peur *f*; **for f. of doing** de peur de faire. **2** *vt* craindre.
**fearless** *a* intrépide.
**feast** festin *m*.
**feat** exploit *m*.
**feather** plume *f*.
**feature** (*of face, person*) trait *m*; (*of thing, place*) caractéristique *f*.
**February** février *m*.
**fed up** *a* **to be f. up** *Fam* en avoir marre (**with** de).
**fee** prix *m*; **fee(s)** (*professional*) honoraires *mpl*; (*for registration*) droits *mpl*; **school** *or* **tuition fees** frais *mpl* de scolarité.
**feeble** *a* faible.
**feed*** *vt* donner à manger à; (*breast-feed*) allaiter; (*bottle-feed*) donner le biberon à (*un bébé*).
**feedback** réaction(s) *f*(*pl*).
**feel 1** *n* toucher *m*; (*feeling*) sensation *f*. **2** *vt** (*be aware of*) sentir; (*experience*) éprouver; (*touch*) tâter; **to f. that** avoir l'impression que. **3** *vi* (*tired, old etc*) se sentir; **I f. hot/sleepy/***etc* j'ai chaud/sommeil/*etc*; **she feels better** elle va mieux; **to f. like sth** (*want*) avoir envie de qch.
**feel around** tâtonner; (*in pocket etc*) fouiller.
**feeling** sentiment *m*; (*physical*) sensation *f*.
**feel up to doing** être en forme pour faire.

**feet** *see* **foot.**
**fell** *pt de* **fall.**
**fellow** (*man*) type *m*.
**felt**[1] *pt & pp de* **feel.**
**felt**[2] feutre *m*.
**felt-tip (pen)** (crayon *m*) feutre *m*.
**female 1** *a* (*voice etc*) féminin; (*animal*) femelle; **f. student** étudiante *f*. **2** *n* femme *f*; (*animal*) femelle *f*.
**feminine** *a* féminin.
**fence 1** *n* barrière *f*; (*in race*) obstacle *m*. **2** *vi* (*with sword*) faire de l'escrime.
**fence (in)** (*land*) clôturer.
**fencing** (*sport*) escrime *f*.
**fend** *vi* **to f. for oneself** se débrouiller.
**fender** (*on car*) aile *f*.
**fern** fougère *f*.
**ferocious** *a* féroce.
**ferry** ferry-boat *m*; (*small, for river*) bac *m*.
**fertile** *a* (*land*) fertile.
**fertilizer** engrais *m*.
**festival** festival *m* (*pl* -als).
**festivities** *npl* festivités *fpl*.
**fetch**[1] *vt* (*bring*) amener (*qn*); (*object*) apporter; **to (go and) f.** aller chercher.
**fetch**[2] *vt* (*be sold for*) rapporter.
**fête** fête *f*.
**fever** fièvre *f*; **to have a f.** avoir de la fièvre.
**feverish** *a* fiévreux.
**few** *a & pron* peu (de); **f. towns**/*etc* peu de villes/*etc*; **a f. towns**/*etc* quelques villes/*etc*; **f. of them** peu d'entre eux; **a f.** quelques-un(e)s (**of** de); **a f. of us** quelques-uns d'entre nous; **quite a f., a good f.** bon nombre (de); **a f. more books**/*etc* encore quelques livres/*etc*; **every f. days** tous les trois ou quatre jours.
**fewer** *a & pron* moins (de) (**than** que).
**fiancé(e)** fiancé, -ée *mf*.
**fiber** fibre *f*.
**fiberboard** (bois) aggloméré *m*.
**fiction (works of) f.** romans *mpl*.
**fiddle** (*dishonest act*) *Fam* combine *f*.
**fiddle (around) with** (*pen etc*) tripoter; (*cars etc*) bricoler.
**fidget** *vi* gigoter.
**field** champ *m*; (*for sports*) terrain *m*.
**fierce** *a* féroce; (*attack*) furieux.
**fifteen** *a & n* quinze (*m*).
**fifteenth** *a & n* quinzième (*mf*).
**fifth** *a & n* cinquième (*mf*).
**fiftieth** *a & n* cinquantième (*mf*).
**fifty** *a & n* cinquante (*m*).
**fig** figue *f*.
**fight 1** *n* bagarre *f*; *Boxing* combat *m*; (*struggle*) lutte *f*; (*quarrel*) dispute *f*. **2** *vi** se battre (**against** contre); (*struggle*) lutter (**for** pour); (*quarrel*) se disputer. **3** *vt* se battre avec (*qn*).
**fight back** *vi* se défendre.
**fighter** (*determined person*) battant, -ante *mf*.
**fight off** (*attacker*) repousser.
**fight over sth** se disputer qch.
**figure**[1] (*numeral*) chiffre *m*; (*price*) prix *m*; (*of woman*) ligne *f*; (*diagram, important person*) figure *f*.
**figure**[2] *vt* **to f. that** (*guess*) penser que.
**figure on doing** compter faire.
**figure out** arriver à comprendre; (*problem*) résoudre.
**file** (*tool*) lime *f*; (*folder, information*) dossier *m*; (*computer data*) fichier *m*; **in single f.** en file.
**file (away)** (*document*) classer.
**file (down)** limer.
**file in/out** entrer/sortir à la queue leu leu.
**filing cabinet** classeur *m*.
**fill 1** *vt* remplir (**with** de); (*tooth*) plomber. **2** *vi* se remplir.
**fillet** filet *m*.
**fill in** (*form, hole*) remplir.
**filling 1** *a* (*meal*) nourrissant. **2** *n* (*in tooth*) plombage *m*; (*in food*) garniture *f*.
**fill out** (*form*) remplir.

**fill up 1** *vt* (*container, form*) remplir. **2** *vi* se remplir; (*with gas*) faire le plein.
**film 1** *n* film *m*; (*for camera*) pellicule *f*. **2** *vt* filmer.
**filter** filtre *m*; **f.-tipped cigarette** cigarette *f* (à bout) filtre.
**filth** saleté *f*.
**filthy** *a* sale.
**fin** (*of fish*) nageoire *f*.
**final 1** *a* (*last*) dernier. **2** *n* (*match*) finale *f*.
**finalize** *vt* mettre au point; (*date*) fixer.
**finally** *adv* enfin.
**finance 1** *n* finance *f*. **2** *vt* financer.
**financial** *a* financier.
**find 1** *n* trouvaille *f*. **2** *vt** trouver; (*sth or s.o. lost*) retrouver.
**find out 1** *vt* (*secret etc*) découvrir; (*person*) démasquer. **2** *vi* (*inquire*) se renseigner (**about** sur); **to f. out about sth** (*discover*) découvrir qch.
**fine[1] 1** *n* amende *f*; (*for driving offense*) contravention *f*. **2** *vt* **to f. s.o. ($100/*etc*)** infliger une amende (de cent dollars/*etc*) à qn.
**fine[2] 1** *a* (*thin, not coarse*) fin; (*very good*) excellent; **he's f.** (*healthy*) il va bien. **2** *adv* (*well*) très bien.
**finger** doigt *m*; **little f.** petit doigt *m*.
**fingernail** ongle *m*.
**fingerprint** empreinte *f* (digitale); (*smudge*) trace *f* de doigt.
**fingertip** bout *m* du doigt.
**finish 1** *n* fin *f*; (*of race*) arrivée *f*. **2** *vt* finir; **to f. doing** finir de faire. **3** *vi* finir; **to have finished with** ne plus avoir besoin de; (*situation, person*) en avoir fini avec.
**finish line** ligne *f* d'arrivée.
**finish off** *vti* finir.
**finish up 1** *vt* finir. **2** *vi* **to f. up in** se retrouver à; **to f. up doing** finir par faire.
**Finn** Finlandais, -aise *mf*.
**Finnish** *a* finlandais.
**fir** sapin *m*.
**fire[1]** feu *m*; (*accidental*) incendie *m*; **to set f. to** mettre le feu à; **on f.** en feu; **(there's a) f.!** au feu!
**fire[2] 1** *vt* **to f. a gun** tirer un coup de fusil *or* de revolver; **to f. s.o.** (*dismiss*) renvoyer qn. **2** *vi* tirer (**at** sur).
**fire alarm** alarme *f* d'incendie.
**firecracker** pétard *m*.
**fire department** pompiers *mpl*.
**fire engine** voiture *f* de pompiers.
**fire escape** escalier *m* de secours.
**fireman** (*pl* **-men**) pompier *m*.
**fireplace** cheminée *f*.
**fire station** caserne *f* de pompiers.
**firewood** bois *m* de chauffage.
**fireworks f. (display)** feu *m* d'artifice.
**firm 1** *n* entreprise *f*. **2** *a* ferme.
**firmly** *adv* fermement.
**first 1** *a* premier. **2** *adv* (*firstly*) premièrement; (*for the first time*) pour la première fois; **(at) f.** d'abord. **3** *n* premier, -ière *mf*; **f. (gear)** (*of vehicle*) première *f*.
**first aid** premiers secours *mpl*.
**first-class 1** *a* excellent; (*ticket, seat*) de première; (*mail*) ordinaire. **2** *adv* (*to travel*) en première.
**first grade** cours *mp* préparatoire.
**firstly** *adv* premièrement.
**first name** prénom *m*.
**fish 1** *n inv* poisson *m*. **2** *vi* pêcher.
**fisherman** (*pl* **-men**) pêcheur *m*.
**fishing** pêche *f*; **to go f.** aller à la pêche.
**fishing rod** canne *f* à pêche.
**fish market** poissonnerie *f*.
**fish sticks** bâtonnets *mpl* de poisson.
**fist** poing *m*.
**fit[1]** *a* en bonne santé; (*in good shape*) en forme; (*suitable*) propre (**for** à, **to do** à faire); (*worthy*) digne (**for** de, **to do** de faire); (*able*) apte (**for** à, **to do** à faire); **f. to eat** bon à manger.
**fit[2] 1** *vt* (*of clothes*) aller (bien) à (*qn*). **2** *vi* **this shirt fits** (*fits me*) cette chemise me va (bien).

**fit**[3] (*attack*) accès *m*.
**fit (in) 1** *vt* (*object*) faire entrer; **to f. s.o. in** (*find time to see*) prendre qn. **2** *vti* **to f. (in) sth** (*go in*) aller dans qch; **he doesn't f. in** il ne peut pas s'intégrer.
**fit (on) 1** *vt* **to f. sth (on) to sth** (*put*) poser qch sur qch; (*fix*) fixer qch à qch. **2** *vti* **to f. (on) sth** (*go on sth*) aller sur qch.
**fitness** (*health*) santé *f*.
**fit (out) with sth** (*house etc*) équiper de qch.
**fitting room** cabine *f* d'essayage.
**five** *a* & *n* cinq (*m*).
**fix** *vt* (*make firm, decide*) fixer; (*mend*) réparer; (*deal with*) arranger; (*prepare, cook*) préparer.
**fix up** (*trip etc*) arranger; **to f. s.o. up with a job**/*etc* procurer un travail/*etc* à qn.
**fizzy** *a* pétillant.
**flag** drapeau *m*; (*on ship*) pavillon *m*.
**flake** (*of snow*) flocon *m*.
**flake (off)** (*of paint*) s'écailler.
**flame** flamme *f*; **to burst into f., go up in flames** prendre feu.
**flammable** *a* inflammable.
**flan** tarte *f*.
**flannel** flanelle *f*.
**flap 1** *vi* (*of wings etc*) battre. **2** *vt* **to f. its wings** battre des ailes. **3** *n* (*of pocket, envelope*) rabat *m*.
**flare up** (*of fire*) prendre; (*of violence*) éclater.
**flash 1** *n* (*of light*) éclat *m*; (*for camera*) flash *m*. **2** *vi* (*shine*) briller; (*on and off*) clignoter. **3** *vt* (*a light*) projeter; (*aim*) diriger (**on, at** sur); **to f. one's headlights** faire un appel de phares.
**flashers** (*of vehicle*) feux *mpl* de détresse.
**flashlight** lampe *f* électrique, lampe *f* de poche.
**flask** (*bottle*) bouteille *f*; (*for pocket*) flasque *f*.
**flat**[1] **1** *a* plat; (*punctured*) crevé; (*deflated*) à plat; (*beer*) éventé; (*rate, fare*) fixe; **to put sth (down) f.** mettre qch à plat; **f. (on one's face)** à plat ventre. **2** *adv* **f. out** (*to work*) d'arrache-pied; (*to run*) à toute vitesse. **3** *n* (*tire*) crevaison *f*.
**flat**[2] (*rooms*) appartement *m*.
**flatly** *adv* (*to deny, refuse*) catégoriquement.
**flatten (out)** aplatir.
**flatter** *vt* flatter.
**flavor** goût *m*; (*of ice cream etc*) parfum *m*.
**flavoring** (*in cake etc*) parfum *m*.
**flaw** défaut *m*.
**flea** puce *f*.
**flea market** marché *m* aux puces.
**flee* 1** *vi* s'enfuir. **2** *vt* (*place*) s'enfuir de.
**fleet** (*of ships*) flotte *f*.
**Flemish 1** *a* flamand. **2** *n* (*language*) flamand *m*.
**flesh** chair *f*.
**flex 1** *vt* (*limb*) fléchir. **2** *n* (*wire*) fil *m* (souple); (*for telephone*) cordon *m*.
**flexible** *a* souple.
**flick** (*with finger*) chiquenaude *f*.
**flick off** enlever (d'une chiquenaude).
**flight** (*of bird, aircraft*) vol *m*; (*escape*) fuite *f*; **f. of stairs** escalier *m*.
**flight attendant** (*male*) steward m; (*female*) hôtesse *f* de l'air.
**flimsy** *a* (*light*) (trop) léger; (*thin*) (trop) mince.
**fling*** *vt* lancer.
**flint** (*for lighter*) pierre *f*.
**flip-flops** *npl* tongs *fpl*.
**flipper** (*of swimmer*) palme *f*.
**flip through** (*book*) feuilleter.
**float 1** *n Fishing* flotteur *m*; (*at carnival*) char *m*. **2** *vi* flotter (**on** sur).
**flock 1** *n* (*of sheep*) troupeau *m*; (*of birds*) volée *f*. **2** *vi* venir en foule.
**flood 1** *n* inondation *f*; (*of letters, tears*) flot *m*. **2** *vt* (*field, house etc*) inonder. **3** *vi* (*of river*) déborder.
**flood in** (*of tourists etc*) affluer.
**flood into** (*of tourists etc*) envahir (*un pays etc*).

**floodlight** projecteur *m*.

**floor** (*ground*) sol *m*; (*wooden etc in building*) plancher *m*; (*story*) étage *m*; **on the f.** par terre; **on the first f.** au rez-de-chaussée.

**floorboard** planche *f*.

**floor lamp** lampadaire *m*.

**flop 1** *vi* (*of play etc*) faire un four. **2** *n* four *m*.

**floppy** *a* (*soft*) mou (*f* molle).

**floppy disk** disquette *f*.

**florist** fleuriste *mf*.

**floss (dental) f.** fil *m* dentaire.

**flour** farine *f*.

**flow 1** *vi* couler; (*of electric current, information*) circuler; (*of traffic*) s'écouler. **2** *n* (*of river*) courant *m*; (*of current, information*) circulation *f*.

**flow chart** tableau *m*.

**flower 1** *n* fleur *f*; **in f.** en fleur(s). **2** *vi* fleurir.

**flower bed** parterre *m* de fleurs, plate-bande *f* (plates-bandes *fpl*).

**flower shop** (boutique *f* de) fleuriste *mf*.

**flu** grippe *f*.

**fluent** *a* **he's f. in Russian, his Russian is f.** il parle couramment le russe.

**fluently** (*to speak a language*) couramment.

**fluff** (*of material*) peluche(s) *f*(*pl*); (*on floor*) moutons *mpl*.

**fluid** *a* & *n* fluide (*m*).

**flunk** *vt* (*exam*) *Fam* être collé à.

**fluorescent** *a* fluorescent.

**flush** *vt* **to f. the toilet** tirer la chasse d'eau.

**flute** flûte *f*.

**flutter** *vi* (*of bird*) voltiger; (*of flag*) flotter.

**fly**[1] (*insect*) mouche *f*.

**fly**[2]* **1** *vi* voler; (*of passenger*) aller en avion; (*of time*) passer vite; (*of flag*) flotter. **2** *vt* (*aircraft*) piloter; (*airline*) voyager par.

**fly**[3] (*on trousers or pants*) braguette *f*.

**fly across** *or* **over** (*country etc*) survoler.

**fly away** *or* **off** s'envoler.

**flying** vol *m*; (*air travel*) l'avion *m*; **f. saucer** soucoupe *f* volante.

**foam** écume *f*; (*on beer*) mousse *f*; **f. rubber** caoutchouc *m* mousse; **f. mattress**/*etc* matelas *m*/*etc* mousse.

**focus 1** *n* (*of attention*) centre *m*; **in f.** au point. **2** *vt* (*image*) mettre au point. **3** *vti* **to f. (one's attention) on** se tourner vers.

**fog** brouillard *m*.

**foggy** *a* **it's f.** il y a du brouillard; **f. weather** brouillard *m*.

**foil** (*for cooking*) papier *m* alu(minium).

**fold 1** *n* (*in paper etc*) pli *m*. **2** *vt* plier; (*wrap*) envelopper (**in** dans); **to f. one's arms** (se) croiser les bras. **3** *vi* (*of chair etc*) se plier.

**fold back** *or* **over 1** *vt* (*blanket etc*) replier. **2** *vi* se replier.

**folder** (*file holder*) chemise *f*.

**folding** *a* (*chair etc*) pliant.

**fold up 1** *vt* (*chair etc*) plier. **2** *vi* se plier.

**folk 1** *a* (*dance etc*) folklorique; **f. music** (musique *f*) folk *m*. **2** *npl* **folks** gens *mpl or fpl*.

**follow 1** *vt* suivre; (*career*) poursuivre; **followed by** suivi de. **2** *vi* suivre.

**follow s.o. around** suivre qn partout.

**follower** partisan *m*.

**following 1** *a* suivant. **2** *prep* à la suite de.

**follow through** (*plan etc*) poursuivre jusqu'au bout.

**follow up** (*idea, story*) creuser; (*clue*) suivre.

**fond** *a* **to be (very) f. of** aimer (beaucoup).

**food** nourriture *f*; (*particular substance*) aliment *m*; (*for cats, dogs*) pâtée *f*.

**fool 1** *n* imbécile *mf*; **to play the f.** faire l'imbécile. **2** *vt* (*trick*) rouler.

**fool around** faire l'imbécile; (*waste time*) perdre son temps.
**foolish** *a* bête.
**foolishly** *adv* bêtement.
**foot** (*pl* **feet**) pied *m*; (*of animal*) patte *f*; (*measure*) pied *m* (= *30,48 cm*); **at the f. of** (*page, stairs*) au bas de; **on f.** à pied.
**football** (*game*) football *m* américain; (*ball*) ballon (de football américain) *m*.
**football player** joueur, -euse *mf* de football américain.
**footbridge** passerelle *f*.
**footpath** sentier *m*.
**footprint** empreinte *f* (de pied *or* de pas).
**footstep** pas *m*.
**footstool** repose-pieds *m inv;* (*cushioned*) pouf *m*.
**for** *prep* pour; (*in exchange for*) contre; (*for a distance of*) pendant; **what's it f.?** ça sert à quoi?; **he was away f. a month** il a été absent pendant un mois; **he won't be back f. a month** il ne sera pas de retour avant un mois; **he's been here/I haven't seen him f. a month** il est ici/je ne l'ai pas vu depuis un mois; **I haven't seen him f. ten years** voilà dix ans que je ne l'ai vu; **it's f. you to say** c'est à toi de dire; **f. that to be done** pour que ça soit fait.
**forbid*** *vt* interdire (**s.o. to do** à qn de faire); **she is forbidden to leave** il lui est interdit de partir.
**force 1** *n* force *f*; **the armed forces** les forces armées. **2** *vt* forcer (*qn*) (**to do** à faire); (*door*) forcer; **forced to do** obligé *or* forcé de faire; **to f. one's way into** entrer de force dans.
**forecast 1** *vt** prévoir. **2** *n* prévision *f*; (*of weather*) prévisions *fpl*.
**forehead** front *m*.
**foreign** *a* étranger; (*trade*) extérieur; (*travel*) à l'étranger.
**foreigner** étranger, -ère *mf*.
**foreman** (*pl* **-men**) (*worker*) contremaître *m*.
**foremost** *a* principal.
**forerunner** précurseur *m*.
**foresee*** *vt* prévoir.
**forest** forêt *f*.
**forever** *adv* pour toujours; (*continually*) sans cesse.
**forge** *vt* (*signature, money*) contrefaire; (*document*) falsifier.
**forge ahead** (*progress*) aller de l'avant.
**forgery** faux *m*.
**forget*** *vti* oublier (**to do** de faire).
**forget about** oublier.
**forgetful** *a* **he's f.** il n'a pas de mémoire.
**forgive*** *vt* pardonner (**s.o. sth** qch à qn).
**fork 1** *n* (*for eating*) fourchette *f*; (*for gardening*) fourche *f*; (*in road*) bifurcation *f*. **2** *vi* (*of road*) bifurquer.
**fork out** (*money*) *Fam* allonger.
**form 1** *n* forme *f*; (*document*) formulaire *m*. **2** *vt* (*group, basis etc*) former; (*habit*) contracter; (*an opinion*) se former; **to f. part of** faire partie de. **3** *vi* (*appear*) se former.
**formal** *a* (*person, tone etc*) cérémonieux; (*stuffy*) compassé; (*official*) officiel; **f. dress** tenue de cérémonie.
**formality** formalité *f*.
**formation** formation *f*.
**former 1** *a* (*previous*) ancien; (*of two*) premier. **2** *pron* **the f.** celui-là, celle-là.
**formerly** *adv* autrefois.
**formula** (*pl* **-as** *or* **-ae**) formule *f*; (*pl* **-as**) (*baby food*) lait *m* maternisé.
**fort** fort *m*.
**fortieth** *a* & *n* quarantième (*mf*).
**fortress** forteresse *f*.
**fortunate** *a* (*choice etc*) heureux; **to be f.** (*of person*) avoir de la chance; **it's f. that** c'est heureux que (+ *subjunctive*).
**fortunately** *adv* heureusement.
**fortune** *n* fortune *f*; **to make one's**

f. faire fortune; **to have the good f. to do** avoir la chance de faire.

**forty** *a* & *n* quarante (*m*).

**forward 1** *adv* **forward(s)** en avant; **to go f.** avancer. **2** *vt* (*letter*) faire suivre; (*goods*) expédier.

**foul 1** *a* (*smell, taste*) infect; (*language*) grossier. **2** *n Football, Basketball* faute *f*.

**found[1]** *pt* & *pp de* **find.**

**found[2]** *vt* (*town etc*) fonder.

**fountain** fontaine *f*.

**fountain pen** stylo(-plume) *m*.

**four** *a* & *n* quatre (*m*).

**fourteen** *a* & *n* quatorze (*m*).

**fourth** *a* & *n* quatrième (*mf*).

**fowl** volaille *f*.

**fox** renard *m*.

**foyer** (*in theater*) foyer *m*.

**fraction** fraction *f*.

**fracture 1** *n* fracture *f*. **2** *vt* **to f. one's leg**/*etc* se fracturer la jambe/*etc*.

**fragile** *a* fragile.

**fragment** fragment *m*.

**fragrance** parfum *m*.

**frail** *a* fragile.

**frame 1** *n* (*of picture, bicycle*) cadre *m*; (*of window*) châssis *m*; **f. of mind** humeur *f*. **2** *vt* (*picture*) encadrer.

**framework** structure *f*; **in the f. of** dans le cadre de.

**franc** franc *m*.

**frank** *a* franc (*f* franche).

**frankly** *adv* franchement.

**frankness** franchise *f*.

**frantic** *a* (*activity*) frénétique; (*rush*) effréné; (*person*) hors de soi.

**frantically** *adv* comme un fou.

**fraud** (*crime*) fraude *f*; (*person*) imposteur *m*.

**fray** *vi* (*of garment*) s'effilocher.

**freckle** tache *f* de rousseur.

**freckled** *a* couvert de taches de rousseur.

**free 1** *a* libre; (*lavish*) généreux (**with** de); **f. (of charge)** gratuit; **to get f.** se libérer; **f. to do** libre de faire; **f. of** (*pain etc*) débarrassé de. **2** *adv* **f. (of charge)** gratuitement. **3** *vt* (*pt* & *pp* **freed**) (*prisoner*) libérer; (*trapped person*) dégager.

**freedom** liberté *f*; **f. from** (*worry*) absence *f* de.

**freely** *adv* librement; (*to give*) libéralement.

**free-range chicken** poulet *m* fermier.

**freeway** autoroute *f*.

**freeze* 1** *vi* geler. **2** *vt* (*food*) congeler; (*prices*) bloquer.

**freezer** congélateur *m*; (*in fridge*) freezer *m*.

**freeze up** *or* **over** *vi* geler; (*of window*) se givrer.

**freezing** *a* (*weather*) glacial; (*hands, person*) gelé; **it's f.** on gèle.

**French 1** *a* français; (*teacher*) de français; (*embassy*) de France; **the F.** les Français *mpl*. **2** *n* (*language*) français *m*.

**French bread a loaf of F.b.** baguette *f*.

**French fries** frites *fpl*.

**Frenchman** (*pl* **-men**) Français *m*.

**French-speaking** *a* francophone.

**Frenchwoman** (*pl* **-women**) Française *f*.

**frequent** *a* fréquent; **f. visitor** habitué, -ée *mf* (**to** de).

**frequently** *adv* fréquemment.

**fresh** *a* frais (*f* fraîche); (*new*) nouveau (*f* nouvelle); **to get some f. air** prendre l'air.

**freshener air f.** désodorisant *m*.

**freshen up** faire un brin de toilette.

**fret** *vi* (*worry*) se faire du souci.

**Friday** vendredi *m*; **Good F.** Vendredi Saint.

**fridge** frigo *m*.

**fried** (*pt* & *pp de* **fry**) *a* (*fish*) frit; **f. egg** œuf *m* sur le plat.

**friend** ami, -ie *mf*; (*from school, work*) camarade *mf*; **to be friends with s.o.** être ami avec qn.

**friendly** *a* aimable (**to** avec); **to be f. with** être ami avec.

**friendship** amitié *f.*
**fright** peur *f*; **to have a f.** avoir peur; **to give s.o. a f.** faire peur à qn.
**frighten** *vt* effrayer.
**frighten away** *or* **off** (*animal, person*) fair fuir.
**frightened** *a* effrayé; **to be f.** avoir peur (**of** de).
**frightening** *a* effrayant.
**frill** (*on dress etc*) volant *m*.
**fro** *adv* **to go to and f.** aller et venir.
**frog** grenouille *f.*
**from** *prep* de; **where are you f.?** d'où êtes-vous?; **a train f.** un train en provenance de. ▪ (*time onwards*) à partir de, dès; **f. today (on), as f. today** à partir d'aujourd'hui, dès aujourd'hui. ▪ (*numbers, prices onwards*) à partir de. ▪ (*away from*) à; **to take/borrow f.** prendre/emprunter à. ▪ (*out of*) dans; sur; **to take f.** (*box*) prendre dans; (*table*) prendre sur; **to drink f. a cup/the bottle** boire dans une tasse/à la bouteille. ▪ (*according to*) d'après. ▪ (*cause*) par. ▪ (*on behalf of*) de la part de; **tell her f. me** dis-lui de ma part.
**front 1** *n* (*of garment, building*) devant *m*; (*of boat, car*) avant *m*; (*of book*) début *m*; **in f. (of)** devant; **in f.** (*ahead*) en avant; (*in race*) en tête; **in the f.** (*in vehicle*) à l'avant. **2** *a* (*tooth*) de devant; (*part, wheel, car seat*) avant *inv*; (*row, page*) premier; **f. door** porte *f* d'entrée.
**frost** gel *m*; (*on window*) givré *m*.
**frostbite** gelure *f.*
**frost up** (*of window etc*) se givrer.
**frosty** *a* (*window*) givré; **it's f.** il gèle.
**froth** mousse *f.*
**frown** *vi* froncer les sourcils.
**frozen** *a* (*vegetables etc*) surgelé; **f. food** surgelés *mpl.*
**fruit** fruit *m*; **(some) f.** (*one item*) un fruit; (*more than one*) des fruits; **f. drink** boisson *f* aux fruits; **f. salad** salade *f* de fruits; **f. tree** arbre *m* fruitier.
**fruitcake** cake *m*.
**frustrated** *a* frustré.
**frustrating** *a* irritant.
**fry 1** *vt* faire frire. **2** *vi* frire.
**frying pan** poêle *f* (à frire).
**fudge** riche dessert *m* au chocolat.
**fuel** combustible *m*; (*for vehicle*) carburant *m*.
**fugitive** fugitif, -ive *mf.*
**fulfill** *vt* (*ambition*) réaliser; (*condition*) remplir; (*desire*) satisfaire.
**fulfilling** *a* satisfaisant.
**full 1** *a* plein (**of** de); (*bus, theater etc*) complet; (*life, day*) rempli; **the f. price** le prix fort; **to pay f. fare** payer plein tarif; **to be f.** (*of person*) n'avoir plus faim; (*of hotel*) être complet; **f. name** (*on form*) nom et prénom. **2** *n* **in f.** (*to read sth etc*) en entier.
**full-scale** *a*, **full-size** *a* (*model*) grandeur nature *inv*.
**full-time** *a* & *adv* à plein temps.
**fully** *adv* entièrement.
**fumes** *npl* vapeurs *fpl*; (*from car exhaust*) gaz *m inv*.
**fun** amusement *m*; **to be f.** être très amusant; **to have (some) f.** s'amuser; **to make f. of** se moquer de; **for f.** pour le plaisir.
**function** fonction *f*; (*meeting*) réunion *f.*
**fund 1** *n* (*for pension etc*) caisse *f*; **funds** (*money resources*) fonds *mpl*. **2** *vt* fournir des fonds à.
**funeral** enterrement *m*.
**funnel** (*of ship*) cheminée *f*; (*for pouring*) entonnoir *m*.
**funny** *a* drôle; (*strange*) bizarre; **a f. idea** une drôle d'idée; **to feel f.** ne pas se sentir très bien.
**fur** fourrure *f.*
**furious** *a* furieux (**with, at** contre).
**furnish** *vt* (*room*) meubler.
**furnished room** pièce *f* meublée.
**furniture** meubles *mpl*; **a piece of f.** un meuble.
**further 1** *adv* = **farther**; (*more*) davantage. **2** *a* supplémentaire; **f. details** de plus amples détails; **a f. case**/*etc* un autre cas/*etc*.

**furthermore** *adv* en outre.
**furthest** *a* & *adv* = **farthest.**
**fury** fureur *f.*
**fuse** (*wire*) plomb *m,* fusible *m*; (*of bomb*) amorce *f;* **to blow a f.** faire sauter un plomb; **we've blown a f.** un plomb a sauté.
**fuss 1** *n* chichis *mpl*; **what a f.!** quelle histoire! **2** *vi* faire des chichis.
**fuss (around)** *vi* s'agiter.
**fuss over s.o.** être aux petits soins pour qn.
**fussy** *a* tatillon; (*difficult*) difficile (**about** sur).
**future 1** *n* avenir *m*; *Grammar* futur *m*; **in f.** à l'avenir; **in the f.** (*one day*) un jour (futur). **2** *a* futur; (*date*) ultérieur.
**fuzzy** *a* (*picture, idea*) flou.

# G

**gadget** gadget *m.*
**Gaelic** *a* & *n* gaélique (*m*).
**gag 1** *n* (*over mouth*) bâillon *m*; (*joke*) gag *m*. **2** *vt* (*victim*) bâillonner. **3** *vi* (*choke*) s'étouffer (**on** avec).
**gaiety** gaieté *f.*
**gaily** *adv* gaiement.
**gain 1** *vt* (*obtain*) gagner; (*experience*) acquérir; **to g. speed/weight** prendre de la vitesse/du poids. **2** *n* (*increase*) augmentation *f* (**in** de); (*profit*) bénéfice *m*.
**gain on** (*catch up with*) rattraper.
**gala** gala *m*.
**galaxy** galaxie *f.*
**gale** grand vent *m*.
**gallant** *a* (*chivalrous*) galant.
**gallery** galerie *f*; (*for public*) tribune *f*; **art g.** (*private*) galerie *f* d'art; (*public*) musée *m* d'art.
**gallivant** *Fam* vadrouiller.
**gallon** gallon *m*.
**gallop 1** *vi* galoper. **2** *n* galop *m*.
**gamble 1** *vi* jouer (**on** sur, **with** avec). **2** *vt* jouer. **3** *n* coup *m* risqué.
**gamble (away)** (*lose*) perdre (au jeu).
**gambler** joueur, -euse *mf.*
**gambling** jeu *m*.
**game** jeu *m*; (*of football, etc*) match *m*; (*of tennis, chess, cards*) partie *f*; **to play a g. of** jouer un match de; faire une partie de.
**game arcade** *f* galerie de jeux.
**gang** (*of children, criminals*) bande *f*, gang *m*; (*of workers*) équipe *f.*
**gangster** gangster *m*.
**gang up on** se mettre à plusieurs contre.
**gangway** (*to ship, aircraft*) passerelle *f.*
**gap** (*empty space*) trou; (*in time*) intervalle *m*; (*in knowledge*) lacune *f*; **the g. between** (*difference*) l'écart *m* entre.
**gape** *vi* rester bouche bée.
**gape at** regarder bouche bée.
**garage** garage *m*.
**garbage** ordures *fpl*; (*nonsense*) idioties *fpl*; **g. bag** sac *m* poubelle; **g. can** poubelle *f*; **g. man** éboueur *m*; **g. truck** camion-benne *m*.
**garden 1** *n* jardin *m*. **2** *vi* jardiner.
**gardener** jardinier, -ière *mf.*
**garden hose** tuyau *m*.
**gardening** jardinage *m*.
**gargle** *vi* se gargariser.
**garland** guirlande *f.*
**garlic** ail *m*.
**garment** vêtement *m*.
**gas 1** *n* gaz *m inv*; (*gasoline*) essence *f*; **g. mask/meter/***etc* masque *m*/compteur *m*/*etc* à gaz; **g. heat** chauffage *m* au gaz; **g. heater** appareil *m* de chauffage à gaz; **g. stove** cuisinière *f* à gaz; (*portable*) réchaud *m* à gaz. **2** *vt* (*poison*) asphyxier (*qn*).
**gash 1** *n* entaille *f*. **2** *vt* entailler.
**gasoline** essence *f.*
**gasp 1** *vi* **to g. (for breath)** haleter. **2** *n* halètement *m*.
**gas station** station-service *f.*
**gassy** *a* (*drink*) gazeux.
**gasworks** usine *f* à gaz.

**gate** (*at grade crossing, field etc*) barrière *f*; (*metal*) grille *f*; (*of castle, in airport*) porte *f*; (*at stadium*) entrée *f*; (*for tickets*) portillon *m*.
**gatecrash** *vi* s'inviter (de force).
**gather 1** *vt* (*people, objects*) rassembler; (*pick up*) ramasser; (*information*) recueillir; **I g. that . . .** je crois comprendre que . . . ; **to g. speed** prendre de la vitesse. **2** *vi* (*of people*) se rassembler.
**gathering** (*group*) réunion *f*.
**gather round** (*come closer*) s'approcher.
**gaudy** *a* voyant.
**gauge 1** *n* (*instrument*) jauge *f*. **2** *vt* (*estimate*) évaluer.
**gaunt** *a* décharné.
**gauze** gaze *f*.
**gave** *pt de* **give.**
**gay 1** *a* homo(sexuel); (*cheerful*) gai. **2** *n* homo(sexuel) *m*.
**gaze 1** *n* regard *m* (fixe). **2** *vi* regarder.
**gaze at** regarder (fixement).
**gear 1** *n* équipement *m*; (*belongings*) affaires *fpl*; (*clothes*) *Fam* vêtements *mpl*; (*speed in vehicle*) vitesse *f*; **in g.** en prise; **not in g.** au point mort. **2** *vt* adapter (**to** à).
**gear up geared up to do** prêt à faire; **to g. oneself up for** se préparer pour.
**geese** *see* **goose.**
**gel** gel *m*.
**gem** pierre *f* précieuse.
**gender** *Grammar* genre *m*.
**general 1** *a* général; **in g.** en général; **the g. public** le (grand) public; **for g. use** à l'usage du public. **2** *n* (*in army*) général *m*.
**generally** *adv* généralement.
**generation** génération *f*.
**generator** groupe *m* électrogène.
**generosity** générosité *f*.
**generous** *a* généreux (**with** de); (*helping*) copieux.
**generously** *adv* généreusement.
**genius** (*ability, person*) génie *m*.
**gentle** *a* (*person, slope etc*) doux (*f* douce); (*touch*) léger; (*exercise, speed*) modéré.
**gentleman** (*pl* **-men**) monsieur *m*.
**gentleness** douceur *f*.
**gently** *adv* doucement.
**genuine** *a* véritable, authentique; (*sincere*) sincère.
**genuinely** *adv* véritablement, sincèrement.
**geographical** *a* géographique.
**geography** géographie *f*.
**geometric(al)** *a* géométrique.
**geometry** géométrie *f*.
**germ** (*in body, food etc*) microbe *m*.
**German 1** *a* allemand. **2** *n* (*person*) Allemand, -ande *mf*; (*language*) allemand *m*.
**German measles** rubéole *f*.
**German shepherd** (*dog*) berger *m* allemand.
**gesture** geste *m*.
**get* 1** *vt* (*obtain*) obtenir; (*find*) trouver; (*buy*) acheter; (*receive*) recevoir; (*catch*) attraper; (*bus, train*) prendre; (*seize*) saisir; (*fetch*) aller chercher (*qn, qch*); (*put*) mettre; (*derive*) tirer (**from** de); (*understand*) comprendre; (*prepare*) préparer; (*hit with fist, stick etc*) atteindre; (*reputation*) se faire; **I have got** j'ai; **to g. s.o. to do sth** faire faire qch à qn; **to g. sth built**/*etc* faire construire/*etc* qch. **2** *vi* (*go*) aller; (*arrive*) arriver (**to** à); (*become*) devenir; **to g. caught/***etc* se faire prendre/*etc*; **to g. cleaned up** se laver; **where have you gotten to?** où en es-tu?; **you've got to stay** (*must*) tu dois rester; **to g. working** se mettre à travailler.
**get across 1** *vt* (*road*) traverser; (*message*) communiquer. **2** *vi* traverser.
**get along** (*manage*) se débrouiller; (*be on good terms*) s'entendre (**with** avec).
**get around** se déplacer; **to g. around to doing** en venir à faire.
**get at** (*reach*) parvenir à.
**get away** (*leave*) partir; (*escape*) s'échapper.

**get back 1** *vt (recover)* récupérer; *(replace)* remettre. **2** *vi (return)* revenir; *(move back)* reculer.

**get by** passer; *(manage)* se débrouiller.

**get down** *vti* descendre.

**get in 1** *vt (laundry etc)* rentrer; *(call for)* faire venir *(qn)*. **2** *vi (enter)* entrer; *(come home)* rentrer; *(enter vehicle or train)* monter; *(of plane, train)* arriver.

**get in(to)** entrer dans; *(vehicle, train)* monter dans; **to g. in(to) bed** se mettre au lit.

**get off 1** *vi (leave)* partir; *(from vehicle or train)* descendre (**from** de); *(in court)* être acquitté. **2** *vt (remove)* enlever; *(send)* expédier; **to g. off a bus** descendre d'un bus.

**get on 1** *vt (shoes, clothes)* mettre; *(bus, train)* monter dans. **2** *vi (progress)* marcher; *(manage)* se débrouiller; *(succeed)* réussir; *(enter bus or train)* monter; **to g. on with** *(task)* continuer.

**get out 1** *vi* sortir; *(from vehicle or train)* descendre (**of** de); **to g. out of** *(danger)* se tirer de; *(habit)* perdre. **2** *vt (remove)* enlever; *(bring out)* sortir *(qch)*, faire sortir *(qn)*.

**get over 1** *vt (road)* traverser; *(obstacle)* surmonter; *(fence)* franchir; *(illness)* se remettre de. **2** *vi (cross)* traverser; *(visit)* passer.

**get through 1** *vi* passer; *(finish)* finir; **to g. through to s.o.** *(on phone)* contacter qn. **2** *vt* passer par; *(meal)* venir à bout de.

**get to** *(send)* faire parvenir *(qch)* à; *(bring)* amener *(qn)* à.

**get-together** réunion *f*.

**get up 1** *vi (rise)* se lever (**from** de); **to g. up to something** *or* **to mischief** faire des bêtises. **2** *vt (bring up)* monter *(qch)*; *(wake up)* réveiller.

**ghastly** *a (horrible)* affreux.

**ghetto** (*pl* **-os**) ghetto *m*.

**ghost** fantôme *m*.

**giant 1** *n* géant *m*. **2** *a (tree, packet)* géant.

**giddy** *a* **to be** *or* **feel g.** avoir le vertige; **to make g.** donner le vertige à.

**gift** cadeau *m*; *(talent)* don *m*.

**gifted** *a* doué.

**gift voucher** bon-cadeau *m*.

**gigantic** *a* gigantesque.

**giggle 1** *vi* pouffer (de rire). **2** *n* **to get/have the giggles** attraper/avoir le fou rire.

**gills** *npl (of fish)* ouïes *fpl*.

**gimmick** truc *m*.

**gin** *(drink)* gin *m*.

**ginger** gingembre *m*.

**giraffe** girafe *f*.

**girl** (jeune) fille *f*; *(daughter)* fille *f*; **American g.** jeune Américaine *f*.

**girlfriend** amie *f*; *(of boy)* petite amie *f*.

**girl scout** éclaireuse *f*.

**give*** *vt* donner (**to** à); *(support)* apporter; *(a smile)* faire; *(a sigh)* pousser; *(a look)* jeter.

**give away** *(free of charge)* donner; *(prizes)* distribuer; *(betray)* trahir *(qn)*.

**give back** *(return)* rendre.

**give in 1** *vi (surrender)* céder (**to** à). **2** *vt (hand in)* remettre.

**give out** *(hand out)* distribuer.

**give over** *(devote)* consacrer (**to** à).

**give up 1** *vi* abandonner. **2** *vt* abandonner; *(seat)* céder (**to** à); *(prisoner)* livrer (**to** à); **to g. up smoking** cesser de fumer.

**give way** *(of branch, person etc)* céder (**to** à); *(in vehicle)* céder la priorité (**to** à).

**glad** *a* content (**of, about** de).

**gladly** *adv* volontiers.

**glamorous** *a* séduisant.

**glamour** *(charm)* enchantement *m*; *(splendor)* éclat *m*.

**glance 1** *n* coup *m* d'œil. **2** *vi* jeter un coup d'œil (**at** à, sur).

**gland** glande *f*.

**glaring** *a (light)* éblouissant; *(injustice)* flagrant.

**glass** verre *m*; *(mirror)* miroir *m*; **a pane of g.** une vitre.

**glasses** *npl (for eyes)* lunettes *fpl*.

**glee** joie *f*.

**glen** vallon *m*.
**glide** *vi* glisser; (*of aircraft, bird*) planer.
**gliding** (*sport*) vol *m* à voile.
**glimmer** (*of hope*) lueur *f*.
**glimpse** aperçu *m*; **to catch** *or* **get a g. of** entrevoir.
**glittering** *a* scintillant.
**globe** globe *m*.
**gloom** (*sadness*) tristesse *f*.
**gloomy** *a* triste; (*pessimistic*) pessimiste.
**glorified** *a* **it's a glorified barn**/*etc* ce n'est guère plus qu'une grange/*etc*.
**glorious** *a* glorieux; (*splendid*) magnifique.
**glory** gloire *f*.
**gloss** (*shine*) brillant *m*.
**glossy** *a* (*paint, finish*) brillant; (*magazine*) de luxe.
**glove** gant *m*.
**glove box** *or* **compartment** (*in car*) boîte *f* à gants.
**glow** *vi* (*of sky, fire*) rougeoyer.
**glue 1** *n* colle *f*. **2** *vt* coller (**to, on** à); **with eyes glued to** les yeux fixés sur.
**glum** *a* triste.
**glut** (*of oil etc*) surplus *m*.
**glutton** glouton, -onne *mf*.
**gnat** (*insect*) cousin *m*.
**gnaw** *vti* ronger.
**go**[1]* *vi* aller (**to** à, **from** de); (*depart*) partir, s'en aller; (*disappear*) disparaître, partir; (*function*) marcher; (*become*) devenir; (*of material*) s'user; **to go well/badly** (*of event*) se passer bien/mal; **she's going to do** (*is about to, intends to*) elle va faire; **it's all gone** il n'y en a plus; **to go and get** aller chercher; **to go riding/on a trip**/*etc* faire du cheval/un voyage/*etc*; **to let go of** lâcher; **to go to a doctor**/*etc* aller voir un médecin/*etc*; **two hours**/*etc* **to go** encore deux heures/*etc*.
**go**[2] (*pl* **goes**) (*attempt*) coup *m*; **to have a go at (doing) sth** essayer (de faire) qch; **on the go** actif.
**go about** *or* **(a)round 1** *vi* se déplacer; (*of news*) circuler. **2** *vt* **to know how to go about it** savoir s'y prendre.
**go across** *vti* (*cross*) traverser.
**go after** (*chase*) poursuivre; (*seek*) (re)chercher.
**go ahead** *vi* avancer; (*continue*) continuer; (*start*) commencer; **go ahead!** allez-y!; **to go ahead with** (*plan etc*) poursuivre.
**go-ahead to get the go-ahead** avoir le feu vert.
**goal** but *m*.
**goalkeeper** gardien *m* de but.
**go along** aller; **to go along with** (*agree*) être d'accord avec.
**go around 1** *vi* (*turn*) tourner; (*be sufficient*) suffire. **2** *vt* (*corner*) tourner; (*world*) faire le tour de.
**goat** chèvre *f*.
**go away** partir, s'en aller.
**go back** retourner; (*in time*) remonter; (*step back*) reculer; **to go back on** (*promise*) revenir sur.
**go-between** intermédiaire *mf*.
**god** dieu *m*; **G.** Dieu *m*.
**goddaughter** filleule *f*.
**godfather** parrain *m*.
**godmother** marraine *f*.
**go down 1** *vi* descendre; (*fall down*) tomber; (*of ship*) couler; (*of sun*) se coucher; (*of price etc*) baisser. **2** *vt* **to go down the stairs/street** descendre l'escalier/la rue.
**godsend to be a g.** tomber à pic.
**godson** filleul *m*.
**goes** *see* **go**[1].
**goggles** *npl* lunettes *fpl* (*de protection, de plongée*).
**go in 1** *vi* (r)entrer; (*of sun*) se cacher. **2** *vt* **to go in a room**/*etc* entrer dans une pièce/*etc*.
**go (in) for** s'intéresser à.
**going 1** *n* (*conditions*) conditions *fpl*; **it's slow** *or* **tough g.** c'est difficile. **2** *a* **the g. price** le prix pratiqué (**for** pour).
**goings-on** *npl* activités *fpl*.
**go into** (*room etc*) entrer dans.
**gold** or *m*; **g. watch**/*etc* montre/*etc* en or.
**golden** *a* (*in color*) doré; (*rule*) d'or.
**goldfish** poisson *m* rouge.

**gold mine** mine *f* d'or.
**gold-plated** *a* plaqué or.
**golf** golf *m*.
**golfer** golfeur, -euse *mf*.
**gone** *pp de* **go**[1].
**good 1** *a* bon (*f* bonne); (*kind*) gentil; (*weather*) beau (*f* belle); (*well-behaved*) sage; **very g.!** (*all right*) très bien!; **to feel g.** se sentir bien; **g. at French**/*etc* bon *or* fort en français/*etc*; **to be g. with** (*children*) savoir s'y prendre avec; **it's a g. thing (that) . . .** heureusement que . . . ; **a g. many, a g. deal (of)** beaucoup (de); **g. morning** bonjour; (*on leaving*) au revoir; **g. evening** bonsoir; **g. night** bonsoir; (*going to bed*) bonne nuit. **2** *n* (*advantage, virtue*) bien *m*; **for her own g.** pour son bien; **it's no g. crying**/*etc* ça ne sert à rien de pleurer/*etc*; **that's no g.** (*worthless*) ça ne vaut rien; (*bad*) ça ne va pas; **what's the g.?** à quoi bon?; **for g.** pour de bon.
**goodbye** *int* au revoir.
**good-looking** *a* beau (*f* belle).
**goods** *npl* marchandises *fpl*; (*articles for sale*) articles *mpl*.
**goodwill** bonne volonté *f*.
**go off** (*leave*) partir; (*of alarm*) se déclencher.
**go on** continuer (**doing** à faire); (*happen*) se passer; (*last*) durer.
**goose** (*pl* **geese**) oie *f*.
**gooseberry** groseille *f* à maquereau.
**goose pimples** *or* **bumps** chair *f* de poule.
**go out** sortir; (*of light, fire*) s'éteindre.
**go over 1** *vi* aller (**to** à); (*to enemy*) passer (**to** à); **to go over to s.o.('s)** faire un saut chez qn. **2** *vt* examiner; (*in one's mind*) repasser.
**gorge** (*ravine*) gorge *f*.
**gorgeous** *a* magnifique.
**gorilla** gorille *m*.
**Gospel** Évangile *m*.
**gossip 1** *n* (*talk*) bavardage(s) *m(pl)*; (*person*) commère *f*. **2** *vi* (*to talk*) bavarder; (*ill-naturedly*) se livrer à des commérages.
**got** *pt & pp de* **get**.
**go through 1** *vi* passer. **2** *vt* (*suffer*) subir; (*examine*) examiner; (*search*) fouiller; (*spend*) dépenser; (*wear out*) user.
**gotten** *pp de* **get**.
**go under** *vi* (*of ship, company*) couler.
**go up 1** *vi* monter; (*of prices*) augmenter. **2** *vt* **to go up the stairs/street** monter l'escalier/la rue.
**gourmet** gourmet *m*.
**govern 1** *vt* (*rule*) gouverner; (*city*) administrer; (*influence*) déterminer. **2** *vi* gouverner.
**government** gouvernement *m*; (*local*) administration *f*.
**governor** gouverneur *m*.
**go without sth** se passer de qch.
**gown** (*of woman*) robe *f*.
**GP** *abbr* (*general practitioner*) généraliste *m*.
**grab** *vt* **to g. (hold of)** saisir; **to g. sth from s.o.** arracher qch à qn.
**grace** (*charm*) grâce *f*.
**graceful** *a* gracieux.
**grade 1** *n* catégorie *f*; (*in exam etc*) note *f*; (*class in school*) classe *f*. **2** *vt* (*classify*) classer; (*school paper*) noter, corriger.
**grade crossing** passage *m* à niveau.
**grade school** école *f* primaire.
**gradual** *a* progressif.
**gradually** *adv* progressivement.
**graduate 1** *vi* obtenir son diplôme. **2** *n n* diplômé, -ée *mf*.
**graduation** remise *f* des diplômes.
**graffiti** *npl* graffiti *mpl*.
**graft 1** *n* greffe *f*. **2** *vt* greffer.
**grain** (*seed*) grain *m*; (*cereal*) céréales *fpl*.
**gram** gramme *m*.
**grammar** grammaire *f*.
**grammar school** = **grade school**.
**grammatical** *a* grammatical.
**grand** *a* (*splendid*) magnifique.
**granddad(dy)** *Fam* papi *m*.
**grandchild** (*pl* **-children**) petit(e)-enfant *mf*.

**granddaughter** petite-fille *f.*
**grandfather** grand-père *m.*
**grandma** *Fam* mamie *f.*
**grandmother** grand-mère *f.*
**grandparents** grands-parents *mpl.*
**grandson** petit-fils *m.*
**granny** *Fam* mamie *f.*
**granola** muesli *m.*
**grant 1** *vt* accorder (**to** à); (*request*) accéder à; **to take sth for granted** considérer qch comme acquis; **I take it for granted that** je présume que. **2** *n* subvention *f*; (*for study*) bourse *f.*
**grape** grain *m* de raisin; **grapes** le raisin, les raisins *mpl*; **to eat (some) grapes** manger du raisin *or* des raisins.
**grapefruit** pamplemousse *m.*
**graph** courbe *f*; **g. paper** papier *m* millimétré.
**grasp 1** *vt* (*seize, understand*) saisir. **2** *n* (*hold*) prise *f*; (*understanding*) compréhension *f.*
**grass** herbe *f*; (*lawn*) gazon *m.*
**grasshopper** sauterelle *f.*
**grate 1** *n* (*for fireplace*) grille *f* de foyer. **2** *vt* (*cheese etc*) râper.
**grateful** *a* reconnaissant (**to** à, **for** de); **I'm g. (to you) for your help** je vous suis reconnaissant de votre aide.
**grater** râpe *f.*
**gratifying** *a* très satisfaisant *or* agréable.
**gratitude** reconnaissance *f*, gratitude *f* (**for** de).
**grave**[1] tombe *f.*
**grave**[2] *a* (*serious*) grave.
**gravel** gravier *m.*
**graveyard** cimetière *m.*
**gravity** (*force*) pesanteur *f.*
**gravy** jus *m* de viande.
**gray** *a* gris; **to be going g.** grissoner.
**graze 1** *vi* (*of cattle*) paître. **2** *vt* (*skin*) écorcher. **3** *n* (*wound*) écorchure *f.*
**grease 1** *n* graisse *f.* **2** *vt* graisser.
**greasy** *a* plein de graisse; (*hair*) gras.
**great** *a* grand; (*excellent*) *Fam* magnifique; **a g. deal (of), a g. many** beaucoup (de); **the greatest team**/*etc* (*best*) la meilleure équipe/*etc.*
**great-grandfather** arrière-grandpère *m.*
**great-grandmother** arrière-grand-mère *f.*
**greatly** (*much*) beaucoup; (*very*) très.
**greed** avidité *f*; (*for food*) gourmandise *f.*
**greedy** *a* avide; (*for food*) gourmand.
**Greek 1** *a* grec (*f* grecque). **2** *n* Grec *m*, Greque *f*; (*language*) grec *m.*
**green 1** *a* vert; **to turn** *or* **go g.** verdir. **2** *n* (*color*) vert *m*; (*lawn*) pelouse *f*; **greens** légumes *mpl* verts.
**greenhouse** serre *f*; **g. effect** effet *m* de serre.
**greet** *vt* saluer.
**greeting** salutation *f*; **greetings** (*for birthday, festival*) vœux *mpl.*
**grenade** (*bomb*) grenade *f.*
**greyhound** lévrier *m.*
**grief** chagrin *m.*
**grieve** *vi* **to g. for s.o.** pleurer qn.
**grill 1** *n* (*utensil*) gril *m*; (*dish*) grillade *f.* **2** *vti* griller.
**grim** *a* (*face, future*) sombre; (*bad*) *Fam* affreux.
**grime** crasse *f.*
**grimy** *a* crasseux.
**grin 1** *vi* avoir un large sourire. **2** *n* large sourire *m.*
**grind*** *vt* moudre; **to g. one's teeth** grincer des dents.
**grinder coffee g.** moulin *m* à café.
**grip 1** *vt* saisir; (*hold*) tenir serré. **2** *n* (*hold*) prise *f*; (*with hand*) poigne *f*; **in the g. of** en proie à.
**gripping** *a* (*book etc*) prenant.
**groan 1** *vi* gémir. **2** *n* gémissement *m.*
**grocer** épicier, -ière *mf.*
**grocery g. store** magasin *m* d'alimentation; **groceries** (*food*) épicerie *f.*

**groin** aine *f.*
**groom** (*bridegroom*) marié *m.*
**groove** (*slot*) rainure *f.*
**grope around** *vi* tâtonner.
**grope for** chercher à tâtons.
**gross** *a* (*total*) (*income etc*) brut.
**grossly** *adv* (*very*) extrêmement.
**ground** terre *f*, sol *m*; (*for camping etc*) terrain *m*; **grounds** (*reasons*) raisons *fpl*; (*gardens*) parc *m*; **on the g.** (*lying, sitting*) par terre.
**ground floor** rez-de-chaussée *m inv.*
**ground meat** hachis *m* (de viande).
**groundwork** préparation *f.*
**group** groupe *m.*
**group (together)** *vti* (se) grouper.
**grow*** **1** *vi* (*of person*) grandir; (*of plant, hair*) pousser; (*increase*) augmenter, grandir; (*of company, town*) se développer. **2** *vt* (*plant, crops*) cultiver; (*beard*) laisser pousser.
**grow into** devenir.
**growl** *vi* grogner (**at** contre).
**grown** *a* (*man, woman*) adulte.
**grown-up** grande personne *f.*
**grow out of** (*clothes*) devenir trop grand pour; (*habit*) perdre.
**growth** croissance *f*; (*increase*) augmentation *f* (**in** de); (*lump*) tumeur *f* (**on** à).
**grow up** devenir adulte.
**grub** (*food*) *Fam* bouffe *f.*
**grubby** *a* sale.
**grudge** rancune *f*; **to have a g. against** garder rancune à.
**grueling** *a* éprouvant.
**gruesome** *a* horrible.
**grumble** *vi* râler, grogner (**about, at** contre).
**grumpy** *a* grincheux.
**grunt** **1** *vti* grogner. **2** *n* grognement *m.*
**guarantee** **1** *n* garantie *f.* **2** *vt* garantir (**against** contre, **s.o. that** à qn que).
**guard** **1** *n* (*vigilance, soldiers*) garde *f*; (*individual person*) garde *m*; **to keep a g. on** surveiller; **under g.** sous surveillance; **on one's g.** sur ses gardes; **on g. (duty)** de garde; **to stand g.** monter la garde. **2** *vt* protéger; (*watch over*) surveiller.
**guess** **1** *n* conjecture *f*; (*intuition*) intuition *f*; **to make a g.** (essayer de) deviner. **2** *vt* deviner (**that** que); (*length, number*) estimer; (*suppose*) supposer; (*think*) croire (**that** que).
**guesswork** hypothèse *f*; **by g.** au jugé.
**guest** invité, -ée *mf*; (*in hotel*) client, -ente *mf*; (*at meal*) convive *mf.*
**guest room** chambre *f* d'amis.
**guidance** conseils *mpl.*
**guide** **1** *n* guide *m*; **g. (book)** guide *m*. **2** *vt* guider; **guided tour** visite *f* guidée.
**guidelines** *npl* indications *fpl* (à suivre).
**guilt** culpabilité *f.*
**guilty** *a* coupable; **g. person** coupable *mf.*
**guinea pig** cobaye *m.*
**guitar** guitare *f.*
**guitarist** guitariste *mf.*
**gulf** (*in sea*) golfe *m*; **a g. between** un abîme entre.
**gull** (*bird*) mouette *f.*
**gulp** (*of drink*) gorgée *f.*
**gulp down** avaler (vite).
**gum¹** (*around teeth*) gencive *f.*
**gum²** **1** *n* (*for chewing*) chewing-gum *m*; (*glue*) colle *f.* **2** *vt* coller.
**gun** pistolet *m*; (*rifle*) fusil *m*; (*firing shells*) canon *m.*
**gun down** abattre.
**gunfire** coups *mpl* de feu.
**gunman** (*pl* **-men**) bandit *m* armé.
**gunpoint at g.** sous la menace d'une arme.
**gunpowder** poudre *f* à canon.
**gunshot** coup *m* de feu.
**gush (out)** jaillir (**of** de).
**gust g. (of wind)** rafale *f* (de vent).
**guts** *npl Fam* (*insides*) ventre *m.*
**gutter** (*on roof*) gouttière *f*; (*in street*) caniveau *m.*

**guy** *Fam* type *m*.
**gym** gym(nastique) *f*; (*gymnasium*) gymnase *m*.
**gymnasium** gymnase *m*.
**gymnastics** gymnastique *f*.
**gynecologist** gynécologue *mf*.

# H

**habit** habitude *f*; **to be in/get into the h. of doing** avoir/prendre l'habitude de faire.
**hack** *vt* (*cut*) tailler.
**hacker (computer) h.** pirate *m* informatique.
**had** *pt & pp de* **have**.
**haddock** (*fish*) aiglefin *m*; **smoked h.** haddock *m*.
**hag (old) h.** (vieille) sorcière *f*.
**haggle** *vi* marchander; **to h. over the price** discuter le prix.
**hail 1** *n* grêle *f*. **2** *vi* grêler; **it's hailing** il grêle.
**hailstone** grêlon *m*.
**hair** (*on head*) cheveux *mpl*; (*on body, of animal*) poils *mpl*; **a h.** (*on head*) un cheveu; (*on body, of animal*) un poil.
**hairbrush** brosse *f* à cheveux.
**haircut** coupe *f* de cheveux; **to get a h.** se faire couper les cheveux.
**hairdo** (*pl* **-dos**) *Fam* coiffure *f*.
**hairdresser** coiffeur, -euse *mf*.
**hair dryer** sèche-cheveux *m inv*.
**-haired** *suffix* **long-/red-h.** aux cheveux longs/roux.
**hairpin** épingle *f* à cheveux.
**hair-raising** *a* effrayant.
**hair spray** (bombe *f* de) laque *f*.
**hairstyle** coiffure *f*.
**hairy** *a* (*person, animal, body*) poilu.
**half 1** *n* (*pl* **halves**) moitié *f*, demi, -ie *mf*; **h. (of) the apple**/*etc* la moitié de la pomme/*etc*; **ten and a h.** dix et demi; **ten and a h. weeks** dix semaines et demie; **to cut in h.** couper en deux. **2** *a* demi; **h. a day, a h.-day** une demi-journée; **h. a dozen, a h.-dozen** une demi-douzaine; **at h. price** à moitié prix. **3** *adv* (*full etc*) à demi, à moitié; **h. past one** une heure et demie.
**half-hour** demi-heure *f*.
**half-time** (*in game*) mi-temps *f*.
**halfway** *adv* à mi-chemin (**between** entre); **to fill**/*etc* **h.** remplir/*etc* à moitié.
**halibut** (*fish*) flétan *m*.
**hall** salle *f*; **lecture h.** amphithéâtre *m*.
**Hallowe'en** la veille de la Toussaint.
**hallway** entrée *f*.
**halt** halte *f*; **to call a h. to** mettre fin à.
**halve** *vt* (*time, expense*) réduire de moitié.
**ham** jambon *m*; **h. and eggs** œufs *mpl* au jambon.
**hamburger** hamburger *m*; (*raw meat*) bœuf *m* haché.
**hammer 1** *n* marteau *m*. **2** *vt* (*nail*) enfoncer (**into** dans).
**hammering** (*defeat*) *Fam* raclée *f*.
**hammock** hamac *m*.
**hamper 1** *vt* gêner. **2** *n* panier *m*; (*laundry basket*) panier *m* à linge.
**hamster** hamster *m*.
**hand**[1] main *f*; (*of clock*) aiguille *f*; *Cards* jeu *m*; **to hold in one's h.** tenir à la main; **to give s.o. a (helping) h.** donner un coup de main à qn; **by h.** (*to make, sew etc*) à la main; **at** *or* **to h.** sous la main; **on h.** disponible; **out of h.** (*situation*) incontrôlable.
**hand**[2] *vt* (*give*) donner, passer (**to** à).
**hand around** (*cookies*) passer.
**handbag** sac *m* à main.
**handbook** manuel *m*; (*guide*) guide *m*.
**handbrake** frein *m* à main.
**handcuff** *vt* passer les menottes à.
**handcuffs** *npl* menottes *fpl*.
**handful** (*group*) poignée *f*.
**handicap 1** *n* handicap *m*. **2** *vt* handicaper; **to be handicapped** (*after an accident etc*) rester handicapé.

**handicapped** *a* handicapé.
**hand in** remettre.
**handkerchief** (*pl* **-fs**) mouchoir *m.*
**handle 1** *n* (*of door*) poignée *f*; (*of knife*) manche *m*; (*of bucket*) anse *f*; (*of saucepan*) queue *f*. **2** *vt* (*manipulate*) manier; (*touch*) toucher à; (*vehicle*) manœuvrer; (*deal with*) s'occuper de.
**handlebars** *npl* guidon *m.*
**hand luggage** bagages *mpl* à main.
**handmade** *a* fait à la main.
**hand out** distribuer.
**handout** (*leaflet*) prospectus *m*; (*money*) aumône *f*; (*papers for course, workshop*) photocopies *fpl*.
**hand over** remettre.
**handrail** rampe *f.*
**handshake** poignée *f* de main.
**handsome** *a* beau (*f* belle); (*profit*) considérable.
**handwriting** écriture *f.*
**handy** *a* commode, pratique; (*skillful*) habile (**at doing** à faire); (*within reach*) sous la main; (*place*) accessible.
**handyman** (*pl* **-men**) bricoleur *m.*
**hang[1]*** **1** *vt* (*pt* & *pp* **hung**) suspendre (**on, from** à); (*let dangle*) laisser pendre (**from, out of** de). **2** *vi* pendre; (*of fog*) flotter. **3** *n* **to get the h. of sth** *Fam* arriver à comprendre qch.
**hang[2]** *vt* (*pt* & *pp* **hanged**) (*criminal*) pendre (**for** pour).
**hangar** hangar *m.*
**hang around** traîner; (*wait*) attendre.
**hang down** *vi* pendre.
**hanger (coat) h.** cintre *m.*
**hang-glider** delta-plane® *m.*
**hanging** *a* suspendu (**from** à).
**hang on** résister; (*wait*) attendre; **to h. on to** ne pas lâcher; (*keep*) garder.
**hang out 1** *vt* (*laundry*) étendre; (*flag*) arborer. **2** *vi* (*of tongue, shirt*) pendre.
**hangover** gueule *f* de bois.
**hang up 1** *vt* (*picture*) accrocher. **2** *vi* (*on phone*) raccrocher.
**hangup** complexe *m.*
**happen** *vi* arriver, se passer; **to h. to s.o./sth** arriver à qn/qch; **I h. to know** il se trouve que je le sais; **do you h. to have . . . ?** est-ce que par hasard vous avez . . . ?
**happening** événement *m.*
**happily** *adv* joyeusement; (*contentedly*) tranquillement; (*fortunately*) heureusement.
**happiness** bonheur *m.*
**happy** *a* heureux (**to do** de faire, **about sth** de qch); **I'm not h. about it** ça ne me plaît pas beaucoup; **H. New Year!** bonne année!
**harass** *vt* harceler.
**harbor** port *m.*
**hard 1** *a* (*not soft, severe, difficult*) dur; **h. worker** gros travailleur *m*; **h. on s.o.** dur avec qn; **h. of hearing** malentendant. **2** *adv* (*to work, hit*) dur; (*to pull*) fort; (*to rain*) à verse; **to think h.** réfléchir bien.
**hard-boiled** *a* (*egg*) dur.
**hard copy** (*document*) papier copie *f.*
**hard core** (*group*) noyau *m.*
**hard disk** disque *m* dur.
**harden** *vti* durcir; **to become hardened to** s'endurcir à.
**hardly** *adv* à peine; **h. anyone** presque personne; **h. ever** presque jamais.
**hardness** dureté *f.*
**hardship** épreuve(s) *f*(*pl*).
**hard up** *a* (*broke*) *Fam* fauché.
**hardware** *n inv* quincaillerie *f*; (*of computer*) matériel *m.*
**hardware store** quincaillerie *f.*
**hard-working** *a* travailleur.
**hare** lièvre *m.*
**harm 1** *n* (*hurt*) mal *m*; (*wrong*) tort *m*. **2** *vt* (*physically*) faire du mal à; (*health, interests etc*) nuire à.
**harmful** *a* nuisible.
**harmless** *a* inoffensif.
**harmonica** harmonica *m.*
**harmonious** *a* harmonieux.

**harmony** harmonie *f.*
**harness** (*for horse*) harnais *m*; (*to carry baby*) porte-bébé *m* ventral.
**harp** harpe *f.*
**harp on sth** *Fam* ne pas s'arrêter de parler de qch.
**harsh** *a* dur, sévère; (*sound, taste*) âpre.
**harshly** *adv* durement.
**harshness** dureté *f.*
**harvest 1** *n* moisson *f*; (*of fruit*) récolte *f.* **2** *vt* moissonner; récolter.
**has** *see* **have.**
**hassle** *Fam* (*trouble*) histoires *fpl*; (*aggravation*) **it's a h.** c'est casse-pieds *inv.*
**haste** hâte *f*; **to make h.** se hâter.
**hasten 1** *vi* se hâter (**to do** de faire). **2** *vt* hâter.
**hastily** *adv* à la hâte.
**hasty** *a* précipité; (*visit*) rapide.
**hat** chapeau *m*; (*of child*) bonnet *m*; (*cap*) casquette *f.*
**hatch** *vi* (*of chick, egg*) éclore.
**hatchback** (*car*) trois-portes *f inv*, cinq-portes *f inv.*
**hate** *vt* détester, haïr; **to h. doing** *or* **to do** détester faire.
**hateful** *a* haïssable.
**hatred** haine *f.*
**haul** *vt* (*pull*) tirer.
**haunted** *a* hanté.
**have* 1** *vt* avoir; (*meal, drink etc*) prendre; **to h. a party/dream** faire une fête/un rêve; **will you h. . . .?** (*some cake, tea etc*) est-ce que tu veux . . .?; **to let s.o. h. sth** donner qch à qn; **you've had it!** *Fam* tu es fichu! **2** *v aux* avoir; (*with* monter, sortir *etc* & *vprs*) être; **to h. decided/been** avoir décidé/été; **to h. gone** être allé; **to h. cut oneself** s'être coupé; **I've got to go, I h. to go** je dois partir, je suis obligé de partir; **to h. sth done** faire faire qch; **he's had his suitcase brought up** il a fait monter sa valise; **haven't I?, hasn't she?** *etc* n'est-ce pas?; **no I haven't!** non!; **yes I h.!** oui!; (*after negative question*) si!
**havoc** ravages *mpl.*
**hawk** faucon *m.*
**hay** foin *m.*
**hay fever** rhume *m* des foins.
**haystack** meule *f* de foin.
**hazard** risque *m.*
**haze** brume *f.*
**hazelnut** noisette *f.*
**hazy** *a* (*weather*) brumeux; (*photo, idea*) flou; **I'm h. about my plans** je ne suis pas sûr de mes projets.
**he** *pron* il; (*stressed*) lui; **he's a happy man** c'est un homme heureux.
**head 1** *n* (*of person, hammer etc*) tête *f*; (*leader*) chef *m*; **it didn't enter my h.** ça ne m'est pas venu à l'esprit; **heads or tails?** pile ou face?; **per h., a h.** (*each*) par personne. **2** *a* (*salesperson etc*) principal. **3** *vt* (*group, company*) être à la tête de; (*list*) être en tête de.
**headache** mal *m* de tête; **to have a h.** avoir mal à la tête.
**head for, be heading** *or* **headed for** (*place*) se diriger vers; (*disaster*) aller à.
**heading** (*of chapter etc*) titre *m*; (*of subject*) rubrique *f.*
**headlight** (*of vehicle*) phare *m.*
**headline** (*of newspaper*) manchette *f*; **the headlines** les titres *mpl.*
**headmaster** (*of school*) directeur *m.*
**headmistress** directrice *f.*
**headphones** *npl* casque *m* (à écouteurs).
**headquarters** *npl* siège *m* (central); (*military*) quartier *m* général.
**headwaiter** maître *m* d'hôtel.
**headway** progrès *mpl.*
**heal** *vi* (*of wound*) se cicatriser; (*of bruise*) disparaître; (*of bone*) se ressouder.
**health** santé *f.*
**health care** soins *mpl* médicaux.
**health food** aliment *m* naturel; **h. food store** magasin *m* diététique.

**health insurance** assurance *f* maladie.
**healthy** *a* (*person*) en bonne santé; (*food, attitude etc*) sain.
**heap 1** *n* tas *m*; **heaps of** (*money, people*) *Fam* des tas de. **2** *vt* entasser.
**heap on s.o.** (*praise*) couvrir qn de; (*insults*) accabler qn de.
**hear* 1** *vt* entendre; (*listen to*) écouter; (*learn*) apprendre (**that** que). **2** *vi* entendre; (*get news*) recevoir des nouvelles (**from** de); **I've heard of** *or* **about him** j'ai entendu parler de lui.
**hearing** (*sense*) ouïe *f*.
**hearing aid** appareil *m* auditif.
**hearse** corbillard *m*.
**heart** cœur *m*; **heart(s)** *Cards* cœur *m*; **by h.** par cœur.
**heart attack** crise *f* cardiaque.
**heartbeat** battement *m* de cœur.
**heartbreaking** *a* navrant.
**heartening** *a* encourageant.
**hearty** *a* (*appetite*) gros (*f* grosse).
**heat** chaleur *f*; (*heating*) chauffage *m*.
**heat (up)** *vti* chauffer.
**heater** radiateur *m*.
**heath** lande *f*.
**heating** chauffage *m*.
**heat wave** vague *f* de chaleur.
**heave 1** *vt* (*lift*) soulever; (*pull*) tirer; (*a sigh*) pousser. **2** (*feel sick*) avoir des haut-le-cœur.
**heaven** ciel *m*; **h. knows when** Dieu sait quand.
**heavily** *adv* lourdement; (*to smoke, drink*) beaucoup; **to rain h.** pleuvoir à verse.
**heavy** *a* lourd; (*rain*) fort; (*traffic*) dense; (*smoker, drinker*) grand.
**Hebrew** (*language*) hébreu *m*.
**hectic** *a* fiévreux; (*period*) très agité.
**hedge** haie *f*.
**hedgehog** hérisson *m*.
**heel** talon *m*.
**hefty** *a* gros (*f* grosse).
**height** hauteur *f*; (*of person*) taille *f*; (*of success etc*) sommet *m*; **at the h. of** (*summer*) au cœur de.
**heir** héritier *m*.
**heiress** héritière *f*.
**held** *pt & pp de* **hold.**
**helicopter** hélicoptère *m*.
**hell** enfer *m*; **a h. of a lot (of)** (*very many, very much*) *Fam* énormément (de); **h.!** *Fam* zut!
**hello!** *int* bonjour!; (*answering phone*) allô!; (*surprise*) tiens!
**helm** (*of boat*) barre *f*.
**helmet** casque *m*.
**help 1** *n* aide *f*, secours *m*; (*cleaning woman*) femme *f* de ménage; (*workers in office, store*) employés, -ées *mfpl*; **h.!** au secours! **2** *vt* aider (**do, to do** à faire); **to h. oneself (to)** se servir (de); **I can't h. laughing**/*etc* je ne peux m'empêcher de rire/*etc*.
**helper** assistant, -ante *mf*.
**helpful** *a* utile; (*person*) serviable.
**helping** (*serving*) portion *f*.
**helpless** *a* (*powerless*) impuissant; (*disabled*) impotent.
**help out** *vti* aider.
**hem** ourlet *m*.
**hemmed in** *a* enfermé; (*surrounded*) cerné.
**hemorrhage** hémorragie *f*.
**hen** poule *f*.
**hepatitis** hépatite *f*.
**her 1** *pron* la, l'; (*after prep, 'than', 'it is'*) elle; **(to) h.** lui; **I see h.** je la vois; **I give it to h.** je le/la lui donne. **2** *poss a* son, sa, *pl* ses.
**herb** herbe *f*; **herbs** (*in cooking*) fines herbes *fpl*.
**herd** troupeau *m*.
**here** *adv* ici; **h. is, h. are** voici; **h. she is** la voici; **summer is h.** l'été est là; **h.!** (*answering roll call*) présent! **h. (you are)!** (*take this*) tenez!
**hermit** solitaire *mf*.
**hero** (*pl* **-oes**) héros *m*.
**heroic** *a* héroïque.
**heroin** (*drug*) héroïne *f*.
**heroine** héroïne *f*.
**herring** hareng *m*.
**hers** *poss pron* le sien, la sienne, *pl* les sien(ne)s; **this hat is h.** ce chapeau est à elle *or* est le sien.

**herself** *pron* elle-même; (*reflexive*) se, s'; (*after prep*) elle.
**hesitant** *a* hésitant.
**hesitate** *vi* hésiter (**about** sur; **to do** à faire).
**hesitation** hésitation *f*.
**hey!** *int* hé!; (*calling attention*) holà!
**hi!** *int Fam* salut!
**hiccups** *npl* **to have (the) h.** avoir le hoquet.
**hide**[1]* **1** *vt* cacher (**from** à). **2** *vi* se cacher (**from** de).
**hide**[2] (*skin*) peau *f*.
**hide-and-seek** cache-cache *m inv*.
**hideous** *a* horrible.
**hideously** *adv* horriblement.
**hide-out** cachette *f*.
**hiding a good h.** (*beating*) une bonne raclée.
**hiding place** cachette *f*.
**hi-fi** hi-fi *f inv*.
**high 1** *a* haut; (*speed*) grand; (*price, number*) élevé; (*on drugs*) *Fam* défoncé; **h. fever** forte fièvre *f*; **to be 16 feet h.** avoir cinq mètres de haut. **2** *adv* **h. (up)** (*to fly, throw etc*) haut. **3** *n* **an all-time h.** un nouveau record.
**high-chair** chaise *f* haute.
**high-class** *a* (*service*) de premier ordre; (*building*) de luxe.
**higher** *a* supérieur (**than** à).
**higher education** enseignement *m* supérieur.
**highlands** *npl* régions *fpl* montagneuses.
**highlight 1** *n* (*of visit, day*) point *m* culminant; (*of show*) clou *m*. **2** *vt* souligner.
**highly** *adv* (*very*) très; (*to recommend*) chaudement; **h. paid** très bien payé.
**high-pitched** *a* (*sound*) aigu.
**high-rise** *a* **h.-rise apartment building** tour *f*.
**high school** = (*ages 11–15*) collège *m*; (*ages 15–18*) lycée *m*.
**high school diploma** = baccalauréat *m*.
**high-speed** *a* ultra-rapide; **h.-speed train** rapide *m*.
**highway** autoroute *f*.
**hijack** *vt* (*aircraft*) détourner.
**hijacker** pirate *m* de l'air.
**hijacking** piraterie *f* aérienne; (*one incident*) détournement *m*.
**hike 1** *n* excursion *f* à pied. **2** *vi* marcher à pied.
**hiker** excursionniste *mf*.
**hilarious** *a* désopilant, hilarant.
**hill** colline *f*.
**hillside on the h.** à flanc de colline.
**hilly** *a* accidenté.
**him** *pron* le, l'; (*after prep, 'than', 'it is'*) lui; **(to) h.** lui; **I see h.** je le vois; **I give it to h.** je le/la lui donne.
**himself** *pron* lui-même; (*reflexive*) se, s'; (*after prep*) lui.
**hinder** *vt* gêner.
**Hindu** *a* & *n* hindou, -oue (*mf*).
**hinge** charnière *f*.
**hint 1** *n* allusion *f*; (*sign*) indication *f*; **hints** (*advice*) conseils *mpl*. **2** *vt* laisser entendre (**that** que).
**hint at** faire allusion à.
**hip** hanche *f*.
**hippopotamus** hippopotame *m*.
**hire** *vt* (*worker*) engager, embaucher.
**his 1** *poss a* son, sa, *pl* ses. **2** *poss pron* le sien, la sienne, *pl* les sien(ne)s; **this hat is h.** ce chapeau est à lui *or* est le sien.
**Hispanic** *a* & *n* hispano-américain, -aine (*mf*).
**hiss 1** *vti* siffler. **2** *n* sifflement *m*.
**historic(al)** *a* historique.
**history** histoire *f*.
**hit* 1** *vt* (*beat etc*) frapper; (*bump into*) heurter; (*reach*) atteindre; (*affect*) toucher. **2** *n* (*blow*) coup *m*; (*play, film*) succès *m*; **h. (song)** chanson *f* à succès.
**hit-and-run driver** chauffard *m*.
**hitch 1** *n* (*snag*) problème *m*. **2** *vti* **to h. (a ride)** *Fam* faire du stop (**to** jusqu'à).
**hitchhike** *vi* faire de l'auto-stop (**to** jusqu'à).
**hitchhiker** auto-stoppeur, -euse *mf*.
**hitchhiking** auto-stop *m*.
**hit (up)on** (*find*) tomber sur.

**hive** ruche *f*.
**hoard** *vt* amasser.
**hoarse** *a* enroué.
**hoax** canular *m*.
**hobby** passe-temps *m inv*.
**hobo** (*pl* **-os**) vagabond, -onde *mf*.
**hockey** hockey *m*; **ice h.** hockey sur glace.
**hold 1** *n* (*grip*) prise *f*; (*of ship*) cale *f*; (*of aircraft*) soute *f*; **to get h. of** saisir; (*contact*) joindre; (*find*) trouver. **2** *vt** tenir; (*breath, interest, attention*) retenir; (*a post*) occuper; (*a record*) détenir; (*possess*) posséder; (*contain*) contenir; **to h. hands** se tenir par la main; **please h.** (*on phone*) ne quittez pas; **to be held** (*of event*) avoir lieu. **3** *vi* (*of nail, rope*) tenir; **if the rain holds off** s'il ne pleut pas.
**hold back** (*crowd*) contenir; (*hide*) cacher.
**hold down** (*price*) maintenir bas; (*job*) garder.
**holder** (*of passport*) titulaire *mf*; (*of record*) détenteur, -trice *mf*; (*container*) support *m*.
**hold on** attendre; (*stand firm*) tenir bon; **h. on!** (*on phone*) ne quittez pas! **h. on (tight)!** tenez bon!
**hold onto** (*cling to*) tenir bien; (*keep*) garder.
**hold out 1** *vt* offrir; (*arm*) étendre. **2** *vi* résister; (*last*) durer.
**hold up** lever; (*support*) soutenir; (*delay*) retarder; (*bank*) attaquer.
**holdup** (*attack*) hold-up *m inv*; (*traffic jam*) bouchon *m*.
**hole** trou *m*.
**holiday** (*legal*) jour férié; **holidays** (*from school, work etc*) vacances *fpl*.
**hollow** *a* creux.
**holy** *a* saint; (*water*) bénit.
**home 1** *n* maison *f*; (*country*) pays *m* (natal); **at h.** à la maison, chez soi; **to make oneself at h.** se mettre à l'aise; **a good h.** une bonne famille; **(retirement) h.** maison *f* de retraite; **h. life/cooking/***etc* la vie/cuisine/*etc* familiale. **2** *adv* à la maison, chez soi; **to go** *or* **come (back) h.** rentrer; **to be h.** être rentré.
**homeless** *a* sans abri.
**homemade** *a* (fait à la) maison *inv*.
**homesick** *a* **to be h.** (*when abroad*) avoir le mal du pays; **to be h.** (*in general*) être nostalgique.
**home town** ville *f* natale.
**homework** devoir(s) *m(pl)*.
**homosexual** *a* & *n* homosexuel, -elle (*mf*).
**honest** *a* honnête; (*frank*) franc (*f* franche) (**with** avec).
**honesty** honnêteté *f*; franchise *f*.
**honey** miel *m*; (*person*) *Fam* chéri, -ie *mf*.
**honeymoon** lune *f* de miel; (*trip*) voyage *m* de noces.
**honk** *vi* (*in vehicle*) klaxonner.
**honor 1** *n* honneur *m*; **in h. of** en l'honneur de; **with honors** (*academic distinction*) avec mention **2** *vt* honorer (**with** de).
**honorable** *a* honorable.
**hood** capuchon *m*; (*mask of robber*) cagoule *f*; (*car or carriage roof*) capote *f*; (*of car engine*) capot *m*.
**hoof** (*pl* **-fs** *or* **-ves**) sabot *m*.
**hook** crochet *m*; (*on clothes*) agrafe *f*; *Fishing* hameçon *m*; **off the h.** (*phone*) décroché.
**hooked** *a* (*nose, object*) recourbé; **h. on** (*drugs, chess etc*) *Fam* accro de.
**hook (on** *or* **up)** accrocher (**to** à).
**hooky to play h.** sécher (la classe).
**hooligan** vandale *m*.
**hoop** cerceau *m*.
**hoot 1** *vi* (*of owl*) hululer. **2** *n* hululement *m*.
**hop 1** *vi* sauter (à cloche-pied); (*of bird*) sautiller; **h. in!** (*in car*) montez! **2** *n* saut *m*.
**hope 1** *n* espoir *m*. **2** *vi* espérer; **I h. so** j'espère que oui. **3** *vt* espérer (**to do** faire, **that** que).
**hope for** espérer.

**hopeful** *a* optimiste; (*promising*) prometteur; **to be h. that** avoir bon espoir que.
**hopefully** (*one hopes*) on espère (que).
**hopeless** *a* désespéré; (*useless*) nul.
**hopelessly** (*extremely*) complètement.
**hops** *npl* houblon *m.*
**hopscotch** marelle *f.*
**horizon** horizon *m*; **on the h.** à l'horizon.
**horizontal** *a* horizontal.
**horn** (*of animal*) corne *f*; (*on vehicle*) klaxon® *m.*
**horrible** *a* horrible.
**horribly** *adv* horriblement.
**horrific** *a* horrible.
**horrify** *vt* horrifier.
**horror** horreur *f.*
**horse** cheval *m.*
**horseback on h.** à cheval.
**horseracing** courses *fpl.*
**horseshoe** fer *m* à cheval.
**hose** tuyau *m*; (*pantyhose*) collant *m.*
**hospitable** *a* accueillant.
**hospital** hôpital *m*; **in the h.** à l'hôpital.
**hospitality** hospitalité *f.*
**hospitalize** *vt* hospitaliser.
**host** hôte *m*; (*of TV show*) présentateur, -trice *mf.*
**hostage** otage *m*; **to take s.o. h.** prendre qn en otage.
**hostel** foyer *m*; **youth h.** auberge *f* de jeunesse.
**hostess** hôtesse *f.*
**hostile** *a* hostile (**to, towards** à).
**hostility** hostilité *f* (**to, towards** envers).
**hot** *a* chaud; (*spice*) fort; **to be** *or* **feel h.** avoir chaud; **it's h.** (*of weather*) il fait chaud.
**hot dog** hot-dog *m.*
**hotel** hôtel *m.*
**hot-water bottle** bouillotte *f.*
**hound** *vt* (*pursue*) traquer.
**hour** heure *f*; **half an h.** une demi-heure; **a quarter of an h.** un quart d'heure.
**hourly 1** *a* (*pay*) horaire; **an h. bus/***etc* un bus/*etc* toutes les heures. **2** *adv* toutes les heures.
**house**[1] (*pl* **-ses**) maison *f*; (*audience in theatre*) salle *f.*
**house**[2] *vt* loger; (*of building*) abriter.
**household** famille *f.*
**housekeeper** *f* gouvernante.
**housekeeping** ménage *m* (*entretien*).
**House of Representatives** Chambre *f* des représentants.
**housewarming to have a h. (party)** pendre la crémaillère.
**housewife** (*pl* **-wives**) ménagère *f.*
**housework** (travaux *mpl* de) ménage *m.*
**housing** logement *m*; (*houses*) logements *mpl.*
**hovel** taudis *m.*
**hover** *vi* (*of bird etc*) planer.
**hovercraft** aéroglisseur *m.*
**how** *adv* comment; **h. kind!** comme c'est gentil!; **h. do you do?** enchanté; **h. long/high is?** quelle est la longueur/hauteur de?; **h. much?, h. many?** combien?; **h. much time/***etc***?** combien de temps/*etc*?; **h. many apples/***etc***?** combien de pommes/*etc*?; **h. about some coffee?** du café?
**however 1** *adv* **h. big he may be** quelque grand qu'il soit; **h. she may do it** de quelque manière qu'elle le fasse. **2** *conj* cependant.
**howl 1** *vi* hurler. **2** *n* hurlement *m.*
**HQ** *abbr* (*headquarters*) QG *m.*
**hubcap** enjoliveur *m.*
**huddle** *vi* se blottir.
**hug 1** *vt* serrer (dans ses bras). **2** *n* **to give s.o. a h.** serrer qn (dans ses bras).
**huge** *a* énorme.
**huh?** *int Fam* hein?
**hull** (*of ship*) coque *f.*
**hum 1** *vi* (*of insect*) bourdonner; (*of person*) fredonner. **2** *vt* (*tune*) fredonner.
**human** *a* humain; **h. being** être *m* humain.

**humanity** humanité *f.*
**humble** *a* humble.
**humid** *a* humide.
**humidity** humidité *f.*
**humiliate** *vt* humilier.
**humiliation** humiliation *f.*
**humorous** *a* (*book etc*) humoristique; (*person*) plein d'humour.
**humor** (*fun*) humour *m.*
**hump** (*lump*) bosse *f.*
**hunch** *Fam* intuition *f.*
**hundred** *a* & *n* cent (*m*); **a h. pages** cent pages; **hundreds of** des centaines de.
**hundredth** *a* & *n* centième (*mf*).
**hunger** faim *f.*
**hungry** *a* **to be** *or* **feel h.** avoir faim; **to make h.** donner faim à.
**hunt 1** *n* (*search*) recherche *f* (**for** de). **2** *vt* (*animals*) chasser; (*pursue*) poursuivre; (*seek*) chercher. **3** *vi* chasser.
**hunt down** traquer.
**hunter** chasseur *m.*
**hunt for sth** (re)chercher qch.
**hunting** chasse *f.*
**hurdle** (*fence*) haie *f*; (*problem*) obstacle *m.*
**hurl** *vt* lancer.
**hurray!** *int* hourra!
**hurricane** ouragan *m.*
**hurry 1** *n* hâte *f*; **in a h.** à la hâte; **to be in a h.** être pressé. **2** *vi* se dépêcher (**to do** de faire); **to h. through a meal** manger à toute vitesse; **to h. towards** se précipiter vers. **3** *vt* (*person*) bousculer.
**hurry up** (*go faster*) se dépêcher.
**hurt* 1** *vt* faire du mal à; (*emotionally*) faire de la peine à; (*reputation etc*) nuire à; **to h. s.o.'s feelings** blesser qn. **2** *vi* faire mal. **3** *n* mal *m.*
**husband** mari *m.*
**hush** silence *m.*
**hustle 1** *vt* (*shove*) bousculer (*qn*). **2** *n* **h. and bustle** tourbillon *m.*
**hut** cabane *f.*
**hygiene** hygiène *f.*
**hygienic** *a* hygiénique.
**hymn** cantique *m.*
**hyphen** trait *m* d'union.
**hyphenated** *a* (*word*) à trait d'union.
**hypocrisy** hypocrisie *f.*
**hypocrite** hypocrite *mf.*
**hysterical** *a* (*upset*) qui a une crise de nerfs; (*funny*) *Fam* désopilant.
**hysterically** *adv* (*to cry*) sans pouvoir s'arrêter.

# I

**I** *pron* je, j'; (*stressed*) moi.
**ice** glace *f*; (*on road*) verglas *m.*
**iceberg** iceberg *m.*
**ice-cold** *a* glacial; (*drink*) glacé.
**ice cream** glace *f.*
**ice cream bar** esquimau® *m.*
**ice cube** glaçon *m.*
**ice-skating** patinage *m* (sur glace).
**ice up** (*of windscreen or windshield*) givrer.
**icicle** glaçon *m.*
**icing** (*on cake*) glaçage *m.*
**icy** *a* glacé; (*weather*) glacial; (*road*) verglacé.
**ID** pièce *f* d'identité.
**idea** idée *f*; **I have an i. that** j'ai l'impression que.
**ideal 1** *a* idéal (*mpl* -aux *or* -als). **2** *n* idéal *m* (*pl* -aux *or* -als).
**ideally** *adv* idéalement; **i. we should stay** l'idéal, ce serait que nous restions.
**identical** *a* identique (**to, with** à).
**identification** (*document*) pièce *f* d'identité.
**identify** *vt* identifier; **to i. (oneself) with** s'identifier avec.
**identity** identité *f.*
**idiom** expression *f* idiomatique.
**idiot** idiot, -ote *mf.*
**idiotic** *a* idiot.
**idle** *a* (*unoccupied*) inactif; (*lazy*) paresseux.
**idler** paresseux, -euse *mf.*
**idol** idole *f.*
**idolize** *vt* (*adore*) traiter comme une idole.

**i.e.** *abbr* c'est-à-dire.
**if** *conj* si; **if he comes** s'il vient; **even if** même si; **if only I were rich** si seulement j'étais riche.
**igloo** igloo *m*.
**ignorance** ignorance *f* (**of** de).
**ignorant** *a* ignorant (**of** de).
**ignore** *vt* ne prêter aucune attention à (*qch*); (*pretend not to recognize*) faire semblant de ne pas reconnaître (*qn*).
**ill 1** *a* (*sick*) malade; (*bad*) mauvais. **2** *n* **ills** maux *mpl*.
**illegal** *a* illégal.
**illegible** *a* illisible.
**illiterate** *a* illettré.
**illness** maladie *f*.
**ill-treat** *vt* maltraiter.
**illusion** illusion *f* (**about** sur).
**illustrate** *vt* illustrer (**with** de).
**illustration** illustration *f*.
**image** image *f*; **(public) i.** (*of firm*) image *f* de marque.
**imaginary** *a* imaginaire.
**imagination** imagination *f*.
**imagine** *vt* (s')imaginer (**that** que).
**imitate** *vt* imiter.
**imitation** imitation *f*; **i. jewelry** bijoux *mpl* fantaisie.
**immaculate** *a* impeccable.
**immature** *a* (*person*) qui manque de maturité.
**immediate** *a* immédiat.
**immediately 1** *adv* (*at once*) tout de suite, immédiatement. **2** *conj* (*as soon as*) dès que.
**immense** *a* immense.
**immensely** *adv* extraordinairement.
**immigrant** *n* & *a* immigré, -ée (*mf*).
**immigration** immigration *f*.
**immortal** *a* immortel.
**immune** *a* (*naturally*) immunisé (**to** contre); (*vaccinated*) vacciné.
**immunize** *vt* vacciner (**against** contre).
**impact** effet *m* (**on** sur).
**impatience** impatience *f*.
**impatient** *a* impatient (**to do** de faire).
**impatiently** *adv* avec impatience.
**imperative** *Grammar* impératif *m*.
**impersonate** *vt* se faire passer pour; (*on TV etc*) imiter.
**impersonator** (*on TV etc*) imitateur, -trice *mf*.
**impertinent** *a* impertinent (**to** envers).
**impetus** impulsion *f*.
**implement[1]** (*tool*) instrument *m*; (*utensil*) ustensile *m*.
**implement[2]** *vt* mettre en œuvre.
**implication** conséquence *f*; (*impact*) portée *f*.
**imply** *vt* laisser entendre (**that** que); (*assume*) impliquer.
**impolite** *a* impoli.
**import 1** *vt* importer (**from** de). **2** *n* importation *f*.
**importance** importance *f*; **of no i.** sans importance.
**important** *a* important.
**importer** importateur, -trice *mf*.
**impose 1** *vt* imposer (**on** à); (*fine*) infliger (**on** à). **2** *vi* (*cause trouble*) déranger; **to i. on s.o.** déranger qn.
**imposing** *a* (*building*) impressionnant.
**imposition** (*inconvenience*) dérangement *m*.
**impossibility** impossibilité *f*.
**impossible** *a* impossible (**to do** à faire); **it is i. (for us) to do it** il (nous) est impossible de le faire.
**impostor** imposteur *m*.
**impractical** *a* peu réaliste.
**impress** *vt* impressionner (*qn*).
**impression** impression *f*.
**impressive** *a* impressionnant.
**imprison** *vt* emprisonner.
**improbable** *a* peu probable.
**improper** *a* (*obscene*) indécent; (*inappropriate*) inopportun, peu approprié.
**improve 1** *vt* améliorer. **2** *vi* s'améliorer; (*of business*) reprendre.
**improvement** amélioration *f*.
**improve on** faire mieux que.
**improvise** *vti* improviser.

**impudent** *a* impudent.
**impulse** impulsion *f*; **on i.** sur un coup de tête.
**impulsive** *a* impulsif.
**impulsively** *adv* de manière impulsive.
**impurity** impureté *f*.
**in 1** *prep* dans; **in the box**/*etc* dans la boîte/*etc*; **in an hour('s time)** dans une heure. ▪ à; **in school** à l'école; **in Paris** à Paris; **in Portugal** au Portugal; **in ink** à l'encre. ▪ en; **in summer/May/French** en été/mai/français; **in Spain** en Espagne; **in an hour** (*within that period*) en une heure; **in doing** en faisant. ▪ de; **in a soft voice** d'une voix douce; **the best in** le meilleur de. ▪ **in the morning** le matin; **one in ten** un sur dix. **2** *adv* **to be in** (*home*) être là, être à la maison; (*of train*) être arrivé; (*in fashion*) être en vogue.
**in-** *prefix* in-.
**inability** incapacité *f* (**to do** de faire).
**inaccessible** *a* inaccessible.
**inaccuracy** (*error*) inexactitude *f*.
**inaccurate** *a* inexact.
**inadequacy** insuffisance *f*.
**inadequate** *a* insuffisant; (*person*) pas à la hauteur.
**inappropriate** *a* peu approprié.
**inaugurate** *vt* (*building*) inaugurer.
**inauguration** inauguration *f*.
**Inc** *abbr* (*Incorporated*) SA, SARL.
**incapable** *a* incapable (**of doing** de faire).
**incense** *vt* mettre en colère.
**incentive** encouragement *m*, motivation *f*.
**inch** pouce *m* (= *2,54 cm*).
**incident** incident *m*; (*in film etc*) épisode *m*.
**incidently** (*by the way*) à propos.
**incite** *vt* inciter (**to do** à faire).
**incitement** incitation *f*.
**inclination** (*desire*) envie *f* (**to do** de faire).
**incline** *vt* (*bend*) incliner; **to be inclined to do** (*feel a wish to*) avoir bien envie de faire; (*tend to*) avoir tendance à faire.
**include** *vt* (*contain*) comprendre; **to be included** être compris; (*on list*) être inclus.
**including** *prep* y compris; **i. service** service *m* compris; **up to and including Monday** jusqu'à lundi inclus.
**inclusive** *a* inclus; **to be i. of** comprendre.
**income** revenu *m* (**from** de); **private i.** rentes *fpl*.
**income tax** impôt *m* sur le revenu.
**incompatible** *a* incompatible (**with** avec).
**incompetent** *a* incompétent.
**incomplete** *a* incomplet.
**inconceivable** *a* inconcevable.
**inconsiderate** *a* (*remark*) irréfléchi; (*person*) pas très gentil (**towards** avec).
**inconsistency** incohérence *f*.
**inconsistent** *a* en contradiction (**with** avec).
**inconspicuous** *a* peu en évidence.
**inconvenience 1** *n* (*bother*) dérangement *m*; (*disadvantage*) inconvénient *m*. **2** *vt* déranger, gêner.
**inconvenient** *a* (*moment, situation etc*) gênant; (*house*) mal situé; **it's i. (for me) to** ça me dérange de.
**incorporate** *vt* (*contain*) contenir.
**incorrect** *a* inexact; **you're i.** vous avez tort.
**increase 1** *vi* augmenter; (*of effort, noise*) s'intensifier. **2** *vt* augmenter; intensifier. **3** *n* augmentation *f* (**in, of** de); intensification *f*; **on the i.** en hausse.
**increasing** *a* (*amount*) croissant.
**increasingly** *adv* de plus en plus.
**incredible** *a* incroyable.
**incredibly** *adv* incroyablement.
**incubator** (*for baby, eggs*) couveuse *f*.
**incur** *vt* (*expenses*) faire; (*loss*) subir.
**incurable** *a* incurable.
**indecent** *a* (*obscene*) indécent.

**indecisive** *a* indécis.
**indeed** *adv* en effet; **very good**/*etc* **i.** vraiment très bon/*etc*; **yes i.!** bien sûr!; **thank you very much i.!** merci infiniment!
**indefinite** *a* indéfini.
**indefinitely** *adv* indéfiniment.
**independence** indépendance *f*.
**independent** *a* indépendant (**of** de).
**independently** *adv* de façon indépendante; **i. of** indépendamment de.
**index 1** *n* (*in book*) index *m*. **2** *vt* (*classify*) classer.
**index card** fiche *f*.
**index finger** index *m*.
**index-linked** *a* indexé (**to** sur).
**Indian** *a* & *n* indien, -ienne (*mf*).
**indicate** *vt* indiquer (**that** que).
**indication** (*sign*) indice *m*, indication *f*.
**indicator** (*instrument*) indicateur *m*; (*in vehicle*) clignotant *m*.
**indifference** indifférence *f* (**to** à).
**indifferent** *a* indifférent (**to** à).
**indigestion** problèmes *mpl* de digestion; **(an attack of) i.** une indigestion.
**indignant** *a* indigné (**at** de).
**indignation** indignation *f*.
**indirect** *a* indirect.
**indirectly** *adv* indirectement.
**indiscreet** *a* indiscret.
**indiscriminately** *adv* (*at random*) au hasard.
**indiscriminate** (*random*) fait, donné *etc* au hasard.
**indistinguishable** *a* indifférenciable (**from** de).
**individual 1** *a* individuel; (*specific*) particulier. **2** *n* (*person*) individu *m*.
**individually** *adv* (*separately*) individuellement.
**indoor** *a* (*games, shoes etc*) d'intérieur; (*swimming pool*) couvert.
**indoors** *adv* à l'intérieur.
**induce** *vt* persuader (**to do** de faire); (*cause*) provoquer.
**indulge** *vt* (*s.o.'s wishes*) satisfaire; (*child etc*) gâter.
**indulge in** (*ice cream etc*) se permettre.
**indulgent** *a* indulgent (**to** envers).
**industrial** *a* industriel; (*conflict*) du travail; **i. park** zone *f* industrielle.
**industry** industrie *f*.
**inedible** *a* immangeable.
**ineffective** *a* (*measure*) inefficace.
**inefficiency** inefficacité *f*.
**inefficient** *a* (*person, measure*) inefficace.
**inept** *a* (*unskilled*) peu habile (**at** à); (*incompetent*) incapable.
**inequality** inégalité *f*.
**inevitable** *a* inévitable.
**inevitably** *adv* inévitablement.
**inexcusable** *a* inexcusable.
**inexpensive** *a* bon marché *inv*.
**inexperience** inexpérience *f*.
**inexperienced** *a* inexpérimenté.
**inexplicable** *a* inexplicable.
**infallible** *a* infaillible.
**infamous** *a* (*evil*) infâme.
**infancy** petite enfance *f*.
**infant** petit(e) enfant *mf*; (*baby*) nourrisson *m*.
**infantry** infanterie *f*.
**infatuated** *a* amoureux (**with** de).
**infatuation** engouement *m* (**for, with** pour).
**infect** *vt* infecter; **to get infected** s'infecter.
**infection** infection *f*.
**infectious** *a* contagieux.
**inferior** *a* inférieur (**to** à); (*goods, work*) de qualité inférieure.
**inferiority** infériorité *f*.
**infernal** *a* infernal.
**infest** *vt* infester (**with** de).
**infinite** *a* infini.
**infinitely** *adv* infiniment.
**infinitive** *Grammar* infinitif *m*.
**infinity** infini *m*.
**infirm** *a* infirme.
**inflamed** *a* (*throat etc*) enflammé.
**inflammation** inflammation *f*.
**inflate** *vt* gonfler.
**inflation** inflation *f*.
**inflexible** *a* inflexible.
**inflict** *vt* (*a wound*) occasionner

(**on** à); **to i. pain on s.o.** faire souffrir qn.
**influence 1** *n* influence *f*; **under the i. (of drink)** en état d'ébriété. **2** *vt* influencer.
**influential** *a* **to be i.** avoir une grande influence.
**influenza** grippe *f*.
**influx** flot *m*.
**info** *Fam* renseignements *mpl* (**on** sur).
**inform** *vt* informer (**of** de, **that** que).
**informal** *a* simple, décontracté; (*expression*) familier; (*meeting*) non-officiel.
**informally** *adv* sans cérémonie; (*to dress*) simplement; (*to discuss*) à titre non-officiel.
**information** renseignements *mpl* (**about, on** sur); **a piece of i.** un renseignement.
**informative** *a* instructif.
**inform on** dénoncer.
**infuriate** *vt* exaspérer.
**infuriating** *a* exaspérant.
**ingenious** *a* ingénieux.
**ingratitude** ingratitude *f*.
**ingredient** ingrédient *m*.
**inhabit** *vt* habiter.
**inhabitant** habitant, -ante *mf*.
**inhale** *vt* aspirer.
**inherit** *vt* hériter (de).
**inheritance** héritage *m*.
**inhibit** *vt* (*hinder*) gêner; **to be inhibited** avoir des inhibitions.
**inhibition** inhibition *f*.
**inhospitable** *a* peu accueillant, inhospitalier.
**inhuman** *a* inhumain.
**initial 1** *a* premier. **2** *n* **initials** initiales *fpl*; (*signature*) paraphe *m*. **3** *vt* parapher.
**initially** *adv* au début.
**inject** *vt* injecter (**into** à).
**injection** injection *f*, piqûre *f*.
**injure** *vt* (*physically*) blesser, faire du mal à.
**injured 1** *a* blessé. **2** *n* **the i.** les blessés *mpl*.
**injury** blessure *f*; (*fracture*) fracture *f*; (*sprain*) foulure *f*.
**injustice** injustice *f*.
**ink** encre *f*.
**inkling** (petite) idée *f*.
**inland 1** *a* intérieur. **2** *adv* à l'intérieur.
**in-laws** *npl* belle-famille *f*.
**inmate** (*of prison*) détenu, -ue *mf*.
**inn** auberge *f*.
**inner** *a* intérieur; **the i. city** les quartiers défavorisés du centre-ville.
**inner tube** (*of tire*) chambre *f* à air.
**innkeeper** aubergiste *mf*.
**innocence** innocence *f*.
**innocent** *a* innocent.
**inoculate** *vt* vacciner (**against** contre).
**inoculation** vaccination *f*.
**input** (*computer operation*) entrée *f*; (*data*) données *fpl*.
**inquire 1** *vi* se renseigner (**about** sur). **2** *vt* demander; **to i. how to get to** demander le chemin de.
**inquire into** faire une enquête sur.
**inquiry** demande *f* de renseignements; (*investigation*) enquête *f*.
**inquisitive** *a* curieux.
**insane** *a* fou (*f* folle).
**insanity** folie *f*.
**inscription** inscription *f*; (*in book*) dédicace *f*.
**insect** insecte *m*.
**insecticide** insecticide *m*.
**insecure** *a* (*not securely fixed*) mal fixé; (*uncertain*) incertain; (*person*) qui manque d'assurance.
**insensitive** *a* insensible (**to** à).
**insensitivity** insensibilité *f*.
**insert** *vt* introduire, insérer (**in, into** dans).
**inside 1** *adv* dedans, à l'intérieur. **2** *prep* à l'intérieur de. **3** *n* dedans *m*, intérieur *m*; **on the i.** à l'intérieur (**of** de); **i. out** (*socks etc*) à l'envers. **4** *a* intérieur.
**insight** (*into question*) aperçu *m* (**into** de).
**insignificant** *a* insignifiant.
**insincere** *a* peu sincère.
**insist 1** *vi* insister (**on doing** pour faire). **2** *vt* (*order*) insister (**that**

pour que +*subjunctive*); (*declare*) affirmer (**that** que).
**insistence** insistance *f*; **her i. on seeing me** l'insistance qu'elle met à vouloir me voir.
**insistent** *a* **to be i.** insister (**that** pour que + *subjunctive*).
**insist on sth** (*demand*) exiger qch; (*assert*) affirmer qch.
**insolence** insolence *f*.
**insolent** *a* insolent.
**insomnia** insomnie *f*.
**inspect** *vt* contrôler.
**inspection** inspection *f*; (*of tickets*) contrôle *m*.
**inspector** inspecteur, -trice *mf*.
**inspiration** inspiration *f*.
**inspire** *vt* inspirer (**s.o. with sth** qch à qn).
**install** *vt* installer.
**installment** (*of money*) acompte *m*; (*of serial*) épisode *m*.
**instance** (*example*) cas *m*; **for i.** par exemple.
**instant 1** *a* immédiat; **i. coffee** café *m* soluble. **2** (*moment*) instant *m*.
**instantly** *adv* immédiatement.
**instead** *adv* plutôt; **i. of (doing) sth** au lieu de (faire) qch; **i. of s.o.** à la place de qn; **i. (of him** *or* **her)** à sa place.
**instinct** instinct *m*.
**instinctive** *a* instinctif.
**instinctively** *adv* instinctivement.
**institution** institution *f*.
**instruct** *vt* (*teach*) enseigner (**s.o. in sth** qch à qn); **to i. s.o. to do** (*order*) charger qn de faire.
**instructions** *npl* (*for use*) mode *m* d'emploi; (*orders*) instructions *fpl*.
**instructive** *a* instructif.
**instructor** (*for skiing etc*) moniteur, -trice *mf*; **driving i.** moniteur, -trice *mf* d'auto-école.
**instrument** instrument *m*.
**insufficient** *a* insuffisant.
**insulate** *vt* (*against cold and electrically*) isoler.
**insulation** (*material*) isolant *m*.
**insult 1** *vt* insulter. **2** *n* insulte *f* (**to** à).
**insurance** assurance *f*; **i. company** compagnie *f* d'assurances.
**insure** *vt* assurer (**against** contre).
**intact** *a* intact.
**intellect** intelligence *f*.
**intellectual** *a* & *n* intellectuel, -elle (*mf*).
**intelligence** intelligence *f*.
**intelligent** *a* intelligent.
**intelligible** *a* compréhensible.
**intend** *vt* (*gift etc*) destiner (**for** à); **to be intended to do/for s.o.** être destiné à faire/à qn; **to i. to do** avoir l'intention de faire.
**intense** *a* intense; (*interest*) vif.
**intensify 1** *vt* intensifier. **2** *vi* s'intensifier.
**intensity** intensité *f*.
**intensive** *a* intensif; **in i. care** en réanimation.
**intent** *a* **i. on doing** résolu à faire.
**intention** intention *f* (**of doing** de faire).
**intentional** *a* **it wasn't i.** ce n'était pas fait exprès.
**intentionally** *adv* exprès.
**intercept** *vt* intercepter.
**interchange** (*on road*) échangeur *m*.
**interchangeable** *a* interchangeable.
**intercom** interphone *m*.
**interconnected** *a* (*facts etc*) liés.
**interest 1** *n* intérêt *m*; (*money*) intérêts *mpl*; **to take an i. in** s'intéresser à; **to be of i. to s.o.** intéresser qn. **2** *vt* intéresser.
**interested** *a* intéressé; **to be i. in sth/s.o.** s'intéresser à qch/qn; **I'm i. in doing** ça m'intéresse de faire.
**interesting** *a* intéressant.
**interfere** *vi* se mêler des affaires d'autrui.
**interfere in** s'ingérer dans.
**interference** ingérence *f*; (*on radio*) parasites *mpl*.
**interfere with** (*upset*) déranger.
**interior 1** *a* intérieur. **2** *n* intérieur *m*.
**interjection** *Grammar* interjection *f*.
**intermediary** intermédiaire *mf*.

**intermediate** *a* intermédiaire; (*course*) de niveau moyen.
**intermission** (*in theater*) entracte *m*.
**intern** interne *mf* (des hôpitaux).
**internal** *a* interne; (*flight*) intérieur.
**Internal Revenue Service** service *m* des impôts.
**international** *a* international.
**interpret** *vt* interpréter.
**interpreter** interprète *mf*.
**interrogate** *vt* interroger.
**interrogation** (*by police*) interrogatoire *m*.
**interrogative** *a* & *n Grammar* interrogatif (*m*).
**interrupt** *vt* interrompre.
**interruption** interruption *f*.
**intersect 1** *vt* couper. **2** *vi* s'entrecouper.
**intersection** (*of roads, lines*) intersection *f*.
**interval** intervalle *m*.
**intervene** *vi* (*of person*) intervenir; (*of event*) survenir.
**intervention** intervention *f*.
**interview 1** *n* entrevue *f* (**with** avec); (*on TV etc*) interview *f*. **2** *vt* avoir une entrevue avec; (*on TV etc*) interviewer .
**interviewer** (*on TV etc*) interviewer *m*.
**intimate** *a* intime.
**intimidate** *vt* intimider.
**into** *prep* dans; **to put i.** mettre dans. ▪ en; **to translate i.** traduire en; **i. pieces** en morceaux. ▪ **to be i. yoga**/*etc Fam* être à fond dans le yoga/*etc*.
**intolerable** *a* intolérable (**that** que +*subjunctive*).
**intoxicate** *vt* enivrer.
**intoxicated** *a* ivre.
**intransitive** *a Grammar* intransitif.
**intricate** *a* complexe.
**introduce** *vt* (*bring in*) introduire (**into** dans); (*program*) présenter; **to i. s.o. to s.o.** présenter qn à qn.
**introduction** introduction *f*; (*of person to person*) présentation *f*; **i. to** (*initiation*) premier contact avec.
**intrude** *vi* déranger (**on s.o.** qn).
**intruder** intrus, -use *mf*.
**intrusion** (*disturbance*) dérangement *m*.
**intuition** intuition *f*.
**inundated** *a* submergé (**with work/letters**/*etc* de travail/lettres/*etc*).
**invade** *vt* envahir.
**invader** envahisseur, -euse *mf*.
**invalid**[1] malade *mf*; (*through injury*) infirme *mf*.
**invalid**[2] *a* non valable.
**invaluable** *a* inestimable.
**invariably** *adv* (*always*) toujours.
**invent** *vt* inventer.
**invention** invention *f*.
**inventor** inventeur, -trice *mf*.
**inventory** inventaire *m*.
**invest** *vt* (*money*) placer, investir (**in** dans).
**investigate** *vt* examiner; (*crime*) enquêter sur.
**investigation** examen *m*; (*inquiry by journalist, police etc*) enquête *f* (**of, into** sur).
**investigator** enquêteur, -euse *mf*.
**invest in** placer son argent dans; (*firm*) investir dans.
**investment** investissement *m*, placement *m*.
**investor** (*in shares*) actionnaire *mf*; (*saver*) épargnant, -ante *mf*.
**invigorating** *a* stimulant.
**invisible** *a* invisible.
**invitation** invitation *f*.
**invite** *vt* inviter (**to do** à faire); (*ask for*) demander; (*give occasion for*) provoquer.
**inviting** *a* engageant.
**invoice 1** *n* facture *f*. **2** *vt* facturer.
**involve** *vt* (*include*) mêler (*qn*) (**in** à); (*entail*) entraîner; **the job involves . . .** le poste nécessite . . . .
**involved** *a* (*concerned*) concerné; (*committed*) engagé (**in** dans); (*complicated*) compliqué; (*at stake*)

en jeu; **the person i.** la personne en question; **to be i. with s.o.** avoir des liens intimes avec qn.

**involvement** participation *f* (**in** à); (*commitment*) engagement *m*; (*emotional*) liaison *f*.

**inward(s)** *adv* vers l'intérieur.

**IOU** *abbr* (*I owe you*) reconnaissance *f* de dette.

**IQ** *abbr* (*intelligence quotient*) QI *m inv*.

**iris** (*plant, of eye*) iris *m*.

**Irish** *a* irlandais; **the I.** les Irlandais *mpl*.

**Irishman** (*pl* **-men**) Irlandais *m*.

**Irishwoman** (*pl* **-women**) Irlandaise *f*.

**iron 1** *n* fer *m*; (*for clothes*) fer *m* (à repasser). **2** *vt* (*clothes*) repasser.

**ironic(al)** *a* ironique.

**ironing** repassage *m*.

**ironing board** planche *f* à repasser.

**irony** ironie *f*.

**irrational** *a* (*person*) peu rationnel.

**irregular** *a* irrégulier.

**irrelevance** manque *m* de rapport.

**irrelevant** *a* sans rapport (**to** avec); **that's i.** ça n'a rien à voir.

**irresistible** *a* irrésistible.

**irrespective of** *prep* sans tenir compte de.

**irrigate** *vt* irriguer.

**irritable** *a* irritable.

**irritate** *vt* (*annoy, inflame*) irriter.

**irritating** *a* irritant.

**irritation** irritation *f*.

**is** *see* **be**.

**Islamic** *a* islamique.

**island** île *f*.

**isolate** *vt* isoler (**from** de).

**isolated** *a* isolé.

**isolation** isolement *m*; **in i.** isolément.

**issue 1** *vt* publier; (*tickets*) distribuer; (*passport*) délivrer; (*an order*) donner; (*warning*) lancer; (*supply*) fournir (**with** de, **to** à). **2** *n* (*matter*) question *f*; (*newspaper*) numéro *m*.

**it** *pron* (*subject*) il, elle; (*object*) le, la, l'; **(to) it** (*indirect object*) lui; **it's ringing** il sonne **I've done it** je l'ai fait. ▪ (*impersonal*) il; **it's snowing** il neige. ▪ (*non specific*) ce, cela, ça; **who is it?** qui est-ce?; **it was Paul who . . .** c'est Paul qui . . . . ▪ **of it, from it, about it** en; **in it, to it, at it** y; **on it** dessus; **under it** dessous.

**Italian 1** *a* & *n* italien, -ienne (*mf*). **2** *n* (*language*) italien *m*.

**italics** *npl* italique *m*.

**itch 1** *n* démangeaison(s) *f*(*pl*). **2** *vi* démanger; **his arm itches** son bras le démange.

**itching** démangeaison(s) *f*(*pl*).

**itchy** *a* **I have an i. hand** j'ai une main qui me démange.

**item** (*object*) article *m*; (*matter*) question *f*; **(news) i.** information *f*.

**its** *poss a* son, sa, *pl* ses.

**itself** *pron* lui-même, elle-même; (*reflexive*) se, s'.

**ivory** ivoire *m*.

**ivy** lierre *m*.

# J

**jab 1** *vt* enfoncer (**into** dans); (*prick*) piquer (*qn*) (**with sth** du bout de qch). **2** *n* (*blow*) coup *m*.

**jack** (*for car*) cric *m*; *Cards* valet *m*; **j. of all trades** homme *m* à tout faire.

**jacket** veste *f*; (*man's suit*) veston *m*; gilet *m*; **j. potato** pomme *f* de terre en robe des champs.

**jackhammer** marteau *m* piqueur.

**jacuzzi** jacousi *m*.

**jagged** *a* déchiqueté.

**jaguar** jaguar *m*.

**jail 1** *n* prison *f*. **2** *vt* emprisonner.

**jam[1]** confiture *f*.

**jam[2] 1** *n* **(traffic) j.** embouteillage *m*. **2** *vt* (*squeeze, make stuck*) coincer; (*street etc*) encombrer. **3** *vi* (*get stuck*) se coincer.

**jam sth/s.o. into** (*cram*) (en)tasser qch/qn dans.

**jammed** *a* (*machine etc*) coincé, bloqué; (*street etc*) encombré.
**jam-packed** *a* bourré de monde.
**January** janvier *m*.
**Japanese 1** *a* & *n inv* japonais, -aise (*mf*). **2** *n* (*language*) japonais *m*.
**jar** pot *m*; (*large, glass*) bocal *m*.
**jaundice** jaunisse *f*.
**javelin** javelot *m*.
**jaw** mâchoire *f*.
**jazz** jazz *m*.
**jealous** *a* jaloux (*f* -ouse) (**of** de).
**jealousy** jalousie *f*.
**jeans** *npl* **(pair of) j.** (blue-)jean *m*.
**jeep**® jeep® *f*.
**jeer (at)** *vti* railler; (*boo*) huer.
**jeering** (*of crowd*) huées *fpl*.
**jeers** *npl* huées *fpl*.
**Jell-O**® *n inv* gelée *f*.
**jelly** (*preserve, dessert*) gelée *f*.
**jeopardize** *vt* mettre en danger.
**jeopardy** danger *m*.
**jerk 1** *vt* donner une secousse à. **2** *n* secousse *f*; **(stupid) j.** *Fam* crétin, -ine *mf*.
**jersey** (*garment*) maillot *m*.
**jet** (*plane*) avion *m* à réaction.
**jet lag** fatigue *f* (due au décalage horaire).
**jet-lagged** *a* qui souffre du décalage horaire.
**jetty** jetée *f*.
**Jew** (*man*) Juif *m*; (*woman*) Juive *f*.
**jewel** bijou *m* (*pl* -oux); (*in watch*) rubis *m*.
**jewel(l)er** bijoutier, -ière *mf*.
**jewelry** bijoux *mpl*.
**Jewish** *a* juif.
**jigsaw j. (puzzle)** puzzle *m*.
**jingle** *vi* (*of keys*) tinter.
**jittery** *a* **to be j.** *Fam* avoir la frousse.
**job** (*task*) travail *m*; (*post*) poste *m*.
**jobless** *a* au chômage.
**jockey** jockey *m*.
**jog 1** *n* (*shake*) secousse *f*. **2** *vt* secouer; (*push*) pousser; (*memory*) rafraîchir. **3** *vi* faire du jogging.
**john** *Slang* cabinets *mpl*.
**join**[1] **1** *vt* (*put together*) joindre; (*wires, pipes*) raccorder; (*words, towns*) relier; **to j. s.o.** (*catch up with, meet*) rejoindre qn; (*go with*) se joindre à qn (**in doing** pour faire). **2** *vi* (*of roads etc*) se rejoindre; (*of objects*) se joindre. **3** *n* raccord *m*.
**join**[2] **1** *vt* (*become a member of*) s'inscrire à (*club, parti*); (*firm, army*) entrer dans. **2** *vi* devenir membre.
**join in** prendre part; **to join in sth** prendre part à qch.
**joint 1** *n* (*in body*) articulation *f*. **2** *a* (*account*) joint; (*effort*) conjugué.
**joke 1** *n* plaisanterie *f*; (*trick*) tour *m*. **2** *vi* plaisanter (**about** sur).
**joker** plaisantin *m*; *Cards* joker *m*.
**jolly** *a* gai.
**jolt** *vti* secouer.
**jostle 1** *vti* (*push*) bousculer. **2** *vi* (*push each other*) se bousculer.
**jot down** noter.
**journalist** journaliste *mf*.
**journey** voyage *m*; (*distance*) trajet *m*.
**joy** joie *f*.
**joyful** *a* joyeux.
**joystick** manche *m* à balai.
**judge 1** *n* juge *m*. **2** *vti* juger.
**judg(e)ment** jugement *m*.
**judo** judo *m*.
**jug** cruche *f*; (*for milk*) pot *m*.
**juggernaut** force *f* irrésistible.
**juggle** *vi* jongler (**with** avec).
**juggler** jongleur, -euse *mf*.
**juice** jus *m*.
**juicy** *a* (*fruit*) juteux.
**July** juillet *m*.
**jumble (up)** mélanger.
**jumbo** *a* géant.
**jumbo jet** gros-porteur *m*.
**jump 1** *n* saut; (*start*) sursaut *m*; (*increase*) hausse *f*. **2** *vi* sauter; (*start*) sursauter; **to j. off sth** sauter de qch. **3** *vt* **to j. rope** sauter à la corde.
**jumper** (*garment*) robe-chasuble *f*.
**jump in** *or* **on 1** *vt* (*train, vehicle*) monter dans. **2** *vi* monter.
**jump rope** corde *f* à sauter.

**jumpy** *a* nerveux.
**junction** carrefour *m*.
**June** juin *m*.
**jungle** jungle *f*.
**junior 1** *a* (*younger*) plus jeune; (*in rank*) subalterne; (*doctor*) jeune. **2** *n* cadet, -ette *mf*; (*in school*) petit(e) élève *mf*.
**junior high (school)** = collège *m* d'enseignement secondaire.
**junk** bric-à-brac *m inv*; (*metal*) ferraille *f*; (*goods*) camelote *f*; (*garbage*) ordures *fpl*.
**jury** jury *m*.
**just** *adv* (*exactly, only*) juste; **she has/had j. left** elle vient/venait de partir; **he'll (only) j. catch the bus** il aura son bus de justesse; **he j. missed it** il l'a manqué de peu; **j. as big**/*etc* tout aussi grand/*etc* (**as** que); **j. over ten** un peu plus de dix; **j. one** un(e) seul(e); **j. about** à peu près; (*almost*) presque; **j. about to do** sur le point de faire.
**justice** justice *f*.
**justify** *vt* justifier; **to be justified in doing** être fondé à faire.
**jut out** faire saillie.

## K

**kangaroo** (*pl* **-oos**) kangourou *m*.
**karate** karaté *m*.
**kebab** brochette *f*.
**keen** *a* (*interest, emotion*) vif; **k. eyesight** vue *f* perçante; **he's a k. athlete** c'est un passionné de sport; **to be k. on doing** (*want*) tenir (beaucoup) à faire.
**keep* 1** *vt* garder; (*shop, car*) avoir; (*diary, promise*) tenir; (*family*) entretenir; (*rule*) respecter; (*delay*) retenir; **to k. doing** continuer à faire; **to k. s.o. waiting/working** faire attendre/travailler qn; **to k. s.o. in/out** empêcher qn de sortir/d'entrer. **2** *vi* (*remain*) rester; (*of food*) se garder; **to k. going** continuer; **to k. (to the) right** tenir sa droite. **3** *n* (*food*) nourriture *f*, subsistance *f*.
**keep away 1** *vt* (*person*) éloigner (**from** de). **2** *vi* ne pas s'approcher (**from** de).
**keep back 1** *vt* (*crowd*) contenir; (*delay*) retenir; (*hide*) cacher (**from** à). **2** *vi* ne pas s'approcher (**from** de).
**keep down** (*restrict*) limiter; (*price*) maintenir bas.
**keeper** (*in park, zoo*) gardien, -ienne *mf*.
**keep from** (*hide*) cacher à; **to k. s.o. from doing** (*prevent*) empêcher qn de faire.
**keep off** (*not go near*) ne pas s'approcher; **the rain kept off** il n'a pas plu.
**keep on** (*hat, employee*) garder; **to k. on doing** continuer à faire.
**keep up** *vti* continuer (**doing sth** à faire qch); **to k. up (with s.o.)** (*follow*) suivre (qn).
**kennel** niche *f*.
**kept** *pt & pp de* **keep**.
**kerosene** pétrole *m* (lampant).
**ketchup** ketchup *m*.
**kettle** bouilloire *f*; **the k. is boiling** l'eau bout.
**key 1** *n* clef *f*; (*of piano, typewriter, computer*) touche *f*. **2** *a* (*industry, post etc*) clef (*f inv*).
**keyboard** clavier *m*.
**key ring** porte-clefs *m inv*.
**kick 1** *n* coup *m* de pied. **2** *vt* donner un coup de pied à. **3** *vi* donner des coups de pied.
**kick down** *or* **in** (*door etc*) démolir à coups de pied.
**kick-off** *Football* coup *m* d'envoi.
**kick out** (*throw out*) *Fam* flanquer dehors.
**kid 1** *n* (*child*) *Fam* gosse *mf*. **2** *vti* (*tease*) *Fam* blaguer.
**kidnap** *vt* kidnapper.
**kidnapper** ravisseur, -euse *mf*.
**kidney** rein *m*; (*as food*) rognon *m*.
**kill** *vti* tuer.
**killer** tueur, -euse *mf*.
**kilo** (*pl* **-os**) kilo *m*.
**kilogram** kilogramme *m*.
**kilometer** kilomètre *m*.
**kind**[1] (*sort*) sorte *f*, genre *m*, espèce

*f* (**of** de); **all kinds of** toutes sortes de; **what k. of drink**/*etc* **is it?** qu'est-ce que c'est comme boisson/*etc*?; **k. of worried**/*etc* plutôt inquiet/*etc*.

**kind**[2] *a* (*pleasant*) gentil (**to** avec).

**kindergarten** jardin *m* d'enfants.

**kindness** gentillesse *f*.

**king** roi *m*.

**kingdom** royaume *m*.

**kiosk** kiosque *m*.

**kiss 1** *n* baiser *m*. **2** *vt* (*person*) embrasser; **to k. s.o.'s hand** baiser la main de qn. **3** *vi* s'embrasser.

**kit** équipement *m*; (*set of articles*) trousse *f*; **(do-it-yourself) k.** kit *m*; **tool k.** trousse *f* à outils.

**kitchen** cuisine *f*.

**kite** (*toy*) cerf-volant *m*.

**kitten** chaton *m*.

**knack to have a** *or* **the k. of doing** avoir le don de faire.

**knee** genou *m* (*pl* genoux).

**kneel* (down)** *vi* s'agenouiller; **to be kneeling (down)** être à genoux.

**knew** *pt de* **know.**

**knickers** culotte *f*.

**knife** (*pl* **knives**) couteau *m*; (*penknife*) canif *m*.

**knight** chevalier *m*; *Chess* cavalier *m*.

**knit** *vti* tricoter.

**knitting** (*activity, material*) tricot *m*; **k. needle** aiguille *f* à tricoter.

**knob** (*on door etc*) bouton *m*.

**knock 1** *vt* (*strike*) frapper; (*collide with*) heurter; **to k. one's head on sth** se cogner la tête contre qch. **2** *vi* frapper. **3** *n* coup *m*; **there's a k. at the door** quelqu'un frappe; **I heard a k.** j'ai entendu frapper.

**knock against** *or* **into** (*bump into*) heurter.

**knock down** (*vase, pedestrian etc*) renverser; (*house, wall etc*) abattre.

**knocker** (*for door*) marteau *m*.

**knock in** (*nail*) enfoncer.

**knock off** (*person, object*) faire tomber (**from** de).

**knock out** (*make unconscious*) assommer; *Boxing* mettre k.-o.; (*beat in competition*) éliminer.

**knock over** (*pedestrian, vase etc*) renverser.

**knot 1** *n* nœud *m*. **2** *vt* nouer.

**know* 1** *vt* (*facts, language etc*) savoir; (*person, place etc*) connaître; (*recognize*) reconnaître (**by** à); **to k. that** savoir que; **to k. how to do** savoir faire; **I'll let you k.** je te le ferai savoir; **to k. (a lot) about** (*person, event*) en savoir long sur; (*cars, sewing etc*) s'y connaître en; **to get to k. s.o.** apprendre à mieux connaître qn. **2** *vi* savoir; **I wouldn't k.** je n'en sais rien; **I k. about that** je suis au courant; **do you k. of a good dentist**/*etc***?** connais-tu un bon dentiste/*etc*?

**know-how** savoir-faire *m inv*.

**knowledge** connaissance *f* (**of** de); (*learning*) connaissances *fpl*.

**known** *a* connu; **well k.** (bien) connu (**that** que); **she is k. to be** on sait qu'elle est.

**knuckle** articulation *f* (du doigt).

**Koran the K.** le Coran *m*.

## L

**lab** *Fam* labo *m*.

**label 1** *n* étiquette *f*. **2** *vt* (*goods*) étiqueter.

**labor 1** *n* (*work*) travail *m*; (*workers*) main-d'œuvre *f*; **in l.** en train d'accoucher. **2** *a* (*market, situation*) du travail.

**laboratory** laboratoire *m*.

**laborer** manœuvre *m*; (*on farm*) ouvrier *m* agricole.

**labor protest** mouvement *m* revendicatif.

**labor union** syndicat *m*.

**lace** (*cloth*) dentelle *f*; (*of shoe*) lacet *m*.

**lace (up)** (*shoe*) lacer.

**lack 1** *n* manque *m*. **2** *vt* manquer de. **3** *vi* **to be lacking** manquer (**in** de).

**lad** gamin *m*.
**ladder** échelle *f*.
**ladle** louche *f*.
**lady** dame *f*; **a young l.** une jeune fille; (*married*) une jeune femme; **l. doctor** femme *f* médecin; **the ladies' room** les toilettes *fpl* pour dames.
**ladybug** coccinelle *f*.
**lager** bière *f* blonde.
**lake** lac *m*.
**lamb** agneau *m*.
**lame** *a* **to be l.** boiter.
**lamp** lampe *f*.
**lamppost** réverbère *m*.
**lampshade** abat-jour *m inv*.
**land 1** *n* terre *f*; (*country*) pays *m*; **(plot of) l.** terrain *m*. **2** *vi* (*of aircraft*) atterrir; (*of passengers*) débarquer. **3** *vt* (*aircraft*) poser.
**landing** (*of aircraft*) atterrissage *m*; (*at top of stairs*) palier *m*.
**landlady** propriétaire *f*; (*of pub*) patronne *f*.
**landlord** propriétaire *m*; (*of pub*) patron *m*.
**landscape** paysage *m*.
**landslide** éboulement *m*.
**lane** (*in country*) chemin *m*; (*in town*) ruelle *f*; (*division of road*) voie *f*.
**language 1** *n* (*English etc*) langue *f*; (*means of expression, style*) langage *m*. **2** *a* (*laboratory*) de langues; (*teacher, studies*) de langue(s).
**lantern** lanterne *f*.
**lap** (*of person*) genoux *mpl*; (*in race*) tour *m* (de piste).
**lapel** (*of coat etc*) revers *m*.
**larder** (*storeroom*) garde-manger *m inv*.
**large** *a* grand; (*in volume*) gros (*f* grosse).
**largely** *adv* en grande mesure.
**lark** (*bird*) alouette *f*; (*joke*) *Fam* rigolade *f*.
**laser** laser *m*.
**last[1] 1** *a* dernier; **next to l.** avant-dernier. **2** *adv* (*lastly*) en dernier lieu; (*on the last occasion*) (pour) la dernière fois; **to leave l.** sortir en dernier. **3** *n* (*person, object*) dernier, -ière *mf*; **the l. of the beer/***etc* le reste de la bière/*etc*; **at (long) l.** enfin.
**last[2]** *vi* durer; (*endure*) tenir.
**lastly** *adv* en dernier lieu, enfin.
**latch** loquet *m*.
**late 1** *a* (*not on time*) en retard (**for** à); (*meal, hour*) tardif; **he's an hour l.** il a une heure de retard; **it's l.** il est tard; **at a later date** à une date ultérieure; **at the latest** au plus tard; **of l.** dernièrement. **2** *adv* (*in the day, season etc*) tard; (*not on time*) en retard; **it's getting l.** il se fait tard; **later (on)** plus tard.
**latecomer** retardataire *mf*.
**lately** *adv* dernièrement.
**Latin 1** *a* latin. **2** *n* (*language*) latin *m*.
**latter 1** *a* (*last-named*) dernier; (*second*) deuxième. **2** *n* dernier, -ière *mf*; second, -onde *mf*.
**laugh 1** *n* rire *m*. **2** *vi* rire (**at, about** de).
**laughter** rire(s) *m*(*pl*).
**launch 1** *vt* (*rocket, fashion etc*) lancer. **2** *n* lancement *m*.
**laundromat** laverie *f* automatique.
**laundry** (*place*) blanchisserie *f*; (*clothes*) linge *m*.
**laundry detergent** lessive *f*.
**lavatory** cabinets *mpl*.
**law** loi *f*; (*study, profession*) droit *m*; **court of l., l. court** cour *f* de justice.
**lawn** pelouse *f*, gazon *m*; **l. mower** tondeuse *f* (à gazon).
**lawsuit** procès *m*.
**lawyer** avocat *m*; (*for wills, sales*) notaire *m*.
**lay*** *vt* (*put down*) poser; (*table*) mettre; (*blanket*) étendre (**over** sur); (*trap*) tendre; (*egg*) pondre.
**lay down** (*put down*) poser.
**layer** couche *f*.
**lay in** (*supplies*) faire provision de.
**lay off** (*worker*) licencier.

**lay out** (*garden*) dessiner; (*display*) disposer; (*money*) *Fam* mettre (**on** dans).
**layout** disposition *f*.
**lazy** *a* paresseux.
**lazybones** *Fam* fainéant, -ante *mf*.
**lead**[1] **1** *vt** (*conduct*) mener, conduire (**to** à); (*team, government etc*) diriger; (*life*) mener; **to l. s.o. in/out/***etc* faire entrer/sortir/*etc* qn; **to l. s.o. to do** amener qn à faire. **2** *vi* (*of street, door etc*) mener (**to** à); (*in race*) être en tête; (*in match*) mener; (*go ahead*) aller devant. **3** *n* (*distance or time ahead*) avance *f* (**over** sur); (*example*) exemple *m*; (*leash*) laisse *f*; (*electric wire*) fil *m*; **to be in the l.** (*in race*) être en tête; (*in match*) mener.
**lead**[2] (*metal*) plomb *m*; (*of pencil*) mine *f*.
**lead s.o. away** *or* **off** emmener qn.
**leader** chef *m*; (*of country, party*) dirigeant, -ante *mf*.
**leading** *a* (*main*) principal.
**lead to** (*result in*) aboutir à; (*cause*) causer.
**lead up to** (*of street etc*) conduire à; (*precede*) précéder.
**leaf** (*pl* **leaves**) feuille *f*; (*of book*) feuillet *m*.
**leaflet** prospectus *m*; (*containing instructions*) notice *f*.
**leaf through** (*book*) feuilleter.
**leak 1** *n* (*of gas etc*) fuite *f*. **2** *vi* (*of liquid, pipe etc*) fuir.
**lean* 1** *vi* (*of object*) pencher; (*of person*) se pencher; **to l. against/on sth** (*of person*) s'appuyer contre/sur qch. **2** *vt* appuyer (**against** contre); **to l. one's head on/out of sth** pencher la tête sur/par qch.
**lean forward** (*of person*) se pencher (en avant).
**lean over** (*of person*) se pencher; (*of object*) pencher.
**leap 1** *n* bond *m*. **2** *vi** bondir.
**leap year** année *f* bissextile.
**learn* 1** *vt* apprendre (**that** que); **to l. (how) to do** apprendre à faire. **2** *vi* apprendre; **to l. about** (*study*) étudier; (*hear about*) apprendre.
**learner** débutant, -ante *mf*.
**learning** (*of language*) apprentissage *m* (**of** de).
**leash** laisse *f*.
**least 1** *a* **the l.** (*smallest amount of*) le moins de; (*slightest*) le *or* la moindre. **2** *n* **the l.** le moins; **at l.** du moins; (*with quantity*) au moins. **3** *adv* (*to work etc*) le moins; (*with adjective*) le *or* la moins.
**leather** cuir *m*.
**leave 1** *n* (*vacation*) congé *m*. **2** *vt** laisser; (*go away from*) quitter; **to be left (over)** rester; **there's no bread/***etc* **left** il ne reste plus de pain/*etc*; **to l. go (of)** (*release*) lâcher. **3** *vi* (*go away*) partir (**from** de, **for** pour).
**leave behind** (*not take*) laisser; (*in race, at school*) distancer.
**leave on** (*hat, gloves*) garder.
**leave out** (*forget to add*) oublier (de mettre) (*accent etc*); (*word, line*) sauter; (*exclude*) exclure.
**lecture 1** *n* (*public speech*) conférence *f*; **to give a l.** faire une conférence. **2** *vt* **to l. s.o.** sermonner qn.
**lecturer** conférencier, -ière *mf*.
**leek** poireau *m*.
**left**[1] *pt & pp de* **leave**.
**left**[2] **1** *a* (*side, hand etc*) gauche. **2** *adv* à gauche. **3** *n* gauche *f*; **on** *or* **to the l.** à gauche (**of** de).
**left-hand** *a* à *or* de gauche; **on the l.-hand side** à gauche (**of** de).
**left-handed** *a* (*person*) gaucher.
**leftovers** *npl* restes *mpl*.
**leg** jambe *f*; (*of dog etc*) patte *f*; (*of table*) pied *m*; **l. (of chicken)** cuisse *f* (de poulet); **l. of lamb** gigot *m* (d'agneau).
**legal** *a* légal.
**legend** légende *f*.
**legible** *a* lisible.
**leisure l. (time)** loisirs *mpl*; **l. activities** loisirs *mpl*.
**lemon** citron *m*; **tea with l.** thé *m* au citron.

**lemonade** citronnade *f.*
**lend*** *vt* prêter (**to** à); (*color, charm etc*) donner (**to** à).
**length** longueur *f*; (*section of rope etc*) morceau *m*; (*duration*) durée *f*; **l. of time** temps *m*.
**lengthen** *vt* allonger; (*in time*) prolonger.
**lenient** *a* indulgent (**to** envers).
**lens** lentille *f*; (*in spectacles*) verre *m*; (*of camera*) objectif *m*.
**lentil** lentille *f* (*graine*).
**leopard** léopard *m*.
**leotard** collant *m* (*de danse*).
**less 1** *a* & *n* moins (de) (**than** que); **l. time**/*etc* moins de temps/*etc*; **l. than a quart/ten** (*with quantity, number*) moins d'un litre/de dix. **2** *adv* moins (**than** que); **l. (often)** moins souvent; **l. and l.** de moins en moins; **one l.** un(e) de moins. **3** *prep* moins.
**lesson** leçon *f*.
**let*** *vt* (*allow*) laisser (**s.o. do** qn faire); **to l. s.o. have sth** donner qch à qn; **l. us** *or* **l.'s eat**/*etc* mangeons/*etc*; **l.'s go for a stroll** allons nous promener; **l. him come** qu'il vienne.
**let down** (*lower*) baisser; **to l. s.o. down** (*disappoint*) décevoir qn.
**letdown** déception *f*.
**let in** (*person*) faire entrer; (*noise, light*) laisser entrer.
**let off** (*firework, gun*) faire partir; **to l. s.o. off** (*not punish*) ne pas punir qn; **to l. s.o. off doing** dispenser qn de faire.
**let out** (*person*) laisser sortir; (*cry, secret*) laisser échapper.
**letter** lettre *f*.
**letterbox** boîte *f* aux *or* à lettres.
**letter opener** coupe-papier *m inv*.
**lettuce** laitue *f*.
**let up** (*of rain etc*) s'arrêter.
**level 1** *n* niveau *m*; (*rate*) taux *m*. **2** *a* (*surface*) plat; (*object on surface*) d'aplomb; (*equal in score*) à égalité (**with** avec); (*in height*) au même niveau (**with** que).
**lever** levier *m*.
**liable** *a* **to be l. to do** être capable *or* susceptible de faire.
**liar** menteur, -euse *mf*.
**liberty** liberté *f*; **at l. to do** libre de faire.
**librarian** bibliothécaire *mf*.
**library** bibliothèque *f*.
**lice** *npl* poux *mpl*.
**license** (*document*) permis *m*; **licence plate/number** plaque *f*/numéro *m* d'immatriculation.
**lick** *vt* lécher.
**licorice** réglisse *f*.
**lid** (*of box etc*) couvercle *m*.
**lie[1]*** *vi* (*in flat position*) s'allonger; (*remain*) rester; (*be*) être; **to be lying** (*on the grass etc*) être allongé.
**lie[2] 1** *vi* (*pt* & *pp* **lied**, *pres p* **lying**) (*tell lies*) mentir. **2** *n* mensonge *m*.
**lie around** (*of objects, person*) traîner.
**lie down** s'allonger; **lying down** allongé.
**life** (*pl* **lives**) vie *f*; **to come to l.** s'animer.
**lifebelt** ceinture *f* de sauvetage.
**lifeboat** canot *m* de sauvetage.
**lifeguard** maître nageur *m* (sauveteur).
**life insurance** assurance-vie *f*.
**life jacket** gilet *m* de sauvetage.
**life preserver** ceinture *f* de sauvetage.
**lifetime in my l.** de mon vivant.
**lift 1** *vt* lever. **2** *n* (*elevator*) ascenseur *m*; **to give s.o. a l.** emmener qn (en voiture) (**to** à).
**lift down** *or* **off** (*take down*) descendre (**from** de).
**lift out** (*take out*) sortir (**of** de).
**lift up** (*arm, object*) lever.
**light[1]** lumière *f*; (*on vehicle*) feu *m*; (*vehicle headlight*) phare *m*; **do you have a l.?** (*for cigarette*) est-ce que vous avez du feu?
**light[2]*** *vt* (*match, fire, gas*) allumer.
**light[3]** *a* (*not dark*) clair; **a l. green jacket** une veste vert clair.
**light[4]** *a* (*in weight, quantity etc*)

léger; **to travel l.** voyager avec peu de bagages.

**light (up)** (*room*) éclairer; (*cigarette*) allumer.

**light bulb** ampoule *f* (électrique).

**lighter** (*for cigarettes*) briquet *m*; (*for stove*) allume-gaz *m inv*.

**lighthouse** phare *m*.

**lighting** (*lights*) éclairage *m*.

**lightning** (*charge*) foudre *f*; **(flash of) l.** éclair *m*.

**like**[1] **1** *prep* comme; **l. this** comme ça; **what's he l.?** comment est-il?; **to be** *or* **look l.** ressembler à; **what was the book l.?** comment as-tu trouvé le livre? **2** *conj* (*as*) *Fam* comme; **do l. I do** fais comme moi.

**like**[2] *vt* aimer (bien) (**to do, doing** faire); **she likes it here** elle se plaît ici; **to l. sth best** aimer mieux qch; **I'd l. to come** je voudrais (bien) *or* j'aimerais (bien) venir; **I'd l. some cake** je voudrais du gâteau; **would you l. an apple?** voulez-vous une pomme?; **if you l.** si vous voulez.

**likeable** *a* sympathique.

**likelihood there's isn't much l. that** il y a peu de chances que (+ *subjunctive*).

**likely 1** *a* probable; (*excuse*) vraisemblable; **it's l. (that) she'll come, she's l. to come** il est probable qu'elle viendra. **2** *adv* **very l.** très probablement; **not l.!** pas question!

**likewise** *adv* de même.

**liking a l. for** (*person*) de la sympathie pour; (*thing*) du goût pour.

**lily** lis *m*.

**limb** membre *m*.

**lime** (*fruit*) citron *m* vert.

**limit 1** *n* limite *f* (**to** à). **2** *vt* limiter (**to** à).

**limousine** (*airport shuttle*) voiture-navette *f*.

**limp 1** *vi* (*of person*) boiter. **2** *n* **to have a l.** boiter.

**line**[1] **1** *n* ligne *f*; (*of poem*) vers *m*; (*wrinkle*) ride *f*; (*track*) voie *f*; (*rope*) corde *f*; (*row*) rangée *f*; (*of vehicles, people*) file *f*; **on the l.** (*phone*) au bout du fil; **to stand in l.** faire la queue; **to drop a l.** (*send a letter*) envoyer un mot (**to** à). **2** *vt* **to l. the street** (*of trees*) border la rue; (*of people*) faire la haie le long de la rue.

**line**[2] *vt* (*clothes*) doubler.

**linen** (*sheets etc*) linge *m*.

**liner (ocean) l.** paquebot *m*.

**line up 1** *vt* (*children, objects*) aligner; (*arrange*) organiser. **2** *vi* s'aligner; (*of people*) faire la queue.

**lining** (*of clothes*) doublure *f*.

**link 1** *vt* (*connect*) relier; (*relate*) lier (**to** à). **2** *n* lien *m*; (*of chain*) maillon *m*; (*by road, rail*) liaison *f*.

**link up** (*of people etc*) s'associer; (*of roads*) se rejoindre.

**lion** lion *m*.

**lip** lèvre *f*.

**lipstick** bâton *m* de rouge; (*substance*) rouge *m* (à lèvres).

**liqueur** liqueur *f*.

**liquid** *n* & *a* liquide (*m*).

**liquor** alcool *m*.

**list 1** *n* liste *f*. **2** *vt* faire la liste de; (*names*) mettre sur la liste, inscrire; (*name one by one*) énumérer.

**listen (to)** écouter.

**listener** (*to radio*) auditeur, -trice *mf*.

**listen (out) for** guetter (*un bruit ou les cris etc de*).

**liter** litre *m*.

**literary** *a* littéraire.

**literature** littérature *f*; (*pamphlets etc*) documentation *f*.

**liter** litre *m*.

**litter** (*rubbish*) détritus *m*; (*papers*) papiers *mpl*; (*young animals*) portée *f*.

**little 1** *a* (*small*) petit. **2** *a* & *n* (*not much*) peu (de); **l. time**/*etc* peu de temps/*etc*; **she eats l.** elle mange peu; **as l. as possible** le moins possible; **a l. money**/*etc* (*some*) un peu d'argent/*etc.* 3 *adv* **a l. heavy**/*etc* un peu lourd/*etc*; **to work**/*etc* **a l.** travailler/*etc* un peu; **l. by l.** peu à peu.

**live**[1] **1** *vi* vivre; (*reside*) habiter, vivre. **2** *vt* (*life*) mener.

**live**[2] **1** *a* (*electric wire*) sous tension; (*switch*) mal isolé. **2** *a* & *adv* (*broadcast*) en direct.

**lively** *a* (*person, style, interest, mind*) vif; (*discussion*) animé.

**live off** *or* **on** (*eat*) vivre de.

**liver** foie *m*.

**live through** (*experience*) vivre; (*survive*) survivre à.

**living 1** *a* (*alive*) vivant. **2** *n* vie *f*; **to make** *or* **earn a** *or* **one's l.** gagner sa vie; **the cost of l.** le coût de la vie.

**living room** salle *f* de séjour.

**lizard** lézard *m*.

**load 1** *n* charge *f*; (*weight*) poids *m*; **a l. of, loads of** (*people, money etc*) *Fam* un tas de. **2** *vt* (*truck, gun etc*) charger (**with** de).

**load up 1** *vt* (*car, ship etc*) charger (**with** de). **2** *vi* charger la voiture, le navire *etc*.

**loaf** (*pl* **loaves**) pain *m*.

**loan 1** *n* (*money lent*) prêt *m*; (*money borrowed*) emprunt *m*. **2** *vt* (*lend*) prêter (**to** à).

**lobby** (*of hotel*) hall *m*.

**lobster** homard *m*.

**local** *a* local; (*regional*) régional; (*of the neighborhood*) du *or* de quartier; (*of the region*) de la région.

**locally** *adv* dans le coin.

**locate** *vt* (*find*) trouver, repérer; **to be located** être situé.

**location** (*site*) emplacement *m*.

**lock 1** *vt* (*door etc*) fermer à clef. **2** *n* (*on door etc*) serrure *f*; (*on canal*) écluse *f*; (*of hair*) mèche *f*.

**lock away** (*prisoner, jewels etc*) enfermer.

**locker** (*for luggage*) casier *m* de consigne automatique; (*for clothes*) vestiaire *m* (métallique).

**locket** médaillon *m*.

**lock s.o. in** enfermer qn; **to l. s.o. in sth** enfermer qn dans qch.

**lock s.o. out** (*accidentally*) enfermer qn dehors.

**lock up 1** *vt* (*house etc*) fermer à clef; (*prisoner, jewels etc*) enfermer. **2** *vi* fermer à clef.

**lodger** (*room and meals*) pensionnaire *mf*; (*room only*) locataire *mf*.

**lodging** hébergement *m*; **lodgings** chambre(s) *f (pl)* meublée(s).

**loft** (*attic*) grenier *m*.

**log** (*tree trunk*) tronc *m* d'arbre; (*for fire*) bûche *f*.

**logical** *a* logique.

**lollipop** sucette *f*.

**loneliness** solitude *f*.

**lonely** *a* solitaire.

**long 1** *a* long (*f* longue); **to be 33 feet l.** avoir dix mètres de long; **to be six weeks l.** durer six semaines; **a l. time** longtemps. **2** *adv* longtemps; **has he been here l.?** il y a longtemps qu'il est ici?; **how l. ago?** il y a combien de temps?; **before l.** sous peu; **she no longer swims** elle ne nage plus; **I won't be l.** je n'en ai pas pour longtemps; **all summer l.** tout l'été; **as l. as, so l. as** (*provided that*) pourvu que (+ *subjunctive*).

**long-distance** (*phone call*) interurbain; (*flight*) long-courrier.

**long johns** caleçon *m* (long).

**long-term** *a* à long terme.

**look 1** *n* regard *m*; (*appearance*) air *m*; **to have a l. (at)** jeter un coup d'œil (à); **to have a l. (for)** chercher; **to have a l. around** regarder; (*walk*) faire un tour; **let me have a l.** fais voir. **2** *vi* regarder; **to l. tired**/*etc* sembler *or* avoir l'air fatigué/*etc*; **you l. like** *or* **as if you're tired** on dirait que tu es fatigué; **to l. well** *or* **good** (*of person*) avoir bonne mine; **you l. good in that hat**/*etc* ce chapeau/*etc* te va très bien.

**look around 1** *vt* visiter. **2** *vi* regarder; (*walk around*) faire un tour; (*look back*) se retourner.

**look at** regarder.
**look down** *vi* baisser les yeux; (*from a height*) regarder en bas.
**look for** chercher.
**look forward to** (*event*) attendre avec impatience; **to l. forward to doing** avoir hâte de faire.
**look into** examiner; (*find out about*) se renseigner sur.
**look (out) on to** (*of window etc*) donner sur.
**look out** (*be careful*) faire attention (**for** à).
**lookout** (*high place*) observatoire *m*; **to be on the l.** faire le guet; **to be on the l. for** guetter.
**look over** *or* **through** examiner; (*briefly*) parcourir; (*region, town*) parcourir.
**look up 1** *vi* lever les yeux; (*into the air*) regarder en l'air; (*improve*) s'améliorer. **2** *vt* (*word*) chercher.
**loose 1** *a* (*screw, belt, knot*) desserré; (*tooth*) branlant; (*page*) détaché; (*clothes*) flottant; (*tea etc*) au poids; (*having escaped*) (*animal*) échappé; (*prisoner*) évadé; **l. change** petite monnaie *f*; **to set** *or* **turn l.** (*dog etc*) lâcher. **2** *n* **on the l.** (*prisoner*) évadé; (*animal*) échappé.
**loosen** *vt* (*knot, belt, screw*) desserrer.
**lord** seigneur *m*.
**lose* 1** *vt* perdre; **to get lost** (*of person*) se perdre; **the ticket/***etc* **got lost** on a perdu le billet/*etc*. **2** *vi* perdre.
**loser** (*in contest etc*) perdant, -ante *mf*.
**lose to s.o.** *vi* être battu par qn.
**loss** perte *f*.
**lost** *a* perdu.
**lost and found** objets *mpl* trouvés.
**lot a l. of, lots of** beaucoup de; **a l.** beaucoup; **quite a l.** pas mal (**of** de); **such a l.** tellement (**of** de); **what a l. of flowers/water/***etc***!** regarde toutes ces fleurs/toute cette eau/*etc*!
**lotion** lotion *f*.
**lottery** loterie *f*.
**loud 1** *a* (*voice, music*) fort; (*noise, cry*) grand; **the radio/TV is too l.** le son de la radio/télé est trop fort. **2** *adv* (*to shout etc*) fort; **out l.** tout haut.
**loudly** *adv* (*to speak etc*) fort.
**loudspeaker** haut-parleur *m*; (*for speaking to crowd*) porte-voix *m inv*.
**lounge** salon *m*; **teachers l.** salle *f* des professeurs.
**lousy** *a* (*food, weather etc*) *Fam* infect.
**love 1** *n* amour *m*; **in l.** amoureux (**with** de); **they're in l.** ils s'aiment. **2** *vt* aimer (beaucoup) (**to do, doing** faire).
**lovely** *a* agréable; (*excellent*) excellent; (*pretty*) joli; (*charming*) charmant; (*kind*) gentil.
**lover a l. of music/***etc* un amateur de musique/*etc*.
**loving** *a* affectueux.
**low 1** *a* bas (*f* basse); (*speed, income, intelligence*) faible; (*opinion, quality*) mauvais; **to feel l.** être déprimé; **in a l. voice** à voix basse; **lower** inférieur. **2** *adv* bas; **to turn down l.** baisser.
**low beams** (*of vehicle*) codes *mpl*.
**lower** *vt* baisser; (*by rope*) descendre.
**low-fat** *a* (*milk*) écrémé; (*cheese*) allégé.
**loyal** *a* fidèle (**to** à), loyal (**to** envers).
**lozenge** (*tablet*) pastille *f*.
**luck** (*chance*) chance *f*; **bad l.** malchance *f*.
**luckily** *adv* heureusement.
**lucky** *a* (*person*) chanceux; (*guess, event*) heureux; **to be l.** avoir de la chance (**to do** de faire); **it's l. that** c'est une chance que; **l. charm** porte-bonheur *m inv*; **l. number/***etc* chiffre *m*/*etc* porte-bonheur.
**ludicrous** *a* ridicule.
**luggage** bagages *mpl*.
**lukewarm** *a* tiède.

**lullaby** berceuse *f.*
**luminous** *a* lumineux.
**lump** morceau *m*; (*bump*) bosse *f*; (*swelling*) grosseur *f.*
**lump sum** somme *f* forfaitaire.
**lunatic** fou *m*, folle *f.*
**lunch** déjeuner *m*; **to have l.** déjeuner; **l. break, l. hour, l. time** heure *f* du déjeuner.
**lung** poumon *m.*
**luxurious** *a* luxueux.
**luxury 1** *n* luxe *m.* **2** *a* (*goods etc*) de luxe.

# M

**MA** *abbr* = **Master of Arts.**
**macaroni** macaroni(s) *m*(*pl*).
**machine** machine *f.*
**machinegun** (*heavy*) mitrailleuse *f*; (*portable*) mitraillette *f.*
**machinery** machines *fpl*; (*works*) mécanisme *m.*
**mackerel** *n inv* maquereau *m.*
**mad** *a* fou (*f* folle); **m. (at)** (*angry*) furieux (contre); **m. about** (*person*) fou de; (*films etc*) passionné de; **like m.** comme un fou *or* une folle.
**madam** madame *f*; (*unmarried*) mademoiselle *f.*
**made** *pt* & *pp de* **make.**
**madman** (*pl* **-men**) fou *m.*
**madness** folie *f.*
**magazine** magazine *m*, revue *f.*
**maggot** ver *m.*
**magic 1** *n* magie *f.* **2** *a* (*wand etc*) magique.
**magical** *a* magique.
**magician** magicien, -ienne *mf.*
**magistrate** magistrat *m.*
**magnet** aimant *m.*
**magnificent** *a* magnifique.
**magnifying glass** loupe *f.*
**mahogany** acajou *m.*
**maid** (*servant*) bonne *f.*
**mail 1** *n* (*system*) poste *f*; (*letters*) courrier *m.* **2** *a* (*bag etc*) postal. **3** *vt* (*letter*) poster.
**mailbox** boîte *f* aux *or* à lettres.
**mailman** (*pl* **-men**) facteur *m.*
**main**[1] *a* principal; **the m. thing is to** l'essentiel est de; **m. road** grand-route *f.*
**main**[2] **water/gas m.** conduite *f* d'eau/de gaz; **the mains** (*electricity*) le secteur.
**mainly** *adv* surtout.
**main street** grand-rue *f.*
**maintain** *vt* (*vehicle etc*) entretenir; (*law and order*) faire respecter; **to m. that** affirmer que.
**maisonette** duplex *m.*
**maitre d'** maître *m* d'hôtel.
**majesty** majesté *f*; **Your M.** Votre Majesté.
**major 1** *a* majeur; **a m. road** une grande route. **2** *n* (*officer*) commandant *m.*
**majorette** majorette *f.*
**majority** majorité *f* (**of** de); **the m. of people** la plupart des gens.
**make* 1** *vt* faire; (*tool, vehicle etc*) fabriquer; (*decision*) prendre; (*friends, salary*) se faire; (*destination*) arriver à; **to m. happy**/*etc* rendre heureux/*etc*; **to m. s.o. do sth** faire faire qch à qn; **to m. do** (*manage*) se débrouiller (**with** avec); **to m. do with** (*be satisfied with*) se contenter de; **to m. it** arriver; (*succeed*) réussir; **what do you m. of it?** qu'en penses-tu? **2** *n* (*brand*) marque *f.*
**make for** aller vers.
**make good** (*loss*) compenser; (*damage*) réparer.
**make off** (*run away*) se sauver.
**make out 1** *vt* (*see*) distinguer; (*understand*) comprendre; (*write*) faire (*chèque, liste*); (*claim*) prétendre (**that** que). **2** *vi* se débrouiller.
**maker** (*of product*) fabricant, -ante *mf.*
**make up 1** *vt* (*story*) inventer; (*put together*) faire (*collection, liste etc*); (*form*) former; (*loss*) compenser; (*quantity*) compléter; (*quarrel*) régler; (*one's face*) maquiller. **2** *vti* **to m. (it) up** (*of friends*) se réconcilier.

**make-up** (*for face*) maquillage *m.*
**make up for** (*loss, damage*) compenser; (*lost time, mistake*) rattraper.
**malaria** malaria *f.*
**male 1** *a* mâle; (*clothes, sex*) masculin. **2** *n* mâle *m.*
**malice** méchanceté *f.*
**malicious** *a* malveillant.
**mall (shopping) m.** galerie *f* marchande; (*large complex*) centre *m* commercial.
**mama** *or* **mamma** *Fam* maman *f.*
**mammal** mammifère *m.*
**man** (*pl* **men**) homme *m.*
**manage 1** *vt* (*run*) diriger; (*handle*) manier; **to m. to do** (*succeed*) réussir à faire; (*by being smart*) se débrouiller pour faire; **I'll m. it** j'y arriverai. **2** *vi* (*succeed*) y arriver; (*make do*) se débrouiller (**with** avec); **to m. without sth** se passer de qch.
**management** (*running, managers*) direction *f.*
**manager** directeur, -trice *mf*; (*of shop, café*) gérant, -ante *mf.*
**managing director** PDG *m.*
**mane** crinière *f.*
**maneuver 1** *n* manœuvre *f.* **2** *vti* manœuvrer.
**maniac** fou *m*, folle *f.*
**man-made** *a* artificiel.
**manner** (*way*) manière *f*; (*behavior*) attitude *f*; **manners** (*social habits*) manières *fpl*; **to have no manners** être mal élevé.
**mantelpiece** (*shelf*) cheminée *f.*
**manual 1** *a* manuel. **2** *n* (*book*) manuel *m.*
**manufacture 1** *vt* fabriquer. **2** *n* fabrication *f.*
**manufacturer** fabricant, -ante *mf.*
**manure** fumier *m.*
**many** *a* & *n* beaucoup (de); **m. things** beaucoup de choses; **I don't have m.** je n'en ai pas beaucoup; **m. came** beaucoup sont venus; (**a good** *or* **great**) **m. of** un (très) grand nombre de; **m. times** bien des fois; **as m. books**/*etc* **as** autant de livres/*etc* que.
**map** (*of country, region*) carte *f*; (*of town etc*) plan *m.*
**marathon** marathon *m.*
**marble** marbre *m*; (*toy*) bille *f.*
**March** mars *m.*
**march 1** *n* marche *f* (*militaire*). **2** *vi* (*of soldiers*) défiler.
**mare** jument *f.*
**margarine** margarine *f.*
**margin** (*of page*) marge *f.*
**mark 1** *n* (*symbol*) marque *f*; (*stain, trace*) trace *f*; (*token, sign*) signe *m*; (*for school exercise etc*) note *f*; (*target*) but *m.* **2** *vt* marquer; (*exam etc*) corriger.
**marker** (*pen*) marqueur *m.*
**market** marché *m.*
**marketing** marketing *m.*
**mark off** (*area*) délimiter.
**marmalade** confiture *f* d'oranges.
**marriage** mariage *m.*
**married** *a* marié; **to get m.** se marier.
**marrow** (*of bone*) moelle *f.*
**marry 1** *vt* épouser, se marier avec; (*of priest etc*) marier. **2** *vi* se marier.
**marsh** marais *m.*
**Martian** *n* & *a* martien, -ienne (*mf*).
**marvelous** *a* merveilleux.
**marzipan** pâte *f* d'amandes.
**mascara** mascara *m.*
**mascot** mascotte *f.*
**masculine** *a* masculin.
**mashed potatoes** purée *f* (de pommes de terre).
**mask** masque *m.*
**mass[1] 1** *n* (*quantity*) masse *f*; **a m. of** (*many*) une multitude de; (*pile*) un tas de; **masses of** des masses de. **2** *a* (*protests, departure*) en masse.
**mass[2]** (*church service*) messe *f.*
**massacre 1** *n* massacre *m.* **2** *vt* massacrer.
**massage 1** *n* massage *m.* **2** *vt* masser.
**masseur** masseur *m.*

**masseuse** masseuse *f.*
**massive** *a* (*huge*) énorme.
**mast** (*of ship*) mât *m.*
**master 1** *n* maître *m*; **M. of Arts/Science** (*person*) Maître *m* ès lettres/sciences; **M. of Ceremonies** animateur, -trice *mf.* **2** *vt* (*control*) maîtriser; (*subject, situation*) dominer; **she has mastered Latin** elle possède le latin.
**masterpiece** chef-d'œuvre *m.*
**mat** tapis *m*; (*of straw*) natte *f*; (*at door*) paillasson *m*; **(place) m.** set *m* (de table).
**match**[1] (*stick*) allumette *f.*
**match**[2] **1** *n* (*game*) match *m*; (*equal*) égal, -ale *mf*; **to be a good m.** (*of colors, people etc*) être bien assortis. **2** *vt* (*of clothes, color etc*) aller (bien) avec; **to be well-matched** être (bien) assortis. **3** *vi* être assortis.
**match (up)** (*plates etc*) assortir.
**match (up to)** égaler; (*s.o.'s hopes or expectations*) répondre à.
**matchbox** boîte *f* d'allumettes.
**matching** *a* (*dress etc*) assorti.
**matchstick** allumette *f.*
**mate** (*friend*) camarade *mf.*
**material** matière *f*; (*cloth*) tissu *m*; **material(s)** (*equipment*) matériel *m*; **building materials** matériaux *mpl* de construction.
**maternal** *a* maternel.
**maternity ward** maternité *f.*
**math** maths *fpl.*
**mathematical** *a* mathématique.
**mathematics** mathématiques *fpl.*
**matinee** (*in theater*) matinée *f.*
**matt** *a* (*paint, paper*) mat.
**matter 1** *n* matière *f*; (*subject, affair*) affaire *f*; **what's the m. with you?** qu'est-ce que tu as?; **there's sth the m.** il y a qch qui ne va pas; **there's sth the m. with my leg** j'ai qch à la jambe. **2** *vi* importer (**to** à); **it doesn't m. if/who/***etc* peu importe si/qui/*etc*; **it doesn't m.!** ça ne fait rien!
**mattress** matelas *m.*
**mature** *a* mûr; (*cheese*) fait.

**maximum** *a* & *n* maximum (*m*).
**May** mai *m.*
**may** *v aux* (*pt* **might**) (*possibility*) pouvoir; **he m. come** il peut arriver; **he might come** il pourrait arriver; **I m.** *or* **might have forgotten it** je l'ai peut-être oublié; **we m.** *or* **might as well go** nous ferions aussi bien de partir. ▪ (*permission*) pouvoir; **m. I stay?** puis-je rester?; **m. I?** vous permettez?; **you m. go** tu peux partir. ▪ (*wish*) **m. you be happy** (que tu) sois heureux.
**maybe** *adv* peut-être.
**mayonnaise** mayonnaise *f.*
**mayor** maire *m.*
**maze** labyrinthe *m.*
**me** *pron* me, m'; (*after prep, 'than', 'it is'*) moi; **(to) me** me, m'; **she knows me** elle me connaît; **he gives (to) me** il me donne.
**meadow** pré *m.*
**meal** repas *m.*
**mean**[1]* *vt* (*signify*) vouloir dire; (*intend*) destiner (**for** à); (*result in*) entraîner; **to m. to do** avoir l'intention de faire; **I m. it** je suis sérieux; **to m. sth to s.o.** avoir de l'importance pour qn; **I didn't m. to!** je ne l'ai pas fait exprès!
**mean**[2] méchant.
**meaning** sens *m.*
**meaningless** *a* qui n'a pas de sens.
**meanness** méchanceté *f.*
**means** *n*(*pl*) (*method*) moyen(s) *m*(*pl*) (**to do, of doing** de faire); (*wealth*) moyens *mpl*; **by m. of** (*stick etc*) au moyen de; (*work etc*) à force de; **by all m.!** très certainement!; **by no m.** nullement.
**meantime** *adv* & *n* **(in the) m.** entre-temps.
**meanwhile** *adv* entre-temps.
**measles** rougeole *f.*
**measure 1** *n* (*action, amount*) mesure *f.* **2** *vt* mesurer.
**measurement** (*of chest etc*) tour *m*; **measurements** mesures *fpl.*

**measure up** (*plank etc*) mesurer.
**measure up to** (*task*) être à la hauteur de.
**meat** viande *f.*
**mechanic** mécanicien, -ienne *mf.*
**mechanical** *a* mécanique.
**mechanism** mécanisme *m.*
**medal** médaille *f.*
**medalist to be a gold m.** être médaille d'or.
**media** *npl* **the (mass) m.** les médias *mpl.*
**median** (*for pedestrians*) refuge *m.*
**medical** *a* médical; (*school*, *studies*) de médecine; (*student*) en médecine.
**medication** médicaments *mpl.*
**medicine** médicament *m*; (*science*) médecine *f.*
**medicine cabinet** *or* **chest** (armoire *f* à) pharmacie *f.*
**medieval** *a* médiéval.
**Mediterranean 1** *a* méditerranéen. **2** *n* **the M.** la Méditerranée.
**medium** *a* moyen.
**medium-sized** *a* moyen.
**meet* 1** *vt* (*person*, *team*) rencontrer; (*person by arrangement*) retrouver; (*pass in street etc*) croiser; (*fetch*) (aller *or* venir) chercher; (*wait for*) attendre; (*be introduced to*) faire la connaissance de. **2** *vi* (*of people*, *teams*) se rencontrer; (*of people by arrangement*) se retrouver; (*be introduced*) se connaître; (*of club etc*) se réunir.
**meeting** réunion *f*; (*large*) assemblée *f*; (*between two people*) rencontre *f*; (*arranged*) rendez-vous *m inv.*
**meet up** (*of people*) se rencontrer; (*by arrangement*) se retrouver.
**meet up with s.o.** rencontrer qn; retrouver qn.
**meet with** (*accident*) avoir; (*difficulty*) rencontrer; (*person*) rencontrer; retrouver.
**melody** mélodie *f.*
**melon** melon *m.*
**melt 1** *vi* fondre. **2** *vt* (faire) fondre.
**member** membre *m.*
**memo** (*pl* **-os**) note *f.*
**memory** mémoire *f*; (*recollection*) souvenir *m*; **in m. of** à la mémoire de.
**men** *see* **man.**
**mend** *vt* réparer; (*clothes*) raccommoder.
**mental** *a* mental.
**mentally** *adv* **he's m. handicapped** c'est un handicapé mental; **she's m. ill** c'est une malade mentale.
**mention 1** *vt* mentionner; **not to m. . . .** sans parler de . . . ; **don't m. it!** il n'y a pas de quoi! **2** *n* mention *f.*
**menu** menu *m.*
**meow** *vi* (*of cat*) miauler.
**mercy** pitié *f*; **at the m. of** à la merci de.
**mere** *a* simple; (*only*) ne . . . que; **she's a m. child** ce n'est qu'une enfant.
**merely** *adv* (tout) simplement.
**merge** *vi* (*blend*) se mêler (**with** à); (*of roads*) se (re)joindre; (*of firms*) fusionner.
**merger** fusion *f.*
**merry** *a* gai.
**merry-go-round** (*at fair*) manège *m.*
**mesh** (*of net*) maille *f.*
**mess** (*confusion*) désordre *m*; (*dirt*) saleté *f*; **in a m.** sens dessus dessous; (*trouble*) dans le pétrin.
**message** message *m.*
**mess around** (*have fun*) s'amuser; (*play the fool*) faire l'idiot.
**mess around with sth** (*fiddle with*) s'amuser avec qch.
**messenger** messager *m*; (*in office*, *hotel*) coursier, -ière *mf.*
**mess up** (*ruin*) gâcher; (*dirty*) salir; (*room*) mettre sens dessus dessous.
**messy** *a* (*untidy*) en désordre; (*dirty*) sale.
**metal** métal *m*; **m. ladder**/*etc* échelle *f*/*etc* métallique.
**meter**[1] (*device*) compteur *m*; **(parking) m.** parcmètre *m.*
**meter**[2] mètre *m.*

**method** méthode *f.*
**methodical** *a* méthodique.
**metric** *a* métrique.
**mice** *see* **mouse.**
**micro-** *prefix* micro-.
**microchip** puce *f.*
**microphone** micro *m.*
**microscope** microscope *m.*
**microwave (oven)** four *m* à micro-ondes.
**mid** *a* **(in) m.-June** (à) la mi-juin; **in m. air** en plein ciel.
**midday** midi *m.*
**middle 1** *n* milieu *m*; (*waist*) taille *f*; **(right) in the m. of** au (beau) milieu de; **in the m. of saying**/*etc* en train de dire/*etc.* **2** *a* du milieu; (*class*) moyen; (*name*) deuxième.
**middle-aged** *a* d'un certain âge.
**middle-class** *a* bourgeois.
**midnight** minuit *m.*
**mid-semester break** vacances *fpl* scolaires.
**midst in the m. of** au milieu de.
**midwife** (*pl* **-wives**) sage-femme *f.*
**might** *see* **may.**
**mild** *a* doux (*f* douce); (*beer, punishment*) léger; (*medicine, illness*) bénin (*f* bénigne).
**mile** mile *m* (= *1,6 km*).
**mileage** = kilométrage *m.*
**military** *a* militaire.
**milk 1** *n* lait *m.* **2** *a* (*chocolate*) au lait; (*bottle*) à lait. **3** *vt* (*cow*) traire.
**milkman** (*pl* **-men**) laitier *m.*
**milk shake** milk-shake *m.*
**mill** moulin *m*; (*factory*) usine *f.*
**millimeter** millimètre *m.*
**million** million *m*; **a m. men**/*etc* un million d'hommes/*etc.*
**millionaire** millionnaire *mf.*
**mime** *vti* mimer.
**mimic** *vt* (**-ck-**) imiter.
**mince** *vt* hacher; **she doesn't m. words** elle ne mâche pas ses mots.
**mind 1** *n* esprit *m*; (*sanity*) raison *f*; (*memory*) mémoire *f*; **to change one's m.** changer d'avis; **to make up one's m.** se décider; **to be on s.o.'s m.** préoccuper qn; **to have in m.** (*person, plan*) avoir en vue. **2** *vti* faire attention à; (*look after*) garder; (*noise etc*) être gêné par; **do you m. if?** (*I smoke*) ça vous gêne si?; (*I leave*) ça ne vous fait rien si?; **I don't m.** ça m'est égal; **I wouldn't m. a cup of tea** j'aimerais bien une tasse de thé; **never m.!** ça ne fait rien!; (*don't worry*) ne vous en faites pas!
**mine[1]** *poss pron* le mien, la mienne, *pl* les mien(ne)s; **this hat is m.** ce chapeau est à moi *or* est le mien.
**mine[2]** (*for coal etc, explosive*) mine *f.*
**miner** mineur *m.*
**mineral** *a* & *n* minéral (*m*).
**mini** *prefix* mini-.
**miniature** *a* (*train etc*) miniature *inv*; **in m.** en miniature.
**minibus** minibus *m.*
**minimum** *a* & *n* minimum (*m*).
**minister** (*clergyman*) pasteur *m.*
**ministry to enter the m.** devenir pasteur.
**minor** *a* (*detail, operation*) petit.
**minority** minorité *f.*
**mint** (*herb*) menthe *f*; (*candy*) bonbon *m* à la menthe; **m. tea**/*etc* thé *m*/*etc* à la menthe.
**minus** *prep* moins; (*without*) sans.
**minute[1]** minute *f.*
**minute[2]** *a* (*tiny*) minuscule.
**miracle** miracle *m.*
**miraculous** *a* miraculeux.
**mirror** miroir *m*, glace *f*; (*in vehicle*) rétroviseur *m.*
**misbehave** *vi* se conduire mal.
**miscellaneous** *a* divers.
**mischief** espièglerie *f*; (*malice*) méchanceté *f*; **to get into m.** faire des bêtises.
**mischievous** *a* espiègle; (*harmful*) méchant, nuisible.
**miser** avare *mf.*
**miserable** *a* (*wretched*) misérable; (*unhappy*) malheureux.
**miserly** *a* avare.
**misery** souffrances *fpl*; (*sadness*) tristesse *f.*
**misfortune** malheur *m.*
**mishap** contretemps *m.*
**mislay*** *vt* égarer.

**mislead*** *vt* tromper.
**misleading** *a* trompeur.
**miss¹ 1** *vt* (*train, opportunity etc*) manquer; (*not see*) ne pas voir; (*not understand*) ne pas comprendre; **he misses Paris/her** Paris/elle lui manque. **2** *vi* manquer.
**miss²** (*woman*) mademoiselle *f*; **Miss Brown** Mademoiselle *or* Mlle Brown.
**missile** (*rocket*) missile *m*; (*object thrown*) projectile *m*.
**missing** *a* absent; (*after disaster*) disparu; (*object*) manquant; **there are two cups m.** il manque deux tasses.
**mission** mission *f*.
**miss out 1** *vt* (*leave out*) sauter. **2** *vi* rater l'occasion.
**miss out on** (*opportunity etc*) rater.
**mist** (*fog*) brume *f*; (*on glass*) buée *f*.
**mistake 1** *n* erreur *f*, faute *f*; **to make a m.** se tromper; **by m.** par erreur. **2** *vt** (*meaning etc*) se tromper sur; **to m. s.o./sth for** prendre qn/qch pour; **you're mistaken** tu te trompes.
**mistakenly** *adv* par erreur.
**mistreat** *vt* maltraiter.
**mistress** maîtresse *f*.
**mistrust 1** *n* méfiance *f*. **2** *vt* se méfier de.
**misty** *a* brumeux.
**misunderstand*** *vt* mal comprendre.
**misunderstanding** malentendu *m*.
**mitten** (*glove*) moufle *f*.
**mix 1** *vt* mélanger, mêler; (*cake*) préparer; (*salad*) remuer. **2** *vi* se mêler; **she doesn't m.** elle n'est pas sociable.
**mixed** *a* (*school*) mixte; (*chocolates etc*) assortis.
**mixer** (*electric, for cooking*) mixe(u)r *m*.
**mixture** mélange *m*.
**mix-up** confusion *f*.
**mix up** (*drink, papers etc*) mélanger; (*make confused*) embrouiller (*qn*); (*mistake*) confondre (**with** avec).
**mix with s.o.** fréquenter qn.
**moan** *vi* (*groan*) gémir; (*complain*) se plaindre (**to** à, **about** de, **that** que).
**mob 1** *n* foule *f*. **2** *vt* assiéger.
**mobile** *a* mobile.
**model 1** *n* (*example etc*) modèle *m*; **(fashion) m.** mannequin *m*; **(scale) m.** modèle *m* (réduit). **2** *a* (*car, plane etc*) modèle réduit *inv*; **m. train** train *m* miniature.
**modeling clay** pâte *f* à modeler.
**moderate** *a* modéré.
**moderation** modération *f*.
**modern** *a* moderne; **m. languages** langues *fpl* vivantes.
**modernize 1** *vt* moderniser. **2** *vi* se moderniser.
**modest** *a* modeste.
**modesty** modestie *f*.
**modification** modification *f*.
**modify** *vt* modifier.
**moist** *a* humide; (*sticky*) moite.
**moisture** humidité *f*; (*on glass*) buée *f*.
**mold 1** *n* (*shape*) moule *m*; (*growth*) moisissure *f*. **2** *vt* (*clay etc*) mouler.
**moldy** *a* moisi; **to get m.** moisir.
**mole** (*on skin*) grain *m* de beauté; (*animal*) taupe *f*.
**mom** *Fam* maman *f*.
**moment** moment *m*; **the m. she leaves** dès qu'elle partira.
**mommy** *Fam* maman *f*.
**Monday** lundi *m*.
**money** argent *m*.
**money order** mandat *m*.
**monitor** (*computer screen*) moniteur *m* (d'ordinateur).
**monk** moine *m*.
**monkey** singe *m*.
**monopolize** *vt* monopoliser.
**monotonous** *a* monotone.
**monotony** monotonie *f*.
**monster** monstre *m*.
**month** mois *m*.
**monthly 1** *a* mensuel. **2** *adv* mensuellement.
**monument** monument *m*.

**moo** *vi* meugler.
**mood** (*of person*) humeur *f*; *Grammar* mode *m*; **in a good/bad m.** de bonne/mauvaise humeur; **to be in the m. to do** être d'humeur à faire.
**moody** *a* (*bad-tempered*) de mauvaise humeur.
**moon** lune *f*.
**moonlight** clair *m* de lune.
**moor** lande *f*.
**mop 1** *n* balai *m* (à laver). **2** *vt* (*floor etc*) essuyer.
**moped** mobylette® *f*.
**mop up** (*liquid*) éponger.
**moral** (*of story*) morale *f*.
**morale** moral *m*.
**more 1** *a* & *n* plus (de) (**than** que); (*other*) d'autres; **m. cars**/*etc* plus de voitures/*etc*; **he has m. (than you)** il en a plus (que toi); **a few m. months** encore quelques mois; **(some) m. tea**/*etc* encore du thé/*etc*; **m. than a quart/ten** (*with quantity, number*) plus d'un litre/de dix; **many m., much m.** beaucoup plus (de). **2** *adv* plus (**than** que); **m. and m.** de plus en plus; **m. or less** plus ou moins; **she doesn't have any m.** elle n'en a plus.
**moreover** *adv* de plus.
**morning** matin *m*; (*duration of morning*) matinée *f*; **in the m.** le matin; (*tomorrow*) demain matin; **at seven in the m.** à sept heures du matin; **every Tuesday m.** tous les mardis matin.
**mortal** *a* & *n* mortel, -elle (*mf*).
**mortgage** prêt-logement *m*.
**Moslem** *a* & *n* musulman, -ane (*mf*).
**mosque** mosquée *f*.
**mosquito** (*pl* **-oes**) moustique *m*.
**moss** mousse *f* (*plante*).
**most 1** *a* & *n* **the m.** le plus (de); **I have the m. books** j'ai le plus de livres; **I have the m.** j'en ai le plus; **m. (of the) books**/*etc* la plupart des livres/*etc*; **m. of the cake**/*etc* la plus grande partie du gâteau/*etc*; **at (the very) m.** tout au plus. **2** *adv* (le) plus; (*very*) très; **the m. beautiful** le plus beau, la plus belle (**in, of** de); **to talk (the) m.** parler le plus; **m. of all** surtout.
**mostly** *adv* surtout.
**motel** motel *m*.
**moth** papillon *m* de nuit; (*in clothes*) mite *f*.
**mother** mère *f*; **M.'s Day** la fête des Mères.
**mother-in-law** (*pl* **mothers-in-law**) belle-mère *f*.
**motion 1** *n* (*of arm etc*) mouvement *m*. **2** *vti* **to m. (to) s.o. to do** faire signe à qn de faire.
**motivated** *a* motivé.
**motive** motif *m* (**for** de).
**motor** (*engine*) moteur *m*.
**motorbike** moto *f*.
**motor boat** canot *m* automobile.
**motorcycle** motocyclette *f*.
**motorcyclist** motocycliste *mf*.
**motorist** automobiliste *mf*.
**mount 1** *n* (*frame for photo*) cadre *m*. **2** *vt* (*horse, photo*) monter. **3** *vi* (*on horse*) se mettre en selle.
**mountain** montagne *f*; **m. bike** VTT *m inv*.
**mountaineer** alpiniste *mf*.
**mountaineering** alpinisme *m*.
**mountainous** *a* montagneux.
**mount up** *vi* (*add up*) chiffrer (**to** à); (*accumulate*) s'accumuler.
**mourn** *vt* **to m. (for) s.o., m. the loss of s.o.** pleurer (la perte de) qn; **she's mourning** elle est en deuil.
**mourning** deuil *m*; **in m.** en deuil.
**mouse** (*pl* **mice**) souris *f*.
**mousse** mousse *f* (*dessert*).
**moustache** moustache *f*.
**mouth** (*pl* **-s**) bouche *f*; (*of dog, lion etc*) gueule *f*; (*of river*) embouchure *f*.
**mouthwash** bain *m* de bouche.
**move 1** *n* mouvement *m*; (*change of house*) déménagement *m*; (*in game*) coup *m*, (*one's turn*) tour *m*; (*act*) démarche *f*; **to make a m.** (*leave*) se préparer à partir; **to get a m. on** se remuer. **2** *vt* déplacer; (*arm, leg*) remuer; (*put*) mettre; (*transport*) transporter; (*piece in game*) jouer; **to m. s.o.** (*emotionally*) émouvoir qn; (*transfer in job*)

muter qn. **3** *vi* bouger; (*go*) aller (**to** à); (*out of house*) déménager; (*change seats*) changer de place; (*play*) jouer; **to m. to a new house**/*etc* aller habiter une nouvelle maison/*etc*; **to m. into a house** emménager dans une maison.

**move along** *vi* avancer.

**move around** *vi* se déplacer; (*fidget*) remuer.

**move away** *vi* s'éloigner; (*to new house*) déménager.

**move back 1** *vt* (*chair etc*) reculer; (*to its position*) remettre. **2** *vi* reculer; (*return*) retourner.

**move sth down** descendre qch.

**move forward** *vti* avancer.

**move in** *vi* (*into house*) emménager.

**movement** (*action, group etc*) mouvement *m*.

**move off** (*go away*) s'éloigner; (*of vehicle*) démarrer.

**move on** *vi* avancer.

**move out** *vi* (*out of house*) déménager.

**move over 1** *vt* pousser. **2** *vi* se pousser.

**mover** *n* déménageur *m*.

**move up 1** *vt* (*meeting*) avancer. **2** *vi* (*on seats etc*) se pousser.

**movie** film *m*; **the movies** (*art, movie theater*) le cinéma.

**movie camera** caméra *f*.

**movie star** vedette *f* (de cinéma).

**movie theater** cinéma *m*.

**moving** *a* en mouvement; (*touching*) émouvant.

**moving van** camion *m* de déménagement.

**mow** *vt* (*pp* **mown** *or* **mowed**) **to m. the lawn** tondre le gazon.

**mower (lawn) m.** tondeuse *f* (à gazon).

**Mr Mr Brown** Monsieur *or* M Brown.

**Mrs Mrs Brown** Madame *or* Mme Brown.

**Ms Ms Brown** Madame *or* Mme Brown.

**MS** *abbr* = **Master of Science.**

**much 1** *a* & *n* beaucoup (de); **not m. time**/*etc* pas beaucoup de temps/*etc*; **I don't have m.** je n'en ai pas beaucoup; **as m. as** autant que; **as m. wine**/*etc* **as** autant de vin/*etc* que; **twice as m.** deux fois plus (de). **2** *adv* **very m.** beaucoup; **not (very) m.** pas beaucoup.

**mud** boue *f*.

**muddle** (*mix-up*) confusion *f*; (*mess*) désordre *m*; **in a m.** (*person*) désorienté; (*mind, ideas*) embrouillé.

**muddle (up)** (*person, facts*) embrouiller; (*papers*) mélanger.

**muddle through** *vi* se tirer d'affaire.

**muddy** *a* (*water, road*) boueux; (*hands etc*) couvert de boue.

**muesli** muesli *m*.

**muffin** *sorte de petite brioche*.

**mug**[1] (*cup*) grande tasse *f*; **(beer) m.** chope *f*.

**mug** *vt* (*in street*) agresser, attaquer.

**mugger** agresseur *m*.

**mule** (*male*) mulet *m*; (*female*) mule *f*.

**multiple** *a* & *n* multiple (*m*).

**multiplication** multiplication *f*.

**multiply** *vt* multiplier.

**mumble** *vti* marmotter.

**mumps** oreillons *mpl*.

**murder 1** *n* meurtre *m*, assassinat *m*. **2** *vt* tuer, assassiner.

**murderer** meurtrier, -ière *mf*, assassin *m*.

**murmur** *vti* murmurer.

**muscle** muscle *m*.

**muscular** *a* (*arm etc*) musclé.

**museum** musée *m*.

**mushroom** champignon *m*.

**music** musique *f*.

**musical 1** *a* musical; (*instrument*) de musique; **to be m.** être musicien. **2** *n* comédie *f* musicale.

**musician** musicien, -ienne *mf*.

**Muslim** *a* & *n* musulman, -ane (*mf*).

**mussel** moule *f*.

**must** *v aux* (*necessity*) devoir; **you m. obey** tu dois obéir, il faut que tu obéisses. ▪ (*certainty*) devoir; **she m. be smart** elle doit être intelligente; **I m. have seen it** j'ai dû le voir.
**mustache** moustache *f.*
**mustard** moutarde *f.*
**musty to smell m.** sentir le moisi.
**mutter** *vti* marmonner.
**mutton** (*meat*) mouton *m.*
**mutual** *a* (*help etc*) mutuel; (*friend*) commun.
**muzzle** (*for animal*) muselière *f.*
**my** *poss a* mon, ma, *pl* mes.
**myself** *pron* moi-même; (*reflexive*) me, m'; (*after prep*) moi.
**mysterious** *a* mystérieux.
**mystery** mystère *m;* (*novel*) roman *m* policier; (*movie*) film *m* policier.

# N

**nail** (*of finger, toe*) ongle *m*; (*metal*) clou *m.*
**nail (down)** *vt* clouer.
**nail file/polish** lime *f*/vernis *m* à ongles.
**naïve** *a* naïf.
**naked** *a* nu.
**name 1** *n* nom *m*; (*reputation*) réputation *f*; **my n. is . . .** je m'appelle . . . ; **first n.** prénom *m*; **last n.** nom *m* de famille. **2** *vt* nommer; (*date, price*) fixer; **he was named after** *or* **for** il a reçu le nom de.
**nana** (*grandmother*) *Fam* mamie *f.*
**nanny** nourrice *f*; (*grandmother*) *Fam* mamie *f.*
**nap** (*sleep*) petit somme *m*; **to have** *or* **take a n.** faire un petit somme.
**napkin** serviette *f.*
**narrow** *a* étroit.
**narrow (down)** (*choice etc*) limiter.
**narrowly he n. escaped being killed/etc** il a failli être tué/*etc.*
**nastily** *adv* (*to behave*) méchamment.
**nasty** *a* mauvais; (*spiteful*) méchant (**to(wards)** avec).
**nation** nation *f.*
**national** *a* national.
**nationality** nationalité *f.*
**native 1** *a* (*country*) natal (*mpl* -als); **to be an English n. speaker** avoir l'anglais comme langue maternelle. **2** *n* **to be a n. of** être originaire de.
**natural** *a* naturel; (*actor etc*) né.
**naturally** *adv* (*as normal, of course*) naturellement; (*to behave etc*) avec naturel.
**nature** (*natural world, character*) nature *f.*
**nature study** sciences *fpl* naturelles.
**naught** rien *m.*
**naughty** *a* (*child*) vilain.
**nauseated** *a* **to feel n.** avoir envie de vomir.
**nauseating** *a* écœurant.
**naval** *a* naval (*mpl* -als); (*officer*) de marine.
**navel** nombril *m.*
**navigate 1** *vi* naviguer. **2** *vt* (*boat*) diriger.
**navigation** navigation *f.*
**navy 1** *n* marine *f.* **2** *a* **n. (blue)** bleu marine *inv.*
**near 1** *adv* près; **very n.** tout près; **n. to** près de; **to come n. to being killed**/*etc* faillir être tué/*etc*; **n. enough** (*more or less*) plus ou moins. **2** *prep* **n. (to)** près de; **n. (to) the end** vers la fin; **to come n. s.o.** s'approcher de qn. **3** *a* proche; **in the n. future** dans un avenir proche.
**nearby 1** *adv* tout près. **2** *a* proche.
**nearly** *adv* presque; **she (very) n. fell** elle a failli tomber; **not n. as smart**/*etc* **as** loin d'être aussi intelligent/*etc* que.
**neat** *a* (*clothes, work*) soigné; (*room*) bien rangé.
**neatly** *adv* avec soin.
**necessarily** *adv* **not n.** pas forcément.
**necessary** *a* nécessaire (**to do** de faire); **to do what's n.** faire le nécessaire.

**necessity** nécessité *f*.
**neck** cou *m*; (*of dress, horse*) encolure *f*.
**necklace** collier *m*.
**nectarine** nectarine *f*.
**need 1** *n* besoin *m*; **to be in n. of** avoir besoin de; **there's no n. (for you) to do** tu n'as pas besoin de faire; **if n. be** si besoin est. **2** *vt* avoir besoin de; **her hair needs cutting** il faut qu'elle se fasse couper les cheveux; **I needn't have rushed** ce n'était pas la peine de me presser.
**needle** aiguille *f*.
**needlessly** *adv* inutilement.
**needlework** couture *f*; (*object*) ouvrage *m*.
**negative 1** *a* négatif. **2** *n* (*of photo*) négatif *m*; *Grammar* forme *f* négative.
**neglect** *vt* (*person, work, duty etc*) négliger; (*garden, car*) ne pas s'occuper de.
**neglected** *a* (*appearance*) négligé; (*garden, house*) mal tenu; **to feel n.** sentir qu'on vous néglige.
**negligence** négligence *f*.
**negligent** *a* négligent.
**negotiate** *vti* (*discuss*) négocier.
**negotiation** négociation *f*.
**neigh** *vi* (*of horse*) hennir.
**neighbor** voisin, -ine *mf*.
**neighborhood** quartier *m*; (*neighbors*) voisinage *m*.
**neighboring** *a* voisin.
**neither 1** *adv* **n. . . . nor** ni . . . ni; **he n. sings nor dances** il ne chante ni ne danse. **2** *conj* (*not either*) **if you won't go, n. will I** si tu n'y vas pas, je n'irai pas non plus. **3** *a* **n. boy (came)** aucun des deux garçons (n'est venu). **4** *pron* **n. (of them)** ni l'un(e) ni l'autre.
**neon** *a* (*lighting etc*) au néon.
**nephew** neveu *m*.
**nerve** nerf *m*; (*courage*) courage *m* (**to do** de faire); (*calm*) sang-froid *m*; (*cheek*) culot *m* (**to do** de faire); **you get on my nerves** tu me tapes sur les nerfs.
**nervous** *a* (*tense*) nerveux; (*worried*) inquiet (**about** de); (*uneasy*) mal à l'aise; **to be** *or* **feel n.** (*before exam etc*) avoir le trac.
**nest** nid *m*.
**net 1** *n* filet *m*. **2** *a* (*profit, weight etc*) net (*f* nette).
**netting (wire) n.** grillage *m*.
**nettle** ortie *f*.
**network** réseau *m*.
**neutral 1** *a* neutre. **2** *n* **in n. (gear)** au point mort.
**never** *adv* (ne . . . ) jamais; **she n. lies** elle ne ment jamais; **n. again** plus jamais.
**never-ending** *a* interminable.
**nevertheless** *adv* néanmoins.
**new** *a* nouveau (*f* nouvelle); (*brand-new*) neuf (*f* neuve); **a n. glass**/*etc* (*different*) un autre verre/*etc*; **what's n.?** *Fam* quoi de neuf?
**newborn** *a* **a n. baby** un nouveau-né, une nouveau-née.
**newcomer** nouveau-venu *m*, nouvelle-venue *f*.
**newly** *adv* (*recently*) nouvellement.
**news** nouvelle(s) *f*(*pl*); (*in the media*) informations *fpl*; **sports n.** (*newspaper column*) chronique *f* sportive; **a piece of n., some n.** une nouvelle; (*in the media*) une information.
**news flash** flash *m*.
**newsletter** bulletin *m*.
**newspaper** journal *m*.
**newsstand** kiosque *m* (à journaux).
**next 1** *a* prochain; (*room, house*) d'à-côté; (*following*) suivant; **n. month** (*in the future*) le mois prochain; **the n. day** le lendemain; **the n. morning** le lendemain matin; **(by) this time n. week** d'ici (à) la semaine prochaine; **to live n. door** habiter à côté (**to** de); **n.-door neighbor** voisin *m* d'à-côté. **2** *n* suivant, -ante *mf*. **3** *adv* (*afterwards*) ensuite; (*now*) maintenant; **when you come n.** la prochaine fois que

tu viendras. **4** *prep* **n. to** (*beside*) à côté de.
**nib** (*of pen*) plume *f.*
**nibble** *vti* (*eat*) grignoter; (*bite*) mordiller.
**nice** *a* (*pleasant*) agréable; (*pretty*) joli; (*kind*) gentil (**to** avec); **it's n. here** c'est bien ici; **n. and warm**/*etc* (*very*) bien chaud/*etc.*
**nicely** *adv* agréablement; (*kindly*) gentiment.
**nickel** (*coin*) pièce *f* de cinq cents.
**nickname** surnom *m.*
**niece** nièce *f.*
**night** nuit *f*; (*evening*) soir *m*; **last n.** (*evening*) hier soir; (*night*) la nuit dernière; **to have an early/late n.** se coucher tôt/tard; **to have a good night('s sleep)** bien dormir.
**nightclub** boîte *f* de nuit.
**nightgown,** *Fam* **nightie** chemise *f* de nuit.
**nightingale** rossignol *m.*
**nightmare** cauchemar *m.*
**nighttime** nuit *f.*
**night watchman** veilleur *m* de nuit.
**nil** zéro *m.*
**nine** *a* & *n* neuf (*m*).
**nineteen** *a* & *n* dix-neuf (*m*).
**ninetieth** *a* & *n* quatre-vingt-dixième (*mf*).
**ninety** *a* & *n* quatre-vingt-dix (*m*).
**ninth** *a* & *n* neuvième (*mf*).
**nip 1** *n* (*bite*) (petite) morsure *f*; (*drink*) petit verre; (*coldness*) **there's a n. in the air** le fond de l'air est frais. **2** *vt* pincer.
**nipple** bout *m* de sein; (*of bottle*) tétine f.
**nitrogen** azote *m.*
**no 1** *adv* & *n* non (*m inv*); **no more than ten**/*etc* pas plus de dix/*etc*; **no more time**/*etc* plus de temps/etc. **2** *a* aucun(e); pas de; **I have no idea** je n'ai aucune idée; **no child came** aucun enfant n'est venu; **I have no time**/*etc* je n'ai pas de temps/*etc*; **of no importance**/*etc* sans importance/*etc*; **'no smoking'** 'défense de fumer'; **no way!** *Fam* pas question!; **no one** = **nobody.**
**noble** *a* noble.
**nobody** *pron* (ne . . .) personne; **n. came** personne n'est venu; **n.!** personne!
**nod 1** *vti* **to n. (one's head)** faire un signe de tête. **2** *n* signe *m* de tête.
**nod off** s'assoupir.
**noise** bruit *m*; (*of bell, drum*) son *m*; **to make a n.** faire du bruit.
**noisily** *adv* bruyamment.
**noisy** *a* bruyant.
**nominate** *vt* (*appoint*) nommer.
**non-** *prefix* non-.
**none** *pron* aucun(e) *mf*; (*in filling out a form*) néant; **she has n. (at all)** elle n'en a pas (du tout); **n. (at all) came** pas un(e) seul(e) n'est venu(e); **n. of the cake**/*etc* pas une seule partie du gâteau/*etc*; **n. of the trees**/*etc* aucun des arbres/*etc.*
**nonetheless** *adv* néanmoins.
**non-existent** *a* inexistant.
**non-fiction** (*in library*) ouvrages *mpl* généraux.
**nonsense** absurdités *fpl*; **that's n.** c'est absurde.
**non-smoker** non-fumeur, -euse *mf.*
**non-stick** *a* (*pan*) anti-adhésif.
**non-stop 1** *a* sans arrêt; (*train, flight*) direct. **2** *adv* sans arrêt; (*to fly*) sans escale.
**noodles** *npl* nouilles *fpl*; (*in soup*) vermicelle(s) *m*(*pl*).
**noon** midi *m*; **at n.** à midi.
**nor** *conj* ni; **neither you n. me/I** ni toi ni moi; **she neither drinks n. smokes** elle ne fume ni ne boit; **I do not know, n. do I care** je ne sais pas et d'ailleurs je men moque.
**normal 1** *a* normal. **2** *n* **above/below n.** au-dessus/au-dessous de la normale.
**normally** *adv* normalement.
**north 1** *n* nord *m*; **(to the) n. of** au nord de. **2** *a* (*coast*) nord *inv.* **3** *adv* au nord.
**North American** *a* & *n* nord-américain, -aine (*mf*).

**northbound** *a* en direction du nord.
**north-east** *n* & *a* nord-est *m* & *a inv.*
**northern** *a* (*coast*) nord *inv*; (*town*) du nord.
**northerner** habitant, -ante *mf* du Nord.
**northward(s)** *a* & *adv* vers le nord.
**north-west** *n* & *a* nord-ouest *m* & *a inv.*
**Norwegian** *a* & *n* norvégien, -ienne (*mf*).
**nose** nez *m*; **her n. is bleeding** elle saigne du nez.
**nosebleed** saignement *m* de nez.
**nostril** (*of person*) narine *f*; (*horse*) naseau *m*.
**nos(e)y** *a* indiscret.
**not** *adv* (ne . . .) pas; **he's n. there, he isn't there** il n'est pas là; **n. yet** pas encore; **why n.?** pourquoi pas?; **n. one reply**/*etc* pas une seule réponse/*etc*; **n. at all** pas du tout; (*after 'thank you'*) je vous en prie. ▪ non; **I think/hope n.** je pense/j'espère que non; **isn't she?, don't you?** *etc* non?
**note 1** *n* (*comment, musical etc*) note *f*; (*money*) billet *m*; (*message*) petit mot *m*; **to make a n. of** prendre note de. **2** *vt* noter.
**notebook** carnet *m*; (*for school*) cahier *m*.
**note down** (*word etc*) noter.
**notepad** bloc-notes *m*.
**notepaper** papier *m* à lettres.
**nothing** *pron* (ne . . .) rien; **he knows n.** il ne sait rien; **n. to eat**/*etc* rien à manger/*etc*; **n. big**/*etc* rien de grand/*etc*; **n. much** pas grand-chose; **I've got n. to do with it** je n'y suis pour rien; **to come to n.** (*of efforts etc*) ne rien donner; **for n.** (*in vain, free of charge*) pour rien; **to have n. on** être tout nu.
**notice 1** *n* avis *m*; (*sign*) pancarte *f*; (*poster*) affiche *f*; **to give n.** donner sa démission; **to give s.o. (advance) n.** avertir qn (**of** de); **to take n.** faire attention (**of** à); **until further n.** jusqu'à nouvel ordre. **2** *vt* remarquer (**that** que).
**noticeable** *a* visible.
**notification** avis *m*.
**notify** *vt* avertir (**s.o. of sth** qn de qch).
**notion** idée *f*.
**noun** nom *m*.
**nourishing** *a* nourrissant.
**novel 1** *n* roman *m*. **2** *a* nouveau (*f* nouvelle).
**novelist** romancier, -ière *mf*.
**November** novembre *m*.
**now 1** *adv* maintenant; **just n., right n.** en ce moment; **I saw her just n.** je l'ai vue à l'instant; **for n.** pour le moment; **from n. on** désormais; **before n.** avant; **n. and then** de temps à autre. **2** *conj* **n. (that)** maintenant que.
**nowadays** *adv* aujourd'hui.
**nowhere** *adv* nulle part; **n. near the house** loin de la maison; **n. near enough** loin d'être assez.
**nozzle** (*hose*) jet *m*.
**nuclear** *a* nucléaire.
**nude in the n.** (tout) nu.
**nudge 1** *vt* pousser du coude. **2** *n* coup *m* de coude.
**nuisance** embêtement *m*; (*person*) peste *f*; **that's a n.** c'est embêtant.
**numb** *a* (*hand etc*) engourdi.
**number 1** *n* nombre *m*; (*of page, house, telephone etc*) numéro *m*; **a n. of** un certain nombre de. **2** *vt* (*page etc*) numéroter.
**numeral** chiffre *m*.
**numerous** *a* nombreux.
**nun** religieuse *f*.
**nurse 1** *n* infirmière *f*; **(male) n.** infirmier *m*. **2** *vt* (*take care of*) soigner; (*baby*) allaiter. **3** *vi* (*of baby*) téter.
**nursery** (*in house*) chambre *f* d'enfants; (*for plants*) pépinière *f*.
**nursery rhyme** chanson *f* enfantine.
**nursery school** école *f* maternelle.

**nut**[1] (*walnut*) noix *f*; (*hazelnut*) noisette *f*; (*peanut*) cacah(o)uète *f*.

**nut**[2] (*for bolt*) écrou *m*.

**nutcracker** *n* casse-noix *m inv*.

**nylon 1** *n* nylon *m*; **nylons** bas *mpl* nylon. **2** *a* (*shirt etc*) en nylon.

# O

**oak** chêne *m*.

**oar** aviron *m*.

**oatmeal** flocons *mpl* d'avoine.

**oats** *npl* avoine *f*.

**obedience** obéissance *f* (**to** à).

**obedient** *a* obéissant.

**obey 1** *vt* obéir à (*qn*); **to be obeyed** être obéi. **2** *vi* obéir.

**object**[1] (*thing, aim*) objet *m*; *Grammar* complément *m* (d'objet).

**object**[2] *vi* **to o. to sth/s.o.** désapprouver qch/qn; **I o. to you(r) doing that** ça me gêne que tu fasses ça.

**objection** objection *f*.

**objective** (*aim*) objectif *m*.

**obligation** obligation *f*.

**oblige** *vt* (*compel*) contraindre (**s.o. to do** qn à faire); (*help*) rendre service à.

**obliging** *a* serviable.

**oblique** *a* oblique.

**obscene** *a* obscène.

**observant** *a* observateur.

**observation** observation *f*.

**observe** *vt* observer; (*say*) remarquer (**that** que).

**obstacle** obstacle *m*.

**obstinate** *a* (*person, resistance*) obstiné.

**obstruct** *vt* (*block*) boucher; (*hinder*) gêner.

**obtain** *vt* obtenir.

**obtainable** *a* disponible.

**obvious** *a* évident (**that** que).

**obviously** *adv* évidemment.

**occasion** (*time, opportunity*) occasion *f*; (*event, ceremony*) événement *m*.

**occasional** *a* (*odd*) qu'on fait, voit *etc* de temps en temps; **she drinks the o. whisky** elle boit un whisky de temps en temps.

**occasionally** *adv* de temps en temps.

**occupant** occupant, -ante *mf*.

**occupation** (*activity*) occupation *f*; (*job*) emploi *m*; (*trade*) métier *m*; (*profession*) profession *f*.

**occupy** *vt* occuper; **to keep oneself occupied** s'occuper (**doing** à faire).

**occur** *vi* (*happen*) avoir lieu; (*be found*) se rencontrer; **it occurs to me that . . .** il me vient à l'esprit que . . .

**occurrence** (*event*) événement *m*.

**ocean** océan *m*.

**o'clock** *adv* **(it's) three o'c.**/*etc* (il est) trois heures/*etc*.

**October** octobre *m*.

**octopus** pieuvre *f*.

**odd** *a* (*strange*) bizarre. ▪ (*number*) impair. ▪ (*left over*) **I have an o. penny** il me reste un penny; **a few o. stamps** quelques timbres (qui restent); **the o. man out** l'exception *f*; **sixty o.** soixante et quelques; **an o. glove**/*etc* un gant/*etc* dépareillé. ▪ = **occasional**; **o. jobs** menus travaux *mpl*.

**oddly** *adv* bizarrement.

**odds** *npl* (*in betting*) cote *f*; (*chances*) chances *fpl*; **at o.** en désaccord (**with** avec); **o. and ends** des petites choses.

**odor** odeur *f*.

**of** *prep* de, d' (de + le = du, de + les = des); **of the table** de la table; **of a book** d'un livre; **she has a lot of it** *or* **of them** elle en a beaucoup; **a friend of his** un ami à lui; **there are ten of us** nous sommes dix; **that's nice of you** c'est gentil de ta part.

**off 1** *adv* (*gone away*) parti; (*light, radio etc*) éteint; (*faucet*) fermé; (*detached*) détaché; (*removed*) enlevé; (*canceled*) annulé; **6 miles o.** à 10 km (d'ici *or* de là); **to be** *ou* **go o.** (*leave*) partir; **a day o.** un jour de congé; **time o.** du temps libre; **5**

**o.** une réduction de 5%; **hands o.!** pas touche!; **to be better o.** être mieux. **2** *prep* (*from*) de; (*distant*) éloigné de; **to get o. the bus**/*etc* descendre du bus/*etc*; **to take sth o. the table**/*etc* prendre qch sur la table/*etc*; **o. New York** au large de New York.

**off-color** *a* risqué.

**offend** *vt* froisser (*qn*); **to be offended (at)** se froisser (de).

**offense** (*crime*) délit *m*; **to take o.** s'offenser (**at** de).

**offensive** *a* (*words etc*) insultant (**to s.o.** pour qn); **o. to s.o.** (*of person*) insultant avec qn.

**offer 1** *n* offre *f*; **special o.** (*in store*) promotion *f*. **2** *vt* offrir (**to do** de faire).

**offhand 1** *a* (*abrupt*) brusque, impoli. **2** *adv* (*to say, know etc*) comme ça.

**office** (*room*) bureau *m* (*of doctor, lawyer*) cabinet *m*; (*post*) fonction *f*; **head o.** siège *m* central; **o. building** immeuble *m* de bureaux.

**officer** (*in the army etc*) officier *m*; **(police) o.** agent *m* (de police).

**official 1** *a* officiel. **2** *n* (*civil servant*) fonctionnaire *mf*.

**officially** *adv* officiellement.

**often** *adv* souvent; **how o.?** combien de fois?; **how o. do they run?** (*train etc*) il y en a tous les combien?; **every so o.** de temps en temps.

**oh!** *int* oh!, ah!; **oh yes!** mais oui!; **oh yes?** ah oui?

**oil 1** *n* huile *f*; (*extracted from ground*) pétrole *m*; (*fuel*) mazout *m*. **2** *vt* (*machine*) graisser.

**oilcan** burette *f*.

**oil change** (*in vehicle*) vidange *f*.

**ointment** pommade *f*.

**OK, okay 1** *a* (*satisfactory*) bien *inv*; (*unharmed*) sain et sauf; (*undamaged*) intact; (*without worries*) tranquille; **it's o.** ça va; **I'm o** (*healthy*) je vais bien. **2** *adv* (*well*) bien; **o.!** (*agreement*) d'accord!

**old** *a* vieux (*f* vieille); (*former*) ancien; **how o. is he?** quel âge a-t-il?; **he's ten years o.** il a dix ans; **he's older than me** il est plus âgé que moi; **an older son** un fils aîné; **the oldest son** le fils aîné; **o. man** vieillard *m*; **o. woman** vieille femme *f*; **to get** *or* **grow old(er)** vieillir; **o. age** vieillesse *f*.

**old-fashioned** *a* démodé; (*person*) rétro *inv*.

**olive** olive *f*; **o. oil** huile *f* d'olive.

**Olympic** *a* (*games etc*) olympique.

**omelet(te)** omelette *f*; **cheese**/*etc* **o.** omelette au fromage/*etc*.

**on 1** *prep* (*position*) sur; **to put on (to)** mettre sur. ▪ (*about*) sur; **to speak on** parler sur. ▪ (*manner, means*) **on foot** à pied; **on the train**/*etc* dans le train/*etc*; **to be on** (*salary*) toucher; (*team*) être membre de; **to keep** *or* **stay on** (*path etc*) suivre. ▪ (*time*) **on Monday** lundi; **on Mondays** le lundi; **on May 3rd** le 3 mai. ▪ (+ *present participle*) en; **on seeing this** en voyant ceci. **2** *adv* (*ahead*) en avant; (*in progress*) en cours; (*lid, brake*) mis; (*light, radio*) allumé; (*gas, faucet*) ouvert; **on (and on)** sans cesse; **to play**/*etc* **on** continuer à jouer/*etc*; **what's on?** (*television*) qu'y a-t-il à la télé?; **from then on** à partir de là.

**once 1** *adv* une fois; (*formerly*) autrefois; **o. a month** une fois par mois; **o. again, o. more** encore une fois; **at o.** tout de suite; **all at o.** tout à coup; (*at the same time*) à la fois. **2** *conj* une fois que.

**one 1** *a* un, une; **o. man** un homme; **o. woman** une femme; **page o.** la page un; **twenty-o.** vingt-et-un. ▪ (*only*) seul; **my o. (and only) aim** mon seul (et unique) but. ▪ (*same*) même; **on the o. bus** dans le même bus. **2** *pron* un, une; **do you want o.?** en veux-tu (un)?; **o. of them** l'un d'eux, l'une d'elles; **a big**/*etc* **o.** un grand/*etc*; **that o.** celui-là, celle-là; **the o. who** *or* **which** celui *or* celle qui; **another o.** un(e) autre. ▪ (*impersonal*) on; **o. knows** on sait; **it helps o.** ça nous *or* vous aide; **one's family** sa famille.

**oneself** *pron* soi-même; (*reflexive*) se, s'.

**one-way** *a* (*street*) à sens unique; (*ticket*) simple.

**onion** oignon *m*.

**onlooker** spectateur, -trice *mf*.

**only 1** *a* seul; **the o. one** le seul, la seule; **an o. son** un fils unique. **2** *adv* seulement, ne . . . que; **I o. have ten** je n'en ai que dix, j'en ai dix seulement; **not o.** non seulement; **I have o. just seen it** je viens tout juste de le voir; **o. he knows** lui seul le sait. **3** *conj* (*but*) *Fam* seulement.

**onto** *prep* = **on to.**

**onward(s)** *adv* en avant; **from that time o.** à partir de là.

**opaque** *a* opaque.

**open 1** *a* ouvert; (*ticket*) open *inv*; **wide o.** grand ouvert. **2** *n* **(out) in the o.** en plein air. **3** *vt* ouvrir. **4** *vi* (*of flower, door, eyes etc*) s'ouvrir; (*of shop, office, person*) ouvrir.

**open-air** *a* (*pool, market etc*) en plein air.

**opening** ouverture *f*; (*career prospect*) débouché *m*.

**openly** *adv* ouvertement.

**openness** franchise *f*.

**open out 1** *vt* ouvrir. **2** *vi* s'ouvrir; (*widen*) s'élargir.

**open up 1** *vt* ouvrir. **2** *vi* s'ouvrir; (*open the door*) ouvrir.

**opera** opéra *m*.

**operate 1** *vi* (*of surgeon*) opérer (**on s.o.** qn, **for** de); (*of machine etc*) fonctionner; (*proceed*) opérer. **2** *vt* faire fonctionner; (*business*) gérer.

**operation** opération *f*; (*working*) fonctionnement *m*.

**operator** (*on phone*) standardiste *mf*.

**opinion** opinion *f*, avis *m*; **in my o.** à mon avis.

**opponent** adversaire *mf*.

**opportunity** occasion *f* (**to do** de faire).

**oppose** *vt* s'opposer à.

**opposed** *a* opposé (**to** à).

**opposing** *a* (*team*) opposé.

**opposite 1** *a* (*direction, opinion etc*) opposé; (*house*) d'en face. **2** *adv* (*to sit etc*) en face. **3** *prep* **o. (to)** en face de. **4** *n* **the o.** le contraire.

**opposition** opposition *f* (**to** à).

**opt** *vi* **to o. for sth** décider pour qch.

**optician** opticien, -ienne *mf*.

**optimist to be an o.** être optimiste.

**optimistic** *a* optimiste.

**option** (*choice*) choix *m*.

**optional** *a* facultatif.

**or** *conj* ou; **he doesn't drink or smoke** il ne boit ni ne fume.

**oral 1** *a* oral. **2** *n* (*exam*) oral *m*.

**orange 1** *n* (*fruit*) orange *f*; **o. juice** jus *m* d'orange. **2** *a* & *n* (*color*) orange *a* & *m inv*.

**orangeade** orangeade *f*.

**orbit** orbite *f*.

**orchard** verger *m*.

**orchestra** orchestre *m*.

**ordeal** épreuve *f*.

**order 1** *n* (*command, arrangement*) ordre *m*; (*purchase*) commande; **in o.** (*passport etc*) en règle; **in o. to do** pour faire; **in o. that** pour que (+ *subjunctive*); **out of o.** (*machine*) en panne; (*telephone*) en dérangement. **2** *vt* ordonner (**s.o. to do** à qn de faire); (*meal, goods etc*) commander; (*taxi*) appeler. **3** *vi* (*in café etc*) commander.

**order s.o. around** commander qn.

**ordinary** *a* (*usual, commonplace*) ordinaire; (*average*) moyen; **it's out of the o.** ça sort de l'ordinaire.

**ore** minerai *m*.

**organ** (*in body*) organe *m*; (*instrument*) orgue *m*, orgues *fpl*.

**organic** *a* (*vegetables etc*) biologique.

**organization** organisation *f*.

**organize** *vt* organiser.

**organizer** organisateur, -trice *mf.*
**oriental** *a* oriental.
**origin** origine *f.*
**original 1** *a* (*idea, artist etc*) original; (*first*) premier; (*copy, version*) original. **2** *n* (*document etc*) original *m.*
**originality** originalité *f.*
**originally** *adv* (*at first*) au départ.
**ornament** (*on dress etc*) ornement *m*; (*vase etc*) bibelot *m.*
**orphan** orphelin, -ine *mf.*
**orphanage** orphelinat *m.*
**ostrich** autruche *f.*
**other 1** *a* autre; **o. doctors** d'autres médecins; **the o. one** l'autre *mf.* **2** *pron* **the o.** l'autre *mf*; **(some) others** d'autres; **some do, others don't** les uns le font, les autres ne le font pas. **3** *adv* **o. than** autrement que.
**otherwise** *adv* autrement.
**ouch!** *int* aïe!
**ought** *v aux* (*obligation, desirability*) devoir; **you o. to leave** tu devrais partir; **I o. to have done it** j'aurais dû le faire; **he said he o. to stay** il a dit qu'il devait rester. ▪ (*probability*) devoir; **it o. to be ready** ça devrait être prêt.
**ounce** once *f* (= *28,35 g*).
**our** *poss a* notre, *pl* nos.
**ours** *pron* le nôtre, la nôtre, *pl* les nôtres; **this book is o.** ce livre est à nous *or* est le nôtre.
**ourselves** *pron* nous-mêmes; (*reflexive & after prep*) nous.
**out 1** *adv* (*outside*) dehors; (*not at home etc*) sorti; (*light, fire*) éteint; (*news, secret*) connu; (*book*) publié; (*eliminated from game*) éliminé; **to be** *or* **go o. a lot** sortir beaucoup; **to have a day o.** sortir pour la journée; **the tide's o.** la marée est basse; **o. there** là-bas. **2** *prep* **o. of** en dehors de; (*danger, water*) hors de; (*without*) sans; **o. of pity**/*etc* par pitié/*etc*; **o. of the window** par la fenêtre; **to drink/take/copy o. of sth** boire/prendre/copier dans qch; **made o. of** (*wood etc*) fait en; **to make sth o. of a box**/*etc* faire qch avec une boîte/*etc*; **she's o. of town** elle n'est pas en ville; **four o. of five** quatre sur cinq; **to feel o. of place** ne pas se sentir intégré.
**outbound** *a* **o. journey** *or* **trip** aller *m.*
**outbreak** (*of war*) début *m*; (*of violence*) éruption *f.*
**outburst** (*of anger, joy*) explosion *f.*
**outcome** résultat *m.*
**outdated** *a* démodé.
**outdo*** *vt* surpasser (**in** en).
**outdoor** *a* (*pool, market*) en plein air; **o. clothes** tenue *f* pour sortir.
**outdoors** *adv* dehors.
**outer** *a* extérieur.
**outer space** l'espace *m* (cosmique).
**outfit** (*clothes*) costume *m*; (*for woman*) toilette *f*; (*toy*) panoplie *f* (*de cow-boy etc*); **ski**/*etc* **o.** tenue *f* de ski/*etc*.
**outing** sortie *f*, excursion *f.*
**outlet** (*market for goods*) débouché *m.*
**outline** (*shape*) contour *m.*
**outlook** *n inv* (*for future*) perspective(s) *f*(*pl*); (*point of view*) perspective *f* (**on** sur).
**outnumber** *vt* être plus nombreux que.
**out-of-date** *a* (*expired*) périmé; (*old-fashioned*) démodé.
**output** rendement *m*; (*computer data*) données *fpl* de sortie.
**outrage 1** *n* scandale *m*; (*anger*) indignation *f.* **2** *vt* **outraged by sth** indigné de qch.
**outrageous** (*shocking*) scandaleux.
**outright** *adv* (*to say, tell*) franchement.
**outside 1** *adv* (au) dehors; **to go o.** sortir. **2** *prep* en dehors de. **3** *n* extérieur *m.* **4** *a* extérieur.
**outskirts** *npl* banlieue *f.*
**outstanding** *a* remarquable; (*problem*) non réglé; (*debt*) impayé.

**outward** *a* (*sign, appearance*) extérieur.
**outward(s)** *adv* vers l'extérieur.
**oval** *a* & *n* ovale (*m*).
**oven** four *m*.
**oven mitt** gant *m* isolant.
**over 1** *prep* (*on*) sur; (*above*) au-dessus de; (*on the other side of*) de l'autre côté de; **to jump/look/***etc* **o. sth** sauter/regarder/*etc* par-dessus qch; **o. it** (*on*) dessus; (*above*) au-dessus; (*to jump etc*) par-dessus; **to be upset/***etc* **o. sth** (*about*) avoir de la peine/*etc* à cause de qch; **o. the phone** au téléphone; **o. the holidays** pendant les vacances; **o. ten days** (*more than*) plus de dix jours; **men o. sixty** les hommes de plus de soixante ans; **all o. Spain** dans toute l'Espagne; **all o. the carpet** partout sur le tapis. **2** *adv* (*above*) (par-)dessus; **o. here** ici; **o. there** là-bas; **to come** *or* **go o.** (*visit*) passer; **to ask o.** inviter (à venir); **all o.** (*everywhere*) partout; **it's (all) o.** (*finished*) c'est fini; **a pound or o.** une livre ou plus; **I have ten o.** il m'en reste dix; **o. and o. (again)** à plusieurs reprises; **o. pleased/***etc* trop content/*etc*.
**overall** *a* (*length etc*) total.
**overalls** *npl* bleus *mpl* de travail.
**overboard** *adv* à la mer.
**overcharge to o. s.o. for sth** faire payer qch trop cher à qn.
**overcoat** pardessus *m*.
**overcome** *vt* (*problem*) surmonter.
**overdo*** *vt* **to o. it** ne pas y aller doucement; **don't o. it!** vas-y doucement!
**overdraft** découvert *m*.
**overdue** *a* (*train etc*) en retard.
**overeat** *vi* manger trop.
**overexcited** *a* surexcité.
**overflow** *vi* (*of river, bath etc*) déborder.
**overhead** *adv* au-dessus.
**overhear** *vt* (*pt* & *pp* **overheard**) surprendre.
**overheat** *vi* (*of engine*) chauffer.
**overjoyed** *a* fou (*f* folle) de joie.
**overlap 1** *vi* se chevaucher. **2** *vt* chevaucher.
**overleaf** *adv* au verso.
**overload** *vt* surcharger.
**overlook** *vt* ne pas remarquer; (*forget*) oublier; (*ignore*) passer sur; (*of window etc*) donner sur.
**overnight 1** *adv* (pendant) la nuit; **to stay o.** passer la nuit. **2** *a* (*train*) de nuit.
**overpass** (*bridge*) toboggan *m*.
**overrated** *a* surfait.
**overseas 1** *adv* (*abroad*) à l'étranger. **2** *a* (*visitor etc*) étranger; (*trade*) extérieur.
**oversight** oubli *m*.
**oversleep** *vi* (*pt* & *pp* **overslept**) dormir trop longtemps.
**overspend** *vi* dépenser trop.
**overtake*** *vti* (*in vehicle*) dépasser.
**overtime 1** *n* heures *fpl* supplémentaires. **2** *adv* **to work o.** faire des heures supplémentaires.
**overturn** *vi* (*of car, boat*) se retourner.
**overweight** *a* **to be o.** (*of person*) avoir des kilos en trop.
**overwhelm** *vt* accabler; **overwhelmed with** (*work, offers*) submergé de.
**overwork 1** *n* surmenage *m*. **2** *vi* se surmener.
**owe** *vt* (*money etc*) devoir (**to** à).
**owing** *prep* **o. to** à cause de.
**owl** hibou *m* (*pl* hiboux).
**own 1** *a* propre; **my o. house** ma propre maison. **2** *pron* **it's my (very) o.** c'est à moi (tout seul); **a house of his o.** sa propre maison; **(all) on one's o.** tout seul; **to get one's o. back** se venger. **3** *vt* posséder; **who owns this ball/***etc***?** à qui appartient cette balle/*etc*?
**owner** propriétaire *mf*.
**own up** avouer (**to sth** qch).
**ox** (*pl* **oxen**) bœuf *m*.
**oxygen** oxygène *m*.
**oyster** huître *f*.

# P

**pa** *Fam* papa *m*.
**pace** pas *m*.
**Pacific 1** *a* pacifique. **2** *n* **the P.** le Pacifique.
**pacifier** (*of baby*) sucette *f*.
**pack 1** *n* paquet *m*; (*backpack*) sac *m* (à dos); (*of wolves*) meute *f*; (*of cards*) jeu *m*; (*of lies*) tissu *m*. **2** *vt* (*fill*) remplir (**with** de); (*suitcase*) faire; (*object into box etc*) emballer; (*object into suitcase*) mettre dans sa valise.
**pack (down)** (*crush*) tasser.
**package** paquet *m*; (*computer programs*) progiciel *m*.
**package tour** voyage *m* organisé.
**packaging** emballage *m*.
**pack away** (*put away*) ranger.
**packed** *a* (*bus etc*) bourré.
**packed lunch** panier-repas *m*.
**packet** paquet *m*.
**pack sth in** *Fam* (*quit*) laisser tomber qch.
**packing** emballage *m*.
**pack into 1** *vt* (*cram*) entasser dans. **2** *vi* (*crowd into*) s'entasser dans.
**pack up 1** *vt* (*put into box*) emballer; (*give up*) *Fam* laisser tomber. **2** *vi Fam* (*stop*) s'arrêter; (*of machine*) tomber en panne.
**pad** (*of cloth etc*) tampon *m*; (*for writing etc*) bloc *m*.
**padded** *a* (*armchair etc*) rembourré.
**paddle 1** *vi* (*dip one's feet*) se mouiller les pieds. **2** *n* (*for boat*) *pagaie f*; (*for Ping-Pong*) raquette *f*. **3** *vt* **to p. a canoe** pagayer.
**paddle boat** pédalo *m*.
**padlock** cadenas *m*; (*on bicycle*) antivol *m*.
**page** (*of book etc*) page *f*.
**pain** douleur *f*; (*grief*) peine *f*; **pains** (*efforts*) efforts *mpl*; **to be in p.** souffrir; **to take (great) pains to do** se donner du mal à faire.
**painful** *a* douloureux.
**painkiller** calmant *m*; **on painkillers** sous calmants.
**paint 1** *n* peinture *f*; **paints** (*in box, tube*) couleurs *fpl*. **2** *vti* peindre; **to p. sth blue**/*etc* peindre qch en bleu/*etc*.
**paintbrush** pinceau *m*.
**painter** peintre *m*.
**painting** (*activity, picture*) peinture *f*.
**paint stripper** décapant *m*.
**pair** (*two*) paire *f*; (*man and woman*) couple *m*.
**pajamas** *npl* pyjama *m*; **a pair of p.** un pyjama.
**Pakistani** *a* & *n* pakistanais, -aise (*mf*).
**pal** *Fam* copain *m*, copine *f*.
**palace** palais *m*.
**palate** (*in mouth*) palais *m*.
**pale** *a* pâle.
**palette** (*of artist*) palette *f*.
**palm** (*of hand*) paume *f*; **p. (tree)** palmier *m*; **p. (leaf)** palme *f*.
**pamphlet** brochure *f*.
**pan** casserole *f*; (*for frying*) poêle *f*.
**pancake** crêpe *f*.
**pane** vitre *f*.
**panel** (*of door etc*) panneau *m*; (*of judges*) jury *m*; (*of experts*) groupe *m*; **(control) p.** console *f*.
**panic 1** *n* panique *f*. **2** *vi* s'affoler.
**pant** *vi* haleter.
**panties** *npl* (*female*) slip *m*.
**pantomime** spectacle *m* de mime.
**pantry** (*larder*) garde-manger *m inv*.
**pants** *npl* (*trousers*) pantalon *m*.
**pantyhose** collant *m*.
**paper 1** *n* papier *m*; (*newspaper*) journal *m*; (*wallpaper*) papier *m* peint; (*in high school, college*) dissertation *f*; **brown p.** papier *m* d'emballage; **to put down on p.** mettre par écrit. **2** *a* (*bag, towel etc*) en papier; (*cup, plate*) en carton.
**paperback** livre *m* de poche.
**paper clip** trombone *m*.
**paper towel** essuie-tout *m inv*.

**parachute** parachute *m*.
**parade** (*procession*) défilé *m*; (*street*) avenue *f*.
**paradise** paradis *m*.
**paragraph** paragraphe *m*; **'new p.'** 'à la ligne'.
**parakeet** perruche *f*.
**parallel** *a* parallèle (**with, to** à).
**paralyze** *vt* paralyser.
**parasite** parasite *m*.
**parasol** (*over table, on beach*) parasol *m*.
**parcel** colis *m*, paquet *m*.
**pardon 1** *n* **I beg your p.** je vous prie de m'excuser; (*not hearing*) vous dites?; **p.?** (*not hearing*) comment?; **p. (me)!** (*sorry*) pardon! **2** *vt* pardonner (**s.o. for sth** qch à qn).
**parent** père *m*, mère *f*; **one's parents** ses parents *mpl*.
**parish** paroisse *f*.
**Parisian** *a* & *n* parisien, -ienne (*mf*).
**park 1** *n* parc *m*. **2** *vt* (*vehicle*) garer. **3** *vi* se garer; (*remain parked*) stationner.
**parka** anorak *m*.
**parking** stationnement *m*; **'no p.'** 'défense de stationner'.
**parking enforcement officer** contractuel, -elle *mf*.
**parking light** (*of vehicle*) veilleuse *f*.
**parking lot** parking *m*.
**parking meter** parcmètre *m*.
**parking place** *or* **space** place *f* de parking.
**parking ticket** contravention *f*.
**parliament** parlement *m*.
**parrot** perroquet *m*.
**parsley** persil *m*.
**parsnip** panais *m*.
**part 1** *n* partie *f*; (*of machine*) pièce *f*; (*of serial*) épisode *m*; (*role*) rôle *m*; (*in hair*) raie *f*. **to take p.** participer (**in** à); **in p.** en partie; **for the most p.** dans l'ensemble; **to be a p. of sth** faire partie de qch; **in these parts** dans ces parages. **2** *adv* (*partly*) en partie. **3** *vi* (*of friends etc*) se quitter; (*of married couple*) se séparer.
**partial** *a* partiel; **to be p. to sth** (*fond of*) *Fam* avoir un faible pour qch.
**participant** participant, -ante *mf*.
**participate** *vi* participer (**in** à).
**participation** participation *f*.
**participle** *Grammar* participe *m*.
**particular 1** *a* particulier; (*fussy*) difficile (**about** sur); (*showing care*) méticuleux; **in p.** en particulier. **2** *npl* **particulars** détails *mpl*; **s.o.'s particulars** les coordonnées *fpl* de qn.
**particularly** *adv* particulièrement.
**partition** (*in room*) cloison *f*.
**partly** *adv* en partie.
**partner** partenaire *mf*; (*in business*) associé, -ée *mf*; **(dancing) p.** cavalier, -ière *mf*.
**partnership** association *f*.
**partridge** perdrix *f*.
**part-time** *a* & *adv* à temps partiel.
**part with sth** (*get rid of*) se séparer de qch.
**party** (*formal*) réception *f*; (*with friends*) soirée *f*; (*for birthday*) fête *f*; (*group*) groupe *m*; (*political*) parti *m*.
**pass 1** *n* (*entry permit*) laissez-passer *m inv*; (*over mountains*) col *m*; *Sports* passe *f*; (*for transportation*) carte *f* d'abonnement. **2** *vi* passer (**to** à, **through** par); (*overtake*) dépasser; (*in exam*) être reçu (**in French**/*etc* en français/*etc*). **3** *vt* passer (**to** à); (*go past*) passer devant (*immeuble etc*); (*vehicle*) dépasser; (*exam*) être reçu à; **to p. s.o.** (*in street*) croiser qn.
**passable** *a* (*not bad*) passable; (*road*) praticable.
**passage** (*of text etc*) passage *m*; (*corridor*) couloir *m*.
**passageway** (*corridor*) couloir *m*.
**pass around** (*cake etc*) faire passer.
**pass away** (*die*) mourir.

**passbook** livret *m* de caisse d'épargne.
**pass by 1** *vi* passer (à côté). **2** *vt* (*building etc*) passer devant; **to p. by s.o.** (*in street*) croiser qn.
**passenger** passager, -ère *mf*; (*on train*) voyageur, -euse *mf*.
**passer-by** (*pl* **passers-by**) passant, -ante *mf*.
**passing grade** (*in school*) moyenne *f*.
**passion** passion *f*.
**passionate** *a* passionné.
**passive 1** *a* passif. **2** *n Grammar* passif *m*.
**pass off to p. oneself off as** se faire passer pour.
**pass on** *vt* (*message etc*) transmettre (**to** à).
**pass out** (*faint*) s'évanouir.
**pass over sth** (*ignore*) passer sur qch.
**passport** passeport *m*.
**pass through** *vi* passer.
**pass up** (*chance*) laisser passer.
**past 1** *n* passé *m*; **in the p.** (*formerly*) dans le temps. **2** *a* (*gone by*) passé; (*former*) ancien; **these p. months** ces derniers mois; **in the p. tense** au passé. **3** *prep* (*in front of*) devant; (*after*) après; (*further than*) plus loin que; **p. four o'clock** quatre heures passées. **4** *adv* devant; **to go p.** passer.
**pasta** pâtes *fpl*.
**paste 1** *n* (*of meat*) pâté *m*; (*of fish*) beurre *m*; (*glue*) colle *f*. **2** *vt* coller.
**pasteurized** *a* (*milk*) pasteurisé.
**pastille** pastille *f*.
**pastime** passe-temps *m inv*.
**pastry** pâte *f*; (*cake*) pâtisserie *f*.
**pasture** pâturage *m*.
**pat** *vt* (*cheek etc*) tapoter; (*animal*) caresser.
**patch** (*for clothes*) pièce *f*; (*over eye*) bandeau *m*; (*of color*) tache *f*; **cabbage p.** carré *m* de choux; **bad p.** mauvaise période *f*.
**patch (up)** (*clothing*) rapiécer.
**path** (*pl* **-s** ) sentier *m*; (*in park*) allée *f*.
**pathetic** *a* (*results etc*) lamentable.
**pathway** sentier *m*.
**patience** patience *f*; **to lose p.** perdre patience (**with s.o.** avec qn).
**patient 1** *a* patient. **2** *n* malade *mf*; (*on doctor's or dentist's list*) patient, -ente *mf*.
**patiently** *adv* patiemment.
**patio** (*pl* **-os**) patio *m*.
**patriotic** *a* patriotique; (*person*) patriote.
**patrol 1** *n* patrouille *f*. **2** *vi* patrouiller. **3** *vt* patrouiller dans.
**pattern** dessin *m*; (*paper model for garment*) patron *m*.
**pause 1** *n* pause *f*; (*in conversation*) silence *m*. **2** *vi* faire une pause; (*hesitate*) hésiter.
**paved** *a* pavé.
**pavement** trottoir *m*; (*roadway*) chaussée *f*.
**pavilion** pavillon *m*.
**paving stone** pavé *m*.
**paw** patte *f*.
**pawn** *Chess* pion *m*.
**pay 1** salaire *m*; (*of workman, soldier*) paie *f*; **p. slip** bulletin *m* de paie. **2** *vt* (*pt* & *pp* **paid**) (*person, sum*) payer; (*deposit*) verser; (*of investment*) rapporter; (*compliment, visit*) faire (**to** à); **to p. s.o. to do** *or* **for doing** payer qn pour faire; **to p. s.o. for sth** payer qch à qn; **to p. money into one's account** verser de l'argent sur son compte. **3** *vi* payer; **to p. a lot** payer cher.
**payable** *a* payable; **a check p. to** un chèque à l'ordre de.
**pay back** (*person, loan*) rembourser.
**paycheck** chèque *m* de règlement de salaire.
**pay for sth** payer qch.
**payment** paiement *m*; (*of deposit*) versement *m*.
**pay off** (*debt, person*) rembourser.
**pay out** (*spend*) dépenser.
**pay phone** téléphone *m* public.

**pay up** *vti* payer.

**PE** *abbr* (*Physical Education*) éducation *f* physique, EPS *f*.

**pea** pois *m*; **(green) peas** petits pois *mpl*; **p. soup** soupe *f* aux pois.

**peace** paix *f*; **p. of mind** tranquillité *f* d'esprit; **in p.** en paix; **to have (some) p. and quiet** avoir la paix.

**peaceful** *a* paisible; (*demonstration*) pacifique.

**peach** pêche *f*.

**peacock** paon *m*.

**peak 1** *n* (*mountain top*) sommet *m*; (*mountain*) pic *m*; **to be at its p.** être à son maximum. **2** *a* (*hours, period*) de pointe.

**peaked** *a Fam* (*ill*) patraque.

**peanut** cacah(o)uète *f*.

**pear** poire *f*; **p. tree** poirier *m*.

**pearl** perle *f*.

**pebble** caillou *m* (*pl* cailloux); (*on beach*) galet *m*.

**pecan** noix *f* de pécan.

**peck** *vti* **to p. (at)** (*of bird*) picorer (*du pain etc*); donner un coup de bec à (*qn*).

**peculiar** *a* bizarre; (*special*) particulier (**to** à).

**peculiarity** (*feature*) particularité *f*.

**pedal 1** *n* pédale *f*. **2** *vi* pédaler. **3** *vt* **to p. a bicycle** faire marcher un vélo; (*ride*) rouler en vélo.

**pedestrian** piéton *m*; **p. crossing** passage *m* pour piétons; **p. street** rue *f* piétonne.

**peek to have a p.** jeter un petit coup d'œil (**at** à).

**peel 1** *n* épluchure(s) *f*(*pl*); **a piece of p., some p.** une épluchure. **2** *vt* (*apple, potato etc*) éplucher. **3** *vi* (*of sunburnt skin*) peler; (*of paint*) s'écailler.

**peeler (potato) p.** éplucheur *m*.

**peel off** (*label etc*) décoller.

**peep 1** *n* coup *m* d'œil (furtif). **2** *vi* **to p. (at)** regarder furtivement.

**peer** *vi* **to p. (at)** regarder attentivement.

**peg** (*for tent*) piquet *m*; (*for clothes*) pince *f* (à linge); (*for coat, hat*) patère *f*.

**pen** (*fountain, ballpoint*) stylo *m*; (*enclosure*) parc *m*.

**penalty** (*prison sentence*) peine *f*; (*fine*) amende *f*; *Sports* penalty *m*.

**pencil** crayon *m*; **in p.** au crayon.

**pencil case** trousse *f*.

**pencil in** (*note down*) noter provisoirement.

**pencil sharpener** taille-crayon(s) *m inv*.

**penetrate** *vt* (*substance*) pénétrer; (*forest*) pénétrer dans.

**penguin** manchot *m*.

**penicillin** pénicilline *f*.

**peninsula** presqu'île *f*.

**penknife** (*pl* **-knives**) canif *m*.

**penniless** *a* sans le sou.

**penny** (*pl* **pennies**) (*coin*) cent *m*; **not a p.!** pas un sou!

**pen pal** correspondant, -ante *mf*.

**pension** pension *f*; **(retirement) p.** retraite *f*.

**pensioner (old age) p.** retraité, -ée *mf*.

**people 1** *npl* gens *mpl or fpl*; (*specific persons*) personnes *fpl*; **the p.** (*citizens*) le peuple; **old p.** les personnes *fpl* âgées; **old people's home** hospice *m* de vieillards; (*private*) maison *f* de retraite; **English p.** les Anglais *mpl*. **2** *n* (*nation*) peuple *m*.

**pepper** poivre *m*; (*vegetable*) poivron *m*.

**peppermint** (*flavor*) menthe *f*; (*candy*) bonbon *m* à la menthe.

**per** *prep* par; **p. year** par an; **p. person** par personne; **p. cent** pour cent; **10 dollars p. pound** 10 dollars la livre.

**percentage** pourcentage *m*.

**perch 1** *n* (*for bird*) perchoir *m*. **2** *vi* (*of bird, person*) se percher.

**percolator** cafetière *f*; (*in café etc*) percolateur *m*.

**perfect 1** *a* parfait. **2** *a* & *n Grammar* **p. (tense)** parfait *m*. **3** *vt* (*tech-*

*nique*) mettre au point; (*one's French etc*) parfaire ses connaissances en.

**perfection** perfection *f.*

**perfectly** *adv* parfaitement.

**perform 1** *vt* (*task, miracle*) accomplir; (*one's duty*) remplir; (*surgical operation*) pratiquer (**on** sur); (*a play, piece of music*) jouer. **2** *vi* (*act, play*) jouer; (*sing*) chanter; (*dance*) danser; (*of machine*) fonctionner.

**performance** (*in theater*) représentation *f*; (*in movie theater, concert hall*) séance *f*; (*of actor, musician*) interprétation *f*; (*of athlete, machine*) performance *f.*

**performer** (*entertainer*) artiste *mf.*

**perfume** parfum *m.*

**perhaps** *adv* peut-être; **p. not** peut-être que non.

**peril** péril *m.*

**period** période *f*; (*historical*) époque *f*; (*lesson*) leçon *f*; (*punctuation mark*) point *m*; **(monthly) period(s)** (*of woman*) règles *fpl.*

**periodical** périodique *m.*

**perk** (*in job*) avantage *m* en nature.

**perk up** (*become livelier*) reprendre du poil de la bête.

**perm 1** *n* permanente *f.* **2** *vt* **to have one's hair permed** se faire faire une permanente.

**permanent** *a* permanent; (*address*) fixe.

**permanently** *adv* à titre permanent.

**permission** *f* (**to do** de faire); **to ask p.** demander la permission.

**permit 1** *vt* permettre (**s.o. to do** à qn de faire). **2** *n* permis *m*; (*entrance pass*) laissez-passer *m inv.*

**perpendicular** *a* perpendiculaire (**to** à).

**persecute** *vt* persécuter.

**persecution** persécution *f.*

**perseverance** persévérance *f.*

**persevere** *vi* persévérer (**in** dans).

**persist** *vi* persister (**in doing** à faire, **in sth** dans qch).

**persistent** *a* (*person*) obstiné; (*noise etc*) continuel.

**person** personne *f*; **in p.** en personne.

**personal** *a* personnel; (*application*) en personne; (*friend*) intime; (*life*) privé; (*indiscreet*) indiscret.

**personality** personnalité *f.*

**personally** *adv* personnellement; (*in person*) en personne.

**personnel** personnel *m.*

**persuade** *vt* persuader (**s.o. to do** qn de faire).

**persuasion** persuasion *f.*

**pessimist to be a p.** être pessimiste.

**pessimistic** *a* pessimiste.

**pest** animal *m or* insecte *m* nuisible; (*person*) casse-pieds *mf inv.*

**pester** *vt* harceler (**with questions** de questions); **to p. s.o. to do sth/for sth** harceler qn pour qu'il fasse qch/jusqu'à ce qu'il donne qch.

**pet 1** *n* animal *m* (domestique); (*favorite person*) chouchou, -oute *mf.* **2** *a* (*dog, cat etc*) domestique; (*favorite*) favori (*f* -ite).

**petal** pétale *m.*

**petition** (*signatures*) pétition *f.*

**petticoat** jupon *m.*

**petty** *a* (*minor*) petit; (*mean*) mesquin; **p. cash** petite caisse *f.*

**pharmacist** pharmacien, -ienne *mf.*

**pharmacy** pharmacie *f.*

**phase** phase *f.*

**phase sth in/out** introduire/supprimer qch progressivement.

**PhD** *abbr* (*university degree*) doctorat *m.*

**pheasant** faisan *m.*

**phenomenal** *a* phénoménal.

**phenomenon** (*pl* **-ena**) phénomène *m.*

**philosopher** philosophe *mf.*

**philosophical** *a* philosophique; (*resigned*) philosophe.

**philosophy** philosophie *f.*

**phlegm** (*in throat*) glaires *fpl*.
**phone 1** *n* téléphone *m*; **on the p.** au téléphone; (*at other end*) au bout du fil. **2** *vt* téléphoner à. **3** *vi* téléphoner.
**phone back** *vti* rappeler.
**phone book** annuaire *m*.
**phone booth** cabine *f* téléphonique.
**phone call** coup *m* de fil; **to make a p. call** téléphoner (**to** à).
**phone number** numéro *m* de téléphone.
**phonetic** *a* phonétique.
**photo** (*pl* **-os**) photo *f*; **to take a p. of** prendre une photo de; **to have one's p. taken** se faire prendre en photo.
**photocopier** photocopieuse *f*.
**photocopy 1** *n* photocopie *f*. **2** *vt* photocopier.
**photograph** photographie *f*.
**photographer** photographe *mf*.
**photographic** *a* photographique.
**photography** photographie *f*.
**phrase** expression *f*; (*idiom*) locution *f*.
**phrasebook** manuel *m* de conversation.
**physical** *a* physique; **p. examination** examen *m* médical; **P. Education** education *f* physique.
**physics** physique *f*.
**pianist** pianiste *mf*.
**piano** (*pl* **-os**) piano *m*.
**pick 1** *n* **to take one's p.** faire son choix. **2** *vt* choisir; (*flower, fruit*) cueillir; (*hole*) faire (**in** dans); **to p. one's nose** se mettre les doigts dans le nez.
**pickax** pioche *f*.
**pickle** cornichon *m*.
**pickled** *a* (*onion etc*) au vinaigre.
**pick sth off** enlever qch.
**pick on s.o.** s'en prendre à qn.
**pick out** choisir; (*identify*) reconnaître.
**pickpocket** pickpocket *m*.
**pick up 1** *vt* (*sth dropped*) ramasser; (*fallen person or chair*) relever; (*person into air, weight*) soulever; (*a cold*) attraper; (*habit, accent, speed*) prendre; (*fetch*) (passer) prendre; (*find*) trouver; (*learn*) apprendre. **2** *vi* (*improve*) s'améliorer; (*of business*) reprendre; (*of patient*) aller mieux.
**picnic** pique-nique *m*.
**picture 1** *n* image *f*; (*painting*) tableau *m*; (*photo*) photo *f*; (*film*) film *m*. **2** *vt* (*imagine*) s'imaginer (**that** que).
**picture frame** cadre *m*.
**picturesque** *a* pittoresque.
**pie** (*open*) tarte *f*; (*with pastry on top*) tourte *f*.
**piece** morceau *m*; (*of fabric, machine, in game*) pièce *f*; (*coin*) pièce *f*; **in pieces** en morceaux; **to take to pieces** (*machine*) démonter; **a p. of news**/*etc* une nouvelle/*etc*; **in one p.** intact; (*person*) indemne.
**pier** jetée *f*.
**pierce** *vt* percer (*qch*).
**piercing** *a* (*cry, cold*) perçant.
**pig** cochon *m*.
**pigeon** pigeon *m*.
**pigeonhole** casier *m*.
**piggyback to give s.o. a p.** porter qn sur le dos.
**piggybank** tirelire *f*.
**pigtail** (*hair*) natte *f*.
**pile 1** *n* tas *m*; (*neatly arranged*) pile *f*; **piles of** *Fam* beaucoup de. **2** *vt* entasser; (*neatly*) empiler.
**pile into** (*crowd into*) s'entasser dans.
**piles** *npl* (*illness*) hémorroïdes *fpl*.
**pile up 1** *vt* entasser; (*neatly*) empiler. **2** *vi* s'accumuler.
**pileup** (*on road*) carambolage *m*.
**pill** pilule *f*; **to be on the p.** prendre la pilule.
**pillar** pilier *m*.
**pillow** oreiller *m*.
**pillowcase** taie *f* d'oreiller.
**pilot** pilote *m*.
**pimple** bouton *m*.
**pin** épingle *f*; (*drawing pin*) punaise *f*.

**pin (on)** épingler (**to** sur, à); (*to wall*) punaiser (**to, on** à).
**pinafore** (*apron*) tablier *m*.
**pinball** flipper *m*; **p. machine** flipper *m*.
**pincers** *npl* (*tool*) tenailles *fpl*.
**pinch 1** *n* (*of salt*) pincée *f*; **to give s.o. a p.** pincer qn. **2** *vt* pincer; (*steal*) *Fam* piquer (**from** à).
**pincushion** pelote *f* (à épingles).
**pine** pin *m*.
**pineapple** ananas *m*.
**pink** *a* & *n* (*color*) rose (*m*).
**pinkie** petit doigt *m*.
**pint** pinte *f* (= *0, 47 litre*); **a p. of beer** = un demi.
**pin up** (*on wall*) punaiser (**on** à); (*notice*) afficher.
**pipe** tuyau *m*; (*of smoker*) pipe *f*; **to smoke a p.** fumer la pipe.
**pirate** pirate *m*.
**pistachio** pistache *f*.
**pistol** pistolet *m*.
**pit** (*hole*) trou *m*; (*coalmine*) mine *f*; (*quarry*) carrière *f*; (*stone of fruit*) noyau *m*; (*smaller*) pépin *m*.
**pitch** *vt* (*tent*) dresser; (*ball*) lancer.
**pitch-black, pitch-dark** *a* noir comme dans un four.
**pity 1** *n* pitié *f*; **(what) a p.!** (quel) dommage!; **it's a p.** c'est dommage (**that** que (+ *subjunctive*), **to do** de faire). **2** *vt* plaindre.
**pizza** pizza *f*.
**placard** (*notice*) affiche *f*.
**place 1** *n* endroit *m*, lieu *m*; (*house*) maison *f*; (*seat, position, rank*) place *f*; **in the first p.** en premier lieu; **to take p.** avoir lieu; **p. of work** lieu *m* de travail; **market p.** place *f* du marché; **at my p., to my p.** (*house*) chez moi; **all over the p.** partout; **to take the p. of** remplacer; **in p. of** à la place de. **2** *vt* placer; (*an order*) passer (**with s.o.** à qn); **to p. s.o.** (*identify*) remettre qn.
**place mat** set *m* (de table).
**place setting** couvert *m*.
**plague 1** *n* peste *f*; (*nuisance*) plaie *f*. **2** *vt* harceler (**with** de).
**plain[1]** *a* (*clear*) clair; (*simple*) simple; (*madness*) pur; (*without pattern*) uni; (*woman, man*) sans beauté; **to make it p. to s.o. that** faire comprendre à qn que.
**plain[2]** plaine *f*.
**plainly** *adv* clairement; (*frankly*) franchement.
**plait 1** *n* tresse *f*. **2** *vt* tresser.
**plan 1** *n* projet *m*; (*economic, of house etc*) plan *m*; **according to p.** comme prévu. **2** *vt* (*foresee*) prévoir; (*organize*) organiser; (*design*) concevoir; **to p. to do** *or* **on doing** avoir l'intention de faire; **as planned** comme prévu.
**plane** (*aircraft*) avion *m*; (*tool*) rabot *m*.
**planet** planète *f*.
**plane tree** platane *m*.
**plan for** (*rain, disaster*) prévoir.
**plank** planche *f*.
**plant 1** *n* plante *f*; (*factory*) usine *f*; **house p.** plante verte. **2** *vt* (*flower etc*) planter.
**plaster** plâtre *m*; **in p.** dans le plâtre.
**plastic 1** *a* (*object*) en plastique. **2** *n* plastique *m*.
**plastic bag** sac *m* en plastique.
**plastic surgery** chirurgie *f* esthétique.
**plastic wrap** film *m* alimentaire.
**plate** (*dish*) assiette *f*; (*metal sheet*) plaque *f*.
**platform** (*at train station*) quai *m*; (*on bus etc*) plate-forme *f*; (*for speaker etc*) estrade *f*.
**play 1** *n* (*in theater*) pièce *f* (de théâtre). **2** *vt* (*part, tune etc*) jouer; (*game*) jouer à; (*instrument*) jouer de; (*team*) jouer contre; (*record, compact disc*) passer; **to p. a part in doing/in sth** contribuer à faire/à qch. **3** *vi* jouer (**at** à); (*of tape recorder etc*) marcher; **what are you playing at?** qu'est-ce que tu fais?; **what's playing?** (*at movies etc*) qu'est-ce qu'on joue?
**play around** *vi* jouer.
**play back** (*tape*) réécouter.

**play down** minimiser.
**player** (*in game, of instrument*) joueur, -euse *mf*; **cassette/CD p.** lecteur *m* de cassettes/CD.
**playground** (*in school*) cour *f* de récréation; (*with swings etc*) terrain *m* de jeux.
**playing card** carte *f* à jouer.
**playing field** terrain *m* de jeux.
**playpen** parc *m* (pour enfants).
**playschool** garderie *f* (d'enfants).
**playtime** récréation *f*.
**pleasant** *a* agréable.
**pleasantly** *adv* agréablement.
**please 1** *adv* s'il vous plaît, s'il te plaît. **2** *vt* **to p. s.o.** plaire à qn; (*satisfy*) contenter qn. **3** *vi* plaire; **do as you p.** fais comme tu veux.
**pleased** *a* content (**with** de, **that** que (+ *subjunctive*), **to do** de faire); **p. to meet you!** enchanté!
**pleasing** *a* agréable.
**pleasure** plaisir *m*.
**pleat** (*in skirt*) pli *m*.
**pleated** *a* plissé.
**plentiful** *a* abondant.
**plenty p. of** beaucoup de; **that's p.** c'est assez.
**pliers** *npl* pince(s) *f*(*pl*).
**plot 1** *n* complot *m* (**against** contre); **p. (of land)** terrain *m*. **2** *vti* comploter (**to do** de faire).
**plot (out)** (*route*) déterminer.
**plow 1** *n* charrue *f*. **2** *vt* (*field*) labourer.
**pluck** *vt* (*fowl*) plumer; (*flower*) cueillir.
**plug** (*of cotton wool*) tampon *m*; (*for sink, bath*) bonde *f*; (*electrical*) fiche *f*, prise *f* (*mâle*); (*socket*) prise *f* de courant; **(wall) p.** (*for screw*) cheville *f*.
**plug (up)** boucher.
**plug in** (*radio etc*) brancher.
**plum** prune *f*.
**plumber** plombier *m*.
**plumbing** plomberie *f*.
**plump** *a* potelé.
**plunge 1** *vt* plonger (**into** dans). **2** *vi* (*dive*) plonger (**into** dans); (*fall*) tomber (**from** de).
**plural 1** *a* (*form*) pluriel; (*noun*) au pluriel. **2** *n* pluriel *m*; **in the p.** au pluriel.
**plus 1** *prep* plus; **two p. two** deux plus deux. **2** *a* **twenty p.** vingt et quelques.
**p.m.** *adv* de l'après-midi; (*evening*) du soir.
**poach** *vt* (*egg*) pocher.
**PO Box** boîte *f* postale.
**pocket** poche *f*; **p. money**/*etc* argent *m*/*etc* de poche.
**pocketbook** (*handbag*) sac *m* à main.
**pocketful a p. of** une pleine poche de.
**pocketknife** (*pl* **-knives**) canif *m*.
**poem** poème *m*.
**poet** poète *m*.
**poetic** *a* poétique.
**poetry** poésie *f*.
**point 1** *n* (*position, score etc*) point *m*; (*decimal*) virgule *f*; (*meaning*) sens *m*; (*of knife etc*) pointe *f*; **points** (*for train*) aiguillage *m*; **p. of view** point *m* de vue; **at this p. (in time)** en ce moment; **what's the p.?** à quoi bon? (**of waiting**/*etc* attendre/*etc*); **there's no p. (in) staying**/*etc* ça ne sert à rien de rester/*etc*. **2** *vt* (*aim*) pointer (**at** sur); **to p. one's finger (at)** montrer du doigt.
**point (at** *or* **to)** (*with finger*) montrer du doigt.
**pointed** *a* pointu.
**pointless** *a* inutile.
**point out** (*show*) indiquer; (*mention*) signaler (**that** que).
**point to** (*indicate*) indiquer.
**poison 1** *n* poison *m*; (*of snake*) venin *m*. **2** *vt* empoisonner.
**poisonous** *a* toxique; (*snake*) venimeux; (*plant*) vénéneux.
**poke** *vt* pousser (*du doigt etc*); (*fire*) tisonner; **to p. sth into sth** fourrer qch dans qch; **to p. one's head out of the window** passer la tête par la fenêtre.
**poke around in** (*drawer etc*) fouiner dans.

**poker** (*for fire*) tisonnier *m*.
**polar bear** ours *m* blanc.
**Pole** *n* Polonais, -aise *mf*.
**pole** (*rod*) perche *f*; (*fixed*) poteau *m*; (*for flag*) mât *m*; **North/South P.** pôle Nord/Sud.
**police** police *f*.
**police car** voiture *f* de police.
**police force** police *f*.
**policeman** (*pl* **-men**) agent *m* de police.
**policewoman** (*pl* **-women**) femme-agent *f*.
**policy** (*plan etc*) politique *f*; **(insurance) p.** police *f* (d'assurance).
**polio** polio *f*.
**Polish 1** *a* polonais. **2** *n* (*language*) polonais *m*.
**polish 1** *vt* cirer; (*metal*) astiquer; (*rough surface*) polir. **2** *n* (*for shoes*) cirage *m*; (*for floor etc*) cire *f*; (*shine*) vernis *m*; **to give sth a p.** faire briller qch.
**polish off** (*food etc*) *Fam* liquider.
**polish up** (*one's French etc*) travailler.
**polite** *a* poli (**to, with** avec).
**politely** *adv* poliment.
**politeness** politesse *f*.
**political** *a* politique.
**politician** homme *m or* femme *f* politique.
**politics** politique *f*.
**poll** (*voting*) scrutin *m*; **to go to the polls** aller aux urnes; **(opinion) p.** sondage *m* (d'opinion).
**pollen** pollen *m*.
**polling place** bureau *m* de vote.
**polls** urnes *fpl*; **to go to the p.** aller aux urnes.
**pollute** *vt* polluer.
**pollution** pollution *f*.
**polo shirt** polo *m*.
**polyester 1** *n* polyester *m*. **2** *a* (*shirt etc*) en polyester.
**polytechnic p. institute** institut *m* universitaire de technologie.
**pomegranate** (*fruit*) grenade *f*.
**pond** étang *m*; (*artificial*) bassin *m*.
**pony** poney *m*.
**ponytail** (*hair*) queue *f* de cheval.
**poodle** caniche *m*.
**pool** (*puddle*) flaque *f*; (*for swimming*) piscine *f*; (*billiards*) billard *m* américain.
**pooped** *a* (*tired*) *Fam* vanné.
**poor 1** *a* pauvre; (*bad*) mauvais; (*weak*) faible. **2** *n* **the p.** les pauvres *mpl*.
**poorly** *adv* (*badly*) mal.
**pop[1] 1** *vti* (*burst*) crever. **2** *vt* (*put*) *Fam* mettre.
**pop[2] 1** *n* (*music*) pop *m*; (*drink*) soda *m*; (*father*) *Fam* papa *m*. **2** *a* (*concert etc*) pop *inv*.
**popcorn** pop-corn *m*.
**pope** pape *m*.
**pop in/out** entrer/sortir un instant.
**pop over** faire un saut (**to** chez).
**poppy** coquelicot *m*.
**popsicle**® glace *f* à eau.
**popular** *a* populaire; (*fashionable*) à la mode; **to be p. with** plaire beaucoup à.
**populated** *a* **highly/sparsely**/*etc* **p.** très/peu/*etc* peuplé; **p. by** peuplé de.
**population** population *f*.
**porch** porche *m*; (*veranda*) véranda *f*.
**pork** (*meat*) porc *m*.
**porridge** porridge *m* (*bouillie de flocons d'avoine*).
**port** (*harbor*) port *m*.
**portable** *a* portable, portatif.
**porter** (*for luggage*) porteur *m*.
**porthole** hublot *m*.
**portion** (*share*) portion *f*; (*of train, book etc*) partie *f*.
**portrait** portrait *m*.
**Portuguese 1** *a* & *n inv* portugais, -aise (*mf*). **2** *n* (*language*) portugais *m*.
**pose 1** *n* (*of model*) pose *f*. **2** *vi* poser (**for** pour).
**posh** *a Fam* (*elegant*) chic *inv*.
**position** position *f*; (*job, circumstances*) situation *f*; **in a p. to do** en mesure de faire.
**positive** *a* positif; (*progress,

*change*) réel; (*answer*) affirmatif; (*sure*) certain (**of** de, **that** que).

**possess** *vt* posséder.

**possessions** *npl* biens *mpl*.

**possessive** *a* & *n Grammar* possessif (*m*).

**possibility** possibilité *f*.

**possible** *a* possible; **it is p. (for us) to do it** il (nous) est possible de le faire; **it is p. that** il est possible que (+ *subjunctive*); **as far as p.** autant que possible; **if p.** si possible; **as much** *or* **as many as p.** le plus possible.

**possibly** *adv* (*perhaps*) peut-être; **if you p. can** si cela t'est possible; **to do all one p. can** faire tout son possible.

**post**[1] (*job, place*) poste *m*.

**post**[2] (*pole*) poteau *m*; (*of door*) montant *m*.

**post (up)** (*notice etc*) afficher.

**postage** tarif *m* (postal) (**to** pour).

**postage stamp** timbre-poste *m*.

**postal** *a* (*services etc*) postal.

**postcard** carte *f* postale.

**poster** affiche *f*; (*for decoration*) poster *m*.

**postgraduate** étudiant, -ante *mf* de troisième cycle.

**postman** (*pl* **-men**) facteur *m*.

**postmark** cachet *m* de la poste.

**post office** (bureau *m* de) poste *f*.

**postpone** *vt* remettre (**for** de, **until** à).

**postponement** remise *f*.

**pot** pot *m*; (*for cooking*) marmite *f*; (*drug*) *Fam* hasch *m*; **pots and pans** casseroles *fpl*.

**potato** (*pl* **-oes**) pomme *f* de terre.

**potential** 1 *a* (*client, sales*) éventuel. 2 *n* **to have p.** (*of firm etc*) avoir de l'avenir.

**potter** potier *m*.

**pottery** (*art*) poterie *f*; (*objects*) poteries *fpl*; **a piece of p.** une poterie.

**potty** pot *m* (de bébé).

**pouch** petit sac *m*; (*of kangaroo*) poche *f*.

**poultry** volaille *f*.

**pounce** *vi* sauter (**on** sur).

**pound** (*weight*) livre *f* (= *453,6 grammes*); (*money*) livre *f* (sterling); (*for cars, dogs*) fourrière *f*.

**pour** *vt* (*liquid*) verser; **to p. money into sth** investir beaucoup d'argent dans qch.

**pour (down) it's pouring (down)** il pleut à verse.

**pour in** 1 *vt* (*liquid*) verser. 2 *vi* (*of water, rain*) entrer à flots; (*of people*) affluer.

**pour off** (*liquid*) vider.

**pour out** 1 *vt* (*liquid*) verser; (*cup etc*) vider. 2 *vi* (*of liquid*) couler à flots; (*of people*) sortir en masse.

**poverty** pauvreté *f*.

**powder** 1 *n* poudre *f*. 2 *vt* **to p. one's face** se poudrer.

**powdered** *a* (*milk, eggs*) en poudre; **p. sugar** sucre *m* glace.

**power** (*ability, authority*) pouvoir *m*; (*strength, nation*) puissance *f*; (*energy*) énergie *f*; (*current*) courant *m*; **in p.** au pouvoir; **p. outage** coupure *f* de courant.

**powerful** *a* puissant.

**power plant** centrale *f* (électrique).

**practical** *a* pratique.

**practical joke** farce *f*.

**practically** *adv* (*almost*) pratiquement.

**practice** 1 *n* (*exercise, way of proceeding*) pratique *f*; (*habit*) habitude *f*; (*sports training*) entraînement *m*; (*rehearsal*) répétition *f*; **to be out of p.** avoir perdu la pratique. 2 *vt* (*sports, art etc*) pratiquer; (*medicine, law*) exercer; (*flute, piano etc*) s'exercer à; (*language*) (s'exercer à) parler (**on** avec). 3 *vi* s'exercer; (*of doctor, lawyer*) exercer.

**praise** 1 *vt* louer (**for sth** de qch); **to p. s.o. for doing** louer qn d'avoir fait. 2 *n* louange(s) *f*(*pl*).

**prank** (*trick*) farce *f*.

**prawn** crevette *f* (rose).

**pray** 1 *vi* prier; **to p. for good weather/a miracle** prier pour avoir du beau temps/pour un miracle. **2** *vt* **to p. that** prier pour que (+ *subjunctive*).

**prayer** prière *f*.

**precaution** précaution *f* (**of doing** de faire); **as a p.** par précaution.

**precede** *vti* précéder.

**preceding** *a* précédent.

**precious** *a* précieux.

**precise** *a* précis; (*person*) minutieux.

**precocious** *a* (*child*) précoce.

**predecessor** prédécesseur *m*.

**predicament** situation *f* fâcheuse.

**predict** *vt* prédire.

**predictable** *a* prévisible.

**prediction** prédiction *f*.

**preface** préface *f*.

**prefer** *vt* préférer (**to** à); **to p. to do** préférer faire.

**preferable** *a* préférable (**to** à).

**preferably** *adv* de préférence.

**preference** préférence *f* (**for** pour).

**prefix** préfixe *m*.

**pregnancy** grossesse *f*.

**pregnant** *a* (*woman*) enceinte; **five months p.** enceinte de cinq mois.

**prehistoric** *a* préhistorique.

**prejudice** préjugé *m*; **to be full of p.** être plein de préjugés.

**preliminary** *a* préliminaire.

**premises** *npl* locaux *mpl*; **on the p.** sur les lieux.

**premium (insurance) p.** prime *f* (d'assurance).

**preparation** préparation *f*; **preparations** préparatifs *mpl* (**for** de).

**prepare 1** *vt* préparer (**sth for** qch pour, **s.o. for** qn à); **to p. to do** se préparer à faire. **2** *vi* **to p. for** (*journey, occasion*) faire des préparatifs pour; (*exam*) préparer.

**prepared** *a* (*ready*) prêt (**to do** à faire); **to be p. for sth** (*expect*) s'attendre à qch.

**preposition** *Grammar* préposition *f*.

**prep school** école *f* secondaire privée.

**prescribe** *vt* (*of doctor*) prescrire.

**prescription** (*for medicine*) ordonnance *f*.

**presence** présence *f*; **in the p. of** en présence de.

**present[1] 1** *a* (*not absent*) présent (**at** à, **in** dans); (*year, state, job, house etc*) actuel. **2** *n* (*gift*) cadeau *m*; **present (tense)** présent *m*; **at p.** à présent.

**present[2]** *vt* présenter (**to** à); **to p. s.o. with** (*gift*) offrir à qn; (*prize*) remettre à qn.

**presentation** présentation *f*; (*of prize*) remise *f*.

**presently** *adv* (*soon*) tout à l'heure; (*now*) à présent.

**preservation** conservation *f*.

**preservative** agent *m* de conservation.

**preserve 1** *vt* (*keep*) conserver. **2** *n* (*jam*) confiture *f*.

**presidency** présidence *f*.

**president** président, -ente *mf*.

**presidential** *a* présidentiel.

**press[1] 1** *n* (*newspapers, machine*) presse *f*. **2** *a* (*conference etc*) de presse.

**press[2] 1** *vt* (*button etc*) appuyer sur; (*clothes*) repasser; **to p. s.o. to do** (*urge*) presser qn de faire. **2** *vi* (*with finger*) appuyer (**on** sur); (*of weight*) faire pression (**on** sur).

**press down** (*button etc*) appuyer sur.

**pressed** *a* **to be p. (for time)** être très bousculé.

**press on** (*carry on*) continuer (**with sth** qch).

**pressure** pression *f*; **the p. of work** le surmenage; **under p.** (*worker, to work*) sous pression.

**pressure cooker** cocotte-minute® *f*.

**presume** *vt* présumer (**that** que).

**pretend** *vti* (*make believe*) faire semblant (**to do** de faire, **that** que).

**pretext** prétexte *m*; **on the p. of/that** sous prétexte de/que.

**pretty 1** *a* joli. **2** *adv* (*rather, quite*) assez; **p. well, p. much** (*almost*) pratiquement.

**prevent** *vt* empêcher (**from doing** de faire).
**prevention** prévention *f*.
**previous** *a* précédent; (*experience*) préalable; **p. to** avant.
**previously** *adv* avant.
**prey** proie *f*; **bird of p.** rapace *m*.
**price** prix *m*.
**price list** tarif *m*.
**prick** *vt* piquer (**with** avec); (*burst*) crever.
**prickly** *a* (*plant, beard*) piquant.
**pride** (*satisfaction*) fierté *f*; (*exaggerated*) orgueil *m*; (*self-respect*) amour-propre *m*; **to take p. in** être fier de; (*take care of*) prendre soin de.
**pride oneself on sth/on doing** s'enorgueillir de qch/de faire.
**priest** prêtre *m*.
**primarily** *adv* essentiellement.
**primary school** école *f* primaire.
**prime minister** premier ministre *m*.
**prime number** nombre *m* premier.
**primitive** *a* primitif.
**primrose** primevère *f*.
**prince** prince *m*.
**princess** princesse *f*.
**principal** (*of school*) directeur, -trice *mf*.
**print 1** *n* (*of finger, foot etc*) empreinte *f*; (*letters*) caractères *mpl*; (*engraving*) gravure *f*; (*photo*) épreuve *f*; **out of p.** épuisé; **p. shop** imprimerie *f*. **2** *vt* (*book etc*) imprimer; (*photo*) tirer; (*write*) écrire en caractères d'imprimerie; **printing plant** imprimerie *f*.
**printer** (*of computer*) imprimante *f*.
**print out** *vti* (*of computer*) imprimer.
**printout** (*of computer*) sortie *f* sur imprimante.
**prior** *a* précédent; (*experience*) préalable.
**priority** priorité *f* (**over** sur).
**prison** prison *f*; **in p.** en prison.
**prisoner** prisonnier, -ière *mf*; **to take s.o. p.** faire qn prisonnier.
**privacy** intimité *f*.
**private 1** *a* privé; (*lesson, car, secretary etc*) particulier; (*report*) confidentiel; (*dinner etc*) intime. **2** *n* (*soldier*) (simple) soldat *m*; **in p.** en privé; (*to have dinner etc*) dans l'intimité.
**privately** *adv* en privé; (*to have dinner etc*) dans l'intimité.
**prize** prix *m*; (*in lottery*) lot *m*.
**prize-winner** lauréat, -ate *mf*; (*in lottery*) gagnant, -ante *mf*.
**probable** *a* probable (**that** que); (*convincing*) vraisemblable.
**probably** *adv* probablement.
**problem** problème *m*; **no p.!** *Fam* pas de problème!; **to have a p. doing** avoir du mal à faire.
**proceed** *vi* (*go*) avancer; (*act*) procéder; (*continue*) continuer.
**process** (*method*) procédé *m* (**for doing** pour faire); (*chemical, economic etc*) processus *m*; **in the p. of doing** en train de faire.
**processed cheese** = fromage *m* fondu.
**procession** cortège *m*.
**produce 1** *vt* (*manufacture, cause etc*) produire; (*bring out*) sortir (*pistolet, mouchoir etc*); (*passport*) présenter. **2** *n* produits *mpl*.
**producer** (*of goods, film*) producteur, -trice *mf*.
**product** produit *m*.
**production** production *f*; (*of play*) mise *f* en scène.
**profession** profession *f*.
**professional 1** *a* professionnel; (*piece of work*) de professionnel. **2** *n* professionnel, -elle *mf*.
**professor** professeur *m* (d'université).
**profit 1** *n* profit *m*, bénéfice *m*; **to sell at a p.** vendre à profit. **2** *vi* **to p. by** *or* **from sth** tirer profit de qch.
**profitable** *a* rentable.
**program 1** *n* (*schedule, of computer*) programme *m*. **2** *vt* programmer.
**program** programme *m*; (*broadcast*) emission *f*.

**progress 1** *n* progrès *m(pl)*; **to make p.** faire des progrès; (*when driving etc*) bien avancer; **in p.** en cours. **2** *vi* progresser; (*of story, meeting*) se dérouler.
**prohibit** *vt* interdire (**s.o. from doing** à qn de faire).
**project** projet *m* (**for sth** pour qch); (*at school*) étude *f*.
**projector** (*for films etc*) projecteur *m*.
**prolong** *vt* prolonger.
**prominent** *a* (*person*) important.
**promise 1** *n* promesse *f*; **to show p.** être prometteur. **2** *vt* promettre (**s.o. sth, sth to s.o.** qch à qn; **to do** de faire; **that** que). **3** *vi* **I p.!** je te le promets!; **p.?** promis?
**promising** *a* (*situation*) prometteur (*f*-euse).
**promote** *vt* **to p. s.o.** (*in job etc*) donner de l'avancement à qn.
**promotion** (*of person*) avancement *m*.
**prompt** *a* (*speedy*) rapide.
**prone** *a* **p. to** (*illnesses, accidents*) prédisposé à.
**pronoun** pronom *m*.
**pronounce** *vt* prononcer.
**pronunciation** prononciation *f*.
**proof** (*evidence*) preuve(s) *f*(*pl*).
**propeller** hélice *f*.
**proper** *a* (*suitable, respectable*) convenable; (*downright*) véritable; (*noun, meaning*) propre; **the p. address/method**/*etc* (*correct*) la bonne adresse/méthode/*etc*.
**properly** *adv* comme il faut, convenablement.
**property** (*building, possessions*) propriété *f*.
**proportion** (*ratio*) proportion *f*; (*portion*) partie *f*; **proportions** (*size*) dimensions *fpl*.
**proposal** proposition *f*; (*of marriage*) demande *f* (en mariage).
**propose 1** *vt* (*suggest*) proposer (**to** à, **that** que (+ *subjunctive*)). **2** *vi* faire une demande (en mariage) (**to** à).
**props** *npl* (*in theater*) accessoires *mpl*.
**prop up** (*ladder etc*) appuyer (**against** contre); (*one's head*) caler; (*wall*) étayer.
**prose** *n* prose *f*.
**prospect** (*outlook, possibility*) perspective *f* (**of** de); **(future) prospects** perspectives *fpl* d'avenir.
**prosperous** *a* riche.
**protect** *vt* protéger (**from** de, **against** contre).
**protection** protection *f*.
**protective** *a* (*clothes etc*) de protection.
**protest 1** *n* protestation *f* (**against** contre); (*demonstration*) manifestation *f*. **2** *vi* protester (**against** contre); (*of students etc*) contester.
**Protestant** *a* & *n* protestant, -ante (*mf*).
**protester** (*student etc*) contestataire *mf*.
**protractor** (*for measuring*) rapporteur *m*.
**proud** *a* fier (**of** de, **to do** de faire); (*superior to others*) orgueilleux.
**proudly** *adv* fièrement; orgueilleusement.
**prove 1** *vt* prouver (**that** que). **2** *vi* **to p. difficult**/*etc* s'avérer difficile/*etc*.
**proverb** proverbe *m*.
**provide** *vt* (*supply*) fournir (**s.o. with sth** qch à qn); **to p. s.o. with sth** (*equip*) pourvoir qn de qch.
**provided, providing** *conj* **p. (that)** pourvu que (+ *subjunctive*).
**provide for s.o.** pourvoir aux besoins de qn; (*s.o.'s future*) assurer l'avenir de qn.
**province** province *f*; **the provinces** la province.
**provincial** *a* provincial.
**provoke** *vt* (*annoy*) agacer.
**prowl (around)** *vi* rôder.
**prowler** rôdeur, -euse *mf*.
**prune 1** *n* pruneau *m*. **2** *vt* (*tree, bush*) tailler.
**pruning shears** sécateur *m*.
**psychiatrist** psychiatre *mf*.
**psychological** *a* psychologique.
**psychologist** psychologue *mf*.
**pub** pub *m* .

**public 1** *a* public (*f* -ique); (*library, swimming pool*) municipal. **2** *n* public *m*; **in p.** en public.
**publication** publication *f.*
**publicity** publicité *f.*
**publish** *vt* publier; (*book, author*) éditer.
**publisher** éditeur, -trice *mf.*
**publishing** (*profession*) édition *f.*
**pudding** pudding *m*; **rice p.** riz *m* au lait.
**puddle** flaque *f* (d'eau).
**puff 1** *n* (*of smoke, wind*) bouffée *f.* **2** *vi* souffler.
**puff at** (*cigar etc*) tirer sur.
**pull 1** *n* **to give sth a p.** tirer qch. **2** *vt* tirer; (*trigger*) appuyer sur; (*tooth*) arracher; (*muscle*) se claquer; **to p. apart** *or* **to pieces** mettre en pièces. **3** *vi* tirer (**at, on** sur); (*go, move*) aller.
**pull along** traîner (**to** jusqu'à).
**pull away 1** *vt* (*move*) éloigner; (*snatch*) arracher (**from** à). **2** *vi* (*in vehicle*) démarrer; **to p. away from** s'éloigner de.
**pull back 1** *vi* se retirer. **2** *vt* retirer; (*curtains*) ouvrir.
**pull down** baisser; (*knock down*) faire tomber; (*demolish*) démolir.
**pull in 1** *vt* (*into room etc*) faire entrer (de force); (*crowd*) attirer. **2** *vi* arriver; (*stop in vehicle*) se garer.
**pull off** (*remove*) enlever.
**pull on** (*boots etc*) mettre.
**pull out 1** *vt* (*tooth, hair*) arracher; (*cork, pin*) enlever; (*from pocket etc*) tirer, sortir (**from** de). **2** *vi* (*move out in vehicle*) déboîter; (*withdraw*) se retirer (**from, of** de).
**pull over 1** *vt* traîner (**to** jusqu'à); (*knock down*) faire tomber. **2** *vi* (*in vehicle*) se ranger (sur le côté).
**pullover** pull(-over) *m.*
**pull through** *vi* s'en tirer.
**pull up 1** *vt* (*socks, sleeve, collar, shade*) remonter, relever; (*plant, tree*) arracher; (*chair*) approcher. **2** *vi* (*in vehicle*) s'arrêter.
**pulse** pouls *m.*
**pump 1** *n* pompe *f*; **(air) p.** (*in service station*) gonfleur *m.* **2** *vt* pomper.
**pumpkin** potiron *m*, citrouille *f.*
**pump up** (*mattress etc*) gonfler.
**punch[1] 1** *n* (*blow*) coup *m* de poing. **2** *vt* donner un coup de poing à (*qn*).
**punch[2] 1** *n* (*for paper*) perforeuse *f.* **2** *vt* (*ticket*) poinçonner; (*with date*) composter; **to p. a hole in sth** faire un trou dans qch.
**punctual** *a* (*on time*) à l'heure; (*regularly*) ponctuel.
**punctuation** ponctuation *f.*
**puncture 1** *n* crevaison *f*; **2** *vti* (*burst*) crever.
**punish** *vt* punir (**for sth** de qch, **for doing** pour avoir fait).
**punishment** punition *f.*
**pupil** élève *mf*; (*of eye*) pupille *f.*
**puppet** marionnette *f.*
**pup(py)** (*dog*) chiot *m.*
**purchase 1** *n* achat *m.* **2** *vt* acheter (**from s.o.** à qn, **for s.o.** à *or* pour qn).
**pure** *a* pur.
**purely** *adv* (*only*) strictement.
**purple 1** *a* violet (*f* -ette). **2** *n* violet *m.*
**purpose** (*aim*) but *m*; **for this p.** dans ce but; **on p.** exprès.
**purposely** *adv* exprès.
**purse** (*for coins*) porte-monnaie *m inv*; (*handbag*) sac *m* à main.
**pursue** *vt* (*inquiry, aim etc*) poursuivre.
**push 1** *n* **to give s.o./sth a p.** pousser qn/qch. **2** *vt* pousser (**to, as far as** jusqu'à); **to p. sth into/between** enfoncer qch dans/entre; **to p. s.o. into doing** pousser qn à faire. **3** *vi* pousser.
**push (down)** (*button*) appuyer sur; (*lever*) abaisser.
**push around** (*bully*) marcher sur les pieds à (*qn*).
**push aside** écarter.
**push away** *or* **back** *vt* repousser.
**push-button** bouton *m*; (*of phone*) touche *f*; **p.-button phone** téléphone *m* à touches.
**push on** continuer (**with sth** qch).

**push over** renverser.
**push (one's way) through** se frayer un chemin (**a crowd** à travers une foule).
**push up** (*lever, sleeve, collar*) relever; (*increase*) augmenter.
**puss** (*cat*) minou *m*.
**put*** *vt* mettre; (*money*) placer (**into** dans); (*question*) poser (**to** à); (*say*) dire.
**put across** *vt* (*message etc*) communiquer (**to** à).
**put aside** (*money, object*) mettre de côté.
**put away** *vt* (*book, car etc*) ranger; (*criminal*) mettre en prison.
**put back** (*replace, postpone*) remettre; (*telephone receiver*) raccrocher.
**put by** (*money*) mettre de côté.
**put down** (*on floor etc*) poser; (*passenger*) déposer; (*a deposit*) verser; (*write down*) inscrire.
**put forward** (*candidate*) proposer (**for** à).
**put in** (*sth into box etc*) mettre dedans; (*insert*) introduire; (*add*) ajouter; (*install*) installer; (*application*) faire.
**put off** renvoyer (à plus tard); (*gas, radio*) fermer; **to p. s.o. off** dissuader qn (**doing** de faire); (*disgust*) dégoûter qn.
**put on** (*clothes etc*) mettre; (*weight*) prendre; (*gas, radio*) mettre; (*record, cassette*) passer; (*clock*) avancer; (*lid*) mettre en place.
**put out** (*take outside*) sortir; (*arm, leg*) étendre; (*hand*) tendre; (*gas, light*) éteindre; (*bother*) déranger.
**put s.o. through** (*on phone*) passer qn (**to** à).
**put together** mettre ensemble; (*assemble*) assembler; (*compose*) composer.
**putty** mastic *m*.
**put up 1** *vi* (*stay*) descendre (**at a hotel** à un hôtel). **2** *vt* (*lift*) lever; (*window*) remonter; (*tent, statue, ladder*) dresser; (*building*) construire; (*umbrella*) ouvrir; (*picture*) mettre; (*price*) augmenter; (*candidate*) proposer (**for** à); (*guest*) loger.
**put up with sth/s.o.** supporter qch/qn.
**puzzle 1** *n* mystère *m*; (*jigsaw*) puzzle *m*. **2** *vt* laisser perplexe.
**puzzled** *a* perplexe.
**puzzling** *a* curieux.
**pylon** pylône *m*.
**pyramid** pyramide *f*.

# Q

**qualification** diplôme *m*; **qualifications** (*skills*) qualités *fpl* nécessaires (**for** pour, **to do** pour faire).
**qualified** *a* (*able*) qualifié (**to do** pour faire); (*teacher etc*) diplômé.
**qualify** *vi* obtenir son diplôme (**as a doctor**/*etc* de médecin/*etc*); (*in sports*) se qualifier (**for** pour).
**quality** qualité *f*.
**quantity** quantité *f*.
**quarrel 1** *n* dispute *f*; **to pick a q.** chercher des histoires (**with s.o.** à qn). **2** *vi* se disputer (**with s.o.** avec qn).
**quarreling** disputes *fpl*.
**quarry** (*to extract stone etc*) carrière *f*.
**quart** litre *m* (*mesure approximative*) ( = *0,95 litre*).
**quarter**[1] quart *m*; (*money*) quart *m* de dollar; (*of fruit*) quartier *m*; (*of school / fiscal year*) trimestre *m*. **to divide sth into quarters** diviser qch en quatre; **q. (of a) pound** quart *m* de livre; **a q. past** *or* **after nine** neuf heures et quart *or* un quart; **a q. to nine** neuf heures moins le quart.
**quarter**[2] (*district*) quartier *m*.
**quartz** *a* (*watch etc*) à quartz.
**quay** quai *m*, débarcadère *m*.
**queen** reine *f*; (*chess, cards*) dame *f*.
**quench** *vt* **to q. one's thirst** se désaltérer.
**query** (*question*) question *f*.
**question 1** *n* question *f*; **it's out of the q.** il n'en est pas question.

2 *vt* interroger (*qn*) (**about** sur); (*doubt*) mettre (*qch*) en question.

**question mark** point *m* d'interrogation.

**questionnaire** questionnaire *m*.

**quibble** *vi* ergoter (**over** sur).

**quiche** quiche *f*.

**quick 1** *a* rapide; **be q.!** fais vite!; **to have a q. meal**/*etc* manger/*etc* en vitesse. **2** *adv* vite.

**quickly** *adv* vite.

**quiet** *a* (*silent, peaceful*) tranquille; (*machine, vehicle*) silencieux; (*voice, sound*) doux (*f* douce); **to be** *or* **keep q.** (*shut up*) se taire; (*make no noise*) ne pas faire de bruit; **q.!** silence!; **to keep q. about sth** ne pas parler de qch.

**quietly** *adv* tranquillement; (*not loudly*) doucement; (*silently*) silencieusement.

**quilt** couverture piquée (américaine).

**quit* 1 to q. doing** arrêter de faire. **2** *vi* abandonner; (*resign*) démissionner.

**quite** *adv* (*entirely*) tout à fait; (*really*) vraiment; (*rather*) assez; **q. a lot** pas mal (**of** de).

**quiz** (*pl* **quizzes**) (*in school*) contrôle *m*; **q. show** jeu(-concours) *m*.

**quotation** citation *f*; (*estimate*) devis *m*.

**quotation marks** guillemets *mpl*; **in q. marks** entre guillemets.

**quote 1** *vt* citer; (*reference*) rappeler; (*price*) indiquer. **2** *vi* **to q. from** citer. **3** *n* = **quotation**.

# R

**rabbi** rabbin *m*.

**rabbit** lapin *m*.

**rabies** rage *f*.

**race¹ 1** *n* (*contest*) course *f*. **2** *vt* (*horse*) faire courir; **to r. (against** *or* **with) s.o.** faire une course avec qn. **3** *vi* (*run*) courir.

**race²** (*group*) race *f*.

**racecar** voiture *f* de course.

**racecar** [illegible] mobile.

**racehorse** cheval *m* de [illegible]

**racetrack** champ *m* de courses [illegible]

**racial** *a* racial.

**racialism, racism** racisme *m*.

**racing** courses *fpl*.

**racist** *a* & *n* raciste (*mf*).

**rack** (*for bottles, letters etc*) casier *m*; (*for drying dishes*) égouttoir *m*; **(luggage) r.** (*on bus, train*) filet *m* à bagages.

**racket** (*for tennis*) raquette *f*; (*din*) vacarme *m*.

**radar** radar *m*.

**radiator** radiateur *m*.

**radio** (*pl* **-os**) radio *f*; (*set*) poste *m* de radio; **on** *or* **over the r.** à la radio.

**radioactive** *a* radioactif.

**radish** radis *m*.

**radius,** (*pl* **-dii**) (*of circle*) rayon *m*.

**raffle** tombola *f*.

**raft** (*boat*) radeau *m*.

**rag** (*old clothing*) haillon *m*; (*for dusting etc*) chiffon *m*; **in rags** (*clothes*) en loques; (*person*) en haillons.

**rage** rage *f*; **to fly into a r.** se mettre en rage.

**ragged** *a* (*clothes*) en loques; (*person*) en haillons.

**raid 1** *n* (*military*) raid *m*; (*by police*) descente *f*; (*by thieves*) hold-up *m inv*; **air r.** raid *m* aérien. **2** *vt* faire un raid *or* une descente *or* un hold-up dans.

**rail** (*for train*) rail *m*; (*rod on balcony*) balustrade *f*; (*on stairs*) rampe *f*; **by r.** (*to travel*) par le train; (*to send*) par chemin de fer.

**railing** (*of balcony*) balustrade *f*; **railings** (*fence*) grille *f*.

**railroad 1** *n* chemin *m* de fer; **r. (track)** voie *f* ferrée. **2** *a* (*ticket*) de chemin de fer; **r. line** ligne *f* de chemin de fer.

**rain 1** *n* pluie *f*; **in the r.** sous la pluie. **2** *vi* pleuvoir; **it's raining** il pleut.

**rainbow** arc-en-ciel *m*.

dy,
aug-
er; to r.
s. 2 n aug-
e).

**ra**... *m*. 2 *vt* (*garden*) rat...

**rake (u**... *aves*) ratisser.

**rally** (*political*) rassemblement *m*.

**rally around** *or* **round (s.o.)** venir en aide (à qn).

**ram 1** *n* (*animal*) bélier *m*. **2** *vt* (*vehicle*) emboutir; **to r. sth into sth** enfoncer qch dans qch.

**ramble** randonnée *f*.

**ramp** (*slope for wheelchair etc*) rampe *f* (d'accès).

**ran** *pt de* **run.**

**ranch** ranch *m*.

**random 1** *n* **at r.** au hasard. **2** *a* (*choice*) (fait) au hasard; (*sample*) prélevé au hasard; **r. check** (*by police*) contrôle-surprise *m*.

**range 1** *n* (*of gun, voice etc*) portée *f*; (*of singer's voice*) étendue *f*; (*of colors, prices, products*) gamme *f*; (*of sizes*) choix *m*; (*of mountains*) chaîne *f*; (*stove*) cuisinière *f*. **2** *vi* (*vary*) varier (**from** de, **to** à).

**rank** rang *m*.

**ransom** (*money*) rançon *f*.

**rape 1** *vt* violer. **2** *n* viol *m*.

**rapid** *a* rapide.

**rapidly** *adv* rapidement.

**rapist** violeur *m*.

**rare** *a* rare; (*meat*) saignant.

**rarely** *adv* rarement.

**rascal** coquin, -ine *mf*.

**rash 1** *n* éruption *f*. **2** *a* irréfléchi.

**rashly** *adv* sans réfléchir.

**raspberry** framboise *f*; **r. jam** confiture *f* de framboises.

**rat** rat *m*.

**rate 1** *n* (*level*) taux *m*; (*speed*) vitesse *f*; (*price*) tarif *m*; **at the r. of** à une vitesse de; (*amount*) à raison de; **at this r.** (*slow speed*) à ce train-là; **at any r.** en tout cas. **2** *vt* évaluer (**at** à); (*regard*) considérer (**as** comme); (*deserve*) mériter.

**rather** *adv* (*preferably, quite*) plutôt; **I'd r. stay** j'aimerais mieux rester (**than** que); **r. than leave**/*etc* plutôt que de partir/*etc*.

**ratio** (*pl* **-os**) proportion *f*.

**ration 1** *n* ration *f*; **rations** (*food*) vivres *mpl*. **2** *vt* rationner.

**rational** *a* (*person*) raisonnable.

**rationing** rationnement *m*.

**rattle 1** *n* (*baby's toy*) hochet *m*. **2** *vi* faire du bruit; (*of window*) trembler. **3** *vt* (*shake*) secouer.

**ravenous** *a* **I'm r.** j'ai une faim de loup.

**raw** *a* (*vegetable etc*) cru; (*skin*) écorché; **r. material** matière *f* première.

**ray** (*of light, sun*) rayon *m*.

**razor** rasoir *m*.

**re -** *prefix* ré-, re-, r-.

**reach 1** *vt* (*place, distant object, aim*) atteindre; (*gain access to*) accéder à; (*of letter*) parvenir à (*qn*); (*contact*) joindre (*qn*); (*conclusion*) arriver à; **to r.s.o. sth** passer qch à qn. **2** *vi* s'étendre (**to** à); (*with arm*) (é)tendre le bras (**for** pour prendre). **3** *n* portée *f*; **within r. of** à portée de; (*near*) à proximité de; **within (easy) r.** (*object*) à portée de main.

**reach out** *vi* (é)tendre le bras (**for** pour prendre).

**react** *vi* réagir (**against** contre, **to** à).

**reaction** réaction *f*.

**reactor** réacteur *m* (*nucléaire*).

**read* 1** *vt* lire; (*meter*) relever; (*of instrument*) indiquer. **2** *vi* lire; **to r. to s.o.** faire la lecture à qn.

**read about s.o./sth** lire qch sur qn/qch.

**read sth aloud** *or* **out loud** lire qch (à haute voix).

**read sth back** *or* **over** relire qch.

**reader** lecteur, -trice *mf*; (*book*) livre *m* de lecture.

**readily** *adv* (*willingly*) volontiers; (*easily*) facilement.

**reading** lecture *f*; (*of meter*) relevé *m*; (*by instrument*) indication *f*.
**read sth through** parcourir qch.
**read up (on) sth** étudier qch.
**ready** *a* prêt (**to do** à faire, **for sth** à *or* pour qch); **to get sth/s.o. r.** préparer qch/qn; **to get r.** se préparer (**for sth** à *or* pour qch, **to do** à faire); **r. cash** argent *m* liquide.
**ready-made** *a* tout fait.
**ready-to-wear** *a* **r. clothes** prêt-à-porter *m inv*.
**real** *a* vrai; (*life, world*) réel.
**real estate** biens *mpl* immobiliers; **r. estate agent** agent *m* immobilier.
**realistic** *a* réaliste.
**reality** réalité *f*.
**realize** *vt* (*know*) se rendre compte de; (*understand*) comprendre (**that** que).
**really** *adv* vraiment.
**rear 1** *n* (*back part*) arrière *m*; **in** *or* **at the r.** à l'arrière. **2** *a* arrière *inv*, de derrière. **3** *vt* (*family, animals*) élever.
**rear (up)** (*of horse*) se cabrer.
**rearrange** *vt* (*hair, room*) réarranger; (*plans*) changer.
**reason 1** *n* raison *f*; **the r. for/why . . .** la raison de/pour laquelle . . . ; **for no r.** sans raison. **2** *vi* raisonner.
**reasonable** *a* raisonnable.
**reasonably** *adv* (*fairly, rather*) assez.
**reasoning** raisonnement *m*.
**reason with s.o.** raisonner qn.
**reassure** *vt* rassurer.
**reassuring** *a* rassurant.
**rebel 1** *n* rebelle *mf*; (*against parents etc*) révolté, -ée *mf*. **2** *vi* se révolter (**against** contre).
**rebellion** révolte *f*.
**rebound 1** *vi* (*of ball*) rebondir; (*of stone*) ricocher. **2** *n* rebond *m*; ricochet *m*.
**rebuild** *vt* reconstruire.
**recall** *vt* (*remember*) se rappeler (**that** que, **doing** avoir fait); **to r. sth to s.o.** rappeler qch à qn.
**receipt** (*for payment, object left etc*) reçu *m* (**for** de); **on r. of** dès réception de.
**receive** *vt* recevoir.
**receiver** (*of phone*) combiné *m*; **to pick up the r.** (*of phone*) décrocher.
**recent** *a* récent; **in r. months** ces mois-ci.
**recently** *adv* récemment.
**reception** (*party, of radio etc*) réception *f*; **r. (desk)** réception *f*, accueil *m*.
**receptionist** secrétaire *mf*, réceptionniste *mf*.
**recharge** *vt* (*battery*) recharger.
**recipe** recette *f* (**for** de).
**recite** *vt* (*poem*) réciter; (*list*) énumérer.
**reckless** *a* (*rash*) imprudent.
**reckon** *vt* (*calculate*) calculer; (*think*) *Fam* penser (**that** que).
**reckon on sth/s.o.** (*rely on*) compter sur qch/qn; **to r. on doing** compter faire.
**reckon with sth/s.o.** (*take into account*) compter avec qch/qn.
**reclaim** *vt* (*luggage at airport*) récupérer.
**recognize** *vt* reconnaître (**by** à).
**recollect** *vt* se souvenir de; **to r. that** se souvenir que.
**recollection** souvenir *m*.
**recommend** *vt* recommander (**to** à, **for** pour); **to r. s.o. to do** recommander à qn de faire.
**recommendation** recommandation *f*.
**record 1** *n* (*best performance*) record *m*; (*register*) registre *m*; (*mention*) mention *f*; (*background*) antécédents *mpl*; **(public) records** archives *fpl*; **to keep a r. of** noter. **2** *a* (*time, number etc*) record *inv*. **3** *vt* (*on tape, in register*) enregistrer; (*in diary*) noter. **4** *vi* enregistrer.
**recorder** flûte *f* à bec; **(tape) r.** magnétophone *m*; **(video) r.** magnétoscope *m*.
**recording** enregistrement *m*.
**recover 1** *vt* (*get back*) retrouver. **2** *vi* (*from illness etc*) se remettre

(**from** de); (*of economy*) se redresser.
**recruit** recrue *f*.
**rectangle** rectangle *m*.
**rectangular** *a* rectangulaire.
**recycle** *vt* recycler.
**red 1** *a* rouge; (*hair*) roux (*f* rousse); **to turn r.** rougir; **r. light** (*traffic light*) feu *m* rouge. **2** *n* (*color*) rouge *m*; **in the r.** (*company, account*) dans le rouge, en déficit.
**red-handed** *a* **caught r.-handed** pris en flagrant délit.
**redhead** roux *m*, rousse *f*.
**red-hot** *a* brûlant.
**redirect** *vt* (*mail*) faire suivre.
**redo*** *vt* (*exercise, house etc*) refaire.
**reduce** *vt* réduire (**to** à, **by** de); **at a reduced price** (*ticket, goods*) à prix réduit.
**reduction** réduction *f* (**in** de).
**redundancy** superfluité *f*.
**redundant** *a* superflu.
**reed** (*plant*) roseau *m*.
**reef** récif *m*.
**reel** (*of thread, film*) bobine *f*; (*film itself*) bande *f*.
**refectory** réfectoire *m*.
**refer 1** *vi* **to r. to** (*mention*) faire allusion à; (*speak of*) parler de; (*apply to*) s'appliquer à. **2** *vt* **to r. sth to s.o.** soumettre qch à qn.
**referee 1** *n Sports* arbitre *m*. **2** *vt* arbitrer.
**reference** (*in book, for job*) référence *f*; (*mention*) mention *f* (**to** de); **with r. to** concernant; **r. book** ouvrage *m* de référence.
**refill 1** *vt* remplir (à nouveau); (*lighter, pen*) recharger. **2** *n* recharge *f*; **a r.** (*drink*) un autre verre.
**reflect** *vt* (*light etc*) refléter; **to be reflected** se refléter.
**reflection** (*image*) reflet *m*.
**reflex** réflexe *m*.
**reform** réforme *f*.
**refrain** *vi* s'abstenir (**from doing** de faire).
**refresh** *vt* (*of bath, drink*) rafraîchir; (*of sleep, rest*) délasser.
**refresher course** cours *m* de recyclage.
**refreshing** *a* (*drink*) rafraîchissant.
**refreshments** *npl* (*drinks*) rafraîchissements *mpl*; (*snacks*) petites choses *fpl* à grignoter.
**refrigerate** *vt* (*food*) conserver au frais.
**refrigerator** réfrigérateur *m*.
**refuge** refuge *m*; **to take r.** se réfugier.
**refugee** réfugié, -ée *mf*.
**refund 1** *vt* rembourser. **2** *n* remboursement *m*.
**refusal** refus *m*.
**refuse 1** *vt* refuser (**s.o. sth** qch à qn, **to do** de faire). **2** *vi* refuser.
**regain** *vt* (*lost ground*) regagner; (*health, strength*) retrouver.
**regard 1** *vt* considérer; **as regards** en ce qui concerne. **2** *n* considération *f* (**for** pour); **to have (a) high r. for s.o.** estimer qn; **to give one's regards to s.o.** transmettre son meilleur souvenir à qn.
**regarding** *prep* en ce qui concerne.
**regardless 1** *a* **r. of** sans tenir compte de. **2** *adv* (*all the same*) quand même.
**regiment** régiment *m*.
**region** région *f*; **in the r. of $50**/*etc* (*about*) dans les 50 dollars/*etc*.
**regional** *a* régional.
**register 1** *n* registre *m*. **2** *vt* (*birth etc*) déclarer; **registered letter** lettre recommandée; **to send by registered mail** envoyer en recommandé. **3** *vi* (*enroll*) s'inscrire (**for a course** à un cours); (*in hotel*) signer le registre.
**registration** (*enrollment*) inscription *f*; **r. (number)** (*of vehicle*) numéro *m* d'immatriculation.
**regret 1** *vt* regretter (**doing, to do** de faire; **that** que (+ *subjunctive*)). **2** *n* regret *m*.
**regular** *a* (*steady*) régulier; (*surface*) uni; (*usual*) habituel; (*price, size*) normal; (*listener*) fidèle.
**regularly** *adv* régulièrement.

**regulations** *npl* (*rules*) règlement *m*.
**rehearsal** répétition *f*.
**rehearse 1** *vt* (*a play etc*) répéter. **2** *vi* répéter.
**reign 1** *n* règne *m*; **in the r. of** sous le règne de. **2** *vi* régner (**over** sur).
**reindeer** *n inv* renne *m*.
**reinforce** *vt* renforcer (**with** de).
**reinforcements** *npl* (*troops*) renforts *mpl*.
**reins** *npl* (*for horse*) rênes *fpl*; (*for baby*) bretelles *fpl* de sécurité (avec laisse).
**reject** *vt* rejeter.
**rejection** rejet *m*; (*of candidate*) refus *m*.
**rejoice** *vi* (*celebrate*) faire la fête; (*be delighted*) se réjouir (**over** *or* **at sth** de qch).
**related** *a* (*linked*) lié (**to** à); **to be r. to s.o.** (*by family*) être parent de qn.
**relate to** (*apply to*) se rapporter à.
**relation** (*relative*) parent, -ente *mf*; (*relationship*) rapport *m*; **international relations** relations *fpl* internationales.
**relationship** (*in family*) lien(s) *m*(*pl*) de parenté; (*relations*) relations *fpl*; (*connection*) rapport *m*.
**relative 1** *n* (*person*) parent, -ente *mf*. **2** *a* relatif; (*qualities etc of two or more people*) respectif.
**relatively** *adv* relativement.
**relax 1** *vt* (*person*) détendre; (*grip, pressure*) relâcher. **2** *vi* se détendre; **r.!** (*calm down*) du calme!
**relaxation** (*rest*) détente *f*.
**relaxed** *a* décontracté.
**release 1** *vt* (*free*) libérer (**from** de); (*bomb*) lâcher; (*brake*) desserrer; (*film, record*) sortir; (*trapped person*) dégager. **2** *n* (*of prisoner*) libération *f*; (*of film etc*) sortie *f*; **press r.** communiqué *m* de presse.
**relevant** *a* pertinent (**to** à); (*useful*) utile; **that's not r.** ça n'a rien à voir.
**reliability** fiabilité *f*; (*of person*) sérieux *m*.
**reliable** *a* fiable; (*person*) sérieux.
**relief** (*from pain etc*) soulagement *m* (**from** à); (*help*) secours *m*; (*in geography etc*) relief *m*.
**relieve** *vt* (*pain, person etc*) soulager; (*take over from*) relayer (*qn*).
**religion** religion *f*.
**religious** *a* religieux.
**relish 1** *n* condiment *m* **2** *vt* (*food, wine*) savourer.
**reload** *vt* (*gun, camera*) recharger.
**reluctance** manque *m* d'enthousiasme (**to do** à faire).
**reluctant** *a* peu enthousiaste (**to do** pour faire).
**reluctantly** *adv* sans enthousiasme.
**rely (up)on** (*count on*) compter sur; (*be dependent on*) dépendre de.
**remain** *vi* rester.
**remaining** *a* qui reste(nt).
**remark 1** *n* remarque *f*. **2** *vt* (faire) remarquer (**that** que). **3** *vi* **to r. on sth** faire des remarques sur qch.
**remarkable** *a* remarquable (**for** par).
**remarkably** *adv* remarquablement.
**rematch** *Sports* revanche *f*.
**remedial** *a* **r. class** cours *m* de rattrapage.
**remember 1** *vt* se souvenir de, se rappeler; **to r. that/doing** se rappeler que/d'avoir fait; **to r. to do** penser à faire. **2** *vi* se souvenir, se rappeler.
**remind** *vt* rappeler (**s.o. of sth** qch à qn, **s.o. that** à qn que); **to r. s.o. to do** faire penser à qn à faire.
**reminder** (*of event & letter*) rappel *m*; **to give s.o. a r. to do** faire penser à qn à faire.
**remorse** remords *m*(*pl*).
**remote** *a* (*far-off*) lointain; (*isolated*) isolé; (*slight*) petit.
**remote control** télécommande *f*.
**removal** enlèvement *m*; suppression *f*.
**remove** *vt* (*clothes, stain etc*) enlever (**from s.o.** à qn, **from sth** de qch); (*obstacle, word*) supprimer.
**renew** *vt* renouveler; (*resume*) re-

prendre; (*library book*) renouveler le prêt de.

**rent 1** *n* (*for house etc*) loyer *m*. **2** *vt* louer.

**rental** *n* (*of house, car*) location *f*.

**rent out** louer.

**reorganize** *vt* (*firm etc*) réorganiser.

**repair 1** *vt* réparer. **2** *n* réparation *f*; **in bad r.** en mauvais état.

**repairman** (*pl* **-men**) réparateur *m*, dépanneur *m*.

**repay** *vt* (*pt & pp* **repaid**) (*pay back*) rembourser; (*reward*) récompenser (**for** de).

**repayment** remboursement *m*; récompense *f*.

**repeat 1** *vt* répéter (**that** que); (*promise, threat*) réitérer; (*class*) redoubler; **to r. oneself** se répéter. **2** *n* (*on TV, radio*) rediffusion *f*.

**repeated** *a* (*attempts etc*) répétés.

**repeatedly** *adv* à maintes reprises, de nombreuses fois.

**repel** *vt* repousser.

**repetition** répétition *f*.

**repetitive** *a* répétitif.

**replace** *vt* (*take the place of*) remplacer (**by, with** par); (*put back*) remettre; (*telephone receiver*) raccrocher.

**replacement** (*person*) remplaçant, -ante *mf*; (*machine part*) pièce *f* de rechange.

**replica** copie *f* exacte.

**reply 1** *vti* répondre (**to** à, **that** que). **2** *n* réponse *f*.

**report 1** *n* (*account*) rapport *m*; (*of meeting*) compte rendu *m*; (*in media*) reportage *m*; (*of pupil*) bulletin *m*; (*rumor*) rumeur *f*. **2** *vt* rapporter; (*announce*) annoncer (**that** que); (*notify*) signaler (**to** à); (*inform on*) dénoncer (**to** à). **3** *vi* faire un rapport; (*of journalist*) faire un reportage (**on** sur); (*go*) se présenter (**to** à, **to s.o.** chez qn).

**report card** bulletin *m* (scolaire).

**reported** *a* (*speech*) indirect.

**reporter** reporter *m*.

**represent** *vt* représenter.

**representative** représentant, -ante *mf*.

**reptile** reptile *m*.

**republic** république *f*.

**reputable** *a* de bonne réputation.

**reputation** réputation *f*; **to have a r. for being** avoir la réputation d'être.

**request 1** *n* demande *f* (**for** de). **2** *vt* demander (**sth from s.o.** qch à qn, **s.o. to do** à qn de faire).

**require** *vt* (*of thing*) demander; (*of person*) avoir besoin de; **if required** s'il le faut.

**required** *a* **the r. qualities**/*etc* les qualités/*etc* qu'il faut.

**rerun** *n* (*on TV, radio*) rediffusion *f*.

**rescue 1** *vt* (*save*) sauver; (*set free*) délivrer (**from** de). **2** *n* sauvetage *m* (**of** de); (*help*) secours *mpl*; **to go to s.o.'s r.** aller au secours de qn.

**research 1** *n* recherches *fpl* (**on, into** sur). **2** *vi* faire des recherches.

**researcher** chercheur, -euse *mf*.

**resemblance** ressemblance *f* (**to** avec).

**resemble** *vt* ressembler à.

**reservation** (*of hotel room etc*) réservation *f*; (*doubt*) réserve *f*.

**reserve 1** *vt* réserver; (*right*) se réserver. **2** *n* **nature r.** réserve *f* naturelle; **in r.** en réserve.

**reserved** *a* (*person, place*) réservé.

**reserve tank** réservoir *m* de secours.

**reside** *vi* **to r. in New York** résider à New York.

**residence** (*home*) résidence *f*; (*of students*) foyer *m*.

**resident** *n* habitant, -ante *mf*; (*of hotel*) pensionnaire *mf*.

**residential** *a* (*district*) résidentiel.

**resign 1** *vt* **to r. oneself to sth/to doing** se résigner à qch/à faire. **2** *vi* démissionner; **to r. from one's job** démissionner.

**resignation** (*from job*) démission *f*.

**resist 1** *vt* (*attack etc*) résister à; **to r. doing sth** se retenir de faire qch; **she can't r. cakes** elle ne peut pas résister devant des gâteaux. **2** *vi* résister.

**resistance** résistance *f* (**to** à).

**resort**[1] **1** *vi* **to r. to doing** en venir à faire; **to r. to sth** avoir recours à qch. **2** *n* **as a last r.** en dernier ressort.

**resort**[2] **(vacation) r.** station *f* de vacances; **beach r.** station *f* balnéaire; **ski r.** station de ski.

**resources** *npl* (*wealth, means*) ressources *fpl*.

**respect 1** *n* respect *m* (**for** pour, de); **with r. to** en ce qui concerne. **2** *vt* respecter.

**respectable** *a* (*honorable, quite good*) respectable; (*clothes, behavior*) convenable.

**respond** *vi* répondre (**to** à); **to r. to treatment** bien réagir au traitement.

**response** réponse *f*.

**responsibility** responsabilité *f*.

**responsible** *a* responsable (**for** de, **to s.o.** devant qn); (*job*) à responsabilités.

**rest**[1] **1** *n* repos *m*; (*support*) support *m*; **to have** *or* **take a r.** se reposer. **2** *vi* (*relax*) se reposer; **to be resting on sth** (*of hand etc*) être posé sur qch. **3** *vt* (*lean*) appuyer (**on** sur, **against** contre).

**rest**[2] (*remaining part*) reste *m* (**of** de); **the r.** (*others*) les autres *mfpl*; **the r. of the men**/*etc* les autres hommes/*etc*.

**restaurant** restaurant *m*.

**restful** *a* reposant.

**restless** *a* agité.

**restore** *vt* (*give back*) rendre (**to** à); (*building etc*) restaurer.

**restrict** *vt* restreindre (**to** à).

**restricted** *a* restreint.

**restriction** restriction *f*.

**restroom** toilettes *fpl*.

**result** résultat *m*; **as a r. of** par suite de.

**resume** *vti* reprendre.

**résumé** curriculum vitae *m inv*.

**retail 1** *a* (*price, shop*) de détail. **2** *adv* (*to sell*) au détail.

**retailer** détaillant, -ante *mf*.

**retain** *vt* (*freshness etc*) conserver.

**retake** *vt* (*exam*) repasser.

**retire** *vi* (*from work*) prendre sa retraite; (*withdraw*) se retirer (**from** de, **to** à); (*go to bed*) aller se coucher.

**retired** *a* (*no longer working*) retraité.

**retiree** retraité, -ée *mf*.

**retirement** retraite *f*.

**return 1** *vi* (*come back*) revenir; (*go back*) retourner; (*go back home*) rentrer. **2** *vt* (*give back*) rendre; (*put back*) remettre; (*send back*) renvoyer. **3** *n* retour *m*; (*on investment*) rendement *m*; **r. (ticket)** (billet *m* d')aller et retour *m*; **tax r.** déclaration *f* de revenus; **in r.** en échange (**for** de). **4** *a* (*flight etc*) (de) retour.

**returnable** *a* (*bottle*) consigné.

**reveal** *vt* (*make known*) révéler (**that** que).

**revenge** vengeance *f*; **to get one's r.** se venger (**on s.o.** de qn, **for sth** de qch); **in r.** pour se venger.

**reverse 1** *a* (*order*) inverse. **2** *n* contraire *m*; **in r. (gear)** en marche arrière. **3** *vti* **to r. (the car)** faire marche arrière; **to r. in/out** rentrer/sortir en marche arrière.

**review 1** *vt* (*book*) faire la critique de. **2** *n* critique *f*.

**revise 1** *vt* (*opinion, notes, text*) réviser. **2** *vi* (*for exam*) réviser (**for** pour).

**revision** révision *f*.

**revive** *vt* (*unconscious person*) ranimer.

**revolt** révolte *f*.

**revolting** *a* dégoûtant.

**revolution** révolution *f*.

**revolutionary** *a* & *n* révolutionnaire (*mf*).

**revolve** *vi* tourner (**around** autour de).

**revolver** revolver *m*.

**revolving door(s)** (porte *f* à) tambour *m*.

**reward 1** *n* récompense *f* (**for** de, pour). **2** *vt* récompenser (**s.o. for sth** qn de *or* pour qch).

**rewind*** **1** *vt* (*tape*) rembobiner. **2** *vi* se rembobiner.

**rheumatism** rhumatisme *m*; **to have r.** avoir des rhumatismes.

**rhinoceros** rhinocéros *m*.

**rhubarb** rhubarbe *f*.

**rhyme 1** *n* rime *f*; (*poem*) vers *mpl*. **2** *vi* rimer (**with** avec).

**rhythm** rythme *m*.

**rhythmical** *a* rythmé.

**rib** (*in body*) côte *f*.

**ribbon** ruban *m*.

**rice** riz *m*.

**rich 1** *a* riche. **2** *n* **the r.** les riches *mpl*.

**riches** *npl* richesses *fpl*.

**rid** *a* **to get r. of** se débarrasser de.

**riddle** (*puzzle*) énigme *f*.

**ride 1** *n* (*on bicycle, by car, on horse etc*) promenade *f*; (*distance*) trajet *m*; **to go for a (car) r.** faire une promenade (en voiture); **to give s.o. a r.** (*in car*) emmener qn en voiture. **2** *vi** aller (à bicyclette, à moto, à cheval *etc*) (**to** à); **to r., go riding** (*on horse*) monter (à cheval). **3** *vt* (*a particular horse*) monter; (*distance*) faire (à cheval *etc*); **to r. a horse** *or* **horses** monter à cheval; **I was riding (on) a bicycle** j'étais à bicyclette; **to r. a bicycle to** aller à bicylette à.

**rider** (*on horse*) cavalier, -ière *mf*.

**ridiculous** *a* ridicule.

**riding (horseback) r.** équitation *f*.

**rifle** fusil *m*.

**rig (oil) r.** derrick *m*; (*at sea*) plateforme *f* pétrolière.

**right**[1] **1** *a* (*correct*) bon (*f* bonne); (*fair*) juste; (*angle*) droit; **to be r.** (*of person*) avoir raison (**to do** de faire); **the r. choice/time** le bon choix/moment; **it's the r. time** (*accurate*) c'est l'heure exacte; **the clock's r.** la pendule est à l'heure; **it's not r. to steal** ce n'est pas bien de voler; **to put r.** (*error*) corriger; **r.!** bien!; **that's r.** c'est ça. **2** *adv* (*straight*) (tout) droit; (*completely*) tout à fait; (*correctly*) juste; (*well*) bien; **she did r.** elle a bien fait; **r. here** ici même; **r. away, r. now** tout de suite. **3** *n* **r. and wrong** le bien et le mal.

**right**[2] **1** *a* (*hand, side etc*) droit. **2** *adv* à droite. **3** *n* droite *f*; **on** *or* **to the r.** à droite (**of** de).

**right**[3] (*claim*) droit *m* (**to do** de faire); **to have a r. to sth** avoir droit à qch.

**right-hand** *a* à *or* de droite; **on the r.-hand side** à droite (**of** de).

**right-handed** *a* (*person*) droitier.

**rightly** *adv* à juste titre.

**rigid** *a* rigide.

**rim** (*of cup etc*) bord *m*.

**rind** (*of cheese*) croûte *f*.

**ring**[1] (*on finger, curtain etc*) anneau *m*; (*with jewel*) bague *f*; (*of people, chairs*) cercle *m*; *Boxing* ring *m*; **diamond r.** bague *f* de diamants; **to make a r. around** entourer (**with** de).

**ring**[2] **1** *n* (*sound*) sonnerie *f*; **to give s.o. a r.** (*phone call*) passer un coup de fil à qn. **2** *vi** (*of bell, phone, person*) sonner. **3** *vt* sonner; **to r. the (door)bell** sonner (à la porte).

**ring out** *vi* (*of bell*) sonner; (*of sound*) retentir.

**rinse 1** *vt* rincer; **to r. one's hands** se rincer les mains. **2** *n* **to give sth a r.** rincer qch.

**rinse out** rincer.

**riot 1** *n* (*uprising*) émeute *f*; (*fight*) bagarre *f*. **2** *vi* faire une émeute; (*fight*) se bagarrer.

**rip 1** *vt* déchirer. **2** *vi* (*of fabric*) se déchirer. **3** *n* déchirure *f*.

**ripe** *a* mûr; (*cheese*) fait.

**ripen** *vti* mûrir.

**rip off** *vt* (*button etc*) arracher (**from** de); **to r. s.o. off** *Fam* rouler qn.

**rip-off** *Fam* **it's a r.-off** c'est du vol organisé.

**rip sth out** arracher qch (**from** de).

**rip sth up** déchirer qch.

**rise 1** *vi** (*of temperature, balloon, price*) monter; (*of sun, curtain, person*) se lever; **to r. in price** augmenter de prix. **2** *n* (*in price etc*) hausse *f* (**in** de); (*slope in ground*) montée *f*; **to give r. to sth** donner lieu à qch.

**risk 1** *n* risque *m* (**of doing** de faire, **in doing** à faire); **at r.** (*person*) en danger; (*job*) menacé. **2** *vt* risquer; **she won't r. leaving** elle ne se risquera pas à partir.

**risky** *a* risqué.

**rival 1** *a* (*company etc*) rival. **2** *n* rival, -ale *mf*. **3** *vt* (*compete with*) rivaliser avec (**in** de); (*equal*) égaler (**in** en).

**river** rivière *f*; (*flowing into sea*) fleuve *m*.

**Riviera the (French) R.** la Côte d'Azur.

**roach** (*cockroach*) cafard *m*.

**road 1** *n* route *f* (**to** qui va à); (*small*) chemin *m*; (*in town*) rue *f*; (*roadway*) chaussée *f*; **across the r.** (*building etc*) en face; **by r.** par la route. **2** *a* (*map, safety*) routier; (*accident*) de la route; **r. sign** panneau *m* (routier).

**roadside** *a* & *n* **(by the) r.** au bord de la route.

**roadway** chaussée *f*.

**roadwork** travaux *mpl*.

**roam** *vt* parcourir; **to r. the streets** (*of child, dog etc*) traîner dans les rues.

**roar 1** *vi* (*of lion*) rugir; (*of person*) hurler. **2** *n* (*of lion*) rugissement *m*.

**roast 1** *vt* rôtir; (*coffee*) griller. **2** *vi* (*of meat*) rôtir. **3** *n* (*meat*) rôti *m*. **4** *a* (*chicken etc*) rôti; **r. beef** rosbif *m*.

**rob** *vt* (*person*) voler; (*bank*) attaquer; (*by breaking in*) cambrioler; **to r. s.o. of sth** voler qch à qn.

**robber** voleur, -euse *mf*.

**robbery** vol *m*.

**robe** (*bathrobe*) robe *f* de chambre.

**robin** rouge-gorge *m*.

**robot** robot *m*.

**rock[1] 1** *vt* (*baby, boat*) bercer. **2** *vi* (*sway*) se balancer; (*of building*) trembler. **3** *n* (*music*) rock *m*.

**rock[2]** (*substance*) roche *f*; (*boulder, rock face*) rocher *m*; (*stone*) pierre *f*; **r. face** paroi *f* rocheuse.

**rocket** fusée *f*.

**rocking chair** fauteuil *m* à bascule.

**rod** (*wooden*) baguette *f*; (*metal*) tige *f*; (*of curtain*) tringle *f*; (*for fishing*) canne *f* (à pêche).

**rogue** (*dishonest*) crapule *f*; (*mischievous*) coquin, -ine *mf*.

**role** rôle *m*.

**roll 1** *n* (*of paper etc*) rouleau *m*; (*small bread loaf*) petit pain *m*; (*of drum*) roulement *m*; (*attendance list*) cahier *m* d'appel; **to call** *or* **take the r.** faire l'appel. **2** *vi* (*of ball etc*) rouler; (*of person, animal*) se rouler. **3** *vt* rouler.

**roll down** (*car window etc*) baisser; (*slope*) descendre (en roulant).

**roller** (*for hair, painting etc*) rouleau *m*.

**roller-skate 1** *n* patin *m* à roulettes. **2** *vi* faire du patin à roulettes.

**rolling pin** rouleau *m* à pâtisserie.

**roll over 1** *vi* (*many times*) se rouler; (*once*) se retourner. **2** *vt* retourner.

**roll up** (*map, cloth*) rouler; (*sleeve, pants*) retrousser.

**Roman** *a* & *n* romain, -aine (*mf*).

**Roman Catholic** *a* & *n* catholique (*mf*).

**romance** (*love*) amour *m*; (*affair*) aventure *f* amoureuse.

**romantic** *a* romantique.

**roof** toit *m*; (*of tunnel, cave*) plafond *m*.

**roof rack** (*of car*) galerie *f*.

**room** (*in house etc*) pièce *f*; (*bedroom*) chambre *f*; (*large, public*) salle *f*; (*space*) place *f* (**for** pour); **men's r., ladies' r.** toilettes *fpl*.

**roommate** camarade *mf* de chambre.

**roomy** *a* spacieux; (*clothes*) ample.

**root** racine *f*; (*origin*) origine *f*; **to take r.** (*of plant*) prendre racine.

**root for** *Fam* encourager.

**rope** corde *f*.

**rope off** (*of police etc*) interdire l'accès de.

**rose** (*flower*) rose *f*; **r. bush** rosier *m*.
**rot (away)** *vti* pourrir.
**rotten** *a* (*fruit, weather etc*) pourri; (*bad*) *Fam* moche; **to feel r.** (*ill*) être mal fichu.
**rough**[1] *a* (*surface, plank*) rugueux; (*ground*) inégal; (*brutal*) brutal; (*sea*) agité.
**rough**[2] *a* (*calculation etc*) approximatif; **r. guess** approximation *f*; **r. draft** brouillon *m*.
**roughly**[1] *adv* (*not gently*) rudement; (*brutally*) brutalement.
**roughly**[2] *adv* (*more or less*) à peu (de choses) près.
**round 1** *a* rond. **2** *n Boxing* round *m*; (*of drinks, visits*) tournée *f*; (*of policeman*) ronde *f*.
**roundabout** *a* indirect.
**round off** (*meal etc*) terminer (**with** par); (*figure*) arrondir.
**round trip** aller (et) retour *m*.
**round up** (*people, animals*) rassembler.
**route** itinéraire *m*; (*of ship, aircraft*) route *f*; **bus r.** ligne *f* d'autobus.
**routine** train-train *m*.
**row**[1] **1** *n* (*line*) rang *m*, rangée *f*; (*one behind another*) file *f*; **two days in a r.** deux jours de suite. **2** *vi* (*in boat*) ramer. **3** *vt* (*boat*) faire aller à la rame.
**row**[2] **1** *n Fam* (*noise*) vacarme *m*; (*quarrel*) dispute *f*. **2** *vi Fam* se disputer (**with** avec).
**row boat** bateau *m* à rames.
**row house** maison *f* attenante aux maisons voisines.
**royal** *a* royal.
**royalty** personnages *mpl* royaux.
**rub** *vti* frotter; (*person*) frictionner.
**rubber** caoutchouc *m*; (*eraser*) gomme *f*.
**rubber band** élastique *m*.
**rubber boots** bottes *fpl* de caoutchouc.
**rubber stamp** tampon *m*.
**rubble** décombres *mpl*.
**rub down** (*person*) frictionner; (*with sandpaper*) poncer (*qch*).
**rub in** (*cream*) faire pénétrer (en massant).
**rub off** *or* **out** (*mark*) effacer.
**ruby** rubis *m*.
**rucksack** sac *m* à dos.
**rudder** gouvernail *m*.
**rude** *a* impoli (**to** envers); (*coarse, insolent*) grossier (**to** envers).
**rudeness** impolitesse *f*; grossièreté *f*.
**rug** carpette *f*.
**rugby** rugby *m*.
**ruin 1** *n* ruine *f*; **in ruins** (*building*) en ruine. **2** *vt* (*health, person etc*) ruiner; (*clothes*) abîmer.
**rule 1** *n* règle *f*; **against the rules** contraire au règlement; **as a r.** en règle générale. **2** *vt* (*country*) gouverner. **3** *vi* (*of king etc*) régner (**over** sur).
**rule sth out** exclure qch.
**ruler** (*for measuring*) règle *f*; (*king, queen etc*) souverain, -aine *mf*.
**rum** rhum *m*.
**rummage sale** vente *f* de charité.
**rumor** bruit *m*, rumeur *f*.
**run 1** *n* (*period*) période *f*; (*for skiing*) piste *f*; **to go for a r.** (aller) faire une course à pied; **on the r.** (*prisoner*) en fuite; **in the long r.** à la longue. **2** *vi** courir; (*of river, nose, faucet*) couler; (*of color in laundry*) déteindre; (*of play, movie*) se jouer; (*function*) marcher; (*of car engine*) tourner; **to r. down/in/***etc* descendre/entrer/*etc* en courant; **to go running** faire du jogging. **3** *vt* (*race, risk*) courir; (*temperature, errand*) faire; (*business, country etc*) diriger; (*bath*) faire couler.
**run across s.o.** (*meet*) tomber sur qn.
**run along!** filez!
**run away** s'enfuir (**from** de).
**run down** (*pedestrian*) renverser.
**rung** (*of ladder*) barreau *m*.
**run into** (*meet*) tomber sur; (*crash into*) percuter.

**runner** (*athlete*) coureur *m*.
**runner-up** second, -onde *mf*.
**running 1** *n* (*on foot*) course *f*. **2** *a* **r. water** eau *f* courante; **six days**/*etc* **r.** six jours/*etc* de suite.
**runny** *a* (*nose*) qui coule.
**run off** (*flee*) s'enfuir.
**run out** (*of inventory*) s'épuiser; (*of lease*) expirer; **to r. out of** (*time, money*) manquer de; **we've r. out of coffee** on n'a plus de café.
**run over** *vt* (*kill pedestrian*) écraser; (*knock down pedestrian*) renverser.
**runway** piste *f* (d'envol).
**rush 1** *vi* se précipiter (**at** sur, **towards** vers); (*hurry*) se dépêcher (**to do** de faire). **2** *vt* (*hurry*) bousculer (*qn*); **to r. s.o. to the hospital** transporter qn d'urgence à l'hôpital; **to r. (through) sth** (*job, meal etc*) faire, manger *etc* qch en vitesse. **3** *n* ruée *f* (**for** vers); (*confusion*) bousculade *f*; (*hurry*) hâte *f*; **in a r.** pressé (**to do** de faire).
**rush hour** heure *f* de pointe.
**rush out** *vi* partir en vitesse.
**Russian 1** *a* & *n* russe (*mf*). **2** *n* (*language*) russe *m*.
**rust 1** *n* rouille *f*. **2** *vi* (se) rouiller.
**rusty** *a* (*metal, memory etc*) rouillé.
**rye bread** pain *m* de seigle.

# S

**sack 1** *n* (*bag*) sac *m*; **to get the s.** (*from one's job*) se faire virer; **to give s.o. the s.** virer qn. **2** *vt* (*dismiss*) virer.
**sacrifice 1** *n* sacrifice *m*. **2** *vt* sacrifier (**to** à, **for** pour).
**sad** *a* triste.
**sadden** *vt* attrister.
**saddle** selle *f*.
**sadly** *adv* tristement; (*unfortunately*) malheureusement.
**sadness** tristesse *f*.
**safe**[1] *a* (*person*) en sécurité; (*equipment, toy, animal*) sans danger; (*place, investment, method*) sûr; (*bridge, ladder*) solide; **s. (and sound)** sain et sauf; **it's s. to go out** on peut sortir sans danger; **s. from** à l'abri de.
**safe**[2] (*for money etc*) coffre-fort *m*.
**safely** *adv* (*without accident*) sans accident; (*without risk*) sans risque; (*in a safe place*) en lieu sûr.
**safety** sécurité *f*.
**safety pin** épingle *f* de sûreté.
**sag** *vi* (*of roof, ground*) s'affaisser.
**said** *pt* & *pp de* **say**.
**sail 1** *vi* naviguer; (*leave*) partir; (*as sport*) faire de la voile; **to s. around the world/an island** faire le tour du monde/d'une île en bateau. **2** *vt* (*boat*) piloter. **3** *n* voile *f*.
**sailboard** planche *f* (à voile).
**sailboat** voilier *m*.
**sailing** navigation *f*; (*sport*) voile *f*; (*departure*) départ *m*.
**sailor** marin *m*.
**saint** saint *m*, sainte *f*.
**sake for my/your/his**/*etc* **s.** pour moi/toi/lui/*etc*; **(just) for the s. of eating**/*etc* simplement pour manger/*etc*.
**salad** salade *f*.
**salad bowl** saladier *m*.
**salad dressing** sauce *f* de salade.
**salary** (*professional*) traitement *m*; (*wage*) salaire *m*.
**sale** vente *f*; **sale(s)** (*at reduced prices*) soldes *mpl*; **on s.** (*cheaply*) en solde; (*available*) en vente; **(up) for s.** à vendre.
**salesclerk** vendeur, -euse *mf*.
**salesman** (*pl* **-men**) (*in store*) vendeur *m*; **(traveling) s.** représentant *m* (de commerce).
**saleswoman** (*pl* **-women**) vendeuse *f*; (*who travels*) représentante *f* (de commerce).
**saliva** salive *f*.
**salmon** saumon *m*.
**salt 1** *n* sel *m*; **bath salts** sels *mpl* de bain. **2** *vt* saler.
**saltcellar** *or* **saltshaker** salière *f*.
**salty** *a* salé.

**same 1** *a* même; **the (very) s. house as** (exactement) la même maison que. **2** *pron* **the s.** le *or* la même, *pl* les mêmes; **it's all the s. to me** ça m'est égal; **all** *or* **just the s.** tout de même; **to do the s.** en faire autant.
**sample 1** *n* échantillon *m*; (*of blood*) prélèvement *m*. **2** *vt* (*wine etc*) goûter.
**sand 1** *n* sable *m*. **2** *vt* (*road*) sabler.
**sandal** sandale *f*.
**sandcastle** château *m* de sable.
**sandpaper** papier *m* de verre.
**sandwich** sandwich *m*; **cheese**/*etc* **s.** sandwich au fromage/*etc*; **s. shop** sandwicherie *f*.
**sandy** *a* (*beach*) de sable; (*road*) sablonneux.
**sanitary napkin** serviette *f* hygiénique.
**Santa Claus** le père Noël.
**sardine** sardine *f*.
**sat** *pt* & *pp de* **sit.**
**satchel** cartable *m*.
**satellite** satellite *m*.
**satin** satin *m*.
**satisfaction** satisfaction *f*.
**satisfactory** *a* satisfaisant.
**satisfy** *vt* satisfaire (*qn*); **to s. oneself that** s'assurer que; **satisfied (with)** satisfait (de).
**satisfying** *a* satisfaisant.
**satsuma** (*fruit*) mandarine *f*, satsuma *f*.
**saturate** *vt* (*soak*) tremper.
**Saturday** samedi *m*.
**sauce** sauce *f*; (*stewed fruit*) compote *f*; **tomato s.** sauce *f* tomate.
**saucepan** casserole *f*.
**saucer** soucoupe *f*.
**sauna** sauna *m*.
**sausage** saucisse *f*; (*dried, for slicing*) saucisson *m*.
**save 1** *vt* (*rescue*) sauver (**from** de); (*keep*) garder; (*money, time*) économiser; (*stamps*) collectionner; **to s. s.o. from doing** empêcher qn de faire; **that will s. him** *or* **her the trouble of going** ça lui évitera d'y aller. **2** *n Sports* arrêt *m*.
**save up 1** *vt* (*money*) économiser. **2** *vi* faire des économies (**for sth, to buy sth** pour acheter qch).
**savings** *npl* (*money*) économies *fpl*.
**savings and loan** = société *f* de crédit immobilier.
**savings bank** caisse *f* d'épargne.
**saw[1] 1** *n* scie *f*. **2** *vt** scier.
**saw[2]** *pt de* **see.**
**sawdust** sciure *f*.
**saw sth off** scier qch.
**saxophone** saxophone *m*.
**say*** *vt* dire (**to** à, **that** que); (*of dial etc*) marquer; **to s. again** répéter; **(let's) s. tomorrow** disons demain; **that is to s.** c'est-à-dire.
**saying** proverbe *m*.
**scab** (*of wound*) croûte *f*.
**scaffolding** échafaudage *m*.
**scald** *vt* ébouillanter.
**scale** (*of map, wages etc*) échelle *f*; (*on fish*) écaille *f*; (*in music*) gamme *f*.
**scales** *npl* (*for weighing*) balance *f*; **(bathroom) s.** pèse-personne *m*.
**scallion** oignon *m* vert.
**scandal** scandale *m*; (*gossip*) médisances *fpl*.
**Scandinavian** *a* & *n* scandinave (*mf*).
**scanner** scanner *m*.
**scar** cicatrice *f*.
**scarce** *a* rare.
**scarcely** *adv* à peine.
**scare** *vt* faire peur à.
**scarecrow** épouvantail *m*.
**scared** *a* effrayé; **to be s. (stiff)** avoir (très) peur.
**scarf** (*pl* **scarves**) (*long*) écharpe *f*; (*square, for women*) foulard *m*.
**scarlet fever** scarlatine *f*.
**scary** *a* **it's s.** ça fait peur.
**scatter 1** *vt* (*crowd, clouds etc*) disperser; (*throw around*) éparpiller (*papiers etc*). **2** *vi* (*of crowd*) se disperser.
**scene** (*setting, fuss, part of play or movie*) scène *f*; (*of crime, accident*) lieu *m*; (*view*) vue *f*.
**scenery** paysage *m*; (*for play or movie*) décor(s) *m*(*pl*).

**scent** (*fragrance, perfume*) parfum *m*.

**schedule 1** *n* (*of work etc*) programme *m*; (*timetable*) horaire *m*; **on s.** (*on time*) à l'heure; **according to s.** comme prévu. **2** *vt* (*to plan*) prévoir; (*event*) fixer le programme de.

**scheduled** *a* (*planned*) prévu; (*service, flight*) régulier.

**scheme** plan *m* (**to do** pour faire); (*dishonest trick*) combine *f*.

**scholarship** (*grant*) bourse *f* (d'études).

**school 1** *n* école *f*; (*teaching, lessons*) classe *f*; **in** *or* **at s.** à l'école; **public s.** école publique; **summer s.** cours *mpl* d'été. **2** *a* (*year etc*) scolaire.

**schoolboy** écolier *m*.

**schoolgirl** écolière *f*.

**schoolteacher** (*primary*) instituteur, -trice *mf*; (*secondary*) professeur *m*.

**science** science *f*; **to study s.** étudier les sciences.

**science fiction** science-fiction *f*.

**scientific** *a* scientifique.

**scientist** scientifique *mf*, savant *m*.

**scissors** *npl* ciseaux *mpl*.

**scold** *vt* gronder (**for doing** pour avoir fait).

**scone** petit pain *m* au lait.

**scooter** (*child's*) trottinette *f*; (*motorcycle*) scooter *m*.

**scope** (*range*) étendue *f*; (*limits*) limites *fpl*; **s. for sth/for doing** (*opportunity*) des possibilités *fpl* de qch/de faire.

**scorch** *vt* roussir.

**score**[1] **1** *n* (*in sports*) score *m*; (*at cards*) marque *f*; (*music*) partition *f*. **2** *vt* (*point, goal*) marquer. **3** *vi* marquer un point *or* un but; (*count points*) marquer les points.

**score**[2] **a s. (of)** (*twenty*) une vingtaine (de).

**scorn** mépris *m*.

**Scot** Écossais, -aise *mf*.

**Scotch** (*whisky*) scotch *m*.

**scotch (tape)**® scotch® *m*.

**Scotsman** (*pl* **-men**) Écossais *m*.

**Scotswoman** (*pl* **-women**) Écossaise *f*.

**Scottish** *a* écossais.

**scoundrel** vaurien *m*.

**scout (boy) s.** scout *m*; **girl s.** éclaireuse *f*.

**scrambled** *a* (*egg*) brouillé.

**scrap 1** *n* petit morceau *m* (**of** de); (*of information*) fragment *m*; (*metal*) ferraille *f*; **scraps** (*food*) restes *mpl*. **2** *vt* se débarrasser de; (*vehicle*) mettre à la ferraille; (*plan*) abandonner.

**scrapbook** album *m* (*pour collages etc*).

**scrape 1** *vt* racler; (*skin, knee etc*) érafler. **2** *vi* **to s. against sth** frotter contre qch. **3** *n* (*on skin*) éraflure *f*.

**scrape away** *or* **off** (*mud etc*) racler.

**scrape through** (*in exam*) réussir de justesse.

**scrape together** (*money, people*) réunir (difficilement).

**scrap metal** ferraille *f*.

**scrap paper** (papier *m*) brouillon *m*.

**scratch 1** *n* (*mark, injury*) éraflure *f*; **to start from s.** (re)partir de zéro; **it isn't up to s.** ce n'est pas au niveau. **2** *vt* (*arm etc that itches*) gratter; (*skin, furniture etc*) érafler; (*one's name*) graver (**on** sur). **3** *vi* (*relieve an itch*) se gratter.

**scratch paper** (*for draft*) (papier) brouillon.

**scream 1** *vti* crier; **to s. at s.o.** crier après qn. **2** *n* cri *m* (perçant).

**screen** écran *m*; **(folding) s.** paravent *m*.

**screw 1** *n* vis *f*. **2** *vt* visser (**to** à).

**screw anchor** cheville *f*.

**screw sth down** *or* **on** visser qch.

**screwdriver** tournevis *m*.

**scribble** *vti* griffonner.

**script** (*of movie*) scénario *m*; (*of play*) texte *m*.

**scrub** *vt* nettoyer (à la brosse); (*pan*) récurer.

**scrub brush** brosse *f* dure.
**scrum** *Rugby* mêlée *f*.
**scuba diving** plongée *f* sous-marine.
**sculptor** sculpteur *m*.
**sculpture** (*art, object*) sculpture *f*.
**sea** mer *f*; **(out) at s.** en mer; **by s.** par mer; **by** *or* **beside the s.** au bord de la mer.
**seafood** fruits *mpl* de mer.
**seafront** bord *m* *or* front *m* de mer.
**seagull** mouette *f*.
**seal 1** *n* (*animal*) phoque *m*; (*mark, design*) sceau *m*; (*of wax*) cachet *m* (de cire). **2** *vt* (*document, container*) sceller; (*envelope*) cacheter; (*with putty*) boucher.
**sea lion** otarie *f*.
**seal off** (*of police etc*) interdire l'accès de.
**seam** (*in cloth*) couture *f*.
**search 1** *n* recherche *f* (**for** de); (*of person, place*) fouille *f*; **in s. of** à la recherche de. **2** *vt* (*person, place*) fouiller (**for** pour trouver); **to s. (through) one's papers**/*etc* **for sth** chercher qch dans ses papiers/*etc*. **3** *vi* chercher; **to s. for sth** chercher qch.
**seashell** coquillage *m*.
**seashore** bord *m* de la mer.
**seasick** *a* **to be s.** avoir le mal de mer.
**seasickness** mal *m* de mer.
**seaside** bord *m* de la mer.
**season 1** *n* saison *f*. **2** *vt* (*food*) assaisonner.
**seasoning** assaisonnement *m*.
**season tickets** abonnement *m*.
**seat 1** *n* siège *m*; (*on train, bus*) banquette *f*; (*in theater*) fauteuil *m*; (*place*) place *f*; **to take** *or* **have a s.** s'asseoir. **2** *vt* (*at table*) placer (*qn*); **the room seats 50** la salle a 50 places (assises); **be seated!** asseyez-vous!
**seat belt** ceinture *f* de sécurité.
**seated** *a* (*sitting*) assis.
**seating** (*seats*) places *fpl* assises.
**seaweed** algue(s) *f*(*pl*).
**second[1] 1** *a* deuxième, second; **every s. week** une semaine sur deux; **in s. (gear)** en seconde. **2** *adv* **to come s.** se classer deuxième. **3** *n* (*person, object*) deuxième *mf*, second, -onde *mf*.
**second[2]** (*part of minute*) seconde *f*.
**secondary** *a* secondaire.
**second-class** *a* (*ticket*) de seconde (classe); (*mail*) non urgent.
**secondhand** *a* & *adv* (*not new*) d'occasion.
**secondly** *adv* deuxièmement.
**secret** *a* & *n* secret (*m*); **in s.** en secret.
**secretary** secrétaire *mf*; (*cabinet official*) ministre *m*; **S. of State** Ministre des Affaires étrangères.
**section** (*of town, book etc*) partie *f*; (*of machine, furniture*) élément *m*; (*in store*) rayon *m*; **the sports**/*etc* **s.** (*of newspaper*) la page des sports/*etc*.
**secure 1** *a* (*person, valuables*) en sûreté; (*place*) sûr; (*solid*) solide; (*door, window*) bien fermé. **2** *vt* (*fasten*) attacher; (*window etc*) bien fermer.
**securely** *adv* (*firmly*) solidement; (*safely*) en sûreté.
**security** sécurité *f*; (*for loan*) caution *f*.
**sedation under s.** sous calmants.
**sedative** calmant *m*.
**see*** *vti* voir; **we'll s.** on verra (bien); **I saw him run(ning)** je l'ai vu courir; **s. you (later)!** à tout à l'heure!; **s. you (soon)!** à bientôt!; **to s. that** (*take care that*) = **to see to it that.**
**see about sth** s'occuper de qch; (*consider*) songer à qch.
**seed** graine *f*; (*in grape*) pépin *m*.
**seeing** *conj* **s. (that)** vu que.
**seek*** *vt* chercher (**to do** à faire); (*ask for*) demander (**from** à).
**seem** *vi* sembler (**to do** faire); **it seems that** (*impression*) il semble que (+ *subjunctive or indicative*); (*rumor*) il paraît que (+ *indica-*

*tive*); **it seems to me that** il me semble que (+ *indicative*).
**see s.o. off** accompagner qn (*à la gare etc*).
**see s.o. out** raccompagner qn.
**seesaw** (jeu *m* de) bascule *f*.
**see to sth** (*deal with*) s'occuper de qch; (*mend*) réparer qch; **to see to it that** veiller à ce que (+ *subjunctive*); (*check*) s'assurer que.
**see s.o. to** (*accompany*) raccompagner qn à.
**segment** segment *m*; (*of orange*) quartier *m*.
**seize** *vt* saisir; (*power, land*) s'emparer de.
**seldom** *adv* rarement.
**select** *vt* choisir (**from** parmi); (*candidates, players etc*) sélectionner.
**selection** sélection *f*.
**self-assurance** assurance *f*.
**self-assured** *a* sûr de soi.
**self-confidence** assurance *f*.
**self-confident** *a* sûr de soi.
**self-conscious** *a* gêné.
**self-control** maîtrise *f* de soi.
**self-defense** légitime défense *f*.
**self-employed** *a* qui travaille à son compte.
**selfish** *a* égoïste.
**self-respect** amour-propre *m*.
**self-service** *n* & *a* libre-service (*m inv*).
**sell*** **1** *vt* vendre; **to have** *or* **be sold out of sth** n'avoir plus de qch. **2** *vi* (*of product*) se vendre.
**seller** vendeur, -euse *mf*.
**semester** semestre *m*.
**semi-** *prefix* demi-, semi-.
**semi(trailer)** semi-remorque *m*.
**semicircle** demi-cercle *m*.
**semicolon** point-virgule *m*.
**semidetached house** maison *f* jumelle.
**semifinal** demi-finale *f*.
**semolina** semoule *f*.
**senator** sénateur *m*.
**send*** *vt* envoyer (**to** à); **to s. s.o. for sth/s.o.** envoyer qn chercher qch/qn.
**send away** *or* **off** **1** *vt* envoyer (**to** à); (*dismiss*) renvoyer. **2** *vi* **to s. away** *or* **off for sth** commander qch (par courrier).
**send back** renvoyer.
**sender** expéditeur, -trice *mf*.
**send for** (*doctor etc*) faire venir; (*by mail*) commander (par courrier).
**send in** (*form etc*) envoyer; (*person*) faire entrer.
**send on** (*letter, luggage*) faire suivre.
**send out** (*invitation etc*) envoyer; (*from room etc*) faire sortir (*qn*); **to s. out for** (*meal*) envoyer chercher.
**send up** (*luggage*) faire monter.
**senior** **1** *a* (*older*) plus âgé; (*position, rank*) supérieur. **2** *n* aîné, -ée *mf*; (*in school*) grand *m*, grande *f*, étudiant, -ante *mf* de dernière année.
**senior high (school)** lycée *m*.
**sensation** sensation *f*.
**sensational** *a* (*terrific*) *Fam* sensationnel.
**sense** **1** *n* (*meaning*) sens *m*; **s. of smell** odorat *m*; **a s. of** (*shame etc*) un sentiment de; **to have a s. of humor** avoir de l'humour; **to have (good) s.** avoir du bon sens; **to have the s. to do** avoir l'intelligence de faire; **to make s.** (*of story*) avoir un sens, tenir debout. **2** *vt* sentir (intuitivement) (**that** que).
**senseless** *a* (*stupid*) insensé.
**sensible** *a* (*wise*) raisonnable.
**sensitive** *a* sensible (**to** à); (*skin*) délicat; (*touchy*) susceptible (**about** à propos de).
**sentence** **1** *n Grammar* phrase *f*; (*punishment, in prison*) peine *f*. **2** *vt* **to s. s.o. to 3 years (in prison)** condamner qn à 3 ans de prison.
**separate** **1** *a* (*distinct*) séparé; (*independent*) indépendant; (*different*) différent. **2** *vt* séparer (**from** de). **3** *vi* se séparer (**from** de).
**separately** *adv* séparément.

**September** septembre *m*.
**sequence** (*order*) ordre *m*; (*series*) succession *f*.
**sequin** paillette *f*.
**sergeant** sergent *m*; (*in police force*) brigadier *m*.
**serial** (*story, film*) feuilleton *m*.
**series** *n inv* série *f*.
**serious** *a* sérieux; (*illness, mistake*) grave.
**seriously** *adv* sérieusement; (*ill*) gravement; **to take s.** prendre au sérieux.
**servant** (*in house etc*) domestique *mf*.
**serve** *vt* servir (**to s.o.** à qn, **s.o. with sth** qch à qn); (*of train, bus etc*) desservir (*un village etc*); **(it) serves you right!** ça t'apprendra!
**serve out** *or* **up** (*meal etc*) servir.
**service 1** *n* service *m*; (*machine or vehicle repair*) révision *f*; **s. charge** (*in restaurant*) service *m*. **2** *vt* (*machine, vehicle*) réviser.
**service area** (*on highway*) aire *f* de service.
**service station** station-service *f*.
**session** séance *f*.
**set 1** *n* (*of keys, tools etc*) jeu *m*; (*of stamps, numbers*) série *f*; (*of people*) groupe *m*; (*in mathematics*) ensemble *m*; (*of books*) collection *f*; (*scenery*) décor *m*; (*hairstyle*) mise *f* en plis; *Tennis* set *m*; **chess s.** jeu *m* d'échecs. **2** *a* (*time, price etc*) fixe; **the s. menu** le plat du jour; **s. on doing** résolu à faire; **to be s. on sth** vouloir qch à tout prix; **all s.** (*ready*) prêt (**to do** pour faire). **3** *vt** (*put*) mettre; (*date, limit etc*) fixer; (*record*) établir; (*mechanism, clock*) régler; (*alarm clock*) mettre (**for** pour); (*arm etc in plaster*) plâtrer; (*task*) donner (**for s.o.** à qn); (*trap*) tendre; **to have one's hair s.** se faire faire une mise en plis. **4** *vi* (*of sun*) se coucher; (*of jelly*) prendre.
**set about sth/doing** (*begin*) se mettre à qch/à faire.
**set back** (*clock*) retarder.
**setback** revers *m*.
**set down** (*object*) déposer.
**set forward** (*clock*) avancer.
**set off 1** *vt* (*bomb*) faire exploser; (*mechanism*) déclencher. **2** *vi* (*leave*) partir.
**set out 1** *vt* (*display, explain*) exposer (**to** à); (*arrange*) disposer. **2** *vi* (*leave*) partir; **to s. out to do** entreprendre de faire.
**settee** canapé *m*.
**setting** (*surroundings*) cadre *m*.
**settle 1** *vt* (*decide, arrange, pay*) régler; (*date*) fixer; **that's (all) settled** c'est décidé. **2** *vi* (*live*) s'installer.
**settle down** (*in chair or house*) s'installer; (*calm down*) se calmer; (*in one's lifestyle*) se ranger.
**settlement** (*agreement*) accord *m*.
**settler** colon *m*.
**settle (up) with s.o.** (*pay*) régler qn.
**set up 1** *vt* (*tent*) dresser; (*business*) créer. **2** *vi* **to s. up shop** monter une affaire.
**seven** *a* & *n* sept (*m*).
**seventeen** *a* & *n* dix-sept (*m*).
**seventh** *a* & *n* septième (*mf*).
**seventieth** *a* & *n* soixante-dixième (*mf*).
**seventy** *a* & *n* soixante-dix (*m*); **s.-one** soixante et onze.
**several** *a* & *pron* plusieurs (**of** d'entre).
**severe** *a* (*tone etc*) sévère; (*winter*) rigoureux; (*test*) dur.
**sew*** *vti* coudre.
**sewer** égout *m*.
**sewing** couture *f*.
**sewing machine** machine *f* à coudre.
**sew on** (*button*) (re)coudre.
**sew up** (*tear*) (re)coudre.
**sex 1** *n* sexe *m*; (*activity*) relations *fpl* sexuelles; **to have s. with s.o.** coucher avec qn. **2** *a* (*education, life etc*) sexuel.
**sexual** *a* sexuel.
**sexy** *a* sexy *inv*.
**sh!** *int* chut!

**shabby** *a* (*room etc*) minable.
**shade** ombre *f*; (*of colour*) ton *m*; (*of lamp*) abat-jour *m inv*; **(window) s.** store *m*; **in the s.** à l'ombre.
**shadow** ombre *f*.
**shady** *a* (*place*) ombragé.
**shake*** **1** *vt* secouer; (*bottle*) agiter; (*upset*) bouleverser; **to s. one's head** (*say no*) secouer la tête; **to s. hands with s.o.** serrer la main à qn; **we shook hands** nous nous sommes serré la main. **2** *vi* trembler (**with** de).
**shall** *v aux* (*future*) **I s. come, I'll come** je viendrai; **we s. not come, we shan't come** nous ne viendrons pas. ▪ (*question*) **s. I leave?** veux-tu que je parte?; **s. we leave?** on part?
**shallow** *a* (*water, river etc*) peu profond.
**shame** (*feeling, disgrace*) honte *f*; **it's a s.** c'est dommage (**to do** de faire); **it's a s. (that)** c'est dommage que (+ *subjunctive*); **what a s.!** (quel) dommage!
**shameful** *a* honteux.
**shampoo** **1** *n* shampooing *m*. **2** *vt* **to s. s.o.'s hair** faire un shampooing à qn.
**shan't** = **shall not.**
**shape** forme *f*; **in (good) s.** (*fit*) en (pleine) forme; **to stay in s.** se maintenir en forme; **to be in good/bad s.** (*of vehicle etc*) être en bon/mauvais état; (*of business*) marcher bien/mal; **to take s.** (*of plan, book etc*) prendre forme; (*progress well*) avancer.
**-shaped** *suffix* **pear-s.**/*etc* en forme de poire/*etc*.
**share** **1** *n* part *f* (**of, in** de); (*of stock*) action *f*. **2** *vt* (*meal, opinion etc*) partager (**with** avec); (*characteristic*) avoir en commun.
**shareholder** actionnaire *mf*.
**share in sth** avoir sa part de qch.
**share sth out** partager *or* répartir qch (**among** entre).
**shark** requin *m*.
**sharp** **1** *a* (*knife etc*) tranchant; (*pointed*) pointu; (*point, pain*) aigu (*f* -uë); (*bend*) brusque. **2** *adv* **five o'clock**/*etc* **s.** cinq heures/*etc* pile.
**sharpen** *vt* (*knife*) aiguiser; (*pencil*) tailler.
**sharply** *adv* (*suddenly*) brusquement.
**shatter** **1** *vt* (*door, arm etc*) fracasser; (*glass*) faire voler en éclats. **2** *vi* se fracasser; (*of glass*) voler en éclats.
**shave** **1** *vt* (*person, head*) raser; **to s. off one's beard** se raser la barbe. **2** *vi* se raser. **3** *n* **to have a s.** se raser.
**shaver** rasoir *m* électrique.
**shaving cream** crème *f* à raser.
**shaving kit** trousse *f* de toilette (d'homme).
**shawl** châle *m*.
**she** *pron* elle; **she's a happy woman** c'est une femme heureuse.
**shed**[1] (*in garden*) abri *m* (de jardin); (*for goods or machines*) hangar *m*.
**shed**[2]***** *vt* (*lose*) perdre; (*tears*) répandre.
**sheep** *n inv* mouton *m*.
**sheepskin** peau *f* de mouton.
**sheet** (*on bed*) drap *m*; (*of paper*) feuille *f*; (*of glass, ice*) plaque *f*.
**shelf** (*pl* **shelves**) étagère *f*; (*in shop*) rayon *m*.
**shell** **1** *n* (*of egg etc*) coquille *f*; (*of tortoise*) carapace *f*; (*seashell*) coquillage *m*; (*explosive*) obus *m*. **2** *vt* (*peas*) écosser.
**shellfish** (*oysters etc*) fruits *mpl* de mer.
**shelter** **1** *n* abri *m*; **to take s.** se mettre à l'abri (**from** de). **2** *vt* abriter (**from** de). **3** *vi* s'abriter.
**shelving** rayonnage(s) *m*(*pl*).
**shepherd** berger *m*.
**sheriff** shérif *m*.
**sherry** sherry *m*.
**shield** **1** *n* bouclier *m*; (*screen*) écran *m*. **2** *vt* protéger (**from** de).
**shift** **1** *n* (*change*) changement *m* (**of, in** de); (*period of work*) poste

*m*; (*workers*) équipe *f*; **gear s.** levier *m* de vitesse. **2** *vt* (*move*) bouger; **to s. gear(s)** changer de vitesse. **3** *vi* bouger.

**shin** tibia *m*.

**shine 1** *vi** briller. **2** *vt* (*polish*) faire briller; **to s. a light on sth** éclairer qch. **3** *n* (*on shoes, cloth*) brillant *m*.

**shiny** *a* brillant.

**ship** navire *m*, bateau *m*; **by s.** en bateau.

**shipping** (*traffic*) navigation *f*.

**shipwreck** naufrage *m*.

**shipwrecked** *a* naufragé; **to be s.** faire naufrage.

**shipyard** chantier *m* naval.

**shirt** chemise *f*; (*of woman*) chemisier *m*; (*of sportsman*) maillot *m*.

**shiver 1** *vi* frissonner (**with** de). **2** *n* frisson *m*.

**shock 1** *n* (*emotional, physical*) choc *m*; **(electric) s.** décharge *f* (électrique); **suffering from s.** en état de choc. **2** *vt* (*offend*) choquer; (*surprise*) stupéfier.

**shock absorber** amortisseur *m*.

**shocking** *a* affreux; (*outrageous*) scandaleux.

**shoe** chaussure *f*, soulier *m*.

**shoelace** lacet *m*.

**shoe polish** cirage *m*.

**shoe repair shop** cordonnerie *f*.

**shoe store** magasin *m* de chaussures.

**shoot* 1** *vt* (*kill*) tuer (d'un coup de feu); (*wound*) blesser (d'un coup de feu); (*execute*) fusiller; (*gun*) tirer un coup de; (*film*) tourner. **2** *vi* (*with gun*) tirer (**at** sur).

**shoot ahead/off** (*rush*) avancer/partir à toute vitesse.

**shooting** (*shots*) coups *mpl* de feu; (*murder*) meurtre *m*.

**shoot up** (*of price*) monter en flèche.

**shop 1** *n* magasin *m*; (*small*) boutique *f*; **at the flower s.** chez le fleuriste. **2** *vi* faire ses courses (**at** chez).

**shopkeeper** commerçant, -ante *mf*.

**shopping to go s.** faire des courses.

**shopping bag** sac *m* à provisions.

**shopping center** (*purpose-built*) centre *m* commercial.

**shopping district** quartier *m* commerçant.

**shop window** vitrine *f*.

**shore** (*of sea, lake*) rivage *m*; (*coast*) côte *f*.

**short 1** *a* court; (*person, distance*) petit; **a s. time** *or* **while (ago)** (il y a) peu de temps; **to be s. of money/time** être à court d'argent/de temps; **we're s. ten men** il nous manque dix hommes; **to be s. for sth** (*of name*) être l'abréviation de qch. **2** *adv* **to cut s.** (*hair*) couper court; (*visit etc*) raccourcir; (*person*) couper la parole à; **to get** *or* **run s.** manquer (**of** de).

**shortage** manque *m*.

**short cut** raccourci *m*.

**shorten** *vt* (*dress, text etc*) raccourcir.

**shortly** *adv* (*soon*) bientôt; **s. after** peu après.

**shorts** *npl* **(a pair of ) s.** un short.

**shortsighted** *a* myope.

**short-term** *a* à court terme.

**shot** (*from gun*) coup *m*; (*with camera*) prise *f* de vues.

**shotgun** fusil *m* (de chasse).

**should** *v aux* (= *ought to*) **you s. do it** vous devriez le faire; **I s. have stayed** j'aurais dû rester; **that s. be Paul** ça doit être Paul. ▪ (= *would*) **it's strange she s. say no** il est étrange qu'elle dise non. ▪ (*possibility*) **if he s. come** s'il vient.

**shoulder** épaule *f*; **(hard) s.** (*of highway*) bas-côté *m*.

**shoulder bag** sac *m* à bandoulière.

**shout 1** *n* cri *m*. **2** *vti* crier; **to s. to s.o. to do** crier à qn de faire.

**shout at s.o.** (*scold*) crier après qn.

**shouting** (*shouts*) cris *mpl*.

**shout out** *vti* crier.

**shove 1** *n* poussée *f*; **to give a s. (to)** pousser. **2** *vt* pousser; (*put*) *Fam* fourrer. **3** *vi* pousser.
**shovel 1** *n* pelle *f*. **2** *vt* (*snow etc*) enlever à la pelle.
**show 1** *n* (*in theater*) spectacle *m*; (*at movies*) séance *f*; **the Auto S.** le Salon de l'Automobile; **on s.** (*painting etc*) exposé. **2** *vt** montrer (**to** à, **that** que); (*in exhibition*) exposer; (*movie*) passer; (*indicate*) indiquer; **to s. s.o. to the door** reconduire qn. **3** *vi* (*be visible*) se voir; (*of movie*) passer.
**show s.o. around** faire visiter qn; **to s. s.o. around the house** faire visiter la maison à qn.
**shower** (*bath*) douche *f*; (*of rain*) averse *f*.
**show in** (*visitor*) faire entrer.
**showing** (*of movie*) séance *f*.
**show off** *vi* crâner.
**show-off** crâneur, -euse *mf*.
**show out** (*visitor*) reconduire.
**show up 1** *vi* (*of person*) arriver. **2** *vt* (*embarrass*) mettre (*qn*) dans l'embarras.
**shrimp** crevette *f* (grise).
**shrink*** *vi* (*of clothes*) rétrécir.
**shrub** arbuste *m*.
**shrug** *vt* **to s. one's shoulders** hausser les épaules.
**shudder** *vi* frémir (**with** de).
**shuffle** *vt* (*cards*) battre.
**shush!** *int* chut!
**shut* 1** *vt* fermer. **2** *vi* (*of door etc*) se fermer; (*of shop etc*) fermer.
**shut down** *vti* fermer.
**shut in** enfermer.
**shut off** (*gas etc*) fermer; (*engine*) arrêter; (*isolate*) isoler.
**shut out** (*light*) empêcher d'entrer; **to s. s.o. out** (*accidentally*) enfermer qn dehors.
**shutter** (*on window*) volet *m*; (*of store*) rideau *m* (métallique).
**shuttle** **s. (service)** navette *f*; **space s.** navette spatiale.
**shut up 1** *vt* (*house etc*) fermer; (*lock up*) enfermer (*personne, objet précieux*). **2** *vi* (*be quiet*) se taire.
**shy** *a* timide.
**shyness** timidité *f*.
**sick 1** *a* malade; **to be s.** (*vomit*) vomir; **off s.** en congé de maladie; **to feel s.** avoir mal au cœur; **to be s. (and tired) of sth/s.o.** *Fam* en avoir marre de qch/qn. **2** *n* **the s.** les malades *mpl*.
**sickness** maladie *f*.
**side** côté *m*; (*of hill, animal*) flanc *m*; (*of road, river*) bord *m*; (*team*) équipe *f*; **at** *or* **by the s. of** à côté de; **at** *or* **by my s.** à côté de moi, à mes côtés; **s. by s.** l'un à côté de l'autre; **to move to one s.** s'écarter; **on this s.** de ce côté; **on the other s.** de l'autre côté; **to take sides with s.o.** se ranger du côté de qn; **on our s.** de notre côté.
**sideboard** buffet *m*.
**sidewalk** trottoir *m*.
**sideways** *adv* & *a* de côté.
**sieve** tamis *m*; (*for liquids*) passoire *f*.
**sift** *vt* (*flour etc*) tamiser.
**sigh 1** *n* soupir *m*. **2** *vi* soupirer.
**sight** vue *f*; (*thing seen*) spectacle *m*; **to lose s. of** perdre de vue; **to catch s. of** apercevoir; **by s.** de vue; **in s.** (*target etc*) en vue; **out of s.** caché; **the (tourist) sights** les attractions *fpl* touristiques.
**sightseeing** **to go s.** faire du tourisme.
**sign 1** *n* signe *m*; (*notice*) panneau *m*; (*over shop, inn*) enseigne *f*; **no s. of** aucune trace de. **2** *vti* (*with signature*) signer.
**signal 1** *n* signal *m*; (*of vehicle*) clignotant *m*; **traffic signals** feux *mpl* de signalisation. **2** *vi* faire signe (**to** à); **to s. (left/right)** (*in car*) mettre son clignotant (à gauche/à droite).
**signature** signature *f*.
**significant** *a* (*important, large*) important.
**significantly** *adv* sensiblement.
**sign in** (*in hotel etc*) signer le registre.
**sign on** *or* **up** (*of soldier, worker*)

s'engager; (*for course*) s'inscrire (for à).
**signpost** poteau *m* indicateur.
**silence 1** *n* silence *m*; **in s.** en silence. **2** *vt* faire taire.
**silent** *a* silencieux; (*movie*) muet (*f* muette); **to keep s.** garder le silence (**about** sur).
**silently** *adv* silencieusement.
**silk** soie *f*.
**sill** (*of window*) rebord *m*.
**silly** *a* bête; **to do something s.** faire une bêtise.
**silver 1** *n* argent *m*; (*plates etc*) argenterie *f*. **2** *a* (*spoon etc*) en argent; **s. paper** papier *m* d'argent.
**silver-plated** *a* plaqué argent.
**silverware** *n inv* argenterie *f*.
**similar** *a* semblable (**to** à).
**similarity** ressemblance *f* (**to** avec).
**simple** *a* simple.
**simplify** *vt* simplifier.
**simply** *adv* (*plainly, merely*) simplement; (*absolutely*) absolument.
**simultaneous** *a* simultané.
**simultaneously** *adv* simultanément.
**sin** péché *m*.
**since 1** *prep* depuis. **2** *conj* depuis que; (*because*) puisque; **s. she's been here** depuis qu'elle est ici; **it's a year s. I saw him** ça fait un an que je ne l'ai pas vu. **3** *adv* **(ever) s.** depuis.
**sincere** *a* sincère.
**sincerely** *adv* sincèrement; **yours s.** (*in letter*) veuillez croire à mes sentiments dévoués.
**sincerity** sincérité *f*.
**sing*** *vti* chanter.
**singer** chanteur, -euse *mf*.
**single** *a* seul; (*room, bed*) pour une personne; (*unmarried*) célibataire; **not a s. book**/*etc* pas un seul livre/*etc*; **every s. day** tous les jours sans exception.
**single out** choisir.
**Single Market** Marché *m* unique.
**singular 1** *a* (*form*) singulier; (*noun*) au singulier. **2** *n* singulier *m*; **in the s.** au singulier.
**sinister** *a* sinistre.
**sink**[1] (*in kitchen*) évier *m*; (*washbasin*) lavabo *m*.
**sink**[2]* *vi* (*of ship, person etc*) couler.
**sink (down) into** (*mud*) s'enfoncer dans; (*armchair*) s'affaler dans.
**sip** *vi* boire à petites gorgées.
**sir** monsieur *m*; **S.** (*title*) sir.
**siren** (*of factory etc*) sirène *f*.
**sister** sœur *f*.
**sister-in-law** (*pl* **sisters-in-law**) belle-sœur *f*.
**sit* 1** *vi* s'asseoir; **to be sitting** être assis; **she was sitting reading** elle était assise à lire. **2** *vt* (*child on chair etc*) asseoir.
**sit (for)** (*exam*) se présenter à.
**sit around** traîner; (*do nothing*) ne rien faire.
**sit down 1** *vi* s'asseoir; **to be sitting down** être assis. **2** *vt* asseoir (*qn*).
**site** (*position*) emplacement *m*; **(building) s.** chantier *m*.
**sitting room** salon *m*.
**situate** *vt* situer; **to be situated** être situé, se situer.
**situation** situation *f*.
**sit up (straight)** *vi* s'asseoir (bien droit).
**six** *a* & *n* six (*m*).
**sixteen** *a* & *n* seize (*m*).
**sixth** *a* & *n* sixième (*mf*).
**sixtieth** *a* & *n* soixantième (*mf*).
**sixty** *a* & *n* soixante (*m*).
**size** (*of person, clothes, packet etc*) taille *f*; (*measurements*) dimensions *fpl*; (*of town, sum*) importance *f*; (*of shoes, gloves*) pointure *f*; (*of shirt*) encolure *f*; **hip/chest s.** tour *m* de hanches/de poitrine.
**skate 1** *n* patin *m*. **2** *vi* patiner.
**skateboard** planche *f* (à roulettes).
**skater** patineur, -euse *mf*.
**skating** patinage *m*; **to go s.** faire du patinage.

**skating rink** (*ice-skating*) patinoire *f*.
**skeleton** squelette *m*.
**sketch 1** *n* (*drawing*) croquis *m*; (*comic play*) sketch *m*. **2** *vi* faire un *or* des croquis.
**skewer** (*for meat etc*) broche *f*; (*for kebab*) brochette *f*.
**ski 1** *n* ski *m*. **2** *vi* (*pt* **skied** ) faire du ski.
**skid 1** *vi* déraper; **to s. into sth** déraper et heurter qch. **2** *n* dérapage *m*.
**skier** skieur, -euse *mf*.
**skiing 1** *n* ski *m*. **2** *a* (*school, clothes, etc*) de ski.
**skillful** *a* habile (**at doing** à faire, **at sth** à qch).
**ski lift** remonte-pente *m*.
**skill** habileté *f* (**at** à); (*technique*) technique *f*.
**skilled worker** ouvrier, -ière qualifié(e).
**skim milk** lait *m* écrémé.
**skin** peau *f*.
**skin diving** plongée *f* sous-marine.
**skinny** *a* maigre.
**skip 1** *vi* (*hop*) sautiller; (*with rope*) sauter à la corde. **2** *vt* (*miss*) sauter (*repas, classe etc*).
**skirt** jupe *f*.
**skull** crâne *m*.
**sky** ciel *m*.
**skyscraper** gratte-ciel *m inv*.
**slack** *a* (*knot, spring*) lâche; **to be s.** (*of rope*) avoir du mou; (*in office etc*) être calme.
**slacken** *vt* (*rope*) relâcher.
**slacks** *npl* pantalon *m*.
**slam 1** *vt* (*door, lid*) claquer. **2** *vi* (*of door*) claquer. **3** *n* claquement *m*.
**slang** argot *m*.
**slant 1** *n* inclinaison *f*. **2** *vi* (*of roof*) être en pente.
**slap 1** *n* tape *f*; (*on face*) gifle *f*. **2** *vt* (*person*) donner une tape à; **to s. s.o.'s face** gifler qn; **to s. s.o.'s bottom** donner une fessée à qn.
**slate** ardoise *f*.
**slaughter 1** *vt* massacrer; (*animal*) abattre. **2** *n* massacre *m*; abattage *m*.
**slave** esclave *mf*.
**slave away** se crever (au travail).
**slavery** esclavage *m*.
**sled** luge *f*; (*horse-drawn*) traîneau *m*.
**sleep 1** *n* sommeil *m*; **to get some s.** dormir. **2** *vi** dormir; (*spend the night*) coucher; **to go** *or* **get to s.** s'endormir.
**sleeper** (*bed in train*) couchette *f*; (*train*) train *m* couchettes.
**sleeping** *a* (*asleep*) endormi.
**sleeping bag** sac *m* de couchage.
**sleeping car** wagon-lit *m*.
**sleeping pill** somnifère *m*.
**sleepy** *a* **to be s.** (*of person*) avoir sommeil.
**sleet 1** *n* neige *f* fondue. **2** *vi* **it's sleeting** il tombe de la neige fondue.
**sleeve** (*of shirt etc*) manche *f*; (*of record*) pochette *f*; **long-/short-sleeved** à manches longues/courtes.
**sleigh** traîneau *m*.
**slept** *pt & pp de* **sleep.**
**slice** tranche *f*.
**slice (up)** *vt* couper (en tranches).
**slide 1** *n* (*in playground*) toboggan *m*; (*film*) diapositive *f*. **2** *vi** glisser. **3** *vt* (*letter etc*) glisser (**into** dans); (*table, chair etc*) faire glisser.
**sliding door** porte *f* à glissière *or* coulissante.
**slight** *a* (*noise, mistake etc*) léger, petit; (*chance*) faible; **the slightest thing** la moindre chose; **not in the slightest** pas le moins du monde.
**slightly** *adv* légèrement.
**slim 1** *a* mince. **2** *vi* maigrir.
**sling** *n* (*for arm*) écharpe *f*; **in a s.** en écharpe.
**slip 1** *n* (*mistake*) erreur *f*; (*woman's undergarment*) combinaison *f*; **a s. of paper** un bout de papier. **2** *vi* glisser. **3** *vt* (*slide*) glisser (*qch*) (**to** à, **into** dans).
**slip away** *vi* s'esquiver.

**slipcover** (*on furniture*) housse *f*.
**slip in** *vi* entrer furtivement.
**slip into** (*room etc*) se glisser dans; (*bathrobe etc*) mettre, passer.
**slip off** (*garment*) enlever.
**slip on** (*garment*) mettre.
**slip out** *vi* sortir furtivement; (*for a moment*) sortir (un instant).
**slipper** pantoufle *f*.
**slippery** *a* glissant.
**slip up** (*make a mistake*) gaffer.
**slit** (*opening*) fente *f*; (*cut*) coupure *f*.
**slogan** slogan *m*.
**slope 1** *n* pente *f*; (*of mountain*) versant *m*; (*for skiing*) piste *f*. **2** *vi* (*of ground, roof etc*) être en pente.
**sloping** *a* en pente.
**slot** (*slit*) fente *f*; (*groove*) rainure *f*.
**slot machine** distributeur *m* automatique; (*gambling*) machine *f* à sous.
**slow 1** *a* lent; **to be s.** (*of clock, watch*) retarder; **to be five minutes s.** retarder de cinq minutes; **in s. motion** au ralenti. **2** *adv* lentement.
**slow down** *or* **up** *vti* ralentir.
**slowly** *adv* lentement; (*bit by bit*) peu à peu.
**slowpoke** *Fam* tortue *f*.
**slug** limace *f*.
**slum** (*house*) taudis *m*; **the slums** les quartiers *mpl* pauvres.
**sly** *a* (*cunning*) rusé.
**smack 1** *n* claque *f*; gifle *f*; (*on bottom*) fessée *f*. **2** *vt* (*person*) donner une claque à; **to s. s.o.'s face** gifler qn; **to s. s.o.('s bottom)** donner une fessée à qn.
**small 1** *a* petit. **2** *adv* (*to cut, chop*) menu.
**smallpox** petite vérole *f*.
**smart** *a* (*fashionable, elegant*) élégant; (*clever*) intelligent.
**smash 1** *vt* (*break*) briser; (*shatter*) fracasser. **2** *vi* se briser.
**smashing** *a Fam* formidable.
**smash into sth** (*of vehicle*) (r)entrer dans qch.
**smash-up** collision *f*.
**smell 1** *n* odeur *f*; **(sense of) s.** odorat *m*. **2** *vt** sentir. **3** *vi* (*stink*) sentir (mauvais); (*have a smell*) avoir une odeur; **to s. of smoke/***etc* sentir la fumée/*etc*.
**smile 1** *n* sourire *m*. **2** *vi* sourire (**at s.o.** à qn).
**smock** blouse *f*.
**smoke 1** *n* fumée *f*; **to have a s.** fumer une cigarette *etc*. **2** *vti* fumer; **'no smoking'** 'défense de fumer'; **smoking compartment** compartiment *m* fumeurs.
**smoker** fumeur, -euse *mf*; (*train compartment*) compartiment *m* fumeurs.
**smooth** *a* (*surface, skin etc*) lisse; (*flight*) agréable.
**smooth down** *or* **out** (*dress, hair etc*) lisser.
**smuggle** *vt* passer (en fraude).
**smuggler** contrebandier, -ière *mf*.
**smuggling** contrebande *f*.
**snack** (*meal*) casse-croûte *m inv*; **snacks** (*things to eat*) petites choses *fpl* à grignoter; (*candies*) friandises *fpl*; **to eat a s.** *or* **snacks** grignoter.
**snack bar** snack(-bar) *m*.
**snail** escargot *m*.
**snake** serpent *m*.
**snap 1** *vt* (*break*) casser (avec un bruit sec). **2** *vi* se casser net. **3** *n* (*fastener*) bouton-pression *m*.
**snap(shot)** photo *f*.
**snatch** *vt* saisir (*d'un geste vif*); **to s. sth from s.o.** arracher qch à qn.
**sneaker** (chaussure *f* de) tennis *m*.
**sneer** *vi* ricaner.
**sneeze 1** *vi* éternuer. **2** *n* éternuement *m*.
**sniff** *vti* **to s. (at)** renifler.
**snip (off)** *vt* couper.
**snooker** snooker *m* (*sorte de jeu de billard*).
**snore** *vi* ronfler.
**snoring** ronflements *mpl*.
**snout** museau *m*.
**snow 1** *n* neige *f*. **2** *vi* neiger; **it's snowing** il neige.

**snowball** boule *f* de neige.
**snowdrift** congère *f*.
**snowflake** flocon *m* de neige.
**snowman** bonhomme *m* de neige.
**snowplow** chasse-neige *m inv*.
**snowstorm** tempête *f* de neige.
**so 1** *adv* (*to such a degree*) si, tellement (**that** que); (*thus*) ainsi; **so that** (*purpose*) pour que (+ *subjunctive*); (*result*) si bien que (+ *indicative*); **so as to do** pour faire; **I think so** je le pense; **if so** si oui; **is that so?** c'est vrai?; **so am I, so do I** *etc* moi aussi; **so much** (*to work etc*) tant (**that** que); **so much courage**/*etc* tant de courage/*etc*; **so many** tant; **so many books**/*etc* tant de livres/*etc*; **ten or so** environ dix; **and so on** et ainsi de suite. **2** *conj* (*therefore*) donc; **so what?** et alors?
**soak 1** *vt* (*drench*) tremper (*qn*); (*laundry, food*) faire tremper. **2** *vi* (*of laundry etc*) tremper.
**soaked through** *a* (*person*) trempé jusqu'aux os.
**soaking** *a* & *adv* **s. (wet)** trempé.
**soak sth up** absorber qch.
**soap** savon *m*.
**soap powder** lessive *f*.
**soapy** *a* savonneux.
**sob 1** *n* sanglot *m*. **2** *vi* sangloter.
**sober** *a* **he's s.** (*not drunk*) il n'est pas ivre.
**soccer** football *m*.
**social** *a* social; **s. club** club *m*; **s. evening** soireé *f*; **to have a good s. life** sortir beaucoup; **s. security** (*pension*) pension *f* de retraite; **s. services, S. Security** = Sécurité *f* sociale; **s. worker** assistant, -ante *mf* social(e).
**socialist** *a* & *n* socialiste (*mf*).
**society** société *f*.
**sock** chaussette *f*.
**socket** (*for electric plug*) prise *f* de courant.
**soda (pop)** soda *m*.
**soda (water)** eau *f* gazeuse.
**sofa** canapé *m*; **s. bed** canapé-lit *m*.
**soft** *a* (*gentle, not stiff*) doux (*f* douce); (*butter, ground*) mou (*f* molle); **s. drink** boisson *f* non alcoolisée.
**softly** *adv* doucement.
**software** *n inv* logiciel *m*.
**soil** sol *m*, terre *f*.
**soldier** soldat *m*.
**sole** (*of shoe*) semelle *f*; (*of foot*) plante *f*; (*fish*) sole *f*; **lemon s.** limande *f*.
**solemn** *a* (*formal*) solennel; (*serious*) grave.
**solid 1** *a* (*car, meal etc*) solide; (*wall, line*) plein; (*gold*) massif; **s. line** ligne *f* continue. **2** *n* solide *m*.
**solution** solution *f* (**to** de).
**solve** *vt* (*problem*) résoudre.
**some 1** *a* (*amount, number*) du, de la, des; **s. wine** du vin; **s. water** de l'eau; **s. dogs** des chiens; **s. pretty flowers** de jolies fleurs. ▪ (*unspecified*) un, une; **s. man (or other)** un homme (quelconque). ▪ (*a few*) quelques; (*a little*) un peu de. **2** *pron* (*number*) quelques-un(e)s (**of** de). ▪ (*a certain quantity*) en; **I want s.** j'en veux.
**somebody** *pron* = **someone.**
**someday** *adv* un jour.
**somehow** *adv* d'une manière ou d'une autre; (*for some reason*) on ne sait pourquoi.
**someone** *pron* quelqu'un; **s. small**/*etc* quelqu'un de petit/*etc*.
**someplace** *adv* quelque part.
**somersault** culbute *f*.
**something** *pron* quelque chose; **s. awful**/*etc* quelque chose d'affreux/*etc*; **s. of a liar**/*etc* un peu menteur/*etc*.
**sometime** *adv* un jour.
**sometimes** *adv* quelquefois.
**somewhat** *adv* quelque peu.
**somewhere** *adv* quelque part.
**son** fils *m*.
**song** chanson *f*.
**son-in-law** (*pl* **sons-in-law**) gendre *m*.
**soon** *adv* bientôt; (*quickly*) vite;

(*early*) tôt; **s. after** peu après; **as s. as she leaves** aussitôt qu'elle partira; **no sooner had he spoken than** à peine avait-il parlé que; **I'd sooner leave** je préférerais partir; **I'd just as s. leave** j'aimerais autant partir; **sooner or later** tôt ou tard.

**soot** suie *f.*

**soothe** *vt* (*pain, nerves*) calmer.

**sore** 1 *a* (*painful*) douloureux; (*angry*) *Fam* fâché (**at** contre); **she has a s. throat** elle a mal à la gorge. 2 *n* plaie *f.*

**sorrow** chagrin *m.*

**sorry** *a* **to be s.** (*regret*) être désolé (**to do** de faire); **I'm s. she can't come** je regrette qu'elle ne puisse pas venir; **I'm s. about the delay** je m'excuse pour ce retard; **s.!** pardon!; **to feel** *or* **be s. for s.o.** plaindre qn.

**sort**[1] sorte *f*, espèce *f* (**of** de); **all sorts of** toutes sortes de; **what s. of drink**/*etc* **is it?** qu'est-ce que c'est comme boisson/*etc*?

**sort**[2] *vt* (*papers etc*) trier.

**sort out** (*classify, select*) trier; (*separate*) séparer (**from** de); (*tidy*) ranger; (*problem*) régler.

**soul** âme *f.*

**sound**[1] 1 *n* son *m*; (*noise*) bruit *m*; **I don't like the s. of it** ça ne me plaît pas du tout. 2 *vt* (*bell, alarm etc*) sonner; **to s. one's horn** klaxonner. 3 *vi* (*of bell etc*) sonner; (*seem*) sembler; **to s. like** sembler être; (*resemble*) ressembler à.

**sound**[2] 1 *a* (*healthy*) sain; (*good, reliable*) solide. 2 *adv* **s. asleep** profondément endormi.

**soundproof** *vt* insonoriser.

**soup** soupe *f*, potage *m.*

**sour** *a* aigre.

**source** source *f.*

**south** 1 *n* sud *m*; **(to the) s. of** au sud de. 2 *a* (*coast*) sud *inv.* 3 *adv* au sud.

**southbound** *a* en direction du sud.

**south-east** *n* & *a* sud-est *m* & *a inv.*

**southern** *a* (*town*) du sud; (*coast*) sud *inv.*

**southerner** habitant, -ante *mf* du Sud.

**southward(s)** *a* & *adv* vers le sud.

**south-west** *n* & *a* sud-ouest *m* & *a inv.*

**souvenir** (*object*) souvenir *m.*

**sow*** *vt* (*seeds*) semer.

**space** (*gap, emptiness, atmosphere*) espace *m*; (*period*) période *f*; (*for parking*) place *f*; **to take up s.** (*room*) prendre de la place.

**space heater** radiateur *m* d'appoint.

**space out** *vt* espacer.

**spaceship** engin *m* spatial.

**spacesuit** combinaison *f* spatiale.

**spacious** *a* spacieux.

**spade** bêche *f*; (*of child*) pelle *f*; **spade(s)** *Cards* pique *m.*

**spaghetti** spaghetti(s) *mpl.*

**Spaniard** Espagnol, -ole *mf.*

**Spanish** 1 *a* espagnol. 2 *n* (*language*) espagnol *m.*

**spank** *vt* donner une fessée à.

**spanking** fessée *f.*

**spare** 1 *a* (*extra*) de trop; (*clothes*) de rechange; (*wheel*) de secours; (*bed, room*) d'ami; **s. time** loisirs *mpl.* 2 *n* **s. (part)** pièce *f* détachée. 3 *vt* (*do without*) se passer de (*qn, qch*); **to s. s.o.** (*details etc*) épargner à qn; (*time*) accorder à qn; (*money*) donner à qn.

**spark** étincelle *f.*

**sparkle** *vi* (*of diamond, star*) étinceler.

**sparkling** *a* (*wine, water*) pétillant.

**spark plug** bougie *f.*

**sparrow** moineau *m.*

**speak*** 1 *vi* parler (**about, of** de); **English-/French-speaking** qui parle anglais/français. 2 *vt* (*language*) parler; (*say*) dire.

**speaker** (*public*) orateur *m*;

(*loudspeaker*) haut-parleur *m*; (*of stereo system*) enceinte *f*.
**speak up** parler plus fort.
**spear** lance *f*.
**special 1** *a* spécial; (*care, attention*) (tout) particulier. **2** *n* **today's s.** (*in restaurant*) le plat du jour.
**specialist** spécialiste *mf* (**in** de).
**specialize** *vi* se spécialiser (**in** dans).
**specially** *adv* spécialement.
**specialty** spécialité *f*.
**species** *n inv* espèce *f*.
**specific** *a* précis.
**specimen** (*example, person*) spécimen *m*.
**spectacular** *a* spectaculaire.
**spectator** spectateur, -trice *mf*.
**speech** (*talk, lecture*) discours *m* (**on, about** sur); (*power of language*) parole *f*; (*spoken language*) langage *m*.
**speed 1** *n* (*rate*) vitesse *f*; (*quickness*) rapidité *f*; **s. limit** limitation *f* de vitesse. **2** *vi* (*drive too fast*) aller trop vite.
**speedboat** vedette *f*.
**speedometer** compteur *m* (de vitesse).
**speed* up 1** *vt* accélérer. **2** *vi* (*of person*) aller plus vite.
**spell[1]** (*period*) (courte) période *f*; (*magic*) charme *m*; **cold s.** vague *f* de froid.
**spell[2]*** *vt* (*write*) écrire; (*say aloud*) épeler; (*of letters*) former (*mot*); **how is it spelled?** comment cela s'écrit-il?
**spelling** orthographe *f*.
**spend* 1** *vt* (*money*) dépenser (**on** pour); (*time etc*) passer (**on sth** sur qch, **doing** à faire). **2** *vi* dépenser.
**sphere** sphère *f*.
**spice 1** *n* épice *f*. **2** *vt* épicer.
**spicy** *a* (*food*) épicé.
**spider** araignée *f*; **s.'s web** toile *f* d'araignée.
**spike** pointe *f*.
**spill* 1** *vt* répandre, renverser. **2** *vi* se répandre, se renverser (**on, over** sur).
**spill out 1** *vt* (*empty*) vider (*café, verre etc*). **2** *vi* (*of coffee etc*) se renverser.
**spill over** déborder.
**spin*** *vt* (*wheel etc*) faire tourner; (*washing*) essorer.
**spinach** (*food*) épinards *mpl*.
**spin (around)** (*of dancer, wheel etc*) tourner.
**spine** (*of back*) colonne *f* vertébrale.
**spiral** spirale *f*.
**spire** flèche *f*.
**spirits** *npl* (*drinks*) alcool *m*.
**spit 1** *vti** cracher. **2** *n* (*for meat*) broche *f*.
**spite in s. of** malgré.
**spiteful** *a* méchant.
**splash 1** *vt* éclabousser (**with** de, **over** sur). **2** *n* (*mark*) éclaboussure *f*.
**splash (around)** *vi* (*in river, mud*) patauger; (*in bath*) barboter.
**splendid** *a* splendide.
**splinter** (*in finger*) écharde *f*.
**split 1** *n* fente *f*; (*tear*) déchirure *f*. **2** *vt** (*break apart*) fendre; (*tear*) déchirer.
**split (up) 1** *vt* (*group*) diviser; (*money, work*) partager (**between** entre). **2** *vi* (*of group*) se diviser (**into** en); (*because of disagreement*) se séparer.
**spoil*** *vt* gâter; (*damage, ruin*) abîmer; (*child, dog etc*) gâter.
**spoke** (*of wheel*) rayon *m*.
**spoke, spoken** *pt & pp de* **speak**.
**spokesman** (*pl* **-men**) porte-parole *m invariable* (**for, of** de).
**sponge** éponge *f*.
**sponge cake** gâteau *m* de Savoie.
**sponge oneself down** se laver à l'éponge.
**spontaneous** *a* spontané.
**spool** bobine *f*.
**spoon** cuillère *f*.
**spoonful** cuillerée *f*.

**sport** sport *m*; **sports** (*in general*) sport *m*; **my favorite s.** mon sport préféré; **to play sports** faire du sport; **sports club** club *m* sportif; **sports car/jacket/ground** voiture *f*/veste *f*/terrain *m* de sport.
**sportsman** (*pl* **-men**) sportif *m*.
**sportswoman** (*pl* **-women**) sportive *f*.
**spot**[1] (*stain, mark*) tache *f*; (*dot*) point *m*; (*place*) endroit *m*; **on the s.** sur place.
**spot**[2] *vt* (*notice*) apercevoir.
**spotless** *a* (*clean*) impeccable.
**spotlight** (*in theater etc*) projecteur *m*; (*for photography*) spot *m*.
**spotted** *a* (*animal*) tacheté.
**spout** (*of teapot etc*) bec *m*.
**sprain 1** *n* foulure *f*. **2** *vt* **to s. one's ankle/wrist** se fouler la cheville/le poignet.
**spray 1** *n* (*can*) bombe *f*; **hair s.** laque *f* à cheveux. **2** *vt* (*liquid, surface*) vaporiser; (*plant*) arroser; (*car*) peindre à la bombe.
**spread 1** *vt** (*stretch, open out*) étendre; (*legs, fingers*) écarter; (*distribute*) répandre (**over** sur); (*paint, payment, visits*) étaler; (*news, germs*) propager. **2** *vi* (*of fire*) s'étendre; (*of news, epidemic*) se propager. **3** *n* (*paste*) pâte *f* (à tartiner); **cheese s.** fromage *m* à tartiner.
**spread out 1** *vt* étendre; écarter; répandre; étaler. **2** *vi* (*of people*) se disperser.
**spring**[1] **1** *n* (*metal device*) ressort *m*. **2** *vi** (*leap*) bondir.
**spring**[2] (*season*) printemps *m*; **in (the) s.** au printemps.
**spring**[3] (*of water*) source *f*.
**springboard** tremplin *m*.
**spring onion** oignon *m* vert.
**springtime** printemps *m*.
**sprinkle** *vt* (*sand etc*) répandre (**on, over** sur); **to s. with water, s. water on** asperger d'eau; **to s. with** (*sugar, salt, flour*) saupoudrer de.
**sprinkler** (*in garden*) arroseur *m*.
**sprout (Brussels) s.** chou *m* (*pl* choux) de Bruxelles.
**spur** (*of horse rider*) éperon *m*.
**spurt (out)** *vi* (*of liquid*) jaillir.
**spy** espion, -onne *mf*.
**spying** espionnage *m*.
**spy on s.o.** espionner qn.
**square 1** *n* carré *m*; (*in town*) place *f*; (*for drawing right angles*) équerre *f*. **2** *a* carré; (*meal*) solide.
**squash 1** *vt* (*crush*) écraser; (*squeeze*) serrer. **2** *n* (*game*) squash *m*; (*vegetable*) courge *f*.
**squat (down)** s'accroupir.
**squatting** *a* accroupi.
**squeak** *vi* (*of door*) grincer; (*of shoe*) craquer.
**squeal 1** *vi* pousser des cris aigus. **2** *n* cri *m* aigu.
**squeeze 1** *vt* (*tube, lemon*) presser; (*hand, arm*) serrer. **2** *vi* (*force oneself*) se glisser (**through/into**/*etc* par/dans/*etc*).
**squeeze (out)** (*juice etc*) faire sortir (**from** de).
**squeeze in** *vi* (*of person*) trouver un peu de place.
**squeeze sth into sth** faire rentrer qch dans qch.
**squeeze up** *vi* se serrer (**against** contre).
**squint 1** *n* **to have a s.** loucher. **2** *vi* loucher; (*in the sunlight etc*) plisser les yeux.
**squirrel** écureuil *m*.
**squirt 1** *vt* (*liquid*) faire gicler. **2** *vi* gicler.
**stab** *vt* (*with knife*) poignarder.
**stable**[1] *a* stable.
**stable**[2] écurie *f*.
**stack** (*heap*) tas *m*; **stacks of** *Fam* un *or* des tas de.
**stack (up)** *vt* entasser.
**stadium** stade *m*.
**staff** personnel *m*; (*of school*) professeurs *mpl*; (*of army*) état-major *m*.
**stag** cerf *m*.
**stage**[1] **1** *n* (*platform*) scène *f*. **2** *vt* (*play*) monter.

**stage**[2] (*phase, of journey*) étape *f.*
**stagecoach** diligence *f.*
**stagger** *vi* chanceler.
**stain 1** *vt* (*to mark*) tacher (**with** de). **2** *n* tache *f.*
**stained glass window** vitrail *m* (*pl* vitraux).
**stainless steel** *a* (*knife etc*) en inox.
**stain remover** détachant *m.*
**staircase** escalier *m.*
**stairs** *npl* escalier *m.*
**stake** (*post*) pieu *m.*
**stale** *a* (*bread etc*) rassis (*f* rassie).
**stalk** (*of plant*) tige *f.*
**stall 1** *n* (*in market*) étal *m* (*pl* étals); (*for newspapers, flowers*) kiosque *m.* **2** *vti* (*of car engine*) caler.
**stammer** *vti* bégayer.
**stamp 1** *n* (*for postage, instrument*) timbre *m*; (*mark*) cachet *m.* **2** *vt* (*document*) tamponner; (*letter*) timbrer; **self-addressed stamped envelope** enveloppe *f* timbrée à votre adresse. **3** *vti* **to s. (one's feet)** taper des pieds.
**stamp collecting** philatélie *f.*
**stand 1** *n* (*support*) support *m*; (*at exhibition*) stand *m*; (*for spectators*) tribune *f*; **news/flower s.** kiosque *m* à journaux/à fleurs. **2** *vt** (*pain, person etc*) supporter; (*put*) mettre (debout); **to s. a chance** avoir une chance. **3** *vi* être *or* se tenir (debout); (*get up*) se lever; (*remain*) rester (debout); (*be situated*) se trouver.
**standard 1** *n* norme *f*; (*level*) niveau *m*; **standards (of behavior)** principes *mpl*; **s. of living** niveau *m* de vie; **up to s.** (*of work etc*) au niveau. **2** *a* (*model, size*) standard *inv.*
**stand around** traîner.
**stand aside** s'écarter.
**stand back** reculer.
**stand by 1** *vi* rester là (sans rien faire); (*be ready*) être prêt. **2** *vt* (*friend*) rester fidèle à.
**standby** *a* (*ticket*) sans garantie.
**stand for** (*mean*) signifier, représenter; (*put up with*) supporter.
**stand in for** remplacer.
**standing** *a* debout *inv.*
**stand out** ressortir (**against** sur).
**standpoint** point *m* de vue.
**standstill to bring to a s.** immobiliser; **to come to a s.** s'immobiliser.
**stand up 1** *vt* mettre debout. **2** *vi* se lever.
**stand up for** défendre.
**stand up to** résister à (*qch*); (*defend oneself*) tenir tête à (*qn*).
**staple 1** *n* (*for paper etc*) agrafe *f.* **2** *vt* agrafer.
**stapler** agrafeuse *f.*
**star 1** *n* étoile *f*; (*person*) vedette *f*; **2** *vi* (*of actor*) être la vedette (**in** de). **3** *vt* (*of movie*) avoir pour vedette.
**stare 1** *n* regard *m* (fixe). **2** *vi* **to s. at** fixer (du regard).
**Star-Spangled Banner** (*flag*) drapeau *m* américain; (*hymn*) hymne *m* national américain.
**start**[1] **1** *n* commencement *m*, début *m*; (*of race*) départ *m*; (*lead*) avance *f* (**on** sur); **to make a s.** commencer. **2** *vt* commencer; **to s. doing** *or* **to do** commencer à faire. **3** *vi* commencer (**with sth** par qch, **by doing** par faire); **starting from** (*price etc*) à partir de.
**start**[2] *vi* (*jump*) sursauter.
**start (off** *or* **out)** partir (**for** pour).
**start (up) 1** *vt* (*engine, vehicle*) mettre en marche; (*business*) fonder. **2** *vi* (of engine, *vehicle*) démarrer.
**starter** (*in vehicle*) démarreur *m.*
**startle** *vt* (*make jump*) faire sursauter.
**start on sth** commencer qch.
**starvation** faim *f.*
**starve** *vi* souffrir de la faim; (*die*) mourir de faim; **I'm starving!** (*hungry*) je meurs de faim!
**state**[1] (*condition*) état *m*; **S.** (*nation etc*) État *m*; **the States** *Fam* les États-Unis *mpl.*
**state**[2] *vt* déclarer (**that** que); (*time, date*) fixer.

**statement** déclaration *f*; **(bank) s.** relevé *m* de compte.

**statesman** (*pl* **-men**) homme *m* d'État.

**station** (*for trains*) gare *f*; (*underground*) station *f*; **(police) s.** commissariat *m* (de police); **bus s.** gare *f* routière; **radio s.** station *f* de radio; **service** *or* **gas s.** station-service *f*.

**stationary** *a* (*vehicle*) à l'arrêt.

**stationery** articles *mpl* de bureau.

**stationery store** papeterie *f*.

**stationmaster** chef *m* de gare.

**station wagon** break *m*, commerciale *f*.

**statistic** (*fact*) statistique *f*.

**statue** statue *f*.

**stay 1** *n* (*visit*) séjour *m*. **2** *vi* rester; (*reside*) loger; (*visit*) séjourner; **to s. put** ne pas bouger.

**stay away** ne pas s'approcher (**from** de); **to s. away from** (*school etc*) ne pas aller à.

**stay in** rester à la maison; (*of nail, screw*) tenir.

**stay out** rester dehors; (*not come home*) ne pas rentrer.

**stay out of sth** (*not interfere in*) ne pas se mêler de qch.

**stay up** ne pas se coucher; (*of fence etc*) tenir; **to s. up late** se coucher tard.

**steadily** *adv* (*gradually*) progressivement; (*regularly*) régulièrement; (*without stopping*) sans arrêt.

**steady** *a* stable; (*hand*) sûr; (*progress, speed*) régulier; **s. (on one's feet)** solide sur ses jambes.

**steak** steak *m*, bifteck *m*.

**steal*** *vti* voler (**from s.o.** à qn).

**steam 1** *n* vapeur *f*; (*on glass*) buée *f*. **2** *vt* (*food*) cuire à la vapeur.

**steamroller** rouleau *m* compresseur.

**steel** acier *m*.

**steep** *a* (*stairs, slope etc*) raide; (*hill, path*) escarpé; (*price*) excessif.

**steeple** clocher *m*.

**steer** *vt* (*vehicle, ship, person*) diriger (**towards** vers).

**steering wheel** volant *m*.

**stem** (*of plant*) tige *f*.

**step 1** *n* pas *m*; (*of stairs*) marche *f*; (*on train, bus*) marchepied *m*; (*doorstep*) pas *m* de la porte; (*action*) mesure *f*; **(flight of) steps** escalier *m*; (*outdoors*) perron *m*; **(pair of) steps** (*ladder*) escabeau *m*. **2** *vi* (*walk*) marcher (**on** sur).

**step aside** s'écarter.

**step back** reculer.

**stepbrother** demi-frère *m*.

**stepdaughter** belle-fille *f*.

**stepfather** beau-père *m*.

**step forward** faire un pas en avant.

**step into /out of** (*car etc*) monter dans/descendre de.

**stepladder** escabeau *m*.

**stepmother** belle-mère *f*.

**step over** (*obstacle*) enjamber.

**stepsister** demi-sœur *f*.

**stepson** beau-fils *m*.

**stereo 1** *n* (*pl* **-os**) (*equipment*) chaîne *f* (stéréo *inv*). **2** *a* stéréo *inv*.

**sterilize** *vt* stériliser.

**stew** ragoût *m*.

**steward** (*on plane, ship*) steward *m*.

**stewardess** hôtesse *f*.

**stewed fruit** compote *f*.

**stick[1]** bâton *m*; (*for walking*) canne *f*.

**stick[2]*** **1** *vt* (*glue*) coller; (*put*) *Fam* mettre, fourrer; **to s. sth into sth** fourrer qch dans qch. **2** *vi* coller (**to** à); (*of food in pan*) attacher (**to** dans); (*of drawer etc*) se coincer, être coincé.

**sticker** autocollant *m*.

**stick on** (*stamp*) coller.

**stick out 1** *vt* (*tongue*) tirer. **2** *vi* (*of petticoat etc*) dépasser.

**stick up** (*notice*) afficher.

**stick up for** défendre.

**sticky** *a* collant; (*label*) adhésif.

**stiff** *a* raide; (*leg etc*) ankylosé; (*brush*) dur; **to have a s. neck** avoir le torticolis; **to feel s.** être courbaturé.

**stifle** *vi* **it's stifling** on étouffe.

**still**[1] *adv* encore, toujours; (*even*) encore; (*nevertheless*) tout de même.

**still**[2] *a* (*not moving*) immobile, (*calm*) calme; **to keep** *or* **stand s.** rester tranquille.

**sting 1** *vti** (*of insect, ointment etc*) piquer. **2** *n* piqûre *f*.

**stingy** *a* avare.

**stink*** *vi* puer; **to s. of smoke**/*etc* empester la fumée/*etc*.

**stink up** (*room*) empester.

**stir** *vt* (*coffee, leaves etc*) remuer.

**stirrup** étrier *m*.

**stitch** point *m*; (*in knitting*) maille *f*; (*in wound*) point *m* de suture.

**stitch (up)** (*sew*) coudre; (*repair*) recoudre.

**stock 1** *n* (*supply*) provision *f*; (*soup*) bouillon *m*; **stock(s)** (*securities*) valeurs *fpl* (boursières); **in s.** en magasin, en stock; **out of s.** épuisé; **the S. Market** la Bourse. **2** *vt* (*sell*) vendre.

**stock (up)** (*store, larder*) approvisionner.

**stocking** bas *m*.

**stock up** *vi* s'approvisionner (**with** de, en).

**stomach** (*for digestion*) estomac *m*; (*front of body*) ventre *m*.

**stomachache** mal *m* de ventre; **to have a s.** avoir mal au ventre.

**stone** pierre *f*; (*pebble*) caillou *m* (*pl* cailloux); (*in fruit*) noyau *m*.

**stood** *pt & pp de* **stand.**

**stool** tabouret *m*.

**stop 1** *n* (*place, halt*) arrêt *m*; (*for plane, ship*) escale *f*; **bus s.** arrêt *m* d'autobus; **to put a s. to sth** mettre fin à qch; **s. sign** (*on road*) stop *m*. **2** *vt* arrêter; (*end*) mettre fin à; (*prevent*) empêcher (**from doing** de faire). **3** *vi* s'arrêter; (*of pain, conversation etc*) cesser; (*stay*) rester; **to s. eating**/*etc* s'arrêter de manger/*etc*; **to s. snowing**/*etc* cesser de neiger/*etc*; **no stopping** (**no standing**) (*street sign*) arrêt interdit.

**stop by** passer (**s.o.'s** chez qn).

**stoplight** (*on vehicle*) stop *m*.

**stop off** *or* **over** (*on journey*) s'arrêter.

**stopoff, stopover** halte *f*.

**stopper** bouchon *m*.

**stop up** (*sink, pipe etc*) boucher.

**stopwatch** chronomètre *m*.

**store** (*supply*) provision *f*; (*warehouse*) entrepôt *m*; (*shop*) magasin *m*.

**store (away)** (*furniture*) entreposer.

**store (up)** (*in warehouse etc*) stocker; (*for future use*) mettre en réserve.

**storekeeper** commerçant, -ante *mf*.

**storeroom** (*in house*) débarras *m*; (*in office, store*) réserve *f*.

**stork** cigogne *f*.

**storm** tempête *f*; (*thunderstorm*) orage *m*.

**stormy** *a* orageux.

**story**[1] histoire *f*; (*newspaper article*) article *m*; (*plot*) intrigue *f*; **short s.** nouvelle *f*.

**story**[2] (*of building*) étage *m*.

**stove** (*for cooking*) cuisinière *f*; (*portable*) réchaud *m*; (*for heating*) poêle *m*.

**straight 1** *a* droit; (*hair*) raide; (*route*) direct; (*tidy*) en ordre; (*frank*) franc (*f* franche). **2** *adv* (*to walk etc*) droit; (*directly*) tout droit; (*to drink whiskey etc*) sec; **s. away** tout de suite; **s. ahead** *or* **on** tout droit.

**straighten (up)** (*tie, hair, room*) arranger.

**straightforward** *a* (*easy, clear*) simple.

**strain 1** *n* (*tiredness*) fatigue *f*; (*mental*) tension *f* nerveuse. **2** *vt* (*eyes*) fatiguer; (*voice*) forcer; **to s. one's back** se faire mal au dos.

**strainer** passoire *f*.

**strange** *a* (*odd*) étrange; (*unknown*) inconnu.

**stranger** (*unknown*) inconnu, -ue *mf*; (*person from outside*) étranger, -ère *mf*.
**strangle** *vt* étrangler.
**strap** sangle *f*, courroie *f*; (*on dress*) bretelle *f*; (*on watch*) bracelet *m*; (*on sandal*) lanière *f*.
**strap (down** *or* **in)** attacher (avec une courroie).
**straw** paille *f*; **a (drinking) s.** une paille.
**strawberry 1** *n* fraise *f*. **2** *a* (*ice cream*) à la fraise; (*jam*) de fraises; (*tart*) aux fraises.
**streak** (*line*) raie *f*; (*of color*) strie *f*; (*of paint*) traînée *f*.
**stream** (*brook*) ruisseau *m*; (*flow*) flot *m*.
**street** rue *f*; **s. door** porte *f* d'entrée.
**streetcar** (*tram*) tramway *m*.
**street lamp** *or* **light** réverbère *m*.
**street map** plan *m* des rues.
**strength** force *f*; (*health, energy*) forces *fpl*; (*of wood etc*) solidité *f*.
**strengthen** *vt* renforcer.
**stress 1** *n* (*mental*) stress *m*; (*emphasis*) & *Grammar* accent *m*; **under s.** stressé. **2** *vt* insister sur; (*word*) accentuer; **to s. that** souligner que.
**stretch 1** *vt* (*rope, neck*) tendre; (*shoe, rubber*) étirer; **to s. one's legs** se dégourdir les jambes. **2** *vi* (*of person, elastic*) s'étirer. **3** *n* (*area*) étendue *f*.
**stretch (out) 1** *vt* (*arm, leg*) étendre; **to s. (out) one's arm** (*reach out*) tendre le bras (**to take** pour prendre). **2** *vi* (*of plain etc*) s'étendre.
**stretcher** brancard *m*.
**strict** *a* strict.
**strictly** *adv* strictement; **s. forbidden** formellement interdit.
**strictness** sévérité *f*.
**stride** (grand) pas *m*, enjambée *f*.
**stride* along/out/***etc* avancer/sortir/*etc* à grands pas.
**strike**[1]***** *vt* (*hit, impress*) frapper; (*collide with*) heurter; (*a match*) frotter; (*of clock*) sonner (*l'heure*); **it strikes me that** il me semble que (+ *indicative*).
**strike**[2] (*of workers*) grève *f*; **to go (out) on s.** se mettre en grève (**for** pour obtenir).
**striker** (*worker*) gréviste *mf*.
**striking** *a* (*impressive*) frappant.
**string** ficelle *f*; (*of parka, apron*) cordon *m*; (*of violin, racket etc*) corde *f*; (*of pearls*) collier *m*.
**strip** (*piece*) bande *f*; **(thin) s.** (*of metal etc*) lamelle *f*.
**strip (off)** *vi* se déshabiller.
**stripe** rayure *f*.
**striped** *a* rayé.
**stroke 1** *n* (*movement*) coup *m*; (*illness*) hémorragie *f* cérébrale; **(swimming) s.** nage *f*; **a s. of luck** un coup de chance. **2** *vt* (*beard, cat etc*) caresser.
**stroll 1** *n* promenade *f*. **2** *vi* se promener.
**stroller** (*for baby*) poussette *f*.
**strong** *a* fort; (*shoes, chair etc*) solide.
**structure** structure *f*; (*building*) construction *f*.
**struggle 1** *n* (*fight*) lutte *f* (**to do** pour faire). **2** *vi* (*fight*) lutter, se battre (**with** avec); (*thrash around*) se débattre; **to s. to do** (*try hard*) s'efforcer de faire; (*have difficulty*) avoir du mal à faire.
**stub** (*of cigarette etc*) bout *m*; (*of ticket, check*) talon *m*, souche *f*.
**stubborn** *a* (*person*) entêté.
**stubbornness** entêtement *m*.
**stub out** (*cigarette*) écraser.
**stuck** (*pt & pp de* **stick**) *a* (*caught, jammed*) coincé; **I'm s.** (*unable to continue*) je ne sais pas quoi faire *or* dire *etc*.
**stud** (*for collar*) bouton *m* de col.
**student 1** *n* étudiant, -ante *mf*; (*at school*) élève *mf*; **music**/*etc* **s.** étudiant, -ante en musique/*etc*. **2** *a* (*life, protest*) étudiant; (*restaurant, housing*) universitaire.
**studio** (*pl* **-os**) (*of artist etc*) studio *m*; **s. apartment** studio *m*.
**study 1** *n* étude *f*; (*office*) bureau *m*. **2** *vt* (*learn, observe*) étudier. **3** *vi*

étudier; **to s. to be a doctor**/*etc* faire des études de médecine *etc*; **to s. for an exam** préparer un examen.

**stuff 1** *n* (*thing*) truc *m*; (*things*) trucs *mpl*; (*possessions*) affaires *fpl*; **it's good s.** c'est bon. **2** *vt* (*fill*) bourrer (**with** de); (*cushion etc*) rembourrer (**with** avec); (*put*) fourrer (**into** dans); (*chicken etc*) farcir.

**stuffed (up)** *a* (*nose*) bouché.

**stuffing** (*for chicken etc*) farce *f*.

**stuffy** *a* (*room etc*) mal aéré; **it smells s.** ça sent le renfermé.

**stumble** *vi* trébucher (**over** sur).

**stump** (*of tree*) souche *f*.

**stun** *vt* (*with punch etc*) étourdir.

**stunned** *a* (*amazed*) stupéfait (**by** par).

**stupid** *a* stupide; **a s. thing** une stupidité; **s. fool** idiot, -ote *mf*.

**stupidity** stupidité *f*.

**sturdy** *a* robuste.

**stutter 1** *vi* bégayer. **2** *n* **to have a s.** être bègue.

**sty** (*for pigs*) porcherie *f*.

**style** style *m*; (*fashion*) mode *f*; (*design of dress etc*) modèle *m*; (*of hair*) coiffure *f*.

**stylish** *a* chic *inv*.

**subject** (*matter*) & *Grammar* sujet *m*; (*at school, university*) matière *f*; (*citizen*) ressortissant, -ante *mf*.

**subjunctive** *Grammar* subjonctif *m*.

**submarine** sous-marin *m*.

**subscriber** abonné, -ée *mf*.

**subscribe to** (*take out subscription*) s'abonner à (*journal etc*); (*be a subscriber*) être abonné à (*journal etc*).

**subscription** (*to newspaper etc*) abonnement *m*.

**subside** *vi* (*of ground*) s'affaisser.

**substance** substance *f*.

**substantial** *a* important; (*meal*) copieux.

**substitute** produit *m* de remplacement; (*person*) remplaçant, -ante *mf* (**for** de).

**subtitle** sous-titre *m*.

**subtle** *a* subtil.

**subtract** *vt* soustraire (**from** de).

**subtraction** soustraction *f*.

**suburb** banlieue *f*; **the suburbs** la banlieue.

**suburban** *a* (*train etc*) de banlieue.

**subway** métro *m*.

**succeed** *vi* réussir (**in doing** à faire, **in sth** dans qch).

**success** succès *m*, réussite *f*; **he was a s.** il a eu du succès; **it was a s.** c'était réussi.

**successful** *a* (*effort etc*) couronné de succès; (*firm*) prospère; (*candidate in exam*) admis; (*writer, film etc*) à succès; **to be s.** réussir (**in** dans, **in an exam** à un examen, **in doing** à faire).

**successfully** *adv* avec succès.

**such 1** *a* tel, telle; **s. a car**/*etc* une telle voiture/*etc*; **s. happiness**/*etc* tant de bonheur/*etc*; **s. as** comme, tel que. **2** *adv* (*so very*) si; (*in comparisons*) aussi; **s. a large helping** une si grosse portion; **s. a kind woman as you** une femme aussi gentille que vous.

**suck** *vt* sucer.

**suck (up)** (*with straw*) aspirer.

**sudden** *a* soudain; **all of a s.** tout à coup.

**suddenly** *adv* subitement.

**suds** *npl* **(soap) s.** mousse *f* de savon.

**suede 1** *n* daim *m*. **2** *a* de daim.

**suffer 1** *vi* souffrir (**from** de). **2** *vt* (*loss*) subir; (*pain*) ressentir.

**suffering** souffrance(s) *f*(*pl*).

**sufficient** *a* (*quantity*) suffisant; **s. money**/*etc* suffisamment d'argent/*etc*.

**sufficiently** *adv* suffisamment.

**suffix** suffixe *m*.

**suffocate** *vti* étouffer.

**sugar 1** *n* sucre *m*; **granulated/lump s.** sucre cristallisé/en morceaux. **2** *vt* sucrer.

**sugar bowl** sucrier *m*.

**suggest** *vt* (*propose*) suggérer, proposer (**to** à, **doing** de faire, **that** que (+ *subjunctive*)); (*imply*) suggérer.

**suggestion** suggestion *f.*
**suicide** suicide *m*; **to commit s.** se suicider.
**suit**[1] (*man's*) costume *m*; (*woman's*) tailleur *m*; *Cards* couleur *f*; **flying/diving/ski s.** combinaison *f* de vol/plongée/ski.
**suit**[2] *vt* (*please, be acceptable to*) convenir à; (*of dress, color etc*) aller (bien) à; **it suits me to stay** ça m'arrange de rester; **suited to** (*job, activity*) fait pour.
**suitable** *a* qui convient (**for** à), convenable (**for** pour); (*dress, color*) qui va (bien).
**suitcase** valise *f.*
**suite** (*rooms*) suite *f*; (*furniture*) mobilier *m.*
**sulk** *vi* bouder.
**sullen** *a* maussade.
**sum** (*amount of money, total*) somme *f*; (*calculation*) calcul *m.*
**summarize** *vt* résumer.
**summary** résumé *m.*
**summer 1** *n* été *m*; **in (the) s.** en été. **2** *a* d'été; **s. vacation** grandes vacances *fpl.*
**summertime** été *m.*
**sum up** *vti* (*facts etc*) résumer.
**sun** soleil *m*; **in the s.** au soleil; **the sun is shining** il fait (du) soleil.
**sunbathe** *vi* prendre un bain de soleil, se faire bronzer.
**sunburn** coup *m* de soleil.
**sunburned** *or* **sunburnt** *a* brûlé par le soleil.
**sundae** glace *f* aux fruits.
**Sunday** dimanche *m.*
**sunglasses** *npl* lunettes *fpl* de soleil.
**sunlamp** lampe *f* à bronzer.
**sunlight** (lumière *f* du) soleil *m.*
**sunny** *a* (*day etc*) ensoleillé; **it's s.** il fait (du) soleil; **s. periods** *or* **intervals** éclaircies *fpl.*
**sunrise** lever *m* du soleil.
**sunroof** toit *m* ouvrant.
**sunset** coucher *m* du soleil.
**sunshine** soleil *m.*
**sunstroke** insolation *f.*
**suntan** bronzage *m*; **s. lotion/oil** crème *f*/huile *f* solaire.
**suntanned** *a* bronzé.
**super** *a Fam* sensationnel.
**superb** *a* superbe.
**superficial** *a* superficiel.
**superglue** colle *f* extra-forte.
**superior** *a* supérieur (**to** à).
**superiority** supériorité *f.*
**supermarket** supermarché *m.*
**superstition** superstition *f.*
**superstitious** *a* superstitieux.
**supervise** *vt* (*person, work*) surveiller; (*office, research*) diriger.
**supervisor** surveillant, -ante *mf*; (*in office*) chef *m* de service; (*in store*) chef *m* de rayon.
**supper** dîner *m*, souper *m*; (*late-night*) souper *m*; **to have s.** dîner, souper.
**supple** *a* souple.
**supply 1** *vt* fournir; (*with electricity, gas, water*) alimenter (**with** en); (*equip*) équiper (**with** de); **to s. s.o. with sth, s. sth to s.o.** fournir qch à qn. **2** *n* (*stock*) provision *f*; **(food) supplies** vivres *mpl.*
**support 1** *vt* (*bear weight of, help, encourage*) soutenir; (*be in favor of*) être en faveur de; (*family etc*) subvenir aux besoins de. **2** *n* (*help*) soutien *m*; (*object*) support *m.*
**supporter** partisan *m*; (*in sport*) supporter *m.*
**suppose** *vti* supposer (**that** que); **I'm supposed to work** *or* **be working** je suis censé travailler; **he's supposed to be rich** on le dit riche; **I s. (so)** je pense; **you're tired, I s.** vous êtes fatigué, je suppose; **s. we go** (*suggestion*) si nous partions; **s.** *or* **supposing you're right** supposons que tu aies raison.
**sure** *a* sûr (**of** de, **that** que); **she's s. to accept** il est sûr qu'elle acceptera; **to make s. of sth** s'assurer de qch; **be s. to do it!** ne manquez pas de le faire!
**surely** *adv* sûrement; **s. he didn't refuse?** (*I hope*) il n'a tout de même pas refusé.
**surface** surface *f*; **s. area** superficie *f*; **s. mail** courrier *m* par voie normale.

**surfboard** planche *f* (de surf).
**surfing** surf *m*; **to go s.** faire du surf.
**surgeon** chirurgien *m*.
**surgery to have s.** avoir une opération (**for** pour).
**surname** nom *m* de famille.
**surprise 1** *n* surprise *f*; **to take s.o. by s.** prendre qn au dépourvu. **2** *a* (*visit etc*) inattendu. **3** *vt* (*astonish*) étonner, surprendre.
**surprised** *a* surpris (**that** que (+ *subjunctive*), **at sth** de qch); **I'm s. to see you** je suis surpris de te voir.
**surprising** *a* surprenant.
**surrender** *vi* se rendre (**to** à).
**surround** *vt* entourer (**with** de); (*of army, police*) encercler; **surrounded by** entouré de.
**surrounding** *a* environnant.
**surroundings** *npl* environs *mpl*; (*setting*) cadre *m*.
**survey** enquête *f*; (*of opinion*) sondage *m*.
**surveyor** (*of land*) géomètre *m*.
**survive 1** *vi* survivre. **2** *vt* survivre à.
**survivor** survivant, -ante *mf*.
**suspect 1** *n* suspect, -ecte *mf*. **2** *vt* soupçonner (**that** que, **of sth** de qch, **of doing** d'avoir fait).
**suspend** *vt* (*postpone, dismiss*) suspendre; (*student*) renvoyer; (*driver's license*) retirer.
**suspenders** *npl* bretelles *fpl*.
**suspense** (*in book etc*) suspense *m*.
**suspension** (*of vehicle*) suspension *f*.
**suspicion** soupçon *m*.
**suspicious** *a* (*person*) méfiant; (*behavior*) suspect; **s.(-looking)** suspect; **to be s. of** se méfier de.
**swallow 1** *vti* avaler. **2** *n* (*bird*) hirondelle *f*.
**swallow sth down** avaler qch.
**swamp** marécage *m*.
**swan** cygne *m*.
**swap 1** *n* échange *m*. **2** *vt* échanger (**for** contre); **to s. seats** changer de place. **3** *vi* échanger.
**swarm** (*of bees etc*) essaim *m*.
**sway** *vi* se balancer.
**swear* 1** *vt* (*promise*) jurer (**to do** de faire, **that** que). **2** *vi* (*curse*) jurer (**at** contre).
**swearword** gros mot *m*.
**sweat 1** *n* sueur *f*. **2** *vi* transpirer, suer; **I'm sweating** je suis en sueur.
**sweater** pull *m*.
**sweat shirt** sweat-shirt *m*.
**Swede** Suédois, -oise *mf*.
**Swedish 1** *a* suédois. **2** *n* (*language*) suédois *m*.
**sweep* 1** *vt* (*with broom*) balayer; (*chimney*) ramoner. **2** *vi* balayer.
**sweep away** (*leaves etc*) balayer; (*carry off*) emporter.
**sweep out** (*room etc*) balayer.
**sweep up** balayer.
**sweet** *a* (*not sour*) doux (*f* douce); (*tea, coffee etc*) sucré; (*child, house, cat*) mignon (*f* mignonne); (*kind*) aimable.
**sweet corn** maïs *m*.
**sweeten** *vt* (*tea etc*) sucrer.
**sweetly** *adv* (*kindly*) aimablement; (*agreeably*) agréablement.
**swell* (up)** *vi* (*of hand, leg etc*) enfler; (*of wood, dough*) gonfler.
**swelling** enflure *f*.
**swerve** *vi* (*of vehicle*) faire une embardée.
**swim 1** *n* **to go for a s.** se baigner. **2** *vi** nager; (*as sport*) faire de la natation; **to go swimming** aller nager. **3** *vt* (*crawl etc*) nager.
**swim meet** (*competition*) concours *m* de natation.
**swimmer** nageur, -euse *mf*.
**swimming** natation *f*.
**swimming pool** piscine *f*.
**swimming trunks** slip *m* de bain.
**swimsuit** maillot *m* de bain.
**swing 1** *n* (*in playground etc*) balançoire *f*. **2** *vi** (*sway*) se balancer. **3** *vt* (*arms etc*) balancer.
**swing around** *vi* (*turn*) virer; (*of person*) se retourner (vivement).
**Swiss 1** *a* suisse. **2** *n inv* Suisse *m*,

Suissesse *f*; **the S.** les Suisses *mpl*.
**switch 1** *n* (*electric*) bouton *m* (électrique). **2** *vt* (*money, employee*) transférer (**to** à); (*exchange*) échanger (**for** contre); **to s. places** *or* **seats** changer de place.
**switch off** (*lamp, gas etc*) éteindre; (*engine*) arrêter.
**switch on** (*lamp, gas etc*) mettre, allumer; (*engine*) mettre en marche.
**swollen** (*pp de* **swell**) *a* (*leg etc*) enflé; (*stomach*) gonflé.
**sword** épée *f*.
**syllable** syllabe *f*.
**syllabus** programme *m* (scolaire).
**symbol** symbole *m*.
**symbolic** *a* symbolique.
**sympathetic** *a* (*showing pity*) compatissant; (*understanding*) compréhensif.
**sympathize** *vi* **I s. (with you)** (*pity*) je suis désolé (pour vous); (*understanding*) je vous comprends.
**sympathy** (*pity*) compassion *f*; (*understanding*) compréhension *f*; (*when s.o. dies*) condoléances *fpl*.
**symphony** symphonie *f*.
**symptom** symptôme *m*.
**synagogue** synagogue *f*.
**synonym** synonyme *m*.
**syringe** seringue *f*.
**syrup** sirop *m*.
**system** système *m*; (*human body*) organisme *m*; (*order*) méthode *f*.

# T

**tab** (*cloth etc flap*) patte *f*.
**table** (*furniture, list*) table *f*; **bedside t.** table *f* de chevet; **to lay** *or* **set/clear the t.** mettre/débarrasser la table.
**tablecloth** nappe *f*.
**tablemat** (*of cloth*) napperon *m*; (*hard*) dessous-de-plat *m inv*.
**tablespoon** = cuillère *f* à soupe.
**tablespoonful** = cuillerée *f* à soupe.
**tablet** (*pill*) comprimé *m*.
**tack** (*nail*) petit clou *m*; (*thumbtack*) punaise *f*.
**tackle** *vt* (*problem etc*) s'attaquer à; *Rugby, Football* plaquer; *Soccer* tacler.
**tacky** *a* (*in appearance*) moche; (*remark etc*) de mauvais goût.
**tact** tact *m*.
**tactful** *a* **to be t.** (*of person*) avoir du tact.
**tactic a t.** une tactique; **tactics** la tactique.
**taffy** caramel *n* (*dur*).
**tag** (*label*) étiquette *f*.
**tail** (*of animal etc*) queue *f*.
**tailor** tailleur *m*.
**take*** *vt* prendre; (*prize*) remporter; (*exam*) passer; (*subtract*) soustraire (**from** de); (*tolerate*) supporter; (*bring*) amener (*qn*) (**to** à); (*by car*) conduire (*qn*) (**to** à); **to t. sth to s.o.** (ap)porter qch à qn; **to t. s.o. (out) to the theater**/*etc* emmener qn au théâtre/*etc*; **to t. sth with one** emporter qch; **to t. s.o. home** ramener qn; **it takes courage**/*etc* il faut du courage/*etc* (**to do** pour faire); **it took me an hour to do it** j'ai mis une heure à le faire.
**take after s.o.** ressembler à qn.
**take along** (*object*) emporter; (*person*) emmener.
**take apart** (*machine*) démonter.
**take away** (*thing*) emporter; (*person*) emmener; (*remove*) enlever; (*subtract*) soustraire (**from** de).
**take back** reprendre; (*return*) rapporter; (*accompany*) ramener (*qn*) (**to** à).
**take down** (*object*) descendre; (*notes*) prendre.
**take in** (*chair, car etc*) rentrer; (*include*) inclure; (*understand*) comprendre; (*deceive*) *Fam* rouler.
**taken** *a* (*seat*) pris.
**take off 1** *vt* (*remove*) enlever; (*lead away*) emmener; (*subtract*) déduire (**from** de). **2** *vi* (*of aircraft*) décoller.
**takeoff** (*of aircraft*) décollage *m*.

**take on** *vt* (*work, staff, passenger*) prendre.

**take out** (*from pocket etc*) sortir; (*stain*) enlever; (*tooth*) arracher; (*insurance*) prendre.

**takeout 1** *a* (*meal*) à emporter; (*restaurant*) qui fait des plats à emporter **2** *n* (*food*) plat *m* à emporter.

**take over 1** *vt* (*company etc*) prendre la direction de; **to t. over s.o.'s job** remplacer qn. **2** *vi* prendre la relève (**from** de); (*permanently*) prendre la succession (**from** de).

**take up** (*carry up*) monter; (*space, time*) prendre; (*hobby*) se mettre à.

**takings** *npl* recette *f*.

**tale** (*story*) conte *m*.

**talent** talent *m*; **to have a t. for** avoir du talent pour.

**talented** *a* doué.

**talk 1** *n* propos *mpl*; (*gossip*) bavardage(s) *m*(*pl*); (*conversation*) conversation *f*; (*lecture*) exposé *m* (**on** sur); **talks** pourparlers *mpl*; **to have a t. with s.o.** parler avec qn; **there's t. of** on parle de. **2** *vi* parler (**to** à; **with** avec; **about, of** de). **3** *vt* (*nonsense*) dire; **to t. s.o. into doing/out of doing** persuader qn de faire/de ne pas faire.

**talkative** *a* bavard.

**talk sth over** discuter (de) qch.

**tall** *a* (*person*) grand; (*tree, house*) haut; **how t. are you?** combien mesures-tu?

**tambourine** tambourin *m*.

**tame 1** *a* (*animal*) apprivoisé. **2** *vt* apprivoiser.

**tampon** tampon *m* hygiénique.

**tan 1** *n* (*suntan*) bronzage *m*. **2** *vti* bronzer.

**tangerine** mandarine *f*.

**tangled** *a* enchevêtré.

**tank** (*storing liquid or gas*) réservoir *m*; (*vehicle*) char *m*; **(fish) t.** aquarium *m*.

**tanker (oil) t.** (*ship*) pétrolier *m*.

**tap 1** *n* (*for water*) robinet *m*; (*blow*) petit coup *m*. **2** *vti* (*hit*) frapper légèrement.

**tape[1] 1** *n* (*of cloth, paper*) ruban *m*; **(adhesive) t.** ruban *m* adhésif. **2** *vt* (*stick*) coller (*avec du ruban adhésif*).

**tape[2] 1** *n* (*for sound/video recording*) bande *f* (magnétique/vidéo). **2** *vt* (*a movie etc*) enregistrer, magnétoscoper; (*music, voice*) enregistrer; (*event*) faire une cassette de. **3** *vi* enregistrer.

**tape measure** mètre *m* (à) ruban.

**tape recorder** magnétophone *m*.

**tar** goudron *m*.

**target** cible *f*; (*objective*) objectif *m*.

**tarpaulin** bâche *f*.

**tart** (*pie*) (*open*) tarte *f*; (*with pastry on top*) tourte *f*.

**tartan** *a* (*skirt etc*) écossais.

**task** travail *m*.

**taste 1** *n* goût *m*. **2** *vt* (*eat, drink*) goûter; (*try*) goûter à; (*make out the taste of*) sentir (le goût de). **3** *vi* **to t. of** *or* **like sth** avoir un goût de qch; **to t. delicious/***etc* avoir un goût délicieux/*etc*.

**tasty** *a* savoureux.

**tattered** *a* (*clothes*) en lambeaux.

**tattle** *vi* rapporter (**on** sur).

**tattletale** *Fam* rapporteur, -euse *mf*.

**tattoo 1** *n* (*pl* **-oos**) (*on body*) tatouage *m*. **2** *vt* tatouer.

**tax 1** *n* taxe *f*, impôt *m*; (*on income*) impôts *mpl*. **2** *vt* (*person*) imposer; (*goods*) taxer.

**taxable** *a* imposable.

**taxi** taxi *m*; **t. stand** station *f* de taxis.

**taxpayer** contribuable *mf*.

**TB** tuberculose *f*.

**tea** thé *m*; **to have t.** prendre le thé; **t. party** thé *m*; **t. set** service *m* à thé.

**teabag** sachet *m* de thé.

**teach* 1** *vt* apprendre (**s.o. sth** qch à qn, **that** que); (*in school etc*) enseigner (**s.o. sth** qch à qn); **to t. s.o. (how) to do** apprendre à qn à faire. **2** *vi* enseigner.

**teacher** professeur *m*; (*in primary school*) instituteur, -trice *mf*.

**teaching** enseignement *m*; **t. staff = teachers**.
**teacup** tasse *f* à thé.
**team** équipe *f*.
**team up** faire équipe (**with** avec).
**teapot** théière *f*.
**tear**[1] **1** *n* (*rip*) déchirure *f*. **2** *vt** déchirer.
**tear**[2] (*in eye*) larme *f*; **in tears** en larmes.
**tear off** *or* **out** (*with force*) arracher; (*receipt, stamp etc*) détacher.
**tear up** (*letter etc*) déchirer.
**tease** *vt* taquiner.
**teaspoon** petite cuillère *f*, cuillère *f* à café.
**teaspoonful** cuillerée *f* à café.
**technical** *a* technique.
**technician** technicien, -ienne *mf*.
**technique** technique *f*.
**technology** technologie *f*.
**teddy bear** ours *m* (en peluche).
**teenager** adolescent, -ente *mf*.
**tee-shirt** tee-shirt *m*.
**teeth** *see* **tooth**.
**tele-** *prefix* télé-.
**telegram** télégramme *m*.
**telegraph pole** poteau *m* télégraphique.
**telephone 1** *n* téléphone *m*; **on the t.** (*speaking*) au téléphone. **2** *a* (*call, line etc*) téléphonique; (*number*) de téléphone; **t. booth** cabine *f* téléphonique; **t. directory** annuaire *m* du téléphone. **3** *vi* téléphoner. **4** *vt* **to t. s.o.** téléphoner à qn.
**telescope** télescope *m*.
**televise** *vt* retransmettre à la télévision.
**television** télévision *f*; **on t.** à la télévision; **t. set** téléviseur *m*.
**tell* 1** *vt* dire (**s.o. sth** qch à qn, **that** que); (*story*) raconter; (*distinguish*) distinguer (**from** de); (*know*) savoir; **to t. s.o. to do** dire à qn de faire; **to t. the difference** voir la différence. **2** *vi* **to t. of** *or* **about sth/s.o.** parler de qch/qn; **to t. on s.o.** rapporter sur qn.
**teller (bank) t.** guichetier, -ière *mf* (*de banque*).
**tell s.o. off** disputer qn.
**temper to lose one's t.** se mettre en colère; **in a bad t.** de mauvaise humeur.
**temperature** température *f*; **to have a t.** avoir de la température.
**temple** (*building*) temple *m*.
**temporary** *a* provisoire; (*job*) temporaire; (*secretary*) intérimaire.
**tempt** *vt* tenter; **tempted to do** tenté de faire.
**temptation** tentation *f*.
**tempting** *a* tentant.
**ten** *a* & *n* dix (*m*).
**tenant** locataire *mf*.
**tend** *vi* **to t. to do** avoir tendance à faire.
**tendency** tendance *f* (**to do** à faire).
**tender** *a* (*soft, loving*) tendre; (*painful*) sensible.
**tennis** tennis *m*; **table t.** tennis *m* de table; **t. court** court *m* (de tennis); **t. shoes** chaussures *fpl* de tennis; tennis *fpl*.
**tense 1** *a* (*person, muscle, situation*) tendu. **2** *n* (*of verb*) temps *m*.
**tension** tension *f*.
**tent** tente *f*.
**tenth** *a* & *n* dixième (*mf*).
**term** (*word*) terme *m*; (*period*) période *f*; (*semester*) semestre *m*; **terms** (*conditions*) conditions *fpl*; (*prices*) prix *mpl*; **on good/bad terms** en bons/mauvais termes (**with** avec).
**terminal (air) t.** aérogare *f*; **(computer) t.** terminal *m* (d'ordinateur).
**terrace** (*next to house etc*) terrasse *f*.
**terrible** *a* affreux.
**terribly** *adv* (*badly, very*) affreusement.
**terrific** *a Fam* (*excellent, very great*) formidable.
**terrify** *vt* terrifier; **to be terrified of** avoir très peur de.
**terrifying** *a* terrifiant.

**territory** territoire *m*.
**terror** terreur *f*.
**terrorist** *n* & *a* terroriste (*mf*).
**terrorize** *vt* terroriser.
**test 1** *vt* (*try*) essayer; (*product, machine*) tester; (*pupil*) interroger; (*of doctor*) examiner (*les yeux etc*); (*analyze*) analyser (*le sang etc*). **2** *n* essai *m*; (*of product*) test *m*; (*in school*) interrogation *f*, test *m*; (*by doctor*) examen *m*; (*of blood etc*) analyse *f*; **eye t.** examen *m* de la vue.
**test tube** éprouvette *f*.
**test-tube baby** bébé-éprouvette *m*.
**text** texte *m*.
**textbook** manuel *m* (scolaire).
**textile** *a* & *n* textile (*m*).
**than** *conj* que; **happier t.** plus heureux que. ▪ (*with numbers*) de; **more t. six** plus de six.
**thank 1** *vt* remercier (**for sth** de qch, **for doing** d'avoir fait); **t. you!** merci!; **no, t. you!** (non) merci! **2** *n* **thanks** remerciements *mpl*; **(many) thanks!** merci (beaucoup)!; **thanks to** (*because of*) grâce à.
**thankful** *a* reconnaissant (**for** de).
**Thanksgiving (day)** jour *m* d'action de grâce(s).
**that 1** *conj* que; **to say t.** dire que. **2** *rel pron* (*subject*) qui; (*object*) que; (*after prep*) lequel, laquelle, *pl* lesquel(le)s; **the boy t. left** le garçon qui est parti; **the book t. I read** le livre que j'ai lu; **the carpet t. I put it on** le tapis sur lequel je l'ai mis; **the house t. she told me about** la maison dont elle m'a parlé; **the day/moment t.** le jour/moment où. **3** *dem a* (*pl see* **those**) ce, cet (*before vowel or mute h*), cette; (*opposed to 'this'*) ce . . . + -là; **t. day** ce jour; ce jour-là; **t. girl** cette fille; cette fille-là. **4** *dem pron* (*pl see* **those**) ça, cela; **t. (one)** celui-là *m*, celle-là *f*; **give me t.** donne-moi ça *or* cela; **t.'s right** c'est juste; **who's t.?** qui est-ce?; **t.'s the house** c'est la maison; (*pointing*) voilà la maison; **t. is (to say)** c'est-à-dire. **5** *adv* (*so*) si; **not t. good** pas si bon; **t. much** (*to cost etc*) (au)tant que ça.
**thaw 1** *n* dégel *m*. **2** *vi* dégeler; (*of snow*) fondre; (*of food*) décongeler; **it's thawing** ça dégèle. **3** *vt* (*food*) (faire) décongeler.
**the** le, l', la, *pl* les; **t. roof** le toit; **t. man** l'homme; **t. moon** la lune; **t. boxes** les boîtes; **of t., from t.** du, de l', de la, *pl* des; **to t., at t.** au, à l', à la, *pl* aux.
**theater** théâtre *m*.
**theft** vol *m*.
**their** *poss a* leur, *pl* leurs.
**theirs** *poss pron* le leur, la leur, *pl* les leurs; **this book is t.** ce livre est à eux *or* est le leur.
**them** *pron* les; (*after prep, 'than', 'it is'*) eux *mpl*, elles *fpl*; **(to) t.** leur; **I see t.** je les vois; **I give (to) t.** je leur donne; **ten of t.** dix d'entre eux *or* elles; **all of t. came** tous sont venus, toutes sont venues; **I like all of t.** je les aime tous *or* toutes.
**themselves** *pron* eux-mêmes *mpl*, elles-mêmes *fpl*; (*reflexive*) se, s'; (*after prep etc*) eux *mpl*, elles *fpl*.
**then 1** *adv* (*at that time*) à cette époque-là; (*just a moment ago*) à ce moment-là; (*next*) ensuite; **from t. on** dès lors; **before t.** avant cela; **until t.** jusque-là. **2** *conj* (*therefore*) donc.
**theory** théorie *f*.
**there** *adv* là; **(down** *or* **over) t.** là-bas; **on t.** là-dessus; **t. is, t. are** il y a; (*pointing*) voilà; **t. he is** le voilà; **that man t.** cet homme-là.
**therefore** *adv* donc.
**thermometer** thermomètre *m*.
**Thermos**® thermos® *m or f*.
**thermostat** thermostat *m*.
**these 1** *dem a* (*sing see* **this**) ces; (*opposed to 'those'*) ces. . . + -ci; **t. men** ces hommes; ces hommes-ci. **2** *dem pron* (*sing see* **this**) **t. (ones)** ceux-ci *mpl*, celles-ci *fpl*; **t. are my friends** ce sont mes amis.

**they** *pron* ils *mpl*, elles *fpl*; (*stressed*) eux *mpl*, elles *fpl*; **t. are doctors** ce sont des médecins. ▪ (*people in general*) on; **t. say** on dit.
**thick 1** *a* épais (*f* épaisse). **2** *adv* (*to spread*) en couche épaisse.
**thicken 1** *vt* épaissir. **2** *vi* (*of fog etc*) s'épaissir; (*of cream etc*) épaissir.
**thickly** *adv* (*to spread*) en couche épaisse.
**thickness** épaisseur *f*.
**thief** (*pl* **thieves**) voleur, -euse *mf*.
**thigh** cuisse *f*.
**thimble** dé *m* (à coudre).
**thin 1** *a* (*slice, paper etc*) mince; (*person, leg*) maigre; (*soup*) peu épais (*f* épaisse). **2** *adv* (*to spread*) en couche mince.
**thin (down)** (*paint etc*) diluer.
**thing** chose *f*; **one's things** (*belongings*) ses affaires *fpl*; **it's a good t. (that)** heureusement que.
**think* 1** *vi* penser (**about, of** à); **to t. (carefully)** réfléchir (**about, of** à); **to t. of doing** penser à faire; **she doesn't t. much of it** ça ne lui dit pas grand-chose. **2** *vt* penser (**that** que); **I t. so** je pense que oui; **what do you t. of him?** que penses-tu de lui?
**think sth over** réfléchir à qch.
**think up** inventer.
**thinly** *adv* (*to spread*) en couche mince.
**third 1** *a* troisième. **2** *n* troisième *mf*; **a t.** (*fraction*) un tiers. **3** *adv* **to come t.** se classer troisième.
**thirdly** *adv* troisièmement.
**thirst** soif *f*.
**thirsty** *a* **to be** *or* **feel t.** avoir soif; **to make s.o. t.** donner soif à qn.
**thirteen** *a* & *n* treize (*m*).
**thirteenth** *a* & *n* treizième (*mf*).
**thirtieth** *a* & *n* trentième (*mf*).
**thirty** *a* & *n* trente (*m*).
**this 1** *dem a* (*pl see* **these**) ce, cet (*before vowel or mute h*), cette; (*opposed to 'that'*) ce. . . + -ci; **t. book** ce livre; ce livre-ci; **t. photo** cette photo; cette photo-ci. **2** *dem pron* (*pl see* **these**) ceci; **t. (one)** celui-ci *m*, celle-ci *f*; **give me t.** donne-moi ceci; **t. is Paul** c'est Paul; (*pointing*) voici Paul. **3** *adv* **t. high** (*pointing*) haut comme ceci; **t. far** jusqu'ici.
**thorn** épine *f*.
**thorough** *a* (*careful*) minutieux; (*knowledge, examination*) approfondi; **to give sth a t. cleaning**/*etc* nettoyer/*etc* qch à fond.
**thoroughly** *adv* (*completely*) tout à fait; (*carefully*) avec minutie; (*to know, clean etc*) à fond.
**those 1** *dem a* (*sing see* **that**) ces; (*opposed to 'these'*) ces. . . + -là; **t. men** ces hommes; ces hommes-là. **2** *dem pron* (*sing see* **that**) **t. (ones)** ceux-là *mpl*, celles-là *fpl*; **t. are my friends** ce sont mes amis.
**though 1** *conj* **(even) t.** bien que (+ *subjunctive*); **as t.** comme si. **2** *adv* (*however*) cependant.
**thought** (*pt* & *pp de* **think**) *n* pensée *f*; **(careful) t.** réflexion *f*.
**thoughtful** *a* (*considerate*) gentil, attentionné.
**thoughtless** *a* (*towards others*) pas très gentil; (*absent-minded*) étourdi.
**thousand** *a* & *n* mille *a* & *m inv*; **a t. pages** mille pages; **two t. pages** deux mille pages; **thousands of** des milliers de.
**thread 1** *n* (*yarn*) fil *m*. **2** *vt* (*needle, beads*) enfiler.
**threat** menace *f*.
**threaten** *vt* menacer (**to do** de faire, **with sth** de qch).
**threatening** *a* menaçant.
**three** *a* & *n* trois (*m*).
**threw** *pt de* **throw**.
**thrill** frisson *m*.
**thrilled** *a* ravi (**with sth** de qch, **to do** de faire).
**thriller** film *m or* roman *m* à suspense.
**thrilling** *a* passionnant.
**thriving** *a* prospère.
**throat** gorge *f*.
**throne** trône *m*.
**through 1** *prep* (*place*) à travers;

(*window, door*) par; (*time*) pendant; (*means*) par; **to go** *or* **get t.** (*forest etc*) traverser; (*hole etc*) passer par; (*wall etc*) passer à travers. **2** *adv* à travers; **to let t.** laisser passer; **to be t.** (*finished*) avoir fini; **t. to** *or* **till** jusqu'à; **I'll put you t. (to him)** (*on phone*) je vous le passe.

**throughout 1** *prep* **t. the neighborhood**/*etc* dans tout le quartier/*etc*; **t. the day**/*etc* pendant toute la journée/*etc*. **2** *adv* (*everywhere*) partout; (*all the time*) tout le temps.

**throw*** *vt* jeter (**to, at** à); (*party*) donner.

**throw away** (*unwanted object*) jeter.

**throw out** (*unwanted object*) jeter; (*expel*) mettre (*qn*) à la porte.

**throw up** *vti* (*vomit*) *Fam* rendre.

**thud** bruit *m* sourd.

**thug** voyou *m*.

**thumb** pouce *m*.

**thumbtack** punaise *f*.

**thunder 1** *n* tonnerre *m*. **2** *vi* tonner; **it's thundering** il tonne.

**thunderstorm** orage *m*.

**Thursday** jeudi *m*.

**tick (off)** (*on list etc*) cocher.

**ticket** billet *m*; (*for bus, subway, cloakroom*) ticket *m*; **(price) t.** étiquette *f*.

**ticket collector** contrôleur, -euse *mf*.

**ticket office** guichet *m*.

**tickle** *vt* chatouiller.

**ticklish** *a* chatouilleux.

**tide** marée *f*.

**tidily** *adv* (*to put away*) soigneusement.

**tidy** *a* (*place, toys etc*) bien rangé; (*clothes, hair*) soigné; (*person*) ordonné; (*in appearance*) soigné.

**tidy sth (up** *or* **away)** ranger qch.

**tie 1** *n* (*around neck*) cravate *f*; (*game*) match *m* nul. **2** *vt* (*fasten*) attacher (**to** à); (*a knot*) faire (**in** à); (*shoe*) lacer.

**tie down** attacher.

**tie up** attacher (*qch*) (**to** à); (*person*) ligoter.

**tiger** tigre *m*.

**tight 1** *a* (*clothes fitting too closely*) (trop) étroit; (*drawer, lid*) dur; (*knot, screw*) serré; (*rope, wire*) raide. **2** *adv* (*to hold, shut*) bien; (*to squeeze*) fort.

**tighten (up)** (*bolt etc*) (res)serrer.

**tightly** *adv* (*to hold*) bien; (*to squeeze*) fort.

**tights** *npl* collant(s) *m*(*pl*).

**tile 1** *n* (*on roof*) tuile *f*; (*on wall or floor*) carreau *m*. **2** *vt* (*wall, floor*) carreler.

**till 1** *prep* & *conj* = **until. 2** *n* (*for money*) caisse *f* (enregistreuse).

**tilt** *vti* pencher.

**timber** bois *m* (de construction).

**time 1** *n* temps *m*; (*point in time*) moment *m*; (*period in history*) époque *f*; (*on clock*) heure *f*; (*occasion*) fois *f*; **some/most of the t.** une partie/la plupart du temps; **all of the t.** tout le temps; **in a year's t.** dans un an; **it's t. (to do)** il est temps (de faire); **to have a good t.** s'amuser; **to have a hard t. doing** avoir du mal à faire; **in t.** (*to arrive*) à temps; **from t. to t.** de temps en temps; **what t. is it?** quelle heure est-il?; **on t.** à l'heure; **at the same t.** en même temps (**as** que); (*simultaneously*) à la fois; **for the t. being** pour le moment; **one at a t.** un à un. **2** *vt* (*athlete etc*) chronométrer; (*activity*) minuter; (*choose the time of*) choisir le moment de.

**timer** (*device*) minuteur *m*; (*built into appliance*) programmateur *m*; (*plugged into socket*) prise *f* programmable.

**timetable** horaire *m*; (*of activities*) emploi *m* du temps.

**timid** *a* (*afraid*) craintif; (*shy*) timide.

**timing what good t.!** quelle synchronisation!

**tin** (*metal*) étain *m*; (*coated steel or iron*) fer-blanc *m*; (*can*) boîte *f*.

**tinfoil** papier *m* (d')alu.

**tiny** *a* tout petit.

**tip 1** *n* (*end*) bout *m*; (*pointed*) pointe *f*; (*money*) pourboire *m*; (*advice*) conseil *m*. **2** *vt* (*waiter etc*) donner un pourboire à.

**tip (out)** (*liquid, load*) déverser (**into** dans).

**tip (up** *or* **over) 1** *vt* (*tilt*) pencher; (*overturn*) faire basculer. **2** *vi* pencher; basculer.

**tiptoe on t.** sur la pointe des pieds.

**tire**[1] **1** *vt* fatiguer. **2** *vi* se fatiguer.

**tire**[2] pneu *m* (*pl* pneus).

**tired** *a* fatigué; **to be t. of sth/s.o./doing** en avoir assez de qch/de qn/de faire.

**tiredness** fatigue *f*.

**tire s.o. out** épuiser qn.

**tiring** *a* fatigant.

**tissue** (*handkerchief etc*) mouchoir *m* en papier.

**title** titre *m*.

**to** *prep* à; (*towards*) vers; (*of attitude*) envers; (*right up to*) jusqu'à; **give it to him** *or* **her** donne-le-lui; **to France** en France; **to Portugal** au Portugal; **to the butcher('s)**/*etc* chez le boucher/*etc*; **the road to Paris** la route de Paris; **the train to Paris** le train pour Paris; **kind/cruel to s.o.** gentil/cruel envers qn; **it's ten (minutes) to one** il est une heure moins dix. ▪ (*with infinitive*) **to say/do**/*etc* dire/faire/*etc*; **(in order) to** pour. ▪ (*with adjective*) de; à; **happy**/*etc* **to do** heureux/*etc* de faire; **it's easy/difficult to do** c'est facile/difficile à faire.

**toad** crapaud *m*.

**toadstool** champignon *m* (vénéneux).

**toast 1** *n* pain *m* grillé; **piece** *or* **slice of t.** tranche *f* de pain grillé, toast *m*. **2** *vt* (faire) griller.

**toaster** grille-pain *m inv*.

**tobacco** tabac *m*.

**tobacco store** (bureau *m* de) tabac *m*.

**toboggan** luge *f*.

**today** *adv* aujourd'hui.

**toddler** enfant *mf* (en bas âge).

**toe** orteil *m*.

**toenail** ongle *m* du pied.

**toffee** caramel *m* (*dur*).

**together** *adv* ensemble; (*at the same time*) en même temps; **t. with** avec.

**toilet** (*room*) toilettes *fpl*; (*bowl, seat*) cuvette *f* *or* siège *m* des cabinets; **to go to the t.** aller aux toilettes.

**toilet paper** papier *m* hygiénique.

**toiletries** *npl* articles *mpl* de toilette.

**toilet water** (*perfume*) eau *f* de toilette.

**token** (*for subway etc*) jeton *m*.

**told** *pt* & *pp de* **tell**.

**tolerant** *a* tolérant (**of** à l'égard de).

**tolerate** *vt* tolérer.

**toll** (*fee*) péage *m*; **t. road/bridge** route *f*/pont *m* à péage.

**tollfree number** = numéro *m* vert.

**tomato** (*pl* **-oes**) tomate *f*.

**tomb** tombeau *m*.

**tomorrow** *adv* demain; **t. morning** demain matin; **the day after t.** après-demain.

**ton** tonne *f* (*= 907 kg*); **tons of** (*lots of*) *Fam* des tonnes de.

**tone** ton *m*; **(dial) t.** tonalité *f*.

**tongs** *npl* pince *f*.

**tongue** langue *f*.

**tonic t. (water)** eau *f* gazeuse (tonique); **gin and t.** gin-tonic *m*.

**tonight** *adv* (*this evening*) ce soir; (*during the night*) cette nuit.

**tonsil** amygdale *f*.

**tonsillitis to have t.** avoir une angine.

**too** *adv* trop; (*also*) aussi; (*moreover*) en plus; **t. tired to play** trop fatigué pour jouer; **t. hard to solve** trop difficile à résoudre; **t. much, t. many** trop; **t. much salt/t. many people**/*etc* trop de sel/gens/*etc*; **one t. many** un de trop.

**took** *pt de* **take.**

**tool** outil *m*.
**tooth** (*pl* **teeth**) dent *f*.
**toothache** mal *m* de dents; **to have a t.** avoir mal aux dents.
**toothbrush** brosse *f* à dents.
**toothpaste** dentifrice *m*.
**toothpick** cure-dent *m*.
**top**[1] **1** *n* (*of mountain, tower, tree*) sommet *m*; (*of wall, ladder, page, garment*) haut *m*; (*of table*) dessus *m*; (*of list*) tête *f*; (*of bottle, tube*) bouchon *m*; (*bottle cap*) capsule *f*; (*of saucepan*) couvercle *m*; (*of pen*) capuchon *m*; **at the t. of the class** le premier de la classe; **on t. of** sur. **2** *a* (*drawer, shelf*) du haut; (*step, layer*) dernier; (*in competition*) premier; (*maximum*) maximum; **on the t. floor** au dernier étage; **at t. speed** à toute vitesse.
**top**[2] **(spinning) t.** toupie *f*.
**topic** sujet *m*.
**top up** (*glass*) remplir; (*coffee, tea*) remettre.
**torch** torche *f*.
**torment** *vt* (*annoy*) agacer.
**tornado** (*pl* **-oes**) tornade *f*.
**tortoise** tortue *f*.
**tortoiseshell** écaille *f*.
**torture 1** *n* torture *f*. **2** *vt* torturer.
**toss 1** *vt* (*throw*) jeter (**to** à); **to t. a coin** jouer à pile ou face. **2** *vi* **let's t.** jouons à pile ou face.
**total** *a* & *n* total (*m*).
**totally** *adv* totalement.
**touch 1** *n* (*contact*) contact *m*; (*sense*) toucher *m*; **in t. with s.o.** en contact avec qn; **to get in t.** se mettre en contact. **2** *vt* toucher. **3** *vi* (*of lines, hands etc*) se toucher; **don't t.!** n'y *or* ne touche pas!
**touch down** (*of aircraft*) atterrir.
**touchy** *a* susceptible.
**tough** *a* (*meat*) dur; (*sturdy*) solide; (*strong*) fort; (*difficult, harsh*) dur.
**tour 1** *n* (*journey*) voyage *m*; (*visit*) visite *f*; (*by artist etc*) tournée *f*. **2** *vt* visiter.
**tourism** tourisme *m*.
**tourist 1** touriste *mf*. **2** *a* touristique.
**tourist (information) office** syndicat *m* d'initiative.
**tournament** tournoi *m*.
**tow** *vt* (*car, boat*) remorquer; (*trailer*) tracter.
**toward(s)** *prep* vers; (*of feelings*) envers; **cruel**/*etc* **t. s.o.** cruel/*etc* envers qn.
**towel** serviette *f* (de toilette); (*for dishes*) torchon *m*.
**tower** tour *f*.
**town** ville *f*; **in t., (in)to t.** en ville.
**town council** conseil *m* municipal.
**town hall** mairie *f*.
**tow truck** dépanneuse *f*.
**toy 1** *n* jouet *m*. **2** *a* (*gun*) d'enfant; (*house, car*) miniature.
**toyshop** magasin *m* de jouets.
**trace 1** *n* trace *f* (**of** de). **2** *vt* (*with tracing paper*) (dé)calquer; (*find*) retrouver.
**tracing paper** papier-calque *m inv*.
**track** (*of animal, sports stadium etc*) piste *f*; (*of record*) plage *f*; (*for train*) voie *f*; (*path*) chemin *m*; (*racetrack*) champ *m* de courses; **tracks** (*of wheels*) traces *fpl*; **on the right t.** sur la bonne voie.
**track shoe** (*running shoe*) jogging *m*.
**tracksuit** survêtement *m*.
**tractor** tracteur *m*.
**tractor-trailer** semi-remorque *m*.
**trade 1** *n* commerce *m*; (*job*) métier *m*. **2** *vi* faire du commerce (**with** avec); (*swap*) échanger; **to t. places** changer de place. **3** *vt* échanger (**for** contre).
**trade-in** (*car etc*) reprise *f*.
**trademark** marque *f* de fabrique; **(registered) t.** marque déposée.
**trade union** syndicat *m*.
**trading** commerce *m*.
**tradition** tradition *f*.
**traditional** *a* traditionnel.
**traffic** circulation *f*; (*air, sea, rail*) trafic *m*.
**traffic jam** embouteillage *m*.

**traffic laws** Code *m* de la route.
**traffic lights** *npl* feux *mpl* (de signalisation); (*when red*) feu *m* rouge.
**traffic sign** panneau *m* de signalisation.
**tragedy** tragédie *f*.
**tragic** *a* tragique.
**trail 1** *n* (*of smoke, blood etc*) traînée *f*. **2** *vti* (*on the ground etc*) traîner.
**trailer** (*for car*) remorque *f*; (camper) caravane *f*.
**train**[1] train *m*; (*underground*) rame *f*; **to go** *or* **come by t.** prendre le train; **t. set** petit train *m*; **t. ticket** billet *m* de train; **t. station** gare *f*; **t. tracks** voie *f* ferrée.
**train**[2] **1** *vt* (*teach*) former (**to do** à faire); (*in sport*) entraîner; (*animal, child*) dresser (**to do** à faire). **2** *vi* recevoir une formation (**as a doctor**/*etc* de médecin/*etc*); (*of athlete*) s'entraîner.
**trained** *a* (*skilled*) qualifié; (*nurse, engineer*) diplômé.
**training** formation *f*; (*in sports*) entraînement *m*.
**traitor** traître *m*.
**tramp** clochard, -arde *mf*.
**tranquilizer** tranquillisant *m*.
**transfer 1** *vt* (*person, goods etc*) transférer (**to** à). **2** *n* transfert *m* (**to** à); (*image*) décalcomanie *f*.
**transfusion (blood) t.** transfusion *f* (sanguine).
**transistor t. (radio)** transistor *m*.
**transitive** *a Grammar* transitif.
**translate** *vt* traduire (**from** de, **into** en).
**translation** traduction *f*.
**translator** traducteur, -trice *mf*.
**transparent** *a* transparent.
**transplant** greffe *f*.
**transport 1** *vt* transporter. **2** *n* transport *m* (**of** de); **means of t.** moyen *m* de transport; **public t.** les transports en commun.
**trap 1** *n* piège *m*. **2** *vt* (*animal*) prendre (au piège); (*jam*) coincer; (*cut off by snow etc*) bloquer (**by** par).
**trap door** trappe *f*.
**trash** (*nonsense*) sottises *fpl*; (*junk*) bric-à-brac *m inv*; (*waste*) ordures *fpl*.
**trashcan** poubelle *f*.
**trashy** *a* (*book, movie*) nul; (*goods*) de mauvaise qualité.
**travel 1** *vi* voyager. **2** *vt* (*country, distance*) parcourir. **3** *n* **travel(s)** voyages *mpl*; **t. agent** agent *m* de voyages; **t. guide** guide *m*.
**traveler** voyageur, -euse *mf*.
**traveler's check** chèque *m* de voyage.
**traveling** voyages *mpl*.
**travel sickness** (*in car*) mal *m* de la route; (*in aircraft*) mal *m* de l'air.
**tray** plateau *m*.
**treacherous** *a* (*road, conditions*) très dangereux.
**tread*** *vi* marcher (**on** sur).
**treasure** trésor *m*.
**treat 1** *vt* traiter; (*consider*) considérer (**as** comme); **to t. s.o. to sth** offrir qch à qn. **2** *n* **(special) t.** petit extra *m*; **to give s.o. a (special) t.** donner une surprise à qn.
**treatment** traitement *m*.
**treble** *vti* tripler.
**tree** arbre *m*.
**tremble** *vi* trembler (**with** de).
**trench** tranchée *f*.
**trial** (*in court*) procès *m*; **to go** *or* **be on t.** être jugé, passer en jugement.
**triangle** triangle *m*.
**triangular** *a* triangulaire.
**tribe** tribu *f*.
**trick 1** *n* (*joke, of magician etc*) tour *m*; (*clever method*) astuce *f*; **to play a t. on s.o.** jouer un tour à qn. **2** *vt* tromper.
**trickle 1** *n* (*of liquid*) filet *m*. **2** *vi* dégouliner.
**tricky** *a* (*problem etc*) difficile.
**tricycle** tricycle *m*.
**trigger** (*of gun*) gâchette *f*.
**trim** *vt* couper (un peu).
**trip** (*journey*) voyage *m*; (*outing*) excursion *f*.
**trip (over** *or* **up)** *vi* trébucher; **to t. over sth** trébucher contre qch.

**triple** *vti* tripler.
**trip s.o. up** faire trébucher qn.
**triumph 1** *n* triomphe *m* (**over** sur). **2** *vi* triompher (**over** de).
**trivial** *a* (*unimportant*) insignifiant.
**trolley** (*streetcar*) tramway *m*.
**trombone** trombone *m*.
**troops** *npl* troupes *fpl*.
**trophy** coupe *f*, trophée *m*.
**tropical** *a* tropical.
**trot 1** *n* trot *m*. **2** *vi* trotter.
**trouble 1** *n* (*difficulty*) ennui(s) *m*(*pl*); (*effort*) peine *f*; (*disorder, illness*) troubles *mpl*; **to be in t.** avoir des ennuis; **to get into t.** s'attirer des ennuis (**with** avec); **to go to the t. of doing, take the t. to do** se donner la peine de faire. **2** *vt* (*inconvenience*) déranger; (*worry, annoy*) ennuyer.
**trousers** *npl* pantalon *m*; **a pair of t., some t.** un pantalon.
**trout** truite *f*.
**truant to play t.** sécher (la classe).
**truck** camion *m*.
**truck driver** *or* **trucker** camionneur *m*; (*over long distances*) routier *m*.
**true** *a* vrai; (*accurate*) exact; **t. to** (*one's promise etc*) fidèle à; **to come t.** se réaliser.
**trump (card)** atout *m*.
**trumpet** trompette *f*.
**trunk** (*of tree, body*) tronc *m*; (*of elephant*) trompe *f*; (*case*) malle *f*; (*of vehicle*) coffre *m*; **trunks** (*for swimming*) slip *m* de bain.
**trust 1** *n* (*faith*) confiance *f* (**in** en). **2** *vt* (*person, judgment*) avoir confiance en; **to t. s.o. with sth, t. sth to s.o.** confier qch à qn.
**truth** vérité *f*.
**try 1** *vt* essayer (**to do, doing** de faire); **to t. one's luck** tenter sa chance. **2** *vi* essayer; **to t. hard** faire un gros effort. **3** *n* (*attempt*) essai *m*; **to give (sth)/ a t.** essayer (qch).
**try (out)** (*car, method etc*) essayer; (*person*) mettre à l'essai.
**try on** (*clothes, shoes*) essayer.
**T-shirt** tee-shirt *m*.
**tub** (*basin*) baquet *m*; (*bath*) baignoire *f*.
**tube** tube *m*.
**tuck in** (*shirt, blanket*) rentrer; (*person in bed*) border.
**Tuesday** mardi *m*.
**tuft** touffe *f*.
**tug** *vti* tirer (**at** sur).
**tug(boat)** remorqueur *m*.
**tuition** enseignement *m*; (*lessons*) leçons *fpl*.
**tulip** tulipe *f*.
**tumble** dégringolade *f*.
**tumble (down)** *vi* dégringoler.
**tumble dryer** sèche-linge *m inv*.
**tumbler** (*glass*) gobelet *m*.
**tummy** *Fam* ventre *m*.
**tuna (fish)** thon *m*.
**tune 1** *n* air *m*; **in t./out of t.** (*instrument*) accordé/désaccordé; **to sing in t./out of t.** chanter juste/faux. **2** *vt* (*instrument*) accorder; (*engine*) régler.
**tuning** (*of engine*) réglage *m*.
**tunnel** tunnel *m*.
**turban** turban *m*.
**turkey** dindon *m*, dinde *f*; (*as food*) dinde *f*.
**turn 1** *n* (*movement, in game*) tour *m*; (*in road*) tournant *m*; **to take turns** se relayer; **it's your t. (to play)** c'est à toi *or* (à) ton tour (de jouer). **2** *vt* tourner; (*mattress, pancake*) retourner; **to t. sth red/***etc* rendre qch rouge/*etc*, rougir/*etc* qch; **she's turned twenty** elle a vingt ans passés. **3** *vi* (*of wheel etc*) tourner; (*turn head or body*) se (re)tourner; (*become*) devenir; **to t. red/***etc* rougir/*etc*.
**turn around 1** *vt* (*head, object*) tourner; (*vehicle*) faire faire demi-tour à. **2** *vi* (*of person*) se retourner.
**turn away 1** *vt* (*eyes*) détourner; (*person*) renvoyer. **2** *vi* se détourner.
**turn back** *vi* retourner.
**turn down** (*gas, radio etc*) baisser; (*offer, person*) refuser.

**turn into sth/s.o. 1** *vt* (*change*) changer en qch/qn. **2** *vi* se changer en qch/qn.
**turnip** navet *m* (*plante*).
**turn off** (*light, radio etc*) éteindre; (*faucet*) fermer; (*machine*) arrêter.
**turn on** (*light, radio etc*) mettre; (*faucet*) ouvrir; (*machine*) mettre en marche.
**turn out 1** *vt* (*light*) éteindre. **2** *vi* (*happen*) se passer.
**turn over 1** *vt* (*page*) tourner. **2** *vi* (*of vehicle, person*) se retourner.
**turn up 1** *vt* (*radio, light etc*) mettre plus fort; (*collar*) remonter. **2** *vi* (*arrive*) arriver.
**turtle** tortue *f;* **sea t.** tortue *f* de mer.
**turtleneck** (*sweater*) col *m* roulé.
**tusk** défense *f*.
**tutor 1** *n* précepteur, -trice *mf*. **2** *vt* donner des cours particuliers à.
**TV** télé *f*.
**tweezers** *npl* pince *f* à épiler.
**twelfth** *a* & *n* douzième (*mf*).
**twelve** *a* & *n* douze (*m*).
**twentieth** *a* & *n* vingtième (*mf*).
**twenty** *a* & *n* vingt (*m*).
**twice** *adv* deux fois; **t. as heavy**/*etc* deux fois plus lourd/*etc*.
**twig** brindille *f*.
**twilight** crépuscule *m*.
**twin** jumeau *m*, jumelle *f*; **t. brother** frère *m* jumeau; **t. sister** sœur *f* jumelle; **t. beds** lits *mpl* jumeaux.
**twine** (grosse) ficelle *f*.
**twinkle** *vi* (*of star*) scintiller.
**twist 1** *vt* (*wire, arm etc*) tordre; (*roll*) enrouler (**around** autour de); (*knob*) tourner; **to t. one's ankle** se tordre la cheville. **2** *n* (*turn*) tour *m*; (*in road*) zigzag *m*.
**twist off** (*lid*) dévisser.
**two** *a* & *n* deux (*m*); **t.-way traffic** circulation *f* dans les deux sens.
**type**[1] (*sort*) genre *m*, type *m*; (*print*) caractères *mpl*.
**type**[2] *vti* (*write*) taper (à la machine).
**typed** *a* tapé à la machine.
**typewriter** machine *f* à écrire.
**typical** *a* typique (**of** de); **that's t. (of him)!** c'est bien lui!
**typist** dactylo *f*.

# U

**UFO** *abbr* (*unidentified flying object*) OVNI *m*.
**ugliness** laideur *f*.
**ugly** *a* laid.
**ulcer** ulcère *m*.
**umbrella** parapluie *m*; (*over table, on beach*) parasol *m*.
**umpire** arbitre *m*.
**un -** *prefix* in-, peu, non, sans.
**unable** *a* **to be u. to do** être incapable de faire; **he's u. to swim** il ne sait pas nager.
**unacceptable** *a* inacceptable.
**unaccustomed to be u. to sth/to doing** ne pas être habitué à qch/à faire.
**unanimous** *a* unanime.
**unanimously** *adv* à l'unanimité.
**unattractive** *a* (*idea, appearance*) peu attrayant; (*ugly*) laid.
**unavailable** *a* (*person*) qui n'est pas disponible; (*product*) épuisé.
**unavoidable** *a* inévitable.
**unavoidably** *adv* inévitablement; (*delayed*) pour une raison indépendante de sa volonté.
**unaware** *a* **to be u. of sth** ignorer qch; **to be u. that** ignorer que.
**unawares** *adv* **to catch s.o. u.** prendre qn au dépourvu.
**unbearable** *a* insupportable.
**unbelievable** *a* incroyable.
**unbreakable** *a* incassable.
**unbutton** *vt* déboutonner.
**uncertain** *a* incertain (**about, of** de); **it's u. whether** il n'est pas certain que (+ *subjunctive*); **I'm u. whether to stay** je ne sais pas très bien si je dois rester.
**uncertainty** incertitude *f*.
**unchanged** *a* inchangé.
**uncle** oncle *m*.

**unclear** *a* (*meaning*) qui n'est pas clair; (*result*) incertain; **it's u. whether** on ne sait pas très bien si.
**uncomfortable** *a* (*chair etc*) inconfortable; (*uneasy*) mal à l'aise.
**uncommon** *a* rare.
**unconnected** *a* (*facts etc*) sans rapport (**with** avec).
**unconscious** *a* (*person*) sans connaissance.
**unconvincing** *a* peu convaincant.
**uncooperative** *a* peu coopératif.
**uncork** *vt* (*bottle*) déboucher.
**uncover** *vt* découvrir.
**undamaged** *a* (*goods*) en bon état.
**undecided** *a* (*person*) indécis (**about** sur).
**undeniable** *a* incontestable.
**under 1** *prep* sous; (*less than*) moins de; (*according to*) selon; **children u. nine** les enfants de moins de neuf ans; **u. the circumstances** dans les circonstances; **u. there** là-dessous; **u. it** dessous. **2** *adv* au-dessous.
**under -** *prefix* sous-.
**undercharge** *vt* **I undercharged him (for it)** je ne (le) lui ai pas fait payer assez.
**underclothes** *npl* sous-vêtements *mpl*.
**underdone** *a* (*steak*) saignant.
**underestimate** *vt* sous-estimer.
**undergo*** *vt* subir.
**undergraduate** étudiant, -ante *mf* (qui prépare la licence).
**underground** *a* souterrain; **u. passage** passage *m* soutterain..
**underline** *vt* (*word etc*) souligner.
**underneath 1** *prep* sous. **2** *adv* (en) dessous; **the book u.** le livre d'en dessous. **3** *n* dessous *m*.
**underpants** *npl* slip *m*.
**underpass** (*on highway*) passage *m* inférieur.
**undershirt** tricot *m* de corps; (*woman's*) chemise *f* (américaine).
**understand*** *vti* comprendre.
**understandable** *a* compréhensible.
**understanding 1** *n* compréhension *f*; (*agreement*) accord *m*; (*sympathy*) entente *f*. **2** *a* (*person*) compréhensif.
**understood** *a* (*agreed*) entendu.
**undertake*** *vt* entreprendre (**to do** de faire).
**undertaker** entrepreneur *m* de pompes funèbres.
**undertaking** (*task*) entreprise *f*.
**underwater 1** *a* sous-marin. **2** *adv* sous l'eau.
**underwear** sous-vêtements *mpl*; (*underpants*) slip *m*.
**undo*** *vt* défaire.
**undone** *a* **to come u.** (*of knot etc*) se défaire.
**undoubtedly** *adv* sans aucun doute.
**undress 1** *vi* se déshabiller. **2** *vt* déshabiller; **to get undressed** se déshabiller.
**uneasy** *a* (*ill at ease*) mal à l'aise.
**unemployed 1** *a* au chômage. **2** *n* **the u.** les chômeurs *mpl*.
**unemployment** chômage *m*; (*payment*) allocation *f* de chômage; **to go on u.** s'inscrire au chômage.
**unemployment office** = agence *f* nationale pour l'emploi, ANPE *f*.
**uneven** *a* inégal.
**uneventful** *a* (*trip etc*) sans histoires.
**unexpected** *a* inattendu.
**unexpectedly** *adv* à l'improviste; (*suddenly*) subitement.
**unfair** *a* injuste (**to s.o.** envers qn).
**unfairly** *adv* injustement.
**unfairness** injustice *f*.
**unfaithful** *a* infidèle (**to** à).
**unfamiliar** *a* inconnu; **to be u. with sth** ne pas connaître qch.
**unfashionable** *a* (*subject etc*) démodé; (*restaurant etc*) peu chic *inv*.
**unfasten** *vt* défaire.
**unfavorable** *a* défavorable.
**unfinished** *a* inachevé.
**unfit** *a* en mauvaise santé; (*in bad shape*) pas en forme; (*unsuitable*)

impropre; (**for** à, **to do** à faire); (*unworthy*) indigne (**for** de, **to do** de faire); (*unable*) inapte (**for** à, **to do** à faire).

**unfold** *vt* déplier.

**unforgettable** *a* inoubliable.

**unforgivable** *a* impardonnable.

**unfortunate** *a* malheureux; **you were u.** tu n'as pas eu de chance.

**unfortunately** *adv* malheureusement.

**unfriendly** *a* froid, peu aimable (**to** avec).

**unfurnished** *a* non meublé.

**ungrateful** *a* ingrat.

**unhappiness** tristesse *f.*

**unhappy** *a* (*sad*) malheureux; **u. with** *or* **about sth** mécontent de qch.

**unharmed** *a* (*person*) indemne.

**unhealthy** *a* (*climate etc*) malsain; (*person*) en mauvaise santé.

**unhelpful** *a* (*person*) peu serviable.

**unhook** *vt* (*picture, curtain*) décrocher; (*dress*) dégrafer.

**unhurt** *a* indemne.

**unhygienic** *a* pas très hygiénique.

**uniform** uniforme *m.*

**unimportant** *a* peu important.

**uninhabited** *a* inhabité.

**uninjured** *a* indemne.

**unintentional** *a* involontaire.

**uninteresting** *a* (*book etc*) peu intéressant.

**union 1** *n* union *f*; (*labor union*) syndicat *m*. **2** *a* syndical; **u. member** syndiqué, -ée *mf.*

**unique** *a* unique.

**unit** unité *f*; (*of furniture etc*) élément *m*; (*team*) groupe *m*.

**unite 1** *vt* unir; (*country, party*) unifier. **2** *vi* (*of students etc*) s'unir.

**universal** *a* universel.

**universe** univers *m.*

**university 1** *n* université *f*; **at u.** à l'université. **2** *a* universitaire; (*student*) d'université.

**unjust** *a* injuste.

**unkind** *a* peu gentil (**to s.o.** avec qn).

**unknown** *a* inconnu.

**unleaded** *a* (*gasoline*) sans plomb.

**unless** *conj* à moins que (+ *subjunctive*); **u. she comes** à moins qu'elle ne vienne.

**unlike** *prep* **u. me, she . . .** à la différence de moi, elle . . . ; **that's u. him** ça ne lui ressemble pas.

**unlikely** *a* peu probable; (*unbelievable*) incroyable; **she's u. to win** il est peu probable qu'elle gagne.

**unlimited** *a* illimité.

**unlisted** *a* (*phone number*) sur la liste rouge.

**unload** *vt* décharger.

**unlock** *vt* ouvrir (*avec une clef*).

**unluckily** *adv* malheureusement.

**unlucky** *a* (*person*) malchanceux; (*number etc*) qui porte malheur; **you're u.** tu n'as pas de chance.

**unmade** *a* (*bed*) défait.

**unmarried** *a* célibataire.

**unnecessary** *a* inutile.

**unnoticed** *a* **to go u.** passer inaperçu.

**unoccupied** *a* (*house*) inoccupé; (*seat*) libre.

**unpack 1** *vt* (*suitcase*) défaire; (*goods, belongings*) déballer. **2** *vi* défaire sa valise.

**unpaid** *a* (*bill, sum*) impayé; (*work, worker*) bénévole.

**unpleasant** *a* désagréable (**to s.o.** avec qn).

**unplug** *vt* (*appliance*) débrancher.

**unpopular** *a* peu populaire; **to be u. with s.o.** ne pas plaire à qn.

**unpredictable** *a* imprévisible; (*weather*) indécis.

**unprepared** *a* **to be u. for sth** (*not expect*) ne pas s'attendre à qch.

**unreasonable** *a* qui n'est pas raisonnable.

**unrecognizable** *a* méconnaissable.

**unrelated** *a* (*facts etc*) sans rapport (**to** avec).

**unreliable** *a* (*person*) peu sûr; (*machine*) peu fiable.

**unrest** agitation *f*.

**unroll 1** *vt* dérouler. **2** *vi* se dérouler.

**unsafe** *a* (*place, machine etc*) dangereux; (*person*) en danger.

**unsatisfactory** *a* peu satisfaisant.

**unscrew** *vt* dévisser.

**unskilled worker** ouvrier, -ière *mf* non qualifié(e).

**unstable** *a* instable.

**unsteadily** *adv* (*to walk*) d'un pas mal assuré.

**unsteady** *a* (*hand, step*) mal assuré; (*table, ladder etc*) instable.

**unsuccessful** *a* (*attempt etc*) vain; (*candidate*) malheureux; **to be u.** ne pas réussir (**in doing** à faire).

**unsuccessfully** *adv* en vain.

**unsuitable** *a* qui ne convient pas (**for** à).

**unsuited** *a* **u. to** (*job, activity*) peu fait pour.

**unsure** *a* incertain (**of, about** de).

**untangle** *vt* démêler.

**untidy** *a* (*clothes, hair*) peu soigné; (*room*) en désordre; (*person*) désordonné; (*in appearance*) peu soigné.

**untie** *vt* (*person, hands*) détacher; (*knot, parcel*) défaire.

**until 1** *prep* jusqu'à; **u. then** jusque-là; **I didn't come u. yesterday** je ne suis venu qu'hier; **not u. tomorrow** pas avant demain. **2** *conj* jusqu'à ce que (+ *subjunctive*); **do nothing u. I come** ne fais rien avant que j'arrive.

**untrue** *a* faux (*f* fausse).

**unused** *a* (*new*) neuf (*f* neuve).

**unusual** *a* exceptionnel; (*strange*) étrange.

**unusually** *adv* exceptionnellement.

**unwell** *a* indisposé.

**unwilling** *a* **he's u. to do** il ne veut pas faire.

**unwillingly** *adv* à contrecœur.

**unworthy** *a* indigne (**of** de).

**unwrap** *vt* ouvrir.

**unzip** *vt* ouvrir (la fermeture éclair® de).

**up 1** *adv* en haut; (*in the air*) en l'air; (*out of bed*) levé, debout; **to come** *or* **go up** monter; **prices are up** les prix ont augmenté; **up there** là-haut; **further** *or* **higher up** plus haut; **up to** (*as far as*) jusqu'à; **it's up to you to do it** c'est à toi de le faire; **that's up to you** ça dépend de toi; **what are you up to?** que fais-tu?; **to walk up and down** marcher de long en large. **2** *prep* (*a hill*) en haut de; (*a tree*) dans; (*a ladder*) sur; **to go up** (*hill, stairs*) monter.

**uphill** *adv* **to go u.** monter.

**upon** *prep* sur.

**upper** *a* supérieur.

**upright** *a* & *adv* (*straight*) droit.

**uproar** vacarme *m*, tapage *m*.

**upset 1** *vt** (*stomach, routine etc*) déranger; **to u. s.o.** (*make sad*) peiner qn; (*offend*) vexer qn. **2** *a* peiné; vexé; (*stomach*) dérangé; **to have an u. stomach** avoir l'estomac dérangé.

**upside down** *adv* à l'envers.

**upstairs 1** *adv* en haut; **to go u.** monter (l'escalier). **2** *a* (*people, room*) du dessus.

**up-to-date** *a* moderne; (*information*) à jour; (*well-informed*) au courant (**on** de).

**upward(s)** *adv* vers le haut; **upwards of five francs** cinq francs et plus.

**urge** *vt* **to u. s.o. to do** conseiller vivement à qn de faire.

**urgency** urgence *f*.

**urgent** *a* urgent.

**urgently** *adv* d'urgence.

**us** *pron* nous; **(to) us** nous; **she sees us** elle nous voit; **he gives (to) us** il nous donne; **all of us** nous tous; **let's** *or* **let us eat!** mangeons!

**use 1** *n* usage *m*, emploi *m*; **to make u. of sth** se servir de qch; **not in u.** hors d'usage; **to be of u.** être utile; **it's no u. crying**/*etc* ça ne sert à rien de pleurer/*etc*; **what's the u. of worrying**/*etc*? à quoi bon s'inquiéter/*etc*? **2** *vt* se servir de, utiliser (**as** comme; **to do, for doing**

pour faire); **it's used to do** *or* **for doing** ça sert à faire; **it's used as** ça sert de.
**use (up)** (*fuel*) consommer; (*supplies*) épuiser; (*money*) dépenser.
**used 1** *a* (*secondhand*) d'occasion. **2** *v aux* **I u. to sing**/*etc* avant, je chantais/*etc*. **3** *a* **u. to sth/to doing** habitué à qch/à faire; **to get u. to** s'habituer à.
**useful** *a* utile (**to** à); **to come in u.** être utile.
**usefulness** utilité *f*.
**useless** *a* inutile; (*person*) nul.
**user** (*of road*) usager *m*; (*of machine, dictionary*) utilisateur, -trice *mf*.
**usual** *a* habituel; **as u.** comme d'habitude.
**usually** *adv* d'habitude.
**utensil** ustensile *m*.
**utter 1** *a* complet; (*idiot*) parfait. **2** *vt* (*a cry*) pousser; (*a word*) dire.
**utterly** *adv* complètement.
**U-turn** (*in vehicle*) demi-tour *m*.

# V

**vacancy** (*post*) poste *m* vacant; (*room*) chambre *f* libre.
**vacant** *a* (*room, seat*) libre; **v. lot** terrain *m* vague.
**vacation** vacances *fpl*; **on v.** en vacances.
**vacationer** vacancier, -ière *mf*.
**vaccinate** *vt* vacciner.
**vaccination** vaccination *f*.
**vaccine** vaccin *m*.
**vacuum** *vt* (*carpet etc*) passer à l'aspirateur.
**vacuum cleaner** aspirateur *m*.
**vague** *a* vague; (*outline*) flou.
**vaguely** *adv* vaguement.
**vain** *a* **in v.** en vain.
**valid** *a* (*ticket etc*) valable.
**valley** vallée *f*.
**valuable 1** *a* (*object*) de (grande) valeur. **2** *npl* **valuables** objets *mpl* de valeur.
**value** valeur *f*; **it's good v. (for money)** ça a un bon rapport qualité/prix.
**van** camionnette *f*, fourgonnette *f*; (*large*) camion *m*.
**vandal** vandale *mf*.
**vandalize** *vt* saccager.
**vanilla 1** *n* vanille *f*. **2** *a* (*ice cream*) à la vanille.
**vanish** *vi* disparaître.
**varied** *a* varié.
**variety** variété *f*; **a v. of reasons**/*etc* diverses raisons/*etc*; **v. show** spectacle *m* de variétés.
**various** *a* divers.
**varnish 1** *vt* vernir. **2** *n* vernis *m*.
**vary** *vti* varier.
**vase** vase *m*.
**Vaseline®** vaseline *f*.
**vast** *a* vaste.
**VAT** *abbr* (*value added tax*) TVA *f*.
**VCR** magnétoscope *m*.
**veal** (*meat*) veau *m*.
**vegetable** légume *m*.
**vegetarian** *a* & *n* végétarien, -ienne (*mf*).
**vegetation** végétation *f*.
**vehicle** véhicule *m*.
**veil** voile *m*.
**vein** (*in body*) veine *f*.
**velvet 1** *n* velours *m*. **2** *a* de velours.
**vending machine** distributeur *m* automatique.
**venetian blind** store *m* vénitien.
**ventilation** (*in room*) aération *f*.
**verb** verbe *m*.
**verdict** verdict *m*.
**verse** (*part of song*) couplet *m*; (*poetry*) poésie *f*; **in v.** en vers.
**version** version *f*.
**vertical** *a* vertical.
**very 1** *adv* très; **v. much** beaucoup; **at the v. latest** au plus tard. **2** *a* (*actual*) même; **his** *or* **her v. brother** son frère même.
**vest** (*waistcoat*) gilet *m*.
**vet(erinarian)** vétérinaire *mf*.
**via** *prep* par.
**vibrate** *vi* vibrer.
**vibration** vibration *f*.
**vicar** pasteur *m*.
**vice** vice *m*; (*tool*) étau *m*.

**vicious** *a* (*spiteful*) méchant; (*violent*) brutal.
**victim** victime *f*; **to be the v. of** être victime de.
**victory** victoire *f*.
**video 1** *n* (*cassette*) cassette *f*; **on v.** sur cassette. **2** *a* (*game, camera etc*) vidéo *inv*. **3** *vt* (*event*) faire une (vidéo)cassette de.
**videocassette** videocassette *f*; **v. recorder** magnetoscope *m*.
**video game** jeu *m* vidéo.
**videotape** bande *f* vidéo.
**view** vue *f*; **to come into v.** apparaître; **in my v.** à mon avis; **in v. of** compte tenu de.
**viewer** (*person*) téléspectateur, -trice *mf*.
**viewpoint** point *m* de vue.
**villa** villa *f*.
**village** village *m*.
**villager** villageois, -oise *mf*.
**vinegar** vinaigre *m*.
**vineyard** vignoble *m*.
**violence** violence *f*.
**violent** *a* violent.
**violently** *adv* violemment.
**violin** violon *m*.
**virus** virus *m*.
**visa** visa *m*.
**vise** étau *m*.
**visible** *a* visible.
**visit 1** *n* visite *f*; (*stay*) séjour *m*. **2** *vt* (*place*) visiter; **to visit s.o.** rendre visite à qn; (*stay with*) faire un séjour chez qn. **3** *vi* être en visite.
**visiting hours** heures *fpl* de visite.
**visitor** visiteur, -euse *mf*; (*guest*) invité, -ée *mf*.
**vital** *a* essentiel; **it's v. that** il est essentiel que (+ *subjunctive*).
**vitamin** vitamine *f*.
**vivid** *a* vif; (*description*) vivant.
**vocabulary** vocabulaire *m*.
**vodka** vodka *f*.
**voice** voix *f*; **at the top of one's v.** à tue-tête.
**volcano** (*pl* **-oes**) volcan *m*.
**volume** (*book, capacity, loudness*) volume *m*.
**voluntary** *a* volontaire; (*unpaid*) bénévole.
**volunteer 1** *n* volontaire *mf*. **2** *vi* se proposer (**for sth** pour qch, **to do** pour faire).
**vomit** *vti* vomir.
**vote 1** *n* vote *m*. **2** *vi* voter; **to v. Republican** voter républicain.
**voter** électeur, -trice *mf*.
**voucher** (*for meal, gift etc*) chèque *m*.
**vowel** voyelle *f*.
**voyage** voyage *m* (par mer).
**vulgar** *a* vulgaire.

# W

**wad** (*of money etc*) liasse *f*; (*of cotton wool*) tampon *m*.
**waddle** *vi* se dandiner.
**wade through** (*mud, water etc*) patauger dans.
**wading pool** (*small, inflatable*) piscine *f* gonflable.
**wad up** (*paper*) chiffonner.
**wafer** gaufrette *f*.
**wag** *vti* (*tail*) remuer.
**wage(s)** *n*(*pl*) salaire *m*.
**wage earner** salarié, -ée *mf*.
**wagon** (*horse-drawn*) charrette *f*, chariot *m*.
**waist** taille *f*; **stripped to the w.** torse nu.
**waistcoat** gilet *m*.
**wait 1** *n* attente *f*. **2** *vi* attendre; **to w. for s.o./sth** attendre qn/qch; **w. until I've gone, w. for me to go** attends que je sois parti; **to keep s.o. waiting** faire attendre qn.
**wait behind** *vi* rester.
**waiter** garçon *m* (de café); **w.!** garçon!
**waiting** attente *f*.
**waiting room** salle *f* d'attente.
**waitress** serveuse *f*; **w.!** mademoiselle!
**wait up** *vi* veiller; **to w. up for s.o.** attendre le retour de qn avant de se coucher.

**wake* (up) 1** *vi* se réveiller. **2** *vt* réveiller.
**walk 1** *n* promenade *f*; (*shorter*) (petit) tour *m*; (*path*) allée *f*; **to go for a w.** faire une promenade; (*shorter*) faire un (petit) tour; **to take for a w.** (*child*) emmener se promener; (*baby, dog*) promener; **five minutes' w. (away)** à cinq minutes à pied. **2** *vi* marcher; (*stroll*) se promener; (*go on foot*) aller à pied. **3** *vt* (*distance*) faire à pied; (*take for a walk*) promener (*chien*).
**walk away** *or* **off** *vi* s'éloigner (**from** de).
**walker** (*for pleasure*) promeneur, -euse *mf*.
**walk in** *vi* entrer.
**walking stick** canne *f*.
**Walkman**® (*pl* **Walkmans**) baladeur *m*.
**walk out** (*leave*) partir.
**wall** mur *m*; (*of cabin, tunnel*) paroi *f*.
**wallet** portefeuille *m*.
**wallpaper 1** *n* papier *m* peint. **2** *vt* tapisser.
**wall-to-wall carpet(ing)** moquette *f*.
**walnut** (*nut*) noix *f*.
**walrus** (*animal*) morse *m*.
**wander (around)** errer; (*stroll*) flâner.
**want** *vt* vouloir (**to do** faire); (*ask for*) demander (*qn*); (*need*) avoir besoin de; **I w. him to go** je veux qu'il parte; **you're wanted** on vous demande.
**war** guerre *f*; **at w.** en guerre (**with** avec).
**ward** (*in hospital*) salle *f*.
**wardrobe** (*built-in*) penderie *f*; (*free-standing*) armoire *f*.
**warehouse,** (*pl* **-ses**) entrepôt *m*.
**warm 1** *a* chaud; **to be** *or* **feel w.** avoir chaud; **it's (nice and) w.** (*of weather*) il fait (agréablement) chaud. **2** *vt* (*person, food etc*) réchauffer.
**warmth** chaleur *f*.
**warm up 1** *vt* (*person, food etc*) réchauffer. **2** *vi* (*of person, room, engine*) se réchauffer; (*of food, water*) chauffer.
**warn** *vt* avertir (**that** que); **to w. s.o. against sth** mettre qn en garde contre qch; **to w. s.o. against doing** conseiller à qn de ne pas faire.
**warning** avertissement *m*; (*advance notice*) (pré)avis *m*; **(hazard) w. flashers** (*of vehicle*) feux *mpl* de détresse.
**warship** navire *m* de guerre.
**wart** verrue *f*.
**was** *pt de* **be.**
**wash 1** *n* **to give sth a w.** laver qch; **in the w.** (*of dirty clothes*) au sale. **2** *vt* laver; **to w. one's hands** se laver les mains.
**washable** *a* lavable.
**wash away** *or* **off** *or* **out 1** *vt* (*stain*) faire partir (en lavant). **2** *vi* partir (au lavage).
**washbasin** lavabo *m*.
**washcloth** gant *m* de toilette.
**washing** (*act*) lavage *m*.
**washing machine** machine *f* à laver.
**wash out** (*bowl etc*) laver.
**washroom** toilettes *fpl*.
**wash up** (*wash hands and face*) se laver.
**wasp** guêpe *f*.
**waste 1** *n* gaspillage *m*; (*of time*) perte *f*. **2** *vt* (*money, food etc*) gaspiller; (*time, opportunity*) perdre.
**wastepaper** vieux papiers *mpl*.
**wastepaper basket** corbeille *f* (à papier).
**watch 1** *n* (*small clock*) montre *f*. **2** *vt* regarder; (*be careful of*) faire attention à. **3** *vi* regarder.
**watchband** bracelet *m* de montre.
**watch (out) for sth/s.o.** (*wait for*) guetter qch/qn.
**watch (over)** (*suspect, baby etc*) surveiller.
**watch out** (*take care*) faire attention (**for** à); **w. out!** attention!
**water 1** *n* eau *f*; **w. pistol** pistolet *m* à eau. **2** *vt* (*plant etc*) arroser.

**watercolor** (*picture*) aquarelle *f*; (*paint*) couleur *f* pour aquarelle.
**watercress** cresson *m* (de fontaine).
**water down** (*wine etc*) couper (d'eau).
**waterfall** chute *f* d'eau.
**waterfront** bord *m* *or* front *m* de mer.
**watering can** arrosoir *m*.
**watermelon** pastèque *f*.
**waterproof** *a* (*material*) imperméable.
**water skiing** ski *m* nautique.
**watertight** *a* étanche.
**wave 1** *n* (*of sea*) vague *f*; (*in hair*) ondulation *f*; **medium/short w.** (*on radio*) ondes *fpl* moyennes/courtes; **long w.** grandes ondes, ondes longues. **2** *vi* (*with hand*) faire signe (de la main); **to w. to s.o.** (*greet*) saluer qn de la main. **3** *vt* (*arm, flag etc*) agiter.
**wavelength** longueur *f* d'ondes.
**wavy** *a* (*hair*) ondulé.
**wax 1** *n* cire *f*. **2** *vt* cirer.
**wax paper** papier *m* sulfurisé.
**way**[1] **1** *n* (*path*) chemin *m* (**to** de); (*direction*) sens *m*; (*distance*) distance *f*; **all the w., the whole w.** (*to talk etc*) pendant tout le chemin; **this w.** par ici; **that way** par là; **which w.?** par où?; **to lose one's w.** se perdre; **the w. there** l'aller *m*; **the w. back** le retour; **the w. in** l'entrée *f*; **the w. out** la sortie; **on the w.** en route (**to** pour); **to be** *or* **stand in s.o.'s w.** être sur le chemin de qn; **to get out of the w.** s'écarter; **a long w. (away** *or* **off)** très loin. **2** *adv* (*behind etc*) très loin; **w. ahead** très en avance (**of** sur).
**way**[2] (*manner*) façon *f*; (*means*) moyen *m*; **(in) this w.** de cette façon; **no w.!** *Fam* pas question!
**we** *pron* nous; **we teachers** nous autres professeurs.
**weak** *a* faible; (*tea, coffee*) léger.
**weaken 1** *vt* affaiblir. **2** *vi* faiblir.
**weakness** faiblesse *f*; (*fault*) point *m* faible.
**wealth** richesse(s) *f*(*pl*).
**wealthy** *a* riche.
**weapon** arme *f*.
**wear* 1** *vt* (*have on body*) porter; (*put on*) mettre. **2** *n* **w. (and tear)** usure *f*.
**wear off** (*of color, effect etc*) disparaître.
**wear out 1** *vt* (*clothes etc*) user; (*person*) épuiser. **2** *vi* s'user.
**weary** *a* fatigué.
**weasel** belette *f*.
**weather** temps *m*; **what's the w. like?** quel temps fait-il?; **it's nice w.** il fait beau; **under the w.** (*ill*) patraque.
**weather forecast** *or* **report** météo *f*.
**weave*** *vt* (*cloth*) tisser.
**web** (*of spider*) toile *f*.
**wedding** mariage *m*.
**wedding ring** *or* **band** alliance *f*.
**wedge 1** *n* (*under wheel etc*) cale *f*. **2** *vt* (*table etc*) caler.
**Wednesday** mercredi *m*.
**weed** mauvaise herbe *f*.
**week** semaine *f*; **a w. from tomorrow** demain en huit.
**weekday** jour *m* de semaine.
**weekend** week-end *m*; **over the w.** ce week-end.
**weekly 1** *a* hebdomadaire. **2** *adv* toutes les semaines. **3** *n* (*magazine*) hebdomadaire *m*.
**weep*** *vi* pleurer.
**weigh** *vti* peser.
**weight** poids *m*; **by w.** au poids; **to put on w.** grossir; **to lose w.** maigrir.
**weird** *a* (*odd*) bizarre.
**welcome 1** *a* **to be w.** (*warmly received, of person*) être bien reçu; **w.!** bienvenue!; **to make s.o. (feel) w.** faire bon accueil à qn; **you're w.!** (*after 'thank you'*) il n'y a pas de quoi!; **some coffee/a break would be w.** un café/une pause ne ferait pas de mal. **2** *n* accueil *m*. **3** *vt* accueillir; (*warmly*) faire bon accueil à; **I w. you!** (*I say welcome to you*) je vous souhaite la bienvenue!

**weld** *vt* souder.

**welfare to be on w.** vivre d'allocations.

**well¹** (*for water*) puits *m*; **(oil) w.** puits *m* de pétrole.

**well²** **1** *adv* bien; **w. done!** bravo!; **as w.** (*also*) aussi; **as w. as** aussi bien que; **as w. as two cats, he has . . .** en plus de deux chats, il a . . . . **2** *a* bien *inv*; **she's w.** (*healthy*) elle va bien; **to get w.** se remettre. **3** *int* eh bien!; **huge, w., very big** énorme, enfin, très grand.

**well-behaved** *a* sage.

**well-informed** *a* bien informé.

**well-known** *a* (bien) connu.

**well-mannered** *a* bien élevé.

**well-off** *a* riche.

**Welsh** **1** *a* gallois; **the W.** les Gallois *mpl*. **2** *n* (*language*) gallois *m*.

**Welshman** (*pl* **-men**) Gallois *m*.

**Welshwoman** (*pl* **-women**) Galloise *f*.

**went** *pt de* **go¹**.

**were** *pt de* **be.**

**west** **1** *n* ouest *m*; **(to the) w. of** à l'ouest de. **2** *a* (*coast*) ouest *inv*. **3** *adv* à l'ouest.

**westbound** *a* en direction de l'ouest.

**western** **1** *a* (*coast*) ouest *inv*; (*culture etc*) occidental. **2** *n* (*film*) western *m*.

**westward(s)** *a* & *adv* vers l'ouest.

**wet** **1** *a* mouillé; (*damp, rainy*) humide; (*day, month*) de pluie; **'w. paint'** 'peinture fraîche'; **to get w.** se mouiller; **to make w.** mouiller; **it's w.** (*raining*) il pleut. **2** *vt* mouiller.

**whale** baleine *f*.

**wharf** quai *m*, débarcadère *m*.

**what** **1** *a* quel, quelle, *pl* quel(le)s; **w. book?** quel livre?; **w. a fool!** quel idiot! **2** *pron* (*in questions*) qu'est-ce qui; (*object*) (qu'est-ce) que; (*after prep*) quoi; **w.'s happening?** qu'est-ce qui se passe?; **w. does he do?** qu'est-ce qu'il fait?, que fait-il?; **w. is it?** qu'est-ce que c'est?; **w.'s that book?** c'est quoi, ce livre?; **w.!** (*surprise*) quoi!; **w.'s it called?** comment ça s'appelle?; **w. for?** pourquoi?; **w. about me?** et moi?; **w. about leaving?** si on partait? **3** *pron* (*indirect, relative*) ce qui; (*object*) ce que; **I know w. will happen/w. she'll do** je sais ce qui arrivera/ce qu'elle fera; **w. I need** ce dont j'ai besoin.

**whatever** **1** *a* **w. (the) mistake**/*etc* quelle que soit l'erreur/*etc*; **no chance w.** pas la moindre chance; **nothing w.** rien du tout. **2** *pron* (*no matter what*) quoi que (+ *subjunctive*); **w. you do** quoi que tu fasses; **w. is important** tout ce qui est important; **do w. you want** fais tout ce que tu veux.

**wheat** blé *m*.

**wheel** **1** *n* roue *f*; **at the w.** (*driving*) au volant. **2** *vt* pousser.

**wheelbarrow** brouette *f*.

**wheelchair** fauteuil *m* roulant.

**when** **1** *adv* quand. **2** *conj* quand; **w. I finish, w. I've finished** quand j'aurai fini; **w. I saw him** *or* **w. I'd seen him, I left** après l'avoir vu, je suis parti; **the day/moment w.** le jour/moment où.

**whenever** *conj* quand; (*each time that*) chaque fois que.

**where** **1** *adv* où; **w. are you from?** d'où êtes-vous? **2** *conj* (là) où; **I found it w. she'd left it** je l'ai trouvé là où elle l'avait laissé; **the place/house w.** l'endroit/la maison où.

**whereabouts** **1** *adv* où (donc). **2** *n* **his w.** l'endroit *m* où il est.

**whereas** *conj* alors que.

**wherever** *conj* **w. you go** partout où tu iras; **I'll go w. you like** j'irai (là) où vous voudrez.

**whether** *conj* si; **I don't know w. to leave** je ne sais pas si je dois partir; **w. she does it or not** qu'elle le fasse ou non.

**which** **1** *a* (*in questions etc*) quel, quelle, *pl* quel(le)s; **w. hat?** quel chapeau?; **in w. case** auquel cas. **2** *rel pron* (*subject*) qui; (*object*) que; (*after prep*) lequel, laquelle, *pl* lesquel(le)s; (*after clause*) ce qui; ce que; **the house w. is old** la maison qui est vieille; **the book w. I like** le livre que j'aime; **the table w. I put it on** la table sur laquelle je l'ai mis; **the film of w.** le film dont; **she's sick, w. is sad** elle est malade, ce qui est triste; **he lies, w. I don't like** il ment, ce que je n'aime pas. **3** *pron* **w. (one)** (*in questions*) lequel, laquelle, *pl* lesquel(le)s; **w. (one) of us?** lequel *or* laquelle d'entre nous *or* de nous? ▪ **w. (one)** (*the one that*) celui qui, celle qui, *pl* ceux qui, celles qui; (*object*) celui *etc* que; **show me w. (one) is red** montrez-moi celui *or* celle qui est rouge; **I know w. (ones) you want** je sais ceux *or* celles que vous désirez.

**whichever** *a* & *pron* **w. book**/*etc* *or* **w. of the books**/*etc* **you buy** quel que soit le livre/*etc* que tu achètes; **take w. books interest you** prenez les livres qui vous intéressent; **take w. (one) you like** prends celui *or* celle que tu veux; **w. (ones) remain** ceux *or* celles qui restent.

**while 1** *conj* (*when*) pendant que; (*although*) bien que (+ *subjunctive*); (*as long as*) tant que; (*whereas*) tandis que; **while eating**/*etc* en mangeant/*etc*. **2** *n* **a w.** un moment; **all the w.** tout le temps.

**whim** caprice *m*.

**whine** *vi* gémir.

**whip 1** *n* fouet *m*. **2** *vt* fouetter.

**whirl (around)** *vi* tourbillonner.

**whisk 1** *n* (*for eggs etc*) fouet *m*. **2** *vt* fouetter.

**whiskers** *npl* (*of cat*) moustaches *fpl*.

**whiskey** whisky *m*.

**whisper 1** *vti* chuchoter. **2** *n* chuchotement *m*.

**whistle 1** *n* sifflement *m*; (*object*) sifflet *m*; **to blow the** *or* **one's w.** siffler. **2** *vti* siffler.

**white 1** *a* blanc (*f* blanche); **to turn w.** blanchir; **w. man** blanc *m*; **w. woman** blanche *f*. **2** *n* (*color, of egg*) blanc *m*.

**whitewash** *vt* (*wall*) badigeonner.

**whiz past** passer à toute vitesse.

**who** *pron* qui; **w. did it?** qui (est-ce qui) a fait ça?

**whoever** *pron* qui que ce soit qui; (*object*) qui que ce soit que; **this man, w. he is** cet homme, quel qu'il soit.

**whole 1** *a* entier; (*intact*) intact; **the w. time/village**/etc tout le temps; **the w. thing** le tout. **2** *n* **on the w.** dans l'ensemble.

**wholesale 1** *a* (*price*) de gros. **2** *adv* (*to sell*) au prix de gros; (*in bulk*) en gros.

**wholesaler** grossiste *mf*.

**wholewheat** *a* (*bread*) complet.

**whom** *pron* (*object*) que; (*in questions and after prep*) qui; **of w.** dont.

**whooping cough** coqueluche *f*.

**whose** *poss pron* & *a* à qui, de qui; **w. book is this?** à qui est ce livre?; **w. daughter are you?** de qui es-tu la fille?; **the woman w. book I have** la femme de qui j'ai le livre.

**why 1** *adv* pourquoi; **w. not?** pourquoi pas? **2** *conj* **the reason w. they . . .** la raison pour laquelle ils . . . .

**wick** mèche *f* (*de bougie*).

**wicked** *a* (*evil*) méchant; (*mischievous*) malicieux.

**wicker 1** *n* osier *m*. **2** *a* (*basket etc*) en osier.

**wide 1** *a* large; (*choice, variety*) grand; **to be three yards w.** avoir trois mètres de large. **2** *adv* (*to open*) tout grand.

**wide-awake** *a* éveillé.

**widely** *adv* (*to travel*) beaucoup.

**widen 1** *vt* élargir. **2** *vi* s'élargir.

**widespread** *a* (très) répandu.

**widow** veuve *f*.

**widower** veuf *m*.

**width** largeur *f*.

**wife** (*pl* **wives**) femme *f*.

**wig** perruque *f*.

**wild** *a* (*animal, flower etc*) sauvage.
**wilderness** désert *m*.
**will**[1] *v aux* **he will come, he'll come** (*future tense*) il viendra (**won't he?** n'est-ce pas?); **you will not come, you won't come** tu ne viendras pas (**will you?** n'est-ce pas?); **w. you have a cup of tea?** veux-tu prendre un thé?; **w. you be quiet!** veux-tu te taire!; **I w.!** (*yes*) oui!
**will**[2] volonté *f*; (*legal document*) testament *m*; **ill w.** mauvaise volonté *f*; **against one's w.** à contrecœur.
**willing** *a* (*helper, worker*) de bonne volonté; **to be w. to do** vouloir bien faire.
**willingly** *adv* (*with pleasure*) volontiers; (*voluntarily*) volontairement.
**willingness** bonne volonté *f*; **his** *or* **her w. to do** son empressement *m* à faire.
**willow** saule *m*.
**win 1** *n* victoire *f*. **2** *vi** gagner. **3** *vt* (*money, prize, race*) gagner.
**wind**[1] vent *m*.
**wind**[2]* **1** *vt* (*roll*) enrouler (**around** autour de); (*clock*) remonter. **2** *vi* (*of river, road*) serpenter.
**windbreaker** blouson *m*.
**windmill** moulin *m* à vent.
**window** fenêtre *f*; (*pane & in vehicle or train*) vitre *f*; (*in store*) vitrine *f*; (*counter*) guichet *m*; **to go w. shopping** faire du lèche-vitrines.
**window box** jardinière *f*.
**windowpane** vitre *f*.
**window screen** grillage *m*.
**windowsill** (*inside*) appui *m* de (la) fenêtre; (*outside*) rebord *m* de (la) fenêtre.
**windshield** pare-brise *m inv*; **w. wiper** essuie-glace *m*.
**windsurfing to go w.** faire de la planche (à voile).
**windy** *a* **it's w.** (*of weather*) il y a du vent.
**wine** vin *m*; **w. bottle** bouteille *f* à vin; **w. list** carte *f* des vins.
**wineglass** verre *m* à vin.
**wing** aile *f*.
**wink 1** *vi* faire un clin d'œil (**at, to** à). **2** *n* clin *m* d'œil.
**winner** gagnant, -ante *mf*; (*of argument, fight*) vainqueur *m*.
**winning 1** *a* (*number, horse etc*) gagnant; (*team*) victorieux. **2** *n* **winnings** gains *mpl*.
**winter 1** *n* hiver *m*; **in (the) w.** en hiver. **2** *a* d'hiver.
**wintertime** hiver *m*.
**wipe** *vt* essuyer; **to w. one's feet/hands** s'essuyer les pieds/les mains.
**wipe off** *or* **up** (*liquid*) essuyer.
**wipe out** (*clean*) essuyer.
**wiper** (*in vehicle*) essuie-glace *m*.
**wire** fil *m*.
**wiring** (*electrical*) installation *f* électrique.
**wise** *a* (*in knowledge*) sage; (*advisable*) prudent.
**wish 1** *vt* souhaiter, vouloir (**to do** faire); **I w. (that) you could help me/could have helped me** je voudrais que/j'aurais voulu que vous m'aidiez; **I w. I hadn't done that** je regrette d'avoir fait ça; **if you w.** si tu veux; **I w. you a happy birthday** je vous souhaite un bon anniversaire; **I w. I could** si seulement je pouvais. **2** *vi* **to w. for sth** souhaiter qch. **3** *n* (*specific*) souhait *m*; (*general*) désir *m*; **best wishes** (*on greeting card*) meilleurs vœux *mpl*; (*in letter*) amitiés *fpl*; **send him** *or* **her my best wishes** fais-lui mes amitiés.
**witch** sorcière *f*.
**with** *prep* avec; **come w. me** viens avec moi; **w. no hat**/*etc* sans chapeau/*etc*. ▪ (*at the house etc of*) chez; **she's staying w. me** elle loge chez moi. ▪ (*cause*) de; **to jump w. joy** sauter de joie. ▪ (*instrument, means*) avec, de; **to write w. a pen** écrire avec un stylo; **to fill w.** remplir de. ▪ (*description*) à; **w. blue eyes** aux yeux bleus.
**withdraw*** **1** *vt* retirer. **2** *vi* se retirer (**from** de).

**wither** *vi* (*of plant etc*) se flétrir.

**within** *prep* (*place, box etc*) à l'intérieur de; **w. 6 miles (of)** (*less than*) à moins de 10 km (de); (*inside an area of*) dans un rayon de 10 km (de); **w. a month** (*to return etc*) avant un mois; (*to finish sth*) en moins d'un mois.

**without** *prep* sans; **w. a tie/***etc* sans cravate/*etc*; **w. doing** sans faire.

**witness 1** *n* (*person*) témoin *m*. **2** *vt* (*accident etc*) être (le) témoin de.

**wobbly** *a* (*table, tooth*) branlant.

**wolf** (*pl* **wolves**) loup *m*.

**woman** (*pl* **women**) femme *f*; **w. doctor** femme *f* médecin; **women's** (*clothes etc*) féminin.

**wonder 1** *n* **(it's) no w.** ce n'est pas étonnant (**that** que (+ *subjunctive*)). **2** *vt* se demander (**if** si, **why** pourquoi). **3** *vi* (*think*) réfléchir; **I was just wondering** je réfléchissais.

**wonderful** *a* merveilleux.

**won't** = **will not.**

**wood** (*material, forest*) bois *m*.

**wooden** *a* de *or* en bois.

**woodwork** (*school subject*) menuiserie *f*.

**wool** laine *f*.

**woolen 1** *a* en laine. **2** *n* **woolens** lainages *mpl*.

**word** mot *m*; (*spoken & promise*) parole *f*; **words** (*of song etc*) paroles *fpl*; **to have a w. with s.o.** parler à qn; (*advise, criticize*) avoir un mot avec qn; **in other words** autrement dit.

**wording** termes *mpl*.

**word processing** traitement *m* de texte.

**word processor** machine *f* de traitement de texte.

**wore** *pt de* **wear**.

**work 1** *n* travail *m*; (*product, book etc*) œuvre *f*; (*building or repair work*) travaux *mpl*; **out of w.** au chômage; **a day off w.** un jour de congé; **he's off w.** il n'est pas allé travailler; **the works** (*of clock etc*) le mécanisme. **2** *vi* travailler; (*of machine etc*) marcher; (*of drug*) agir. **3** *vt* (*machine*) faire marcher; **to get worked up** s'exciter.

**work at** *or* **on sth** (*improve*) travailler qch.

**workbench** établi *m*.

**worker** travailleur, -euse *mf*; (*manual*) ouvrier, -ière *mf*; **(office) w.** employé, -ée *mf* (de bureau).

**working** *a* **w. class** classe *f* ouvrière; **in w. order** en état de marche.

**workman** (*pl* **-men**) ouvrier *m*.

**work on** (*book, problem etc*) travailler à.

**work out 1** *vi* (*succeed*) marcher; (*do exercises*) s'entraîner; **it works out to 50 francs** ça fait 50 francs. **2** *vt* calculer; (*problem*) résoudre; (*scheme*) préparer; (*understand*) comprendre.

**workout** séance *f* d'entraînement.

**workshop** atelier *m*.

**world 1** *n* monde *m*; **all over the w.** dans le monde entier. **2** *a* (*war etc*) mondial; (*champion, cup, record*) du monde.

**worm** ver *m*.

**worn** (*pp de* **wear**) *a* (*clothes etc*) usé.

**worn-out** *a* (*object*) complètement usé; (*person*) épuisé.

**worrisome** *a* inquiétant.

**worry 1** *n* souci *m*. **2** *vi* s'inquiéter (**about sth** de qch, **about s.o.** pour qn). **3** *vt* inquiéter; **to be worried** être inquiet.

**worse 1** *a* pire, plus mauvais (**than** que); **to get w.** se détériorer; **he's getting w.** (*in health*) il va de plus en plus mal. **2** *adv* plus mal (**than** que); **to be w. off** aller moins bien financièrement.

**worsen** *vti* empirer.

**worship** *vt* (*person, god*) adorer.

**worst 1** *a* pire, plus mauvais. **2** *adv* **(the) w.** le plus mal. **3** *n* **the w. (one)** le *or* la pire, le *or* la plus mauvais(e); **at w.** au pire.

**worth 1** *n* valeur *f*; **to buy 50 fr w. of chocolates** acheter po quante francs de chocolats. **2** *a* **to be w. sth** valoir qch; **how much** *or* **what is it w.?** ça vaut combien?; **the movie's w. seeing** le film vaut la peine d'être vu; **it's w. (one's) while** ça (en) vaut la peine; **it's w. (while) waiting** ça vaut la peine d'attendre.

**worthy** *a* **w. of sth/s.o.** digne de qch/qn.

**would** *v aux* **I w. stay, I'd stay** (*conditional tense*) je resterais; **he w. have done it** il l'aurait fait; **w. you help me, please?** voulez-vous m'aider, s'il vous plaît?; **w. you like some tea?** voudriez-vous (prendre) du thé?; **I w. see her every day** (*in the past*) je la voyais chaque jour.

**wound 1** *vt* blesser; **the wounded** les blessés *mpl*. **2** *n* blessure *f*.

**wrap (up) 1** *vt* envelopper; (*parcel*) emballer. **2** *vti* **to w. (oneself) up** (*dress warmly*) se couvrir. **3** *n* **plastic w.** film *m* plastique.

**wrapper** (*of candy*) papier *m*.

**wrapping** (*action, material*) emballage *m*; **w. paper** papier *m* d'emballage.

**wreath** (*pl* **-s**) couronne *f*.

**wreck 1** *n* (*ship*) épave *f*; (*sinking*) naufrage *m*; (*train etc*) train *m etc* accidenté; (*accident*) accident m. **2** *vt* détruire.

**wrench** (*tool*) clef *f* (à écrous), clef *f* à molette.

**wrestle** *vi* lutter (**with s.o.** avec qn).

**wrestler** lutteur, -euse *mf*; catcheur, -euse *mf*.

**wrestling** (*sport*) lutte *f*; (*no holds barred*) catch *m*.

**wring* (out)** (*clothes by hand*) tordre.

**wrinkle** (*on skin*) ride *f*.

**wrist** poignet *m*.

**wristwatch** montre *f*.

**write*** *vti* écrire.

**write away** *or* **off for** (*details etc*) écrire pour demander.

**write back** *vi* répondre.

**write sth down** noter qch.

**write sth out** écrire qch; (*copy*) recopier qch.

**writer** auteur *m* (**of** de); (*literary*) écrivain *m*.

**writing** (*handwriting*) écriture *f*; **to put sth (down) in w.** mettre qch par écrit; **some w.** (*on page*) quelque chose d'écrit.

**writing desk** secrétaire *m*.

**writing pad** bloc *m* de papier à lettres; (*for notes*) bloc-notes *m*.

**writing paper** papier *m* à lettres.

**wrong 1** *a* (*sum, idea etc*) faux (*f* fausse); (*direction, time etc*) mauvais; (*unfair*) injuste; **to be w.** (*of person*) avoir tort (**to do** de faire); (*mistaken*) se tromper; **it's w. to swear**/*etc* c'est mal de jurer/*etc*; **the clock's w.** la pendule n'est pas à l'heure; **something's w.** quelque chose ne va pas; **something's w. with the phone** le téléphone ne marche pas bien; **something's w. with her arm** elle a quelque chose au bras; **what's w. with you?** qu'est-ce que tu as?; **the w. way around** *or* **up** à l'envers. **2** *adv* mal; **to go w.** (*of plan*) mal tourner. **3** *n* **to be in the w.** être dans son tort.

**wrongly** *adv* (*incorrectly*) mal.

## X

**Xmas** *Fam* Noël *m*.

**X-ray 1** *n* (*photo*) radio(graphie) *f*; (*beam*) rayon *m* X; **to have an X-ray** passer une radio. **2** *vt* radiographier.

## Y

**yacht** yacht *m*.

**yard** (*of farm, school etc*) cour *f*; (*for storage*) dépôt *m*; (*measure*) yard *m* (= *91,44 cm*).

**yarn** (*thread*) fil *m*.
**yawn 1** *vi* bâiller. **2** *n* bâillement *m*.
**year** an *m*, année *f*; **school/tax y.** année *f* scolaire/fiscale; **this y.** cette année; **in the y. 1992** en (l'an) 1992; **he's ten years old** il a dix ans; **New Y.** Nouvel An; **New Year's Day** le jour de l'An; **New Year's Eve** la Saint-Sylvestre.
**yearly** *a* annuel.
**yeast** levure *f*.
**yell** hurlement *m*.
**yell (out)** *vti* hurler.
**yell at s.o.** (*scold*) crier après qn.
**yellow** *a* & *n* (*color*) jaune (*m*).
**yes** *adv* oui; (*contradicting negative question*) si.
**yesterday** *adv* hier; **y. morning** hier matin; **the day before y.** avant-hier.
**yet 1** *adv* encore; (*already*) déjà; **she hasn't come (as) y.** elle n'est pas encore venue; **has he come y.?** est-il déjà arrivé? **2** *conj* (*nevertheless*) pourtant.
**yield** *vi* **'y.'** (*road sign*) 'cédez la priorité'.
**yogurt** yaourt *m*.
**yolk** jaune *m* (d'œuf).
**you** *pron* (*polite form singular*) vous; (*familiar form singular*) tu; (*polite and familar form plural*) vous; (*object*) vous; te, t'; *pl* vous; (*after prep, 'than', 'it is'*) vous; toi; *pl* vous; **(to) y.** vous; te, t'; *pl* vous; **y. are** vous êtes; tu es; **I see y.** je vous vois; je te vois; **y. teachers** vous autres professeurs; **y. idiot!** espèce d'imbécile! ▪ (*indefinite*) on; (*object*) vous; te, t'; *pl* vous; **y. never know** on ne sait jamais.
**young 1** *a* jeune; **my young(er) brother** mon (frère) cadet; **his** *or* **her youngest brother** le cadet de ses frères; **the youngest son** le cadet. **2** *n* (*of animals*) petits *mpl*; **the y.** (*people*) les jeunes *mpl*.
**youngster** jeune *mf*.
**your** *poss a* (*polite form singular, polite and familiar form plural*) votre, *pl* vos; (*familiar form singular*) ton, ta, *pl* tes; (*one's*) son, sa, *pl* ses.
**yours** *poss pron* le vôtre, la vôtre, *pl* les vôtres; (*familiar form singular*) le tien, la tienne, *pl* les tien(ne)s; **this book is y.** ce livre est à vous *or* est le vôtre; ce livre est à toi *or* est le tien.
**yourself** *pron* (*polite form*) vous-même; (*familiar form*) toi-même; (*reflexive*) vous; te, t'; (*after prep*) vous; toi.
**yourselves** *pron pl* vous-mêmes; (*reflexive* & *after prep*) vous.
**youth** jeunesse *f*; (*young man*) jeune *m*; **y. center** maison *f* des jeunes.

# Z

**zebra** zèbre *m*.
**zero** (*pl* **-os**) zéro *m*.
**zigzag 1** *n* zigzag *m*. **2** *a* en zigzag. **3** *vi* zigzaguer.
**zip (up)** fermer (avec une fermeture éclair®).
**zip code** code *m* postal; (*geographic area*) division *f* postale.
**zipper** fermeture *f* éclair®.
**zit** (*pimple*) *Fam* bouton *m*.
**zone** zone *f*.
**zoo** (*pl* **zoos**) zoo *m*.
**zucchini** (*pl* **-ni** *or* **-nis**) courgette *f*.

# French verb conjugations

## Regular verbs

| | -ER Verbs | -IR Verbs | -RE Verbs |
|---|---|---|---|
| *Infinitive* | *donn/er* | *fin/ir* | *vend/re* |
| 1 Present | je donne<br>tu donnes<br>il donne<br>nous donnons<br>vous donnez<br>ils donnent | je finis<br>tu finis<br>il finit<br>nous finissons<br>vous finissez<br>ils finissent | je vends<br>tu vends<br>il vend<br>nous vendons<br>vous vendez<br>ils vendent |
| 2 Imperfect | je donnais<br>tu donnais<br>il donnait<br>nous donnions<br>vous donniez<br>ils donnaient | je finissais<br>tu finissais<br>il finissait<br>nous finissions<br>vous finissiez<br>ils finissaient | je vendais<br>tu vendais<br>il vendait<br>nous vendions<br>vous vendiez<br>ils vendaient |
| 3 Past historic | je donnai<br>tu donnas<br>il donna<br>nous donnâmes<br>vous donnâtes<br>ils donnèrent | je finis<br>tu finis<br>il finit<br>nous finîmes<br>vous finîtes<br>ils finirent | je vendis<br>tu vendis<br>il vendit<br>nous vendîmes<br>vous vendîtes<br>ils vendirent |
| 4 Future | je donnerai<br>tu donneras<br>il donnera<br>nous donnerons<br>vous donnerez<br>ils donneront | je finirai<br>tu finiras<br>il finira<br>nous finirons<br>vous finirez<br>ils finiront | je vendrai<br>tu vendras<br>il vendra<br>nous vendrons<br>vous vendrez<br>ils vendront |
| 5 Subjunctive | je donne<br>tu donnes<br>il donne<br>nous donnions<br>vous donniez<br>ils donnent | je finisse<br>tu finisses<br>il finisse<br>nous finissions<br>vous finissiez<br>ils finissent | je vende<br>tu vendes<br>il vende<br>nous vendions<br>vous vendiez<br>ils vendent |

# Regular verbs

| | -ER Verbs | -IR Verbs | -RE Verbs |
|---|---|---|---|
| *Infinitive* | *donn/er* | *fin/ir* | *vend/re* |
| 6 Imperative | donne<br>donnons<br>donnez | finis<br>finissons<br>finissez | vends<br>vendons<br>vendez |
| 7 Present participle | donnant | finissant | vendant |
| 8 Past participle | donné | fini | vendu |

*Note* The conditional is formed by adding the following endings to the infinitive: -ais, -ais, -ait, -ions, -iez, -aient. Final 'e' is dropped in infinitives ending '-re'.

## Spelling anomalies of -er verbs

Verbs in **-ger** (eg **manger**) take an extra **e** before endings beginning with **o** or **a:** *Present* je mange, nous mangeons; *Imperfect* je mangeais, nous mangions; *Past historic* je mangeai, nous mangeâmes; *Present participle* mangeant. Verbs in **-cer** (eg **commencer**) change **c** to **ç** before endings beginning with **o** or **a:** *Present* je commence, nous commençons; *Imperfect* je commençais, nous commencions; *Past historic* je commençai, nous commençâmes; *Present participle* commençant. Verbs containing mute **e** in their penultimate syllable fall into two groups. In the first (eg **mener, peser, lever**), **e** becomes **è** before an unpronounced syllable in the present and subjunctive, and in the future and conditional tenses (eg je mène, ils mèneront). The second group contains most verbs ending in **-eler** and **-eter** (eg **appeler, jeter**). These verbs change **l** to **ll** and **t** to **tt** before an unpronounced syllable (eg j'appelle, ils appelleront; je jette, ils jetteront). However, the following four verbs in **-eler** and **-eter** fall into the first group in which **e** changes to **è** before mute **e** (eg je pèle, ils pèleront; j'achète, ils achèteront): **geler, peler; acheter, haleter.** Derived verbs (eg **dégeler, racheter**) are conjugated in the same way. Verbs containing **é** in their penultimate syllable change **é** to **è** before the unpronounced endings of the present and subjunctive only (eg je cède but je céderai). Verbs in **-yer** (eg **essuyer**) change **y** to **i** before an unpronounced syllable in the present and subjunctive, and in the future and conditional tenses (eg j'essuie, ils essuieront). In verbs in **-ayer** (eg **balayer**), **y** may be retained before mute **e** (eg je balaie or balaye, ils balaieront or balayeront).

# Irregular verbs

Listed below are those verbs considered to be the most useful. Forms and tenses not given are fully derivable, such as the third person singular of the present tense which is normally formed by substituting 't' for the final 's' of the first person singular, eg 'crois' becomes 'croit', 'dis' becomes 'dit'. Note that the endings of the past historic fall into three categories, the 'a' and 'i' categories shown at *donner,* and at *finir* and *vendre,* and the 'u' category which has the following endings: -us, -ut, -ûmes, -ûtes, -urent. Most of the verbs listed below form their past historic with 'u'. The imperfect may usually be formed by adding -ais, -ait, -ions, -iez, -aient to the stem of the first person plural of the present tense, eg 'je buvais' etc may be derived from 'nous buvons' (stem 'buv-' and ending '-ons'); similarly, the present participle may generally be formed by substituting -ant for -ons (eg buvant). The future may usually be formed by adding -ai, -as, -a, -ons, -ez, -ont to the infinitive or to an infinitive without final 'e' where the ending is -re (eg conduire). The imperative usually has the same forms as the second persons singular and plural and first person plural of the present tense.

1 = Present 2 = Imperfect 3 = Past historic 4 = Future

5 = Subjunctive 6 = Imperative 7 = Present participle

8 = Past participle n = nous v = vous

† verbs conjugated with **être** only.

# Irregular French verbs

**abattre** *like* **battre**
**†s'abstenir** like **tenir**
**accourir** *like* **courir**
**accueillir** *like* **cueillir**
**acquérir** 1 j'acquiers, n acquérons 2 j'acquérais 3 j'acquis 4 j'acquerrai 5 j'acquière 7 acquérant 8 acquis
**admettre** *like* **mettre**
**†aller** 1 je vais, ta vas, il va, n allons, v allez, ils vont 4 j'irai 5 j'aille, nous allions, ils aillent 6 va, allons, allez (*but note* vas-y)
**apercevoir** *like* **recevoir**
**apparaître** *like* **connaître**
**appartenir** *like* **tenir**
**apprendre** *like* **prendre**
**asseoir** 1 j'assieds, il assied, n asseyons, ils asseyent 2 j'asseyais 3 j'assis 4 j'assiérai 5 j'asseye 7 asseyant 8 assis
**atteindre** 1 j'atteins, n atteignons, ils atteignent 2 j'atteignais 3 j'atteignis 4 j'atteindrai 5 j'atteigne 7 atteignant 8 atteint
**avoir** 1 j'ai, tu as, il a, n avons, v avez, ils ont 2 j'avais 3 j'eus 4 j'aurai 5 j'aie, il ait, n ayons, ils aient 6 aic, ayons, ayez 7 ayant 8 eu
**battre** 1 je bats, il bat, n battons 5 je batte
**boire** 1 je bois, n buvons, ils boivent 2 je buvais 3 je bus 5 je boive, n buvions 7 buvant 8 bu
**bouillir** 1 je bous, n bouillons, ils bouillent

2 je bouillais 3 *not used* 5 je bouille 7 bouillant

| | |
|---|---|
| **combattre** | *like* **battre** |
| **commettre** | *like* **mettre** |
| **comprendre** | *like* **prendre** |
| **conclure** | 1 je conclus, n concluons, ils concluent 5 je conclue |
| **conduire** | 1 je conduis, n conduisons 3 je conduisis 5 je conduise 8 conduit |
| **connaître** | 1 je connais, il connaît, n connaissons 3 je connus 5 je connaisse 7 connaissant 8 connu |
| **conquérir** | *like* **acquérir** |
| **consentir** | *like* **conduire** |
| **contenir** | *like* **tenir** |
| **contraindre** | *like* **atteindre** |
| **contredire** | *like* **dire** *except* 1 v contredisez |
| **convaincre** | *like* **vaincre** |
| **convenir** | *like* **tenir** |
| **coudre** | 1 je couds, il coud, no cousons, ils cousent 3 je cousis 5 je couse 7 cousant 8 cousu |
| **courir** | 1 je cours, n courons 3 je courus 4 je courrai 5 je coure 8 couru |
| **couvrir** | 1 je couvre, n couvrons 2 je couvrais 5 je couvre 8 couvert |
| **craindre** | *like* **atteindre** |
| **croire** | 1 je crois, n croyons, ils croient 2 je croyais 3 je crus 5 je croie, n croyions 7 croyant 8 cru |
| **cueillir** | 1 je cueille, n cueillons 2 je cueillais 4 je cueillerai 5 je cueille 7 cueillant |
| **cuire** | 1 je cuis, n cuisons 2 je cuisais 3 je cuisis 5 je cuise 7 cuisant 8 cuit |

# Irregular French verbs

**débattre** *like* **battre**
**décevoir** *like* **recevoir**
**découvrir** *like* **couvrir**
**décrire** *like* **écrire**
**déduire** *like* **conduire**
**défaire** *like* **faire**
**déplaire** *like* **plaire**
**déteindre** *like* **atteindre**
**détruire** *like* **conduire**
**†devenir** *like* **tenir**
**devoir** 1 je dois, n devons, ils doivent 2 je devais 3 je dus 4 je devrai 5 je doive, n devions 6 *not used* 7 devant 8 dû, due, *pl* dus, dues
**dire** 1 je dis, n disons, v dites 2 je disais 3 je dis 5 je dise 7 disant 8 dit
**disparaître** *like* **connaître**
**dissoudre** 1 je dissous, n dissolvons 2 je dissolvais 5 je dissolve 7 dissolvant 8 dissous, dissoute
**distraire** 1 je distrais, n distrayons 2 je distrayais 3 *none* 5 je distraie 7 distrayant 8 distrait
**dormir** *like* **mentir**
**éclore** 1 il éclôt, ils éclosent 8 éclos
**écrire** 1 j'écris, n écrivons 2 j'écrivais 3 j'écrivis 5 j'écrive 7 écrivant 8 écrit
**élire** *like* **lire**
**émettre** *like* **mettre**
**émouvoir** 1 j'émeus, n émouvons, ils émeuvent 2 j'émouvais 3 j'émus (*rare*)

| | |
|---|---|
| | 4 j'émouvrai 5 j'émeuve, n émouvions 8 ému |
| **endormir** | *like* **mentir** |
| **enfreindre** | *like* **atteindre** |
| **†s'enfuir** | *like* **fuir** |
| **entreprendre** | *like* **prendre** |
| **entretenir** | *like* **tenir** |
| **envoyer** | 4 j'enverrai |
| **éteindre** | *like* **atteindre** |
| **être** | 1 je suis, tu es, il est, n sommes, v êtes, ils sont 2 j'étais 3 je fus 4 je serai 5 je sois, n soyons, ils soient 6 sois, soyons, soyez 7 étant 8 été |
| **exclure** | *like* **conclure** |
| **extraire** | *like* **distraire** |
| **faillir** | (*defective*) 3 je faillis 4 je faillirai 8 failli |
| **faire** | 1 je fais, n faisons, v faites, ils font 2 je faisais 3 je fis 4 je ferai 5 je fasse 7 faisant 8 fait |
| **falloir** | (*impersonal*) 1 il faut 2 il fallait 3 il fallut 4 il faudra 5 il faille 6 *none* 7 *none* 8 fallu |
| **frire** | (*defective*) 1 je fris, tu fris, il frit 4 je frirai (*rare*) 6 fris (*rare*) 8 frit (*for other persons and tenses use* faire frire) |
| **fuir** | 1 je fuis, n fuyons, ils fuient 2 je fuyais 3 je fuis 5 je fuie 7 fuyant 8 fui |
| **haïr** | 1 je hais, il hait, n haïssons |
| **inscrire** | *like* **écrire** |
| **instruire** | *like* **conduire** |
| **interdire** | *like* **dire** *except* 1 v interdisez |

## Irregular French verbs

| | |
|---|---|
| **interrompre** | *like* **rompre** |
| **intervenir** | *like* **tenir** |
| **introduire** | *like* **conduire** |
| **joindre** | *like* **atteindre** |
| **lire** | 1 je lis, n lisons 2 je lisais 3 je lus 5 je lise 7 lisant 8 lu |
| **maintenir** | *like* **tenir** |
| **mentir** | 1 je mens, n mentons 2 je mentais 5 je mente 7 mentant |
| **mettre** | 1 je mets, n mettons 2 je mettais 3 je mis 5 je mette 7 mettant 8 mis |
| **moudre** | je mouds, il moud, n moulons 2 je moulais 3 je moulus 5 je moule 7 moulant 8 moulu |
| **†mourir** | 1 je meurs, n mourons, ils meurent 2 je mourais 3 je mourus 4 je mourrai 5 je meure, n mourions |
| **†naître** | 1 je nais, il naît, n naissons 2 je naissais 3 je naquis 4 je naîtrai 5 je naisse 7 naissant 8 né |
| **nuire** | 1 je nuis, n nuisons 2 je nuisais 3 je nuisis 5 je nuise 7 nuisant 8 nui |
| **obtenir** | *like* **tenir** |
| **offrir** | *like* **couvrir** |
| **ouvrir** | *like* **couvrir** |
| **paître** | (*defective*) 1 il paît 2 il paissait 3 *none* 4 il paîtra 5 il paisse 7 paissant 8 *none* |
| **paraître** | *like* **connaître** |
| **parcourir** | *like* **courir** |
| **†partir** | *like* **mentir** |
| **†parvenir** | *like* **tenir** |
| **peindre** | *like* **atteindre** |

# Irregular French verbs

| | |
|---|---|
| **permettre** | *like* **mettre** |
| **plaindre** | *like* **atteindre** |
| **plaire** | 1 je plais, il plaît, n plaisons 2 je plaisais 3 je plus 5 je plaise 7 plaisant 8 plu |
| **pleuvoir** | (*impersonal*) 1 il pleut 2 il pleuvait 3 il plut 4 il pleuvra 5 il pleuve 6 *none* 7 pleuvant 8 plu |
| **poursuivre** | *like* **suivre** |
| **pouvoir** | 1 je peux *or* je puis, tu peux, il peut, n pouvons, ils peuvent 2 je pouvais 3 je pus 4 je pourrai 5 je pouisse 6 *not used* 7 pouvant 8 pu |
| **prédire** | *like* **dire** *except* 1 v prédisez |
| **prendre** | 1 je prends, il prend, n prenons, ils prennent 2 je prenais 3 je pris 5 je prenne 7 prenant 8 pris |
| **prescrire** | *like* **écrire** |
| **pressentir** | *like* **mentir** |
| **prévenir** | *like* **tenir** |
| **prévoir** | *like* **voire** *except* 4 je prévoirai |
| **produire** | *like* **conduire** |
| **promettre** | *like* **mettre** |
| **†provenir** | *like* **tenir** |
| **rabattre** | *like* **battre** |
| **recevoir** | 1 je reçois, n recevons, ils reçoivent 2 je recevais 3 je reçus 4 je recevrai 5 je reçoive, n recevions, ils reçoivent 7 recevant 8 reçu |
| **reconduire** | *like* **conduire** |
| **reconnaître** | *like* **connaître** |
| **reconstruire** | *like* **conduire** |
| **recoudre** | *like* **coudre** |
| **recouvrir** | *like* **couvrir** |

# Irregular French verbs

| | |
|---|---|
| **recueillir** | *like* **cueillir** |
| **redire** | *like* **dire** |
| **réduire** | *like* **conduire** |
| **refaire** | *like* **faire** |
| **rejoindre** | *like* **atteindre** |
| **relire** | *like* **lire** |
| **reluire** | *like* **nuire** |
| **rendormir** | *like* **mentir** |
| **renvoyer** | *like* **envoyer** |
| †**repartir** | *like* **mentir** |
| **repentir** | *like* **mentir** |
| **reprendre** | *like* **prendre** |
| **reproduire** | *like* **conduire** |
| **résoudre** | 1 je résous, n résolvons 2 je résolvais 3 je résolus 5 je résolve 7 résolvant 8 résolu |
| **ressentir** | *like* **mentir** |
| **resservir** | *like* **mentir** |
| **ressortir** | *like* **mentir** |
| **restreindre** | *like* **atteindre** |
| **retenir** | *like* **tenir** |
| †**revenir** | *like* **tenir** |
| **revivre** | *like* **vivre** |
| **revoir** | *like* **voir** |
| **rire** | 1 je ris, n rions 2 je riais 3 je ris 5 je rie, n riions 7 riant 8 ri |
| **rompre** | *regular except* 1 il rompt |
| **satisfaire** | *like* **faire** |
| **savoir** | 1 je sais, n savons, il savent 2 je savais 3 je sus 4 je saurai 5 je sache 6 sache, sachons, sachez 7 sachant 8 su |
| **sentir** | *like* **mentir** |
| **servir** | *like* **mentir** |

# Irregular French verbs

**sortir** *like* **mentir**
**souffrir** *like* **couvrir**
**sourire** *like* **rire**
**soustraire** *like* **distraire**
**soutenir** *like* **tenir**
**†se souvenir** *like* **tenir**
**suffire** 1 je suffis, n suffisons 2 je suffisais 3 je suffis 5 je suffise 7 suffisant 8 suffi
**suivre** 1 je suis, n suivons 2 je suivais 3 je suivis 5 je suive 7 suivant 8 suivi
**surprendre** *like* **prendre**
**survivre** *like* **vivre**
**taire** 1 je tais, n taisons 2 je taisais 3 je tus 5 je taise 7 taisant 8 tu
**teindre** *like* **atteindre**
**tenir** 1 je tiens, n tenons, ils tiennent 2 je tenais 3 je tins, tu tins, il tint, n tînmes, v tîntes, ils tinrent 4 je teindrai 5 je tienne 7 tenant 8 tenu
**traduire** *like* **conduire**
**traire** *like* **distraire**
**transmettre** *like* **mettre**
**vaincre** 1 je vaincs, il vainc, n vainquons 2 je vainquais 3 je vainquis 5 je vainque 7 vainquant 8 vaincu
**valoir** 1 je vaux, il vaut, n valons 2 je valais 3 je valus 4 je vaudrai 5 je vaille 6 *not* used 7 valant 8 valu
**†venir** *like* **tenir**
**vivre** 1 je vis, n vivons 2 je vivais 3 je vécus 5 je vive 7 vivant 8 vécu
**voir** 1 je vois, n voyons 2 je voyais 3 je

vis 4 je verrai 5 je voie, n voyions 7 voyant 8 vu

**vouloir** 1 je veux, il veut, n voulons, ils veulent 2 je voulais 3 je voulus 4 je voudrai 5 je veuille 6 veuille, veuillons, veuillez 7 voulant 8 voulu

| Countries and regions | Pays et régions |
|---|---|
| Africa (*African*) | Afrique *f* (africain) |
| South/North Africa (*South/North African*) | A. du Sud/Nord (*sud-/nord-africain*) |
| Algeria (*Algerian*) | Algérie *f* (*algérien*) |
| America (*American*) | Amérique *f* (*américain*) |
| South/North America (*South/North American*) | A. du Sud/Nord (*sud-/nord-américain*) |
| Argentina (*Argentinian*) | Argentine *f* (*argentin*) |
| Asia (*Asian*) | Asie *f* (*asiatique*) |
| Australia (*Australian*) | Australie *f* (*australien*) |
| Austria (*Austrian*) | Autriche *f* (*autrichien*) |
| Belgium (*Belgian*) | Belgique *f* (*belge*) |
| Brazil (*Brazilian*) | Brésil *m* (*brésilien*) |
| Canada (*Canadian*) | Canada *m* (*canadien*) |
| Caribbean (the) | Antilles *fpl* (les) |
| China (*Chinese*) | Chine *f* (*chinois*) |
| CIS (*abbr* Commonwealth of Independent States) | CEI *f* (*abrév* Communauté des États Indépendants) |
| Cuba (*Cuban*) | Cuba *m* (*cubain*) |
| Cyprus (*Cypriot*) | Chypre *f* (*c(h)ypriote*) |
| Czech Republic (*Czech*) | Républiqe *f* (*tehèque*) |
| Denmark (*Danish*) | Danemark *m* (*danois*) |
| Egypt (*Egyptian*) | Égypte *f* (*égyptien*) |
| England (*English*) | Angleterre *f* (*anglais*) |
| Europe (*European*) | Europe *f* (*européen*) |
| Finland (*Finnish*) | Finlande *f* (*finlandais*) |
| France (*French*) | France *f* (*français*) |
| Germany (*German*) | Allemagne *f* (*allemand*) |
| Great Britain (*British*) | Grande-Bretagne *f* (*britannique*) |
| Greece (*Greek*) | Grèce *f* (*grec*) |
| Holland (*Dutch*) | Pays-Bas *mpl* (*hollandais*) |

| Countries and regions | Pays et régions |
|---|---|
| Hungary (*Hungarian*) | Hongrie *f* (*hongrois*) |
| Indian (*Indian*) | Inde *f* (*indien*) |
| Indonesia (*Indonesian*) | Indonésie *f* (*indonésien*) |
| Iran (*Iranian*) | Iran *m* (*iranien*) |
| Iraq (*Iraqi*) | Irak *m* (*irakien*) |
| Ireland (*Irish*) | Irlande *f* (*irlandais*) |
| Israel (*Israeli*) | Israël *m* (*israélien*) |
| Italy (*Italian*) | Italie *f* (*italien*) |
| Jamaica (*Jamaican*) | Jamaïque *f* (*jamaïcain*) |
| Japan (*Japanese*) | Japon *m* (*japonais*) |
| Kenya (*Kenyan*) | Kenya *m* (*kényan*) |
| Korea (*Korean*) | Corée *f* (*coréen*) |
| North/South Korea | C. du Sud/Nord |
| Lebanon (*Lebanese*) | Liban *m* (*libanais*) |
| Libya (*Libyan*) | Libye *f* (*libyen*) |
| Luxembourg | Luxembourg *m* (*luxembourgeois*) |
| Malaysia (*Malaysian*) | Malaisie (*malais*) |
| Mexico (*Mexican*) | Mexique *m* (*mexicain*) |
| Morocco (*Moroccan*) | Maroc *m* (*marocain*) |
| New Zealand | Nouvelle-Zélande *f* (*néo-zélandais*) |
| Nigeria (*Nigerian*) | Nigéria *m* (*nigérian*) |
| Norway (*Norwegian*) | Norvège *f* (*norvégien*) |
| Pakistan (*Pakistani*) | Pakistan *m* (*pakistanais*) |
| Philippines (*Filipino*) | Philippines *fpl* (*philippin*) |
| Poland (*Polish*) | Pologne *f* (*polonais*) |
| Portugal (*Portuguese*) | Portugal *m* (*portugais*) |
| Romania (*Romanian*) | Roumanie *f* (*roumain*) |
| Russia (*Russian*) | Russie *f* (*russe*) |
| Saudi Arabia (*Saudi*) | Arabie *f* Séoudite (*saoudien*) |
| Scotland (*Scottish*) | Écosse *f* (*écossais*) |

| Countries and regions | Pays et régions |
|---|---|
| Slovakia (*Slovak*) | Slovaquie (*slovaque*) |
| Spain (*Spanish*) | Espagne *f* (*espagnol*) |
| Sweden (*Swedish*) | Suède *f* (*suédois*) |
| Switzerland (*Swiss*) | Suisse *f* (*suisse*) |
| Syria (*Syrian*) | Syrie *f* (*syrien*) |
| Thailand (*Thai*) | Thaïlande *f* (*thaïlandais*) |
| Tunisia (*Tunisian*) | Tunisie *f* (*tunisien*) |
| Turkey (*Turkish*) | Turquie *f* (*turc*) |
| United Kingdom (*British*) | Royaume-Uni *m* (*britannique*) |
| United States (*American*) | États-Unis *mpl* (*américain*) |
| Vietnam (*Vietnamese*) | Viêt-nam *m* (*vietnamien*) |
| Wales (*Welsh*) | Pays *m* de Galles (*gallois*) |
| West Indies (*West Indian*) | Antilles *fpl* (*antillais*) |

# A

**a** *voir* **avoir.**

**à** *prép* (**à** + **le** = **au** [o], **à** + **les** = **aux** [o]) (*direction: lieu*) to; (*temps*) till, to; **aller à Paris** to go to Paris; **de 3 à 4 h** from 3 till *ou* to 4 (o'clock). ▪ (*position: lieu*) at, in; (*surface*) on; (*temps*) at; **être au bureau/à la ferme/au jardin/à Paris** to be at *ou* in the office/on *ou* at the farm/in the garden/in Paris; **à 8 h** at 8 (o'clock); **à mon arrivée** on (my) arrival; **à lundi!** see you (on) Monday! ▪ (*description*) **l'homme à la barbe** the man with the beard; **verre à liqueur** liqueur glass. ▪ (*attribution*) **donner qch à qn** to give sth to s.o., give s.o. sth. ▪ (*devant infinitif*) **apprendre à lire** to learn to read; **travail à faire** work to do; **maison à vendre** house for sale. ▪ (*appartenance*) **c'est** (**son livre**) **à lui** it's his (book); **c'est à vous de** (*décider, protester etc*) it's up to you to; (*lire, jouer etc*) it's your turn to. ▪ (*prix*) for; **pain à 2F** loaf for 2F. ▪ (*poids*) by; **vendre au poids** to sell by the weight. ▪ (*moyen, manière*) **à bicyclette** by bicycle; **à la main** by hand; **à pied** on foot; **au crayon** with a pencil, in pencil; **au galop** at a gallop; **deux à deux** two by two. ▪ (*appel*) **au voleur!** (stop) thief!

**abaisser** *vt* to lower.

**abaisser (s')** *vpr* (*barrière*) to lower; (*température*) to drop.

**abandon** *m* (*de sportif*) withdrawal; **à l'a.** in a neglected state.

**abandonner 1** *vt* (*travail*) to give up; (*endroit*) to desert. **2** *vi* to give up; (*sportif*) to withdraw.

**abat-jour** *m inv* lampshade.

**abattoir** *m* slaughterhouse.

**abattre*** *vt* (*mur*) to knock down; (*arbre*) to cut down; (*animal*) to slaughter; (*avion*) to shoot down; (*personne*) to shoot.

**abattre (s')** *vpr* **s'a. sur** (*pluie*) to come down on; (*tempête*) to hit.

**abbaye** *f* abbey.

**abbé** *m* (*prêtre*) priest.

**abcès** *m* abscess.

**abdomen** *m* stomach, abdomen.

**abeille** *f* bee.

**abîmer** *vt* to ruin.

**abîmer (s')** *vpr* to get ruined.

**aboiement** *m* bark; **aboiements** barking.

**abominable** *a* terrible.

**abondance** *f* **une a. de** plenty of.

**abondant, -ante** *a* plentiful.

**abonné, -ée** *mf* (*à un journal, au téléphone*) subscriber.

**abonnement** *m* subscription; (**carte d'**) **a.** (*de train*) season pass.

**abonner (s')** *vpr* to subscribe, take out a subscription (**à** to).

**abord (d')** *adv* first.

**abordable** *a* (*prix, marchandises*) affordable.

**abordage** *m* (*assaut*) boarding.

**aborder 1** *vi* to land. **2** *vt* (*personne*) to approach; (*problème*) to tackle; (*attaquer*) to board (*ship*).

**aboutir** *vi* to succeed; **a. à** lead to; **n'a. à rien** to come to nothing.

**aboyer** *vi* to bark.

**abréger** *vt* (*récit*) to shorten.

**abreuvoir** *m* (*récipient*) drinking trough.

**abréviation** *f* abbreviation.

**abri** *m* shelter; **a. (de jardin)** (garden) shed; **à l'a. de** (*vent*) sheltered from; (*besoin*) safe from; **sans a.** homeless.

**abricot** *m* apricot.

**abricotier** *m* apricot tree.

**abriter** *vt* to shelter.

**abriter (s')** *vpr* to (take) shelter.

**abrupt, -e** *a* (*pente etc*) steep.

**abrutir** *vt* (*télévision*) to stupefy, numb; (*travail*) exhaust.

**absence** *f* absence.

**absent, -ente 1** *a* absent, away. **2** *mf* absentee.

**absenter (s')** *vpr* to go away (**de** from).

**absolu, -ue** *a* absolute.

**absolument** *adv* absolutely.

**absorbant, -ante** *a* (*papier*) absorbent; (*travail, lecture*) absorbing.

**absorber** *vt* to absorb; (*manger*) to eat.

**abstenir* (s')** *vpr* to refrain (**de faire** from doing).

**absurde** *a* absurd.

**abus** *m* abuse; (*de nourriture*) overindulgence (**de** in).

**abuser** *vi* to go too far; **a. de** (*situation, personne*) to take unfair advantage of; (*friandises*) to overindulge in.

**acajou** *m* mahogany.

**accabler** *vt* to overwhelm (**de** with).

**accéder** *vi* **a. à** (*lieu*) to reach.

**accélérateur** *m* accelerator.

**accélérer** *vi* to accelerate.

**accélérer (s')** *vpr* to speed up.

**accent** *m* accent; (*sur une syllabe*) stress.

**accepter** *vt* to accept; **a. de faire** to agree to do.

**accès** *m* access (**à** to); (*de folie, colère, toux*) fit; (*de fièvre*) bout; **'a. interdit'** 'no entry'.

**accessoires** *mpl* (*de voiture etc*) accessories; (*de théâtre*) props.

**accident** *m* accident; **a. d'avion/de train** plane/train crash.

**accidentel, -elle** *a* accidental.

**acclamations** *fpl* cheers.

**acclamer** *vt* to cheer.

**accommoder** *vt* (*assaisonner*) to prepare.

**accompagnateur, -trice** *mf* (*musical*) accompanist; (*d'un groupe*) guide.

**accompagnement** *m* (*musical*) accompaniment.

**accompagner** *vt* (*personne*) to go *ou* come with; (*chose, musique*) to accompany.

**accomplir** *vt* to carry out.

**accord** *m* agreement; (*musical*) chord; **tomber d'a.** to reach an agreement; **être d'a.** to agree (**avec** with); **d'a.!** all right!

**accordéon** *m* accordion.

**accorder** *vt* (*donner*) to grant; (*instrument*) to tune; (*verbe*) to make agree.

**accorder (s')** *vpr* (*s'entendre*) to get along.

**accotement** *m* (*of road*) shoulder.

**accouchement** *m* delivery.

**accoucher** *vi* to give birth (**de** to).

**accouder (s')** *vpr* **s'a. à** *ou* **sur** to lean on (*with one's elbows*).

**accourir*** *vi* to come running.

**accroc** *m* tear (**à** in).

**accrochage** *m* (*de voitures*) minor collision.

**accrocher** *vt* (*déchirer*) to catch; (*fixer*) to hook; (*suspendre*) to hang up (*on a hook*); (*heurter*) to hit.

**accrocher (s')** *vpr* (*se cramponner*) to cling (**à** to); (*ne pas céder*) to persevere.

**accroupi, -ie** *a* squatting.

**accroupir (s')** *vpr* to squat (down).

**accueil** *m* welcome.

**accueillant, -ante** *a* welcoming.

**accueillir*** *vt* to welcome.

**accumuler** *vt,* **s'accumuler** *vpr* to pile up.

**accusation** *f* accusation; (*au tribunal*) charge.

**accusé, -ée** *mf* accused; (*cour d'assises*) defendant.

**accuser** *vt* to accuse (**de** of); (*rendre responsable*) to blame (**de** for).

**acharnement** *m* (stubborn) determination.

**acharner (s')** *vpr* **s'a. sur** (*attaquer*) to lay into; **s'a. à faire** to struggle to do.

**achat** *m* purchase; **faire des achats** to go shopping.

**acheter** *vti* to buy; **a. à qn** to buy from s.o.; (*pour qn*) to buy for s.o.

**acheteur, -euse** *mf* buyer; (*dans un magasin*) shopper.

**achever** *vt* to finish (off); **a. de faire qch** (*personne*) to finish doing sth; **a. qn** (*tuer*) to finish s.o. off.

**acide 1** *a* sour. **2** *m* acid.

**acier** *m* steel.

**acompte** *m* deposit.

**acquérir*** *vt* (*acheter*) to purchase; (*obtenir*) to acquire.
**acquisition** *f* (*achat*) purchase.
**acquittement** *m* (*d'un accusé*) acquittal.
**acquitter** *vt* (*dette*) to pay; (*accusé*) to acquit; **s'a. envers qn** to repay s.o.
**acrobate** *mf* acrobat.
**acrobatie(s)** *f*(*pl*) acrobatics.
**acrobatique** *a* acrobatic.
**acte** *m* (*action, de pièce de théâtre*) act.
**acteur, -trice** *mf* actor, actress.
**actif, -ive 1** *a* active. **2** *m Grammaire* active.
**action** *f* action; (*en Bourse*) share, stock.
**actionnaire** *mf* shareholder.
**activer** *vt* (*feu*) to boost.
**activer (s')** *vpr* (*se dépêcher*) *Fam* to get a move on.
**activité** *f* activity.
**actualité** *f* (*événements*) current events; **actualités** (*à la télévision etc*) news.
**actuel, -elle** *a* (*présent*) present; (*contemporain*) topical.
**actuellement** *adv* at the present time.
**adaptation** *f* adjustment; (*de roman*) adaptation.
**adapter** *vt* to adapt; (*ajuster*) to fit (**à** to); **s'a. à** (*s'habituer*) to adapt to, adjust to; (*tuyau etc*) to fit.
**additif** *m* additive.
**addition** *f* addition; (*au restaurant*) check.
**additionner** *vt* to add (**à** to); (*nombres*) to add up.
**adhérent, -ente** *mf* member.
**adhérer** *vi* **a. à** (*coller*) to stick to; (*s'inscrire*) to join.
**adhésif, -ive** *a* & *m* adhesive.
**adieu, -x** *int* & *m* farewell.
**adjectif** *m* adjective.
**adjoint, -ointe** *mf* assistant; **a. au maire** deputy mayor.
**admettre*** *vt* (*laisser entrer, accueillir, reconnaître*) to admit; (*autoriser, tolérer*) to allow; (*candidat*) to pass; **être admis à** (*examen*) to have passed.
**administratif, -ive** *a* administrative.
**administration** *f* administration; **l'A.** (*service public*) the Civil Service.
**administrer** *vt* (*gérer, donner*) to administer.
**admirable** *a* admirable.
**admirateur, -trice** *mf* admirer.
**admiratif, -ive** *a* admiring.
**admiration** *f* admiration.
**admirer** *vt* to admire.
**adolescent, -ente** *mf* adolescent, teenager.
**adopter** *vt* to adopt.
**adoptif, -ive** *a* (*fils, patrie*) adopted.
**adoption** *f* adoption.
**adorable** *a* adorable.
**adoration** *f* worship.
**adorer** *vt* to love, adore (**faire** doing); (*dieu*) to worship.
**adosser (s')** *vpr* to lean back (**à** against).
**adoucir** *vt* (*voix, traits*) to tone down.
**adoucir (s')** *vpr* (*temps*) to turn milder.
**adresse** *f* (*domicile*) address; (*habileté*) skill.
**adresser** *vt* (*lettre*) to send; (*compliment, remarque*) to address; **a. la parole à** to speak to; **s'a. à** to speak to; (*aller trouver*) to go and see; (*bureau*) to (go and) ask at; (*être destiné à*) to be aimed at.
**adroit, -oite** *a* skillful.
**adulte** *mf* adult, grown-up.
**adverbe** *m* adverb.
**adversaire** *mf* opponent.
**aération** *f* ventilation.
**aérer** *vt* to air (out).
**aérien, -ienne** *a* (*photo*) aerial; **attaque/transport aérien(ne)** air attack/transport.
**aérobic** *m* aerobics.
**aérogare** *f* air terminal.
**aéroglisseur** *m* hovercraft.

**aéroport** *m* airport.
**aérosol** *m* aerosol.
**affaiblir** *vt,* **s'affaiblir** *vpr* to weaken.
**affaire** *f (question)* matter; **affaires** business; *(effets)* things; **avoir a. à** to have to deal with; **c'est mon a.** that's my business; **faire une bonne a.** to get a bargain.
**affamé, -ée** *a* starving.
**affection** *f (attachement)* affection.
**affectueux, -euse** *a* affectionate, loving.
**affichage** *m* **panneau d'a.** billboard.
**affiche** *f* poster.
**afficher** *vt (affiche)* to stick up.
**affirmatif, -ive** *a (ton, réponse)* positive, affirmative.
**affirmation** *f* assertion.
**affirmer** *vt* to assert.
**affliger** *vt* to distress.
**affluence** *f* crowd; **heure(s) d'a.** rush hour(s).
**affluent** *m* tributary.
**affolement** *m* panic.
**affoler** *vt* to drive crazy.
**affoler (s')** *vpr* to panic.
**affranchir** *vt* (lettre) to stamp.
**affreux, -euse** *a* horrible.
**affront** *m* insult; **faire un a. à** to insult.
**affronter** *vt* to confront; *(mauvais temps, difficultés etc)* to brave.
**affûter** *vt* to sharpen.
**afin 1** *prép* **a. de** *(+ infinitif)* in order to. **2** *conj* **a. que** *(+ subjonctif)* so that.
**africain, -aine** *a* & *mf* African.
**agacer** *vt* to irritate.
**âge** *m* age; **quel â. as-tu?** how old are you?; **d'un certain â.** middle-aged; **le moyen â.** the Middle Ages.
**âgé, -ée** *a* elderly; **â. de six ans** six years old; **enfant â. de six ans** six-year-old child.
**agence** *f* agency; *(succursale)* branch office; **a. immobilière** real estate office.
**agenda** *m* appointment book.
**agenouiller (s')** *vpr* to kneel (down); **être agenouillé** to be kneeling (down).
**agent** *m* agent; **a. (de police)** policeman; **a. immobilier** real estate agent.
**agglomération** *f* built-up area; *(ville)* town.
**aggloméré** *m* fiberboard.
**aggraver** *vt,* **s'aggraver** *vpr* to worsen.
**agile** *a* agile.
**agilité** *f* agility.
**agir** *vi* to act.
**agir (s')** *vi* **il s'agit d'argent**/*etc* it's a question *ou* matter of money/*etc*; **de quoi s'agit-il?** what is it?, what's it about?
**agitation** *f (de la mer)* roughness; *(d'une personne)* restlessness.
**agité, -ée** *a (mer)* rough; *(personne)* restless.
**agiter** *vt (remuer)* to stir; *(secouer)* to shake; *(brandir)* to wave.
**agiter (s')** *vpr (enfant)* to fidget.
**agneau, -x** *m* lamb.
**agrafe** *f* hook; *(pour papiers)* staple.
**agrafer** *vt (robe)* to do up; *(papiers)* to staple.
**agrafeuse** *f* stapler.
**agrandir** *vt* to enlarge.
**agrandir (s')** *vpr* to expand.
**agrandissement** *m (de ville)* expansion; *(de maison)* extension; *(de photo)* enlargement.
**agréable** *a* pleasant.
**agréer** *vt* **veuillez a. (l'expression de) mes salutations distinguées** *(dans une lettre)* sincerely yours.
**agresser** *vt* to attack.
**agresseur** *m* attacker; *(dans la rue)* mugger.
**agressif, -ive** *a* aggressive.
**agression** *f (dans la rue)* mugging.
**agressivité** *f* aggressiveness.
**agricole** *a* **ouvrier/machine a.** farm worker/machine; **travaux agricoles** farm work.

**agriculteur** *m* farmer.
**agriculture** *f* farming.
**aguets (aux)** *adv* on the look-out.
**ah!** *int* ah!, oh!
**ai** *voir* **avoir.**
**aide 1** *f* help; **à l'a. de** with the aid of. **2** *mf* (*personne*) assistant.
**aider** *vt* to help (**à faire** to do); **s'a. de** to make use of.
**aïe!** *int* ouch!
**aie(s), aient** *voir* **avoir.**
**aigle** *m* eagle.
**aigre** *a* sour.
**aigu, -uë** *a* (*douleur*) acute; (*dents*) sharp; (*voix*) shrill.
**aiguillage** *m* (*pour train*) switches.
**aiguille** *f* (*à coudre, de pin*) needle; (*de montre*) hand.
**aiguiller** *vt* (*train*) to switch.
**aiguilleur** *m* signalman; **a. du ciel** air traffic controller.
**aiguiser** *vt* to sharpen.
**ail** *m* garlic.
**aile** *f* wing; (*de moulin à vent*) sail; (*d'automobile*) fender.
**ailier** *m Football* wing.
**aille(s), aillent** *voir* **aller**[1]**.**
**ailleurs** *adv* somewhere else; **d'a.** (*du reste*) anyway.
**aimable** *a* (*gentil*) kind; (*sympathique*) likeable.
**aimant** *m* magnet.
**aimanter** *vt* to magnetize.
**aimer** *vt* to love; **a. (bien)** (*apprécier*) to like, be fond of; **a. faire** to like doing *ou* to do; **a. mieux** to prefer; **ils s'aiment** they're in love.
**aîné, -ée 1** *a* (*de deux frères etc*) elder, older; (*de plus de deux*) eldest, oldest. **2** *mf* elder *ou* older (child); eldest *ou* oldest (child).
**ainsi** *adv* (*comme ça*) (in) this *ou* that way; **a. que** as well as; **et a. de suite** and so on.
**air**[1] *m* air; (*mélodie*) tune; **en plein a.** in the open (air), outdoors; **ficher en l'a.** *Fam* (*jeter*) to chuck, to pitch; (*gâcher*) to mess up; **en l'a.** (*jeter*) (up) in the air; (*paroles*) empty.
**air**[2] *m* (*expression*) look; **avoir l'a.** to look, seem; **avoir l'a. de** to look like.
**aire** *f* area; **a. de stationnement** parking area.
**aise** *f* **à l'a.** (*dans un vêtement etc*) comfortable; (*dans une situation*) at ease; **mal à l'a.** uncomfortable.
**aisé, -ée** *a* (*riche*) comfortably off; (*facile*) easy.
**ait** *voir* **avoir.**
**ajouter** *vti* to add (**à** to).
**ajuster** *vt* (*pièce, salaires*) to adjust; **a. à** (*adapter*) to fit to.
**alaise** *f* (waterproof) undersheet.
**alarme** *f* (*signal*) alarm; **a. antivol/d'incendie** burglar/fire alarm.
**alarmer** *vt* to alarm.
**album** *m* (*de timbres etc*) album.
**alcool** *m* alcohol; (*spiritueux*) spirits; **a. à 90**° rubbing alcohol.
**alcoolique** *a* & *mf* alcoholic.
**alcoolisé, -ée** *a* alcoholic.
**alcootest**® *m* breath test; (*appareil*) breathalyzer.
**alentours** *mpl* surroundings.
**alerte** *f* alarm; **en état d'a.** on the alert.
**alerter** *vt* to warn.
**algèbre** *f* algebra.
**algérien, -ienne** *a* & *mf* Algerian.
**algue(s)** *f*(*pl*) seaweed.
**alibi** *m* alibi.
**aliéné, -ée** *mf* insane person.
**alignement** *m* alignment.
**aligner** *vt*, **s'aligner** *vpr* to line up.
**aliment** *m* food.
**alimentaire** *a* **ration**/*etc* **a.** food rations/*etc*; **produits alimentaires** foods.
**alimentation** *f* (*action*) feeding; (*régime*) diet; (*nourriture*) food; **magasin d'a.** grocery store.
**alimenter** *vt* (*nourrir*) to feed.
**allaiter** *vti* to breastfeed.
**allécher** *vt* to tempt.
**allée** *f* (*de parc etc*) path; (*de cinéma, supermarché etc*) aisle.
**allégé, -ée** *a* (*fromage etc*) low-fat.

**alléger** *vt* to make lighter.
**allemand, -ande 1** *a* & *mf* German. **2** *m* (*langue*) German.
**aller**[1]* *vi* (*aux* **être**) to go; **a. à** (*convenir à*) to suit; **a. avec** (*vêtement*) to go with; **a. bien/mieux** (*personne*) to be well/better; **il va savoir**/*etc* he'll know/*etc*, he's going to know/*etc*; **il va partir** he's about to leave, he's going to leave; **va voir!** go and see!; **comment vas-tu?, (comment) ça va?** how are you?; **ça va!** all right!, fine!; **allez-y!** go on!, go ahead!; **allez! au lit!** come on *ou* go on to bed!
**aller**[2] *m* outward journey; **a. (simple)** one-way (ticket); **a. (et) retour** round-trip (ticket).
**aller (s'en)** *vpr* to go away; (*tache*) to come out.
**allergie** *f* allergy.
**allergique** *a* allergic (**à** to).
**alliance** *f* (*anneau*) wedding ring; (*de pays*) alliance.
**allié, -ée** *mf* ally.
**allier** *vt* to combine (**à** with); (*pays*) to ally (**à** with).
**allier (s')** *vpr* (*pays*) to become allied (**à** with, to).
**allô!** *int* hello!
**allocation** *f* allowance, benefit; **a. (de) chômage** unemployment benefit; **allocations familiales** child benefit.
**allongé, -ée** *a* (*étiré*) elongated.
**allonger 1** *vt* (*bras*) to stretch out; (*jupe*) to lengthen. **2** *vi* (*jours*) to get longer.
**allonger (s')** *vpr* to stretch out.
**allumage** *m* (*de voiture*) ignition.
**allumer** *vt* (*feu, cigarette, gaz*) to light; (*électricité*) to turn *ou* switch on.
**allumer (s')** *vpr* (*lumière*) to come on.
**allumette** *f* match.
**allure** *f* (*vitesse*) pace; (*de véhicule*) speed; (*air*) look.
**allusion** *f* allusion; **faire a. à** to refer to.
**alors** *adv* (*en ce cas-là*) so; **a. que** (*tandis que*) whereas.
**alouette** *f* (sky)lark.
**alourdir** *vt* to weigh down.
**alourdir (s')** *vpr* to become heavy *ou* heavier.
**Alpes (les)** *fpl* the Alps.
**alphabet** *m* alphabet.
**alphabétique** *a* alphabetical.
**alpinisme** *m* mountain climbing.
**alpiniste** *mf* mountain climber.
**alterner** *vti* to alternate.
**altitude** *f* height.
**alu** *m* **papier (d')a.** tinfoil.
**aluminium** *m* aluminum; **papier a.** tinfoil.
**amabilité** *f* kindness.
**amaigri, -ie** *a* thin(ner).
**amaigrissant** *a* **régime a.** (weight-loss) diet.
**amande** *f* almond.
**amarrer** *vt* to moor.
**amarres** *fpl* moorings.
**amas** *m* heap, pile.
**amasser** *vt*, **s'amasser** *vpr* to pile up.
**amateur** *m* (*d'art etc*) lover; (*sportif*) amateur; **une équipe a.** an amateur team.
**ambassade** *f* embassy.
**ambassadeur, -drice** *mf* ambassador.
**ambiance** *f* atmosphere.
**ambitieux, -euse** *a* ambitious.
**ambition** *f* ambition.
**ambulance** *f* ambulance.
**ambulant, -ante** *a* traveling.
**âme** *f* soul.
**amélioration** *f* improvement.
**améliorer** *vt*, **s'améliorer** *vpr* to improve.
**aménagement** *m* fitting out; conversion.
**aménager** *vt* (*arranger*) to fit out (**en** as); (*transformer*) to convert (**en** into).
**amende** *f* fine.
**amener** *vt* to bring.
**amer, -ère** *a* bitter.

**américain, -aine** *a* & *mf* American.
**amertume** *f* bitterness.
**ameublement** *m* furniture.
**ami, -ie** *mf* friend; (*de la nature etc*) lover (**de** of); **petit a.** boyfriend; **petite amie** girlfriend.
**amical, -e, -aux** *a* friendly.
**amiral, -aux** *m* admiral.
**amitié** *f* friendship.
**amonceler (s')** *vpr* to pile up.
**amont (en)** *adv* upstream.
**amorce** *f* (*de pêcheur*) bait; (*de pistolet d'enfant*) cap.
**amortir** *vt* (*coup*) to cushion; (*bruit*) to deaden.
**amortisseur** *m* shock absorber.
**amour** *m* love; **pour l'a. de** for the sake of.
**amoureux, -euse 1** *mf* lover. **2** *a* **a. de qn** in love with s.o.
**amour-propre** *m* self-respect.
**amovible** *a* removable.
**amphithéâtre** *m* (*romain*) amphitheater; (*à l'université*) lecture hall.
**ample** *a* (*vêtement*) full, ample.
**ampleur** *f* (*de robe*) fullness.
**amplificateur** *m* amplifier.
**amplifier** *vt* (*son, courant*) to amplify.
**ampoule** *f* (*électrique*) (light) bulb; (*aux pieds etc*) blister; (*de médicament*) phial.
**amputer** *vt* to amputate.
**amusant, -ante** *a* amusing.
**amusement** *m* amusement.
**amuser** *vt* to entertain.
**amuser (s')** *vpr* to enjoy oneself, have fun; **s'a. avec** to play with; **s'a. à faire** to amuse oneself doing.
**amygdales** *fpl* tonsils.
**an** *m* year; **il a dix ans** he's ten (years old); **Nouvel A.** New Year.
**analogue** *a* similar.
**analyse** *f* analysis.
**analyser** *vt* to analyze.
**ananas** *m* pineapple.
**anarchie** *f* anarchy.
**anatomie** *f* anatomy.
**ancêtre** *m* ancestor.
**anchois** *m* anchovy.
**ancien, -ienne** *a* old; (*meuble*) antique; (*qui n'est plus*) former; (*antique*) ancient; (*dans une fonction*) senior.
**ancre** *f* anchor.
**ancrer** *vt* to anchor.
**andouille** *f* **espèce d'a.!** *Fam* (you) nitwit!
**âne** *m* (*animal*) donkey; (*personne*) ass.
**anéantir** *vt* to wipe out.
**anecdote** *f* anecdote.
**ânesse** *f* female donkey.
**anesthésie** *f* anesthesia; **a. générale** general anesthetic.
**anesthésier** *vt* to anesthetize.
**ange** *m* angel.
**angine** *f* throat infection.
**anglais, -aise 1** *a* English. **2** *mf* Englishman, Englishwoman; **les A.** the English. **3** *m* (*langue*) English.
**angle** *m* angle; (*de rue*) corner.
**angoissant, -ante** *a* distressing.
**angoisse** *f* (great) anxiety, anguish.
**anguille** *f* eel.
**animal, -e, -aux** *m* & *a* animal.
**animateur, -trice** *mf* (*de télévision*) emcee; (*de club*) leader, organizer.
**animation** *f* (*des rues*) activity; (*de réunion*) liveliness.
**animé, -ée** *a* lively.
**animer** *vt* (*débat*) to lead; (*soirée*) to liven up; (*mécanisme*) to drive.
**animer (s')** *vpr* (*rue etc*) to come to life.
**ankylosé, -ée** *a* stiff.
**anneau, -x** *m* ring.
**année** *f* year; **bonne a.!** Happy New Year!
**annexe** *f* (*bâtiment*) annex(e).
**anniversaire** *m* (*d'événement*) anniversary; (*de naissance*) birthday.
**annonce** *f* (*publicitaire*) advertisement; **petites annonces** classified advertisements.
**annoncer** *vt* to announce; (*vente*)

to advertise; **s'a. pluvieux/difficile**/*etc* to look rainy/difficult/*etc*.
**annuaire** *m* (*téléphonique*) directory, phone book.
**annuel, -elle** *a* yearly.
**annulaire** *m* ring finger.
**annuler** *vt* to cancel.
**ânonner** *vt* to stumble through.
**anonyme** *a* & *mf* anonymous (person).
**anorak** *m* parka.
**anormal, -e, -aux** *a* abnormal.
**anse** *f* (*de tasse etc*) handle.
**Antarctique (l')** *m* the Antarctic.
**antenne** *f* (*de radio etc*) antenna; (*d'insecte*) antenna.
**antérieur, -eure** *a* (*précédent*) former; (*placé devant*) front.
**antibiotique** *m* antibiotic.
**antibrouillard** *a* & *m* **(phare) a.** fog light.
**antichoc** *a inv* shockproof.
**anticorps** *m* antibody.
**antilope** *f* antelope.
**antipathique** *a* disagreeable.
**antiquaire** *mf* antique dealer.
**antique** *a* ancient.
**antiquité** *f* (*temps, ancienneté*) antiquity; (*objet ancien*) antique.
**antivol** *m* anti-theft device.
**anxiété** *f* anxiety.
**anxieux, -euse** *a* anxious.
**août** *m* August.
**apaiser** *vt* to calm.
**apercevoir*** *vt* to see; (*brièvement*) to catch a glimpse of; **s'a. de** to realize.
**apéritif** *m* aperitif.
**aplanir** *vt* (*terrain*) to level; (*difficulté*) to iron out, smooth out.
**aplati, -ie** *a* flat.
**aplatir** *vt* to flatten (out).
**aplomb (d')** *adv* (*meuble etc*) level, straight.
**apostrophe** *f* (*signe*) apostrophe.
**apparaître*** *vi* to appear.
**appareil** *m* (*électrique*) appliance; (*téléphonique*) telephone; (*avion*) aircraft; (*dentaire*) braces; (*digestif*) system; **a. (photo)** camera.
**apparemment** *adv* apparently.
**apparence** *f* appearance.
**apparent, -ente** *a* apparent; (*visible*) conspicuous, noticeable.
**apparition** *f* appearance; (*spectre*) apparition.
**appartement** *m* & apartment.
**appartenir*** *vi* to belong (**à** to).
**appât** *m* bait.
**appâter** *vt* to lure.
**appauvrir (s')** *vpr* to become impoverished.
**appel** *m* (*cri*) call; (*en justice*) appeal; **faire l'a.** to call the roll; **faire a. à** to call upon.
**appeler** *vt* (*personne, nom etc*) to call; (*en criant*) to call out to (*s.o*); **a. à l'aide** to call for help.
**appeler (s')** *vpr* to be called; **il s'appelle Paul** his name is Paul.
**appendicite** *f* appendicitis.
**appétissant, -ante** *a* appetizing.
**appétit** *m* appetite (**de** for); **bon a.!** enjoy your meal!
**applaudir** *vti* to applaud.
**applaudissements** *mpl* applause.
**application** *f* application.
**applique** *f* wall lamp.
**appliqué, -ée** *a* painstaking.
**appliquer (s')** *vpr* **s'a. à** (*un travail*) to apply oneself to; (*concerner*) to apply to; **s'a. à faire** to take pains to do.
**apporter** *vt* to bring.
**appréciation** *f* (*de professeur*) comment (**sur** on).
**apprécier** *vt* (*aimer, percevoir*) to appreciate.
**appréhender** *vt* (*craindre*) to dread (**de faire** doing).
**apprendre*** *vti* (*étudier*) to learn; (*événement, fait*) to hear of; (*nouvelle*) to hear; **a. à faire** to learn to do; **a. qch à qn** to teach s.o. sth; (*informer*) to tell s.o. sth; **a. à qn à faire** to teach s.o. to do; **a. que** to learn that; (*être informé*) to hear that.
**apprenti, -ie** *mf* apprentice.

**apprentissage** *m* apprenticeship; (*d'une langue*) learning (**de** of).
**apprêter (s')** *vpr* to get ready (**à faire** to do).
**apprivoisé, -ée** *a* tame.
**apprivoiser** *vt* to tame.
**approcher 1** *vt* (*chaise etc*) to draw up (**de** to); (*personne*) to come *ou* get close to, approach. **2** *vi* to draw near(er), get close(r) (**de** to).
**approcher (s')** *vpr* to come *ou* get near(er) (**de** to); **il s'est approché de moi** he came up to me.
**approfondir** *vt* (*trou*) to dig deeper; (*question*) to go into thoroughly.
**approprier (s')** *vpr* to take, help oneself to.
**approuver** *vt* to approve.
**approvisionner (s')** *vpr* to get one's supplies (**de** of).
**appui** *m* support; (*pour coude etc*) rest.
**appuyer 1** *vt* (*soutenir*) to support; **a. qch sur** (*poser*) to rest sth on; **s'a. sur** to lean on, rest on. **2** *vi* **a. sur** to rest on; (*bouton*) to press.
**après 1** *prép* (*temps*) after; (*espace*) beyond; **a. un an** after a year; **a. le pont** beyond the bridge; **a. avoir mangé** after eating. **2** *adv* after(wards); **l'année d'a.** the following year.
**après (d')** *prép* according to.
**après-demain** *adv* the day after tomorrow.
**après-midi** *m ou f inv* afternoon.
**apte** *a* capable (**à** of).
**aptitudes** *fpl* aptitude (**pour** for).
**aquarelle** *f* watercolor.
**aquarium** *m* aquarium.
**aquatique** *a* aquatic.
**arabe 1** *a* & *mf* Arab. **2** *a* & *m* (*langue*) Arabic; **chiffres arabes** Arabic numerals.
**arachide** *f* peanut.
**araignée** *f* spider.
**arbitre** *m Football*, *Boxe* referee; *Tennis* umpire.
**arbitrer** *vt* to referee; to umpire.
**arbre** *m* tree.
**arbuste** *m* (small) shrub.
**arc** *m* (*arme*) bow; (*voûte*) arch; (*de cercle*) arc.
**arcades** *fpl* arcade, arches.
**arc-en-ciel** *m* (*pl* **arcs-en-ciel**) rainbow.
**arche** *f* (*voûte*) arch.
**archer** *m* archer.
**archiplein, -pleine** *a* jam-packed.
**architecte** *m* architect.
**architecture** *f* architecture.
**archives** *fpl* records.
**Arctique (l')** *m* the Arctic.
**ardent, -ente** *a* (*passionné*) ardent.
**ardeur** *f* (*énergie*) enthusiasm.
**ardoise** *f* slate.
**are** *m* = 100 square meters.
**arène** *f* (*pour taureaux*) bullring; **arènes** (*romaines*) amphitheater.
**arête** *f* (*de poisson*) bone; (*de cube*) edge, ridge.
**argent** *m* (*métal*) silver; (*monnaie*) money; **a. comptant** cash.
**argenterie** *f* silverware.
**argile** *f* clay.
**argot** *m* slang.
**argument** *m* argument.
**arithmétique** *f* arithmetic.
**armature** *f* (*de lunettes*, *tente*) frame.
**arme** *f* arm, weapon; **a. à feu** firearm.
**armée** *f* army; **a. de l'air** air force.
**armement(s)** *m*(*pl*) arms.
**armer** *vt* (*personne*) to arm (**de** with); (*fusil*) to cock; **s'a.** to arm oneself (**de** with).
**armoire** *f* (*penderie*) wardrobe, closet; **a. à pharmacie** medicine chest *ou* cabinet.
**armure** *f* armor.
**arôme** *m* (*goût*) flavor; (*odeur*) (pleasant) smell.
**arracher** *vt* (*clou*, *dent*, *cheveux*, *page*) to pull out; (*plante*) to pull up; **a. qch à qn** to snatch sth from s.o.

**arranger** *vt* (*chambre*, *visite etc*) to fix up; (*voiture*, *texte*) to put right; **ça m'arrange** that suits me.

**arranger (s')** *vpr* to come to an agreement; (*finir bien*) to turn out fine; **s'a. pour faire** to manage to do.

**arrestation** *f* arrest.

**arrêt** *m* (*halte*, *endroit*) stop; (*action*) stopping; **temps d'a.** pause; **sans a.** constantly; **'a. interdit'** (*panneau de signalisation*) 'no stopping (no standing).'

**arrêté** *m* order.

**arrêter 1** *vt* to stop; (*voleur etc*) to arrest. **2** *vi* to stop; **il n'arrête pas de critiquer**/*etc* he's always criticizing/*etc*.

**arrêter (s')** *vpr* to stop (**de faire** doing).

**arrière 1** *adv* **en a.** (*marcher*) backwards; (*rester*) behind. **2** *m* & *a inv* rear, back; **faire marche a.** to reverse, back. **3** *m Sports* (full) back.

**arrière-boutique** *f* back (room) (*of a shop*).

**arrière-goût** *m* aftertaste.

**arrière-grand-mère** *f* great-grandmother.

**arrière-grand-père** *m* great-grandfather.

**arrivage** *m* shipment.

**arrivée** *f* arrival; **ligne d'a.** finish line.

**arriver** *vi* (*aux* **être**) to arrive; (*survenir*) to happen; **a. à** to reach; **a. à qn** to happen to s.o.; **a. à faire** to manage to do; **il m'arrive d'oublier**/*etc* I (sometimes) forget/*etc*.

**arrondir** *vt* (*chiffre*, *angle*) to round off.

**arrondissement** *m* (*d'une ville*) district.

**arrosage** *m* watering.

**arroser** *vt* (*terre*) to water.

**arrosoir** *m* watering can.

**art** *m* art.

**artère** *f* artery; (*rue*) main road.

**artichaut** *m* artichoke.

**article** *m* (*de presse*, *de commerce*, *en grammaire*) article; **articles de toilette** toiletries.

**articulation** *f* (*de membre*) joint; **a. (du doigt)** knuckle.

**articuler** *vt* (*mot etc*) to articulate.

**artifice** *m* **feu d'a.** firework display.

**artificiel, -elle** *a* artificial.

**artisan** *m* craftsman.

**artiste** *mf* artist.

**artistique** *a* artistic.

**as**[1] *voir* **avoir.**

**as**[2] *m* (*carte*, *champion*) ace.

**ascenseur** *m* elevator.

**ascension** *f* ascent; **l'A.** Ascension Day.

**asiatique** *a* & *mf* Asian.

**asile** *m* (*abri*) shelter.

**aspect** *m* (*air*) appearance.

**asperge** *f* asparagus.

**asperger** *vt* to spray (**de** with).

**asphyxie** *f* suffocation.

**asphyxier** *vt* to suffocate.

**aspirateur** *m* vacuum cleaner; **passer (à) l'a.** to vacuum.

**aspirer** *vt* (*liquide*) to suck up.

**aspirine** *f* aspirin.

**assaisonnement** *m* seasoning.

**assaisonner** *vt* to season.

**assassin** *m* murderer.

**assassinat** *m* murder.

**assassiner** *vt* to murder.

**assaut** *m* onslaught; **prendre d'a.** to (take by) storm.

**assemblée** *f* (*personnes réunies*) gathering; (*parlement*) assembly.

**assembler** *vt* to put together.

**assembler (s')** *vpr* to gather.

**asseoir* (s')** *vpr* to sit (down).

**assez** *adv* enough; **a. de pain/gens** enough bread/people; **j'en ai a.** I've had enough; **a. grand**/*etc* (*suffisamment*) big/*etc* enough (**pour faire** to do); **a. fatigué**/*etc* (*plutôt*) fairly *ou* quite tired/*etc*.

**assiéger** *vt* (*magasin*, *vedette*) to mob.

**assiette** *f* plate; **a. anglaise** (assorted) cold cuts.

**assis, -ise** (*pp of* **asseoir**) *a* sitting (down).

**assises** *fpl* **(cour d')a.** court of assizes.
**assistance** *f* (*assemblée*) audience; (*aide*) assistance.
**assistant, -ante** *mf* assistant; **assistant(e) social(e)** social worker; **assistante maternelle** (*dans une garderie*) daycare worker; (*à domicile*) babysitter.
**assister 1** *vt* (*aider*) to help. **2** *vi* **a. à** (*réunion, cours etc*) to attend; (*accident*) to witness.
**association** *f* association.
**associé, -ée** *mf* partner.
**associer (s')** *vpr* to associate (**à** with).
**assoiffé, -ée** *a* thirsty.
**assombrir (s')** *vpr* (*ciel*) to cloud over.
**assommer** *vt* (*personne*) to knock unconscious.
**assortiment** *m* assortment.
**assortir** *vt*, **s'assortir** *vpr* to match.
**assoupir (s')** *vpr* to doze off.
**assouplir** *vt* (*corps*) to limber up, to stretch.
**assouplissement** *m* **exercices d'a.** stretching exercises.
**assourdir** *vt* to deafen.
**assourdissant, -ante** *a* deafening.
**assurance** *f* (*aplomb*) self-assurance; (*contrat*) insurance.
**assurer** *vt* (*par un contrat*) to insure; (*travail*) to carry out; **s'a.** to insure oneself (**contre** against); **a. à qn que** to assure s.o. that; **a. qn de qch** to assure s.o. of sth; **s'a. que/de** to make sure that/of.
**astérisque** *m* asterisk.
**asthmatique** *a* & *mf* asthmatic.
**asthme** *m* asthma.
**asticot** *m* maggot.
**astiquer** *vt* to polish.
**astre** *m* star.
**astrologie** *f* astrology.
**astronaute** *mf* astronaut.
**astronomie** *f* astronomy.
**astuce** *f* (*pour faire qch*) knack, trick.
**astucieux, -euse** *a* clever.
**atelier** *m* (*d'ouvrier etc*) workshop; (*de peintre*) studio.
**athlète** *mf* athlete.
**athlétique** *a* athletic.
**athlétisme** *m* athletics.
**atlantique 1** *a* Atlantic. **2** *m* **l'A.** the Atlantic.
**atlas** *m* atlas.
**atmosphère** *f* atmosphere.
**atome** *m* atom.
**atomique** *a* (*bombe etc*) atomic.
**atout** *m* trump (card).
**atroce** *a* atrocious.
**atrocités** *fpl* atrocities.
**attabler (s')** *vpr* to sit down at the table.
**attachant, -ante** *a* (*enfant etc*) likeable.
**attaché-case** *m* attaché case, briefcase.
**attacher** *vt* (*lier*) to tie (up) (**à** to); (*boucler, fixer*) to fasten; **s'a. à qn** to become attached to s.o.
**attaquant, -ante** *mf* attacker.
**attaque** *f* attack.
**attaquer** *vti* to attack; **s'a. à** to attack.
**attarder (s')** *vpr* (*en chemin*) to dawdle.
**atteindre*** *vt* to reach; **être atteint de** (*maladie*) to be suffering from.
**attelage** *m* (*crochet*) hook (*for towing*).
**atteler** *vt* (*bêtes*) to harness; (*remorque*) to hook up.
**attendre 1** *vt* to wait for; **elle attend un bébé** she's expecting a baby. **2** *vi* to wait; **s'a. à** to expect; **a. que qn vienne** to wait for s.o. to come; **faire a. qn** to keep s.o. waiting; **en attendant** meanwhile; **en attendant que** (+ *subjonctif*) until.
**attendrir (s')** *vpr* to be moved (**sur** by).
**attentat** *m* attempt on s.o.'s life; **a. (à la bombe)** (bomb) attack.
**attente** *f* wait(ing); **salle d'a.** waiting room.
**attentif, -ive** *a* (*personne*) attentive; (*travail, examen*) careful.

**attention** *f* attention; **faire a. à** to pay attention to; **a.!** watch out!, be careful!; **a. à la voiture!** watch out for the car!
**attentivement** *adv* attentively.
**atterrir** *vi* to land.
**atterrissage** *m* landing.
**attirer** *vt* to attract; (*attention*) to draw (**sur** to).
**attitude** *f* attitude.
**attraction** *f* attraction.
**attraper** *vt* (*ballon, maladie, voleur, train etc*) to catch; (*accent, contravention etc*) to pick up; **se laisser a.** (*duper*) to get taken in.
**attrayant, -ante** *a* attractive.
**attribuer** *vt* (*donner*) to assign (**à** to); (*décerner*) to award (**à** to).
**attribut** *m* attribute.
**attrister** *vt* to sadden.
**attroupement** *m* (disorderly) crowd.
**attrouper** *vt*, **s'attrouper** *vpr* to gather.
**au** *voir* **à, le**.
**aube** *f* dawn.
**auberge** *f* inn; **a. de jeunesse** youth hostel.
**aubergine** *f* eggplant.
**aucun, -une 1** *a* no, not any; **il n'a a. talent** he has no talent, he doesn't have any talent; **a. professeur n'est venu** no teacher has come. **2** *pron* none, not any; **il n'en a a.** he has none (at all), he doesn't have any (at all).
**audace** *f* (*courage*) daring.
**audacieux, -euse** *a* daring.
**au-dessous de** *prép* under, below.
**au-dessus 1** *adv* above; over; (*à l'étage supérieur*) upstairs. **2** *prép* **au-d. de** above; (*âge, température, prix*) over.
**audio** *a inv* audio.
**auditeur, -trice** *mf* listener; **les auditeurs** the audience.
**auditoire** *m* audience.
**auge** *f* (feeding) trough.
**augmentation** *f* increase (**de** in, of); **a. de salaire** (pay) raise.
**augmenter** *vti* to increase (**de** by).
**aujourd'hui** *adv* today.
**auprès de** *prép* by, close to.
**auquel** *voir* **lequel**.
**aura, aurai(t)** *etc voir* **avoir**.
**aurore** *f* dawn.
**ausculter** *vt* to examine (*with a stethoscope*).
**aussi** *adv* (*comparaison*) as; **a. sage que** as wise as. ▪ (*également*) too, also, as well; **moi a.** so do, can, am *etc* I. ▪ (*tellement*) so; **un repas a. délicieux** so delicious a meal, such a delicious meal.
**aussitôt** *adv* immediately; **a. que** as soon as; **a. levé, il partit** as soon as he was up, he left.
**australien, -ienne** *a* & *mf* Australian.
**autant** *adv* **a. de . . . que** (*quantité*) as much . . . as; (*nombre*) as many . . . as. ▪ **a. de** (*tant de*) so much; (*nombre*) so many. ▪ **a. (que)** (*souffrir, lire etc*) as much (as); **en faire a.** to do the same; **j'aimerais a. aller au cinéma** I'd just as soon go to the movies.
**autel** *m* altar.
**auteur** *m* (*de livre*) author; (*de chanson*) composer.
**authentique** *a* genuine.
**auto** *f* car; **autos tamponneuses** bumper cars.
**autobus** *m* bus.
**autocar** *m* bus, coach.
**autocollant** *m* sticker.
**auto-école** *f* driving school.
**autographe** *m* autograph.
**automatique** *a* automatic.
**automatiquement** *adv* automatically.
**automne** *m* autumn, fall.
**automobile** *f* & *a* car, automobile.
**automobiliste** *mf* motorist, driver.
**autoradio** *m* car radio.
**autorisation** *f* permission.
**autoriser** *vt* to permit (**à faire** to do).
**autoritaire** *a* authoritarian.
**autorité** *f* authority.

**autoroute** *f* highway.

**auto-stop** *m* hitchhiking; **faire de l'a.** to hitchhike.

**auto-stoppeur, -euse** *mf* hitchhiker.

**autour 1** *adv* around. **2** *prép* **a. de** around.

**autre** *a* & *pron* other; **un a. livre** another book; **un a.** another (one); **d'autres** others; **d'autres médecins** other doctors; **d'autres questions?** any other questions?; **qn/personne/rien d'a.** s.o./no one/nothing else; **a. chose/part** something/somewhere else; **qui/quoi d'a.?** who/what else?; **l'un l'a., les uns les autres** each other; **l'un et l'a.** both (of them); **l'un ou l'a.** either (of them); **ni l'un ni l'a.** neither (of them); **les uns . . . les autres** some . . . others; **d'un moment à l'a.** any moment.

**autrefois** *adv* in the past.

**autrement** *adv* differently; (*sinon*) otherwise.

**autrichien, -ienne** *a* & *mf* Austrian.

**autruche** *f* ostrich.

**aux** *voir* **à, le.**

**auxiliaire** *a* & *m* **(verbe) a.** auxiliary (verb).

**auxquel(le)s** *voir* **lequel.**

**aval (en)** *adv* downstream.

**avalanche** *f* avalanche.

**avaler** *vti* to swallow.

**avance** *f* **à l'a., d'a.** in advance; **en a.** (*arriver, partir*) early; (*avant l'horaire prévu*) ahead (of time); **en a. sur** ahead of; **avoir une heure d'a.** (*train etc*) to be an hour early.

**avancement** *m* (*de personne*) promotion.

**avancer 1** *vt* (*date*) to move up; (*main, chaise*) to move forward; (*travail*) to speed up. **2** *vi* to advance, move forward; (*montre*) to be fast.

**avancer (s')** *vpr* to move forward.

**avant 1** *prép* before; **a. de voir** before seeing; **a. qu'il (ne) parte** before he leaves; **a. tout** above all. **2** *adv* before; **en a.** (*mouvement*) forward; (*en tête*) ahead; **la nuit d'a.** the night before. **3** *m* & *a inv* front. **4** *m* (*joueur*) forward.

**avantage** *m* advantage.

**avantager** *vt* to favor.

**avant-bras** *m inv* forearm.

**avant-dernier, -ière** *a* & *mf* last but one.

**avant-hier** *adv* the day before yesterday.

**avant-veille** *f* **l'a.-veille (de)** two days before.

**avare 1** *a* miserly, stingy. **2** *mf* miser.

**avarice** *f* miserliness, avarice.

**avarié, -ée** *a* (*aliment*) rotting, rotten.

**avec** *prép* with; (*envers*) to(wards); **et a. ça?** (*dans un magasin*) anything else?

**avenir** *m* future; **à l'a.** in future.

**aventure** *f* adventure.

**aventurer (s')** *vpr* to venture.

**aventurier, -ière** *mf* adventurer.

**avenue** *f* avenue.

**averse** *f* shower.

**avertir** *vt* (*mettre en garde*) to warn; (*informer*) to notify.

**avertissement** *m* warning; notification.

**avertisseur** *m* (*klaxon®*) horn; **a. d'incendie** fire alarm.

**aveu, -x** *m* confession.

**aveugle 1** *a* blind. **2** *mf* blind man, blind woman; **les aveugles** the blind.

**aveugler** *vt* to blind.

**aveuglette (à l')** *adv* **chercher qch à l'a.** to grope for sth.

**aviateur, -trice** *mf* airman, airwoman.

**aviation** *f* (*armée de l'air*) air force; (*avions*) aircraft *inv*; **l'a.** (*activité*) flying; **base d'a.** air base.

**avion** *m* aircraft *inv*, (air)plane; **a. à réaction** jet; **a. de ligne** airliner; **par a.** (*lettre*) airmail; **en a., par a.** (*voyager*) by plane, by air.

**aviron** *m* oar; **l'a.** (*sport*) rowing.
**avis** *m* opinion; (*communiqué*) notice; **à mon a.** in my opinion; **changer d'a.** to change one's mind.
**avocat, -ate 1** *mf* attorney. **2** *m* (*fruit*) avocado (pear).
**avoine** *f* oats.
**avoir* 1** *v aux* to have; **je l'ai vu** I've seen him. **2** *vt* (*posséder*) to have; (*obtenir*) to get; **qu'est-ce que tu as?** what's the matter with you?; **il n'a qu'à essayer** all he has to do is try; **a. faim/chaud/***etc* to be *ou* feel hungry/hot/*etc*; **a. cinq ans** to be five (years old); **j'en ai pour dix minutes** this will take me ten minutes. **3** (*locution*) **il y a** there is, *pl* there are; **il y a six ans** six years ago; (*voir* **il**).
**avouer** *vti* to confess (**que** that).
**avril** *m* April.
**axe** *m* (*ligne*) axis; (*essieu*) axle; **grands axes** (*routes*) main roads.
**ayant, ayez, ayons** *voir* **avoir**.
**azote** *m* nitrogen.
**azur** *m* (sky) blue; **la Côte d'A.** the (French) Riviera.

# B

**baby-foot** *m inv* foosball.
**bac 1** *m* (*bateau*) ferry(boat); (*cuve*) tank. **2** *abrév* = **baccalauréat.**
**baccalauréat** *m* = high school diploma.
**bâche** *f* tarpaulin.
**bachelier, -ière** *mf* holder of the *baccalauréat*.
**bâcher** *vt* to cover over (with a tarpaulin).
**badaud, -aude** *mf* onlooker.
**badigeonner** *vt* (*mur*) to whitewash; (*écorchure*) to coat, paint.
**bafouiller** *vti* to stammer.
**bagage** *m* piece of luggage *ou* baggage; **bagages** luggage, baggage.
**bagarre** *f* fight(ing).
**bagarrer (se)** *vpr* to fight.
**bagnole** *f Fam* car.
**bague** *f* (*anneau*) ring.
**baguette** *f* stick; (*de chef d'orchestre*) baton; (*pain*) (long thin) loaf; **baguettes** (*de tambour*) drumsticks; (*pour manger*) chopsticks; **b. (magique)** (magic) wand.
**baie** *f* (*de côte*) bay.
**baignade** *f* (*bain*) bath, swim; (*endroit*) swimming place.
**baigner 1** *vt* to bathe; **2** *vi* **b. dans** (*aliment*) to be steeped in.
**baigner (se)** *vpr* to go swimming.
**baigneur, -euse 1** *mf* bather, swimmer. **2** *m* (*poupée*) baby doll.
**baignoire** *f* bath (tub).
**bâillement** *m* yawn.
**bâiller** *vi* to yawn.
**bâillon** *m* gag.
**bâillonner** *vt* to gag.
**bain** *m* bath; **prendre un b. de soleil** to sunbathe; **salle de bain(s)** bathroom; **être dans le b.** *Fam* to have gotten into the swing of things; **b. de bouche** mouthwash.
**baiser** *m* kiss.
**baisse** *f* fall, drop (**de** in); **en b.** falling.
**baisser 1** *vt* to lower, drop; (*tête*) to bend; (*radio, chauffage*) to turn down. **2** *vi* to go down, drop.
**baisser (se)** *vpr* to bend down.
**bal,** *pl* **bals** *m* ball; (*populaire*) dance.
**balade** *f Fam* walk; (*en auto*) drive.
**balader (se)** *vpr Fam* (*à pied*) to (go for a) walk; **se b. (en voiture)** to go for a drive.
**baladeur** *m* Walkman®.
**balai** *m* broom; **manche à b.** broomstick.
**balance** *f* (pair of) scales.
**balancer** *vt* to sway; (*lancer*) *Fam* to pitch; (*se débarrasser de*) *Fam* to chuck, to pitch.
**balancer (se)** *vpr* to swing (from side to side).
**balançoire** *f* (*suspendue*) swing.
**balayer** *vt* to sweep (up); (*enlever*) to sweep away.

**balayette** *f* (hand) brush.
**balayeur, -euse 1** *mf* (*personne*) roadsweeper. **2** *f* (*véhicule*) roadsweeper.
**balbutier** *vti* to stammer.
**balcon** *m* balcony.
**baleine** *f* whale.
**balisage** *m* beacons.
**balise** *f* (*pour naviguer*) beacon.
**baliser** *vt* to mark with beacons.
**ballast** *m* ballast.
**balle** *f* (*de tennis, golf etc*) ball; (*projectile*) bullet.
**ballerine** *f* ballerina.
**ballet** *m* ballet.
**ballon** *m* (*jouet d'enfant, appareil*) balloon; (*sports*) ball; **b. de football** soccer ball.
**ballot** *m* bundle.
**ballottage** *m* (*scrutin*) second ballot.
**balnéaire** *a* **station b.** beach resort.
**balustrade** *f* (hand)rail.
**bambin** *m* tiny tot.
**bambou** *m* bamboo.
**ban** *m* (*applaudissements*) round of applause; **un (triple) b. pour . . .** three cheers for . . . .
**banane** *f* banana.
**banc** *m* (*siège*) bench; **b. de sable** sandbank.
**bancaire** *a* **compte b.** bank account.
**bandage** *m* bandage.
**bande**[1] *f* (*de terrain, papier etc*) strip; (*de film*) reel; (*rayure*) stripe; (*pansement*) bandage; (*sur la chaussée*) line; **b. (magnétique)** tape; **b. vidéo** videotape; **b. dessinée** comic strip.
**bande**[2] *f* (*groupe*) gang.
**bandeau, -x** *m* (*sur les yeux*) blindfold; (*pour la tête*) headband.
**bander** *vt* (*blessure*) to bandage; (*yeux*) to blindfold.
**banderole** *f* (*sur montants*) banner.
**bandit** *m* robber.
**banlieue** *f* **la b.** the outskirts (of town).
**banque** *f* bank; (*activité*) banking.
**banquette** *f* (*de véhicule, train*) seat.
**banquier** *m* banker.
**banquise** *f* ice floe.
**baptême** *m* christening, baptism.
**baptiser** *vt* (*enfant*) to christen, baptize.
**baquet** *m* tub, basin.
**bar** *m* (*lieu, comptoir*) bar.
**baraque** *f* hut, shack.
**baraquement** *m* (makeshift) huts.
**barbare** *a* (*cruel*) barbaric.
**barbe** *f* beard; **se faire la b.** to shave; **quelle b.!** *Fam* what a bore!
**barbecue** *m* barbecue.
**barbelé** *a* **fil de fer b.** barbed wire.
**barboter** *vi* to splash around.
**barbouillage** *m* smear(ing); (*gribouillage*) scribble, scribbling.
**barbouiller** *vt* (*salir*) to smear; (*gribouiller*) to scribble.
**barbu, -ue** *a* bearded.
**baril** *m* barrel; **b. de poudre** powder keg.
**barman,** *pl* **-men** *ou* **-mans** *m* bartender.
**baromètre** *m* barometer.
**baron** *m* baron.
**baronne** *f* baroness.
**barque** *f* (small) boat.
**barrage** *m* (*sur une route*) roadblock; (*sur un fleuve*) dam.
**barre** *f* bar; (*de bateau*) helm; (*trait*) stroke.
**barreau, -x** *m* (*de fenêtre*) bar; (*d'échelle*) rung.
**barrer** *vt* (*route etc*) to block; (*mot, phrase*) to cross out.
**barrette** *f* barrette.
**barricade** *f* barricade.
**barricader** *vt* to barricade; **se b.** to barricade oneself (in).
**barrière** *f* (*porte*) gate; (*clôture*) fence; (*obstacle*) barrier.
**barrique** *f* (large) barrel.
**bas, basse 1** *a* low. **2** *adv* low; (*parler*) in a whisper; **plus b.** further *ou* lower down. **3** *m* (*de côte, page, mur etc*) bottom; **tiroir**/*etc* **du b.** bottom drawer/*etc*; **en b.** down

(below); (*par l'escalier*) downstairs; **en** *ou* **au b. de** at the bottom of.

**bas** *m* (*chaussette*) stocking.

**bas-côté** *m* roadside, verge, shoulder.

**bascule** *f* weighing machine; (*jeu d'enfant*) seesaw.

**basculer** *vti* to topple over.

**base** *f* base; **bases** (*d'un argument, accord etc*) basis; **salaire de b.** base pay; **à b. de lait/citron** milk-/lemon-based.

**baser** *vt* to base (**sur**, on).

**basket(-ball)** *m* basketball.

**basque** *a* & *mf* Basque.

**basse** *voir* **bas.**

**basse-cour** *f* (*pl* **basses-cours**) farmyard.

**bassin** *m* pond; (*rade*) dock; (*du corps*) pelvis; **b. houiller** coalfield.

**bassine** *f* bowl.

**bataille** *f* battle.

**batailleur, -euse 1** *mf* fighter. **2** *a* fond of fighting, belligerent.

**bateau, -x** *m* boat; (*grand*) ship.

**bâtiment** *m* building; (*navire*) vessel; **le b.** (*industrie*) the construction industry.

**bâtir** *vt* to build; **bien bâti** well-built.

**bâton** *m* stick; (*d'agent*) baton; **b. de rouge** lipstick; **donner des coups de b. à qn** to beat s.o. (with a stick).

**battante** *af* **pluie b.** driving rain.

**battement** *m* beat(ing); (*de paupières*) blink(ing); (*délai*) interval; **b. de cœur** heartbeat.

**batterie** *f* battery; **la b.** (*d'un orchestre*) the drums.

**batteur** *m* (*d'orchestre*) drummer.

**battre* 1** *vt* to beat. **2** *vi* to beat; **b. des mains** to clap (one's hands); **b. des paupières** to blink; **b. des ailes** (*oiseau*) to flap its wings.

**battre (se)** *vpr* to fight.

**bavard, -arde** *a* talkative.

**bavardage** *m* chatting.

**bavarder** *vi* to chat.

**baver** *vi* to drool; **en b.** *Fam* to have a rough time of it.

**bavoir** *m* bib.

**bavure** *f* (*tache*) smudge.

**bazar** *m* (*magasin*) bazaar; (*désordre*) mess.

**beau** (*or* **bel** *before vowel or mute h*), **belle,** *pl* **beaux, belles** *a* beautiful, attractive; (*voyage, temps etc*) fine, lovely; **au b. milieu** right in the middle; **j'ai b. crier**/*etc* it's no use (my) shouting/*etc*.

**beaucoup** *adv* (*lire etc*) a lot; **aimer b.** to like very much *ou* a lot; **b. de** (*livres etc*) many, a lot of; (*courage etc*) a lot of; **pas b. d'argent**/*etc* not much money/*etc*; **j'en ai b.** (*quantité*) I have a lot; (*nombre*) I have lots; **b. plus** much more; many more (**que** than).

**beau-frère** *m* (*pl* **beaux-frères**) brother-in-law.

**beau-père** *m* (*pl* **beaux-pères**) father-in-law.

**beauté** *f* beauty.

**beaux-parents** *mpl* parents-in-law.

**bébé** *m* baby.

**bec** *m* (*d'oiseau*) beak; (*de cruche*) spout; **coup de b.** peck.

**bécane** *f Fam* bike.

**bêche** *f* spade.

**bêcher** *vt* (*cultiver*) to dig.

**becquée** *f* **donner la b. à** (*oiseau*) to feed.

**bedonnant, -ante** *a* potbellied.

**bégayer** *vi* to stutter.

**bègue 1** *mf* stutterer. **2** *a* **être b.** to stutter.

**beige** *a* & *m* beige.

**beignet** *m* (*pâtisserie*) fritter.

**bel** *voir* **beau.**

**bêler** *vi* to bleat.

**belette** *f* weasel.

**belge** *a* & *mf* Belgian.

**belle** *voir* **beau.**

**belle-fille** *f* (*pl* **belles-filles**) (*épouse d'un fils*) daughter-in-law.

**belle-mère** *f* (*pl* **belles-mères**) mother-in-law.

**belle-sœur** *f* (*pl* **belles-sœurs**) sister-in-law.

**belliqueux, -euse** *a* (*agressif*) aggressive.

**bénédiction** *f* blessing.
**bénéfice** *m* (*gain*) profit; (*avantage*) benefit.
**bénéficier** *vi* to benefit (**de** from).
**bénéfique** *a* beneficial.
**bénévole** *a* & *mf* voluntary (worker).
**bénir** *vt* to bless; (*remercier*) to give thanks to.
**bénit, -ite** *a* (*pain*) consecrated; **eau bénite** holy water.
**benjamin, -ine** *mf* youngest child.
**benne** *f* (*de camion*) (movable) container; **camion à b. basculante** dump truck.
**béquille** *f* (*canne*) crutch; (*de moto*) stand.
**berceau, -x** *m* cradle.
**bercer** *vt* (*balancer*) to rock; (*apaiser*) to soothe, lull.
**berceuse** *f* lullaby.
**béret** *m* beret.
**berge** *m* (*rive*) (raised) bank.
**berger** *m* shepherd; **b. allemand** German shepherd.
**bergère** *f* shepherdess.
**bergerie** *f* sheepfold.
**besogne** *f* job, task.
**besoin** *m* need; **avoir b. de** to need.
**bestiole** *f* (*insecte*) bug.
**bétail** *m* livestock.
**bête**[1] *f* animal; (*insecte*) bug; **b. noire** pet peeve.
**bête**[2] *a* stupid.
**bêtement** *adv* stupidly; **tout b.** quite simply.
**bêtise** *f* stupidity; (*action, parole*) stupid thing.
**béton** *m* concrete; **mur**/*etc* **en b.** concrete wall/*etc*.
**betterave** *f* beet.
**beurre** *m* butter.
**beurrer** *vt* to butter.
**beurrier** *m* butter dish.
**bibelot** *m* (small) ornament, trinket.
**biberon** *m* (feeding) bottle.
**bible** *f* bible; **la B.** the Bible.
**bibliothécaire** *mf* librarian.
**bibliothèque** *f* library; (*meuble*) bookcase.
**bic**® *m* ballpoint.
**biceps** *m* (*muscle*) biceps.
**biche** *f* doe.
**bicyclette** *f* bicycle.
**bidon 1** *m* (jerry) can. **2** *a inv Fam* phoney.
**bidonville** *m* shantytown.
**bidule** *m* (*chose*) *Fam* whatchamacallit.
**bien 1** *adv* well; **b. fatigué/souvent**/*etc* (*très*) very tired/often/*etc*; **merci b.!** thanks very much!; **b.!** fine!, right!; **b. des fois/des gens**/*etc* lots of *ou* many times/people/*etc*; **je l'ai b. dit** (*intensif*) I *did* say so; **tu as b. fait** you did right; **c'est b. fait (pour lui)** it serves him right. **2** *a inv* (*convenable, compétent etc*) fine. **3** *m* (*avantage*) good; (*chose*) possession; **ça te fera du b.** it will do you good; **pour ton b.** for your own good; **le b. et le mal** good and evil.
**bien-être** *m* wellbeing.
**bienfaisant, -ante** *a* beneficial.
**bien que** *conj* (+ *subjonctif*) although.
**bientôt** *adv* soon; **à b.!** see you soon!; **il est b. midi**/*etc* it's nearly twelve/*etc*.
**bienvenu, -ue 1** *a* welcome. **2** *f* welcome; **souhaiter la bienvenue à** to welcome.
**bière** *f* beer; **b. pression** draft beer.
**bifteck** *m* steak.
**bifurcation** *f* (*route etc*) fork.
**bifurquer** *vi* to fork.
**bigoudi** *m* (hair) roller.
**bijou, -x** *m* jewel.
**bijouterie** *f* (*commerce*) jewelry store, jeweler's.
**bijoutier, -ière** *mf* jeweler.
**bilan** *m* (*financier*) balance sheet; (*résultat*) outcome; (*d'un accident*) (casualty) toll; **b. de santé** checkup; **déposer le b.** to file for bankruptcy.
**bile** *f* bile; **se faire de la b.** *Fam* to worry.
**bilingue** *a* bilingual.
**billard** *m* (*jeu*) billiards; (*table*) billiard table.

**bille** *f* (*d'enfant*) marble; **stylo à b.** ballpoint (pen).
**billet** *m* ticket; **b. (de banque)** bill; **b. aller, b. simple** one-way ticket; **b. (d')aller et retour** round trip ticket.
**biologique** *a* biological; (*légumes etc*) organic.
**bip(-bip)** *m* beeper.
**biscotte** *f* Melba toast.
**biscuit** *m* cookie.
**bison** *m* (American) buffalo.
**bissextile** *af* **année b.** leap year.
**bistouri** *m* scalpel.
**bitume** *m* (*revêtement*) asphalt.
**bizarre** *a* peculiar, odd.
**blague** *f* (*plaisanterie, farce*) joke; **b. à part** seriously.
**blaguer** *vi* to be joking.
**blâmer** *vt* to criticize, blame.
**blanc, blanche 1** *a* white; (*page*) blank. **2** *mf* (*personne*) white man *ou* woman. **3** *m* (*couleur*) white; (*de poulet*) breast; (*espace*) blank; **b. (d'œuf)** (egg) white; **laisser en b.** to leave blank; **chèque en b.** blank check; **donner carte blanche à qn** to give s.o. free rein.
**blancheur** *f* whiteness.
**blanchir** *vi* to turn white.
**blanchisserie** *f* (*lieu*) laundry.
**blé** *m* wheat.
**blessant, -ante** *a* hurtful.
**blessé, -ée** *mf* casualty.
**blesser** *vt* to injure, hurt; (*avec un couteau, une balle etc*) to wound; (*offenser*) to hurt; **se b. le** *ou* **au bras**/*etc* to hurt one's arm/*etc*.
**blessure** *f* injury; wound.
**bleu, -e 1** *a* (*mpl* **bleus**) blue. **2** *m* (*pl* **-s**) (*couleur*) blue; (*contusion*) bruise; (*vêtement*) overalls.
**blindé, -ée** *a* (*voiture etc*) armoured; **porte blindée** reinforced steel door; **une vitre blindée** bulletproof glass.
**bloc** *m* block; (*de papier*) pad; **à b.** (*visser etc*) tight.
**bloc-notes** *m* (*pl* **blocs-notes**) writing pad.
**blond, -onde 1** *a* fair(-haired), blond. **2** *mf* fair-haired *ou* blond man *ou* woman; **(bière) blonde** lager.
**bloquer** *vt* (*obstruer*) to block; (*coincer*) to jam; (*roue*) to lock; (*prix*) to freeze.
**bloquer (se)** *vpr* to jam; (*roue*) to lock.
**blottir (se)** *vpr* to crouch; (*dans son lit*) to snuggle in; **se b. contre** to snuggle up to.
**blouse** *f* (*tablier*) smock.
**blouson** *m* windbreaker.
**blue-jean** *m* jeans.
**bobine** *f* reel, spool.
**bocal, -aux** *m* glass jar; (*à poissons*) bowl.
**bœuf,** *pl* **-fs** *m* ox (*pl* oxen); (*viande*) beef.
**boire*** *vti* to drink; **offrir à b. à qn** to offer s.o. a drink.
**bois** *m* wood; (*de construction*) timber; **en** *ou* **de b.** wooden; **b. de chauffage** firewood.
**boisé, -ée** *a* wooded.
**boisson** *f* drink.
**boîte** *f* box; (*de conserve*) can; **b. aux** *ou* **à lettres** mailbox.
**boiter** *vi* to limp.
**boîtier** *m* (*de montre*) case.
**bol** *m* bowl; **un b. d'air** a breath of fresh air.
**bombardement** *m* bombing; shelling.
**bombarder** *vt* to bomb; (*avec des obus*) to shell.
**bombe** *f* bomb; (*de laque etc*) spray.
**bon, bonne** *a* good; (*qui convient*) right; (*apte*) fit; **b. anniversaire!** happy birthday!; **le b. choix/moment** the right choice/time; **b. à manger** fit to eat; **c'est b. à savoir** it's worth knowing; **croire b. de** to think it wise to; **b. en français**/*etc* good at French/*etc*; **un b. moment** (*intensif*) a good while; **pour de b.** really (and truly); **ah b.?** is that so?
**bon** *m* (*billet*) coupon, voucher.
**bonbon** *m* candy.
**bond** *m* leap.
**bondé, -ée** *a* packed.

**bondir** *vi* to leap.
**bonheur** *m* happiness; (*chance*) good luck; **par b.** luckily.
**bonhomme,** *pl* **bonshommes** *m* fellow; **b. de neige** snowman.
**bonjour** *m* & *int* good morning; (*après-midi*) good afternoon; **donner le b. à, dire b. à** to say hello to.
**bonne**[1] *voir* **bon**.
**bonne**[2] *f* maid.
**bonnet** *m* (*de ski etc*) cap; (*de femme, d'enfant*) bonnet, hat.
**bonsoir** *m* & *int* (*en rencontrant qn*) good evening; (*en quittant qn*) goodbye; (*au coucher*) good night.
**bonté** *f* kindness.
**bord** *m* (*rebord*) edge; (*rive*) bank; **au b. de la mer**/at the beach; **au b. de la route** by the roadside; **b. du trottoir** curb; **à bord (de)** (*avion, bateau*) on board.
**border** *vt* (*vêtement*) to edge; (*lit, personne*) to tuck in; **b. la rue**/*etc* (*maisons, arbres*) to line the street/*etc*.
**bordure** *f* border.
**borne** *f* boundary mark; **b. kilométrique** = milestone.
**bosse** *f* (*dans le dos*) hump; (*enflure, de terrain*) bump.
**bosser** *vi Fam* to work (hard).
**bossu, -ue 1** *a* hunchbacked. **2** *mf* hunchback.
**botte** *f* (*chaussure*) boot; (*de fleurs etc*) bunch.
**bottine** *f* (ankle) boot.
**bouc** *m* billy goat; (*barbe*) goatee.
**bouche** *f* mouth; **b. de métro** métro entrance; **b. d'égout** drain opening.
**bouchée** *f* mouthful.
**boucher**[1] *vt* (*évier, nez etc*) to stop up; (*bouteille*) to cork; (*vue, rue etc*) to block; **se b. le nez** to hold one's nose.
**boucher**[2] *m* butcher.
**boucherie** *f* butcher's (shop).
**bouchon** *m* stopper; (*de liège*) cork; (*de tube, bidon*) cap; (*embouteillage*) traffic jam.
**boucle** *f* (*de ceinture*) buckle; **b. d'oreille** earring; **b. (de cheveux)** curl.
**bouclé, -ée** *a* (*cheveux*) curly.
**boucler 1** *vt* (*attacher*) to fasten; (*cheveux*) to curl. **2** *vi* to be curly.
**bouclier** *m* shield.
**bouder** *vi* to sulk.
**boudin** *m* blood sausage.
**boue** *f* mud.
**bouée** *f* buoy; **b. de sauvetage** lifebuoy.
**boueux, -euse** *a* muddy.
**bouffée** *f* (*de fumée*) puff.
**bougeoir** *m* candlestick.
**bouger** *vti* to move.
**bougie** *f* candle; (*d'automobile*) spark plug.
**bouillie** *f* porridge.
**bouillir*** *vi* to boil.
**bouilloire** *f* kettle.
**bouillon** *m* (*aliment*) broth; (*bulles*) bubbles.
**bouillonner** *vi* to bubble.
**boulanger, -ère** *mf* baker.
**boulangerie** *f* baker's (shop).
**boule** *f* ball; **boules** (French) bowling game; **b. de neige** snowball.
**bouleau, -x** *m* (silver) birch.
**bouledogue** *m* bulldog.
**boulet** *m* **b. de canon** cannonball.
**boulette** *f* (*de papier*) ball; (*de viande*) meatball.
**boulevard** *m* boulevard.
**bouleversement** *m* upheaval.
**bouleverser** *vt* (*déranger*) to turn upside down; (*émouvoir*) to upset (greatly).
**boulon** *m* bolt.
**bouquet** *m* (*de fleurs*) bunch.
**bouquin** *m Fam* book.
**bourdon** *m* (*insecte*) bumblebee.
**bourdonnement** *m* buzzing.
**bourdonner** *vi* to buzz.
**bourg** *m* (small) market town.
**bourgeois, -oise** *a* & *mf* middle-class (person).
**bourgeon** *m* bud.
**bourgeonner** *vi* to bud.
**bourrasque** *f* squall, gust of wind.
**bourrer** *vt* to stuff, cram (**de** with); (*pipe*) to fill.
**bourse** *f* (*sac*) purse; (*d'études*)

grant, scholarship; **la B.** the Stock Exchange.

**bousculade** *f* jostling.

**bousculer** *vt* (*heurter, pousser*) to jostle.

**boussole** *f* compass.

**bout** *m* end; (*de langue, canne, doigt*) tip; (*de papier, pain, ficelle*) piece; **un b. de temps** a little while; **au b. d'un moment** after a moment; **à b.** exhausted; **à b. de souffle** out of breath.

**bouteille** *f* bottle; (*de gaz*) cylinder.

**boutique** *f* shop.

**bouton** *m* (*bourgeon*) bud; (*au visage etc*) pimple; (*de vêtement*) button; (*poussoir*) (push-)button; (*de porte, télévision*) knob.

**bouton-d'or** *m* (*pl* **boutons-d'or**) buttercup.

**boutonner** *vt,* **se boutonner** *vpr* to button (up).

**boutonnière** *f* buttonhole.

**bouton-pression** *m* (*pl* **boutons-pression**) snap (fastener).

**box,** *pl* **boxes** *m* (*garage*) garage facility; (*de cheval*) stall; (*au bureau*) cubicle.

**boxe** *f* boxing.

**boxer** *vi* to box.

**boxeur** *m* boxer.

**boycotter** *vt* to boycott.

**bracelet** *m* bracelet; (*de montre*) strap, band.

**braconner** *vi* to poach.

**braconnier** *m* poacher.

**braguette** *f* (*de pantalon*) fly.

**brailler** *vti* to bawl.

**braise(s)** *f* (*pl*) embers.

**brancard** *m* (*civière*) stretcher.

**branchages** *mpl* (cut) branches.

**branche** *f* (*d'arbre*) branch; (*de compas*) arm, leg.

**branchement** *m* connection.

**brancher** *vt* to plug in.

**brandir** *vt* to flourish.

**branlant, -ante** *a* (*table etc*) wobbly, shaky.

**braquer 1** *vt* (*arme etc*) to point (**sur** at). **2** *vi* to turn the steering wheel, steer.

**bras** *m* arm; **b. dessus b. dessous** arm in arm; **à b. ouverts** with open arms.

**brasier** *m* blaze.

**brassard** *m* armband.

**brasse** *f* (*nage*) breaststroke.

**brasserie** *f* (*usine*) brewery; (*café*) brasserie.

**brassière** *f* (*de bébé*) undershirt.

**brave** *a* & *m* brave (man).

**bravement** *adv* bravely.

**bravo 1** *int* bravo. **2** *m* cheer.

**bravoure** *f* bravery.

**brebis** *f* ewe.

**brèche** *f* gap.

**bredouille** *a* **rentrer b.** to come back empty-handed.

**bref, brève 1** *a* brief, short. **2** *adv* **(enfin) b.** in a word.

**bretelle** *f* strap; (*d'accès*) access road; **bretelles** (*pour pantalon*) suspenders.

**breton, -onne** *a* & *mf* Breton.

**brevet** *m* diploma; **b. (des collèges)** = exam at end of junior high school; **b. (d'invention)** patent.

**bricolage** *m* (*passe-temps*) do-it-yourself.

**bricoler 1** *vi* to do odd jobs. **2** *vt* (*fabriquer*) to put together.

**bricoleur, -euse** *mf* handyman, handywoman.

**bride** *f* bridle.

**brider** *vt* to hold in *ou* back.

**bridés** *a* **avoir les yeux bridés** to have slit eyes.

**brièvement** *adv* briefly.

**brièveté** *f* shortness, brevity.

**brigand** *m* robber; (*enfant*) rascal.

**brillamment** *adv* brilliantly.

**brillant, -ante 1** *a* (*luisant*) shining; (*astiqué*) shiny; (*couleur*) bright; (*doué*) brilliant. **2** *m* shine; (*couleur*) brightness.

**briller** *vi* to shine; **faire b.** (*meuble*) to polish (up).

**brin** *m* (*d'herbe*) blade; (*de corde, fil*) strand; (*de muguet*) spray.

**brindille** *f* twig.

**brioche** *f* brioche (*light sweet bun*).

**brique** *f* brick; (*de lait, jus de fruit*) carton.
**briquet** *m* (cigarette) lighter.
**brise** *f* breeze.
**briser** *vt,* **se briser** *vpr* to break.
**britannique 1** *a* British. **2** *mf* Briton; **les Britanniques** the British.
**broc** *m* pitcher, jug.
**brocanteur, -euse** *mf* second-hand dealer (*in furniture etc*).
**broche** *f* (*pour rôtir*) spit; (*bijou*) brooch.
**brochet** *m* pike.
**brochette** *f* (*tige*) skewer; (*plat*) kebab.
**brochure** *f* brochure, booklet.
**broder** *vt* to embroider (**de** with).
**broderie** *f* embroidery.
**bronchite** *f* bronchitis.
**bronzage** *m* (sun)tan.
**bronze** *m* bronze.
**bronzer 1** *vt* to tan; **se (faire) b.** to sunbathe, get a (sun)tan. **2** *vi* to get (sun)tanned.
**brosse** *f* brush; **b. à dents** toothbrush.
**brosser** *vt* to brush; **se b. les dents/cheveux** to brush one's teeth/hair.
**brouette** *f* wheelbarrow.
**brouhaha** *m* hubbub.
**brouillard** *m* fog; **il y a du b.** it's foggy.
**brouiller** *vt* (*œufs*) to scramble; **b. la vue à qn** to blur s.o.'s vision.
**brouiller (se)** *vpr* (*temps*) to cloud over; (*vue*) to get blurred; (*amis*) to fall out (**avec** with).
**brouillon** *m* rough draft.
**broussailles** *fpl* bushes.
**brousse** *f* **la b.** the bush.
**brouter** *vti* to graze.
**broyer** *vt* to grind.
**bruit** *m* noise, sound; (*nouvelle*) rumor; **faire du b.** to make noise.
**brûlant, -ante** *a* (*objet, soleil*) burning (hot).
**brûlé** *m* **odeur de b.** smell of burning.
**brûler** *vti* to burn; **se b.** to burn oneself; **b. un feu (rouge)** to go through the lights.
**brûlure** *f* burn.
**brume** *f* mist, haze.
**brumeux, -euse** *a* misty, hazy.
**brun, brune 1** *a* brown; (*cheveux*) dark, brown; (*personne*) dark-haired. **2** *m* (*couleur*) brown. **3** *mf* dark-haired person.
**brunir** *vi* to turn brown; (*cheveux*) to get darker.
**brushing** *m* blow-dry.
**brusque** *a* (*manière, personne*) abrupt; (*subit*) sudden.
**brusquement** *adv* suddenly.
**brusquerie** *f* abruptness.
**brut** *a* (*pétrole*) crude; (*poids, salaire*) gross.
**brutal, -e, -aux** *a* (*violent*) brutal; (*enfant*) rough.
**brutaliser** *vt* to ill-treat.
**brutalité** *f* brutality.
**brute** *f* brute.
**bruyamment** *adv* noisily.
**bruyant, -ante** *a* noisy.
**bu, bue** *pp of* **boire**.
**bûche** *f* log.
**bûcheron** *m* lumberjack.
**budget** *m* budget.
**buée** *f* mist.
**buffet** *m* (*armoire*) sideboard; (*table, repas*) buffet.
**buisson** *m* bush.
**bulldozer** *m* bulldozer.
**bulle** *f* bubble; (*de B. D.*) balloon.
**bulletin** *m* (*météo*) report; (*scolaire*) report card; **b. de paie** pay slip; **b. de vote** ballot paper.
**bureau, -x** *m* (*table*) desk; (*lieu*) office; **b. de change** foreign exchange office, bureau de change; **b. de tabac** tobacco store.
**burette** *f* oilcan.
**bus** *m Fam* bus.
**but** *m* (*objectif*) aim, goal; *Football* goal.
**buter** *vi* **b. contre** to stumble over.
**butoir** *m* (*de porte*) stop(per).
**butte** *f* mound.
**buvard** *m* blotting paper.

**buvette** *f* refreshment bar.
**buveur, -euse** *mf* drinker.

# C

**ça** *pron dém* (*abrév de* **cela**) (*pour désigner*) that; (*plus près*) this; (*sujet indéfini*) it, that; **ça m'amuse que . . .** it amuses me that . . . ; **où/quand/comment/***etc* **ça?** where?/when?/how?/*etc*; **ça va (bien)?** how's it going?; **ça va!** fine!, OK!; **ça alors!** (*surprise, indignation*) I'll be!, how about that!; **c'est ça** that's right.
**cabane** *f* hut, cabin; (*à outils*) shed; (*à lapins*) hutch.
**cabine** *f* (*de bateau*) cabin; (*téléphonique*) phone booth *ou* box; (*à la piscine*) cubicle; **c. (de pilotage)** cockpit; (*d'un grand avion*) flight deck; **c. d'essayage** fitting room.
**cabinet** *m* (*de médecin*) office; (*de ministre*) department; **cabinets** (*toilettes*) toilet, lavatory; **c. de toilette** (small) bathroom; **c. de travail** study.
**câble** *m* cable; (*cordage*) rope; **la télévision par c.** cable television.
**cabosser** *vt* to dent.
**cabrer (se)** *vpr* (*cheval*) to rear (up).
**cacah(o)uète** *f* peanut.
**cacao** *m* cocoa.
**cachalot** *m* sperm whale.
**cache-cache** *m inv* hide-and-seek.
**cache-nez** *m inv* scarf, muffler.
**cacher** *vt* to hide (**à** from); **je ne cache pas que . . .** I don't hide the fact that . . .
**cacher (se)** *vpr* to hide.
**cachet** *m* (*de la poste*) postmark; (*comprimé*) tablet.
**cacheter** *vt* to seal.
**cachette** *f* hiding place; **en c.** in secret.
**cachot** *m* dungeon.
**cactus** *m* cactus.
**cadavre** *m* corpse.
**caddie®** *m* (supermarket) cart.
**cadeau, -x** *m* present, gift.
**cadenas** *m* padlock.
**cadence** *f* (*vitesse*) rate; **en c.** in time.
**cadet, -ette 1** *a* (*de deux frères etc*) younger; (*de plus de deux*) youngest. **2** *mf* younger (child); youngest (child); (*sportif*) junior.
**cadran** *m* (*de téléphone*) dial; (*de montre*) face.
**cadre** *m* (*de photo, vélo etc*) frame; (*décor*) setting; (*sur un imprimé*) box; (*chef*) executive, manager.
**cafard** *m* **avoir le c.** to be in the dumps; **ça me donne le c.** it depresses me.
**café** *m* coffee; (*bar*) café; **c. au lait, c. crème** coffee with milk; **c. noir, c. nature** black coffee; **c. soluble** *ou* **instantané** instant coffee; **tasse de c.** cup of black coffee.
**cafétéria** *f* cafeteria.
**cafetière** *f* coffeepot; (*électrique*) percolator.
**cage** *f* cage; (*d'escalier*) well; *Sport* goal (area).
**cageot** *m* crate, box.
**cagoule** *f* ski mask; (*de bandit, moine*) hood.
**cahier** *m* exercise book; **c. de brouillon** scratch pad; **c. d'appel** roll (*in school*).
**cahot** *m* jolt, bump.
**cailler** *vti* (*sang*) to clot; (*lait*) to curdle; **faire c.** (*lait*) to curdle.
**caillot** *m* (blood) clot.
**caillou, -x** *m* stone.
**caisse** *f* case, box; (*guichet*) cash desk; (*de supermarché*) checkout; (*tambour*) drum; **c. (enregistreuse)** till, cash register; **c. d'épargne** savings bank.
**caissier, -ière** *mf* cashier; (*de supermarché*) checkout assistant.
**cake** *m* fruit cake.
**calcaire** *a* (*eau*) hard.
**calciné, -ée** *a* charred.
**calcul** *m* calculation; (*discipline*) arithmetic.
**calculatrice** *f* calculator.

**calculer** *vt* to calculate.
**cale** *f* (*pour maintenir*) wedge; (*de bateau*) hold.
**caleçon** *m* underpants; **c. de bain** bathing trunks.
**calendrier** *m* calendar.
**caler 1** *vt* (*meuble etc*) to wedge; (*appuyer*) to prop (up). **2** *vti* (*moteur*) to stall.
**calfeutrer** *vt* to draftproof; **se c. (chez soi)** to shut oneself away.
**calibre** *m* (*diamètre*) caliber; (*d'œuf*) grade.
**califourchon (à)** *adv* astride; **se mettre à c. sur** to straddle.
**câlin, -ine 1** *a* affectionate. **2** *m* cuddle.
**calmant** *m* (*pour la nervosité*) sedative; (*la douleur*) painkiller; **sous calmants** under sedation; on painkillers.
**calme 1** *a* calm. **2** *m* calm(ness); **du c.!** keep quiet!; (*pas de panique*) keep calm!; **dans le c.** (*travailler, étudier*) in peace and quiet.
**calmer** *vt* (*douleur*) to soothe; (*inquiétude*) to calm; **c. qn** to calm s.o. (down).
**calmer (se)** *vpr* to calm down.
**calorie** *f* calorie.
**calque** *m* (*dessin*) tracing; **(papier-)c.** tracing paper.
**camarade** *mf* friend; **c. de jeu** playmate.
**camaraderie** *f* friendship.
**cambouis** *m* (dirty) oil.
**cambriolage** *m* burglary.
**cambrioler** *vt* to burglarize.
**cambrioleur, -euse** *mf* burglar.
**camelote** *f* junk.
**camembert** *m* Camembert (cheese).
**caméra** *f* (TV *ou* film) camera.
**caméscope** *m* camcorder.
**camion** *m* truck.
**camion-benne** *m* (*pl* **camions-bennes**) garbage truck.
**camionnette** *f* van.
**camp** *m* camp; **feu de c.** campfire; **lit de c.** camp bed; **dans mon c.** (*jeu*) on my side.
**campagnard, -arde** *mf* countryman, countrywoman.
**campagne** *f* country(side); (*électorale, militaire etc*) campaign; **à la c.** in the country.
**camper** *vi* to camp.
**campeur, -euse** *mf* camper.
**camping** *m* camping; (*terrain*) camp(ing) site.
**camping-car** *m* camper.
**canadien, -ienne** *a* & *mf* Canadian.
**canal, -aux** *m* (*pour bateaux*) canal.
**canalisation** *f* (*de gaz etc*) mains.
**canaliser** *vt* (*foule*) to channel.
**canapé** *m* (*siège*) sofa, couch, settee.
**canard** *m* duck.
**canari** *m* canary.
**cancer** *m* cancer.
**cancéreux, -euse** *mf* cancer patient.
**candidat, -ate** *mf* candidate; **être** *ou* **se porter c. à** to apply for.
**candidature** *f* application; (*aux élections*) candidacy; **poser sa c.** to apply (**à** for).
**cane** *f* (female) duck.
**caneton** *m* duckling.
**canette** *f* (*de bière*) (small) bottle.
**caniche** *m* poodle.
**canif** *m* penknife.
**canine** *f* canine (tooth).
**caniveau, -x** *m* gutter (*in street*).
**canne** *f* (walking) stick; **c. à pêche** fishing rod.
**cannibale** *mf* cannibal.
**canoë** *m* canoe; (*sport*) canoeing.
**canon** *m* (big) gun; (*de fusil etc*) barrel.
**canot** *m* boat; **c. de sauvetage** lifeboat; **c. pneumatique** rubber dinghy.
**canoter** *vi* to go boating.
**cantine** *f* canteen; (*à l'école*) cafeteria.
**cantique** *m* hymn.
**cantonnier** *m* road mender.
**caoutchouc** *m* rubber; **balle**/*etc* **en c.** rubber ball/*etc*.

**CAP** *m abrév* (*certificat d'aptitude professionnelle*) technical and vocational diploma.
**cap** *m* (*pointe de terre*) cape; (*direction*) course; **mettre le c. sur** to steer a course for.
**capable** *a* capable, able; **c. de faire** able to do, capable of doing.
**capacité** *f* ability; (*contenance*) capacity.
**cape** *f* cape; (*grande*) cloak.
**capitaine** *m* captain.
**capital** *m* (*argent*) capital.
**capitale** *f* (*lettre, ville*) capital.
**capitulation** *f* surrender.
**capituler** *vi* to surrender.
**capot** *m* (*de véhicule*) hood.
**capote** *f* (*de véhicule*) (convertible) top.
**caprice** *m* (passing) whim.
**capricieux, -euse** *a* temperamental.
**capsule** *f* (*spatiale*) capsule; (*de bouteille*) cap.
**capter** *vt* (*signal, radio*) to pick up.
**captiver** *vt* to fascinate.
**capture** *f* capture.
**capturer** *vt* to capture.
**capuche** *f* hood.
**capuchon** *m* hood; (*de stylo*) cap.
**car 1** *conj* because, for. **2** *m* bus, coach; **c. de police** police van.
**carabine** *f* rifle; **c. à air comprimé** airgun.
**caractère**[1] *m* (*lettre*) character; **petits caractères** small letters; **caractères d'imprimerie** capitals.
**caractere**[2] *m* (*tempérament, nature*) character; **avoir bon c.** to be good-natured.
**caractéristique** *a* & *f* characteristic.
**carafe** *f* decanter.
**carambolage** *m* pileup (*of vehicles*).
**caramel** *m* caramel; (*bonbon dur*) taffy.
**carapace** *f* shell.
**caravane** *f* (*pour camper*) trailer.
**carbone** *m* **(papier) c.** carbon (paper).
**carboniser** *vt* to burn (to ashes).
**carburant** *m* fuel.
**carburateur** *m* carburetor.
**carcasse** *f* carcass; (*d'immeuble etc*) frame, shell.
**cardiaque** *a* **être c.** to have a weak heart; **crise/problème c.** heart attack/trouble.
**cardinal, -aux 1** *a* (*nombre, point*) cardinal. **2** *m* cardinal.
**caressant, -ante** *a* loving.
**caresse** *f* caress.
**caresser** *vt* to stroke.
**cargaison** *f* cargo.
**cargo** *m* cargo boat.
**carie** *f* **la c. (dentaire)** tooth decay; **une c.** a cavity.
**cariée** *af* **dent c.** decayed *ou* bad tooth.
**carillon** *m* (*cloches*) chimes; (*horloge*) chiming clock.
**carlingue** *f* (*d'avion*) cabin.
**carnaval,** *pl* **-als** *m* carnival.
**carnet** *m* notebook; (*de timbres, chèques, adresses*) book; **c. de notes** report card.
**carotte** *f* carrot.
**carpe** *f* carp.
**carpette** *f* rug.
**carré, -ée** *a* & *m* square.
**carreau, -x** *m* (*vitre*) (window) pane; (*pavé*) tile; *Cartes* (*couleur*) diamonds; **à carreaux** (*nappe etc*) check.
**carrefour** *m* crossroads.
**carrelage** *m* (*sol*) tiled floor.
**carrément** *adv* (*dire etc*) bluntly; (*complètement*) downright.
**carrière** *f* (*terrain*) quarry; (*métier*) career.
**carrosse** *m* (horse-drawn) carriage.
**carrosserie** *f* body(work).
**carrure** *f* build.
**cartable** *m* satchel.
**carte** *f* card; (*routière*) map; (*menu*) menu; **c. (postale)** (post)card; **c. à jouer** playing card; **jouer aux cartes** to play cards; **c. de visite** business card; **c. de crédit** credit card; **c. des vins** wine list; **c. grise** vehicle registration document.

**carton** *m* cardboard; (*boîte*) cardboard box.
**cartonné** *a* **livre c.** hardback.
**cartouche** *f* cartridge; (*de cigarettes*) carton.
**cas** *m* case; **en tout c.** in any case; **en aucun c.** on no account; **en c. de besoin** if need be; **en c. d'accident** in the event of an accident; **en c. d'urgence** in an emergency; **au c. où elle tomberait** if she should fall; **pour le c. où il pleuvrait** in case it rains.
**cascade** *f* waterfall; (*de cinéma*) stunt.
**cascadeur, -euse** *mf* stunt man, stunt woman.
**case** *f* pigeonhole; (*de tiroir*) compartment; (*d'échiquier etc*) square; (*de formulaire*) box; (*hutte*) hut, cabin.
**caserne** *f* barracks; **c. de pompiers** fire station.
**casier** *m* pigeonhole; (*fermant à clef*) locker; **c. à bouteilles/à disques** bottle/record rack; **c. judiciaire** criminal record.
**casino** *m* casino.
**casque** *m* helmet; (*de coiffeur*) (hair) dryer; **c. (à écouteurs)** headphones.
**casqué, -ée** *a* helmeted.
**casquette** *f* (*coiffure*) cap.
**casse-croûte** *m inv* snack.
**casse-noisettes** *m inv*, **casse-noix** *m inv* nut-cracker(s).
**casse-pieds** *mf inv* (*personne*) *Fam* pain in the neck.
**casser 1** *vt* to break; (*noix*) to crack; **elle me casse les pieds** *Fam* she's getting on my nerves. **2** *vi*, **se casser** *vpr* to break; **se c. la figure** (*tomber*) *Fam* to take a spill.
**casserole** *f* (sauce)pan.
**cassette** *f* (*audio*) cassette *f*; (*vidéo*) video, cassette; **sur c.** (*film*) on video.
**cassis** *m* (*fruit*) blackcurrant; (*obstacle*) dip (*across road*).
**castor** *m* beaver.
**catalogue** *m* catalog.
**catastrophe** *f* disaster; **atterrir en c.** to make an emergency landing.
**catastrophique** *a* disastrous.
**catch** *m* (all-in) wrestling.
**catcheur, -euse** *mf* wrestler.
**catéchisme** *m* catechism.
**catégorie** *f* category.
**cathédrale** *f* cathedral.
**catholique** *a* & *mf* Catholic.
**cauchemar** *m* nightmare.
**cause** *f* cause; **à c. de** because of, on account of.
**causer 1** *vt* (*provoquer*) to cause. **2** *vi* (*bavarder*) to chat (**de** about).
**cavalier, -ière** *mf* rider; (*pour danser*) partner.
**cave** *f* cellar.
**caveau, -x** *m* (burial) vault.
**caverne** *f* cave.
**cavité** *f* hollow.
**CCP** *m abrév* (*compte chèque postal*) Post Office checking account.
**ce**[1] (**c'** *before e and é*) *pron dém* it, that; **c'est toi/bon**/*etc* it's *ou* that's you/good/*etc*; **c'est mon médecin** he's my doctor; **ce sont eux qui . . .** they are the ones who . . . ; **c'est à elle de jouer** it's her turn to play; **est-ce que tu viens?** are you coming? ▪ **ce que, ce qui** what; **je sais ce qui est bon/ce que tu veux** I know what is good/what you want; **ce que c'est beau!** how beautiful it is!, it's so beautiful!
**ce**[2], **cette**, *pl* **ces** (**ce** *becomes* **cet** *before a vowel or mute h*) *a dém* this, that, *pl* these, those; (+ *-ci*) this, *pl* these; (+ *-là*) that, *pl* those; **cet homme** this *ou* that man; **cet homme-ci** this man; **cet homme-là** that man.
**ceci** *pron dém* this.
**céder 1** *vt* to give up (**à** to). **2** *vi* (*personne*) to give in (**à** to); (*branche, chaise etc*) to give way.
**cédille** *f Grammaire* cedilla.
**ceinture** *f* belt; (*taille*) waist; **c. de sécurité** seatbelt; **c. de sauvetage** life preserver.

**cela** *pron dém* (*pour désigner*) that; (*sujet indéfini*) it, that; **c. m'attriste que . . .** it saddens me that . . . ; **quand/comment/***etc* **c.?** when?/how?/*etc*.

**célèbre** *a* famous.

**célébrer** *vt* to celebrate.

**célébrité** *f* fame.

**céleri** *m* (*en branches*) celery.

**célibataire 1** *a* single, unmarried. **2** *m* bachelor. **3** *f* unmarried woman.

**cellophane®** *f* cellophane®.

**cellule** *f* cell.

**celui, celle,** *pl* **ceux, celles** *pron dém* the one, *pl* those, the ones; **c. de Jean** John's (one); **ceux de Jean** John's (ones). ▪ (+ *-ci*) this one, *pl* these (*ones*); (*dont on vient de parler*) the latter; (+ *-là*) that one, *pl* those (ones); the former; **ceux-ci sont gros** these (ones) are big.

**cendre** *f* ash.

**cendrier** *m* ashtray.

**cent** *a* & *m* hundred; **c. pages** a *ou* one hundred pages; **cinq pour c.** five percent.

**centaine** *f* **une c.** a hundred (or so); **des centaines de** hundreds of.

**centième** *a* & *mf* hundredth.

**centigrade** *a* centigrade.

**centime** *m* centime.

**centimètre** *m* centimeter; (*ruban*) tape measure.

**central, -e, -aux 1** *a* central. **2** *m* **c. (téléphonique)** (telephone) exchange.

**centrale** *f* (*usine*) power plant.

**centre** *m* center; **c. commercial** shopping center *ou* mall.

**centre-ville** *m inv* downtown area.

**cependant** *conj* however, yet.

**céramique** *f* (*matière*) ceramic; **de c.** ceramic.

**cerceau, -x** *m* hoop.

**cercle** *m* circle.

**cercueil** *m* coffin.

**céréale** *f* cereal.

**cérémonie** *f* ceremony.

**cerf** *m* deer *inv*.

**cerf-volant** *m* (*pl* **cerfs-volants**) kite.

**cerise** *f* cherry.

**cerisier** *m* cherry tree.

**cerner** *vt* to surround; **avoir les yeux cernés** to have rings under one's eyes.

**certain[1], -aine** *a* (*sûr*) certain, sure; **c'est c. que tu réussiras** you're certain *ou* sure to succeed; **je suis c. de réussir** I'm certain *ou* sure I'll succeed; **être c. de qch** to be certain *ou* sure of sth.

**certain[2], -aine** *a* (*difficile à fixer*) certain; **un c. temps** a certain (amount of) time.

**certainement** *adv* certainly.

**certains** *pron pl* some (people).

**certificat** *m* certificate.

**certifier** *vt* to certify.

**certitude** *f* certainty; **avoir la c. que** to be certain that.

**cerveau, -x** *m* brain; **rhume de c.** head cold.

**cervelle** *f* brain; (*plat*) brains.

**ces** *voir* **ce[2]**.

**CES** *m abrév* (*collège d'enseignement secondaire*) = (junior) high school.

**cesse** *f* **sans c.** constantly.

**cesser** *vti* to stop; **faire c.** to put a stop to; **il ne cesse (pas) de parler** he doesn't stop talking.

**cessez-le-feu** *m inv* ceasefire.

**c'est-à-dire** *conj* that is (to say).

**cet, cette** *voir* **ce[2]**.

**ceux** *voir* **celui**.

**chacun, -une** *pron* each (one), every one; (*tout le monde*) everyone.

**chagrin** *m* grief; **avoir du c.** to be very upset.

**chahut** *m* racket.

**chahuter** *vi* to create a racket.

**chahuteur, -euse** *mf* rowdy.

**chaîne** *f* chain; (*de télévision*) channel; (*de montagnes*) chain, range; **travail à la c.** assembly-line work; **c. hi-fi** hi-fi system.

**chaînette** *f* (small) chain.

**chair** *f* flesh; **(couleur) c.** flesh-col-

ored; **en c. et en os** in the flesh; **la c. de poule** goose pimples *or* bumps; **c. à saucisses** sausage meat.
**chaise** *f* chair; **c. longue** deckchair; **c. haute** high-chair.
**châle** *m* shawl.
**chalet** *m* chalet.
**chaleur** *f* heat; (*douce*) warmth.
**chaleureux, -euse** *a* warm.
**chaloupe** *f* (*bateau*) launch.
**chalumeau, -x** *m* blowtorch.
**chalutier** *m* trawler.
**chamailler (se)** *vpr* to squabble.
**chambouler** *vt Fam* to make topsy-turvy.
**chambre** *f* (bed)room; **c. à coucher** bedroom; (*mobilier*) bedroom suite *ou* set; **c. à air** (*de pneu*) inner tube; **c. de commerce** chamber of commerce; **c. d'amis** guest room; **garder la c.** to stay indoors.
**chameau, -x** *m* camel.
**chamois** *m* **peau de c.** chamois.
**champ** *m* field; **c. de bataille** battlefield; **c. de courses** racetrack.
**champagne** *m* champagne.
**champignon** *m* mushroom.
**champion, -onne** *mf* champion.
**championnat** *m* championship.
**chance** *f* luck; (*probabilité, occasion*) chance; **avoir de la c.** to be lucky; **c'est une c. que** it's lucky that.
**chanceler** *vi* to stagger.
**chandail** *m* (thick) sweater.
**chandelier** *m* candlestick.
**chandelle** *f* candle; **en c.** (*tir*) straight into the air.
**change** *m* (*de devises*) exchange.
**changement** *m* change.
**changer** *vti* to change; **c. qn en** to change s.o. into; **ça la changera de ne pas travailler** it'll be a change for her not to be working; **c. de train/voiture/***etc* to change trains/one's car/*etc*; **c. de vitesse/sujet** to change gear/change the subject.
**changer (se)** *vpr* to change (one's clothes).
**chanson** *f* song.
**chant** *m* singing; (*chanson*) song; **c. de Noël** Christmas carol.
**chantage** *m* blackmail.
**chanter 1** *vi* to sing; (*coq*) to crow; **si ça te chante** *Fam* if you feel like it. **2** *vt* to sing.
**chanteur, -euse** *mf* singer.
**chantier** *m* (building) site; **c. naval** shipyard, dockyard.
**chantonner** *vti* to hum.
**chaos** *m* chaos.
**chapeau, -x** *m* hat.
**chapelet** *m* rosary; **un c. de** (*saucisses etc*) a string of.
**chapelle** *f* chapel.
**chapelure** *f* breadcrumbs.
**chapiteau, -x** *m* (*de cirque*) big top; (*pour expositions etc*) marquee, tent.
**chapitre** *m* chapter.
**chaque** *a* each, every.
**char** *m* (*romain*) chariot; (*de carnaval*) float; **c. (d'assaut)** tank.
**charade** *f* (*énigme*) riddle.
**charbon** *m* coal; **c. de bois** charcoal.
**charcuterie** *f* pork butcher's shop; (*aliments*) cooked pork meats.
**charcutier, -ière** *mf* pork butcher.
**chardon** *m* thistle.
**charge** *f* (*poids*) load; (*fardeau*) burden; **à la c. de qn** (*personne*) dependent on s.o.; (*frais*) payable by s.o.; **prendre en c.** to take charge of.
**chargé, -ée** *a* (*véhicule, arme etc*) loaded; (*journée*) busy.
**chargement** *m* loading; (*objet*) load.
**charger** *vt* to load; (*soldats, batterie*) to charge; **se c. de** (*enfant, travail etc*) to take charge of; **c. qn de** (*travail etc*) to entrust s.o. with; **c. qn de faire** to instruct s.o. to do.
**chariot** *m* (*à bagages etc*) cart.
**charité** *f* (*secours*) charity.
**charmant, -ante** *a* charming.
**charme** *m* charm; (*magie*) spell.
**charmer** *vt* to charm.
**charnière** *f* hinge.
**charpente** *f* frame(work).

**charpentier** *m* carpenter.
**charrette** *f* cart.
**charrier** *vt* (*transporter*) to cart; (*rivière*) to carry along (*sand etc*).
**charrue** *f* plow.
**charter** *m* charter (flight).
**chasse[1]** *f* hunting, hunt; **c. à courre** hunting; **avion de c.** fighter plane; **faire la c. à** to hunt for.
**chasse[2]** *f* **c. d'eau** toilet flush; **tirer la c.** to flush the toilet.
**chasse-neige** *m inv* snowplow.
**chasser 1** *vt* (*animal*) to hunt; (*faire partir*) to chase (*s.o., smell etc*) away; (*mouche*) to brush away. **2** *vi* to hunt.
**chasseur, -euse** *mf* hunter.
**châssis** *m* frame; (*d'automobile*) chassis.
**chat** *m* cat; **pas un c.** not a soul; **c. perché** (*jeu*) tag.
**châtaigne** *f* chestnut.
**châtaignier** *m* chestnut tree.
**châtain** *a inv* (chestnut) brown.
**château, -x** *m* castle; (*palais*) palace; **c. fort** fortified castle; **c. d'eau** water tower.
**châtiment** *m* punishment.
**chaton** *m* kitten.
**chatouiller** *vt* to tickle.
**chatouilleux, -euse** *a* ticklish.
**chatte** *f* (she-)cat.
**chatterton** *m* electrician's tape.
**chaud, chaude 1** *a* hot; (*doux*) warm. **2** *m* **avoir c.** to be hot; to be warm; **il fait c.** it's hot; it's warm; **être au c.** to be in the warm.
**chaudement** *adv* warmly.
**chaudière** *f* boiler.
**chauffage** *m* heating.
**chauffant, -ante** *a* (*couverture*) electric; **plaque chauffante** hot plate.
**chauffé, -ée** *a* (*piscine etc*) heated.
**chauffe-eau** *m inv* water heater.
**chauffer 1** *vt* to heat (up). **2** *vi* to heat (up); (*moteur*) to overheat.
**chauffeur** *m* driver; (*employé*) chauffeur.
**chaume** *m* (*pour toiture*) thatch; **toit de c.** thatched roof.
**chaumière** *f* thatched cottage.
**chaussée** *f* road(way).
**chausse-pied** *m* shoehorn.
**chausser** *vt* **c. qn** to put shoes on (to) s.o.; **se c.** to put on one's shoes; **c. du 40** to take a size 40 shoe.
**chaussette** *f* sock.
**chausson** *m* slipper; (*de danse*) shoe.
**chaussure** *f* shoe.
**chauve** *a* & *mf* bald (person).
**chauve-souris** *f* (*pl* **chauves-souris**) (*animal*) bat.
**chaux** *f* lime.
**chavirer** *vti* to capsize.
**chef** *m* leader, head; **c. d'entreprise** head of (a) company; **c. de gare** stationmaster; **c. d'orchestre** conductor; **en c.** (*commandant, rédacteur*) in chief.
**chef-d'œuvre** *m* (*pl* **chefs-d'œuvre**) masterpiece.
**chef-lieu** *m* (*pl* **chefs-lieux**) chief town (*of a département*).
**chemin** *m* road, path; (*trajet, direction*) way; **beaucoup de c. à faire** a long way to go; **se mettre en c.** to set out.
**chemin de fer** *m* railroad.
**cheminée** *f* fireplace; (*encadrement*) mantelpiece; (*sur le toit*) chimney; (*de navire*) funnel.
**cheminot** *m* railroad employee.
**chemise** *f* shirt; (*cartonnée*) folder; **c. de nuit** (*de femme*) nightgown; (*d'homme*) nightshirt.
**chemisette** *f* short-sleeved shirt.
**chemisier** *m* blouse.
**chêne** *m* oak.
**chenil** *m* kennel.
**chenille** *f* caterpillar.
**chèque** *m* check; **c. de voyage** traveler's check.
**chèque-repas** *m* (*pl* **chèques-repas**) meal voucher.
**chéquier** *m* checkbook.
**cher, chère** *a* (*aimé*) dear (**à** to); (*coûteux*) expensive; **payer c.** (*objet*) to pay a lot for; (*erreur etc*) to pay dearly for.
**chercher** *vt* to look for; (*dans un dictionnaire*) to look up; **aller c.** to

(go and) fetch *ou* get; **c. à faire** to attempt to do.

**chercheur, -euse** *mf* research worker.

**chéri, -ie 1** *a* dearly loved. **2** *mf* darling.

**chétif, -ive** *a* puny.

**cheval, -aux** *m* horse; **à c.** on horseback; **faire du c.** to go horseback riding; **chevaux de bois** merry-go-round.

**chevalier** *m* knight.

**chevaline** *af* **boucherie c.** horse butcher's (shop).

**chevelure** *f* (head of) hair.

**chevet** *m* **table/livre de c.** bedside table/book; **au c. de** at the bedside of.

**cheveu, -x** *m* **un c.** a hair; **cheveux** hair; **tiré par les cheveux** far-fetched.

**cheville** *f* ankle; (*pour vis*) (wall) plug.

**chèvre** *f* goat.

**chevreau, -x** *m* (*petit de la chèvre*) kid.

**chez** *prép* **c. qn** at s.o.'s house, flat *etc*; **il est c. Jean/c. le médecin** he's at John's (place)/at the doctor's; **il va c. Jean/c. le médecin** he's going to John's (place)/to the doctor's; **c. moi, c. nous** at home; **je vais c. moi** I'm going home; **une habitude c. elle** a habit with her; **c. Mme Dupont** (*adresse*) care of Mme Dupont.

**chic 1** *a inv* smart; (*gentil*) *Fam* nice. **2** *int* **c. (alors)!** great! **3** *m* style.

**chicorée** *f* (*à café*) chicory; (*pour salade*) endive.

**chien** *m* dog; **un mal de c.** an awful lot of trouble; **temps de c.** rotten weather.

**chien-loup** *m* (*pl* **chiens-loups**) wolfhound.

**chienne** *f* dog, bitch.

**chiffon** *m* rag; **c. (à poussière)** dust cloth.

**chiffonner** *vt* to crumple.

**chiffre** *m* figure, number; (*romain, arabe*) numeral; **c. d'affaires** sales.

**chimie** *f* chemistry.

**chimique** *a* chemical.

**chimpanzé** *m* chimpanzee.

**chinois, -oise 1** *a* Chinese. **2** *mf* Chinese man *ou* woman, Chinese *inv*; **les C.** the Chinese. **3** *m* (*langue*) Chinese.

**chiot** *m* pup(py).

**chips** *mpl* (potato) chips.

**chirurgical, -e, -aux** *a* surgical.

**chirurgie** *f* surgery.

**chirurgien** *m* surgeon.

**choc** *m* (*d'objets, émotion*) shock.

**chocolat** *m* chocolate; **c. à croquer** bittersweet chocolate; **c. au lait** milk chocolate.

**chocolaté, -ée** *a* chocolate-flavored.

**chœur** *m* (*chanteurs, nef*) choir; **en c.** (all) together.

**choisir** *vt* to choose, pick.

**choix** *m* choice; (*assortiment*) selection.

**cholestérol** *m* cholesterol.

**chômage** *m* unemployment; **au c.** unemployed.

**chômer** *vi* to be unemployed.

**chômeur, -euse** *mf* unemployed person; **les chômeurs** the unemployed.

**choquant, -ante** *a* shocking.

**choquer** *vt* to shock.

**chorale** *f* choral society.

**chose** *f* thing; **monsieur C.** Mr What's-his-name.

**chou, -x** *m* cabbage; **choux de Bruxelles** Brussels sprouts.

**choucroute** *f* sauerkraut.

**chouette 1** *f* owl. **2** *a Fam* super, great.

**chou-fleur** *m* (*pl* **choux-fleurs**) cauliflower.

**choyer** *vt* to pamper.

**chrétien, -ienne** *a & mf* Christian.

**chrome** *m* chrome.

**chromé, -ée** *a* chrome-plated.

**chronique** *f* (*à la radio*) report; (*dans le journal*) column.

**chronomètre** *m* stopwatch.

**chronométrer** *vt* to time.

**chrysanthème** *m* chrysanthemum.

**chuchotement** *m* whisper(-ing).
**chuchoter** *vti* to whisper.
**chut!** *int* sh!, shush!
**chute** *f* fall; **c. d'eau** waterfall; **c. de neige** snowfall; **c. de pluie** rainfall.
**ci 1** *adv* **par-ci par-là** here and there. **2** *pron dém* **comme ci comme ça** so so.
**cible** *f* target.
**cicatrice** *f* scar.
**cicatrisation** *f* healing (up).
**cicatriser** *vt*, **se cicatriser** *vpr* to heal up (*leaving a scar*).
**cidre** *m* cider.
**Cie** *abrév* (*compagnie*) Co.
**ciel** *m* (*pl* **ciels**) sky; (*pl* **cieux**) (*paradis*) heaven.
**cierge** *m* candle.
**cigale** *f* (*insecte*) cicada.
**cigare** *m* cigar.
**cigarette** *f* cigarette.
**cigogne** *f* stork.
**cil** *m* (eye)lash.
**cime** *f* (*d'un arbre*) top; (*d'une montagne*) peak.
**ciment** *m* cement.
**cimenter** *vt* to cement.
**cimetière** *m* cemetery.
**ciné** *m Fam* movies.
**ciné-club** *m* film club.
**cinéma** *m* (*art, industrie*) movies; (*bâtiment*) movie theater; **faire du c.** to make movies.
**cinglé, -ée** *a Fam* crazy.
**cinq** *a* & *m* five.
**cinquantaine** *f* about fifty.
**cinquante** *a* & *m* fifty.
**cinquantième** *a* & *mf* fiftieth.
**cinquième** *a* & *mf* fifth.
**cintre** *m* coathanger.
**cirage** *m* (shoe) polish.
**circonférence** *f* circumference.
**circonflexe** *a Grammaire* circumflex.
**circonstance** *f* circumstance; **pour la c.** for this occasion.
**circonstanciel, -ielle** *a Grammaire* adverbial.
**circuit** *m* (*électrique, sportif etc*) circuit; (*voyage*) tour.
**circulaire 1** *a* circular. **2** *f* (*lettre*) circular.
**circulation** *f* circulation; (*automobile*) traffic.
**circuler** *vi* to circulate; (*véhicule, train*) to travel; (*passant*) to walk around; (*rumeur*) to go around; **faire c.** (*piétons etc*) to move on.
**cire** *f* wax.
**cirer** *vt* to polish.
**cirque** *m* circus.
**ciseau, -x** *m* chisel; **(une paire de) ciseaux** (a pair of) scissors.
**citadin, -ine** *mf* city dweller.
**citation** *f* quotation.
**cité** *f* city; **c. universitaire** (university) dormitory complex.
**citer** *vt* to quote.
**citerne** *f* (*réservoir*) tank.
**citoyen, -enne** *mf* citizen.
**citron** *m* lemon; **c. pressé** (fresh) lemon juice.
**citronnade** *f* lemonade.
**citrouille** *f* pumpkin.
**civière** *f* stretcher.
**civil, -e 1** *a* civil; (*non militaire*) civilian; **année civile** calendar year. **2** *m* civilian; **en c.** (*policier*) in plain clothes.
**civilisation** *f* civilization.
**civilisé, -ée** *a* civilized.
**civique** *a* civic; **instruction c.** civics.
**clair, -e 1** *a* (*distinct, limpide, évident*) clear; (*éclairé*) light; (*pâle*) light(-colored); **bleu/vert c.** light blue/green. **2** *adv* (*voir*) clearly. **3** *m* **c. de lune** moonlight.
**clairement** *adv* clearly.
**clairière** *f* clearing.
**clairon** *m* bugle.
**clairsemé, -ée** *a* sparse.
**clandestin, -ine** *a* (*journal, mouvement*) underground; **passager c.** stowaway.
**claque** *f* smack, slap.
**claquement** *m* (*de porte*) slam(ming).
**claquer 1** *vt* (*porte*) to slam, bang; **se c. un muscle** to tear a muscle. **2** *vi* (*porte*) to slam, bang; (*coup de*

*feu*) to ring out; **c. des mains** to clap one's hands; **elle claque des dents** her teeth are chattering.
**clarinette** *f* clarinet.
**clarté** *f* light; (*précision*) clarity.
**classe** *f* class; **aller en c.** to go to school.
**classement** *m* classification; filing; grading; (*rang*) place; (*en sport*) placing.
**classer** *vt* to classify; (*papiers*) to file; (*candidats*) to grade; **se c. premier** to come first.
**classeur** *m* (*meuble*) filing cabinet; (*portefeuille*) (loose leaf) binder.
**classique** *a* classical.
**clavicule** *f* collarbone.
**clavier** *m* keyboard.
**clé, clef** *f* key; (*outil*) wrench; **fermer à c.** to lock; **sous c.** under lock and key; **c. de contact** ignition key.
**clémentine** *f* tangerine.
**clergé** *m* clergy.
**cliché** *m* (*de photo*) negative.
**client, -ente** *mf* customer; (*d'un avocat*) client; (*d'un médecin*) patient; (*d'hôtel*) guest.
**clientèle** *f* customers; (*d'un avocat, d'un médecin*) practice.
**cligner** *vi* **c. des yeux** to blink; (*fermer à demi*) to squint; **c. de l'œil** to wink.
**clignotant** *m* (*de voiture*) turn signal.
**clignoter** *vi* to blink; (*lumière*) to flicker.
**climat** *m* climate.
**climatisation** *f* air conditioning.
**climatiser** *vt* to air-condition.
**clin d'œil** *m* wink; **en un c. d'œil** in no time (at all).
**clinique** *f* (private) clinic.
**clochard, -arde** *mf* down-and-out, tramp.
**cloche** *f* bell.
**cloche-pied (à)** *adv* **sauter à c.-pied** to hop on one foot.
**clocher** *m* bell tower; (*en pointe*) steeple.
**clochette** *f* (small) bell.
**cloison** *f* partition.
**clope** *m ou f Fam* smoke, cigarette.
**clopin-clopant** *adv* **aller c.-clopant** to hobble.
**cloque** *f* blister.
**clos, close** *a* closed.
**clôture** *f* (*barrière*) fence.
**clôturer** *vt* to enclose.
**clou** *m* nail; **les clous** (*passage*) crosswalk.
**clouer** *vt* to nail; **cloué au lit** confined to bed.
**clouté, -ée** *a* (*pneus*) studded; **passage c.** crosswalk.
**clown** *m* clown.
**club** *m* (*association*) club.
**cm** *abrév* (*centimètre*) cm.
**coaguler** *vti*, **se coaguler** *vpr* to clot.
**coalition** *f* coalition.
**cobaye** *m* guinea pig.
**coca** *m* (*Coca-Cola®*) coke.
**cocaïne** *f* cocaine.
**coccinelle** *f* ladybug.
**cocher**[1] *vt* to tick (off), to check (off).
**cocher**[2] *m* coachman.
**cochon, -onne 1** *m* pig; **c. d'Inde** guinea pig. **2** *mf* (*personne sale*) (dirty) pig.
**cocorico** *int* & *m* cock-a-doodle-doo.
**cocotier** *m* coconut palm.
**cocotte** *f* casserole; **c. minute®** pressure cooker.
**code** *m* code; **codes, phares c.** low beams; **C. de la route** traffic laws.
**cœur** *m* heart; (*couleur*) *Cartes* hearts; **au c. de** (*ville, hiver etc*) in the middle *ou* heart of; **par c.** by heart; **avoir mal au c.** to feel sick; **avoir le c. gros** to have a heavy heart; **avoir bon c.** to be kind-hearted; **de bon c.** (*offrir*) willingly; (*rire*) heartily.
**coffre** *m* chest; (*de banque*) safe; (*de voiture*) trunk.
**coffre-fort** *m* (*pl* **coffres-forts**) safe.
**coffret** *m* (*à bijoux etc*) box.

**cogner** *vti* to knock, bang; **se c. la tête**/*etc* to knock *ou* bang one's head/*etc*; **se c. à qch** to knock *ou* bang into sth.

**cohue** *f* crowd.

**coiffer** *vt* **c. qn** to do s.o.'s hair; **se c.** to do one's hair.

**coiffeur, -euse** *mf* hairdresser.

**coiffure** *f* hat; (*arrangement*) hairstyle.

**coin** *m* (*angle*) corner; (*endroit*) spot; **du c.** (*magasin etc*) local; **dans le c.** in the (local) area.

**coincé, -ée** *a* stuck.

**coincer** *vt* (*mécanisme etc*) to jam; **se c.** to get stuck *ou* jammed; **se c. le doigt** to get one's finger stuck.

**coïncidence** *f* coincidence.

**coing** *m* quince.

**col** *m* collar; (*de montagne*) pass; **c. roulé** turtleneck.

**colère** *f* anger; **une c.** a fit of anger; **en c.** angry (**contre** with); **se mettre en c.** to lose one's temper.

**coléreux, -euse** *a* quick-tempered.

**colique** *f* diarrhea.

**colis** *m* parcel.

**collaboration** *f* collaboration.

**collaborer** *vi* collaborate (**à** on).

**collant, -ante 1** *a* (*papier*) sticky; (*vêtement*) skin-tight. **2** *m* pantyhose; (*opaque*) tights; (*de danse*) leotard.

**colle** *f* glue; (*blanche*) paste.

**collecte** *f* (*quête*) collection.

**collectif, -ive** *a* collective; **billet c.** group ticket.

**collection** *f* collection.

**collectionner** *vt* to collect.

**collectionneur, -euse** *mf* collector.

**collège** *m* = (junior) high school.

**collégien, -enne** *mf* = (junior) high school student.

**collègue** *mf* colleague.

**coller** *vt* to stick; (*à la colle transparente*) to glue; (*à la colle blanche*) to paste; (*affiche*) to stick up; (*papier peint*) to hang; (*mettre*) *Fam* to stick; **c. contre** (*nez, oreille etc*) to press against.

**collier** *m* (*bijou*) necklace; (*de chien*) collar.

**colline** *f* hill.

**collision** *f* collision; **entrer en c. avec** to collide with.

**colombe** *f* dove.

**colonel** *m* colonel.

**colonie** *f* colony; **c. de vacances** summer camp.

**colonne** *f* column; **c. vertébrale** spine.

**coloré, -ée** *a* colorful; (*verre, liquide*) colored.

**colorer** *vt* to color.

**coloriage** *m* **album de coloriages** coloring book.

**colorier** *vt* (*dessin*) to color (in).

**coloris** *m* (*nuance*) shade.

**colosse** *m* giant.

**coma** *m* coma; **dans le c.** in a coma.

**combat** *m* fight.

**combatif, -ive** *a* eager to fight; (*instinct, esprit*) fighting.

**combattant** *m* fighter, brawler.

**combattre*** *vti* to fight.

**combien 1** *adv* (*quantité*) how much; (*nombre*) how many; **c. de** (*temps, argent etc*) how much; (*gens, livres etc*) how many. ▪ (*à quel point*) how; **c. y a-t-il d'ici à . . . ?** how far is it to . . . ? **2** *m inv* **le c. sommes-nous?** *Fam* what is the date?; **tous les c.?** *Fam* how often?

**combinaison** *f* combination; (*vêtement de femme*) slip; (*de mécanicien*) overalls; **c. de vol/plongée/ski** flying/diving/ski suit; **c. spatiale** spacesuit.

**combiné** *m* (*de téléphone*) receiver.

**combiner** *vt* (*assembler*) to combine.

**comble 1** *m* **le c. de** (*la joie etc*) the height of; **c'est un** *ou* **le c.!** that's the limit! **2** *a* (*bondé*) packed.

**combler** *vt* (*trou etc*) to fill; **c. son retard** to make up lost time.

**combustible** *m* fuel.

**comédie** *f* comedy; **c. musicale** musical; **jouer la c.** to put on an act, pretend.

**comédien** *m* actor.

**comédienne** *f* actress.

**comestible** *a* edible.

**comique** *a* (*amusant*) funny; (*acteur etc*) comic.

**comité** *m* committee.

**commandant** *m* (*d'un navire*) captain; **c. de bord** (*d'un avion*) captain.

**commande** *f* (*achat*) order; **sur c.** to order; **les commandes** (*d'un avion etc*) the controls.

**commandement** *m* (*autorité*) command.

**commander 1** *vt* to command; (*acheter*) to order. **2** *vi* **c. à qn de faire** to command s.o. to do.

**comme 1** *adv* & *conj* like; **c. moi** like me; **c. cela** like that; **qu'as-tu c. vins?** what kind of wines do you have? ▪ as; **blanc c. neige** (as) white as snow; **c. si** as if; **c. pour faire** as if to do; **c. par hasard** as if by chance. **2** *adv* (*exclamatif*) **regarde c. il pleut!** look how (hard) it's raining!; **c. c'est petit!** how small it is! **3** *conj* (*temps, cause*) as; **c. elle entrait** as she was coming in.

**commencement** *m* beginning, start.

**commencer** *vti* to begin, start (**à faire** to do, doing; **par** with; **par faire** by doing); **pour c.** to begin with.

**comment** *adv* how; **c. le sais-tu?** how do you know?; **c.?** (*répétition, surprise*) what?; **c. est-il?** what is he like?; **c. faire?** what's to be done?; **c. t'appelles-tu?** what's your name?; **c. allez-vous?** how are you?

**commerçant, -ante** *mf* merchant; **rue commerçante** shopping street.

**commerce** *m* trade, commerce; (*magasin*) store, business; **dans le c.** (*objet*) (on sale) in stores.

**commercial, -e, -aux** *a* commercial.

**commettre*** *vt* (*délit etc*) to commit; (*erreur*) to make.

**commissaire** *m* **c. (de police)** police chief.

**commissariat** *m* **c. (de police)** (central) police station.

**commission** *f* (*course*) errand; (*pourcentage*) commission (**sur** on); **faire les commissions** to go shopping, run (the) errands.

**commode 1** *a* (*pratique*) handy. **2** *f* chest of drawers, dresser.

**commun, -une** *a* (*collectif, habituel etc*) common; (*frais, cuisine*) shared; **ami c.** mutual friend; **en c.** in common; **avoir** *ou* **mettre en c.** to share.

**commune** *f* commune.

**communication** *f* communication; **c. (téléphonique)** (telephone) call.

**communier** *vi* to receive Holy Communion.

**communion** *f* (Holy) Communion.

**communiqué** *m* (official) statement; (*publicitaire*) message; **c. de presse** press release.

**communiquer** *vti* to communicate.

**communiste** *a* & *mf* communist.

**compact, -e** *a* dense.

**compagne** *f* friend; (*épouse*) companion.

**compagnie** *f* (*présence, société*) company; **tenir c. à qn** to keep s.o. company.

**compagnon** *m* companion; **c. de jeu** playmate; **c. de travail** coworker.

**comparable** *a* comparable.

**comparaison** *f* comparison (**avec** with).

**comparer** *vt* to compare (**à** to, with).

**compartiment** *m* compartment.

**compas** *m* compass.

**compatriote** *mf* compatriot.

**compenser 1** *vt* to compensate for. **2** *vi* to compensate.

**compétence** *f* competence.
**compétent, -ente** *a* competent.
**compétition** *f* competition; (*épreuve sportive*) event; **de c.** (*esprit, sport*) competitive.
**complaisance** *f* kindness.
**complaisant, -ante** *a* kind.
**complément** *m Grammaire* complement.
**complet, -ète 1** *a* complete; (*train, hôtel etc*) full; (*aliment*) whole. **2** *m* suit.
**complètement** *adv* completely.
**compléter** *vt* to complete; (*somme*) to make up.
**complexe 1** *a* complex. **2** *m* (*sentiment, construction*) complex.
**complication** *f* complication.
**complice** *m* accomplice.
**compliment** *m* compliment; **mes compliments!** congratulations!
**complimenter** *vt* to compliment (**sur, pour** on).
**compliqué, -ée** *a* complicated.
**compliquer** *vt* to complicate; **se c.** to get complicated.
**complot** *m* plot.
**comploter** *vti* to plot (**de faire** to do).
**comporter (se)** *vpr* to behave; (*joueur, voiture*) to perform.
**composé, -ée** *a* & *m* (*mot, en chimie etc*) compound; **temps c.** compound tense; **passé c.** perfect (tense).
**composer** *vt* to make up, compose; (*numéro*) to dial; **se c. de, être composé de** to be made up *ou* composed of.
**compositeur, -trice** *mf* composer.
**composter** *vt* (*billet*) to cancel.
**compote** *f* stewed fruit, sauce; **c. de pommes** applesauce.
**compréhensible** *a* understandable.
**compréhensif, -ive** *a* (*personne*) understanding.
**comprendre*** *vt* to understand; (*comporter*) to include; **je n'y comprends rien** I don't understand anything about it; **ça se comprend** that's understandable.
**comprimé** *m* tablet.
**comprimer** *vt* to compress.
**compris, -ise** *a* (*inclus*) included (**dans** in); **tout c.** (all) inclusive; **y c.** including.
**comptable** *mf* bookkeeper; (*expert*) accountant.
**comptant 1** *a* **argent c.** (hard) cash. **2** *adv* **payer c.** to pay (in) cash.
**compte** *m* account; (*calcul*) count; (*nombre*) (right) number; **avoir un c. en banque** to have a bank(ing) account; **c. chèque** checking account; **c. à rebours** countdown; **tenir c. de** to take into account; **c. tenu de** considering; **se rendre c. de** to realize; **à son c.** (*travailler*) for oneself; (*s'installer*) on one's own; **en fin de c.** all things considered.
**compte-gouttes** *m inv* dropper.
**compter 1** *vt* (*calculer*) to count; **c. faire** to expect to do; (*avoir l'intention de*) to intend to do; **c. qch à qn** (*facturer*) to charge s.o. for sth. **2** *vi* (*calculer, avoir de l'importance*) to count; **c. sur** to rely on.
**compte rendu** *m* report; (*de livre, film*) review.
**compteur** *m* meter; **c. (de vitesse)** speedometer; **c. (kilométrique)** odometer.
**comptoir** *m* (*de magasin*) counter; (*de café*) bar; (*de bureau*) (reception) desk.
**comte** *m* count; *Br* earl.
**comtesse** *f* countess.
**concentré, -ée 1** *a* (*lait*) condensed; (*attentif*) concentrating (hard). **2** *m* **c. de tomates** tomato purée.
**concentrer** *vt*, **se concentrer** *vpr* to concentrate.
**concerner** *vt* to concern.
**concert** *m* concert.
**concessionnaire** *mf* (authorized) dealer.
**concevoir** *vt* to conceive.

**concierge** *mf* caretaker, janitor.
**concitoyen, -enne** *mf* fellow citizen.
**conclure*** *vti* to conclude (**que** that).
**conclusion** *f* conclusion.
**concombre** *m* cucumber.
**concordant, -ante** *a* in agreement.
**concorder** *vi* to agree; **c. avec** to match.
**concours** *m* (*examen*) competitive examination; (*jeu*) competition; **c. hippique** horse show.
**concret, -ète** *a* concrete.
**conçu, -ue** *a* **c. pour faire/pour qn** designed to do/for s.o.; **bien c.** (*maison etc*) well designed.
**concurrence** *f* competition; **faire c. à** to compete with.
**concurrencer** *vt* to compete with.
**concurrent, -ente** *mf* competitor.
**condamnation** *f* sentence; (*censure*) condemnation.
**condamné, -ée** *mf* condemned man *ou* woman.
**condamner** *vt* to condemn; (*accusé*) to sentence (**à** to); (*porte*) to block up; **c. à une amende** to fine.
**condition** *f* condition; **conditions** (*clauses, tarifs*) terms; **à c. de faire, à c. que l'on fasse** providing *ou* provided (that) one does.
**conditionné** *a* **à air c.** (*pièce etc*) air-conditioned.
**conditionnel** *m Grammaire* conditional.
**condoléances** *fpl* sympathy.
**conducteur, -trice** *mf* driver.
**conduire*** *vt* to lead; (*voiture*) to drive; (*eau*) to carry; **c. qn à** (*accompagner*) to take s.o. to.
**conduire (se)** *vpr* to behave.
**conduite** *f* behavior; (*de voiture*) driving (**de** of); (*d'eau, de gaz*) main.
**cône** *m* cone.
**confection** *f* making (**de** of); **vêtements de c.** ready-to-wear clothes.
**confectionner** *vt* to make.
**conférence** *f* conference.
**confesser** *vt*, **se confesser** *vpr* to confess.
**confession** *f* confession.
**confettis** *mpl* confetti.
**confiance** *f* trust; **faire c. à qn, avoir c. en qn** to trust s.o.; **c. en soi** (self-)confidence.
**confiant, -ante** *a* trusting; (*sûr de soi*) confident.
**confidence** *f* (*secret*) confidence; **faire une c. à qn** to confide in s.o.
**confidentiel, -ielle** *a* confidential.
**confier** *vt* **c. à qn** (*enfant, objet*) to give s.o. to take care of; **c. un secret**/*etc* **à qn** to confide a secret/*etc* to s.o.; **se c. à qn** to confide in s.o.
**confirmation** *f* confirmation.
**confirmer** *vt* to confirm (**que** that).
**confiserie** *f* candy store; **confiseries** (*produits*) candy.
**confiseur, -euse** *mf* confectioner.
**confisquer** *vt* to confiscate (**à qn** from s.o.).
**confit** *a* **fruits confits** candied fruit.
**confiture** *f* jam.
**conflit** *m* conflict.
**confondre** *vt* (*choses, personnes*) to mix up, confuse; **c. avec** to mistake for.
**confort** *m* comfort.
**confortable** *a* comfortable.
**confrère** *m* colleague.
**confus, -fuse** *a* confused; (*gêné*) embarrassed; **je suis c.!** (*désolé*) I'm terribly sorry!
**confusion** *f* confusion; (*gêne, honte*) embarrassment.
**congé** *m* (*vacances*) vacation; **c. de maladie** sick leave; **congés payés** paid vacation.
**congélateur** *m* freezer, deep-freeze.
**congeler** *vt* to freeze.
**congère** *f* snowdrift.
**congrès** *m* congress.
**conjoint** *m* spouse.
**conjonction** *f Grammaire* conjunction.
**conjugaison** *f* conjugation.

**conjuguer** *vt* (*verbe*) to conjugate.

**connaissance** *f* knowledge; (*personne*) acquaintance; **connaissances** knowledge (**en** of); **faire la c. de qn, faire c. avec qn** to meet s.o.; **perdre c.** to lose consciousness; **sans c.** unconscious.

**connaître*** *vt* to know; (*rencontrer*) to meet; **nous nous connaissons déjà** we've met before; **s'y c. à** *ou* **en qch** to know (all) about sth.

**connu, -ue** (*pp of* **connaître**) *a* (*célèbre*) well-known.

**conquérant, -ante** *mf* conqueror.

**conquérir*** *vt* to conquer.

**conquête** *f* conquest; **faire la c. de** to conquer.

**consacrer** *vt* (*temps, vie etc*) to devote (**à** to); **se c. à** to devote oneself to.

**conscience** *f* (*psychologique*) consciousness; (*morale*) conscience; **avoir/prendre c. de** to be/become conscious *ou* aware of; **c. professionnelle** conscientiousness.

**consciencieux, -euse** *a* conscientious.

**conscient, -ente** *a* **c. de** aware of.

**conseil[1]** *m* **un c.** a piece of advice; **des conseils** advice.

**conseil[2]** *m* (*assemblée*) council; **c. d'administration** board of directors; **c. des ministres** (*réunion*) cabinet meeting.

**conseiller** *vt* to advise; **c. qch à qn** to recommend sth to s.o.; **c. à qn de faire** to advise s.o. to do.

**conseiller, -ère** *mf* (*expert*) consultant, adviser; (*d'un conseil*) councilor; **c. municipal** city councilman *ou* -woman.

**consentement** *m* consent.

**consentir*** *vi* **c. à** to consent to.

**conséquence** *f* consequence.

**conservation** *f* preservation.

**conservatoire** *m* school (*of music, drama*).

**conserve** *f* **conserves** canned food; **de** *ou* **en c.** canned; **mettre en c.** to can.

**conserver** *vt* to keep; (*fruits, vie, tradition etc*) to preserve

**conserver (se)** *vpr* (*aliment*) to keep.

**considérable** *a* considerable.

**considérer** *vt* to consider (**que** that, **comme** to be).

**consigne** *f* (*instruction*) orders; (*de gare*) baggage check; (*somme*) deposit; **c. automatique** luggage *ou* baggage lockers.

**consigner** *vt* (*bouteille etc*) to charge a deposit on.

**consistant, -ante** *a* (*sauce etc*) thick; (*repas*) solid.

**consister** *vi* **c. en/dans** to consist of/in; **c. à faire** to consist in doing.

**consolation** *f* comfort.

**console** *f* console.

**consoler** *vt* to comfort, console (**de** for); **se c. de** (*la mort de qn etc*) to get over.

**consolider** *vt* to strengthen.

**consommateur, -trice** *mf* consumer; (*au café*) customer.

**consommation** *f* consumption; (*boisson*) drink.

**consommer 1** *vt* (*aliment etc*) to consume. **2** *vi* (*au café*) to drink; **c. beaucoup/peu** (*véhicule*) to get good/bad mileage.

**consonne** *f* consonant.

**conspirateur, -trice** *mf* conspirator.

**conspiration** *f* plot.

**conspirer** *vi* to plot (**contre** against).

**constamment** *adv* constantly.

**constat** *m* (official) report.

**constatation** *f* observation.

**constater** *vt* to note, observe (**que** that); (*enregistrer*) to record.

**consternation** *f* distress.

**consterner** *vt* to distress.

**constipé, -ée** *a* constipated.

**constituer** *vt* (*composer*) to make up; (*représenter*) to represent; **constitué de** made up of; **se c. prisonnier** to give oneself up.

**constitution** *f* constitution; (*composition*) composition.

**construction** *f* construction; **matériaux/jeu de c.** construction materials/set.

**construire*** *vt* to build.

**consul** *m* consul.

**consulat** *m* consulate.

**consultation** *f* consultation; **cabinet de c.** (doctor's) office.

**consulter** *vt*, **se consulter** *vpr* to consult.

**contact** *m* contact; (*toucher*) touch; (*de voiture*) ignition; **être en c. avec** to be in touch *ou* contact with; **entrer en c. avec** to come into contact with; **mettre/couper le c.** (*dans une voiture*) to turn on/off the ignition; **lentilles** *ou* **verres de c.** contact lenses.

**contacter** *vt* to contact.

**contagieux, -euse** *a* contagious, infectious.

**contagion** *f* infection.

**conte** *m* tale; **c. de fée** fairy tale.

**contempler** *vt* to gaze at.

**contemporain, -aine** *a* & *mf* contemporary.

**contenance** *f* (*d'un récipient*) capacity.

**contenir*** *vt* to contain; (*avoir comme capacité*) to hold.

**content, -ente** *a* pleased, happy (**de faire** to do, **de qn/qch** with s.o./sth); **c. de soi** self-satisfied.

**contenter** *vt* to satisfy, please; **se c. de** to be content *or* happy with.

**contenu** *m* (*de récipient*) contents.

**conter** *vt* (*histoire etc*) to tell.

**contestataire** *mf* protester.

**contestation** *f* protest.

**contester 1** *vi* (*étudiants etc*) to protest. **2** *vt* to protest against.

**conteur, -euse** *mf* storyteller.

**contexte** *m* context.

**continent** *m* continent; (*opposé à une île*) mainland.

**continu, -ue** *a* continuous.

**continuel, -elle** *a* continual.

**continuellement** *adv* continually.

**continuer 1** *vt* to continue, carry on (**à** *ou* **de faire** doing). **2** *vi* to continue, go on.

**contour** *m* outline.

**contourner** *vt* (*colline etc*) to go around.

**contraceptif, -ive** *a* & *m* contraceptive.

**contracter** *vt*, **se contracter** *vpr* to contract.

**contractuel, -elle** *mf* parking enforcement officer.

**contradiction** *f* contradiction.

**contradictoire** *a* contradictory; (*théories*) conflicting.

**contraindre*** *vt* to compel (**à faire** to do).

**contrainte** *f* compulsion.

**contraire 1** *a* opposite; **c. à** contrary to. **2** *m* opposite; **au c.** on the contrary.

**contrairement** *adv* **c. à** contrary to.

**contrariant, -ante** *a* (*action etc*) annoying; (*personne*) difficult.

**contrarier** *vt* (*projet etc*) to spoil; (*personne*) to annoy.

**contrariété** *f* annoyance.

**contraste** *m* contrast.

**contrat** *m* contract.

**contravention** *f* (*pour stationnement interdit*) (parking) ticket.

**contre** *prép* & *adv* against; (*en échange de*) (in exchange) for; **échanger c.** to exchange for; **fâché c.** angry with; **six voix c. deux** six votes to two; **Nîmes c. Arras** (*match*) Nîmes versus Arras; **un médicament c.** (*toux etc*) medicine for; **par c.** on the other hand; **tout c. qch/qn** close to sth/s.o.

**contre-** *préfixe* counter-.

**contre-attaque** *f* counterattack.

**contrebande** *f* (*fraude*) smuggling; **de c.** (*tabac etc*) smuggled; **passer qch en c.** to smuggle sth.

**contrebandier, -ière** *mf* smuggler.

**contrecœur (à)** *adv* reluctantly.

**contredire*** *vt* to contradict; **se c.** to contradict oneself.

**contre-jour (à)** *adv* against the (sun)light.

**contremaître** *m* foreman.

**contre-plaqué** *m* plywood.
**contretemps** *m* hitch.
**contribuable** *mf* taxpayer.
**contribuer** *vi* to contribute (**à** to).
**contribution** *f* contribution; (*impôt*) tax.
**contrôle** *m* inspection, check(ing) (**de** of); (*des prix, de la qualité*) control; (*maîtrise*) control.
**contrôler** *vt* (*examiner*) to inspect, check; (*maîtriser, surveiller*) to control.
**contrôleur, -euse** *mf* (*de train*) conductor; (*au quai*) ticket collector; (*de bus*) conductor.
**contrordre** *m* change of orders.
**contusion** *f* bruise.
**convaincant, -ante** *a* convincing.
**convaincre*** *vt* to convince (**de** of); **c. qn de faire** to persuade s.o. to do.
**convaincu, -ue** *a* (*certain*) convinced (**de** of).
**convalescence** *f* convalescence; **être en c.** to convalesce.
**convalescent, -ente 1** *mf* convalescent. **2** *a* **être c.** to convalesce.
**convenable** *a* suitable; (*correct*) decent.
**convenablement** *adv* suitably; decently.
**convenir*** *vi* **c. à** (*être fait pour*) to be suitable for; (*plaire à, aller à*) to suit; **ça convient** (*date etc*) that's suitable.
**convenu, -ue** *a* (*prix etc*) agreed.
**conversation** *f* conversation.
**convertir** *vt* to convert (**à** to, **en** into).
**conviction** *f* (*certitude*) conviction.
**convive** *mf* guest (*at table*).
**convocation** *f* (*lettre*) (written) notice to attend.
**convoi** *m* (*véhicules*) convoy.
**convoquer** *vt* to summon (**à** to).
**coopération** *f* cooperation.
**coopérer** *vi* to cooperate (**à** in, **avec** with).
**coordonnées** *fpl* (*adresse, téléphone*) *Fam* contact address and phone number, particulars.
**copain** *m Fam* (*camarade*) pal; (*petit ami*) boyfriend; **être c. avec** to be pals with.
**copeau, -x** *m* (*de bois*) shaving.
**copie** *f* copy; (*devoir, examen*) paper.
**copier** *vti* to copy (**sur** from).
**copieux, -euse** *a* plentiful.
**copine** *f Fam* (*camarade*) pal; (*petite amie*) girlfriend; **être c. avec** to be pals with.
**copropriété** *f* **(immeuble en) c.** condominium.
**coq** *m* rooster, cock.
**coque** *f* (*de navire*) hull; (*de noix*) shell; (*fruit de mer*) cockle; **œuf à la c.** soft-boiled egg.
**coquelicot** *m* poppy.
**coqueluche** *f* whooping cough.
**coquet, -ette** *a* (*chic*) stylish, chic.
**coquetier** *m* egg cup.
**coquetterie** *f* (*élégance*) style, elegance.
**coquillage** *m* (*mollusque*) shellfish; (*coquille*) shell.
**coquille** *f* shell; **c. Saint-Jacques** scallop.
**coquin, -ine** *a* mischievous.
**cor** *m* (*instrument*) horn; **c. (au pied)** corn.
**corail, -aux** *m* coral.
**Coran** *m* **le C.** the Koran.
**corbeau, -x** *m* crow.
**corbeille** *f* basket; **c. à papier** waste paper basket.
**corbillard** *m* hearse.
**corde** *f* rope; (*plus mince*) cord; (*de raquette, violon etc*) string; **c. à linge** clothesline; **c. à sauter** jump rope.
**cordial, -e, -aux** *a* warm.
**cordon** *m* (*de tablier, sac etc*) string; (*de rideau*) cord.
**cordon-bleu** *m* (*pl* **cordons-bleus**) cordon-bleu cook.
**cordonnerie** *f* shoe repair shop.
**cordonnier** *m* shoe repairman.
**coriace** *a* tough.
**corne** *f* (*de chèvre etc*) horn; (*de cerf*) antler; (*matière, instrument*) horn.

**corneille** *f* crow.

**cornet** *m* (*de glace*) cornet, cone; **c. (de papier)** (paper) cone.

**cornichon** *m* (*concombre*) pickle.

**corps** *m* body; **lutter c. à c.** to fight hand-to-hand; **prendre c.** (*projet*) to take shape.

**correct, -e** *a* (*exact*, *décent*) correct.

**correctement** *adv* correctly.

**correction** *f* correction; (*punition*) whipping; (*exactitude*, *décence*) correctness; **la c. de** (*devoirs*, *examen*) the marking of.

**correspondance** *f* correspondence; (*de train*, *d'autocar*) connection, transfer.

**correspondant, -ante 1** *a* corresponding. **2** *mf* (*d'un adolescent etc*) pen pal; (*au téléphone*) caller.

**correspondre** *vi* to correspond (**à** to, with); (*écrire*) to correspond (**avec** with).

**corrida** *f* bullfight.

**corriger** *vt* to correct; (*devoir*) to mark; **c. qn de** (*défaut*) to cure s.o. of.

**corrompu, -ue** *a* corrupt.

**corsage** *m* (*chemisier*) blouse.

**cortège** *m* procession; **c. officiel** (*automobiles*) motorcade.

**corvée** *f* chore.

**cosmonaute** *mf* cosmonaut.

**cosmos** *m* (*univers*) cosmos; (*espace*) outer space.

**cosse** *f* (*de pois etc*) pod.

**costaud, -aude** *a Fam* brawny.

**costume** *m* (*déguisement*) costume; (*complet*) suit.

**costumé** *a* **bal c.** costume ball.

**côte** *f* rib; (*de mouton*) chop; (*de veau*) cutlet; (*montée*) hill; (*littoral*) coast; **c. à c.** side by side.

**côté** *m* side; (*direction*) way; **de l'autre c.** on the other side (**de** of); (*direction*) the other way; **du c. de** (*vers*, *près de*) towards; **de c.** (*mettre de l'argent etc*) to one side; (*regarder*) sideways; **à c.** nearby; (*pièce*) in the other room; (*maison*) next door; **à c. de** next to, beside; (*comparaison*) compared to; **à mes côtés** by my side.

**coteau, -x** *m* (small) hill.

**côtelette** *f* (*d'agneau*, *de porc*) chop; (*de veau*) cutlet.

**côtier, -ière** *a* coastal.

**cotisation** *f* (*de club*) dues.

**cotiser (se)** *vpr* to club together (**pour acheter** to buy).

**coton** *m* cotton; **c. (hydrophile)** cotton wool.

**cou** *m* neck.

**couchage** *m* **sac de c.** sleeping bag.

**couchant** *a* (*soleil*) setting.

**couche** *f* (*épaisseur*) layer; (*de peinture*) coat; (*linge de bébé*) diaper.

**couché, -ée** *a* **être c.** to be in bed; (*étendu*) to be lying (down).

**coucher 1** *vt* to put to bed; (*héberger*) to put up; (*allonger*) to lay (down *ou* out). **2** *vi* to sleep (**avec** with).

**coucher (se)** *vpr* to go to bed; (*s'allonger*) to lie flat *ou* down; (*soleil*) to set.

**couchette** *f* (*de train*) sleeper, sleeping berth; (*de bateau*) bunk.

**coucou** *m* (*oiseau*) cuckoo; (*fleur*) cowslip.

**coude** *m* elbow; **se serrer les coudes** to help one another; **c. à c.** side by side; **coup de c.** nudge; **pousser du c.** to nudge.

**coudre*** *vti* to sew.

**couette** *f* duvet, down comforter.

**couler[1]** *vi* (*eau etc*) to flow; (*robinet*, *nez*, *sueur*) to run; (*fuir*) to leak.

**couler[2]** *vti* (*bateau*, *nageur*) to sink.

**couleur** *f* color; *Cartes* suit; **couleurs** (*teint*) color; **de c.** colored; **photo/***etc* **en couleurs** color photo/*etc*; **téléviseur c.** *ou* **en couleurs** color TV set.

**couleuvre** *f* (grass) snake.

**coulisses** *fpl* **dans les c.** in the wings, backstage.

**couloir** *m* corridor; (*de circulation*, *d'une piste*) lane.

**coup** *m* blow, knock; (*léger*) tap; (*choc moral*) blow; (*de fusil etc*) shot; (*de crayon, d'horloge*) stroke; (*aux échecs etc*) move; (*fois*) *Fam* time; **donner des coups à** to hit; **c. de brosse** brush(-up); **c. de chiffon** wipe (with a rag); **c. de sonnette** ring (on a bell); **c. de dents** bite; **c. de chance** stroke of luck; **tenter le c.** *Fam* to give it a try; **tenir le c.** to hold out; **sous le c. de** (*émotion*) under the influence of; **après c.** afterwards; **tué sur le c.** killed outright; **à c. sûr** for sure; **tout à c., tout d'un c.** suddenly; **d'un seul c.** all at once; **du c.** (*de ce fait*) as a result.

**coupable 1** *a* guilty (**de** of). **2** *mf* guilty person, culprit.

**coupant, -ante** *a* sharp.

**coupe** *f* (*trophée*) cup; (*à boire*) goblet; (*de vêtement etc*) cut; **c. de cheveux** haircut.

**coupe-ongles** *m inv* (finger nail) clippers.

**coupe-papier** *m inv* letter opener.

**couper 1** *vt* to cut; (*arbre*) to cut down; (*téléphone*) to cut off; (*courant etc*) to switch off; (*morceler*) to cut up; (*croiser*) to cut across; **c. la parole à qn** to cut s.o. short. **2** *vi* to cut; **ne coupez pas!** (*au téléphone*) hold on!

**couper (se)** *vpr* (*routes*) to intersect; **se c. au doigt** to cut one's finger.

**couple** *m* pair, couple.

**couplet** *m* verse.

**coupure** *f* cut; (*de journal*) clipping; **c. d'électricité** blackout, power outage.

**cour** *f* court (yard); (*de roi*) court; **c. (de récréation)** playground.

**courage** *m* courage; **bon c.!** good luck!

**courageux, -euse** *a* courageous.

**couramment** *adv* (*parler*) fluently; (*souvent*) frequently.

**courant, -ante 1** *a* (*fréquent*) common; (*eau*) running; (*modèle, taille*) standard. **2** *m* (*de l'eau, électrique*) current; **c. d'air** draft; **coupure de c.** blackout, power outage; **être/mettre au c.** to know/tell (**de** about).

**courbaturé, -ée** *a* aching (all over).

**courbe 1** *a* curved. **2** *f* curve.

**courber** *vti* to bend.

**coureur** *m* runner; (*cycliste*) cyclist; (*automobile*) racecar driver.

**courgette** *f* zucchini.

**courir* 1** *vi* to run; (*se hâter*) to rush; (*à bicyclette, en auto*) to race; **le bruit court que . . .** there's a rumor going around that . . . **2** *vt* (*risque*) to run; (*épreuve sportive*) to run (in); (*danger*) to face.

**couronne** *f* crown; (*de fleurs*) wreath.

**couronnement** *m* (*de roi etc*) coronation.

**couronner** *vt* to crown.

**courrier** *m* mail; **c.électronique** e-mail.

**courroie** *f* strap; (*de transmission*) belt.

**cours** *m* course; (*d'une monnaie etc*) rate; (*leçon*) class; (*série de leçons*) course; **c. d'eau** river, stream; **en c.** (*travail*) in progress; (*année*) current; **en c. de route** on the way; **au c. de** during.

**course**[1] *f* (*action*) run(ning); (*épreuve de vitesse*) race; **courses** (*de chevaux*) races; **cheval de c.** racehorse; **voiture de c.** racecar.

**course**[2] *f* (*commission*) errand; **courses** (*achats*) shopping; **faire une c.** to run an errand; **faire les courses** to go shopping.

**coursier, -ière** *mf* messenger.

**court, courte 1** *a* short. **2** *adv* (*couper, s'arrêter*) short; **à c. de** (*argent etc*) short of. **3** *m Tennis* court.

**couscous** *m* couscous.

**cousin, -ine** *mf* cousin.

**coussin** *m* cushion.

**couteau, -x** *m* knife.

**coûter** *vti* to cost; **ça coûte com-**

**bien?** how much does it cost?; **coûte que coûte** at all costs.

**coûteux, -euse** *a* costly, expensive.

**coutume** *f* custom; **avoir c. de faire** to be accustomed to doing.

**couture** *f* sewing; (*métier*) dressmaking; (*raccord*) seam.

**couturier** *m* fashion designer.

**couturière** *f* dressmaker.

**couvée** *f* (*oiseaux*) brood.

**couvent** *m* convent.

**couver 1** *vt* (*œufs*) to sit on. **2** *vi* (*poule*) to brood.

**couvercle** *m* lid, cover.

**couvert** *m* (set of) cutlery; **mettre le c.** to set *ou* lay the table.

**couvert, -erte** *a* covered (**de** with, in); (*ciel*) overcast.

**couverture** *f* (*de lit*) blanket; (*de livre etc*) cover.

**couveuse** *f* incubator.

**couvrir*** *vt* to cover (**de** with).

**couvrir (se)** *vpr* (*s'habiller*) to wrap up; (*ciel*) to cloud over.

**cow-boy** *m* cowboy.

**crabe** *m* crab.

**crachat** *m* spit, spittle.

**cracher 1** *vi* to spit. **2** *vt* to spit (out).

**craie** *f* chalk.

**craindre*** *vt* to be afraid of, fear; (*chaleur, froid*) to be sensitive to; **c. de faire** to be afraid of doing; **ne craignez rien** don't be afraid.

**crainte** *f* fear.

**craintif, -ive** *a* timid.

**crampe** *f* cramp.

**cramponner (se)** *vpr* **se c. à** to hold on to, cling to.

**crampons** *mpl* (*de chaussures*) cleats.

**cran** *m* (*entaille*) notch; (*de ceinture*) hole; **couteau à c. d'arrêt** switchblade; **c. de sûreté** safety catch.

**crâne** *m* skull.

**crapaud** *m* toad.

**craquement** *m* snapping *ou* cracking (sound).

**craquer** *vi* (*branche*) to snap; (*bois sec*) to crack; (*sous la dent*) to crunch; (*se déchirer*) to split, rip; (*personne*) to break down.

**crasse** *f* filth.

**crasseux, -euse** *a* filthy.

**cratère** *m* crater.

**cravate** *f* tie.

**crawl** *m* (*nage*) crawl.

**crayon** *m* pencil; **c. de couleur** colored pencil; (*en cire*) crayon; **c. à bille** ballpoint (pen).

**crayonner** *vt* to pencil.

**création** *f* creation.

**créature** *f* creature.

**crèche** *f* (*de Noël*) crib; (*pour bébé*) daycare (center).

**crédit** *m* credit; **à c.** on credit; **faire c.** (*prêter*) to give credit (**à** to).

**créditeur** *a* **compte c.** account in credit.

**créer** *vt* to create.

**crémaillère** *f* **pendre la c.** to have a house-warming (party).

**crématorium** *m* crematorium.

**crème** *f* cream; (*dessert*) cream dessert; **c. Chantilly** whipped cream; **c. glacée** ice cream; **c. à raser** shaving cream; **c. anglaise** custard sauce.

**créneau, -x** *m* **faire un c.** to parallel park.

**crêpe** *f* pancake, crepe.

**crépiter** *vi* to crackle.

**crépu, -ue** *a* frizzy.

**crépuscule** *m* twilight, dusk.

**cresson** *m* (water)cress.

**crête** *f* (*de montagne etc*) crest.

**creuser** *vt* to dig; **se c. la tête** to rack one's brains.

**creux, -euse 1** *a* hollow; (*estomac*) empty; **assiette creuse** soup plate. **2** *m* hollow; (*de l'estomac*) pit.

**crevaison** *f* (*de pneu*) flat.

**crevasse** *f* (*trou*) crevice.

**crevé, -ée** *a* (*fatigué*) *Fam* worn out; (*mort*) *Fam* dead.

**crever 1** *vi* (*bulle etc*) to burst; (*pneu*) to go flat; (*mourir*) *Fam* to die. **2** *vt* to burst; (*œil*) to put out.

**crevette** *f* (*grise*) shrimp; (*rose*) prawn.

**cri** *m* (*de joie, surprise*) cry, shout; (*de peur*) scream; (*de douleur*) cry; (*appel*) call, cry.
**cric** *m* (*de voiture*) jack.
**crier 1** *vi* to shout (out), cry (out); (*de peur*) to scream; **c. après qn** *Fam* to shout at s.o. **2** *vt* (*injure, ordre*) to shout (out).
**crime** *m* crime; (*assassinat*) murder.
**criminel, -elle 1** *a* criminal. **2** *mf* criminal; (*assassin*) murderer.
**crinière** *f* mane.
**crise** *f* crisis; (*accès*) attack; (*de colère etc*) fit; **c. cardiaque** heart attack.
**crisper** *vt* (*visage*) to make tense; (*poing*) to clench.
**cristal, -aux** *m* crystal.
**critique 1** *a* critical. **2** *f* (*reproche*) criticism.
**critiquer** *vt* to criticize.
**croc** *m* (*dent*) fang.
**croche-pied** *m* **faire un c.-pied à qn** to trip s.o. up.
**crochet** *m* hook; (*aiguille*) crochet hook; (*travail*) crochet; **faire qch au c.** to crochet sth; **faire un c.** (*personne*) to make a detour.
**crochu, -ue** *a* (*nez*) hooked.
**crocodile** *m* crocodile.
**croire* 1** *vt* to believe; (*estimer*) to think, believe (**que** that); **j'ai cru la voir** I thought I saw her. **2** *vi* to believe (**à, en** in).
**croisement** *m* (*de routes*) crossroads.
**croiser** *vt* (*jambes, ligne etc*) to cross; **c. qn** to pass *ou* meet s.o.
**croiser (se)** *vpr* (*voitures etc*) to pass (each other); (*routes*) to cross.
**croisière** *f* cruise.
**croissant** *m* crescent; (*pâtisserie*) croissant.
**croix** *f* cross.
**croque-monsieur** *m inv* = toasted cheese and ham sandwich.
**croquer** *vti* to crunch.
**croquis** *m* sketch.
**crosse** *f* (*de fusil*) butt.
**crotte** *f* (*de lapin etc*) droppings, dung.
**crottin** *m* (horse) dung.
**croustillant, -ante** *a* (*pain*) crusty.
**croustiller** *vi* to be crusty.
**croûte** *f* (*de pain etc*) crust; (*de fromage*) rind; (*de plaie*) scab.
**croûton** *m* crust (*at end of loaf*).
**croyant, -ante 1** *a* **être c.** to be a believer. **2** *mf* believer.
**CRS** *abrév mpl* (*Compagnies républicaines de sécurité*) riot police.
**cru[1], crue** *pp of* **croire.**
**cru[2], crue** *a* (*aliment etc*) raw.
**cruauté** *f* cruelty (**envers** to).
**cruche** *f* pitcher, jug.
**crudités** *fpl* assorted raw vegetables.
**cruel, -elle** *a* cruel (**envers, avec** to).
**cube 1** *m* cube; **cubes** (*jeu*) building blocks. **2** *a* (*mètre etc*) cubic.
**cueillette** *f* picking; (*fruits cueillis*) harvest.
**cueillir*** *vt* to pick.
**cuiller, cuillère** *f* spoon; **petite c., c. à café** teaspoon; **c. à soupe** soup spoon, tablespoon.
**cuillerée** *f* spoonful; **c. à café** teaspoonful; **c. à soupe** tablespoonful.
**cuir** *m* leather.
**cuire* 1** *vt* to cook; (*à l'eau*) to boil; **c. (au four)** to bake; (*viande*) to roast. **2** *vi* to cook; to boil; to bake; to roast; **faire c.** to cook.
**cuisine** *f* (*pièce*) kitchen; (*art, aliments*) cooking; **faire la c.** to cook, do the cooking; **livre de c.** cook book.
**cuisiner** *vti* to cook.
**cuisinier, -ière 1** *mf* cook. **2** *f* (*appareil*) stove, range.
**cuisse** *f* thigh; (*de poulet*) leg.
**cuisson** *m* cooking.
**cuit, cuite** (*pp of* **cuire**) *a* cooked; **bien c.** well done.
**cuivre** *m* (*rouge*) copper; (*jaune*) brass.
**culbute** *f* (*saut*) sommersault; (*chute*) (backward) tumble.
**culbuter** *vi* to tumble over (backwards).

**culotte** *f* (*de femme*) (pair of) panties; **culottes (courtes)** knickers.
**culte** *m* (*de dieu*) worship; (*religion*) form of worship.
**cultivateur, -trice** *mf* farmer.
**cultivé, -ée** *a* (*personne*) cultivated.
**cultiver** *vt* (*terre*) to farm; (*plantes*) to grow.
**cultiver (se)** *vpr* to improve one's mind.
**culture** *f* culture; (*agriculture*) farming; (*de légumes*) growing.
**culturel, -elle** *a* cultural.
**cure** *f* (course of) treatment, cure.
**curé** *m* (parish) priest.
**cure-dent** *m* toothpick.
**curer** *vt* (*fossé etc*) to clean out.
**curieux, -euse 1** *a* (*bizarre*) curious; (*indiscret*) inquisitive, curious (**de** about). **2** *mf* inquisitive person; (*badaud*) onlooker.
**curiosité** *f* curiosity.
**curriculum (vitae)** *m inv* résumé.
**curseur** *m* (*d'ordinateur*) cursor.
**cuve** *f* (*réservoir*) tank.
**cuvette** *f* (*récipient*) basin, bowl; (*des toilettes*) bowl.
**cycle** *m* (*série*) cycle.
**cyclisme** *m* cycling.
**cycliste** *mf* cyclist; **course c.** cycling *ou* bicycle race; **champion c.** cycling champion.
**cyclomoteur** *m* moped.
**cyclone** *m* cyclone.
**cygne** *m* swan.
**cylindre** *m* cylinder.
**cylindrée** *f* (engine) capacity.
**cylindrique** *a* cylindrical.
**cymbale** *f* cymbal.
**cyprès** *m* (*arbre*) cypress.

# D

**d'abord** *adv* first.
**dactylo** *f* (*personne*) typist; (*action*) typing.
**daim** *m* fallow deer; (*cuir*) suede.
**dallage** *m* paving.
**dalle** *f* paving stone.
**dallé, -ée** *a* paved.
**dame** *f* lady; (*mariée*) married lady; (*Échecs, Cartes*) queen; (*au jeu de dames*) king; **(jeu de) dames** checkers.
**damier** *m* checkerboard.
**dandiner (se)** *vpr* to waddle.
**danger** *m* danger; **en d.** in danger; **mettre en d.** to endanger; **en cas de d.** in an emergency; **en d. de mort** in peril of death; **'d. de mort'** (*panneau*) 'danger'; **être sans d.** to be safe.
**dangereusement** *adv* dangerously.
**dangereux, -euse** *a* dangerous (**pour** to).
**danois, -oise 1** *a* Danish. **2** *mf* Dane. **3** *m* (*langue*) Danish.
**dans** *prép* in; (*changement de lieu*) into; (*à l'intérieur de*) inside; **entrer d.** to go in(to); **boire/prendre/***etc* **d.** to drink/take/*etc* from *ou* out of; **d. deux jours/***etc* (*temps futur*) in two days/*etc*; **d. les dix francs/***etc* about ten francs/*etc*.
**danse** *f* dance; (*art*) dancing.
**danser** *vti* to dance.
**danseur, -euse** *mf* dancer.
**date** *f* date; **en d. du . . .** dated the . . . ; **d. d'expiration** expiry date; **d. limite** deadline.
**dater 1** *vt* (*lettre etc*) to date. **2** *vi* **d. de** to date from; **à d. de** as from.
**datte** *f* (*fruit*) date.
**dauphin** *m* dolphin.
**davantage** *adv* (*quantité*) more; (*temps*) longer; **d. de temps/***etc* more time/*etc*; **d. que** more than; longer than.
**de**[1] (**d'** *before a vowel or mute h*; **de + le = du, de + les = des**) *prép* (*complément d'un nom*) of; **les rayons du soleil** the rays of the sun; **le livre de Paul** Paul's book; **un pont de fer** an iron bridge; **une augmentation d'impôts/***etc* an increase in taxes/*etc*. ▪ (*complément d'un adjectif*) **digne de** worthy of; **heureux de** happy to; **content de qch/qn** pleased with sth/s.o. ▪ (*complément d'un verbe*) **parler** to speak of *ou* about; **décider**

**faire** to decide to do. ▪ (*provenance*: *lieu & temps*) from; **mes amis du village** my friends from the village. ▪ (*agent*) **accompagné de** accompanied by. ▪ (*moyen*) **armé de** armed with; **se nourrir de** to live on. ▪ (*manière*) **d'une voix douce** in *ou* with a gentle voice. ▪ (*cause*) **mourir de faim** to die of hunger. ▪ (*temps*) **travailler de nuit** to work by night; **six heures du matin** six o'clock in the morning. ▪ (*mesure*) **avoir** *ou* **faire six mètres de haut** to be 20 feet high; **homme de trente ans** thirty-year-old man; **gagner cent francs de l'heure** to earn a hundred francs an hour.

**de**[2] *art partitif* some; **elle boit du vin** she drinks (some) wine; **il ne boit pas de vin** (*négation*) he doesn't drink (any) wine; **des fleurs** (some) flowers; **de jolies fleurs** (some) pretty flowers; **il y en a six de tués** (*avec un nombre*) there are six killed.

**dé** *m* (*à jouer*) dice; (*à coudre*) thimble; **jouer aux dés** to play dice.

**déballer** *vt* to unpack.

**débarbouiller (se)** *vpr* to wash one's face.

**débarcadère** *m* quay, wharf.

**débarquement** *m* landing; unloading.

**débarquer 1** *vt* (*passagers*) to land; (*marchandises*) to unload. **2** *vi* (*passagers*) to land.

**débarras** *m* storeroom; **bon d.!** *Fam* good riddance!

**débarrasser** *vt* (*table etc*) to clear (**de** of); **d. qn de** (*ennemi*, *soucis etc*) to rid s.o. of; (*manteau etc*) to relieve s.o. of; **se d. de** to get rid of.

**débat** *m* discussion, debate.

**débattre*** *vt* to discuss, debate.

**débattre (se)** *vpr* to struggle (to get free).

**débile 1** *a* (*esprit*, *enfant etc*) weak; *Fam* idiotic. **2** *mf Fam* idiot.

**débit** *m* (*vente*) sales; (*compte*) debit; (*de fleuve*) flow; **d. de boissons** bar, café.

**débiter** *vt* (*découper*) to cut up (**en** into); (*vendre*) to sell; (*compte*) to debit.

**débiteur, -trice 1** *mf* debtor. **2** *a* **compte d.** debit account.

**déblayer** *vt* (*terrain*, *décombres*) to clear.

**débloquer** *vt* (*mécanisme*) to unjam; (*crédits*) to release.

**déboîter 1** *vt* (*tuyau*) to disconnect; (*os*) to dislocate. **2** *vi* (*véhicule*) to pull out, change lanes.

**déborder 1** *vi* (*fleuve*, *liquide*) to overflow; **l'eau déborde du vase** the water is overflowing the vase. **2** *vt* (*dépasser*) to go beyond; **débordé de travail** snowed under with work.

**débouché** *m* (*carrière*) opening; (*marché pour produit*) outlet.

**déboucher** *vt* (*bouteille*) to open, uncork; (*lavabo*, *tuyau*) to unclog.

**débourser** *vti* to pay out.

**debout** *adv* standing (up); **mettre d.** (*planche etc*) to stand up, put upright; **se mettre d.** to stand *ou* get up; **rester d.** to remain standing; **être d.** (*levé*) to be up; **d.!** get up!

**déboutonner** *vt* to unbutton, undo.

**débraillé, -ée** *a* (*tenue etc*) slovenly, sloppy.

**débrancher** *vt* to unplug, disconnect.

**débrayer** *vi* (*conducteur*) to depress the clutch.

**débris** *mpl* fragments; (*restes*) remains; (*détritus*) garbage.

**débrouillard, -arde** *a* smart, resourceful.

**débrouiller (se)** *vpr* to manage (**pour faire** to do).

**début** *m* start, beginning; **au d.** at the beginning.

**débutant, -ante** *mf* beginner.

**débuter** *vi* to start, begin.

**décaféiné, -ée** *a* decaffeinated.

**décalage** *m* (*écart*) gap; **d. horaire** time difference.

**décalcomanie** *f* (*image*) decal.

**décaler** *vt* to shift.
**décalquer** *vt* (*dessin*) to trace.
**décapant** *m* cleaning agent; (*pour enlever la peinture*) paint stripper.
**décaper** *vt* (*métal*) to clean; (*surface peinte*) to strip.
**décapiter** *vt* to behead.
**décapotable** *a* (*voiture*) convertible.
**décapsuler** *vt* **d. une bouteille** to take the top off a bottle.
**décapsuleur** *m* bottle-opener.
**décéder** *vi* to die.
**déceler** *vt* (*trouver*) to detect.
**décembre** *m* December.
**décemment** *adv* decently.
**décent, -ente** *a* (*convenable*) decent.
**déception** *f* disappointment.
**décerner** *vt* (*prix*) to award.
**décès** *m* death.
**décevant, -ante** *a* disappointing.
**décevoir*** *vt* to disappoint.
**déchaîné, -ée** *a* (*foule*) wild.
**déchaîner** *vt* **d. l'enthousiasme/les rires** to set off wild enthusiasm/a storm of laughter.
**déchaîner (se)** *vpr* (*tempête, rires*) to break out; (*foule*) to run riot; (*personne*) to fly into a rage.
**décharge** *f* **d. (publique)** (garbage) dump; **d. (électrique)** (electric) shock.
**déchargement** *m* unloading.
**décharger** *vt* to unload; (*batterie*) to discharge.
**décharger (se)** *vpr* (*batterie*) to go dead.
**déchausser (se)** *vpr* to take one's shoes off.
**déchet** *m* **déchets** (*restes*) waste; **il y a du d.** there's some waste.
**déchiffrer** *vt* to decipher.
**déchiqueter** *vt* to tear to shreds.
**déchirer** *vt* (*page etc*) to tear (up); (*vêtement*) to tear; (*ouvrir*) to tear open.
**déchirer (se)** *vpr* (*robe etc*) to tear.
**déchirure** *f* tear.
**décidé, -ée** *a* (*air, ton*) determined; **d. à faire** determined to do.
**décidément** *adv* undoubtedly.
**décider 1** *vt* (*opération*) to decide on; **d. que** to decide that. **2** *vi* **d. de faire** to decide to do.
**décider (se)** *vpr* **se d. à faire** to make up one's mind to do.
**décimal, -e, -aux** *a* decimal.
**décimètre** *m* decimeter; **double d.** ruler.
**décisif, -ive** *a* decisive.
**décision** *f* decision; (*fermeté*) determination.
**déclaration** *f* declaration; (*de vol etc*) notification; (*commentaire*) statement; **d. de revenus** tax return.
**déclarer** *vt* to declare (**que** that); (*vol etc*) to notify.
**déclarer (se)** *vpr* (*incendie*) to break out.
**déclencher** *vt* (*mécanisme, réaction*) to trigger, start (off); (*attaque*) to launch.
**déclencher (se)** *vpr* (*alarme etc*) to go off.
**déclic** *m* (*bruit*) click.
**décoiffer** *vt* **d. qn** to mess up s.o.'s hair.
**décollage** *m* (*d'avion*) takeoff.
**décoller 1** *vi* (*avion*) to take off. **2** *vt* (*timbre*) to unstick; **se d.** to come unstuck.
**décolorer (se)** *vpr* to fade.
**décombres** *mpl* rubble.
**décongeler 1** *vt* **(faire) d.** (*aliment*) to thaw. **2** *vi* to thaw.
**déconseiller** *vt* **d. qch à qn** to advise s.o. against sth; **d. à qn de faire** to advise s.o. against doing.
**décontracter (se)** *vpr* to relax.
**décor** *m* (*théâtre, paysage*) scenery; (*d'intérieur*) decoration.
**décorateur, -trice** *mf* (interior) decorator.
**décoratif, -ive** *a* decorative.
**décoration** *f* decoration.
**décorer** *vt* (*maison, soldat*) to decorate (**de** with).
**découdre** *vt* to unstitch; **se d.** to come unstitched.
**découpage** *m* (*image*) cutout.

**découper** *vt* (*viande*) to carve; (*article*) to cut out.
**découragement** *m* discouragement.
**décourager** *vt* to discourage; **se d.** to get discouraged.
**découvert** *m* (*d'un compte*) overdraft.
**découverte** *f* discovery.
**découvrir*** *vt* to discover (**que** that).
**découvrir (se)** *vpr* (*dans son lit*) to push the bedcovers off; (*ciel*) to clear (up); (*enlever son chapeau*) to remove one's hat.
**décrasser** *vt* (*nettoyer*) to clean.
**décrire*** *vt* to describe.
**décroché** *a* (*téléphone*) off the hook.
**décrocher** *vt* (*détacher*) to unhook; (*tableau*) to take down; **se d.** (*tableau*) to fall down; **d. (le téléphone)** to pick up the phone.
**décrotter** *vt* to clean (the mud off).
**déçu, -ue** (*pp of* **décevoir**) *a* disappointed.
**déculotter (se)** *vpr* to take off one's pants.
**dédaigner** *vt* to scorn, despise.
**dédaigneux, -euse** *a* scornful.
**dédain** *m* scorn.
**dedans 1** *adv* inside; **en d.** on the inside; **tomber d.** (*trou*) to fall in (it); **je me suis fait rentrer d.** (*accident de voiture*) someone crashed into me. **2** *m* **le d.** the inside.
**dédommagement** *m* compensation.
**dédommager** *vt* to compensate (**de** for).
**déduction** *f* deduction.
**déduire*** *vt* (*soustraire*) to deduct (**de** from).
**déesse** *f* goddess.
**défaire*** *vt* (*nœud etc*) to undo; **se d.** to come undone.
**défait** *a* (*lit*) unmade.
**défaite** *f* defeat.
**défaut** *m* (*faiblesse*) fault; (*de fabrication*) defect.
**défavorable** *a* unfavorable (**à** to).
**défavoriser** *vt* to put at a disadvantage.
**défectueux, -euse** *a* faulty, defective.
**défendre**[1] *vt* (*protéger*) to defend; **se d.** to defend oneself.
**défendre**[2] *vt* (*interdire*) **d. à qn de faire** to forbid s.o. to do; **d. qch à qn** to forbid s.o. sth.
**défense**[1] *f* (*protection*) defense; (*d'éléphant*) tusk.
**défense**[2] *f* (*interdiction*) **'d. de fumer'** 'no smoking'; **'d. (absolue) d'entrer'** '(strictly) no entry'.
**défenseur** *m* defender.
**défi** *m* challenge; **lancer un d. à qn** to challenge s.o.
**défier** *vt* to challenge (**à** to); **d. qn de faire** to challenge s.o. to do.
**défiguré, -ée** *a* disfigured.
**défilé** *m* (*militaire*) parade; (*gorge*) pass.
**défiler** *vi* (*soldats*) to march.
**définir** *vt* to define; **article défini** *Grammaire* definite article.
**définitif, -ive** *a* final, definitive.
**définition** *f* definition; (*de mots croisés*) clue.
**défoncé, -ée** *a* (*route*) bumpy; (*drogué*) *Fam* high.
**défoncer** *vt* (*porte, mur*) to smash in, knock down; (*trottoir, route*) to dig up.
**déformé, -ée** *a* misshapen; **chaussée déformée** uneven road surface, bumpy road.
**déformer** *vt* to put out of shape; **se d.** to lose its shape.
**défouler (se)** *vpr* to let off steam.
**défricher** *vt* (*terrain*) to clear.
**défroisser** *vt* to smooth out.
**dégagé, -ée** *a* (*ciel*) clear.
**dégagement** *m* (*action*) clearing; *Football* kick (down the field); **itinéraire de d.** alternative route (*to ease traffic congestion*).
**dégager 1** *vt* (*table etc*) to clear (**de** of); (*odeur*) to give off; **d. qn de** (*décombres etc*) to pull s.o. out

of. **2** *vi Football* to clear the ball (down the field); **dégagez!** clear the way!

**dégager (se)** *vpr* (*ciel*) to clear; **se d. de** (*personne*) to pull oneself free from (*rubble*); (*odeur*) to come out of (*kitchen*).

**dégainer** *vti* (*arme*) to draw.

**dégarni, -ie** *a* bare; **front d.** receding hairline.

**dégarnir** *vt* (*arbre de Noël*) to take down the decorations from.

**dégarnir (se)** *vpr* (*crâne*) to go bald.

**dégâts** *mpl* damage.

**dégel** *m* thaw.

**dégeler** *vti* to thaw (out).

**dégivrer** *vt* (*réfrigérateur*) to defrost.

**déglingué, -ée** *a* falling to pieces.

**dégonflé, -ée 1** *a* (*pneu*) flat; (*lâche*) *Fam* yellow. **2** *mf Fam* yellow-belly.

**dégonfler** *vt* (*pneu*) to deflate.

**dégonfler (se)** *vpr* (*pneu*) to deflate; (*se montrer lâche*) *Fam* to chicken out.

**dégouliner** *vi* to trickle.

**dégourdi, -ie 1** *a* (*malin*) smart. **2** *mf* smart boy *ou* girl.

**dégourdir (se)** *vpr* **se d. les jambes** to stretch one's legs.

**dégoût** *m* disgust; **avoir du d. pour qch** to have a (strong) dislike for sth.

**dégoûtant, -ante** *a* disgusting.

**dégoûté, -ée** *a* disgusted (**de**, with, by); **il n'est pas d.** (*difficile*) he's not fussy.

**dégoûter** *vt* to disgust; **d. qn de qch** to (be enough to) make s.o. sick of sth.

**degré** *m* (*angle*, *température*) degree.

**dégringolade** *f* tumble.

**dégringoler** *vi* to tumble (down).

**déguerpir** *vi* to clear out, make tracks.

**dégueulasse** *a Fam* disgusting.

**déguisement** *m* disguise; (*de bal costumé*) costume.

**déguiser** *vt* to disguise; **d. qn (en)** (*costumer*) to dress s.o. up **(as); se d. (en)** to dress oneself up (as).

**déguster** *vt* (*goûter*) to taste.

**dehors 1** *adv* out(side); **en d.** on the outside; **en d. de la maison** outside the house; **en d. de la ville** out of town; **au-d. (de), au d. (de)** outside. **2** *m* (*extérieur*) outside.

**déjà** *adv* already; **elle l'a d. vu** she's seen it before, she's already seen it; **quand partez-vous, d.?** when did you say you are leaving?

**déjeuner 1** *vi* (*à midi*) to have lunch; (*le matin*) to have breakfast. **2** *m* lunch; **petit d.** breakfast.

**delà** *adv* **au-d. (de), au d. (de) beyond.**

**délabré, -ée** *a* dilapidated.

**délacer** *vt* (*chaussures*) to undo, untie.

**délai** *m* time limit; **sans d.** without delay; **dernier d.** final date.

**délasser (se)** *vpr* to relax.

**délayer** *vt* (*mélanger*) to mix (with liquid).

**délégation** *f* delegation.

**délégué, -ée** *mf* delegate.

**délibérer** *vi* (*se consulter*) to deliberate (**de** about).

**délicat, -ate** *a* (*santé, travail*) delicate; (*geste*) tactful; (*exigeant*) particular.

**délicatement** *adv* (*doucement*) delicately.

**délice** *m* delight.

**délicieux, -euse** *a* (*plat*) delicious.

**délier** *vt* to undo; **se d.** (*paquet*) to come undone.

**délimiter** *vt* (*terrain*) to mark off.

**délinquant, -ante** *mf* delinquent.

**délirer** *vi* (*dire n'importe quoi*) to rave.

**délit** *m* offense.

**délivrer** *vt* (*prisonnier*) to release, (set) free; (*billet*) to issue.

**déloger** *vt* to drive out.

**deltaplane**® *m* hang glider.

**déluge** *m* flood; (*de pluie*) downpour.

**demain** *adv* tomorrow; **à d.!** see you tomorrow!

**demande** *f* request (**de qch** for sth); **demandes d'emploi** positions wanted.

**demander** *vt* to ask for; (*nécessiter*) to require; **d. le chemin/l'heure** to ask the way/the time; **d. qch à qn** to ask s.o. for sth; **d. à qn de faire** to ask s.o. to do; **ça demande du temps** it takes time; **être très demandé** to be in great demand.

**demander (se)** *vpr* to wonder (**pourquoi** why, **si** if).

**démangeaison** *f* itch; **avoir des démangeaisons** to be itching.

**démanger** *vti* to itch; **son bras le démange** his arm itches.

**démaquiller (se)** *vpr* to take off one's makeup.

**démarche** *f* walk; **faire des démarches** to go through the process (**pour faire** of doing).

**démarrage** *m* start.

**démarrer** *vi* (*moteur*) to start (up); (*voiture*) to move off.

**démarreur** *m* starter.

**démasquer** *vt* to expose.

**démêler** *vt* (*cheveux*) to untangle.

**déménagement** *m* move, moving; **camion de d.** moving van.

**déménager** *vi* to move.

**déménageur** *m* mover.

**démettre** *vt* **se d. le pied**/*etc* to dislocate one's foot/*etc*.

**demeure** *f* (*belle maison*) mansion.

**demeurer** *vi* (*aux* **être**) (*rester*) to remain; (*aux* **avoir**) (*habiter*) to live.

**demi, -ie 1** *a* half; **d.-journée** half-day; **une heure et demie** an hour and a half; (*horloge*) half past one. **2** *adv* **(à) d. plein**/*etc* half-full/*etc*. **3** *m* (*verre*) (half-pint) glass of beer.

**demi-cercle** *m* semicircle.

**demi-douzaine** *f* **une d.-douzaine (de)** half a dozen.

**demi-finale** *f* semifinal.

**demi-frère** *m* stepbrother.

**demi-heure** *f* **une d.-heure** a half-hour, half an hour.

**demi-pension** *f* breakfast and one meal.

**demi-pensionnaire** *mf* day student.

**démission** *f* resignation.

**démissionner** *vi* to resign.

**demi-sœur** *f* stepsister.

**demi-tarif** *a inv* (*billet*) half-price.

**demi-tour** *m* (*en voiture*) U-turn; **faire d.-tour** (*à pied*) to turn back; (*en voiture*) to make a U-turn.

**démocratie** *f* democracy.

**démocratique** *a* democratic.

**démodé, -ée** *a* old-fashioned.

**demoiselle** *f* (*célibataire*) single woman; **d. d'honneur** (*à un mariage*) bridesmaid.

**démolir** *vt* (*maison*) to demolish, knock *ou* pull down.

**démolition** *f* demolition.

**démonstratif, -ive** *a & m Grammaire* demonstrative.

**démonstration** *f* demonstration, proof.

**démonter** *vt* (*mécanisme*) to take apart; (*tente*) to take down; **se d.** to come apart; to come down.

**démontrer** *vt* to show.

**démoraliser** *vt* to demoralize; **se d.** to become demoralized.

**déneiger** *vt* to clear of snow.

**dénicher** *vt* (*trouver*) to dig up.

**dénoncer** *vt* **d. qn** (*au professeur*) to tell on s.o. (**à** to); **se d.** to own up (**à** to).

**dénouer** *vt* (*corde*) to undo, untie; **se d.** (*nœud*) to come undone *ou* untied.

**denrées** *fpl* **d. alimentaires** foods.

**dense** *a* dense.

**dent** *f* tooth (*pl* teeth); (*de fourchette*) prong; **faire ses dents** (*enfant*) to be teething; **coup de d.** bite.

**dentaire** *a* dental.

**dentelle** *f* lace.

**dentier** *m* (set of) false teeth.

**dentifrice** *m* toothpaste.

**dentiste** *mf* dentist.
**déodorant** *m* deodorant.
**dépannage** *m* (emergency) repair.
**dépanner** *vt* (*voiture*) to repair.
**dépanneur** *m* (*de télévision*) repairman; (*de voiture*) roadside mechanic.
**dépanneuse** *f* (*voiture*) tow truck.
**départ** *m* departure; (*d'une course*) start; **ligne de d.** starting post; **au d.** at the start.
**département** *m* department.
**départementale** *af* **route d.** secondary road.
**dépasser 1** *vt* (*véhicule*) to overtake; **d. qn** (*en hauteur*) to be taller than s.o.; (*surclasser*) to be ahead of s.o. **2** *vi* (*clou etc*) to stick out.
**dépêcher (se)** *vpr* to hurry (up).
**dépeigné, -ée** *a* **être d.** to have untidy hair.
**dépendre** *vi* to depend (**de** on, upon).
**dépense** *f* (*frais*) expense.
**dépenser** *vt* (*argent*) to spend.
**dépenser (se)** *vpr* to exert oneself.
**dépensier, -ière** *a* wasteful.
**dépister** *vt* (*criminel*) to track down; (*maladie*) to detect.
**dépit** *m* **en d. de** in spite of; **en d. du bon sens** (*mal*) atrociously.
**déplacement** *m* (*voyage*) (business) trip.
**déplacer** *vt* to shift, move.
**déplacer (se)** *vpr* (*voyager*) to travel (about).
**déplaire*** *vi* **ça me déplaît** I don't like it.
**dépliant** *m* (*prospectus*) leaflet.
**déplier** *vt*, **se déplier** *vpr* to unfold.
**déplorable** *a* regrettable, deplorable.
**déplorer** *vt* (*regretter*) to deplore; **d. que** (+ *subjonctif*) to regret that.
**déployer** *vt* (*ailes*) to spread.
**déporter** *vt* (*dévier*) to carry (off course).
**déposer** *vt* (*poser*) to put down; (*laisser*) to leave; (*plainte*) to lodge; (*ordures*) to dump; **d. qn** (*en voiture*) to drop s.o. (off).
**déposer (se)** *vpr* (*poussière*) to settle.
**dépôt** *m* (*d'ordures*) dump; (*dans une bouteille*) deposit.
**dépotoir** *m* garbage dump.
**dépouillé, -ée** *a* (*arbre*) bare.
**dépression** *f* depression; **d. nerveuse** nervous breakdown.
**déprimé, -ée** *a* depressed.
**déprimer** *vt* to depress.
**depuis 1** *prép* since; **d. lundi** since Monday; **d. qu'elle est partie** since she left; **j'habite ici d. un mois** I've been living here for a month; **d. quand êtes-vous là?** how long have you been here?; **d. Paris** from Paris. **2** *adv* since (then).
**député** *m* (*à l'Assemblée Nationale*) = congressman, congresswoman.
**déraciner** *vt* (*arbre*) to uproot.
**déraillement** *m* derailment.
**dérailler** *vi* (*train*) to jump the rails.
**dérangement** *m* **en d.** (*téléphone*) out of order.
**déranger** *vt* (*affaires*) to disturb, upset; **d. qn** to disturb *ou* bother s.o.; **ça vous dérange si je fume?** do you mind if I smoke?
**déranger (se)** *vpr* (*se déplacer*) to bother to come *ou* go; **ne te dérange pas!** don't bother!
**dérapage** *m* skid.
**déraper** *vi* to skid.
**déréglé, -ée** *a* out of order.
**dérégler** *vt* (*télévision etc*) to put out of order; **se d.** (*montre etc*) to go wrong.
**dériver** *vi* (*bateau*) to drift.
**dernier, -ière 1** *a* last; (*mode*) latest; (*étage*) top; **en d.** last. **2** *mf* last (person *ou* one); **ce d.** the latter; **être le d. de la classe** to be (at the) bottom of the class.
**dernièrement** *adv* recently.
**dérober** *vt* (*voler*) to steal (**à** from).

**dérouiller** *vt* **se d. les jambes** to stretch one's legs.
**dérouler** *vt* (*tapis*) to unroll; (*fil*) to unwind.
**dérouler (se)** *vpr* (*événement*) to take place.
**derrick** *m* oil rig.
**derrière 1** *prép* & *adv* behind; **assis d.** (*dans une voiture*) sitting in the back; **par d.** (*attaquer*) from behind. **2** *m* back; (*fesses*) behind; **pattes de d.** hind legs.
**des** *voir* **de**[1,2], **le.**
**dès** *prép* from; **d. le début** (right) from the start; **d. qu'elle viendra** as soon as she comes.
**désaccord** *m* disagreement.
**désaccordé, -ée** *a* (*violon etc*) out of tune.
**désaffecté, -ée** *a* (*gare etc*) disused.
**désagréable** *a* unpleasant.
**désaltérer** *vt* **d. qn** to quench s.o.'s thirst; **se d.** to quench one's thirst.
**désapprouver** *vt* to disapprove of.
**désarmer** *vt* to disarm.
**désastre** *m* disaster.
**désastreux, -euse** *a* disastrous.
**désavantage** *m* disadvantage.
**désavantager** *vt* to handicap.
**desceller (se)** *vpr* to come loose.
**descendre 1** *vi* (*aux* **être**) to come *ou* go down; (*d'un train*) to get off; (*d'un arbre*) to climb down (**de** from); (*thermomètre*) to fall; (*marée*) to go out; **d. de cheval** to dismount; **d. en courant** to run down. **2** *vt* (*aux* **avoir**) (*escalier*) to come *ou* go down; (*objet*) to bring *ou* take down.
**descente** *f* (*d'avion etc*) descent; (*pente*) slope; **d. de lit** (*tapis*) bedside rug.
**description** *f* description.
**désenfler** *vi* to go down.
**déséquilibre (en)** *adv* (*meuble*) unsteady.
**déséquilibrer** *vt* to throw off balance.
**désert -erte** *a* deserted; **île déserte** desert island.
**désert** *m* desert.
**désespérant, -ante** *a* (*enfant*) hopeless.
**désespéré, -ée** *a* (*personne*) in despair; (*situation*) hopeless; (*efforts*) desperate.
**désespérer** *vt* to drive to despair.
**désespoir** *m* despair.
**déshabiller** *vt*, **se déshabiller** *vpr* to undress.
**désherbant** *m* weed killer.
**désherber** *vti* to weed.
**désigner** *vt* (*montrer*) to point to; (*élire*) to appoint; (*signifier*) to indicate.
**désinfectant** *m* disinfectant.
**désinfecter** *vt* to disinfect.
**désirer** *vt* to want; **je désire que tu viennes** I want you to come.
**désobéir** *vi* to disobey; **d. à qn** to disobey s.o.
**désobéissant, -ante** *a* disobedient.
**désodorisant** *m* air freshener.
**désolé, -ée** *a* **être d.** (*navré*) to be sorry (**que** (+ *subjonctif*) that, **de faire** to do).
**désoler** *vt* to upset (very much).
**désordonné, -ée** *a* (*personne*) messy, untidy.
**désordre** *m* (*dans une chambre*) mess; (*dans une classe*) disturbance; **en d.** messy, untidy.
**désorganisé, -ée** *a* disorganized.
**désormais** *adv* from now on.
**desquel(le)s** *voir* **lequel.**
**dessécher** *vt* (*bouche*) to parch.
**désssécher (se)** *vpr* (*plante*) to wither; (*peau*) to get dry.
**desserrer** *vt* (*ceinture*) to loosen; (*poing*) to open; (*frein*) to release; **se d.** to come loose.
**dessert** *m* dessert.
**desservir** *vt* (*table*) to clear; **le car dessert ce village** the bus stops at this village.
**dessin** *m* drawing; **d. (humoristique)** cartoon; **d. animé** (*film*) cartoon; **école de d.** art school.
**dessinateur, -trice** *mf* drawer; **d. humoristique** cartoonist.

**dessiner** *vt* to draw.

**dessous 1** *adv* under(neath), below; **en d.** under(neath); **par-d.** (*passer*) under(neath). **2** *m* underside, underneath; **drap de d.** bottom sheet; **les gens du d.** the people downstairs.

**dessous-de-plat** *m inv* tablemat.

**dessus 1** *adv* (*marcher, monter*) on it; (*passer*) over it; **par-d.** (*sauter*) over (it). **2** *m* top; **drap de d.** top sheet; **les gens du d.** the people upstairs.

**dessus-de-lit** *m inv* bedspread.

**destin** *m* fate.

**destination** *f* (*lieu*) destination; **à d. de** (*train*) to, for.

**destiner** *vt* **d. qch à qn** to intend sth for s.o.

**destruction** *f* destruction.

**détachant** *m* stain remover.

**détacher**[1] *vt* (*ceinture*) to undo; (*personne*) to untie; (*ôter*) to take off; **se d.** (*chien*) to break loose; (*se dénouer*) to come undone; **se d. (de qch)** (*fragment*) to come off (sth).

**détacher**[2] *vt* (*linge*) to remove the stains from.

**détail**[1] *m* detail; **en d.** in detail.

**détail**[2] *m* **de d.** (*magasin, prix*) retail; **vendre au d.** to sell retail.

**détaillant, -ante** *mf* retailer.

**détaillé, -ée** *a* (*récit etc*) detailed.

**détaler** *vi* to run off.

**détecteur** *m* detector.

**détective** *m* **d. (privé)** (private) detective.

**déteindre*** *vi* (*couleur*) to run; **ton tablier bleu a déteint sur ma chemise** the blue of your apron has come off on my shirt.

**détendre** *vt* **d. qn** to relax s.o.

**détendre (se)** *vpr* (*se reposer*) to relax; (*corde etc*) to slacken.

**détendu, -ue** *a* relaxed; (*ressort etc*) slack.

**détente** *f* (*repos*) relaxation.

**détenu, -ue** *mf* prisoner.

**détergent** *m* detergent.

**détérioration** *f* deterioration (**de** in).

**détériorer (se)** *vpr* to deteriorate.

**déterminer** *vt* (*préciser*) to determine.

**déterrer** *vt* to dig up.

**détester** *vt* to hate (**faire** doing, to do).

**détonation** *f* explosion.

**détour** *m* (*crochet*) detour.

**détourné, -ée** *a* (*chemin*) roundabout, indirect.

**detournement** *m* (*d'avion*) hijacking.

**détourner** *vt* (*dévier*) to divert; (*tête*) to turn (away); (*avion*) to hijack; **d. les yeux** to look away.

**détourner (se)** *vpr* to turn away; **se d. de** (*chemin*) to stray from.

**détraqué, -ée** *a* out of order.

**détraquer** *vt* (*mécanisme*) to put out of order.

**détraquer (se)** *vpr* (*machine*) to break down.

**détresse** *f* distress; **en d.** (*navire*) in distress.

**détritus** *mpl* garbage.

**détroit** *m* strait(s).

**détruire*** *vt* to destroy.

**dette** *f* debt; **avoir des dettes** to be in debt.

**deuil** *m* (*vêtements*) mourning; **en d.** in mourning.

**deux** *a* & *m* two; **d. fois** twice; **tous (les) d.** both.

**deuxième** *a* & *mf* second.

**deuxièmement** *adv* secondly.

**deux-pièces** *m inv* (*maillot de bain*) bikini.

**deux-points** *m inv Grammaire* colon.

**deux-roues** *m inv* two-wheeled vehicle.

**dévaler 1** *vt* (*escalier*) to race down. **2** *vi* (*tomber*) to tumble down.

**dévaliser** *vt* to rob.

**devancer** *vt* to get *ou* be ahead of.

**devant 1** *prép* & *adv* in front (of); **d. (l'hôtel/***etc*) in front (of the hotel/*etc*); **passer d. (l'église/***etc*) to go past (the church/*etc*); **assis d.** (*dans une voiture*) sitting in the

front. **2** *m* front; **roue de d.** front wheel; **patte de d.** foreleg.
**devanture** *f* (*vitrine*) shop *ou* store window.
**dévaster** *vt* to ruin, devastate.
**développer** *vt* (*muscles, photos etc*) to develop; **se d.** to develop.
**devenir*** *vi* (*aux* **être**) to become; **qu'est-il devenu?** what's become of him?
**déverser** *vt*, **se déverser** *vpr* (*liquide*) to pour out (**dans** into).
**déviation** *f* (*itinéraire provisoire*) detour.
**dévier** **1** *vt* (*circulation*) to divert. **2** *vi* (*de sa route*) to veer (off course).
**deviner** *vt* to guess.
**devinette** *f* riddle.
**devis** *m* estimate (*of cost of work to be done*).
**devise** *f* (*légende*) motto; **devises** (*argent*) (foreign) currency.
**dévisser** *vt* to unscrew.
**dévisser (se)** *vpr* (*bouchon*) to unscrew; (*se desserrer*) to come loose.
**dévoiler** *vt* (*secret*) to disclose.
**devoir***[1] *v aux* (*nécessité*) **je dois refuser** I must refuse, I have (got) to refuse; **j'ai dû refuser** I had to refuse. ▪ (*probabilité*) **il doit être tard** it must be late; **elle a dû oublier** she must have forgotten; **il ne doit pas être bête** he can't be stupid. ▪ (*obligation*) **tu dois apprendre tes leçons** you must study your lessons; **il aurait dû venir** he should have come; **vous devriez rester** you should stay. ▪ (*événement prévu*) **elle doit venir** she's supposed to be coming, she's due to come.
**devoir***[2] **1** *vt* (*argent etc*) to owe (**à** to). **2** *m* (*obligation*) duty; (*exercice*) exercise; **devoirs** (*à faire à la maison*) homework; **d. sur table** exam(ination) in class.
**dévorer** *vt* (*manger*) to eat up.
**dévoué, -ée** *a* (*soldat etc*) dedicated.
**dévouement** *m* dedication.
**dévouer (se)** *vpr* **se d. (pour qn)** to sacrifice oneself (for s.o.).
**diabète** *m* diabetes.
**diabétique** *mf* diabetic.
**diable** *m* devil; **habiter au d.** to live miles from anywhere.
**diagnostic** *m* diagnosis.
**diagonale** *f* diagonal (line); **en d.** diagonally.
**dialecte** *m* dialect.
**dialogue** *m* conversation; (*de film*) dialogue.
**diamant** *m* diamond.
**diamètre** *m* diameter.
**diapositive,** *Fam* **diapo** *f* (color) slide.
**diarrhée** *f* diarrhea.
**dictée** *f* dictation.
**dicter** *vt* to dictate (**à** to).
**dictionnaire** *m* dictionary.
**dicton** *m* saying.
**diesel** *a* & *m* **(moteur) d.** diesel (engine).
**diète** *f* (*jeûne*) **à la d.** on a diet.
**diététique** *a* **produit d.** health food.
**dieu, -x** *m* god; **D.** God.
**différence** *f* difference (**de** in).
**différent, -ente** *a* different (**de** from, to).
**difficile** *a* difficult; (*exigeant*) fussy; **d. à faire** difficult to do; **il nous est d. de** it's difficult for us to.
**difficulté** *f* difficulty; **en d.** in a difficult situation.
**diffuser** *vt* (*émission*) to broadcast.
**digérer** *vti* to digest.
**digestif, -ive** **1** *a* digestive. **2** *m* after-dinner liqueur.
**digestion** *f* digestion.
**digne** *a* **d. de** worthy of.
**digue** *f* dike; (*en bord de mer*) sea wall.
**dilater** *vt*, **se dilater** *vpr* to expand.
**diligence** *f* (*véhicule*) stagecoach.
**dimanche** *m* Sunday.
**dimension** *f* dimension.
**diminuer** **1** *vt* to reduce. **2** *vi* (*réserves*) to decrease; (*jours*) to get shorter; (*prix*) to drop.
**diminutif** *m* (*prénom*) nickname.
**dinde** *f* turkey.

**dindon** *m* turkey (cock).
**dîner 1** *vi* to have dinner; (*au Canada, en Belgique*) to have lunch. **2** *m* dinner.
**dînette** *f* (*jouet*) doll's dinner service *ou* set.
**dinosaure** *m* dinosaur.
**diphtongue** *f* diphthong.
**diplôme** *m* certificate, diploma.
**dire*** *vt* (*mot*) to say; (*vérité, secret, heure*) to tell; **d. des bêtises** to talk nonsense; **d. qch à qn** to tell s.o. sth, say sth to s.o.; **d. à qn que** to tell s.o. that, say to s.o. that; **d. à qn de faire** to tell s.o. to do; **on dirait un château/du Mozart** it looks like a castle/sounds like Mozart; **ça ne me dit rien** (*envie*) I don't feel like it; (*souvenir*) it doesn't ring a bell; **ça ne se dit pas** that's not said.
**direct, -e 1** *a* direct; **train d.** fast train. **2** *m* **en d.** (*émission*) live.
**directement** *adv* directly.
**directeur, -trice** *mf* director; (*d'école*) principal.
**direction** *f* (*sens*) direction; **en d. de** (*train*) to, for; **sous la d. de** (*orchestre*) conducted by; **la d.** (*équipe dirigeante*) the management.
**dirigeable** *a* & *m* **(ballon) d.** airship, dirigible.
**dirigeant** *m* (*de parti etc*) leader; (*d'entreprise, club*) manager.
**diriger** *vt* (*société*) to run; (*parti, groupe*) to lead; (*véhicule*) to steer; (*orchestre*) to conduct; (*arme etc*) to point (**vers** towards); **se d. vers** (*lieu*) to make one's way towards.
**dis, disant** *voir* **dire.**
**discipline** *f* (*règle*) discipline.
**discipliné, -ée** *a* well-disciplined.
**discipliner (se)** *vpr* to discipline oneself.
**disco** *f* disco.
**discothèque** *f* (*club*) discotheque.
**discours** *m* speech.
**discret, -ète** *a* (*personne*) discreet.
**discrètement** *adv* discreetly.
**discrétion** *f* discretion.
**discrimination** *f* discrimination.
**discussion** *f* discussion; (*conversation*) talk; **pas de d.!** no argument!
**discuter** *vi* (*parler*) to talk (**de** about); (*répliquer*) to argue; **d. sur qch** to discuss sth.
**dise (nt)** *etc voir* **dire.**
**disloquer (se)** *vpr* (*meuble*) to fall apart.
**disparaître*** *vi* to disappear; (*être porté manquant*) to be reported missing.
**disparition** *f* disappearance.
**disparu, -ue** *a* (*soldat*) missing.
**dispense** *f* exemption.
**dispenser** *vt* **d. qn de** (*obligation*) to exempt s.o. from.
**disperser** *vt* (*objets*) to scatter.
**disperser (se)** *vpr* (*foule*) to disperse.
**disponible** *a* (*article, place etc*) available.
**disposé, -ée** *a* **bien d.** in a good mood; **d. à faire** prepared to do.
**disposer 1** *vt* (*objets*) to arrange; **se d. à faire** to prepare to do. **2** *vi* **d. de qch** to make use of sth.
**dispositif** *m* (*mécanisme*) device.
**disposition** *f* arrangement; **à la d. de qn** at s.o.'s disposal; **prendre ses dispositions** to make arrangements.
**dispute** *f* quarrel.
**disputer** *vt* (*match*) to play; (*rallye*) to compete in; **d. qn** (*gronder*) *Fam* to tell s.o. off.
**disputer (se)** *vpr* to quarrel (**avec** with).
**disqualifier** *vt* (*équipe*) to disqualify.
**disque** *m* disk; **d. compact** compact disk.
**disquette** *f* (*d'ordinateur*) floppy (disk), diskette.
**dissertation** *f* (*au lycée etc*) essay.
**dissimuler** *vt* (*cacher*) to hide (**à** from); **se d.** to hide (oneself).
**dissipé, -ée** *a* (*élève*) unruly.
**dissiper** *vt* (*brouillard*) to dispel; **d. qn** to distract s.o.
**dissiper (se)** *vpr* (*brume*) to lift; (*élève*) to misbehave.

**dissoudre*** *vt,* **se dissoudre** *vpr* to dissolve.
**distance** *f* distance; **à deux mètres de d.** seven feet apart.
**distancer** *vt* to leave behind.
**distinct, -incte** *a* distinct.
**distinctement** *adv* clearly.
**distinguer** *vt* to distinguish; (*voir*) to make out; **d. le blé de l'orge** to tell wheat from barley; **se d. de** to be distinguishable from.
**distraction** *f* amusement; (*étourderie*) absent-mindedness.
**distraire*** *vt* (*divertir*) to entertain; **se d.** to amuse oneself.
**distrait, -aite** *a* absent-minded.
**distribuer** *vt* (*donner*) to hand out; (*courrier*) to deliver; (*cartes*) to deal.
**distributeur** *m* **d. (automatique)** vending machine; **d. de billets** ticket machine; (*de banque*) automatic teller machine, ATM.
**distribution** *f* distribution; (*du courrier*) delivery.
**dit, dite, dites** *voir* **dire**.
**divan** *m* couch.
**divers, -erses** *apl* (*distincts*) varied; (*plusieurs*) various.
**divertir** *vt* to entertain.
**divertir (se)** *vpr* to enjoy oneself.
**divertissement** *m* entertainment.
**diviser** *vt,* **se diviser** *vpr* to divide (**en** into).
**division** *f* division.
**divorce** *m* divorce.
**divorcé, -ée** *a* divorced.
**divorcer** *vi* to get divorced.
**dix** *a* & *m* ten.
**dix-huit** *a* & *m* eighteen.
**dixième** *a* & *mf* tenth.
**dix-neuf** *a* & *m* nineteen.
**dix-sept** *a* & *m* seventeen.
**dizaine** *f* **une d. (de)** about ten.
**docile** *a* docile.
**docker** *m* docker.
**docteur** *m* doctor.
**doctorat** *m* doctorate, = PhD.
**document** *m* document.
**documentaire** *m* (*film*) documentary.
**documentaliste** *mf* (*à l'école*) (school) librarian.
**documentation** *f* (*documents*) documentation.
**documenter (se)** *vpr* to collect information.
**dodo** *m* (*langage enfantin*) **faire d.** to sleep.
**doigt** *m* finger; **d. de pied** toe; **petit d.** little finger, pinkie.
**dois, doit, doive(nt)** *voir* **devoir**[1,2].
**dollar** *m* dollar.
**domaine** *m* (*terres*) estate.
**dôme** *m* dome.
**domestique 1** *a* (*animal*) domestic; **travaux domestiques** housework. **2** *mf* servant.
**domicile** *m* home; **livrer à d.** to deliver (to the house).
**domination** *f* domination.
**dominer 1** *vt* to dominate. **2** *vi* (*être le plus fort*) to dominate.
**domino** *m* domino; **dominos** (*jeu*) dominoes.
**dommage** *m* **(c'est) d.!** it's a pity *ou* a shame! (**que** + *subjonctif* that); **dommages** (*dégâts*) damage.
**dompter** *vt* (*animal*) to tame.
**dompteur, -euse** *mf* (*de lions*) lion tamer.
**don** *m* (*cadeau, aptitude*) gift; (*charité*) donation.
**donc** *conj* (*par conséquent*) so; **asseyez-vous d.!** won't you sit down!
**données** *fpl* (*information*) data.
**donner 1** *vt* to give; (*récolte*) to produce; (*sa place*) to give up; (*cartes*) to deal; **d. un coup à** to hit; **d. à réparer** to take (in) to be repaired; **ça donne soif/faim** it makes you thirsty/hungry; **se d. du mal** to go to a lot of trouble (**pour faire** to do). **2** *vi* **d. sur** (*fenêtre*) to overlook; (*porte*) to open onto.
**dont** *pron rel* (= **de qui, duquel, de quoi** *etc*) (*personne*) of whom; (*chose*) of which; (*appartenance*:

*personne, chose*) whose; **une mère d. le fils est malade** a mother whose son is ill; **la fille d. il est fier** the daughter he is proud of *ou* of whom he is proud; **la façon d.** the way in which.

**doré, -ée** *a* (*objet*) gilt, gold; (*couleur*) golden.

**dorer** *vt* (*objet*) to gild; **se d. au soleil** to sunbathe.

**dormir*** *vi* to sleep.

**dortoir** *m* dormitory.

**dos** *m* (*de personne, d'animal*) back; **à d. d'âne** (riding) on a donkey; **'voir au d.'** (*verso*) 'see over.'

**dose** *f* dose.

**dossier** *m* (*de siège*) back; (*papiers*) file.

**douane** *f* customs.

**douanier** *m* customs officer.

**double 1** *a* & *adv* double. **2** *m* **le d. (de)** (*quantité*) twice as much (as), double; **je l'ai en d.** I have two of them.

**doubler 1** *vt* (*vêtement*) to line; (*film*) to dub. **2** *vti* (*augmenter*) to double; (*en voiture*) to overtake.

**doublure** *f* (*étoffe*) lining.

**douce** *voir* **doux**.

**doucement** *adv* (*délicatement*) gently; (*à voix basse*) softly; (*lentement*) slowly.

**douceur** *f* (*de miel*) sweetness; (*de peau*) softness; (*de temps*) mildness.

**douche** *f* shower.

**doucher** *vt* **d. qn** to give s.o. a shower; **se d.** to take a shower.

**doué, -ée** *a* gifted (**en** at); (*intelligent*) clever.

**douillet, -ette** *a* (*lit*) soft, cozy; **tu es d.** (*délicat*) you're such a baby.

**douleur** *f* (*mal*) pain; (*chagrin*) sorrow.

**douloureux, -euse** *a* painful.

**doute** *m* doubt; **sans d.** probably, no doubt.

**douter** *vi* to doubt; **se d. de qch** to suspect sth; **je m'en doute** I would think so.

**doux, douce** *a* (*miel etc*) sweet; (*peau*) soft; (*temps*) mild.

**douzaine** *f* dozen; (*environ*) about twelve; **une d. d'œufs**/*etc* a dozen eggs/*etc*.

**douze** *a* & *m* twelve.

**douzième** *a* & *mf* twelfth.

**dragée** *f* sugared almond.

**dragon** *m* (*animal*) dragon.

**draguer** *vt* (*rivière*) to dredge; (*personne*) *Fam* to come on to.

**dramatique** *a* dramatic; **film d.** drama.

**drame** *m* drama; (*catastrophe*) tragedy.

**drap** *m* (*de lit*) sheet; **d. housse** fitted sheet; **d. de bain** bath towel.

**drapeau, -x** *m* flag.

**dressage** *m* training.

**dresser** *vt* (*échelle*) to put up; (*animal*) to train.

**dresser (se)** *vpr* (*personne*) to stand up; (*montagne*) to stand.

**dribbler** *vti Sport* to dribble.

**drogue** *f* **une d.** (*stupéfiant*) a drug; **la d.** drugs.

**drogué, -ée** *mf* drug addict.

**droguer (se)** *vpr* to take drugs.

**droguerie** *f* hardware store.

**droit[1]** *m* (*privilège*) right (**de faire** to do); (*d'inscription etc*) fee(s); **le d.** (*science*) law; **avoir d. à** to be entitled to.

**droit[2], droite 1** *a* (*route etc*) straight; (*vertical*) upright; (*angle*) right. **2** *adv* straight; **tout d.** straight ahead.

**droit[3], droite** *a* (*côté etc*) right.

**droite** *f* **la d.** (*côté*) the right (side); **à d.** (*tourner*) (to the) right; (*rouler etc*) on the right; **de d.** (*fenêtre etc*) right-hand; **à d. de** on *ou* to the right of.

**droitier, -ière** *a* & *mf* right-handed (person).

**drôle** *a* odd, strange; **d. d'air/de type** strange look/guy.

**drôlement** *adv* (*extrêmement*) terribly.

**du** *voir* **de[1,2], le.**

**dû, due** (*pp of* **devoir**[1,2]) *a* **d. à** due to.
**duc** *m* duke.
**duchesse** *f* duchess.
**duel** *m* duel.
**dune** *f* (sand) dune.
**duplex** *m* duplex.
**duquel** *voir* **lequel**.
**dur, -e 1** *a* (*substance*) hard; (*difficile*) hard, tough; (*hiver, personne, ton*) harsh; (*œuf*) hard-boiled. **2** *adv* (*travailler*) hard.
**durant** *prép* during.
**durcir** *vti*, **se durcir** *vpr* to harden.
**durée** *f* (*de film etc*) length.
**durer** *vi* to last; **ça dure depuis** it's been going on for.
**dureté** *f* hardness; (*de ton etc*) harshness.
**duvet** *m* (*d'oiseau*) down; (*sac*) sleeping bag.
**dynamique** *a* dynamic.
**dynamite** *f* dynamite.
**dynamo** *f* dynamo.
**dyslexique** *a* & *mf* dyslexic.

# E

**eau, -x** *f* water; **e. douce/salée** fresh/salt water; **e. de Cologne** cologne; **tomber à l'e.** (*projet*) to fall through.
**eau-de-vie** *f* (*pl* **eaux-de-vie**) brandy.
**ébéniste** *m* cabinet-maker.
**éblouir** *vt* to dazzle.
**éboueur** *m* garbage collector.
**ébouillanter (s')** *vpr* to scald oneself.
**éboulement** *m* landslide.
**ébouler (s')** *vpr* (*falaise*) to crumble; (*roches*) to fall.
**ébouriffé, -ée** *a* (*cheveux*) disheveled.
**ébranler** *vt* to shake; (*santé*) to weaken.
**ébranler (s')** *vpr* (*train etc*) to move off.
**ébrécher** *vt* (*assiette*) to chip.
**ébullition** *f* **être en é.** (*eau*) to be boiling.
**écaille** *f* (*de poisson*) scale; (*de tortue*) shell; (*pour lunettes*) tortoiseshell; (*de peinture*) flake.
**écailler** *vt* (*poisson*) to scale; (*huître*) to shell.
**écailler (s')** *vpr* (*peinture*) to flake (off), peel.
**écarlate** *a* scarlet.
**écarquiller** *vt* **é. les yeux** to open one's eyes wide.
**écart** *m* (*intervalle*) gap; (*embardée*) swerve; (*différence*) difference (**de** in, **entre** between); **à l'é.** out of the way; **à l'é. de** away from.
**écarté, -ée** *a* (*endroit*) remote; **les jambes écartées** with legs apart.
**écarter** *vt* (*objets*) to move apart; (*jambes, rideaux*) to open; **é. qch de qch** to move sth away from sth; **é. qn de** (*exclure*) to keep s.o. out of.
**écarter (s')** *vpr* (*s'éloigner*) to move away (**de** from).
**échafaud** *m* scaffold.
**échafaudage** *m* (*de peintre etc*) scaffold(ing).
**échalote** *f* shallot.
**échange** *m* exchange; **en é.** in exchange (**de** for).
**échanger** *vt* to exchange (**contre** for).
**échangeur** *m* (*autoroute*) interchange.
**échantillon** *m* sample.
**échapper** *vi* **é. à qn** to escape from s.o.; **é. à la mort** to escape death; **son nom m'échappe** her name escapes me.
**échapper (s')** *vpr* (*s'enfuir*) to escape (**de** from); (*gaz, eau*) to escape.
**écharde** *f* splinter.
**écharpe** *f* scarf; (*de maire*) sash; **en é.** (*bras*) in a sling.
**échauffer (s')** *vpr* (*sportif*) to warm up.
**échec** *m* failure; **les échecs** (*jeu*) chess; **é.!** check!; **é. et mat!** checkmate!

**échelle** *f* (*marches*) ladder; (*dimension*) scale; **faire la courte é. à qn** to give s.o. a leg up *ou* a boost.
**échelon** *m* (*d'échelle*) rung; (*de fonctionnaire*) grade.
**échiquier** *m* chessboard.
**écho** *m* (*d'un son*) echo.
**échouer** *vi* to fail; **é. à** (*examen*) to fail.
**échouer (s')** *vpr* (*navire*) to run aground.
**éclabousser** *vt* to splash (**de** with).
**éclaboussure** *f* splash.
**éclair** *m* (*lumière*) flash; (*d'orage*) flash of lightning.
**éclairage** *m* (*de pièce etc*) lighting.
**éclaircie** *f* (*durée*) sunny interval.
**éclaircir** *vt* (*couleur etc*) to make lighter; (*mystère*) to clear up.
**éclaircir (s')** *vpr* (*ciel*) to clear (up); (*situation*) to become clear.
**éclaircissement** *m* explanation.
**éclairé, -ée** *a* **bien/mal é.** well/badly lit.
**éclairer** *vt* (*pièce etc*) to light (up); **é. qn** (*avec une lampe*) to give s.o. some light.
**éclairer (s')** *vpr* (*visage*) to brighten up; (*situation*) to become clear; **s'é. à la bougie** to use candlelight.
**éclaireur, -euse** *mf* boy/girl scout.
**éclat**[1] *m* (*de la lumière*) brightness; (*de phare*) glare.
**éclat**[2] *m* (*de verre ou de bois*) splinter; (*de rire*) (out)burst.
**éclatant, -ante** *a* (*lumière, succès*) brilliant.
**éclatement** *m* (*de ballon etc*) bursting; (*de bombe*) explosion.
**éclater** *vi* (*ballon etc*) to burst; (*bombe*) to go off; (*verre*) to shatter; (*guerre, incendie*) to break out; (*orage*) to break; **é. de rire** to burst out laughing; **é. en sanglots** to burst into tears.
**éclore*** *vi* (*œuf*) to hatch.
**éclosion** *f* hatching.
**écluse** *f* (*de canal*) lock.
**écœurer** *vt* **é. qn** to make s.o. feel sick.
**école** *f* school; **à l'é.** in *ou* at school; **aller à l'é.** to go to school.
**écolier, -ière** *mf* schoolboy, schoolgirl.
**écologiste** *mf* environmentalist.
**économe** *a* thrifty.
**économie** *f* economy; **économies** (*argent*) savings; **une é. de temps** time saved; **faire des économies** to save (up).
**économique** *a* (*bon marché*) economical.
**économiser** *vti* to economize (**sur** on).
**écorce** *f* (*d'arbre*) bark; (*de fruit*) peel, skin.
**écorcher** *vt* (*érafler*) to scrape; **s'é.** to scrape oneself; **é. les oreilles** to grate on one's ears.
**écorchure** *f* scrape.
**écossais, -aise 1** *a* Scottish; (*tissu*) tartan; (*whisky*) Scotch. **2** *mf* Scot.
**écosser** *vt* (*pois*) to shell.
**écoulement** *m* (*de liquide*) flow; (*de temps*) passage.
**écouler (s')** *vpr* (*eau*) to flow out; (*temps*) to pass.
**écouter 1** *vt* to listen to. **2** *vi* to listen.
**écouteur** *m* (*de téléphone*) earpiece; **écouteurs** (*casque*) earphones.
**écran** *m* screen; **le petit é.** television.
**écrasant, -ante** *a* overwhelming.
**écraser** *vt* to crush; (*cigarette*) to put *ou* stub out; (*piéton*) to run over; **se faire é.** to get run over.
**écraser (s')** *vpr* to crash (**contre** into).
**écrémé** *a* (*lait*) skim.
**écrier (s')** *vpr* to exclaim (**que** that).
**écrire* 1** *vt* to write; (*en toutes lettres*) to spell; **é. à la machine** to type. **2** *vi* to write.
**écrire (s')** *vpr* (*mot*) to be spelled *ou* spelt.
**écrit** *m* **par é.** in writing.

**écriteau, -x** *m* notice, sign.
**écriture** *f* writing.
**écrivain** *m* author, writer.
**écrou** *m* (*de boulon*) nut.
**écrouler (s')** *vpr* to collapse.
**écueil** *m* reef; (*obstacle*) pitfall.
**écuelle** *f* bowl.
**écume** *f* (*de mer etc*) foam.
**écureuil** *m* squirrel.
**écurie** *f* stable.
**écusson** *m* (*en étoffe*) badge.
**édifice** *m* building.
**édifier** *vt* to erect.
**éditer** *vt* to publish.
**éditeur, -trice** *mf* publisher.
**édition** *f* (*livre, journal*) edition; (*métier*) publishing.
**édredon** *m* eiderdown.
**éducatif, -ive** *a* educational.
**éducation** *f* education; **avoir de l'é.** to have good manners.
**éduquer** *vt* to educate.
**effacer** *vt* to rub out, erase; (*en lavant*) to wash out; (*avec un chiffon*) to wipe away.
**effectif** *m* (*de classe etc*) total number.
**effectivement** *adv* actually.
**effectuer** *vt* (*expérience etc*) to carry out; (*trajet etc*) to make.
**effet** *m* effect (**sur** on); **faire de l'e.** (*remède*) to be effective; **en e.** indeed, in fact; **sous l'e. de la colère** in anger.
**efficace** *a* (*mesure etc*) effective; (*personne*) efficient.
**efficacité** *f* effectiveness; efficiency.
**effilocher (s')** *vpr* to fray.
**effleurer** *vt* to skim, touch (lightly).
**effondrer (s')** *vpr* to collapse.
**efforcer (s')** *vpr* **s'e. de faire** to try (hard) to do.
**effort** *m* effort; **sans e.** (*réussir etc*) effortlessly.
**effrayant, -ante** *a* frightening.
**effrayer** *vt* to frighten, scare.
**effroyable** *a* dreadful.
**égal, -e, -aux 1** *a* equal (**à** to); (*uniforme, régulier*) even; **ça m'est é.** I don't care. **2** *mf* (*personne*) equal.
**également** *adv* (*aussi*) also, as well.
**égaler** *vt* to equal.
**égaliser** *vi* to equalize.
**égalité** *f* equality; (*regularité*) evenness; **à é. (de score)** even, equal (in points).
**égard** *m* **à l'é. de** (*envers*) towards.
**égarer** *vt* (*objet*) to mislay.
**égarer (s')** *vpr* to lose one's way.
**égayer** *vt* (*pièce*) to brighten up; **é. qn** to cheer s.o. up.
**église** *f* church.
**égoïste** *a* & *mf* selfish (person).
**égorger** *vt* to cut the throat of.
**égout** *m* sewer; **eaux d'é.** sewage.
**égoutter 1** *vt* to drain. **2** *vi*, **s'égoutter** *vpr* to drain; (*linge*) to drip.
**égouttoir** *m* (dish) drainer.
**égratigner** *vt* to scratch.
**égratignure** *f* scratch.
**eh!** *int* hey!; **eh bien!** well!
**élan** *m* (*vitesse*) momentum; (*impulsion*) impulse; **prendre son é.** to get a running start.
**élancer (s')** *vpr* (*bondir*) to leap *ou* rush (forward).
**élargir (s')** *vpr* (*route etc*) to widen.
**élastique 1** *a* (*objet*) elastic. **2** *m* (*lien*) elastic *ou* rubber band.
**électeur, -trice** *mf* voter.
**élection** *f* election.
**électoral, -e, -aux** *a* **campagne électorale** election campaign.
**électricien** *m* electrician.
**électricité** *f* electricity.
**électrique** *a* electric.
**électrocuter** *vt* to electrocute.
**électronique** *a* electronic.
**électrophone** *m* record player.
**élégance** *f* elegance; **avec é.** elegantly.
**élégant, -ante** *a* elegant.
**élément** *m* element; (*de meuble*) unit; **éléments** (*notions*) rudiments.
**élémentaire** *a* basic; (*cours, école etc*) elementary.
**éléphant** *m* elephant.
**élevage** *m* breeding, raising.

**élève** *mf* pupil.

**élevé, -ée** *a* (*haut*) high; **bien/mal é.** well-/bad-mannered.

**élever** *vt* (*prix, voix etc*) to raise; (*enfant*) to bring up, raise; (*animal*) to breed, raise.

**élever (s')** *vpr* (*prix, ton etc*) to rise; **s'é. à** (*prix*) to amount to.

**éleveur, -euse** *mf* breeder.

**éliminatoire** *a* & *f* **(épreuve) é.** heat.

**éliminer** *vt* to eliminate.

**élire*** *vt* to elect (**à** to).

**elle** *pron* (*sujet*) she; (*chose, animal*) it; **elles** they. ▪ (*complément*) her; (*chose, animal*) it; **elles** them.

**elle-même** *pron* herself; (*chose, animal*) itself; **elles-mêmes** themselves.

**éloigné, -ée** *a* (*lieu*) far away; (*date*) distant; **é. de** (*village etc*) far (away) from.

**éloigner** *vt* (*chose, personne*) to move *ou* take away (**de** from).

**éloigner (s')** *vpr* (*partir*) to move *ou* go away (**de** from).

**émail, -aux** *m* enamel.

**emballage** *m* (*action*) packing; wrapping; (*caisse*) packaging; (*papier*) wrapping (paper).

**emballer** *vt* (*dans une caisse etc*) to pack; (*dans du papier*) to wrap (up); **e. qn** (*passionner*) *Fam* to thrill s.o.

**emballer (s')** *vpr* (*personne*) *Fam* to get carried away; (*cheval*) to bolt.

**embarcadère** *m* quay, wharf.

**embarcation** *f* (small) b[illegible]

**embardée** [illegible]barrass-

[illegible]**ante** *a* (*paquet*) [illegible]; (*question*) embarras-[illegible]

**embarrasser** *vt* **e. qn** to be in s.o.'s way; (*question etc*) to embarrass s.o.; **s'e. de** to burden oneself with.

**embaucher** *vt* (*ouvrier*) to hire.

**embêtant, -ante** *a* annoying; boring.

**embêtement** *m* trouble.

**embêter** *vt* (*agacer*) to bother; (*ennuyer*) to bore.

**embêter (s')** *vpr Fam* to get bored.

**emboîter** *vt* **s'emboîter** *vpr* (*tuyau(x)*) to fit together.

**embouchure** *f* (*de fleuve*) mouth.

**embourber (s')** *vpr* to get bogged down.

**embouteillage** *m* traffic jam.

**embouteillé, -ée** *a* (*rue*) congested.

**emboutir** *vt* (*voiture*) to crash into.

**embranchement** *m* (*de voie*) junction.

**embrasser** *vt* (*donner un baiser à*) to kiss; **s'e.** to kiss (each other).

**embrayage** *m* (*de véhicule*) clutch.

**embrocher** *vt* to skewer.

**embrouiller** *vt* (*fils*) to tangle (up); (*papiers etc*) to mix up; **e. qn** to confuse s.o.

**embrouiller (s')** *vpr* to get confused (**dans** in, with).

**embuscade** *f* ambush.

**émerger** *vi* to emerge (**de** from).

**émerveiller** *vt* to amaze, fill with wonder.

**émetteur** *m* **(poste) é.** transmitter.

**émettre*** *vt* (*lu*[illegible]) [illegible] to broad-[illegible]; [illegible] to issue.

**émietter (s')** *vpr* to [illegible]

[illegible]**grer** *vi* to emigrate.

**émission** *f* (*de radio etc*) broadcast; (*diffusion*) transmission; (*de timbre, monnaie*) issue.

**emmanchure** *f* arm hole.

**emmêler** *vt* to tangle (up).

**emménager** *vi* (*dans un logement*) to move in; **e. dans** to move into.

**emmener** *vt* to take (**à** to); **e. qn en promenade** to take s.o. for a walk.
**emmitoufler (s')** *vpr* to wrap (oneself) up.
**émotion** *f* emotion; (*trouble*) excitement; **une é.** (*peur*) a scare.
**émouvant, -ante** *a* moving.
**émouvoir*** *vt* to move, touch.
**empailler** *vt* to stuff.
**emparer (s')** *vpr* **s'e. de** to take, grab.
**empêchement** *m* **avoir un e.** to have something come up at the last minute (*to prevent or delay an action*).
**empêcher** *vt* to prevent, stop (**de faire** (from) doing); **elle ne peut pas s'e. de rire** she can't help laughing.
**empereur** *m* emperor.
**empester 1** *vt* (*tabac etc*) to stink of; **e. qn** to stink s.o. out. **2** *vi* to stink.
**empiler** *vt,* **empiler (s')** *vpr* to pile up (**sur** on).
**empire** *m* empire.
**emplacement** *m* site; (*de stationnement*) place.
**emplir** *vt,* **emplir (s')** *vpr* to fill (**de** with).
**emploi** *m* (*usage*) use; (*travail*) job, employment; **e. du temps** schedule; **sans e.** (*au chômage*) unemployed.
**employé, -ée** *mf* employee; (*de bureau, banque*) clerk, employee.
**employer** *vt* (*utiliser*) to use; **e. qn** to employ s.o.
**employer (s')** *vpr* (*expression*) to be ...
**emplo...** ...*mf* employer.
**empoign...**
**empoisonn...** poison oneself; ... be poisoned.
**emporter** *vt* (*prend...*) (**avec soi**) with ... (away) to carry away; (*p... traîner*) ... *vent*) to blow off *ou* away.
**emporter (s')** *vpr* to lose one's temper (**contre** with).
**empreinte** *f* mark; **e. (digitale)** fingerprint; **e. (de pas)** footprint.

**empresser (s')** *vpr* **s'e. de faire** to hasten to do.
**emprisonner** *vt* to jail.
**emprunt** *m* (*argent etc*) loan.
**emprunter** *vt* (*argent*) to borrow (**à** from); (*route*) to use.
**ému, -ue** *a* moved; (*attristé*) upset.
**en**[1] *prép* (*lieu*) in; (*direction*) to; **être/aller en France** to be in/go to France. ▪ (*temps*) in; **en février** in February; **d'heure en heure** from hour to hour. ▪ (*moyen, état etc*) by; in; on; **en avion** by plane; **en groupe** in a group; **en congé** on leave *ou* vacation. ▪ (*matière*) in; **en bois** in wood; **chemise en nylon** nylon shirt; **c'est en or** it's (made of) gold. ▪ (*comme*) **en cadeau** as a present. ▪ (+ *participe présent*) **en mangeant/***etc* while eating/*etc*; **en apprenant que** on hearing that; **en souriant** smiling, with a smile. ▪ (*transformation*) into; **traduire en** to translate into.
**en**[2] *pron & adv* (= *de là*) from there; **j'en viens** I've just come from there. ▪ (= *de ça, lui etc*) **il en est content** he's pleased with it *ou* him *ou* them; **en parler** to talk about it; **en mourir** to die of *ou* from it. ▪ (*partitif*) some; **j'en ai** I have some.
**encadrer** *vt* (*tableau*) to frame; (*entourer d'un trait*) to circle (*word*).
**encaisser** *vt* (*argent, loyer etc*) to collect.
**enceinte** *a* (*femme*) pregnant; **e. de six mois** six months pregnant.
**encens** *m* incense.
**encercler** *vt* to surround.
**enchaîner** *vt* to chain (up); (*idées* ...) to link (up).
...**(s')** *vpr* (*idées etc*) to be ...
**enc...**
...delighted

**enchanteur** *m* magician.
**enclos** *m* enclosure.
**encoche** *f* nick (**à** in).
**encolure** *f* neck; (*tour du cou*) collar (size).
**encombrant, -ante** *a* (*paquet*) bulky.
**encombrement** *m* (*d'objets*) clutter; (*de rue*) traffic jam.
**encombrer** *vt* (*pièce etc*) to clutter up (**de** with); (*rue*) to congest (**de** with); **e. qn** to hamper s.o.
**encore** *adv* (*toujours*) still; **e. là** still here. ▪ (*avec négation*) yet; **pas e.** not yet. ▪ (*de nouveau*) again; **essaie e.** try again. ▪ (*de plus*) **e. un café** another coffee, one more coffee; **e. une fois** (once) again, once more; **e. un** another (one), one more; **e. du pain** (some) more bread; **e. quelque chose** something else; **qui/quoi e.?** who/what else? ▪ (*avec comparatif*) even, still; **e. mieux** even better, better still.
**encourageant, -ante** *a* encouraging.
**encouragement** *m* encouragement.
**encourager** *vt* to encourage (**à faire** to do).
**encrasser** *vt* to clog up (with dirt).
**encre** *f* ink; **e. de Chine** India ink.
**encrier** *m* inkpot.
**encyclopédie** *f* encyclopedia.
**endetter (s')** *vpr* to get into debt.
**endive** *f* chicory, endive.
**endommager** *vt* to damage.
**endormi, -ie** *a* asleep, sleeping.
**endormir*** *vt* to put to sleep.
**endormir (s')** *vpr* to fall asleep, go to sleep.
**endroit** *m* (*lieu*) place; **à l'e.** (*vêtement*) right side out.
**endurant, -ante** *a* tough.
**endurcir** *vt* **e. qn** to harden s.o.; **s'e. à** to become hardened to (*pain etc*).
**endurer** *vt* to endure.
**énergie** *f* energy.
**énergique** *a* energetic; (*remède*) powerful; (*mesure, ton*) forceful.
**énergiquement** *adv* energetically.
**énervé, -ée** *a* on edge.
**énerver** *vt* **é. qn** (*irriter*) to get on s.o.'s nerves; (*rendre énervé*) to make s.o. nervous.
**énerver (s')** *vpr* to get worked up.
**enfance** *f* childhood.
**enfant** *mf* child (*pl* children); **e. en bas âge** infant; **e. de chœur** altar boy.
**enfantin, -ine** *a* (*voix, joie*) childlike; (*simple*) easy.
**enfer** *m* hell; **d'e.** (*bruit etc*) infernal; **à un train d'e.** at breakneck speed.
**enfermer** *vt* to lock up; **s'e. dans** (*chambre etc*) to lock oneself (up) in.
**enfiler** *vt* (*aiguille*) to thread; (*perles etc*) to string; (*vêtement*) to pull on.
**enfin** *adv* (*à la fin*) finally, at last; (*en dernier lieu*) lastly; **e. bref** in a word; **(mais) e.!** for heaven's sake!
**enflammer** *vt* to set fire to; (*allumette*) to light; (*irriter*) to inflame (*throat etc*).
**enflammer (s')** *vpr* to catch fire.
**enfler** *vti* to swell.
**enflure** *f* swelling.
**enfoncer 1** *vt* (*clou*) to knock in, hammer in; (*porte, voiture*) to smash in; **e. dans qch** (*couteau, mains etc*) to plunge into sth. **2** *vi*, **s'enfoncer** *vpr* (*s'enliser*) to sink (**dans** into).
**enfouir** *vt* to bury.
**enfuir* (s')** *vpr* to run away *ou* off (**de** from).
**enfumer** *vt* (*pièce*) to fill with smoke.
**engagement** *m* (*promesse*) commitment; (*dans une compétition*) entry; **prendre l'e. de** to undertake to.
**engager** *vt* (*discussion, combat*) to start; **e. qn** (*embaucher*) to hire s.o.
**engager (s')** *vpr* (*dans l'armée*) to enlist; (*sportif*) to enter (**pour** for); (*action, jeu*) to start; **s'e. à faire** to undertake to do.

**engelure** *f* chilblain.
**engin** *m* machine; **e. spatial** spaceship.
**engloutir** *vt* (*nourriture*) to wolf down; (*faire disparaître*) to swallow up.
**engouffrer (s')** *vpr* **s'e. dans** to sweep *ou* rush into.
**engourdir (s')** *vpr* to go numb.
**engrais** *m* fertilizer; (*naturel*) manure.
**engraisser 1** *vt* (*animal*) to fatten (up). **2** *vi* to get fat.
**engrenage** *m* gears.
**engueuler** *vt* **e. qn** *Fam* to give s.o. hell, bawl s.o. out.
**énigme** *f* riddle.
**enivrer (s')** *vpr* to get drunk (**de** on).
**enjambée** *f* stride.
**enjamber** *vt* to step over; (*pont etc*) to span (*river etc*).
**enjoliveur** *m* hubcap.
**enlèvement** *m* (*d'enfant*) kidnapping.
**enlever** *vt* to take away (**à qn** from s.o.); (*vêtement*) to take off; (*tache*) to take out; (*enfant etc*) to kidnap.
**enlever (s')** *vpr* (*tache*) to come out.
**enliser (s')** *vpr* to get bogged down (**dans** in).
**enneigé, -ée** *a* (*montagne, route*) snow-covered; (*bloqué par la neige*) snowed in.
**enneigement** *m* **bulletin d'e.** snow report.
**ennemi, -ie 1** *mf* enemy. **2** *a* **pays/soldat e.** enemy country/soldier.
**ennui** *m* boredom; **un e.** (*tracas*) trouble; **l'e., c'est que** the annoying thing is that.
**ennuyé, -ée** *a* (*air*) bored; **je suis e.** that bothers me.
**ennuyer** *vt* (*agacer, préoccuper*) to bother; (*fatiguer*) to bore.
**ennuyer (s')** *vpr* to get bored.
**ennuyeux, -euse** *a* boring; (*contrariant*) annoying.
**énorme** *a* enormous, huge.
**énormément** *adv* enormously; **e. de** an enormous amount of.
**enquête** *f* (*de police*) investigation; (*judiciaire*) inquiry; (*sondage*) survey.
**enquêter** *vi* to investigate; **e. sur** to investigate.
**enquêteur, -euse** *mf* investigator.
**enragé, -ée** *a* (*chien*) rabid; (*furieux*) furious.
**enregistrement** *m* (*des bagages*) check-in; (*sur bande etc*) recording.
**enregistrer 1** *vt* (*par écrit, sur bande etc*) to record; **(faire) e.** (*bagages*) to check. **2** *vi* to record; **ça enregistre** it's recording.
**enrhumer (s')** *vpr* to catch a cold.
**enrichir (s')** *vpr* to get rich.
**enrobé, -ée** *a* **e. de chocolat** chocolate-covered.
**enroué, -ée** *a* hoarse.
**enrouler** *vt* to wind; (*tapis*) to roll up; **s'e. dans** (*couvertures*) to wrap oneself up in.
**enseignant, -ante** *mf* teacher.
**enseigne** *f* sign; **e. lumineuse** neon sign.
**enseignement** *m* education; (*action, métier*) teaching.
**enseigner 1** *vt* to teach; **e. qch à qn** to teach s.o. sth. **2** *vi* to teach.
**ensemble 1** *adv* together. **2** *m* (*d'objets*) set; (*vêtement féminin*) outfit; **l'e. du personnel** the whole staff; **l'e. des enseignants** all of the teachers; **dans l'e.** on the whole; **d'e.** (*vue etc*) general.
**ensevelir** *vt* to bury.
**ensoleillé, -ée** *a* sunny.
**ensuite** *adv* (*puis*) next; (*plus tard*) afterwards.
**entaille** *f* (*fente*) notch; (*blessure*) gash.
**entailler** *vt* to notch; to gash.
**entamer** *vt* (*pain, peau etc*) to cut (into); (*bouteille etc*) to start (on).
**entasser** *vt*, **s'entasser** *vpr* (*objets*) to pile up; **(s')e. dans** (*passagers etc*) to crowd *ou* pile into.
**entendre** *vt* to hear; **e. parler de** to hear of; **e. dire que** to hear (it said) that.

**entendre (s')** *vpr* (*être d'accord*) to agree (**sur** on); **s'e. (avec qn)** to get on (with s.o.).

**entendu, -ue** *a* (*convenu*) agreed; **e.!** all right!; **bien e.** of course.

**entente** *f* (*accord*) agreement; **(bonne) e.** (*amitié*) good relationship.

**enterrement** *m* burial; (*funérailles*) funeral.

**enterrer** *vt* to bury.

**entêtement** *m* stubbornness; (*à faire qch*) persistence.

**entêter (s')** *vpr* to persist (**à faire** in doing).

**enthousiasme** *m* enthusiasm.

**enthousiasmer** *vt* to fill with enthusiasm; **s'e. pour** to be *ou* get enthusiastic about.

**enthousiaste** *a* enthusiastic.

**entier, -ière 1** *a* (*total*) whole; (*intact*) intact; **le pays tout e.** the whole country. **2** *m* **en e.** completely.

**entièrement** *adv* entirely.

**entonnoir** *m* (*ustensile*) funnel.

**entorse** *f* sprain.

**entortiller** *vt* **e. qch autour de qch** to wrap sth around sth.

**entourage** *m* circle of family and friends.

**entourer** *vt* to surround (**de** with); **entouré de** surrounded by.

**entracte** *m* (*au théâtre*) intermission.

**entraider (s')** *vpr* to help each other.

**entrain** *m* **plein d'e.** lively.

**entraînant, -ante** *a* (*musique*) lively.

**entraînement** *m* (*sportif*) training.

**entraîner** *vt* to carry away; (*causer*) to bring about; (*emmener de force*) to drag (*s.o.*) (away); (*athlète etc*) to train (**à** for).

**entraîner (s')** *vpr* (*sportif*) to train.

**entraîneur** *m* (*d'athlète*) coach.

**entre** *prép* between; **l'un d'e. vous** one of you.

**entrebâillé, -ée** *a* slightly open.

**entrebâiller** *vt* to open slightly.

**entrechoquer (s')** *vpr* to chink.

**entrecôte** *f* (filleted) rib steak.

**entrée** *f* (*action*) entry; (*porte*) entrance; (*accès*) admission (**de** to); (*vestibule*) entrance hall; (*billet*) ticket (for admission); (*plat*) first course; (*en informatique*) input; **à son e.** as he *ou* she came in; **'e. interdite'** 'no entry'; **'e. libre'** 'admission free'.

**entreposer** *vt* to store.

**entrepôt** *m* warehouse.

**entreprendre*** *vt* to undertake (**de faire** to do).

**entrepreneur** *m* (*en bâtiment*) contractor.

**entreprise** *f* company, firm.

**entrer** *vi* (*aux* **être**) to go in; (*venir*) to come in; **e. dans** (*pièce*) to come *ou* go into; (*arbre etc*) to crash into; **faire/laisser e. qn** to show/let s.o. in.

**entre-temps** *adv* meanwhile.

**entretenir*** *vt* to maintain; **e. sa forme** to stay in shape.

**entretenir (s')** *vpr* **s'e. de** to talk about (**avec** with).

**entretien** *m* maintenance; (*dialogue*) conversation; (*entrevue*) interview.

**entrevue** *f* interview.

**entrouvert, -erte** *a* half-open.

**énumération** *f* list(ing).

**énumérer** *vt* to list.

**envahir** *vt* to invade; (*herbe etc*) to overrun (*garden*).

**envahisseur** *m* invader.

**enveloppe** *f* (*pour lettre*) envelope; **e. timbrée à votre adresse** self-addressed stamped envelope.

**envelopper** *vt* to wrap (up) (**dans** in).

**envers 1** *prép* toward(s), to. **2** *m* **à l'e.** (*chaussette*) inside out; (*pantalon*) back to front; (*la tête en bas*) upside down.

**envie** *f* (*jalousie*) envy; (*désir*) desire; **avoir e. de qch** to want sth; **j'ai e. de faire** I feel like doing.

**envier** *vt* to envy (**qch à qn** s.o. sth).

**environ** *adv* (*à peu près*) about.

**environnant, -ante** *a* surrounding.
**environnement** *m* environment.
**environner** *vt* to surround.
**environs** *mpl* surroundings; **aux environs de** around.
**envisager** *vt* to consider (**de faire** doing).
**envoi** *m* sending; (*paquet*) package; **coup d'e.** *Sport* kick-off.
**envoler (s')** *vpr* (*oiseau*) to fly away; (*avion*) to take off; (*chapeau etc*) to blow away.
**envoyé, -ée** *mf* (*reporter*) correspondent.
**envoyer*** *vt* to send; (*lancer*) to throw.
**épais, -aisse** *a* thick.
**épaisseur** *f* thickness.
**épaissir** *vti*, **s'épaissir** *vpr* to thicken.
**épanoui, -ie** *a* in full bloom; (*visage*) beaming.
**épanouir (s')** *vpr* to blossom; (*visage*) to beam.
**épargner** *vt* (*argent*) to save; (*ennemi etc*) to spare; **e. qch à qn** (*ennuis etc*) to spare s.o. sth.
**éparpiller** *vt*, **s'éparpiller** *vpr* to scatter.
**épatant, -ante** *a* marvelous.
**épaule** *f* shoulder.
**épave** *f* wreck.
**épée** *f* sword.
**épeler** *vt* (*mot*) to spell.
**éperon** *m* spur.
**épi** *m* (*de blé etc*) ear.
**épice** *f* spice.
**épicé, -ée** *a* spicy.
**épicer** *vt* to spice.
**épicerie** *f* grocery store; (*produits*) groceries.
**épicier, -ière** *mf* grocer.
**épidémie** *f* epidemic.
**épinards** *mpl* spinach.
**épine** *f* (*de plante*) thorn.
**épineux, -euse** *a* thorny.
**épingle** *f* pin; **é. de nourrice** safety pin; **é. à linge** clothes pin; **é. à cheveux** hairpin.
**épisode** *m* episode.
**épithète** *f* (*adjectif*) attribute.
**éplucher** *vt* (*carotte, pomme etc*) to peel.
**épluchure** *f* peeling.
**éponge** *f* sponge.
**éponger** *vt* to sponge up.
**époque** *f* (*date*) time; (*historique*) age.
**épouse** *f* wife.
**épouser** *vt* **é. qn** to marry s.o.
**épousseter** *vt* to dust.
**épouvantable** *a* terrifying; (*mauvais*) appalling.
**épouvantail** *m* scarecrow.
**épouvante** *f* terror; **film d'é.** horror movie.
**épouvanter** *vt* to terrify.
**époux** *m* husband.
**épreuve** *f* (*examen*) test; (*sportive*) event; (*malheur*) ordeal.
**éprouver** *vt* to test; (*sentiment etc*) to feel.
**éprouvette** *f* test tube; **bébé-e.** test-tube baby.
**épuisant, -ante** *a* exhausting.
**épuisé, -ée** *a* exhausted; (*marchandise*) out of stock.
**épuiser** *vt* to exhaust; **s'é. à faire** to exhaust oneself doing.
**épuiser (s')** *vpr* (*réserves*) to run out.
**équateur** *m* equator.
**équation** *f* equation.
**équerre** *f* (*pour tracer*) square.
**équilibre** *m* balance; **tenir** *ou* **mettre en é.** to balance (**sur** on); **perdre l'é.** to lose one's balance.
**équilibrer** *vt* (*budget*) to balance.
**équipage** *m* crew.
**équipe** *f* team; (*d'ouvriers*) crew; **é. de secours** search party.
**équipement** *m* equipment; (*de camping, ski*) gear.
**équiper** *vt* to equip (**de** with).
**équipier, -ière** *mf* team member.
**équitable** *a* fair.
**équitation** *f* (horseback) riding.
**équivalent, -ente** *a* & *m* equivalent.
**érafler** *vt* to scrape, scratch.
**éraflure** *f* scrape, scratch.

**errer** *vi* to wander.
**erreur** *f* mistake.
**éruption** *f* (*de boutons*) rash.
**es** *voir* **être.**
**escabeau, -x** *m* stepladder.
**escadrille** *f* (*groupe d'avions*) flight.
**escalade** *f* climbing.
**escalader** *vt* to climb.
**escale** *f* **faire e. à** (*avion*) to stop (over) at; (*navire*) to put in at.
**escalier** *m* stairs; **e. roulant** escalator.
**escalope** *f* escalope (*thin slice of meat*).
**escargot** *m* snail.
**escarpé, -ée** *a* steep.
**esclave** *mf* slave.
**escorte** *f* escort.
**escorter** *vt* to escort.
**escrime** *f* fencing.
**escrimeur, -euse** *mf* fencer.
**escroc** *m* crook.
**espace** *m* space; **e. vert** garden, park.
**espacer** *vt* to space out.
**espagnol, -ole 1** *a* Spanish. **2** *mf* Spaniard. **3** *m* (*langue*) Spanish.
**espèce** *f* (*race*) species; (*genre*) kind, sort; **e. d'idiot!** (you) silly fool!
**espérance** *f* hope.
**espérer 1** *vt* to hope for; **e. que** to hope that; **e. faire** to hope to do. **2** *vi* to hope.
**espiègle** *a* mischievous.
**espion, -onne** *mf* spy.
**espionnage** *m* spying.
**espionner** *vt* to spy on.
**espoir** *m* hope; **sans e.** (*cas etc*) hopeless.
**esprit** *m* spirit; (*intellect*) mind; (*humour*) wit; **venir à l'e. de qn** to cross s.o.'s mind.
**Esquimau, -de, -aux** *mf* Eskimo.
**esquiver** *vt* to dodge.
**essai** *m* (*épreuve*) test; (*tentative*) try, attempt.
**essaim** *m* swarm (*of bees etc*).
**essayage** *m* (*de costume*) fitting.
**essayer** *vt* to try (**de faire** to do); (*vêtement*) to try on.
**essence** *f* gas.
**essentiel, -ielle 1** *a* essential. **2** *m* **l'e.** the main thing.
**essentiellement** *adv* essentially.
**essieu, -x** *m* axle.
**essoufflé, -ée** *a* out of breath.
**essuie-glace** *m* windshield wiper.
**essuie-mains** *m inv* (hand) towel.
**essuyer** *vt* to wipe.
**est**[1] *voir* **être.**
**est**[2] *m & a inv* east; **d'e.** (*vent*) east(erly); **de l'e.** eastern.
**estime** *f* regard.
**estimer** *vt* (*objet*) to value; (*juger*) to consider (**que** that); **e. qn** to have a high regard for s.o.; **s'e. heureux**/*etc* to consider oneself happy/*etc*.
**estomac** *m* stomach.
**estrade** *f* platform.
**estropier** *vt* to cripple.
**estuaire** *m* estuary.
**et** *conj* and; **vingt et un**/*etc* twenty-one/*etc*.
**étable** *f* cowshed.
**établi** *m* (work)bench.
**établir** *vt* (*installer*) to set up; (*plan, liste*) to draw up.
**établir (s')** *vpr* (*habiter*) to settle.
**établissement** *m* establishment; **é. scolaire** school.
**étage** *m* (*d'immeuble*) floor; **à l'é.** upstairs; **au premier é.** on the second floor.
**étagère** *f* shelf.
**étais, était** *etc voir* **être.**
**étalage** *m* (*vitrine*) display window.
**étaler** *vt* to lay out; (*en vitrine*) to display; (*beurre etc*) to spread.
**étanche** *a* watertight; (*montre*) waterproof.
**étang** *m* pond.
**étant** *voir* **être.**
**étape** *f* stage; (*lieu*) stop(over).
**État** *m* (*nation*) State; **homme d'É.** statesman.
**état** *m* (*condition*) state; **en bon é.** in good condition; **être en é. de faire** to be up to doing.
**étau, -x** *m* vise.

**été**[1] *pp of* **être.**
**été**[2] *m* summer; **en é.** in (the) summer.
**éteindre* 1** *vt* (*feu etc*) to put out; (*lampe etc*) to turn *ou* switch off. **2** *vi* to switch off.
**éteindre (s')** *vpr* (*feu*) to go out.
**éteint, -einte** *a* (*feu, bougie*) out; (*lampe*) off.
**étendre** *vt* (*nappe*) to spread (out); (*linge*) to hang out; **é. le bras**/*etc* to stretch out one's arm/*etc*.
**étendre (s')** *vpr* (*personne*) to stretch out; (*plaine*) to stretch; (*feu*) to spread.
**étendu, -ue** *a* (*forêt etc*) extensive; (*personne*) stretched out.
**étendue** *f* (*importance*) extent; (*surface*) area.
**éternité** *f* eternity.
**éternuement** *m* sneeze.
**éternuer** *vi* to sneeze.
**êtes** *voir* **être.**
**étinceler** *vi* to sparkle.
**étincelle** *f* spark.
**étiqueter** *vt* to label.
**étiquette** *f* label.
**étirer (s')** *vpr* to stretch (oneself).
**étoffe** *f* material.
**étoile** *f* star; **à la belle é.** in the open.
**étoilé, -ée** *a* (*ciel*) starry.
**étonnant, -ante** *a* surprising.
**étonnement** *m* surprise.
**étonner** *vt* to surprise.
**étonner (s')** *vpr* to be surprised (**de qch** at sth, **que** (+ *subjonctif*) that).
**étouffant, -ante** *a* (*air*) stifling.
**étouffer 1** *vt* (*tuer*) to suffocate, smother; (*bruit*) to muffle; (*feu*) to smother; **é. qn** (*chaleur*) to stifle s.o. **2** *vi* **on étouffe!** it's stifling!
**étouffer (s')** *vpr* (*en mangeant*) to choke (**sur, avec** on).
**étourderie** *f* thoughtlessness; **une é.** a thoughtless blunder.
**étourdi, -ie** *a* thoughtless.
**étourdir** *vt* to stun; (*vertige*) to make dizzy.
**étourdissant, -ante** *a* (*bruit*) deafening.
**étourdissement** *m* (*malaise*) dizzy spell.
**étrange** *a* strange, odd.
**étranger, -ère 1** *a* (*d'un autre pays*) foreign; (*non familier*) strange (**à** to). **2** *mf* foreigner; (*inconnu*) stranger; **à l'é.** abroad; **de l'é.** from abroad.
**étrangler** *vt* (*tuer*) to strangle.
**étrangler (s')** *vpr* to choke.
**être* 1** *vi* to be; **il est tailleur** he's a tailor; **est-ce qu'elle vient?** is she coming?; **il vient, n'est-ce pas?** he's coming, isn't he?; **est-ce qu'il aime le thé?** does he like tea?; **nous sommes dix** there are ten of us; **nous sommes le dix** today is the tenth (of the month); **il a été à Paris** he has been to Paris. **2** *v aux* (*avec venir, partir etc*) to have; **elle est arrivée** she has arrived. **3** *m* **ê. humain** human being.
**étrennes** *fpl* New Year's gift.
**étrier** *m* stirrup.
**étroit, -oite** *a* narrow; (*vêtement*) tight; **être à l'é.** to be cramped.
**étroitement** *adv* (*surveiller etc*) closely.
**étude** *f* study; (*salle*) study hall; **à l'é.** (*projet*) under consideration; **faire des études de** (*médecine etc*) to study.
**étudiant, -ante** *mf* & *a* student.
**étudier** *vti* to study.
**étui** *m* (*à lunettes etc*) case.
**eu, eue** *pp of* **avoir.**
**euh!** *int* hem!, er!
**euro-** *préfixe* Euro-.
**européen, -enne** *a* & *mf* European.
**eux** *pron* (*sujet*) they; (*complément*) them; (*réfléchi, emphase*) themselves.
**eux-mêmes** *pron* themselves.
**évacuer** *vt* to evacuate.
**évadé, -ée** *mf* escaped prisoner.
**évader (s')** *vpr* to escape (**de** from).
**évaluer** *vt* to estimate.
**Évangile** *m* Gospel.
**évanouir (s')** *vpr* to faint, pass *ou* black out.
**évanouissement** *m* blackout.

**évasion** *f* escape (**de** from).
**éveiller** *vt* (*susciter*) to arouse.
**événement** *m* event.
**éventail** *m* fan; (*choix*) range.
**éventrer** *vt* (*sac, oreiller*) to rip open; (*animal*) to open up.
**éventuellement** *adv* possibly.
**évêque** *m* bishop.
**évidemment** *adv* obviously.
**évident** *a* obvious (**que** that); (*facile*) *Fam* easy.
**évier** *m* (kitchen) sink.
**éviter** *vt* to avoid (**de faire** doing); **é. qch à qn** to spare s.o. sth.
**ex-** *préfixe* ex-; **ex-mari** ex-husband.
**exact, -e** *a* (*précis*) exact, accurate; (*juste, vrai*) correct.
**exactement** *adv* exactly.
**exactitude** *f* accuracy; correctness.
**ex aequo** *adv* **être classés ex ae.** to tie.
**exagération** *f* exaggeration.
**exagéré, -ée** *a* excessive.
**exagérer** *vti* to exaggerate.
**examen** *m* examination; (*bac etc*) exam(ination).
**examinateur, -trice** *mf* examiner.
**examiner** *vt* to examine.
**excédent** *m* **e. de bagages** excess baggage.
**excellent, -ente** *a* excellent.
**excepté** *prép* except.
**exception** *f* exception; **à l'e. de** except (for).
**exceptionnel, -elle** *a* exceptional.
**exceptionnellement** *adv* exceptionally.
**excès** *m* excess; **e. de vitesse** speeding.
**excessif, -ive** *a* excessive.
**excitant, -ante** *a Fam* exciting.
**excitation** *f* excitement.
**excité, -ée** *a* excited.
**exciter** *vt* to excite.
**exclamation** *f* exclamation.
**exclamer (s')** *vpr* to exclaim.
**exclure*** *vt* to exclude (**de** from).
**excursion** *f* trip, outing; (*à pied*) hike.
**excuse** *f* (*prétexte*) excuse; **excuses** (*regrets*) apology; **faire des excuses** to apologize (**à** to).
**excuser** *vt* to excuse (**qn d'avoir fait, qn de faire** s.o. for doing).
**excuser (s')** *vpr* to apologize (**de** for, **auprès de** to).
**exécuter** *vt* (*travail etc*) to carry out; (*jouer*) to perform; **e. qn** (*tuer*) to execute s.o.
**exécution** *f* (*mise à mort*) execution.
**exemplaire** *m* copy.
**exemple** *m* example; **par e.** for example; **donner l'e.** to set an example (**à** to).
**exercer** *vt* (*muscles, droits*) to exercise.
**exercer (s')** *vpr* to practice (**à qch** sth, **à faire** doing).
**exercice** *m* exercise; **faire de l'e.** to (take) exercise.
**exigeant, -eante** *a* demanding.
**exigence** *f* demand.
**exiger** *vt* to demand (**de** from, **que** (+ *subjonctif*) that).
**existence** *f* existence.
**exister** *vi* to exist; **il existe** there is; (*plural*) there are.
**exorbitant, -ante** *a* exorbitant.
**expédier** *vt* (*envoyer*) to send off.
**expéditeur, -trice** *mf* sender.
**expédition** *f* (*envoi*) dispatch; (*voyage*) expedition.
**expérience** *f* (*connaissance*) experience; (*scientifique*) experiment; **faire l'e. de qch** to experience sth.
**expérimenté, -ée** *a* experienced.
**expert** *m* expert (**en** on, in).
**expirer** *vi* to breathe out; (*mourir*) to pass away.
**explication** *f* explanation; (*mise au point*) discussion.
**expliquer** *vt* to explain (**à** to, **que** that).
**expliquer (s')** *vpr* (*discuter*) to talk things over (**avec** with).
**exploit** *m* feat, exploit.
**exploitation** *f* (*agricole*) farm.
**exploiter** *vt* (*champs*) to farm; (*profiter de*) to exploit.
**explorateur, -trice** *mf* explorer.

**exploration** *f* exploration.
**explorer** *vt* to explore.
**exploser** *vi* to explode.
**explosif** *m* explosive.
**explosion** *f* explosion.
**exportation** *f* export.
**exporter** *vt* to export (**vers** to, **de** from).
**exposé, -ée** *a* **e. au sud**/*etc* facing south/*etc*.
**exposer** *vt* to expose (**à** to); (*tableau etc*) to exhibit; (*vie*) to risk; **s'e. à** to expose oneself to.
**exposition** *f* (*salon*) exhibition.
**exprès** *adv* on purpose; (*spécialement*) specially.
**express** *m inv* (*train*) express; (*café*) espresso.
**expression** *f* (*phrase, mine*) expression.
**exprimer** *vt* to express; **s'e.** to express oneself.
**exquis, -ise** *a* (*nourriture*) delicious.
**exténué, -ée** *a* exhausted.
**extérieur, -e 1** *a* outside; (*surface*) outer, external; (*signe*) outward. **2** *m* outside; **à l'e. (de)** outside.
**externe** *mf* (*élève*) day student.
**extincteur** *m* fire extinguisher.
**extra-** *préfixe* extra-.
**extraire*** *vt* to extract (**de** from).
**extrait** *m* extract.
**extraordinaire** *a* extraordinary.
**extrême** *a* & *m* extreme.
**extrêmement** *adv* extremely.
**extrémité** *f* end.

# F

**fable** *f* fable.
**fabricant, -ante** *mf* manufacturer.
**fabrication** *f* manufacture.
**fabriquer** *vt* to make; (*en usine*) to manufacture; **qu'est-ce qu'il fabrique?** *Fam* what's he up to?
**fabuleux, -euse** *a* fabulous.
**fac** *f* university.
**façade** *f* (*de bâtiment*) front.
**face** *f* face; (*de cube etc*) side; **en f.** opposite; **en f. de** opposite, facing; (*en présence de*) in front of, face to face with; **f. à un problème** faced with a problem; **regarder qn en f.** to look s.o. in the face; **f. à f.** face to face.
**fâché, -ée** *a* (*air*) angry; (*amis*) on bad terms.
**fâcher** *vt* to anger.
**fâcher (se)** *vpr* to get angry (**contre** with); **se f. avec qn** to fall out with s.o.
**facile** *a* easy; **c'est f. à faire** it's easy to do; **il nous est f. de** it's easy for us to.
**facilement** *adv* easily.
**facilité** *f* easiness; (*à faire qch*) ease.
**faciliter** *vt* to make easier.
**façon** *f* way; **la f. dont elle parle** the way (in which) she talks; **f. (d'agir)** behavior; **façons** (*manières*) manners; **de toute f.** anyway; **à ma f.** my way.
**facteur** *m* mailman, postal carrier.
**factrice** *f* postal carrier.
**facture** *f* bill, invoice.
**facultatif, -ive** *a* optional.
**faculté** *f* university; **à la f.** at the university, at school.
**fade** *a* (*nourriture*) bland.
**faible 1** *a* weak; (*bruit*) faint; (*vent*) slight; **f. en anglais**/*etc* poor at English/*etc*. **2** *m* **avoir un f. pour** to have a soft spot for.
**faiblement** *adv* weakly; (*légèrement*) slightly; (*éclairer*) faintly.
**faiblesse** *f* weakness; faintness; slightness.
**faiblir** *vi* (*forces*) to weaken.
**faillir*** *vi* **il a failli tomber** he almost fell.
**faillite** *f* **faire f.** to go bankrupt.
**faim** *f* hunger; **avoir f.** to be hungry; **donner f. à qn** to make s.o. hungry.
**fainéant, -ante** *mf* lazy bones.
**faire* 1** *vt* (*bruit, faute, gâteau etc*) to make; (*devoir, ménage etc*) to do; (*rêve*) to have; (*sourire*) to give;

(*promenade, chute*) to take; **ça fait dix mètres/francs** (*mesure, prix*) it's *ou* that's 33 feet/ten francs; **qu'a-t-il fait (de)?** what's he done (with)?; **que f.?** what should I/you/we/*etc* do?; **f. du tennis**/*etc* to play tennis/*etc*; **f. l'idiot** to play the fool; **ça ne fait rien** that doesn't matter. **2** *vi* (*agir*) to do; (*paraître*) to look; **il fait vieux** he looks old; **elle ferait bien de partir** she'd do well to leave; **il fait beau/froid**/*etc* it's sunny/cold/*etc*; **ça fait deux ans que je ne l'ai pas vu** I haven't seen him for two years; **ça fait un an que je suis là** I've been here for a year. **3** *v aux* (+ *infinitif*); **f. construire une maison** to have *ou* get a house built; **f. crier**/*etc* **qn** to make s.o. shout/*etc*; **se f. obéir**/*etc* to make oneself obeyed/*etc*; **se f. tuer**/*etc* to get *ou* be killed/*etc*.

**faire (se)** *vpr* **se f. des amis** to make friends; **se f. vieux**/*etc* to get old/*etc*; **il se fait tard** it's getting late; **se f. à** to get used to; **ne t'en fais pas!** don't worry!

**faire-part** *m inv* announcement.

**fais, fait, faites** *voir* **faire**.

**faisan** *m* pheasant.

**faisceau, -x** *m* (*rayons*) beam.

**fait, faite** (*pp of* **faire**) **1** *a* (*fromage*) ripe; (*yeux*) made up; **tout f.** ready made; **c'est bien f.!** it serves you right! **2** *m* event; (*réalité*) fact; **prendre sur le f.** to catch red-handed; **f. divers** news item; **au f.** by the way; **en f.** in fact.

**falaise** *f* cliff.

**falloir*** *vi* **il faut qch/qn** I, you, we *etc* need sth/s.o.; **il lui faut un stylo** he *ou* she needs a pen; **il faut partir** I, you, we *etc* have to go; **il faut que je parte** I have to go; **il faudrait qu'elle reste** she ought to stay; **il faut un jour** it takes a day (**pour faire** to do).

**fameux, -euse** *a* famous; (*excellent*) first-class.

**familiarité** *f* familiarity (**avec** with).

**familier, -ière** *a* familiar (**à** to); **f. avec qn** (over)familiar with s.o.; **animal f.** pet.

**familièrement** *adv* (*parler*) informally.

**famille** *f* family; **en f.** with one's family.

**fan** *m* fan.

**fana** *mf* **être f. de** to be crazy about.

**fané, -ée** *a* faded.

**faner (se)** *vpr* to fade.

**fantaisie** *f* (*caprice*) whim; **(de) f.** (*bouton etc*) novelty.

**fantastique** *a* fantastic.

**fantôme** *m* ghost.

**farce**[1] *f* practical joke.

**farce**[2] *f* (*viande*) stuffing.

**farceur, -euse** *mf* practical joker.

**farcir** *vt* to stuff.

**fardeau, -x** *m* burden.

**farine** *f* flour.

**farouche** *a* (*animal*) easily scared; (*violent*) fierce.

**fascination** *f* fascination.

**fasciner** *vt* to fascinate.

**fasse(s), fassent** *etc voir* **faire.**

**fatal, -e,** *mpl* **-als** *a* fatal; (*inévitable*) inevitable.

**fatalement** *adv* inevitably.

**fatigant, -ante** *a* tiring; (*ennuyeux*) tiresome.

**fatigue** *f* tiredness.

**fatigué, -ée** *a* tired (**de** of).

**fatiguer** *vt* to tire.

**fatiguer (se)** *vpr* to get tired (**de** of).

**fauché, -ée** *a Fam* (flat) broke.

**faucher** *vt* (*herbe*) to mow; (*blé*) to reap.

**faucon** *m* hawk.

**faufiler (se)** *vpr* to edge one's way (**dans** through, into).

**fausse** *voir* **faux.**

**faut** *voir* **falloir.**

**faute** *f* mistake; (*responsabilité*) fault; (*péché*) sin; **c'est ta f.** it's your fault.

**fauteuil** *m* armchair; **f. roulant** wheelchair.

**fauve** *m* wild animal, big cat.

**faux, fausse 1** *a* false; (*pas exact*)

wrong; (*monnaie*) forged. **2** *adv* (*chanter*) out of tune.
**faux** *f* scythe.
**faux-filet** *m* sirloin.
**faveur** *f* **en f. de** in aid *ou* favor of.
**favorable** *a* favorable (**à** to).
**favori, -ite** *a* & *mf* favorite.
**favoriser** *vt* to favor.
**fax** *m* (*appareil, message*) fax.
**faxer** *vt* (*message*) to fax.
**fée** *f* fairy.
**féerique** *a* fairy(-like).
**fêler** *vt*, **se fêler** *vpr* to crack.
**félicitations** *fpl* congratulations (**pour** on).
**féliciter** *vt* to congratulate (**qn de** *ou* **sur** s.o. on).
**fêlure** *f* crack.
**femelle** *a* & *f* (*animal*) female.
**féminin, -ine** *a* (*prénom etc*) female; (*trait, pronom etc*) feminine; (*mode, revue etc*) women's.
**femme** *f* woman (*pl* women); (*épouse*) wife; **f. médecin** woman doctor; **f. de ménage** cleaning woman.
**fendre** *vt* (*bois etc*) to split.
**fendre (se)** *vpr* to crack.
**fenêtre** *f* window.
**fente** *f* slit.
**fer** *m* iron; **barre de f.** iron bar; **f. forgé** wrought iron; **f. à cheval** horseshoe; **santé de f.** cast-iron constitution.
**fer (à repasser)** *m* iron (*for clothes*).
**fera, ferai(t)** *etc voir* **faire.**
**fer-blanc** *m* (*pl* **fers-blancs**) tin.
**férié** *a* **jour f.** holiday.
**ferme**[1] *f* farm.
**ferme**[2] **1** *a* firm; (*pas, voix*) steady. **2** *adv* (*travailler, boire*) hard.
**fermé, -ée** *a* (*porte etc*) closed, shut; (*route etc*) closed; (*gaz etc*) off.
**fermement** *adv* firmly.
**fermer 1** *vt* to close, shut; (*gaz etc*) to turn *ou* switch off; (*vêtement*) to do up; **f. (à clef)** to lock. **2** *vi*, **se fermer** *vpr* to close, shut.
**fermeture** *f* closing; (*heure*) closing time; **f. éclair**® zipper.
**fermier, -ière** *mf* farmer.
**féroce** *a* fierce, savage.
**feront** *voir* **faire**.
**ferraille** *f* scrap metal, old iron; **mettre à la f.** to scrap.
**ferrée** *af* **voie ferrée** railroad; (*rails*) track.
**ferroviaire** *a* **compagnie f.** railroad company.
**fertile** *a* fertile.
**fesse** *f* buttock; **les fesses** one's behind.
**fessée** *f* spanking.
**festin** *m* (*banquet*) feast.
**festival,** *pl* **-als** *m* festival.
**fête** *f* (*civile*) holiday; (*religieuse*) feast (day); (*entre amis*) party; **f. foraine** fair, carnival; **f. de famille** family celebration; **c'est sa f.** it's his *ou* her saint's *ou* feast day; **f. des Mères** Mother's Day; **jour de f.** holiday; **faire la f.** to have a good time.
**fêter** *vt* to celebrate.
**feu, -x** *m* fire; (*de réchaud*) burner; **feux (tricolores)** traffic lights; **feux de détresse** (hazard) warning flashers; **f. rouge** red light; (*objet*) traffic lights; **mettre le f. à** to set fire to; **en f.** on fire; **faire du f.** to light *ou* make a fire; **avez-vous du f.?** have you got a light?; **à f. doux** on low heat; **au f.!** fire!; **coup de f.** (*bruit*) gunshot.
**feuillage** *m* leaves.
**feuille** *f* leaf; (*de papier etc*) sheet; **f. d'impôt** tax form; **f. de paye** pay slip.
**feuilleter** *vt* to flip through; **pâte feuilletée** puff pastry *ou* paste.
**feuilleton** *m* serial.
**feutre** *m* **crayon f.** felt-tip (pen).
**février** *m* February.
**fiançailles** *fpl* engagement.
**fiancé** *m* fiancé.
**fiancée** *f* fiancée.
**fiancer (se)** *vpr* to become engaged (**avec** to).
**ficeler** *vt* to tie up.
**ficelle** *f* string.
**fiche** *f* (*carte*) index card; (*papier*) form.
**fiche(r)** *vt* (*pp* **fichu**) *Fam* **f. le**

**camp** to shove off; **fiche-moi la paix!** leave me alone!; **se f. de qn** to make fun of s.o.; **je m'en fiche!** I don't give a damn!
**fichier** *m* card index.
**fichu, -ue** *a* **c'est f.** (*abîmé*) *Fam* it's had it.
**fidèle** *a* faithful (**à** to); (*client*) regular.
**fier (se)** *vpr* **se f. à** to trust.
**fier, fière** *a* proud (**de** of).
**fièrement** *adv* proudly.
**fierté** *f* pride.
**fièvre** *f* fever; **avoir de la f.** to have a temperature *ou* a fever.
**fiévreux, -euse** *a* feverish.
**figer** *vti*, **se figer** *vpr* to congeal.
**figue** *f* fig.
**figure** *f* (*visage*) face; (*géométrique*) figure.
**figurer** *vi* to appear.
**figurer (se)** *vpr* to imagine.
**fil**[1] *m* thread; **f. dentaire** dental floss.
**fil**[2] *m* (*métallique*) wire; **f. de fer** wire; **passer un coup de f. à qn** to give s.o. a ring, call s.o. up.
**file** *f* line; (*couloir*) lane; **f. d'attente** line; **en f. (indienne)** in single file.
**filer 1** *vt* **f. qn** (*suivre*) to shadow s.o. **2** *vi* (*partir*) to rush off; (*aller vite*) to speed along.
**filet** *m* (*à bagages*) rack; (*d'eau*) trickle; (*de poisson*) fillet; **f. (à provisions)** string bag.
**fille** *f* girl; (*parenté*) daughter; **petite f.** (little *ou* young) girl; **jeune f.** girl, young lady.
**fillette** *f* little girl.
**filleul** *m* godson.
**filleule** *f* goddaughter.
**film** *m* film, movie; (*pellicule*) film; **f. plastique** plastic wrap.
**filmer** *vt* to film.
**fils** *m* son.
**filtre** *m* filter; **(à bout) f.** (*cigarette*) (filter-)tipped; **(bout) f.** filter tip.
**filtrer** *vt* to filter.
**fin** *f* end; **mettre f. à** to put an end to; **prendre f.** to come to an end; **sans f.** endless; **à la f.** in the end; **f. mai** at the end of May.
**fin, fine 1** *a* (*pointe etc*) fine; (*peu épais*) thin; (*esprit*, *oreille*) sharp. **2** *adv* (*couper etc*) finely.
**final, -e, -aux** *ou* **-als** *a* final.
**finale** *f* final.
**finalement** *adv* finally.
**finance** *f* finance.
**financer** *vt* to finance.
**financier, -ière** *a* financial.
**finir** *vti* to finish; **f. de faire** to finish doing; (*cesser*) to stop doing; **f. par faire** to end up doing; **c'est fini** it's over.
**finlandais, -aise 1** *a* Finnish. **2** *mf* Finn.
**fissure** *f* crack.
**fissurer (se)** *vpr* to crack.
**fixe** *a* fixed; **idée f.** obsession; **regard f.** stare.
**fixement** *adv* **regarder f.** to stare at.
**fixer** *vt* (*attacher*) to fix (**à** to); (*date etc*) to fix; **f. (du regard)** to stare at; **être fixé** (*décidé*) to be decided.
**flacon** *m* (small) bottle.
**flair** *m* (*d'un chien etc*) (sense of) smell; (*intuition*) insight.
**flairer** *vt* to smell.
**flamand, -ande 1** *a* Flemish. **2** *m* (*langue*) Flemish.
**flamber** *vi* to burn.
**flamme** *f* flame; **en flammes** on fire.
**flan** *m* (*dessert*) custard tart, baked custard.
**flanc** *m* side.
**flâner** *vi* to stroll.
**flaque** *f* puddle.
**flash**, *pl* **flashes** *m* (*de photographie*) flash(light); (*dispositif*) flash(gun); (*d'informations*) (news)flash.
**flatter** *vt* to flatter.
**flatterie** *f* flattery.
**fléau, -x** *m* (*catastrophe*) scourge.
**flèche** *f* arrow; (*d'église*) spire; **monter en f.** (*prix*) to shoot up.
**flécher** *vt* to mark (with arrows).
**fléchette** *f* dart; **fléchettes** (*jeu*) darts.
**fléchir 1** *vt* (*membre*) to flex. **2** *vi* (*poutre*) to sag.

**flétrir** *vt,* **se flétrir** *vpr* to wither.
**fleur** *f* flower; (*d'arbre*) blossom; **en fleur(s)** in flower; **à fleurs** (*tissu*) flowered, flowery.
**fleuri, -ie** *a* in bloom; (*tissu*) flowered, flowery.
**fleurir** *vi* to flower; (*arbre*) to blossom.
**fleuriste** *mf* florist.
**fleuve** *m* river.
**flexible** *a* pliable.
**flic** *m Fam* cop.
**flipper** *m* (*jeu*) pinball; (*appareil*) pinball machine.
**flocon** *m* (*de neige*) flake.
**flot** *m* (*de souvenirs etc*) flood; **à f.** afloat; **les flots** the waves.
**flotte** *f* (*de bateaux*) fleet; (*pluie*) *Fam* rain; (*eau*) *Fam* water.
**flotter** *vi* to float; (*drapeau*) to fly.
**flotteur** *m Pêche* float.
**flou, -e** *a* fuzzy, blurred.
**fluide** *a* & *m* fluid.
**fluo** *a inv* (*couleur etc*) luminous, fluorescent.
**fluorescent, -ente** *a* fluorescent.
**flûte 1** *f* flute; (*verre*) champagne glass. **2** *int* heck!
**foi** *f* faith; **être de bonne/mauvaise f.** to be/not to be (completely) sincere.
**foie** *m* liver.
**foin** *m* hay.
**foire** *f* fair.
**fois** *f* time; **une f.** once; **deux f.** twice; **chaque f. que** whenever; **une f. qu'il sera arrivé** once he has arrived; **à la f.** at the same time; **des f.** sometimes; **une f. pour toutes** once and for all.
**fol** *voir* **fou.**
**folie** *f* madness.
**folklore** *m* folklore.
**folklorique** *a* **musique f.** folk music.
**folle** *voir* **fou.**
**foncé, -ée** *a* (*couleur*) dark.
**foncer** *vi* (*aller vite*) to tear along; **f. sur qn** to charge at s.o.
**fonction** *f* function; **la f. publique** public *ou* civil service.
**fonctionnaire** *mf* civil servant.
**fonctionnement** *m* working.
**fonctionner** *vi* (*machine etc*) to work; **faire f.** to operate.
**fond** *m* (*de boîte, jardin etc*) bottom; (*de salle etc*) back; (*arrière-plan*) background; **au f. de** at the bottom of; at the back of; **f. de teint** foundation (makeup); **à f.** (*connaître etc*) thoroughly.
**fonder** *vt* (*ville etc*) to found.
**fondre 1** *vt* to melt; (*métal*) to melt down; **faire f.** (*sucre etc*) to dissolve. **2** *vi* to melt; (*sucre etc*) to dissolve; **f. en larmes** to burst into tears.
**fonds** *mpl* (*argent*) funds.
**font** *voir* **faire.**
**fontaine** *f* fountain.
**fonte** *f* (*des neiges*) melting; (*fer*) cast iron.
**football** *m* soccer; **f. américain** football.
**footballeur, -euse** *mf* soccer player.
**footing** *m* jogging.
**force** *f* force; (*physique, morale*) strength; **ses forces** one's strength; **de f.** by force; **à f. de lire/***etc* through reading/*etc*, after much reading/*etc*.
**forcément** *adv* obviously; **pas f.** not necessarily.
**forcer** *vt* (*porte etc*) to force; **f. qn à faire** to force s.o. to do; **se f.** to force oneself (**à faire** to do).
**forêt** *f* forest.
**forfait** *m* **déclarer f.** to withdraw from the game.
**formalité** *f* formality.
**format** *m* size.
**formation** *f* education, training.
**forme** *f* (*contour*) shape, form; **en f. de poire/***etc* pear/*etc*-shaped; **en (pleine) f.** in good shape *ou* form.
**formel, -elle** *a* (*absolu*) formal.
**former** *vt* to form; (*apprenti etc*) to train.
**former (se)** *vpr* (*apparaître*) to form.
**formidable** *a* terrific, tremendous.

**formulaire** *m* (*feuille*) form.
**formule** *f* formula; (*phrase*) (set) expression; **f. de politesse** polite form of address.
**fort, forte 1** *a* strong; (*pluie, mer*) heavy; (*voix, radio*) loud; (*fièvre*) high; (*élève*) bright; **f. en** (*maths etc*) good at; **c'est plus f. qu'elle** she can't help it. **2** *adv* (*frapper, pleuvoir*) hard; (*parler*) loud(ly); (*serrer*) tight; **sentir f.** to have a strong smell.
**fort** *m* fort.
**forteresse** *f* fortress.
**fortifiant** *m* tonic.
**fortune** *f* fortune; **faire f.** to make one's fortune.
**fosse** *f* (*trou*) pit; (*tombe*) grave.
**fossé** *m* ditch.
**fou** (*or* **fol** *before vowel or mute h*), **folle 1** *a* crazy; (*succès, temps*) tremendous; **f. de** (*musique etc*) crazy about; **f. de joie** wildly happy. **2** *mf* madman, madwoman. **3** *m Échecs* bishop; **faire le f.** to play the fool.
**foudre** *f* **la f.** lightning.
**foudroyant, -ante** *a* (*succès etc*) staggering.
**foudroyer** *vt* (*tuer*) to electrocute.
**fouet** *m* whip; (*de cuisine*) whisk.
**fouetter** *vt* to whip; (*œufs*) to whisk.
**fougère** *f* fern.
**fouiller 1** *vt* (*personne, maison etc*) to search. **2** *vi* **f. dans** (*tiroir etc*) to search through.
**fouillis** *m* jumble, mess.
**foulard** *m* (head) scarf.
**foule** *f* crowd; **une f. de** (*objets etc*) a mass of.
**fouler** *vt* **se f. la cheville**/*etc* to sprain one's ankle/*etc*.
**foulure** *f* sprain.
**four** *m* oven.
**fourche** *f* fork.
**fourchette** *f* fork (*used for eating or cooking*).
**fourgon** *m* van; (*mortuaire*) hearse.
**fourgonnette** *f* (small) van.
**fourmi** *f* ant; **avoir des fourmis** to have pins and needles (**dans** in).
**fourneau, -x** *m* (*poêle*) stove.
**fournée** *f* batch.
**fournir** *vt* to supply; (*effort*) to make; **f. qch à qn** to supply s.o. with sth.
**fourré, -ée** *a* (*gant etc*) fur-lined.
**fourrer** *vt Fam* (*mettre*) to stick.
**fourre-tout** *m inv* (*sac*) carryall.
**fourrière** *f* (*lieu*) pound.
**fourrure** *f* fur.
**foyer** *m* (*maison, famille*) home; (*résidence de jeunes etc*) hostel.
**fracas** *m* din.
**fracasser** *vt,* **se fracasser** *vpr* to smash.
**fraction** *f* fraction.
**fracture** *f* fracture; **se faire une f. au bras**/*etc* to fracture one's arm/*etc*.
**fracturer** *vt* (*porte etc*) to break (open); **se f. la jambe**/*etc* to fracture one's leg/*etc*.
**fragile** *a* fragile.
**fragment** *m* fragment.
**fraîcheur** *f* freshness; coolness.
**frais, fraîche 1** *a* fresh; (*temps*) cool; (*boisson*) cold; **servir f.** (*vin etc*) to serve chilled. **2** *m* **il fait f.** it's cool; **mettre au f.** to put in a cool place; (*au frigo*) to refrigerate.
**frais** *mpl* expenses; **à mes f.** at my (own) expense.
**fraise** *f* strawberry.
**framboise** *f* raspberry.
**franc, franche** *a* (*personne etc*) frank; **coup f.** *Football* free kick; *Basketball* foul shot.
**franc** *m* (*monnaie*) franc.
**français, -aise 1** *a* French. **2** *mf* Frenchman, Frenchwoman; **les F.** the French. **3** *m* (*langue*) French.
**franchement** *adv* frankly; (*vraiment*) really.
**franchir** *vt* (*fossé*) to jump (over), clear; (*frontière etc*) to cross; (*porte*) to go through; (*distance*) to cover.
**franchise** *f* frankness.
**francophone** *mf* French speaker.
**frange** *f* (*de cheveux*) bangs.
**frappant, -ante** *a* striking.

**frapper 1** *vt* to hit, strike; **f. qn** (*surprendre*) to strike s.o. **2** *vi* (*à la porte etc*) to knock (**à** at); **f. du pied** to stamp (one's foot).
**fraude** *f* (*à un examen*) cheating; (*crime*) fraud; **passer qch en f.** to smuggle sth.
**frauder** *vi* (*à un examen*) to cheat (**à** on).
**frayer** *vt* **se f. un passage** to clear a way (**à travers, dans** through).
**frayeur** *f* fright.
**fredonner** *vt* to hum.
**freezer** *m* freezer.
**frein** *m* brake; **donner un coup de f.** to brake.
**freinage** *m* braking.
**freiner** *vi* to brake.
**frémir** *vi* (*trembler*) to shudder (**de** with).
**fréquemment** *adv* frequently.
**fréquent, -ente** *a* frequent.
**fréquenter** *vt* (*école, église*) to attend; **f. qn** to see s.o.; **se f.** to see each other.
**frère** *m* brother.
**friandises** *fpl* candies.
**fric** *m* (*argent*) *Fam* cash.
**frictionner** *vt* to rub (down).
**frigo** *m* fridge.
**frileux, -euse** *a* sensitive to cold.
**frire*** *vti* to fry; **faire f.** to fry.
**frisé, -ée** *a* curly.
**friser** *vti* (*cheveux*) to curl.
**frisson** *m* shiver; shudder.
**frissonner** *vi* (*de froid*) to shiver; (*de peur etc*) to shudder (**de** with).
**frit, frite** (*pp of* **frire**) *a* fried.
**frites** *fpl* French fries.
**friteuse** *f* (deep) fryer.
**froid, froide 1** *a* cold. **2** *m* cold; **avoir/prendre f.** to be/catch cold; **il fait f.** it's cold.
**froisser** *vt* (*tissu*) to crumple; (*personne*) to offend.
**froisser (se)** *vpr* (*tissu*) to crumple; (*personne*) to take offense (**de** at).
**frôler** *vt* (*toucher*) to brush against.
**fromage** *m* cheese; **f. blanc** soft white cheese.
**fromagerie** *f* (*magasin*) cheese shop.
**froncer** *vt* **f. les sourcils** to frown.
**front** *m* forehead, brow; (*de bataille*) front.
**frontière** *f* border.
**frotter** *vti* to rub; (*pour nettoyer*) to scrub.
**frousse** *f Fam* fear; **avoir la f.** to be scared.
**fruit** *m* fruit; **des fruits, les fruits** fruit; **fruits de mer** seafood.
**fruitier** *a* **arbre f.** fruit tree.
**fuel** *m* (fuel) oil.
**fugitif, -ive** *mf* fugitive.
**fuir*** *vi* to run away; (*gaz, robinet etc*) to leak.
**fuite** *f* flight (**de** from); (*de gaz etc*) leak; **en f.** on the run; **prendre la f.** to run away *ou* off.
**fumé, -ée** *a* smoked.
**fumée** *f* smoke; (*vapeur*) fumes.
**fumer 1** *vi* to smoke; (*liquide brûlant*) to steam. **2** *vt* to smoke.
**fumeur, -euse** *mf* smoker; **compartiment fumeurs** smoking compartment.
**fumier** *m* manure.
**funérailles** *fpl* funeral.
**fur et à mesure (au)** *adv* as one goes along; **au f. et à m. que** as.
**fureur** *f* fury; **faire f.** (*mode etc*) to be all the rage.
**furie** *f* fury.
**furieux, -euse** *a* furious (**contre** with, at); (*vent*) raging.
**furoncle** *m* boil.
**fuseau, -x** *m* (*pantalon*) ski pants; **f. horaire** time zone.
**fusée** *f* rocket.
**fusible** *m* fuse.
**fusil** *m* rifle, gun; (*de chasse*) shotgun; **coup de f.** gunshot.
**fusillade** *f* (*tirs*) gunfire.
**fusiller** *vt* (*exécuter*) to shoot; **f. qn du regard** to glare at s.o.
**fût** *m* (*tonneau*) barrel, cask.
**futé, -ée** *a* cunning.
**futur, -ure** *a* & *m* future.

# G

**gâcher** *vt* to spoil; (*argent etc*) to waste.

**gâchette** *f* trigger.

**gâchis** *m* (*gaspillage*) waste.

**gadget** *m* gadget.

**gag** *m* gag.

**gage** *m* (*garantie*) security; **mettre en g.** to pawn.

**gagnant, -ante 1** *a* winning. **2** *mf* winner.

**gagner 1** *vt* to earn; (*par le jeu*) to win; (*atteindre*) to reach; **g. une heure**/*etc* to save an hour/*etc*. **2** *vi* to win.

**gai, -e** *a* cheerful.

**gaiement** *adv* cheerfully.

**gaieté** *f* cheerfulness.

**gain** *m* **un g. de temps** a saving of time; **gains** (*salaire*) earnings; (*au jeu*) winnings.

**gaine** *f* (*sous-vêtement*) girdle; (*étui*) sheath.

**gala** *m* gala.

**galant, -ante** *a* gallant.

**galerie** *f* gallery; (*porte-bagages*) roof rack.

**galet** *m* pebble.

**gallois, -oise 1** *a* Welsh. **2** *m* (*langue*) Welsh. **3** *mf* Welshman, Welshwoman.

**galon** *m* (*ruban*) braid; (*de soldat*) stripe.

**galop** *m* gallop; **aller au g.** to gallop.

**galoper** *vi* to gallop.

**gambade** *f* leap.

**gambader** *vi* to leap around.

**gamelle** *f Fam* pan; (*de chien*) bowl; (*d'ouvrier*) lunch box.

**gamin, -ine** *mf* (*enfant*) kid.

**gamme** *f* (*de notes*) scale; (*série*) range.

**gangster** *m* gangster.

**gant** *m* glove; **g. de toilette** facecloth; **boîte à gants** glove compartment.

**ganté, -ée** *a* (*main*) gloved; (*personne*) wearing gloves.

**garage** *m* garage.

**garagiste** *mf* garage mechanic.

**garantie** *f* guarantee; **garantie(s)** (*d'assurance*) cover.

**garantir** *vt* to guarantee (**contre** against); **g. à qn que** to assure *ou* guarantee s.o. that.

**garçon** *m* boy; (*jeune homme*) young man; **g. (de café)** waiter.

**garde 1** *m* guard; **g. du corps** bodyguard. **2** *f* (*d'enfants, de bagages etc*) care (**de** of); **avoir la g. de** to be in charge of; **prendre g.** to pay attention (**à qch** to sth); **prendre g. de ne pas faire** to be careful not to do; **mettre en g.** to warn (**contre** against); **mise en g.** warning; **de g.** on duty; **monter la g.** to stand guard; **sur ses gardes** on one's guard; **chien de g.** watchdog.

**garde-chasse** *m* (*pl* **gardes-chasses**) gamekeeper.

**garder** *vt* to keep; (*vêtement*) to keep on; (*surveiller*) to watch (over); (*enfant*) to take care of; **g. la chambre** to stay in one's room.

**garder (se)** *vpr* (*aliment*) to keep.

**garderie** *f* daycare center.

**gardien, -ienne** *mf* (*d'immeuble etc*) caretaker, janitor; (*de prison*) (prison) guard; (*de zoo, parc*) keeper; (*de musée*) attendant, guard; **g. de but** goalkeeper, goalie.

**gare** *f* station; **g. routière** bus station.

**garer** *vt* to park; (*au garage*) to put in the garage.

**garer (se)** *vpr* to park.

**garnement** *m* rascal.

**garnir** *vt* (*équiper*) to outfit, equip (**de** with); (*magasin*) to stock; (*orner*) to trim (**de** with).

**garniture** *f* (*de légumes*) garnish.

**gars** *m* fellow, guy.

**gas-oil** *m* diesel (oil).

**gaspillage** *m* waste.

**gaspiller** *vt* to waste.

**gâté, -ée** *a* (*dent etc*) bad.

**gâteau, -x** *m* cake; **g. de riz** rice pudding; **g. sec** cookie.

**gâter** *vt* to spoil.
**gâter (se)** *vpr* (*aliment, dent*) to go bad; (*temps, situation*) to get worse.
**gauche 1** *a* left. **2** *f* **la g.** (*côté*) the left (side); **à g.** (*tourner*) (to the) left; (*marcher etc*) on the left; **de g.** (*fenêtre etc*) left-hand; **à g. de** on *ou* to the left of.
**gaucher, -ère** *a* & *mf* left-handed (person).
**gaufre** *f* waffle.
**gaufrette** *f* wafer.
**Gaulois** *mpl* **les G.** the Gauls.
**gaver (se)** *vpr* to stuff oneself (**de** with).
**gaz** *m inv* gas; **réchaud à g.** gas stove.
**gaze** *f* gauze.
**gazeux, -euse** *a* (*boisson, eau*) fizzy, carbonated.
**gazinière** *f* gas stove.
**gazole** *m* diesel (oil).
**gazon** *m* grass, lawn.
**géant, -ante** *a* & *mf* giant.
**gel** *m* frost; (*pour cheveux etc*) gel.
**gelé, -ée** *a* frozen.
**gelée** *f* frost; (*de fruits*) jelly.
**geler** *vti* to freeze; **il gèle** it's freezing.
**gémir** *vi* to groan.
**gémissement** *m* groan.
**gênant, -ante** *a* (*objet*) cumbersome; (*situation*) awkward; (*bruit*) annoying.
**gencive** *f* gum.
**gendarme** *m* gendarme.
**gendarmerie** *f* (*local*) police headquarters.
**gendre** *m* son-in-law.
**gêne** *f* (*trouble physique*) discomfort; (*confusion*) embarrassment.
**gêné, -ée** *a* (*mal à l'aise*) awkward.
**gêner** *vt* to bother; (*troubler*) to embarrass; (*mouvement*) to hamper; (*circulation*) to hold up; **g. qn** (*par sa présence*) to be in s.o.'s way.
**général, -e, -aux 1** *a* general; **en g.** in general. **2** *m* (*officier*) general.
**généralement** *adv* generally.
**génération** *f* generation.
**généreusement** *adv* generously.
**généreux, -euse** *a* generous (**de** with).
**générosité** *f* generosity.
**génial, -e, -aux** *a* brilliant.
**génie** *m* genius.
**genou, -x** *m* knee; **à genoux** kneeling (down); **se mettre à genoux** to kneel (down); **sur ses genoux** on one's lap.
**genre** *m* (*espèce*) kind, sort; (*d'un nom*) gender.
**gens** *mpl* people; **jeunes g.** young people; (*hommes*) young men.
**gentil, -ille** *a* nice; **g. avec qn** nice *ou* kind to s.o.; **sois g.** (*sage*) be good.
**gentillesse** *f* kindness.
**gentiment** *adv* kindly; (*sagement*) nicely.
**géographie** *f* geography.
**géographique** *a* geographical.
**géomètre** *m* surveyor.
**géométrie** *f* geometry.
**géométrique** *a* geometric(al).
**gerbe** *f* (*de blé*) sheaf; (*de fleurs*) bunch.
**gercer** *vti*, **se gercer** *vpr* to chap.
**gerçure** *f* **avoir des gerçures aux mains/lèvres** to have chapped hands/lips.
**germe** *m* (*microbe*) germ; (*de plante*) shoot.
**germer** *vi* (*graine*) to start to grow; (*pomme de terre*) to sprout.
**geste** *m* gesture; **ne pas faire un g.** not to make a move.
**gesticuler** *vi* to gesticulate.
**gibier** *m* (*animaux etc*) game.
**giboulée** *f* shower.
**gicler** *vi* (*liquide*) to spurt; **faire g.** to spurt.
**gifle** *f* slap (in the face).
**gifler** *vt* **g. qn** to slap s.o.
**gigantesque** *a* gigantic.
**gigot** *m* leg of mutton *ou* lamb.
**gigoter** *vi* to wriggle, fidget.
**gilet** *m* cardigan; (*de costume*) vest; **g. de sauvetage** life jacket.
**girafe** *f* giraffe.
**giratoire** *a* **sens g.** traffic circle.
**girouette** *f* weather vane.

**gitan, -ane** *mf* (Spanish) gipsy.
**givre** *m* frost.
**givré, -ée** *a* frost-covered.
**glace** *f* (*eau gelée*) ice; (*crème glacée*) ice cream; (*vitre*) window; (*miroir*) mirror.
**glacé, -ée** *a* (*eau, main etc*) icy.
**glacer** *vt* to chill.
**glacial, -e, -aux** *a* icy.
**glacier** *m* (*vendeur*) ice-cream man.
**glacière** *f* icebox.
**glaçon** *m* ice cube.
**gland** *m* acorn.
**glande** *f* gland.
**glissant, -ante** *a* slippery.
**glisser 1** *vi* (*involontairement*) to slip; (*volontairement*) (*sur la glace etc*) to slide; (*coulisser*) (*tiroir etc*) to slide; **ça glisse** it's slippery. **2** *vt* to slip (**dans** into).
**glissière** *f* **porte à g.** sliding door.
**globe** *m* globe.
**gloire** *f* glory.
**glorieux, -euse** *a* glorious.
**gloussement** *m* cluck(ing).
**glousser** *vi* to cluck.
**glouton, -onne 1** *a* greedy. **2** *mf* glutton.
**gluant, -ante** *a* sticky.
**goal** *m* goalkeeper.
**gobelet** *m* (*de plastique, papier*) cup.
**godet** *m* pot.
**golf** *m* golf; (*terrain*) golf course.
**golfe** *m* gulf, bay.
**golfeur, -euse** *mf* golfer.
**gomme** *f* (*à effacer*) eraser.
**gommer** *vt* (*effacer*) to rub out, erase.
**gond** *m* hinge.
**gonflable** *a* inflatable.
**gonflé, -ée** *a* swollen.
**gonfler 1** *vt* (*pneu*) to pump up; (*en soufflant*) to blow up. **2** *vi*, **se gonfler** *vpr* to swell.
**gonfleur** *m* (air) pump.
**gorge** *f* throat; (*vallée*) gorge.
**gorgée** *f* mouthful (*of wine etc*); **petite g.** sip.
**gorille** *m* gorilla.
**gosier** *m* throat.
**gosse** *mf* (*enfant*) *Fam* kid.
**gouache** *f* gouache.
**goudron** *m* tar.
**goudronner** *vt* to tar.
**goulot** *m* (*de bouteille*) neck; **boire au g.** to drink from the bottle.
**gourde** *f* water bottle.
**gourdin** *m* club, cudgel.
**gourmand, -ande 1** *a* (over)fond of food; **g. de** fond of. **2** *mf* hearty eater.
**gourmandise** *f* (over)fondness for food.
**gourmet** *m* gourmet.
**gourmette** *f* identity bracelet.
**gousse** *f* **g. d'ail** clove of garlic.
**goût** *m* taste; **de bon g.** in good taste; **sans g.** tasteless.
**goûter 1** *vt* to taste; **g. à qch** to taste (a little of) sth. **2** *vi* to have an afternoon snack, have tea. **3** *m* afternoon snack, tea.
**goutte** *f* drop.
**gouttelette** *f* droplet.
**goutter** *vi* to drip (**de** from).
**gouttière** *f* (*d'un toit*) gutter.
**gouvernail** *m* rudder; (*barre*) helm.
**gouvernement** *m* government.
**gouverner** *vti* to govern.
**grâce 1** *f* grace; (*avantage*) favor. **2** *prép* **g. à** thanks to.
**gracieux, -euse** *a* (*élégant*) graceful.
**grade** *m* rank.
**gradin** *m* tier (of seats).
**graffiti** *mpl* graffiti.
**grain** *m* grain; (*de café*) bean; (*de poussière*) speck; **g. de beauté** mole; (*sur le visage*) beauty spot.
**graine** *f* seed.
**graisse** *f* fat; (*pour machine*) grease.
**graisser** *vt* to grease.
**graisseux, -euse** *a* (*vêtement etc*) greasy.
**grammaire** *f* grammar; **livre de g.** grammar (book).
**gramme** *m* gram.
**grand, grande 1** *a* big, large; (*en hauteur*) tall; (*chaleur, découverte etc*) great; (*bruit*) loud; (*différence*)

big, great; **g. frère**/*etc* (*plus âgé*) big brother/*etc*; **il est g. temps** it's high time (**que** that). **2** *adv* **g. ouvert** wide-open; **ouvrir g.** to open wide.

**grand-chose** *pron* **pas g.-chose** not much.

**grandeur** *f* (*importance*) greatness; (*dimension*) size; **g. nature** life-size.

**grandir** *vi* to grow.

**grand-mère** *f* (*pl* **grands-mères**) grandmother.

**grand-père** *m* (*pl* **grands-pères**) grandfather.

**grand-route** *f* main road.

**grands-parents** *mpl* grandparents.

**grange** *f* barn.

**graphique** *m* graph.

**grappe** *f* cluster; **g. de raisin** bunch of grapes.

**gras, grasse 1** *a* fat; (*aliment*) fatty; (*graisseux*) greasy; **matières grasses** fat. **2** *m* (*de viande*) fat.

**gratin** *m* **macaronis/chou-fleur au g.** macaroni and/cauliflower with cheese.

**gratitude** *f* gratitude.

**gratte-ciel** *m inv* skyscraper.

**gratter** *vt* to scrape; (*avec les ongles etc*) to scratch; **se g.** to scratch oneself; **ça me gratte** it itches.

**gratuit, -uite** *a* free.

**gratuitement** *adv* free (of charge).

**gravats** *mpl* rubble.

**grave** *a* serious; (*voix*) deep; **ce n'est pas g.!** it's not important!; **accent g.** grave accent.

**gravement** *adv* seriously.

**graver** *vt* (*sur métal etc*) to engrave; (*sur bois*) to carve.

**graveur** *m* engraver.

**gravier** *m* gravel.

**gravillons** *mpl* gravel.

**gravir** *vt* to climb (*with effort*).

**gravité** *f* (*de situation etc*) seriousness.

**gravure** *f* (*image*) print.

**grec, grecque 1** *a* & *mf* Greek. **2** *m* (*langue*) Greek.

**greffe** *f* (*de peau, d'arbre*) graft; (*d'organe*) transplant.

**greffer** *vt* (*peau etc*) to graft (**à** on to); (*organe*) to transplant.

**grêle** *f* hail.

**grêler** *vi* to hail.

**grêlon** *m* hailstone.

**grelot** *m* (small round) bell (*that jingles*).

**grelotter** *vi* to shiver (**de** with).

**grenade** *f* (*fruit*) pomegranate; (*projectile*) grenade.

**grenadine** *f* pomegranate syrup, grenadine.

**grenier** *m* attic.

**grenouille** *f* frog.

**grève** *f* strike; **g. de la faim** hunger strike; **se mettre en g.** to go (out) on strike.

**gréviste** *mf* striker.

**gribouiller** *vti* to scribble.

**gribouillis** *m* scribble.

**grièvement** *adv* **g. blessé** seriously injured.

**griffe** *f* (*ongle*) claw; (*de couturier*) (designer) label.

**griffer** *vt* to scratch.

**griffonner** *vt* to scribble.

**grignoter** *vti* to nibble.

**gril** *m* grill.

**grillade** *f* (*viande*) grill.

**grillage** *m* window screen, chicken wire.

**grille** *f* (*clôture*) railing.

**grille-pain** *m inv* toaster.

**griller 1** *vt* (*viande*) to grill; (*pain*) to toast; **g. un feu rouge** to run a red light. **2** *vi* **mettre à g.** to put on the grill.

**grillon** *m* (*insecte*) cricket.

**grimace** *f* **faire des grimaces/la g.** to make faces/a face.

**grimacer** *vi* to make faces *ou* a face.

**grimpant, -ante** *a* climbing.

**grimper 1** *vi* to climb (**à qch** up sth). **2** *vt* to climb.

**grincement** *m* creaking; grinding.

**grincer** *vi* to creak; **g. des dents** to grind one's teeth.

**grincheux, -euse** *a* grumpy.

**grippe** *f* flu.
**grippé, -ée** *a* **être g.** to have (the) flu.
**gris, grise 1** *a* gray. **2** *m* gray.
**grisaille** *f* grayness.
**grisâtre** *a* grayish.
**grognement** *m* growl; grunt.
**grogner** *vi* to growl (**contre** at); (*cochon*) to grunt.
**grognon, -onne** *a* grumpy.
**grondement** *m* growl; rumble.
**gronder 1** *vi* to growl; (*tonnerre*) to rumble. **2** *vt* to scold, tell off.
**groom** *m* bellboy.
**gros, grosse 1** *a* big; (*gras*) fat; (*épais*) thick; (*effort, progrès*) great; (*somme*) large; (*averse, rhume*) heavy; **g. mot** swear word. **2** *adv* **en g.** roughly; (*écrire*) in big letters; (*vendre*) wholesale.
**groseille** *f* (white *ou* red) currant.
**grossesse** *f* pregnancy.
**grosseur** *f* size; (*tumeur*) lump.
**grossier, -ière** *a* rough; (*personne*) rude (**envers** to).
**grossièrement** *adv* roughly; (*répondre*) rudely.
**grossièreté** *f* roughness; (*insolence*) rudeness; (*mot*) rude word.
**grossir** *vi* to put on weight.
**grotte** *f* cave, grotto.
**grouiller** *vi* to be swarming (**de** with).
**groupe** *m* group.
**grouper** *vt*, **se grouper** *vpr* to group (together).
**grue** *f* crane.
**grumeau, -x** *m* lump.
**gruyère** *m* gruyère (cheese).
**guenilles** *fpl* rags (and tatters).
**guêpe** *f* wasp.
**guère** *adv* **(ne) . . . g.** hardly; **il ne sort g.** he hardly goes out.
**guéri, -ie** *a* cured, better.
**guérir 1** *vt* to cure (**de** of). **2** *vi* to recover (**de** from).
**guérison** *f* recovery.
**guerre** *f* war; **en g.** at war (**avec** with).
**guerrier, -ière** *mf* warrior.
**guet** *m* **faire le g.** to be on the lookout.
**guetter** *vt* to be on the lookout for.
**gueule** *f* mouth.
**guichet** *m* ticket office; (*de banque etc*) window.
**guichetier, -ière** *mf* (*de banque etc*) teller; (*à la gare*) ticket agent.
**guide** *m* (*personne, livre*) guide.
**guider** *vt* to guide; **se g. sur un manuel**/*etc* to use a handbook/*etc* as a guide.
**guidon** *m* handlebar(s).
**guignol** *m* (*spectacle*) = Punch and Judy show.
**guillemets** *mpl* quotation marks; **entre g.** in quotation marks.
**guirlande** *f* garland.
**guitare** *f* guitar.
**guitariste** *mf* guitarist.
**gymnase** *m* gymnasium.
**gymnastique** *f* gymnastics.
**gynécologue** *mf* gynecologist.

# H

**habile** *a* skillful (**à qch** at sth, **à faire** at doing).
**habileté** *f* skill.
**habillé, -ée** *a* dressed (**de** in, **en** as a).
**habiller** *vt* to dress (**de** in).
**habiller (s')** *vpr* to dress, get dressed; (*avec élégance*) to dress up.
**habitable** *a* (*maison*) fit to live in.
**habitant, -ante** *mf* (*de pays etc*) inhabitant; (*de maison*) occupant.
**habitation** *f* house.
**habité, -ée** *a* (*région*) inhabited; (*maison*) occupied.
**habiter 1** *vi* to live (**à, en, dans** in). **2** *vt* (*maison etc*) to live in.
**habits** *mpl* (*vêtements*) clothes.
**habitude** *f* habit; **avoir l'h. de qch/faire** to be used to sth/doing; **d'h.** usually; **comme d'h.** as usual.
**habituel, -elle** *a* usual.
**habituellement** *adv* usually.
**habituer** *vt* **h. qn à** to accustom s.o. to.

**habituer (s')** *vpr* to get accustomed (**à** to).
**hache** *f* ax.
**hacher** *vt* to chop (up); (*avec un appareil*) to grind.
**hachis** *m* ground meat.
**haie** *f* (*clôture*) hedge; **course de haies** (*coureurs*) hurdle race.
**haine** *f* hatred.
**haïr*** *vt* to hate.
**haleine** *f* breath; **hors d'h.** out of breath.
**haleter** *vi* to pant.
**hall** *m* (*de gare*) main hall; (*de maison*) hall(way).
**halte 1** *f* (*arrêt*) stop. **2** *int* stop!
**haltères** *mpl* weights.
**hamac** *m* hammock.
**hameçon** *m* (fish) hook.
**hamster** *m* hamster.
**hanche** *f* hip.
**handicapé, -ée** *a* & *mf* handicapped (person).
**hangar** *m* shed; (*pour avions*) hangar.
**hanté, -ée** *a* haunted.
**harassé, -ée** *a* (*fatigué*) exhausted.
**hardi, -ie** *a* bold.
**hareng** *m* herring.
**hargneux, -euse** *a* bad-tempered.
**haricot** *m* (*blanc*) (haricot) bean; (*vert*) green bean.
**harmonica** *m* harmonica.
**harmonie** *f* harmony.
**harmonieux, -euse** *a* harmonious.
**harnais** *m* harness.
**harpe** *f* harp.
**hasard** *m* **le h.** chance; **un h.** a coincidence; **par h.** by chance; **au h.** at random; **à tout h.** just in case.
**hasardeux, -euse** *a* risky.
**hâte** *f* haste; **à la h.** in a hurry; **avoir h. de faire** to be eager to do.
**hâter (se)** *vpr* to hurry (**de faire** to do).
**hausse** *f* rise (**de** in); **en h.** rising.
**haut, haute 1** *a* high; (*de taille*) tall; **à haute voix** aloud; **h. de 5 mètres** 16 feet high *ou* tall. **2** *adv* (*voler etc*) high (up); (*parler*) loud; **tout h.** (*lire etc*) aloud; **h. placé** (*personne*) in a high position. **3** *m* top; **en h. de** at the top of; **en h.** (*loger*) upstairs; (*regarder*) up; (*mettre*) on (the) top; **avoir 5 mètres de h.** to be 16 feet high *ou* tall.
**hauteur** *f* height.
**haut-parleur** *m* loudspeaker.
**hayon** *m* (*porte*) hatchback.
**hé!** *int* (*appel*) hey!
**hebdomadaire** *a* & *m* weekly.
**héberger** *vt* to put up.
**hectare** *m* hectare (= *2.47 acres*).
**hein!** *int Fam* eh!
**hélas!** *int* unfortunately.
**hélice** *f* propeller.
**hélicoptère** *m* helicopter.
**hémorragie** *f* hemorrhage; **h. cérébrale** stroke.
**hennir** *vi* to neigh.
**hépatite** *f* hepatitis.
**herbe** *f* grass; (*pour soigner etc*) herb; **mauvaise h.** weed; **fines herbes** herbs.
**hérisser (se)** *vpr* (*poils*) to bristle (up).
**hérisson** *m* hedgehog.
**héritage** *m* (*biens*) inheritance.
**hériter** *vti* to inherit (**qch de qn** sth from s.o.); **h. de qch** to inherit sth.
**héritier** *m* heir.
**héritière** *f* heiress.
**hermétique** *a* airtight.
**héroïne** *f* (*femme*) heroine; (*drogue*) heroin.
**héroïque** *a* heroic.
**héros** *m* hero.
**hésitant, -ante** *a* hesitant; (*pas, voix*) unsteady.
**hésitation** *f* hesitation; **avec h.** hesitantly.
**hésiter** *vi* to hesitate (**sur** over, about; **à faire** to do).
**hêtre** *m* (*arbre, bois*) beech.
**heu!** *int* er!
**heure** *f* hour; (*moment*) time; **quelle h. est-il?** what time is it?; **il est six heures** it's six (o'clock); **six heures moins cinq** five to six; **six**

**heures cinq** five past *ou* after six; **à l'h.** (*arriver*) on time; **dix kilomètres à l'h.** six miles an hour; **de bonne h.** early; **tout à l'h.** (*futur*) later; (*passé*) a moment ago; **heures supplémentaires** overtime; **l'h. de pointe** (*circulation etc*) rush hour.

**heureusement** *adv* (*par chance*) fortunately (**pour** for).

**heureux, -euse 1** *a* happy; (*chanceux*) lucky; **h. de qch/de voir qn** happy *ou* glad about sth/to see s.o. **2** *adv* (*vivre etc*) happily.

**heurter** *vt* to hit; **se h. à** to bump into, hit.

**hibou, -x** *m* owl.

**hier** *adv* & *m* yesterday; **h. soir** last night.

**hi-fi** *a inv* & *f inv Fam* hi-fi.

**hippopotame** *m* hippopotamus.

**hirondelle** *f* swallow.

**histoire** *f* history; (*récit, mensonge*) story; **des histoires** (*ennuis*) trouble; **sans histoires** (*voyage etc*) uneventful.

**historique** *a* historical; (*lieu, événement*) historic.

**hiver** *m* winter.

**HLM** *m ou f abrév* (*habitation à loyer modéré*) = low-income housing.

**hocher** *vt* **h. la tête** (*pour dire oui*) to nod one's head; (*pour dire non*) to shake one's head.

**hochet** *m* (*jouet*) rattle.

**hockey** *m* hockey; **h. sur glace** ice hockey.

**hold-up** *m inv* (*attaque*) holdup.

**hollandais, -aise 1** *a* Dutch. **2** *mf* Dutchman, Dutchwoman; **les H.** the Dutch. **3** *m* (*langue*) Dutch.

**homard** *m* lobster.

**homme** *m* man (*pl* men); **l'h.** (*espèce*) man(kind); **des vêtements d'h.** men's clothes; **h. d'affaires** businessman.

**homosexuel, -elle** *a* & *mf* homosexual.

**honnête** *a* honest; (*satisfaisant*) decent.

**honnêtement** *adv* honestly; decently.

**honnêteté** *f* honesty.

**honneur** *m* honor; **en l'h. de** in honor of; **faire h. à** (*sa famille etc*) to be a credit to; (*repas*) to do justice to.

**honorable** *a* honorable; (*convenable*) respectable.

**honte** *f* shame; **avoir h.** to be *ou* feel ashamed (**de qch/de faire** of sth/to do, of doing).

**honteux, -euse** *a* ashamed; (*scandaleux*) shameful.

**hôpital, -aux** *m* hospital; **à l'h.** in the hospital.

**hoquet** *m* **avoir le h.** to have (the) hiccups.

**horaire** *m* timetable.

**horizon** *m* horizon; **à l'h.** on the horizon.

**horizontal, -e, -aux** *a* horizontal.

**horloge** *f* clock.

**horreur** *f* horror; **faire h. à** to disgust; **avoir h. de** to hate.

**horrible** *a* horrible.

**horriblement** *adv* horribly.

**horrifiant, -ante** *a* horrifying.

**horrifié, -ée** *a* horrified.

**hors** *prép* **h. de** out of.

**hors-bord** *m inv* speedboat.

**hors-d'œuvre** *m inv* (*à table*) hors d'oeuvre, appetizer.

**hors-taxe** *a inv* duty-free.

**hospitaliser** *vt* to hospitalize.

**hospitalité** *f* hospitality.

**hostile** *a* hostile (**à** to, towards).

**hostilité** *f* hostility (**envers** to, towards).

**hôte 1** *m* (*qui reçoit*) host. **2** *mf* (*invité*) guest.

**hôtel** *m* hotel; **h. de ville** city hall.

**hôtesse** *f* hostess; **h. (de l'air)** flight attendant.

**hotte** *f* basket (*carried on back*).

**hourra!** *int* hurray!

**housse** *f* (protective) cover.

**HT** *abrév* (*hors taxe*) before tax, exclusive of tax.

**hublot** *m* porthole.

**huile** *f* oil.

**huit** *a* & *m eight;* **h. jours** a week.
**huitième** *a* & *mf* eighth.
**huître** *f* oyster.
**humain, -aine** *a* human.
**humanité** *f* humanity.
**humble** *a* humble.
**humblement** *adv* humbly.
**humecter** *vt* to moisten.
**humeur** *f* mood; (*caractère*) temperament; **bonne h.** (*gaieté*) good humor; **de bonne/mauvaise h.** in a good/bad mood.
**humide** *a* damp.
**humidité** *f* humidity; (*plutôt froide*) damp(ness).
**humiliation** *f* humiliation.
**humilier** *vt* to humiliate.
**humoristique** *a* humorous.
**humour** *m* humor; **avoir de l'h.** to have a sense of humor.
**hurlement** *m* howl; scream.
**hurler 1** *vi* (*loup, vent*) to howl; (*personne*) to scream. **2** *vt* to scream.
**hygiène** *f* hygiene.
**hygiénique** *a* hygienic; **papier h.** toilet paper.
**hymne** *m* **h. national** national anthem.
**hypermarché** *m* hypermarket.
**hypocrisie** *f* hypocrisy.
**hypocrite 1** *a* hypocritical. **2** *mf* hypocrite.
**hypothèse** *f* (*supposition*) assumption.

# I

**iceberg** *m* iceberg.
**ici** *adv* here; **par i.** (*passer*) this way; (*habiter*) around here; **jusqu'i.** (*temps*) up to now; (*lieu*) as far as this *ou* here; **d'i. peu** before long.
**idéal, -e, -aux** *ou* **-als** *a* & *m* ideal.
**idée** *f* idea; **changer d'i.** to change one's mind.
**identifier** *vt* to identify; **s'i. à** *ou* **avec** to identify (oneself) with.
**identique** *a* identical (**à** to, with).
**identité** *f* identity; **carte d'i.** identity card, ID.
**idiot, -ote 1** *a* silly. **2** *mf* idiot.
**idiotie** *f* **une i.** a silly thing.
**idole** *m* idol.
**igloo** *m* igloo.
**ignifugé, -ée** *a* fireproof(ed).
**ignorance** *f* ignorance.
**ignorant, -ante** *a* ignorant (**de** of).
**ignorer** *vt* not to know; **i. qn** to ignore s.o.
**il** *pron* (*personne*) he; (*chose, animal*) it; **il pleut** it's raining; **il y a** there is; *pl* there are; **il y a six ans** six years ago; **il y a une heure qu'il travaille** he's been working for an hour; **qu'est-ce qu'il y a?** what's the matter?
**île** *f* island.
**illégal, -e, -aux** *a* illegal.
**illettré, -ée** *a* illiterate.
**illisible** *a* (*écriture*) illegible.
**illuminer** *vt*, **s'illuminer** *vpr* to light up.
**illusion** *f* illusion; **se faire des illusions** to delude oneself (**sur** about).
**illustration** *f* illustration.
**illustré** *m* comic.
**illustrer** *vt* to illustrate (**de** with).
**ils** *pron* they.
**image** *f* picture; (*dans une glace*) reflection.
**imaginaire** *a* imaginary.
**imagination** *f* imagination.
**imaginer** *vt*, **s'imaginer** *vpr* to imagine (**que** that).
**imbattable** *a* unbeatable.
**imbécile** *mf* idiot.
**imitateur, -trice** *mf* (*artiste*) impersonator.
**imitation** *f* imitation.
**imiter** *vt* to imitate; **i. qn** (*pour rire*) to mimic s.o.; (*faire comme*) to do the same as s.o.
**immangeable** *a* inedible.
**immatriculation** *f* registration.
**immédiat, -ate** *a* immediate.
**immédiatement** *adv* immediately.
**immense** *a* immense.

**immeuble** *m* building; (*d'habitation*) apartment building; (*de bureaux*) office building.
**immigration** *f* immigration.
**immigré, -ée** *a* & *mf* immigrant.
**immobile** *a* still.
**immobiliser** *vt* to bring to a stop.
**immobiliser (s')** *vpr* to come to a stop.
**immortel, -elle** *a* immortal.
**impair, -e** *a* (*nombre*) odd.
**impardonnable** *a* unforgivable.
**imparfait** *m* (*temps*) *Grammaire* imperfect.
**impartial, -e, -aux** *a* fair, unbiased.
**impasse** *f* dead end.
**impatience** *f* impatience.
**impatient, -ente** *a* impatient (**de faire** to do).
**impatienter (s')** *vpr* to get impatient.
**impeccable** *a* (*propre*) immaculate.
**impératif** *m* *Grammaire* imperative.
**imperméable 1** *a* (*tissu*) waterproof. **2** *m* raincoat.
**impitoyable** *a* ruthless.
**impoli, -ie** *a* rude.
**impolitesse** *f* rudeness.
**importance** *f* importance; **ça n'a pas d'i.** it doesn't matter.
**important, -ante 1** *a* important; (*quantité etc*) big. **2** *m* **l'i., c'est de** the important thing is to.
**importation** *f* import; **d'i.** (*article*) imported.
**importer 1** *vi* **n'importe qui/quoi/où/quand/comment** anyone/anything/anywhere/anytime/anyhow. **2** *vt* to import (**de** from).
**imposer** *vt* to impose (**à** on).
**impossibilité** *f* impossibility.
**impossible** *a* impossible (**à faire** to do); **il (nous) est i. de le faire** it is impossible (for us) to do it.
**impôt** *m* tax; **i. sur le revenu** income tax; **(service des) impôts** tax authorities.
**impression** *f* impression.
**impressionnant, -ante** *a* impressive.
**impressionner** *vt* (*émouvoir*) to make a strong impression on.
**imprévisible** *a* unforeseeable.
**imprévu, -ue** *a* unexpected.
**imprimante** *f* (*d'ordinateur*) printer.
**imprimé** *m* printed form.
**imprimer** *vt* (*livre etc*) to print.
**imprimerie** *f* printing plant.
**improviser** *vti* to improvise.
**improviste (à l')** *adv* unexpectedly.
**imprudence** *f* carelessness, foolishness; **commettre une i.** to do something foolish.
**imprudent, -ente** *a* careless, foolish.
**impuissant, -ante** *a* helpless.
**impulsif, -ive** *a* impulsive.
**inabordable** *a* (*prix*) prohibitive.
**inacceptable** *a* unacceptable.
**inachevé, -ée** *a* unfinished.
**inadmissible** *a* unacceptable, inadmissible.
**inanimé, -ée** *a* (*mort*) lifeless; (*évanoui*) unconscious.
**inaperçu, -ue** *a* **passer i.** to go unnoticed.
**inattendu, -ue** *a* unexpected.
**inattention** *f* lack of attention; **un moment d'i.** a moment of distraction.
**inauguration** *f* inauguration.
**inaugurer** *vt* to inaugurate.
**incapable** *a* **i. de faire** unable to do.
**incassable** *a* unbreakable.
**incendie** *m* fire.
**incendier** *vt* to set fire to.
**incertain, -aine** *a* uncertain; (*temps*) unsettled.
**incertitude** *f* uncertainty.
**incessant, -ante** *a* continual.
**inchangé, -ée** *a* unchanged.
**incident** *m* incident.
**incisive** *f* incisor (tooth).
**incliner** *vt* (*courber*) to bend; (*pencher*) to tilt.
**incliner (s')** *vpr* (*se courber*) to bow (down).

**inclus, -use** *a* inclusive; **jusqu'à lundi i.** up to and including Monday.
**incolore** *a* colorless; (*vernis*) clear.
**incommoder** *vt* to bother.
**incompatible** *a* incompatible.
**incompétent, -ente** *a* incompetent.
**incomplet, -ète** *a* incomplete.
**incompréhensible** *a* incomprehensible.
**inconnu, -ue 1** *a* unknown (**à** to). **2** *mf* (*étranger*) stranger.
**inconscient, -ente** *a* unconscious (**de** of); (*imprudent*) thoughtless.
**inconsolable** *a* heartbroken, cut up.
**incontestable** *a* undeniable.
**inconvénient** *m* drawback.
**incorrect, -e** *a* (*grossier*) impolite.
**incroyable** *a* incredible.
**inculpé, -ée** *mf* **l'i.** the accused.
**inculper** *vt* to charge (**de** with).
**incurable** *a* incurable.
**indécis, -ise** *a* (*hésitant*) undecided.
**indéfini, -ie** *a* indefinite.
**indéfiniment** *adv* indefinitely.
**indemne** *a* unhurt.
**indemnité** *f* compensation; (*allocation*) allowance.
**indépendance** *f* independence.
**indépendant, -ante** *a* independent (**de** of).
**indescriptible** *a* indescribable.
**index** *m* (*doigt*) index finger, forefinger.
**indicatif** *m* (*à la radio*) theme song *ou* music; (*téléphonique*) area code; *Grammaire* indicative.
**indication** *f* (piece of) information; **indications** (*pour aller quelque part*) directions.
**indice** *m* (*dans une enquête*) clue.
**indien, -ienne** *a* & *mf* Indian.
**indifférence** *f* indifference (**à** to).
**indifférent, -ente** *a* indifferent (**à** to).
**indigestion** *f* (attack of) indigestion.
**indignation** *f* indignation.
**indigner (s')** *vpr* to be *ou* become indignant (**de** at).
**indiquer** *vt* (*montrer*) to show; (*dire*) to tell; **i. du doigt** to point to *ou* at.
**indirect, -e** *a* indirect.
**indirectement** *adv* indirectly.
**indiscipliné, -ée** *a* unruly.
**indiscret, -ète** *a* inquisitive.
**indiscrétion** *f* indiscretion.
**indispensable** *a* essential.
**indistinct, -incte** *a* unclear.
**individu** *m* individual.
**individuel, -elle** *a* individual.
**indolore** *a* painless.
**indulgent, -ente** *a* indulgent (**envers** to).
**industrialisé, -ée** *a* industrialized.
**industrie** *f* industry.
**industriel, -elle** *a* industrial.
**inefficace** *a* (*mesure etc*) ineffective; (*personne*) inefficient.
**inépuisable** *a* inexhaustible.
**inestimable** *a* priceless.
**inévitable** *a* inevitable, unavoidable.
**inexact, -e** *a* inaccurate.
**inexcusable** *a* inexcusable.
**inexplicable** *a* inexplicable.
**inexpliqué, -ée** *a* unexplained.
**infaillible** *a* infallible.
**infarctus** *m* **un i.** a coronary.
**infatigable** *a* tireless.
**infect, -e** *a* (*odeur*) foul; (*café etc*) vile.
**infecter (s')** *vpr* to get infected.
**infection** *f* infection; (*odeur*) stench.
**inférieur, -e** *a* lower; (*qualité etc*) inferior (**à** to); **l'étage i.** the floor below.
**infériorité** *f* inferiority.
**infernal, -e, -aux** *a* infernal.
**infesté, -ée** *a* **i. de requins**/*etc* shark/*etc*-infested.
**infiltrer (s')** *vpr* (*liquide*) to seep (through) (**dans** into).
**infini, -ie 1** *a* infinite. **2** *m* infinity.
**infiniment** *adv* (*regretter, remercier*) very much.

**infinitif** *m Grammaire* infinitive.
**infirme** *a* & *mf* disabled (person).
**infirmerie** *f* sick room, sickbay.
**infirmier** *m* male nurse.
**infirmière** *f* nurse.
**inflammable** *a* (in)flammable.
**inflammation** *f* inflammation.
**inflation** *f* inflation.
**inflexible** *a* inflexible.
**influence** *f* influence.
**influencer** *vt* to influence.
**information** *f* information; (*nouvelle*) piece of news; **les informations** the news.
**informatique** *f* (*science*) computer science; (*technique*) data processing.
**informatisé, -ée** *a* computerized.
**informer** *vt* to inform (**de** of, about; que that).
**informer (s')** *vpr* to inquire (**de** about; **si** if, whether).
**infraction** *f* offense.
**infusion** *f* herbal *ou* herb tea.
**ingénieur** *m* engineer; **femme i.** woman engineer.
**ingénieux, -euse** *a* ingenious.
**ingrat, -ate** *a* ungrateful (**envers** to).
**ingratitude** *f* ingratitude.
**ingrédient** *m* ingredient.
**inhabité, -ée** *a* uninhabited.
**inhabituel, -elle** *a* unusual.
**inhumain, -aine** *a* inhuman.
**inimaginable** *a* unimaginable.
**ininflammable** *a* non-flammable.
**ininterrompu, -ue** *a* continuous.
**initiale** *f* (*lettre*) initial.
**injecter** *vt* to inject.
**injection** *f* injection.
**injure** *f* insult.
**injurier** *vt* to insult.
**injuste** *a* (*contraire à la justice*) unjust; (*non équitable*) unfair.
**injustice** *f* injustice.
**innocence** *f* innocence.
**innocent, -ente** 1 *a* innocent (**de** of). 2 *mf* innocent person.
**innombrable** *a* countless.
**inoccupé, -ée** *a* unoccupied.
**inoffensif, -ive** *a* harmless.
**inondation** *f* flood.
**inonder** *vt* to flood.
**inoubliable** *a* unforgettable.
**inox** *m* stainless steel.
**inoxydable** *a* **acier i.** stainless steel.
**inquiet, -iète** *a* worried (**de** about).
**inquiétant, -ante** *a* worrying.
**inquiéter** *vt* to worry; **s'i. (de)** to worry (about).
**inquiétude** *f* worry.
**inscription** *f* (*enrollment*) registration; (*sur écriteau etc*) inscription; **frais d'i.** (*à l'université*) tuition fees.
**inscrire*** *vt* to write *ou* put down; **i. qn** to enroll s.o.
**inscrire (s')** *vpr* to put one's name down; **s'i. à** (*club*) to join; (*examen*) to enroll for, register for.
**insecte** *m* insect.
**insecticide** *m* insecticide.
**insensible** *a* insensitive (**à** to).
**inséparable** *a* inseparable (**de** from).
**insigne** *m* badge.
**insignifiant, -ante** *a* insignificant.
**insistance** *f* insistence.
**insister** *vi* to insist (**pour faire** on doing); **i. sur** (*détail etc*) to stress.
**insolation** *f* sunstroke.
**insolence** *f* insolence.
**insolent, -ente** *a* insolent.
**insomnie** *f* insomnia.
**insonoriser** *vt* to soundproof.
**insouciant, -ante** *a* carefree.
**inspecter** *vt* to inspect.
**inspecteur, -trice** *mf* inspector.
**inspection** *f* inspection.
**inspiration** *f* inspiration.
**inspirer** *vt* to inspire (**qch à qn** s.o. with sth).
**instable** *a* (*meuble*) shaky.
**installation** *f* putting in; moving in.
**installer** *vt* (*appareil etc*) to install, put in; (*étagère*) to put up.
**installer (s')** *vpr* (*s'asseoir, s'établir*) to settle (down); **s'i. dans** (*maison*) to move into.

**instant** *m* moment; **à l'i.** a moment ago; **pour l'i.** for the moment.
**instinct** *m* instinct.
**instinctif, -ive** *a* instinctive.
**instituteur, -trice** *mf* elementary school teacher.
**institution** *f* (*organisation, structure*) institution.
**instructif, -ive** *a* instructive.
**instruction** *f* education; **instructions** (*ordres*) instructions.
**instruire*** *vt* to teach, educate; **s'i.** to educate oneself.
**instrument** *m* instrument; (*outil*) implement.
**insuffisant, -ante** *a* inadequate.
**insulte** *f* insult (**à** to).
**insulter** *vt* to insult.
**insupportable** *a* unbearable.
**intact, -e** *a* intact.
**intégralement** *adv* in full.
**intellectuel, -elle** *a* & *mf* intellectual.
**intelligemment** *adv* intelligently.
**intelligence** *f* intelligence.
**intelligent, -ente** *a* intelligent.
**intempéries** *fpl* **les i.** bad weather.
**intense** *a* intense; (*circulation*) heavy.
**intensifier** *vt*, **s'intensifier** *vpr* to intensify.
**intensité** *f* intensity.
**intention** *f* intention; **avoir l'i. de faire** to intend to do.
**interchangeable** *a* interchangeable.
**interdiction** *f* ban (**de** on); **'i. de fumer'** 'no smoking'.
**interdire*** *vt* to forbid, not to allow (**qch à qn** s.o. sth); **i. à qn de faire** not to allow s.o. to do.
**interdit, -ite** *a* forbidden; **'stationnement i.'** 'no parking'.
**intéressant, -ante** *a* interesting; (*prix etc*) attractive.
**intéresser** *vt* to interest; **s'i. à** to take an interest in.
**intérêt** *m* interest; **intérêts** (*argent*) interest; **tu as i. à faire** you'd do well to do.
**intérieur, -e 1** *a* inner; (*poche*) inside; (*politique*) domestic. **2** *m* inside (**de** of); **à l'i. (de)** inside.
**interlocuteur, -trice** *mf* **mon i.** the person I am, was *etc* speaking to.
**intermédiaire** *mf* **par l'i. de** through (the medium of).
**interminable** *a* endless.
**international, -e, -aux** *a* international.
**interne** *mf* (*élève*) boarder.
**interpeller** *vt* (*appeler*) to shout at.
**interphone** *m* intercom.
**interposer (s')** *vpr* to intervene (**dans** in).
**interprète** *mf* interpreter; (*chanteur*) singer.
**interpréter** *vt* (*expliquer*) to interpret; (*chanter*) to sing.
**interrogatif, -ive** *a* & *m Grammaire* interrogative.
**interrogation** *f* question; (*à l'école*) test.
**interrogatoire** *m* interrogation.
**interroger** *vt* to question.
**interrompre*** *vt* to interrupt.
**interrupteur** *m* (*électrique*) switch.
**interruption** *f* interruption.
**intersection** *f* intersection.
**intervalle** *m* (*écart*) gap; (*temps*) interval.
**intervenir*** *vi* to intervene; (*survenir*) to occur.
**intervention** *f* intervention; **i. (chirurgicale)** operation.
**interview** *f* interview.
**interviewer** *vt* to interview.
**intestin** *m* bowel.
**intime** *a* intimate; (*journal, mariage*) private.
**intimider** *vt* to intimidate.
**intituler (s')** *vpr* to be entitled.
**intolérable** *a* intolerable (**que** (+ *subjonctif*) that).
**intraduisible** *a* impossible to translate.
**intransitif, -ive** *a Grammaire* intransitive.
**intrépide** *a* fearless.
**introduction** *f* introduction.
**introduire*** *vt* (*insérer*) to put in

(**dans** to); (*faire entrer*) to show in; **s'i. dans** to get into.
**introuvable** *a* nowhere to be found.
**inusable** *a* durable.
**inutile** *a* useless.
**inutilement** *adv* needlessly.
**inutilisable** *a* unusable.
**invariable** *a* invariable.
**invasion** *f* invasion.
**inventer** *vt* to invent; (*imaginer*) to make up.
**inventeur, -trice** *mf* inventor.
**invention** *f* invention.
**inverse** *a* (*sens*) opposite; (*ordre*) reverse.
**inverser** *vt* (*ordre*) to reverse.
**investir** *vti* to invest (**dans** in).
**investissement** *m* investment.
**invisible** *a* invisible.
**invitation** *f* invitation.
**invité, -ée** *mf* guest.
**inviter** *vt* to invite; **s'i. (chez qn)** to (gate)crash.
**involontaire** *a* (*geste etc*) unintentional.
**ira, irai(t)** *voir* **aller**[1].
**irlandais, -aise 1** *a* Irish. **2** *mf* Irishman, Irishwoman; **les I.** the Irish. **3** *m* (*langue*) Irish.
**ironie** *f* irony.
**ironique** *a* ironic(al).
**iront** *voir* **aller**[1].
**irrégulier, -ière** *a* irregular.
**irremplaçable** *a* irreplaceable.
**irréparable** *a* (*véhicule etc*) beyond repair.
**irrésistible** *a* irresistible.
**irriguer** *vt* to irrigate.
**irritable** *a* irritable.
**irritation** *f* irritation.
**irriter** *vt* to irritate.
**islamique** *a* Islamic.
**isolant** *m* insulation (material).
**isolé, -ée** *a* isolated (**de** from).
**isoler** *vt* to isolate (**de** from); (*du froid etc*) to insulate.
**issue** *f* exit; **rue** *etc* **sans i.** dead end.
**italien, -ienne 1** *a* & *mf* Italian. **2** *m* (*langue*) Italian.
**italique** *m* italics.
**itinéraire** *m* route.
**ivoire** *m* ivory.
**ivre** *a* drunk.
**ivresse** *f* drunkenness.
**ivrogne** *mf* drunk(ard).

# J

**jaillir** *vi* (*liquide*) to spurt (out); (*lumière*) to beam out, shine (forth).
**jalousie** *f* jealousy.
**jaloux, -ouse** *a* jealous (**de** of).
**jamais** *adv* never; **elle ne sort j.** she never goes out; **j. de la vie!** (absolutely) never!; **si j.** if ever.
**jambe** *f* leg.
**jambon** *m* ham.
**janvier** *m* January.
**japonais, -aise 1** *a* Japanese. **2** *mf* Japanese man *ou* woman, Japanese *inv*; **les J.** the Japanese. **3** *m* (*langue*) Japanese.
**jardin** *m* garden; **j. public** park.
**jardinage** *m* gardening.
**jardinier** *m* gardener.
**jardinière** *f* (*caisse à fleurs*) window box.
**jaune 1** *a* yellow. **2** *m* yellow; **j. d'œuf** (egg) yolk.
**jaunir** *vti* to turn yellow.
**jaunisse** *f* jaundice.
**Javel (eau de)** *f* bleach.
**jazz** *m* jazz.
**je** *pron* (**j'** *before vowel or mute h*) I.
**jean** *m* (pair of) jeans.
**jeep**® *f* jeep®.
**jerrycan** *m* gasoline can; (*pour l'eau*) water can.
**jet** *m* (*de vapeur*) burst; (*de tuyau d'arrosage*) nozzle; **j. d'eau** fountain.
**jetable** *a* disposable.
**jetée** *f* pier.
**jeter** *vt* to throw (**à** to, **dans** into); (*à la poubelle*) to throw away; **se j. sur** to pounce on; **le fleuve se jette dans** the river flows into.
**jeton** *m* (*pièce*) token; (*de jeu*) chip.
**jeu, -x** *m* game; (*amusement*) play; (*d'argent*) gambling; (*série com-*

*plète*) set; (*de cartes*) deck; **j. de mots** play on words; **jeux de société** parlor *ou* indoor games; **j. télévisé** (television) quiz show.

**jeudi** *m* Thursday.

**jeun (à)** *adv* **être à j.** to have eaten no food.

**jeune 1** *a* young. **2** *mf* young person; **les jeunes** young people.

**jeunesse** *f* youth; **la j.** (*jeunes*) the young.

**jockey** *m* jockey.

**jogging** *m* jogging; **faire du j.** to jog.

**joie** *f* joy.

**joindre*** *vt* to join; (*envoyer avec*) to enclose (**à** with); **j. qn** to get in touch with s.o.; **se j. à** (*un groupe etc*) to join.

**joker** *m Cartes* joker.

**joli, -ie** *a* nice; (*femme, enfant*) pretty.

**jongler** *vi* to juggle (**avec** with).

**jongleur, -euse** *mf* juggler.

**jonquille** *f* daffodil.

**joue** *f* cheek.

**jouer 1** *vi* to play; (*acteur*) to act; (*au tiercé etc*) to gamble, bet; **j. au tennis/aux cartes/***etc* to play tennis/cards/*etc*; **j. du piano/***etc* to play the piano/*etc*. **2** *vt* to play; (*risquer*) to bet (**sur** on); (*pièce, film*) to put on.

**jouet** *m* toy.

**joueur, -euse** *mf* player; (*au tiercé etc*) gambler; **bon j.** good loser.

**jour** *m* day; (*lumière*) (day)light; **il fait j.** it's light; **en plein j.** in broad daylight; **de nos jours** nowadays; **du j. au lendemain** overnight; **le j. de l'An** New Year's Day.

**journal, -aux** *m* (news)paper; (*intime*) diary; **j. (télévisé)** television news.

**journaliste** *mf* journalist.

**journée** *f* day; **toute la j.** all day (long).

**joyeux, -euse** *a* merry, happy; **j. Noël!** merry Christmas!; **j. anniversaire!** happy birthday!

**judo** *m* judo.

**juge** *m* judge.

**jugement** *m* judg(e)ment; (*verdict*) sentence; **passer en j.** to stand trial.

**juger** *vt* to judge; (*au tribunal*) to try; (*estimer*) to consider (**que** that).

**juif, juive 1** *a* Jewish. **2** *mf* Jew.

**juillet** *m* July.

**juin** *m* June.

**jumeau, -elle,** *pl* **-eaux, -elles** *mf* & *a* twin; **frère j.** twin brother; **sœur jumelle** twin sister; **lits jumeaux** twin beds.

**jumelles** *fpl* (*pour regarder*) binoculars.

**jument** *f* mare.

**jungle** *f* jungle.

**jupe** *f* skirt.

**jupon** *m* petticoat.

**jurer 1** *vi* (*dire un gros mot*) to swear (**contre** at). **2** *vt* (*promettre*) to swear (**que** that, **de faire** to do).

**juron** *m* swearword.

**jury** *m* jury.

**jus** *m* juice; (*de viande*) gravy.

**jusque 1** *prép* **jusqu'à** (*espace*) as far as; (*temps*) until; **jusqu'à dix francs** (*limite*) up to ten francs; **jusqu'en mai** until May; **jusqu'où?** how far?; **jusqu'ici** (*temps*) up till now. **2** *conj* **jusqu'à ce qu'il vienne** until he comes.

**juste 1** *a* (*équitable*) fair; (*légitime*) just; (*exact*) right; (*étroit*) tight. **2** *adv* (*deviner etc*) right; (*chanter*) in tune; (*seulement*) just.

**justement** *adv* exactly.

**justice** *f* justice; (*autorités*) law.

**justifier** *vt* to justify.

**juteux, -euse** *a* juicy.

# K

**kangourou** *m* kangaroo.

**karaté** *m* karate.

**képi** *m* cap, kepi.

**kidnapper** *vt* to kidnap.

**kilo** *m* kilo.

**kilogramme** *m* kilogram.

**kilométrage** *m* = mileage.

**kilomètre** *m* kilometer.
**kiosque** *m* (*à journaux*) kiosk.
**kit** *m* **meuble en k.** (piece of) flat-pack furniture.
**klaxon®** *m* horn.
**klaxonner** *vi* to honk.
**k.-o.** *a inv* **mettre k.-o.** to knock out.

## L

**l', la** *voir* **le.**
**là 1** *adv* (*lieu*) there; (*chez soi*) in; (*temps*) then; **je reste là** I'll stay here; **c'est là que** that's where; **à cinq mètres de là** 16 feet away; **jusque-là** (*lieu*) as far as that; (*temps*) up till then. **2** *int* **oh là là!** oh dear!
**là-bas** *adv* over there.
**laboratoire** *m* laboratory.
**labourer** *vt* to plow.
**labyrinthe** *m* maze.
**lac** *m* lake.
**lacet** *m* (shoe-)lace; (*de route*) twist.
**lâche 1** *a* cowardly. **2** *mf* coward.
**lâcher 1** *vt* to let go of; (*bombe*) to drop. **2** *vi* (*corde*) to give way.
**lâcheté** *f* cowardice.
**là-dedans** *adv* in there.
**là-dessous** *adv* underneath.
**là-dessus** *adv* on there.
**là-haut** *adv* up there; (*à l'étage*) upstairs.
**laid, laide** *a* ugly.
**laideur** *f* ugliness.
**lainage** *m* woolen garment.
**laine** *f* wool; **en l.** woolen.
**laisse** *f* lead, leash.
**laisser** *vt* to leave; **l. qn partir/***etc* to let s.o. go/*etc*; **l. qch à qn** to let s.o. have sth.
**lait** *m* milk.
**laitier** *a* **produit l.** dairy product.
**laitue** *f* lettuce.
**lambeau, -x** *m* shred, bit.
**lame** *f* (*de couteau etc*) blade; (*vague*) wave.
**lamentable** *a* (*mauvais*) terrible.
**lampadaire** *m* floor lamp; (*de rue*) street lamp.
**lampe** *f* lamp; (*au néon*) light; **l. de poche** flashlight.
**lance** *f* spear; (*extrémité de tuyau*) nozzle; **l. d'incendie** fire hose.
**lancement** *m* (*de fusée etc*) launch(ing).
**lancer** *vt* to throw (**à** to); (*avec force*) to hurl; (*fusée, produit etc*) to launch; (*appel etc*) to issue.
**lancer (se)** *vpr* (*se précipiter*) to rush.
**landau** *m* (*pl* **-s**) baby carriage.
**langage** *m* language.
**langouste** *f* (spiny) lobster.
**langue** *f* tongue; (*langage*) language; **l. maternelle** mother tongue; **langues vivantes** modern languages.
**lanière** *f* strap.
**lanterne** *f* lantern; **lanternes** (*de véhicule*) parking lights.
**lapin** *m* rabbit.
**laque** *f* lacquer.
**lard** *m* (*fumé*) bacon; (*gras*) (pig's) fat.
**large 1** *a* wide, broad; (*vêtement*) loose; **l. de six mètres** 20 feet wide. **2** *m* breadth, width; **avoir six mètres de l.** to be 20 feet wide; **le l.** (*mer*) the open sea; **au l. de Cherbourg** off Cherbourg.
**largement** *adv* (*ouvrir*) wide; (*au moins*) easily; **avoir l. le temps** to have plenty of time.
**largeur** *f* width, breadth.
**larme** *f* tear; **en larmes** in tears.
**laser** *m* laser.
**lasser** *vt*, **se lasser** *vpr* to tire (**de** of).
**latin** *m* (*langue*) Latin.
**lavabo** *m* washbasin, sink.
**lave-auto** *m* car wash.
**laver** *vt* to wash; **se l.** to wash up; **se l. les mains** to wash one's hands.
**laverie** *f* (*automatique*) laundromat.
**lavette** *f* dishcloth.
**lave-vaisselle** *m* dishwasher.
**layette** *f* baby clothes.

**le, la,** *pl* **les** (**le** & **la** *become* **l'** *before a vowel or mute h*) **1** *art déf* (**à** + **le** = **au, à** + **les** = **aux; de** + **le** = **du, de** + **les** = **des**) the. ▪ (*généralisation*) **la beauté** beauty; **la France** France; **les hommes** men; **aimer le café** to like coffee. ▪ (*possession*) **il ouvrit la bouche** he opened his mouth; **avoir les cheveux blonds** to have blond hair. ▪ (*mesure*) **dix francs la livre** ten francs a pound. ▪ (*temps*) **elle vient le lundi** she comes on Monday(s); **l'an prochain** next year; **une fois l'an** once a year. **2** *pron* (*homme*) him; (*femme*) her; (*chose*, *animal*) it; *pl* them; **es-tu fatigué?—je le suis** are you tired?—I am; **je le crois** I think so.

**lécher** *vt* to lick; **se l. les doigts** to lick one's fingers.

**leçon** *f* lesson.

**lecteur, -trice** *mf* reader; **l. de cassettes/CD** cassette/CD player.

**lecture** *f* reading; **lectures** (*livres*) books.

**légal, -e, -aux** *a* legal.

**légende** *f* (*histoire*) legend; (*de plan*) key; (*de photo*) caption.

**léger, -ère** *a* light; (*bruit*, *fièvre etc*) slight; (*café*, *thé*) weak; (*bière*, *tabac*) mild.

**légèrement** *adv* (*un peu*) slightly.

**légèreté** *f* lightness.

**légitime** *a* **être en état de l. défense** to act in self-defense.

**légume** *m* vegetable.

**lendemain** *m* **le l.** the next day; **le l. de** the day after; **le l. matin** the next morning.

**lent, lente** *a* slow.

**lentement** *adv* slowly.

**lenteur** *f* slowness.

**lentille** *f* (*graine*) lentil.

**léopard** *m* leopard.

**lequel, laquelle,** *pl* **lesquels, lesquelles** (+ **à** = **auquel, à laquelle, auxquel(le)s;** + **de** = **duquel, de laquelle, desquel(le)s**) *pron* (*chose*, *animal*) which; (*personne*) who, (*indirect*) whom; (*interrogatif*) which (one); **dans l.** in which; **parmi lesquels** (*choses*, *animaux*) among which; (*personnes*) among whom.

**les** *voir* **le**.

**lessive** *f* (laundry) detergent; (*linge*) laundry; **faire la l.** to do the laundry.

**lettre** *f* letter; **en toutes lettres** (*mot*) in full.

**leur 1** *a poss* their. **2** *pron poss* **le l., la l., les leurs** theirs. **3** *pron inv* (*indirect*) (to) them; **il l. est facile de** it's easy for them to.

**levé, -ée** *a* **être l.** (*debout*) to be up.

**lever 1** *vt* to lift (up); **l. les yeux** to look up. **2** *m* **le l. du soleil** sunrise.

**lever (se)** *vpr* to get up; (*soleil*, *rideau*) to rise; (*jour*) to break.

**levier** *m* lever; (*pour soulever*) crowbar.

**lèvre** *f* lip.

**lézard** *m* lizard.

**liaison** *f* (*routière etc*) link; (*entre mots*) liaison.

**liasse** *f* bundle.

**libération** *f* freeing, release.

**libérer** *vt* to (set) free, release (**de** from); **se l.** to free oneself (**de** from).

**liberté** *f* freedom; **en l. provisoire** on bail; **mettre en l.** to free.

**libraire** *mf* bookseller.

**librairie** *f* bookshop.

**libre** *a* free (**de qch** from sth, **de faire** to do); (*voie*) clear.

**librement** *adv* freely.

**libre-service** *m* (*pl* **libres-services**) self-service.

**licence** *f* (*diplôme*) (Bachelor's) degree; (*sportive*) license.

**licencié, -ée** *a* & *mf* graduate; **l. ès lettres/sciences** Bachelor of Arts/Science.

**licenciement** *m* dismissal.

**licencier** *vt* (*ouvrier*) to lay off, dismiss.

**liège** *m* (*matériau*) cork.

**lien** *m* (*rapport*) link; (*ficelle*) tie; **l. de parenté** family tie.

**lier** *vt* (*attacher*) to tie (up); (*relier*) to link (up).

**lieu, -x** *m* place; (*d'un accident*) scene; **les lieux** (*locaux*) the premises; **avoir l.** to take place; **au l. de** instead of.
**lièvre** *m* hare.
**ligne** *f* line; (*belle silhouette*) figure; **(se) mettre en l.** to line up; **en l.** (*au téléphone*) connected; **grandes lignes** (*de train*) main line (services); **à la l.** new paragraph; **l. d'arrivée** finish line.
**ligoter** *vt* to tie up.
**lilas** *m* lilac.
**lime** *f* file.
**limer** *vt* to file.
**limitation** *f* (*de vitesse, poids*) limit.
**limite 1** *f* limit (**à** to); (*frontière*) boundary. **2** *a* (*cas*) extreme; (*vitesse etc*) maximum; **date l.** latest date; **date l. de vente** sell-by date.
**limiter** *vt* to limit (**à** to).
**limonade** *f* lemon-lime soda.
**limpide** *a* (crystal) clear.
**linge** *m* linen; (*à laver*) laundry.
**lingerie** *f* underwear.
**lion** *m* lion.
**lionne** *f* lioness.
**liqueur** *f* liqueur.
**liquide 1** *a* liquid; **argent l.** ready cash. **2** *m* liquid; **du l.** (*argent*) ready cash.
**lire*** *vti* to read.
**lis** *m* lily.
**lis, lisant, lise(nt)** *etc voir* **lire**.
**lisible** *a* (*écriture*) legible.
**lisse** *a* smooth.
**lisser** *vt* to smooth.
**liste** *f* list; **sur la l. rouge** (*numéro de téléphone*) unlisted.
**lit**[1] *m* bed; **l. d'enfant** crib; **lits superposés** bunk beds.
**lit**[2] *voir* **lire**.
**literie** *f* bedding.
**litre** *m* liter.
**littéraire** *a* literary.
**littérature** *f* literature.
**littoral** *m* coast(line).
**livraison** *f* delivery.
**livre**[1] *m* book; **l. de poche** paperback (book).
**livre**[2] *f* (*monnaie, poids*) pound.
**livrer** *vt* to deliver (**à** to); **l. qn à** (*la police etc*) to give s.o. over to.
**livret** *m* **l. scolaire** report card; **l. de caisse d'épargne** bankbook, passbook.
**livreur, -euse** *mf* delivery man, delivery woman.
**local, -ale, -aux** *a* local.
**local, -aux** *m* room; **locaux** premises.
**locataire** *mf* tenant.
**location** *f* (*de maison voiture*) rental; (*par propriétaire*) renting (out), letting; (*loyer*) rental.
**locomotive** *f* (*de train*) engine.
**locution** *f* phrase.
**loge** *f* (*de concierge*) lodge; (*d'acteur*) dressing room; (*de spectateur*) box.
**logement** *m* accommodation; (*appartement*) apartment; (*maison*) house; **le l.** housing.
**loger 1** *vt* to accommodate; (*héberger*) to put up. **2** *vi* (*à l'hôtel etc*) to put up; (*habiter*) to live.
**logiciel** *m* software *inv*.
**logique** *a* logical.
**logiquement** *adv* logically.
**loi** *f* law; (*du Parlement*) act; **projet de l.** bill.
**loin** *adv* far (away *ou* off); **Boston est l. (de Paris)** Boston is a long way away (from Paris); **plus l.** further, farther; **de l.** from a distance.
**lointain, -aine** *a* distant.
**loisirs** *mpl* spare time, leisure (time); (*distractions*) leisure activities.
**long, longue 1** *a* long; **être l. (à faire)** to be a long time *ou* slow (in doing); **l. de deux mètres** seven feet long. **2** *m* **avoir deux mètres de l.** to be seven feet long; **(tout) le l. de** (*espace*) (all) along; **de l. en large** (*marcher*) up and down; **à la longue** in the long run.
**longer** *vt* to go along; (*forêt, mer*) to skirt; (*mur*) to hug.
**longtemps** *adv* (for) a long time; **trop l.** too long.
**longueur** *f* length; **à l. de journée**

all day long; **l. d'ondes** wavelength.
**lors** *adv* **l. de** at the time of.
**lorsque** *conj* when.
**losange** *m* (*forme*) diamond.
**lot** *m* (*de loterie*) prize; **gros l.** grand prize, jackpot.
**loterie** *f* lottery.
**lotion** *f* lotion.
**lotissement** *m* (*habitations*) housing development.
**louche** *f* ladle.
**loucher** *vi* to squint.
**louer** *vt* (*prendre en location*) to rent; (*donner en location*) to rent (out), let; **maison à l.** house to let.
**loup** *m* wolf; **avoir une faim de l.** to be ravenous.
**loupe** *f* magnifying glass.
**lourd, lourde 1** *a* heavy; (*temps*) close; (*faute*) gross. **2** *adv* **peser l.** to be heavy.
**loyal, -e, -aux** *a* (*honnête*) fair (**envers** to).
**loyauté** *f* fairness.
**loyer** *m* rent.
**lu, lue** *pp of* **lire**.
**lucarne** *f* (*fenêtre*) skylight.
**lueur** *f* glimmer.
**lui 1** *pron mf* (*complément indirect*) (to) him; (*femme*) (to) her; (*chose, animal*) (to) it; **il lui est facile de** it's easy for him *ou* her to. **2** *pron m* (*complément direct*) him; (*chose, animal*) it; (*sujet emphatique*) he.
**lui-même** *pron* himself; (*chose, animal*) itself.
**luisant, -ante** *a* shiny.
**lumière** *f* light.
**lumineux, -euse** *a* (*idée, ciel etc*) bright.
**lundi** *m* Monday.
**lune** *f* moon; **l. de miel** honeymoon.
**lunettes** *fpl* glasses, spectacles; (*de protection, de plongée*) goggles; **l. de soleil** sunglasses.
**lustre** *m* (*éclairage*) chandelier.
**lutte** *f* fight, struggle; (*sport*) wrestling.
**lutter** *vi* to fight, struggle.
**luxe** *m* luxury; **article de l.** luxury article.
**luxueux, -euse** *a* luxurious.
**lycée** *m* = high school.
**lycéen, -enne** *mf* = high school student

# M

**ma** *voir* **mon**.
**macaroni(s)** *m*(*pl*) macaroni.
**macédoine** *f* **m. (de légumes)** mixed vegetables.
**mâcher** *vt* to chew.
**machin** *m Fam* (*chose*) whatchamacallit.
**machinal, -e, -aux** *a* instinctive.
**machinalement** *adv* instinctively.
**machine** *f* machine; **m. à coudre** sewing machine; **m. à écrire** typewriter; **m. à laver** washing machine.
**mâchoire** *f* jaw.
**maçon** *m* bricklayer.
**madame,** *pl* **mesdames** *f* madam; **bonjour mesdames** good morning (ladies); **Madame** *ou* **Mme Legras** Mrs Legras; **Madame** (*dans une lettre*) Dear Madam.
**madeleine** *f* (small) sponge cake.
**mademoiselle,** *pl* **mesdemoiselles** *f* miss; **bonjour mesdemoiselles** good morning (ladies); **Mademoiselle** *ou* **Mlle Legras** Miss Legras; **Mademoiselle** (*dans une lettre*) Dear Madam.
**magasin** *m* store; **grand m.** department store; **en m.** in stock.
**magazine** *m* magazine.
**magicien, -ienne** *mf* magician.
**magie** *f* magic.
**magique** *a* (*baguette etc*) magic; (*mystérieux*) magical.
**magnétophone** (*Fam* **magnéto**) *m* tape recorder; **m. à cassettes** cassette recorder.
**magnétoscope** *m* video (recorder), VCR.

**magnétoscoper** *vt* (*film etc*) to tape, record (*on a video recorder*).
**magnifique** *a* magnificent.
**mai** *m* May.
**maigre** *a* (*personne*) thin; (*viande*) lean.
**maigrir** *vi* to get thin(ner).
**maille** *f* (*de tricot*) stitch; (*de filet*) mesh.
**maillon** *m* (*de chaîne*) link.
**maillot** *m* (*de sportif*) jersey, shirt; **m. (de corps)** undershirt; **m. (de bain)** (*de femme*) swimsuit; (*d'homme*) (swim) trunks.
**main** *f* hand; **tenir à la m.** to hold in one's hand; **à la m.** (*faire, coudre etc*) by hand; **haut les mains!** hands up!; **donner un coup de m. à qn** to lend s.o. a (helping) hand; **sous la m.** handy.
**maintenant** *adv* now; **m. que** now that.
**maintenir*** *vt* (*conserver*) to keep; (*retenir*) to hold.
**maire** *m* mayor.
**mairie** *f* city hall.
**mais** *conj* but; **m. oui, m. si** yes of course; **m. non** definitely not.
**maïs** *m* (*céréale*) corn.
**maison** *f* (*bâtiment*) house; (*chez-soi*) home; (*entreprise*) firm; **à la m.** at home; **aller à la m.** to go home; **m. de la culture** arts center; **m. des jeunes** youth center.
**maître** *m* (*d'un chien etc*) master; **m. d'école** teacher; **m. d'hôtel** (*restaurant*) head waiter; **m. nageur** swimming instructor (and lifeguard).
**maîtresse** *f* mistress; **m. d'école** teacher.
**maîtrise** *f* (*diplôme*) Master's degree (**de** in).
**maîtriser** *vt* (*incendie*) to (bring under) control; **m. qn** to overpower s.o.
**majesté** *f* **Votre M.** (*titre*) Your Majesty.
**majeur, -e 1** *a* **être m.** to be of age. **2** *m* (*doigt*) middle finger.
**majorette** *f* majorette.
**majorité** *f* majority (**de** of); (*âge*) coming of age.
**majuscule** *f* capital letter.
**mal, maux 1** *m* (*douleur*) pain; **dire du m. de qn** to say bad things about s.o.; **m. de dents** toothache; **m. de gorge** sore throat; **m. de tête** headache; **m. de ventre** stomachache; **avoir le m. de mer** to be seasick; **avoir m. à la tête/gorge/***etc* to have a headache/sore throat/*etc*; **ça (me) fait m., j'ai m.** it hurts (me); **faire du m. à** to hurt; **avoir du m. à faire** to have trouble doing; **le bien et le m.** good and evil. **2** *adv* (*travailler etc*) badly; (*entendre, comprendre*) not too well; **pas m.!** not bad!; **c'est m. de mentir** it's wrong to lie.
**malade 1** *a* ill, sick; **être m. du cœur** to have a bad heart. **2** *mf* sick person; (*d'un médecin*) patient.
**maladie** *f* illness.
**maladresse** *f* clumsiness.
**maladroit, -droite** *a* clumsy.
**malaise** *m* **avoir un m.** to feel dizzy.
**malaria** *f* malaria.
**malchance** *f* bad luck.
**mâle** *a* & *m* male.
**malentendu** *m* misunderstanding.
**malfaiteur** *m* criminal.
**malgré** *prép* in spite of; **m. tout** after all.
**malheur** *m* (*événement, malchance*) misfortune.
**malheureusement** *adv* unfortunately.
**malheureux, -euse 1** *a* (*triste*) miserable. **2** *mf* (*pauvre*) poor man *ou* woman.
**malhonnête** *a* dishonest.
**malice** *f* mischievousness.
**malicieux, -euse** *a* mischievous.
**malin, -igne** *a* (*astucieux*) clever.
**malle** *f* (*coffre*) trunk; (*de véhicule*) trunk.
**mallette** *f* small suitcase; (*pour documents*) attaché case.
**malpoli, -ie** *a* rude.
**malsain, -saine** *a* unhealthy.

**maltraiter** *vt* to ill-treat.
**maman** *f* mama, mom(my).
**mamie** *f Fam* grandma.
**mammifère** *m* mammal.
**manche[1]** *f* (*de vêtement*) sleeve; (*d'un match*) round; **la M.** the English Channel.
**manche[2]** *m* (*d'outil*) handle; **m. à balai** broomstick; (*d'avion etc*) joystick.
**manchette** *f* (*de chemise*) cuff.
**manchot** *m* (*oiseau*) penguin.
**mandarine** *f* tangerine.
**mandat** *m* (*postal*) money order.
**manège** *m* (*à la foire*) merry-go-round.
**manette** *f* lever.
**mangeoire** *f* (feeding) trough.
**manger** *vti* to eat; **donner à m. à** to feed.
**maniable** *a* easy to handle.
**maniaque 1** *a* fussy. **2** *mf* fussbudget.
**manie** *f* craze.
**manier** *vt* to handle.
**manière** *f* way; **de toute m.** anyway; **à ma m.** (in) my own way; **la m. dont elle parle** the way (in which) she talks; **faire des manières** (*chichis*) to make a fuss.
**manifestant, -ante** *mf* demonstrator.
**manifestation** *f* (*défilé*) demonstration.
**manifester 1** *vt* (*sa colère etc*) to show; **se m.** (*maladie*) to show itself. **2** *vi* (*dans la rue*) to demonstrate.
**manipuler** *vt* (*manier*) to handle.
**mannequin** *m* (*personne*) (fashion) model; (*statue*) dummy, mannequin.
**manœuvre 1** *m* (*ouvrier*) laborer. **2** *f* (*action*) maneuver.
**manœuvrer** *vti* (*véhicule*) to maneuver.
**manque** *m* lack (**de** of).
**manquer 1** *vt* (*cible, train etc*) to miss. **2** *vi* (*faire défaut*) to be short; (*être absent*) to be absent (**à** from); **m. de** (*pain, argent etc*) to be short of; (*attention*) to lack; **ça manque de sel** there isn't enough salt; **elle/cela lui manque** he misses her/that; **elle a manqué (de) tomber** she nearly fell; **il manque/il nous manque dix tasses** there are/we are ten cups short.
**mansarde** *f* attic.
**manteau, -x** *m* coat.
**manuel, -elle 1** *a* (*travail*) manual. **2** *m* handbook, manual; (*scolaire*) textbook.
**mappemonde** *f* map of the world; (*sphère*) globe.
**maquereau, -x** *m* (*poisson*) mackerel.
**maquette** *f* (scale) model.
**maquillage** *m* (*fard*) makeup.
**maquiller** *vt* (*visage*) to make up; **se m.** to make (oneself) up.
**marais** *m* marsh.
**marathon** *m* marathon.
**marbre** *m* marble.
**marchand, -ande** *mf* shopkeeper; (*de voitures, meubles*) dealer; **m. de journaux** (*dans un magasin*) newspaper vendor; **m. de légumes** grocer.
**marchander** *vi* to haggle.
**marchandise(s)** *f* (*pl*) goods.
**marche** *f* (*d'escalier*) step; (*trajet*) walk; **la m.** (*sport*) walking; **faire m. arrière** (*en voiture*) to reverse; **un train en m.** a moving train; **mettre qch en m.** to start sth (up).
**marché** *m* (*lieu*) market; **faire son** *ou* **le m.** to do one's shopping (*in the market*); **bon m.** cheap.
**marcher** *vi* (*à pied*) to walk; (*poser le pied*) to step (**dans** in); (*fonctionner*) to work; **faire m.** (*machine*) to work; **ça marche?** *Fam* how's it going?
**mardi** *m* Tuesday; **M. gras** Shrove Tuesday, Mardi Gras.
**mare** *f* (*étang*) pond.
**marécage** *m* swamp.
**marécageux, -euse** *a* swampy.
**marée** *f* tide; **m. noire** oil slick.
**marelle** *f* hopscotch.
**margarine** *f* margarine.
**marge** *f* (*de cahier etc*) margin.
**marguerite** *f* daisy.

**mari** *m* husband.
**mariage** *m* marriage; (*cérémonie*) wedding.
**marié, -ée 1** *a* married. **2** *m* (bride)-groom; **les mariés** the bride and (bride)groom. **3** *f* bride.
**marier** *vt* **m. qn** (*prêtre etc*) to marry s.o.
**marier (se)** *vpr* to get married (**avec qn** to s.o.).
**marin, -ine 1** *a* **air**/*etc* **m.** sea air/*etc*. **2** *m* sailor.
**marine 1** *f* **m. (de guerre)** navy. **2** *m* & *a inv* (*couleur*) **(bleu) m.** navy (blue).
**marionnette** *f* puppet.
**marmelade** *f* **m. (de fruits)** stewed fruit.
**marmite** *f* (cooking) pot.
**marmonner** *vti* to mutter.
**maroquinerie** *f* (*magasin*) leather goods shop.
**marque** *f* (*trace*) mark; (*de produit*) make, brand; (*points*) score; **m. de fabrique** trademark; **m. déposée** (registered) trademark.
**marquer 1** *vt* (*par une marque*) to mark; (*écrire*) to note down; (*but*) to score; **m. les points** to keep (the) score. **2** *vi* (*trace*) to leave a mark; (*joueur*) to score.
**marqueur** *m* (*crayon*) marker.
**marraine** *f* godmother.
**marrant, -ante** *a Fam* funny.
**marre** *f* **en avoir m.** *Fam* to be fed up (**de** with).
**marron 1** *m* chestnut. **2** *m* & *a inv* (*couleur*) brown.
**mars** *m* March.
**marteau, -x** *m* hammer; **m. piqueur** jackhammer.
**martien, -ienne** *mf* & *a* Martian.
**martyriser** *vt* (*enfant*) to batter, abuse.
**mascara** *m* mascara.
**mascotte** *f* mascot.
**masculin, -ine 1** *a* male. **2** *a* & *m* *Grammaire* masculine.
**masque** *m* mask.
**massacre** *m* slaughter.
**massacrer** *vt* to slaughter.
**massage** *m* massage.
**masse** *f* (*volume*) mass; **en m.** in large numbers.
**masser** *vt* (*frotter*) to massage.
**masser (se)** *vpr* (*gens*) to (form a) crowd.
**masseur** *m* masseur.
**masseuse** *f* masseuse.
**massif, -ive 1** *a* (*or, bois etc*) solid. **2** *m* (*de fleurs*) clump; (*de montagnes*) massif.
**mastic** *m* (*pour vitres*) putty.
**mastiquer** *vt* (*vitre*) to putty; (*mâcher*) to chew.
**mat, mate** *a* (*papier, couleur*) mat(t).
**mât** *m* (*de navire*) mast; (*poteau*) pole.
**match** *m Sport* match, game.
**matelas** *m* mattress; **m. pneumatique** air mattress.
**matelot** *m* sailor.
**matériaux** *mpl* (building) materials.
**matériel, -ielle 1** *a* (*dégâts*) material. **2** *m* (*de camping etc*) equipment; (*d'ordinateur*) hardware *inv*.
**maternel, -elle 1** *a* (*amour, femme etc*) maternal. **2** *f* **(école) maternelle** nursery school.
**maternité** *f* (*hôpital*) maternity ward.
**mathématiques** *fpl* mathematics.
**maths** *fpl* math.
**matière** *f* (*à l'école*) subject; (*substance*) material; **m. première** raw material.
**matin** *m* morning; **le m.** (*chaque matin*) in the morning; **à sept heures du m.** at seven in the morning.
**matinal, -e, -aux** *a* **être m.** to be an early riser.
**matinée** *f* morning; **faire la grasse m.** to sleep late.
**matraque** *f* (*de policier*) truncheon, billy club; (*de malfaiteur*) club.
**maussade** *a* (*personne*) bad-tempered, moody; (*temps*) gloomy.
**mauvais, -aise** *a* bad; (*méchant*)

wicked; (*mal choisi*) wrong; (*mer*) rough; **plus m.** worse; **le plus m.** the worst; **il fait m.** the weather's bad; **m. en** (*anglais etc*) bad at.

**mauve** *a* & *m* (*couleur*) mauve.

**maximal, -e** *a* maximum.

**maximum** *m* maximum; **le m. de** (*force etc*) the maximum (amount of); **au m.** (*tout au plus*) at most.

**mayonnaise** *f* mayonnaise.

**mazout** *m* (fuel) oil.

**me (m'** *before vowel or mute h*) *pron* (*complément direct*) me; (*indirect*) (to) me; (*réfléchi*) myself.

**mécanicien** *m* mechanic; (*de train*) engineer.

**mécanique** *a* mechanical; **jouet m.** wind-up toy.

**mécanisme** *m* mechanism.

**méchanceté** *f* malice; **une m.** (*parole*) a malicious word.

**méchant, -ante** *a* (*cruel*) wicked; (*enfant*) naughty.

**mèche** *f* (*de cheveux*) lock; (*de bougie*) wick; (*de pétard*) fuse.

**méconnaissable** *a* unrecognizable.

**mécontent, -ente** *a* dissatisfied (**de** with).

**mécontentement** *m* dissatisfaction.

**mécontenter** *vt* to displease.

**médaille** *f* (*décoration*) medal; (*bijou*) medallion; **être m. d'or** to be a gold medallist.

**médecin** *m* doctor.

**médecine** *f* medicine; **étudiant en m.** medical student.

**médias** *mpl* (mass) media.

**médical, -e, -aux** *a* medical.

**médicament** *m* medicine.

**médiéval, -e, -aux** *a* medieval.

**médiocre** *a* second-rate.

**médisance(s)** *f* (*pl*) malicious gossip.

**Méditerranée** *f* **la M.** the Mediterranean.

**méditerranéen, -enne** *a* Mediterranean.

**meeting** *m* meeting.

**méfiance** *f* distrust.

**méfiant, -ante** *a* suspicious.

**méfier (se)** *vpr* **se m. de** to distrust; (*faire attention à*) to watch out for; **méfie-toi!** watch out!; **je me méfie** I'm suspicious.

**mégot** *m* cigarette butt.

**meilleur, -e 1** *a* better (**que** than); **le m. résultat**/*etc* the best result/*etc*. **2** *mf* **le m., la meilleure** the best (one).

**mélange** *m* mixture.

**mélanger** *vt*, **se mélanger** *vpr* (*mêler*) to mix.

**mêlée** *f* fight, scuffle; *Rugby* scrum.

**mêler** *vt* to mix (**à** with).

**mêler (se)** *vpr* to mix (**à** with); **se m. à** (*la foule*) to join; **mêle-toi de ce qui te regarde!** mind your own business!

**mélodie** *f* melody.

**melon** *m* (*fruit*) melon; **(chapeau) m.** bowler (hat).

**membre** *m* (*bras, jambe*) limb; (*d'un groupe*) member.

**même 1** *a* same; **en m. temps** at the same time (**que** as). **2** *pron* **le m., la m.** the same (one); **les mêmes** the same (ones). **3** *adv* even; **m. si** even if; **ici m.** in this very place.

**mémoire** *f* memory; **à la m. de** in memory of.

**mémorable** *a* memorable.

**menaçant, -ante** *a* threatening.

**menace** *f* threat.

**menacer** *vt* to threaten (**de faire** to do).

**ménage** *m* housekeeping; (*couple*) couple; **faire le m.** to do the housework.

**ménager, -ère** *a* (*appareil*) domestic; **travaux ménagers** housework.

**ménagère** *f* housewife.

**mendiant, -ante** *mf* beggar.

**mendier 1** *vi* to beg. **2** *vt* to beg for.

**mener 1** *vt* (*personne, vie etc*) to lead; (*enquête etc*) to carry out; **m. qn à** to take s.o. to. **2** *vi* (*en sport*) to lead.

**menottes** *fpl* handcuffs.

**mensonge** *m* lie.

**mensuel, -elle** *a* monthly.
**mental, -e, -aux** *a* mental.
**menteur, -euse** *mf* liar.
**menthe** *f* mint.
**mention** *f* (*à un examen*) distinction.
**mentir*** *vi* to lie (**à** to).
**menton** *m* chin.
**menu** *m* menu.
**menuiserie** *f* carpentry.
**menuisier** *m* carpenter.
**mépris** *m* contempt (**pour** for).
**méprisant, -ante** *a* contemptuous.
**mépriser** *vt* to despise.
**mer** *f* sea; **en m.** at sea; **aller à la m.** to go to the seaside.
**mercerie** *f* (*magasin*) (sewing) notions store.
**merci** *int* & *m* thank you (**de, pour** for).
**mercredi** *m* Wednesday.
**merde!** *int Fam* shit!
**mère** *f* mother; **m. de famille** mother (of a family).
**mériter** *vt* (*être digne de*) to deserve.
**merle** *m* blackbird.
**merveille** *f* wonder.
**merveilleux, -euse** *a* wonderful.
**mes** *voir* **mon.**
**mésaventure** *f* slight mishap.
**mesdames** *voir* **madame.**
**mesdemoiselles** *voir* **mademoiselle.**
**message** *m* message.
**messager** *m* messenger.
**messe** *f* mass (*church service*).
**messieurs** *voir* **monsieur.**
**mesure** *f* (*dimension*) measurement; (*action*) measure; (*cadence*) time.
**mesurer** *vt* to measure; **m. 1 mètre 83** (*personne*) to be six feet tall; (*objet*) to measure six feet.
**métal, -aux** *m* metal.
**métallique** *a* **échelle**/*etc* **m.** metal ladder/*etc.*
**métallurgie** *f* (*industrie*) steel industry.
**météo** *f* (*bulletin*) weather forecast.
**météorologique** *a* **bulletin**/*etc* **m.** weather report/*etc.*
**méthode** *f* (*manière, soin*) method.
**méthodique** *a* methodical.
**métier** *m* (*travail*) job.
**mètre** *m* (*mesure*) meter; (*règle*) (meter) stick; **m. carré** square meter; **m. (à ruban)** tape measure.
**métrique** *a* metric.
**métro** *m* subway.
**metteur** *m* **m. en scène** (*de cinéma*) director.
**mettre*** *vt* to put; (*table*) to set, lay; (*vêtement*) to put on; (*chauffage etc*) to put on, switch on; (*réveil*) to set (**à** for); **j'ai mis une heure** it took me an hour; **m. en colère** to make angry.
**mettre (se)** *vpr* to put oneself; (*debout*) to stand; (*assis*) to sit; (*objet*) to go; **se m. en short**/*etc* to put on one's shorts/*etc*; **se m. à faire** to start doing; **se m. à table** to sit (down) at the table.
**meuble** *m* piece of furniture; **meubles** furniture.
**meubler** *vt* to furnish.
**meugler** *vi* (*vache*) to moo.
**meule** *f* (*de foin*) haystack.
**meurtre** *m* murder.
**meurtrier, -ière** *mf* murderer.
**mi-** *préfixe* **la mi-mars**/*etc* mid March/*etc.*
**miauler** *vi* to miaow.
**miche** *f* round loaf.
**mi-chemin (à)** *adv* halfway.
**mi-côte (à)** *adv* halfway up *ou* down (the hill).
**micro** *m* microphone.
**microbe** *m* germ.
**micro-onde** *f* **four à micro-ondes** microwave oven.
**microscope** *m* microscope.
**midi** *m* (*heure*) twelve o'clock, noon; (*heure du déjeuner*) lunchtime.
**mie** *f* **la m.** the soft part of the bread; **pain de m.** sandwich loaf.
**miel** *m* honey.
**mien, mienne** *pron poss* **le m., la**

**mienne, les miens, les miennes** mine; **les deux miens** my two.
**miette** *f* (*de pain*) crumb.
**mieux** *adv* & *a inv* better (**que** than); **le m., la m., les m.** the best; (*de deux*) the better; **tu ferais m. de partir** you had better leave.
**mignon, -onne** *a* (*joli*) cute; (*agréable*) nice.
**migraine** *f* headache.
**mil** *m inv* (*dans les dates*) **l'an deux m.** the year two thousand.
**milieu, -x** *m* (*centre*) middle; **au m. de** in the middle of.
**militaire 1** *a* military. **2** *m* soldier.
**mille** *a* & *m inv* thousand; **m. hommes/***etc* a *ou* one thousand men/*etc*.
**mille-pattes** *m inv* centipede.
**milliard** *m* billion.
**millième** *a* & *mf* thousandth.
**millier** *m* thousand; **un m. (de)** a thousand or so.
**millimètre** *m* millimeter.
**million** *m* million; **un m. de francs/***etc* a million francs/*etc*; **deux millions** two million.
**millionnaire** *mf* millionaire.
**mime** *mf* (*acteur*) mime.
**mimer** *vti* to mime.
**minable** *a* shabby.
**mince** *a* thin; (*élancé*) slim.
**mincir** *vi* to get thin.
**mine**[1] *f* appearance; **avoir bonne m.** to look well.
**mine**[2] *f* (*de charbon etc*) mine; (*de crayon*) lead; (*engin explosif*) mine.
**miner** *vt* (*terrain*) to mine.
**minerai** *m* ore.
**minéral, -e, -aux** *a* & *m* mineral.
**mineur** *m* (*ouvrier*) miner.
**miniature** *a inv* (*train etc*) miniature.
**minimal, -e** *a* minimum.
**minimum** *m* minimum; **le m. de** (*force etc*) the minimum (amount of); **au (grand) m.** at the very least.
**ministère** *m* ministry.
**ministre** *m* minister.
**minorité** *f* minority.
**minou** *m* (*chat*) kitty.
**minuit** *m* midnight.
**minuscule** *a* (*petit*) tiny.
**minute** *f* minute.
**minuterie** *f* timer (*for lighting in a stairway*).
**minuteur** *m* timer.
**minutieux, -euse** *a* meticulous.
**miracle** *m* miracle; **par m.** miraculously.
**miraculeux, -euse** *a* miraculous.
**miroir** *m* mirror.
**mis, mise** *pp of* **mettre.**
**mise**[1] *f* (*action*) putting; **m. en marche** starting up; **m. en scène** (*de film*) direction.
**mise**[2] (*argent*) stake.
**misérable 1** *a* (*très pauvre*) destitute. **2** *mf* (*personne pauvre*) pauper.
**misère** *f* (grinding) poverty.
**missile** *m* (*fusée*) missile.
**mission** *f* mission.
**mite** *f* (clothes) moth.
**mi-temps** *f* (*pause*) (*en sport*) half-time; (*période*) (*en sport*) half; **à mi-t.** (*travailler*) part-time.
**mitraillette** *f* machinegun (*portable*).
**mitrailleuse** *f* machinegun (*heavy*).
**mixe(u)r** *m* (*pour mélanger*) (food) mixer.
**mixte** *a* (*école*) co-educational, mixed.
**mobile** *a* (*pièce*) moving; (*personne*) mobile.
**mobilier** *m* furniture.
**mobylette**® *f* moped.
**moche** *a* (*laid*) ugly.
**mode 1** *f* fashion; **à la m.** fashionable. **2** *m Grammaire* mood; **m. d'emploi** directions (for use).
**modèle** *m* model; **m. (réduit)** (scale) model.
**modération** *f* moderation.
**modéré, -ée** *a* moderate.
**modérer** *vt* (*vitesse, chaleur etc*) to reduce.
**moderne** *a* modern.
**moderniser** *vt*, **se moderniser** *vpr* to modernize.
**modeste** *a* modest.

**modestie** *f* modesty.
**modification** *f* alteration.
**modifier** *vt* to alter.
**moelle** *f* (*d'os*) marrow; **m. épinière** spinal cord.
**moelleux, -euse** *a* (*lit, tissu*) soft.
**moi** *pron* (*complément direct*) me; (*indirect*) (to) me; (*sujet emphatique*) I.
**moi-même** *pron* myself.
**moindre** *a* **la m. erreur**/*etc* the slightest mistake/*etc*; **le m.** (*de mes problèmes etc*) the least (**de** of).
**moine** *m* monk.
**moineau, -x** *m* sparrow.
**moins 1** *adv* less (**que** than); **m. de** (*temps, travail*) less (**que** than); (*gens, livres*) fewer (**que** than); (*cent francs*) less than; **m. grand** not as big (**que** as); **de m. en m.** less and less; **le m.** (*travailler*) the least; **le m. grand, la m. grande, les m. grand(e)s** the smallest; **au m., du m.** at least; **de m., en m.** (*qui manque*) missing; **dix ans de m.** ten years less; **en m.** (*personne, objet*) less; (*personnes, objets*) fewer; **à m. que** (+ *subjonctif*) unless. **2** *prép* (*en calcul*) minus; **deux heures m. cinq** five to two; **il fait m. dix (degrés)** it's minus ten (degrees).
**mois** *m* month; **au m. de juin** in (the month of) June.
**moisi, -ie 1** *a* moldy. **2** *m* mold; **sentir le m.** to smell musty.
**moisir** *vi* to get moldy.
**moisson** *f* harvest.
**moissonner** *vt* to harvest.
**moite** *a* sticky.
**moitié** *f* half; **la m. de la pomme** half (of) the apple; **à m. fermé** half closed; **à m. prix** (at) half-price; **de m.** by half.
**mol** *voir* **mou.**
**molaire** *f* back tooth.
**molette** *f* **clé à m.** adjustable wrench.
**molle** *voir* **mou**.
**mollet** *m* (*de jambe*) calf.
**moment** *m* (*instant*) moment; (*période*) time; **en ce m.** at the moment; **par moments** at times; **au m. de partir** when just about to leave; **au m. où** just as; **du m. que** (*puisque*) seeing that.
**mon, ma,** *pl* **mes** (**ma** *becomes* **mon** *before a vowel or mute h*) *a poss* my; **mon père** my father; **ma mère** my mother; **mon ami(e)** my friend.
**monde** *m* world; **du m.** (*beaucoup de gens*) a lot of people; **le m. entier** the whole world; **tout le m.** everybody.
**mondial, -e, -aux** *a* (*crise etc*) worldwide; **guerre mondiale** world war.
**moniteur, -trice** *mf* instructor; (*de colonie de vacances*) camp counselor.
**monnaie** *f* (*devise*) currency; (*pièces*) change; **faire de la m.** to get change; **faire de la m. à qn** to give s.o. change (**sur un billet** for a bill).
**monopoliser** *vt* to monopolize.
**monotone** *a* monotonous.
**monotonie** *f* monotony.
**monsieur,** *pl* **messieurs** *m* (*homme*) man, gentleman; **oui m.** yes sir; **oui messieurs** yes gentlemen; **M. Legras** Mr Legras; **Monsieur** (*dans une lettre*) Dear Sir.
**monstre** *m* monster.
**monstrueux, -euse** *a* (*abominable*) hideous.
**mont** *m* (*montagne*) mount.
**montagne** *f* mountain; **la m.** (*zone*) the mountains.
**montagneux, -euse** *a* mountainous.
**montant** *m* (*somme*) amount; (*de barrière*) post.
**montée** *f* (*ascension*) climb, (*chemin*) slope.
**monter 1** *vi* (*aux* **être**) (*personne*) to go *ou* come up; (*s'élever*) (*ballon, prix etc*) to go up; (*grimper*) to climb (up) (**sur** onto); (*marée*) to come in; **m. dans un véhicule** to get in(to) a vehicle; **m. dans un train** to get on(to) a train; **m. sur** *ou* **à** (*échelle*) to climb up; **m. en**

**courant**/*etc* to run/*etc* up; **m. (à cheval)** to ride (a horse). **2** *vt* (*aux* **avoir**) (*côte*) to climb (up); (*objet*) to bring *ou* take up; (*cheval*) to ride; (*tente*) to set up; **m. l'escalier** to go *ou* come up the stairs.
**montre** *f* (wrist)watch.
**montrer** *vt* to show (**à** to); **m. du doigt** to point to; **se m.** to show oneself.
**monture** *f* (*de lunettes*) frame.
**monument** *m* monument; **m. aux morts** war memorial.
**moquer (se)** *vpr* **se m. de** to make fun of; **je m'en moque!** I couldn't care less!
**moquette** *f* wall-to-wall carpeting.
**moral** *m* spirits, morale.
**morale** *f* (*d'histoire*) moral.
**morceau, -x** *m* piece; (*de sucre*) lump.
**mordiller** *vt* to nibble.
**mordre** *vti* to bite.
**morse** *m* (*animal*) walrus.
**morsure** *f* bite.
**mort** *f* death.
**mort, morte** (*pp of* **mourir**) **1** *a* (*personne, plante etc*) dead. **2** *mf* dead man, dead woman; **les morts** the dead; **de nombreux morts** (*victimes*) many casualties *ou* dead.
**mortel, -elle** *a* (*hommes, ennemi etc*) mortal; (*accident*) fatal.
**morue** *f* cod.
**mosquée** *f* mosque.
**mot** *m* word; **envoyer un m. à** to drop a line to; **mots croisés** crossword (puzzle); **m. de passe** password.
**motard** *m* motorcyclist.
**moteur** *m* (*de véhicule etc*) engine, motor.
**motif** *m* (*raison*) reason (**de** for).
**motivé, -ée** *a* motivated.
**moto** *f* motorcycle, motorbike.
**motocycliste** *mf* motorcyclist.
**motte** *f* (*de terre*) lump.
**mou** (*or* **mol** *before vowel or mute h*), **molle** *a* soft; (*sans énergie*) feeble.
**mouche** *f* (*insecte*) fly.
**moucher (se)** *vpr* to blow one's nose.
**mouchoir** *m* handkerchief; (*en papier*) tissue.
**moudre*** *vt* (*café*) to grind.
**moue** *f* long face; **faire la m.** to pull a (long) face.
**mouette** *f* (sea)gull.
**moufle** *f* mitten.
**mouillé, -ée** *a* wet (**de** with).
**mouiller** *vt* to (make) wet; **se faire m.** to get wet; **se m.** to get (oneself) wet.
**moule**[1] *m* mold; **m. à gâteaux** cake pan.
**moule**[2] *f* (*animal*) mussel.
**mouler** *vt* to mold; **m. qn** (*vêtement*) to fit s.o. tightly.
**moulin** *m* mill; **m. à vent** windmill; **m. à café** coffee grinder.
**moulu** (*pp of* **moudre**) *a* (*café*) ground.
**mourir*** *vi* (*aux* **être**) to die (**de** of, from); **m. de froid** to die of exposure; **je meurs de faim!** I'm starving!
**mousse** *f* (*plante*) moss; (*écume*) foam; (*de bière*) froth; (*de savon*) lather; (*dessert*) mousse.
**mousser** *vi* (*bière*) to froth; (*savon*) to lather; (*eau*) to foam.
**moustache** *f* mustache; **moustaches** (*de chat*) whiskers.
**moustachu, -ue** *a* wearing a mostache.
**moustique** *m* mosquito.
**moutarde** *f* mustard.
**mouton** *m* sheep *inv*; (*viande*) mutton.
**mouvement** *m* (*geste, groupe etc*) movement; (*de colère*) outburst.
**mouvementé, -ée** *a* (*vie, voyage etc*) eventful.
**moyen, -enne 1** *a* average; (*format etc*) medium(-sized); **classe moyenne** middle class. **2** *f* average; (*dans un examen, un devoir*) passing grade; **en moyenne** on average.
**moyen** *m* (*procédé, façon*) means, way (**de faire** of doing, to do); **il n'y a pas m. de faire** it's not possible to

do; **je n'ai pas les moyens** (*argent*) I can't afford it.

**muer** *vi* (*animal*) to molt; (*voix*) to break.

**muet, -ette 1** *a* (*infirme*) mute; (*film, voyelle*) silent. **2** *mf* mute person.

**mufle** *m* (*d'animal*) muzzle.

**mugir** *vi* (*bœuf*) to bellow.

**mugissement(s)** *m*(*pl*) bellow(-ing).

**muguet** *m* lily of the valley.

**mule** *f* (*pantoufle*) mule; (*animal*) (she-)mule.

**multicolore** *a* multicolored.

**multiple** *m* (*nombre*) multiple.

**multiplication** *f* multiplication.

**multiplier** *vt* to multiply.

**municipal, -e, -aux** *a* municipal; **conseil m.** city council.

**munir** *vt* **m. de** to equip with; **se m. de** to provide oneself with.

**munitions** *fpl* ammunition.

**mur** *m* wall; **m. du son** sound barrier.

**mûr, mûre** *a* (*fruit*) ripe.

**muraille** *f* (high) wall.

**mûre** *f* (*baie*) blackberry.

**mûrir** *vti* (*fruit*) to ripen.

**murmure** *m* murmur.

**murmurer** *vti* to murmur.

**muscle** *m* muscle.

**musclé, -ée** *a* (*bras*) muscular.

**museau, -x** *m* (*de chien, chat*) nose, muzzle.

**musée** *m* museum.

**muselière** *f* (*appareil*) muzzle.

**musical, -e, -aux** *a* musical.

**musicien, -ienne** *mf* musician.

**musique** *f* music.

**musulman, -ane** *a* & *mf* Muslim.

**mutuel, -elle** *a* (*réciproque*) mutual.

**myope** *a* & *mf* shortsighted (person).

**mystère** *m* mystery.

**mystérieux, -euse** *a* mysterious.

# N

**nage** *f* (swimming) stroke; **traverser à la n.** to swim across; **en n.** sweating.

**nageoire** *f* (*de poisson*) fin.

**nager 1** *vi* to swim. **2** *vt* (*crawl etc*) to swim.

**nageur, -euse** *mf* swimmer.

**naïf, -ïve** *a* naïve.

**nain, naine** *mf* dwarf.

**naissance** *f* (*de personne, animal*) birth.

**naître*** *vi* to be born.

**nappe** *f* (*sur une table*) table cloth.

**napperon** *m* (*pour vase etc*) (cloth) mat, doily.

**narine** *f* nostril.

**naseau, -x** *m* (*de cheval*) nostril.

**natal, -e,** *mpl* **-als** *a* (*pays*) native; **sa maison natale** the house where he *ou* she was born.

**natation** *f* swimming.

**nation** *f* nation.

**national, -e, -aux** *a* national; **(route) nationale** highway.

**nationalité** *f* nationality.

**natte** *f* (*de cheveux*) braid; (*tapis*) mat.

**nature 1** *f* (*monde naturel, caractère*) nature. **2** *a inv* (*omelette, yaourt etc*) plain; (*café*) black.

**naturel, -elle** *a* natural.

**naufrage** *m* (ship)wreck; **faire n.** to be (ship)wrecked.

**naufragé, -ée** *a* & *mf* shipwrecked (person).

**nautique** *a* **ski**/*etc* **n.** water skiing/*etc*.

**naval, -e,** *mpl* **-als** *a* naval.

**navet** *m* (*plante*) turnip.

**navette** *f* **faire la n.** to shuttle back and forth (**entre** between); **n. spatiale** space shuttle.

**navigation** *f* (*trafic de bateaux*) shipping.

**naviguer** *vi* (*bateau*) to sail.

**navire** *m* ship.

**navré, -ée** *a* **je suis n.** I'm (terribly) sorry (**de faire** to do).

**ne (n'** *before vowel or mute h; used to form negative verb with* **pas, jamais, personne, rien, que** *etc*) *adv* (+ *pas*) not; **il ne boit pas** he does not *ou* doesn't drink.

**né, -ée** *a* (*pp of* **naître**) born; **elle est née** she was born.

**nécessaire 1** *a* necessary. **2** *m* **n. de toilette** (*d'homme*) shaving kit; (*de femme*) cosmetic case; **faire le n.** to do what's necessary.
**nécessité** *f* necessity.
**nécessiter** *vt* to require.
**nectarine** *f* nectarine.
**négatif, -ive 1** *a* negative. **2** *m* (*de photo*) negative.
**négation** *f Grammaire* negation; (*mot*) negative.
**négligence** *f* (*défaut*) carelessness.
**négligent, -ente** *a* careless.
**négliger** *vt* (*personne, travail etc*) to neglect; **n. de faire** to neglect to do.
**négociation** *f* negotiation.
**négocier** *vti* to negotiate.
**neige** *f* snow; **n. fondue** sleet.
**neiger** *vi* to snow.
**nénuphar** *m* water lily.
**néon** *m* **éclairage au n.** neon lighting.
**nerf** *m* nerve; **du n.!** buck up!; **ça me tape sur les nerfs** it gets on my nerves.
**nerveux, -euse** *a* (*agité*) nervous.
**nescafé**® *m* instant coffee.
**n'est-ce pas?** *adv* isn't he?, don't you? *etc*.
**net, nette 1** *a* (*image, refus*) clear; (*coupure, linge*) clean; (*soigné*) neat; (*poids, prix*) net. **2** *adv* (*s'arrêter*) dead; (*casser, couper*) clean.
**nettement** *adv* (*bien plus*) definitely.
**nettoyage** *m* cleaning; **n. à sec** dry cleaning.
**nettoyer** *vt* to clean (up).
**neuf, neuve 1** *a* new; **quoi de n.?** what's new(s)? **2** *m* **remettre à n.** to make as good as new.
**neuf** *a* & *m* nine.
**neutre** *a* (*pays*) neutral.
**neuvième** *a* & *mf* ninth.
**neveu, -x** *m* nephew.
**nez** *m* nose; **n. à n.** face to face (**avec** with).
**ni** *conj* **ni . . . ni** (+ *ne*) neither . . . nor; **il n'a ni faim ni soif** he's neither hungry nor thirsty; **sans manger ni boire** without eating or drinking; **ni l'un(e) ni l'autre** neither (of them).
**niche** *f* (*de chien*) doghouse.
**nicher** *vi*, **se nicher** *vpr* (*oiseau*) to nest.
**nid** *m* nest.
**nièce** *f* niece.
**nier** *vt* to deny (**que** that).
**niveau, -x** *m* level; **au n. de qn** (*élève etc*) up to s.o.'s standard.
**noble 1** *a* noble. **2** *mf* nobleman, noblewoman.
**noce(s)** *nf* (*pl*) wedding.
**nocif, -ive** *a* harmful.
**Noël** *m* Christmas; **le père N.** Father Christmas, Santa Claus.
**nœud** *m* knot; (*ruban*) bow; **n. coulant** slipknot, noose; **n. papillon** bow tie.
**noir, noire 1** *a* black; (*nuit, lunettes etc*) dark; **il fait n.** it's dark. **2** *m* (*couleur*) black; (*obscurité*) dark; **N.** (*homme*) black. **3** *f* **Noire** (*femme*) black.
**noircir 1** *vt* to make black. **2** *vi*, **se noircir** *vpr* to turn black.
**noisetier** *m* hazel (tree).
**noisette** *f* hazelnut.
**noix** *f* (*du noyer*) walnut; **n. de coco** coconut.
**nom** *m* name; *Grammaire* noun; **n. de famille** last name, surname; **n. propre** *Grammaire* proper noun.
**nombre** *m* number.
**nombreux, -euse** *a* (*amis, livres*) numerous, many; (*famille*) large; **peu n.** few; **venir n.** to come in large numbers.
**nombril** *m* navel.
**nommer** *vt* (*appeler*) to name; **n. qn** (*désigner*) to appoint s.o. (**à un poste** to a post).
**nommer (se)** *vpr* to be called.
**non** *adv* & *m inv* no; **tu viens ou n.?** are you coming or not?; **n. seulement** not only; **je crois que n.** I

don't think so; **(ni) moi n. plus** neither do, am, can *etc* I.

**nonante** *a* (*en Belgique, en Suisse*) ninety.

**non-fumeur, -euse** *mf* non-smoker.

**nord** *m* north; **au n. de** north of; **du n.** (*vent*) northerly; (*ville*) northern.

**nord-africain, -aine** *a* & *mf* North African.

**nord-américain, -aine** *a* & *mf* North American.

**nord-est** *m* & *a inv* northeast.

**nord-ouest** *m* & *a inv* northwest.

**normal, -e, -aux** *a* normal.

**normale** *f* **au-dessus/au-dessous de la n.** above/below normal.

**normalement** *adv* normally.

**norvégien, -ienne** *a* & *mf* Norwegian.

**nos** *voir* **notre.**

**notaire** *m* lawyer.

**notamment** *adv* particularly.

**note** *f* (*de musique, remarque*) note; (*à l'école*) grade; (*facture*) bill; **prendre n. de** to make a note of.

**noter** *vt* to note; (*un devoir*) to grade.

**notice** *f* (*mode d'emploi*) instructions.

**notre,** *pl a poss* **nos** our.

**nôtre** *pron poss* **le** *ou* **la n., les nôtres** ours.

**nouer** *vt* (*chaussure etc*) to tie.

**nouilles** *fpl* noodles.

**nounours** *m* teddy bear.

**nourrice** *f* (*assistante maternelle*) nanny.

**nourrir** *vt* to feed.

**nourrissant, -ante** *a* nourishing.

**nourrisson** *m* infant.

**nourriture** *f* food.

**nous** *pron* (*sujet*) we; (*complément direct*) us; (*indirect*) (to) us; (*réfléchi*) ourselves; (*réciproque*) each other.

**nous-mêmes** *pron* ourselves.

**nouveau** (*or* **nouvel** *before vowel or mute h*), **nouvelle,** *pl* **nouveaux, nouvelles 1** *a* new. **2** *mf* (*dans une classe*) new boy, new girl. **3** *m* **de n., à n.** again.

**nouveau-né, -ée** *mf* new-born baby.

**nouvelle** *f* (*information*) **nouvelle(s)** news; **une n.** a piece of news.

**novembre** *m* November.

**noyade** *f* drowning.

**noyau, -x** *m* (*fruit*) pit.

**noyé, -ée** *mf* drowned man *ou* woman.

**noyer**[1] *vt*, **se noyer** *vpr* to drown.

**noyer**[2] *m* (*arbre*) walnut tree.

**nu, nue** *a* (*personne*) naked; (*mains*) bare; **tout nu** (stark) naked; **tête nue, nu-tête** bareheaded.

**nuage** *m* cloud.

**nuageux, -euse** *a* cloudy.

**nuance** *f* (*de couleurs*) shade.

**nucléaire** *a* nuclear.

**nuire*** *vi* **n. à qn** to harm s.o.

**nuisible** *a* harmful.

**nuit** *f* night; (*obscurité*) dark(ness); **il fait n.** it's dark; **la n.** (*se promener etc*) at night; **cette n.** (*aujourd'hui*) tonight; (*hier*) last night; **bonne n.** (*au coucher*) good night.

**nul, nulle** *a* (*médiocre*) hopeless; **faire match n.** to tie; **nulle part** nowhere.

**numéro** *m* number; (*de journal*) issue; (*au cirque*) act; **un n. de danse** a dance number; **n. vert** (*au téléphone*) = tollfree number.

**numéroter** *vt* (*page etc*) to number.

**nuque** *f* back of the neck.

**nylon** *m* nylon; **chemise**/*etc* **en n.** nylon shirt/*etc*.

# O

**obéir** *vi* to obey; **o. à qn** to obey s.o.

**obéissance** *f* obedience.

**obéissant, -ante** *a* obedient.

**objectif** *m* (*but*) objective; (*d'appareil photo*) lens.

**objet** *m* (*chose*) object; **objets trouvés** (*bureau*) lost and found.
**obligation** *f* obligation.
**obligatoire** *a* compulsory.
**obliger** *vt* to force, compel (**à faire** to do); **être obligé de faire** to have to do.
**oblique** *a* oblique.
**obscène** *a* obscene.
**obscur, -e** *a* (*noir*) dark.
**obscurcir** *vt* (*pièce*) to make dark(er).
**obscurcir (s')** *vpr* (*ciel*) to get dark(er).
**obscurité** *f* dark(ness).
**obsèques** *fpl* funeral.
**observation** *f* (*étude*) observation; (*reproche*) (critical) remark.
**observatoire** *m* (*endroit élevé*) lookout (post).
**observer** *vt* (*regarder*) to watch; (*remarquer, respecter*) to observe.
**obstacle** *m* obstacle.
**obstiné, -ée** *a* stubborn, obstinate.
**obstiner (s')** *vpr* **s'o. à faire** to persist in doing.
**obtenir*** *vt* to get, obtain.
**obus** *m* (*arme*) shell.
**occasion** *f* chance (**de faire** to do); (*prix avantageux*) bargain; **d'o.** second-hand, used.
**occidental, -e, -aux** *a* western.
**occupation** *f* (*activité etc*) occupation.
**occupé, -ée** *a* busy (**à faire** doing); (*place, maison etc*) occupied; (*téléphone*) busy; (*taxi*) hired.
**occuper** *vt* (*maison, pays etc*) to occupy; (*place, temps*) to take up; **o. qn** (*travail, jeu*) to keep s.o. busy.
**occuper (s')** *vpr* to keep (oneself) busy (**à faire** doing); **s'o. de** (*affaire, problème*) to deal with; **s'o. de qn** (*malade etc*) to take care of s.o.; **occupe-toi de tes affaires!** mind your own business!
**océan** *m* ocean.
**octobre** *m* October.
**oculiste** *mf* eye specialist.
**odeur** *f* smell.
**odieux, -euse** *a* horrible.
**odorat** *m* sense of smell.
**œil,** *pl* **yeux** *m* eye; **lever/baisser les yeux** to look up/down; **coup d'o.** look, glance; **jeter un coup d'o. sur** to (have a) look at; **o. poché, o. au beurre noir** black eye.
**œillet** *m* (*fleur*) carnation.
**œuf,** *pl* **œufs** *m* egg; **o. sur le plat** fried egg.
**œuvre** *f* (*travail, livre etc*) work.
**offenser** *vt* to offend.
**office** *m* (*messe*) service.
**officiel, -ielle** *a* official.
**officier** *m* (*dans l'armée etc*) officer.
**offre** *f* offer; **l'o. et la demande** supply and demand; **offres d'emploi** job vacancies, positions vacant.
**offrir*** *vt* to offer (**de faire** to do); (*cadeau*) to give; **s'o. qch** to treat oneself to sth.
**oh!** *int* oh!
**oie** *f* goose (*pl* geese).
**oignon** *m* (*légume*) onion; (*de fleur*) bulb.
**oiseau, -x** *m* bird.
**oisif, -ive** *a* (*inactif*) idle.
**oisiveté** *f* idleness.
**olive** *f* olive; **huile d'o.** olive oil.
**olivier** *m* olive tree.
**olympique** *a* (*jeux*) Olympic.
**ombragé, -ée** *a* shady.
**ombre** *f* (*d'arbre etc*) shade; (*de personne, objet*) shadow; **à l'o.** in the shade.
**omelette** *f* omelet(te); **o. au fromage/***etc* cheese/*etc* omelet(te).
**omnibus** *a* & *m* **(train) o.** slow *ou* local train.
**omoplate** *f* shoulder blade.
**on** *pron* (*les gens*) they, people; (*nous*) we; (*vous*) you; **on frappe** someone's knocking; **on m'a dit que** I was told that.
**oncle** *m* uncle.
**onde** (*de radio*) wave; **grandes ondes** long wave; **ondes courtes** short wave.
**ondulation** *f* (*de cheveux*) wave.

**onduler** *vi* (*cheveux*) to be wavy.
**ongle** *m* (finger) nail.
**ont** *voir* **avoir.**
**onze** *a* & *m* eleven.
**onzième** *a* & *mf* eleventh.
**opaque** *a* opaque.
**opéra** *m* (*musique*) opera; (*édifice*) opera house.
**opération** *f* operation.
**opérer** *vt* (*en chirurgie*) to operate on (**de** for); **se faire o.** to have an operation.
**opinion** *f* opinion (**sur** about, on).
**opposé, -ée 1** *a* (*direction, opinion etc*) opposite; (*équipe*) opposing; **o. à** opposed to. **2** *m* **l'o.** the opposite (**de** of); **à l'o.** (*côté*) on the opposite side (**de** from, to).
**opposer** *vt* (*résistance*) to put up (**à** against); (*équipes*) to bring together; **o. qn à qn** to set s.o. against s.o.
**opposer (s')** *vpr* (*équipes*) to play against each other; **s'o. à** (*mesure, personne*) to be opposed to, oppose.
**opposition** *f* opposition (**à** to).
**opticien, -ienne** *mf* optician.
**optimiste** *a* optimistic.
**or 1** *m* gold; **montre**/*etc* **en or** gold watch/*etc*; **d'or** (*règle*) golden; **mine d'or** goldmine. **2** *conj* (*cependant*) now, well.
**orage** *m* (thunder)storm.
**orageux, -euse** *a* stormy.
**oral, -e, -aux 1** *a* oral. **2** *m* (*examen*) oral.
**orange 1** *f* (*fruit*) orange. **2** *a* & *m inv* (*couleur*) orange.
**orangeade** *f* orangeade.
**orbite** *f* (*d'astre*) orbit; (*d'œil*) socket.
**orchestre** *m* (*classique*) orchestra, (*jazz, pop*) band; (*places*) orchestra.
**ordinaire** *a* (*habituel, normal*) ordinary, regular; (*médiocre*) ordinary; **d'o.** usually.
**ordinateur** *m* computer.
**ordonnance** *f* (*de médecin*) prescription.
**ordonné, -ée** *a* tidy.
**ordonner** *vt* to order (**que** (+ *subjonctif*) that); (*médicament etc*) to prescribe; **o. à qn de faire** to order s.o. to do.
**ordre** *m* (*commandement, classement*) order; (*absence de désordre*) tidiness (*of room, person etc*); **en o.** (*chambre etc*) tidy; **mettre en o., mettre de l'o. dans** to tidy (up); **jusqu'à nouvel o.** until further notice.
**ordures** *fpl* (*débris*) garbage.
**oreille** *f* ear; **faire la sourde o.** to take no notice, refuse to listen.
**oreiller** *m* pillow.
**oreillons** *mpl* mumps.
**organe** *m* (*de corps*) organ.
**organisateur, -trice** *mf* organizer.
**organisation** *f* organization.
**organiser** *vt* to organize; **s'o.** to get organized.
**organisme** *m* (*corps*) body; (*bureaux etc*) organization.
**orge** *f* barley.
**orgue 1** *m* (*instrument*) organ. **2** *fpl* **grandes orgues** great organ.
**orgueil** *m* pride.
**orgueilleux, -euse** *a* proud.
**oriental, -e, -aux** *a* (*côte, pays etc*) eastern; (*du Japon, de la Chine*) far-eastern, oriental.
**orientation** *f* direction; (*de maison*) orientation; **o. professionnelle** career counseling.
**orienté, -ée** *a* (*appartement etc*) **o. à l'ouest** facing west.
**orienter** *vt* (*lampe etc*) to position; (*voyageur, élève*) to direct.
**orienter (s')** *vpr* to find one's bearings *ou* direction.
**original, -e, -aux 1** *a* (*idee, artiste etc*) original. **2** *m* (*texte*) original.
**originalité** *f* originality.
**origine** *f* origin; **à l'o.** originally; **d'o.** (*pneu etc*) original; **pays d'o.** country of origin.
**ornement** *m* ornament.
**orner** *vt* to decorate (**de** with).
**orphelin, -ine** *mf* orphan.

**orphelinat** *m* orphanage.
**orteil** *m* toe; **gros o.** big toe.
**orthographe** *f* spelling.
**ortie** *f* nettle.
**os** *m* bone; **trempé jusqu'aux os** soaked to the skin.
**oser** *vti* to dare; **o. faire** to dare (to) do.
**osier** *m* wicker; **panier d'o.** wicker basket.
**otage** *m* hostage; **prendre qn en o.** to take s.o. hostage.
**otarie** *f* (*animal*) sea lion.
**ôter** *vt* to take away (**à qn** from s.o.); (*vêtement*) to take off; (*déduire*) to take away.
**ou** *conj* or; **ou bien** or else; **ou elle ou moi** either her or me.
**où** *adv* & *pron* where; **le jour où** the day when; **la table où** the table on which; **par où?** which way?; **d'où?** where from?; **le pays d'où** the country from which.
**oubli** *m* **l'o. de qch** forgetting sth; **un o.** (*dans une liste etc*) an oversight.
**oublier** *vt* to forget (**de faire** to do).
**ouest** *m* & *a inv* west; **d'o.** (*vent*) west(erly); **de l'o.** western.
**ouf!** *int* (whew) what a relief!
**oui** *adv* & *m inv* yes; **tu viens, o. ou non?** are you coming or aren't you?; **je crois que o.** I think so.
**ouïe** *f* hearing.
**ouïes** *fpl* (*de poisson*) gills.
**ouille!** *int* ouch!
**ouragan** *m* hurricane.
**ourlet** *m* hem.
**ours** *m* bear; **o. blanc** polar bear.
**outil** *m* tool.
**outillage** *m* tools.
**outre 1** *prép* besides. **2** *adv* **en o.** besides.
**outré, -ée** *a* (*révolté*) outraged.
**ouvert, -erte** (*pp of* **ouvrir**) *a* open; (*robinet, gaz*) on.
**ouvertement** *adv* openly.
**ouverture** *f* opening; (*trou*) hole.
**ouvrage** *m* (*travail, livre*) work; (*couture*) (needle)work; **un o.** (*travail*) a piece of work.
**ouvre-boîtes** *m inv* can opener.
**ouvre-bouteilles** *m inv* bottle opener.
**ouvrier, -ière 1** *mf* worker; **o. qualifié/spécialisé** skilled/unskilled worker. **2** *a* (*quartier*) working-class; **classe ouvrière** working class.
**ouvrir* 1** *vt* to open (up); (*gaz, radio etc*) to turn on, switch on. **2** *vi* to open; (*ouvrir la porte*) to open (up).
**ouvrir (s')** *vpr* (*porte, boîte etc*) to open (up).
**ovale** *a* & *m* oval.
**OVNI** *m abrév* (*objet volant non identifié*) UFO.
**oxygène** *m* oxygen.

# P

**pacifique 1** *a* (*manifestation etc*) peaceful; (*côte etc*) Pacific. **2** *m* **le P.** the Pacific.
**pagaie** *f* paddle.
**pagaille** *f* (*désordre*) mess; **en p.** in a mess.
**pagayer** *vi* to paddle.
**page** *f* (*de livre etc*) page.
**paie** *f* pay, wages.
**paiement** *m* payment.
**paillasson** *m* (door)mat.
**paille** *f* straw; (*pour boire*) (drinking) straw; **tirer à la courte p.** to draw lots *ou* straws.
**paillette** *f* (*d'habit*) sequin; **paillettes** (*de savon*) flakes.
**pain** *m* bread; **un p.** a loaf (of bread); **p. grillé** toast; **p. complet** whole-wheat bread; **p. d'épice** gingerbread; **p. de seigle** rye bread; **petit p.** roll.
**pair, -e** *a* (*numéro*) even.
**paire** *f* pair (**de** of).
**paisible** *a* (*vie, endroit*) peaceful.
**paître*** *vi* to graze.
**paix** *f* peace; (*traité*) peace treaty; **en p.** in peace; **avoir la p.** to have (some) peace and quiet.
**palais**[1] *m* (*château*) palace; **P. de**

**justice** courthouse; **p. des sports** sports stadium.
**palais**[2] *(dans la bouche)* palate.
**pâle** *a* pale.
**paletot** *m* (knitted) cardigan.
**palette** *f (de peintre)* palette.
**pâleur** *f* paleness.
**palier** *m (d'escalier)* landing; **être voisins de p.** to live on the same floor.
**pâlir** *vi* to turn pale (**de** with).
**palissade** *f* fence *(of stakes)*.
**palme** *f* palm (leaf); *(de nageur)* flipper.
**palmier** *m* palm (tree).
**palper** *vt* to feel.
**palpitant, -ante** *a* thrilling.
**palpiter** *vi (cœur)* to throb.
**pamplemousse** *m* grapefruit.
**pan!** *int* bang!
**panaché** *a* & *m* **(demi) p.** shandy *(beer and lemonade)*.
**pancarte** *f* sign; *(de manifestant)* placard.
**pané, -ée** *a* breaded.
**panier** *m* basket; **p. à salade** *(ustensile)* salad basket.
**panique** *f* panic.
**paniqué, -ée** *a* panic-stricken.
**paniquer** *vi* to panic.
**panne** *f* breakdown; **tomber en p.** to break down; **être en p.** to have broken down; **p. d'électricité** blackout, power outage.
**panneau, -x** *m (écriteau)* sign; *(de porte etc)* panel; **p. (de signalisation)** road sign; **p. (d'affichage)** billboard.
**panoplie** *f (jouet)* outfit.
**panorama** *m* view.
**pansement** *m* dressing, bandage; **p. adhésif** Band-Aid®.
**panser** *vt (main etc)* to dress, bandage.
**pantalon** *m* (pair of) trousers *ou* pants; **en p.** in trousers, in pants.
**pantin** *m* puppet, jumping jack.
**pantoufle** *f* slipper.
**paon** *m* peacock.
**papa** *m* dad(dy).
**pape** *m* pope.
**papeterie** *f (magasin)* stationery store.
**papi** *m Fam* grand(d)ad.
**papier** *m (matière)* paper; **un p.** *(feuille)* a sheet of paper; *(formulaire)* a form; **sac/***etc* **en p.** paper bag/*etc*; **papiers (d'identité)** (identity) papers; **p. hygiénique** toilet paper; **p. à lettres** writing paper; **du p. journal** (some) newspaper; **p. peint** wallpaper; **p. de verre** sandpaper.
**papillon** *m* butterfly; **p. (de nuit)** moth.
**paquebot** *m* (ocean) liner.
**pâquerette** *f* daisy.
**Pâques** *m sing* & *fpl* Easter.
**paquet** *m (de bonbons etc)* packet; *(colis)* package; *(de cigarettes)* pack; *(de cartes)* pack, deck.
**par** *prép (agent, manière, moyen)* by; **choisi p.** chosen by; **p. le train** by train; **p. le travail** by *ou* through work; **apprendre p. un ami** to learn from *ou* through a friend; **commencer p. qch** to begin with sth. ▪ *(lieu)* through; **p. la porte** through *ou* by the door; **jeter p. la fenêtre** to throw out (of) the window; **p. ici/là** *(aller)* this/that way; *(habiter)* around here/there. ▪ *(motif)* out of, from; **p. pitié** out of *ou* from pity. ▪ *(temps)* on; **p. un jour d'hiver** on a winter day; **p. ce froid** in this cold. ▪ *(distributif)* **dix fois p. an** ten times a year; **deux p. deux** two by two.
**parachute** *m* parachute.
**paradis** *m* heaven, paradise.
**paragraphe** *m* paragraph.
**paraître*** *vi (sembler)* to seem; *(livre)* to come out; **il paraît qu'il va partir** it appears *ou* seems he's leaving.
**parallèle** *a* parallel (**à** with, to).
**paralyser** *vt* to paralyze.
**parapluie** *m* umbrella.
**parasite** *m* parasite; **parasites** *(à la radio)* interference.
**parasol** *m* sunshade.
**paravent** *m* (folding) screen.

**parc** *m* park; (*de château*) grounds; (*de bébé*) playpen; **p. (de stationnement)** parking lot.
**parce que** *conj* because.
**parcelle** *f* fragment; (*terrain*) plot.
**par-ci par-là** *adv* here, there and everywhere.
**parcmètre** *m* parking meter.
**parcourir*** *vt* (*région*) to travel all over; (*distance*) to cover; (*texte*) to glance through.
**parcours** *m* (*itinéraire*) route; (*distance*) distance.
**par-dessous** *prép* & *adv* under(neath).
**pardessus** *m* overcoat.
**par-dessus** *prép* & *adv* over (the top of); **p.-dessus tout** above all.
**pardon** *m* **p.!** (*excusez-moi*) sorry!; **demander p.** to apologize (**à** to).
**pardonner** *vt* to forgive; **p. qch à qn/à qn d'avoir fait qch** to forgive s.o. for sth/for doing sth.
**pare-brise** *m inv* windshield.
**pare-chocs** *m inv* bumper.
**pareil, -eille 1** *a* similar; **p. à** the same as; **être pareils** to be the same; **un p. désordre**/*etc* such a mess/*etc*. **2** *adv Fam* the same.
**parent, -ente 1** *mf* relative. **2** *mpl* (*père et mère*) parents. **3** *a* related (**de** to).
**parenthèse** *f* (*signe*) bracket.
**paresse** *f* laziness.
**paresseux, -euse** *a* & *mf* lazy (person).
**parfait, -aite** *a* perfect; **p.!** excellent!
**parfaitement** *adv* perfectly; (*certainement*) certainly.
**parfois** *adv* sometimes.
**parfum** *m* (*odeur*) fragrance; (*goût*) flavor; (*liquide*) perfume.
**parfumé, -ée** *a* (*savon, fleur*) scented; **p. au café**/*etc* coffee-/*etc* flavored.
**parfumer** *vt* to perfume; (*glace, crème*) to flavor (**à** with).
**parfumer (se)** *vpr* to put on perfume.
**parfumerie** *f* perfume shop.
**pari** *m* bet; **p. mutuel urbain** = pari-mutuel.
**parier** *vti* to bet (**sur** on, **que** that).
**parisien, -ienne 1** *a* Parisian; **la banlieue parisienne** the outskirts of Paris. **2** *mf* Parisian.
**parking** *m* parking lot.
**parlement** *m* parliament.
**parlementaire** *mf* member of parliament.
**parler 1** *vi* to talk, speak (**de** about, of; **à** to). **2** *vt* (*langue*) to speak.
**parler (se)** *vpr* (*langue*) to be spoken.
**parmi** *prép* among(st).
**paroi** *f* (inside) wall; (*de rocher*) (rock) face.
**paroisse** *f* parish.
**paroissial, -e, -aux** *a* **église**/*etc* **paroissiale** parish church/*etc*.
**parole** *f* (*mot, promesse*) word; **adresser la p. à** to speak to; **prendre la p.** to speak; **demander la p.** to ask to speak.
**parquet** *m* (parquet) floor.
**parrain** *m* godfather.
**parrainer** *vt* (*course etc*) to sponsor.
**parsemé, -ée** *a* **p. de** (*sol*) strewn (all over) with.
**part** *f* (*portion*) share; (*de gâteau*) portion; **prendre p. à** (*activité*) to take part in; (*la joie etc de qn*) to share; **de toutes parts** from *ou* on all sides; **de p. et d'autre** on both sides; **d'autre p.** (*d'ailleurs*) moreover; **de la p. de** (*provenance*) from; **quelque p.** somewhere; **nulle p.** nowhere; **autre p.** somewhere else; **à p.** (*mettre*) aside; (*excepté*) apart from; (*personne*) different.
**partage** *m* (*de gâteau, trésor etc*) sharing.
**partager** *vt* (*repas, joie etc*) to share (**avec** with).
**partenaire** *mf* partner.
**parterre** *m* (*de jardin*) flower bed.
**parti** *m* (*politique*) party.

**participant, -ante** *mf* participant.

**participation** *f* participation; **p. (aux frais)** contribution (*towards expenses*).

**participe** *m Grammaire* participle.

**participer** *vi* **p. à** (*jeu etc*) to take part in; (*frais, joie*) to share (in).

**particularité** *f* peculiarity.

**particulier, -ière** *a* (*spécial*) particular; (*privé*) private; (*bizarre*) peculiar; **en p.** (*surtout*) in particular.

**particulièrement** *adv* particularly.

**partie** *f* part; (*de cartes, tennis etc*) game; **en p.** partly; **faire p. de** to be a part of; (*club etc*) to belong to.

**partir*** *vi* (*aux* **être**) (*aller*) to go; (*s'en aller*) to go, leave; (*coup de feu*) to go off; (*tache*) to come out; **à p. de** (*date, prix*) from.

**partisan** *m* supporter; **être p. de qch/de faire** to be in favor of sth/of doing.

**partition** *f* (*musique*) score.

**partout** *adv* everywhere; **p. où tu vas** *ou* **iras** everywhere *ou* wherever you go.

**parvenir*** *vi* (*aux* **être**) **p. à** (*lieu*) to reach; **p. à faire** to manage to do.

**pas**[1] *adv* (*négatif*) not; **(ne) . . . p.** not; **je ne sais p.** I don't know; **p. de pain**/*etc* no bread/*etc*; **p. encore** not yet; **p. du tout** not at all.

**pas**[2] *m* step; (*allure*) pace; (*bruit*) footstep; (*trace*) footprint; **rouler au p.** (*véhicule*) to go dead slow; **au p. (cadencé)** in step; **faire les cent p.** to walk up and down, pace; **faux p.** (*en marchant*) stumble; (*erreur*) blunder; **le p. de la porte** the doorstep.

**passable** *a* (*travail, résultat*) (just) average.

**passage** *m* passing; (*traversée en bateau*) crossing; (*extrait, couloir*) passage; (*droit*) right of way; (*chemin*) path; **p. clouté** *ou* **pour piétons** (pedestrian) crosswalk; **p. souterrain** underground passage (for pedestrians); **p. à niveau** grade crossing; **'p. interdit'** 'no through traffic'; **'cédez le p.'** (*au carrefour*) 'yield'.

**passager, -ère** *mf* passenger.

**passant, -ante** *mf* passer-by.

**passe** *f Sport* pass; **mot de p.** password.

**passé, -ée 1** *a* (*temps*) past; (*couleur*) faded; **la semaine passée** last week; **dix heures passées** after ten (o'clock); **être passé** (*personne*) to have been here/there; (*orage*) to be over; **avoir vingt ans passés** to be over twenty. **2** *m* past; *Grammaire* past (tense).

**passe-passe** *m inv* **tour de p.-passe** magic trick.

**passeport** *m* passport.

**passer 1** *vi* (*aux* **être** *ou* **avoir**) to pass (**à** to, **de** from); (*traverser*) to go through *ou* over; (*facteur*) to come; (*temps*) to pass, go by; (*film*) to be shown; (*douleur*) to pass; (*couleur*) to fade; **p. devant** (*maison etc*) to go past, pass (by); **p. à la boulangerie** *ou* **chez le boulanger** to go to *ou* by the bakery; **laisser p.** (*personne, lumière*) to let through; **p. prendre** to pick up; **p. voir qn** to drop in on s.o.; **p. pour** (*riche etc*) to be taken for; **p. en** (*seconde etc*) (*à l'école*) to advance to; (*en voiture*) to shift into. **2** *vt* (*aux* **avoir**) (*frontière etc*) to cross; (*donner*) to pass, hand (**à** to); (*temps*) to spend (**à faire** doing); (*CD, chemise, film*) to put on; (*examen*) to take; (*thé*) to strain; (*café*) to filter; (*limites*) to go beyond; (*visite médicale*) to have; **p. qch à qn** (*caprice etc*) to grant s.o. sth; **p. un coup d'éponge**/*etc* **à qch** to go over sth with a sponge/*etc*.

**passer (se)** *vpr* to take place, happen; (*douleur*) to go (away); **se p. de** to do *ou* go without; **ça s'est bien passé** it went off well.

**passerelle** *f* footbridge; (*d'avion, de bateau*) gangway.
**passe-temps** *m inv* pastime.
**passif, -ive 1** *a* passive. **2** *m Grammaire* passive.
**passion** *f* passion; **avoir la p. des voitures/d'écrire** to have a passion for cars/writing.
**passionnant, -ante** *a* thrilling.
**passionné, -ée** *a* passionate; **p. de qch** passionately fond of sth.
**passionner** *vt* to thrill; **se p. pour** to have a passion for.
**passoire** *f* (*à thé*) strainer; (*à légumes*) colander.
**pasteurisé, -ée** pasteurized.
**pastille** *f* pastille, lozenge.
**patauger** *vi* to wade (*in the mud etc*); (*barboter*) to splash around.
**pâte** *f* paste; (*à pain*) dough; (*à tarte*) pastry; **pâtes (alimentaires)** pasta; **p. à modeler** modeling clay.
**pâté** *m* (*charcuterie*) pâté; **p. (en croûte)** meat pie; **p. (de sable)** sand castle; **p. de maisons** block of houses.
**pâtée** *f* (*pour chien, chat*) dog food, cat food.
**paternel, -elle** *a* paternal.
**patiemment** *adv* patiently.
**patience** *f* patience.
**patient, -ente 1** *a* patient. **2** *mf* (*malade*) patient.
**patin** *m* **p. (à glace)** (ice) skate; **p. à roulettes** roller skate.
**patinage** *m* skating.
**patiner** *vi* (*en sport*) to skate; (*roue*) to spin round.
**patinoire** *f* skating rink.
**pâtisserie** *f* pastry; (*magasin*) pastry shop.
**pâtissier, -ière** *mf* pastry cook.
**patrie** *f* (native) country.
**patriote 1** *mf* patriot. **2** *a* patriotic.
**patriotique** *a* (*chant etc*) patriotic.
**patron, -onne 1** *mf* (*chef*) boss. **2** *m* (*modèle de papier*) pattern.
**patrouille** *f* patrol.
**patrouiller** *vi* to patrol.
**patte** *f* leg; (*de chat, chien*) paw; **marcher à quatre pattes** to crawl.
**pâturage** *m* pasture.
**paume** *f* (*de main*) palm.
**paupière** *f* eyelid.
**pause** *f* (*arrêt*) break.
**pauvre 1** *a* poor. **2** *mf* poor man *ou* woman; **les pauvres** the poor.
**pauvreté** *f* (*besoin*) poverty.
**pavé** *m* (*de rue*) paving stone.
**paver** *vt* to pave.
**pavillon** *m* (*maison*) (detached) house; (*drapeau*) flag.
**payant, -ante** *a* (*hôte, spectateur*) paying; (*place, entrée*) that one has to pay for.
**paye** *f* pay, wages.
**payer 1** *vt* (*personne, somme*) to pay; (*service, objet*) to pay for; **p. qn pour faire** to pay s.o. to do *ou* for doing. **2** *vi* (*personne, métier*) to pay.
**pays** *m* country; **du p.** (*vin, gens*) local.
**paysage** *m* landscape.
**paysan, -anne** *mf* (small) farmer.
**PCV** *abrév* (*paiement contre vérification*) **téléphoner en PCV** to reverse the charges, call collect.
**PDG** *abrév m* (président directeur général) CEO.
**péage** *m* (*droit*) toll; (*lieu*) tollbooth.
**peau, -x** *f* skin; (*de fruit*) peel, skin; (*cuir*) hide.
**pêche**[1] *f* fishing; (*poissons*) catch; **p. (à la ligne)** angling; **aller à la p.** to go fishing.
**pêche**[2] *f* (*fruit*) peach.
**péché** *m* sin.
**pêcher**[1] **1** *vi* to fish. **2** *vt* (*attraper*) to catch.
**pêcher**[2] *m* peach tree.
**pêcheur** *m* fisherman; (*à la ligne*) angler.
**pédale** *f* pedal; **p. de frein** footbrake (pedal).
**pédaler** *vi* to pedal.
**pédalo** *m* paddle boat.
**pédiatre** *mf* children's doctor.

**pédicure** *mf* chiropodist.
**peigne** *m* comb; **se donner un coup de p.** to give one's hair a comb.
**peigner** *vt* (*cheveux*) to comb; **p. qn** to comb s.o.'s hair.
**peigner (se)** *vpr* to comb one's hair.
**peignoir** *m* bathrobe; **p. (de bain)** bathrobe.
**peindre*** *vti* to paint; **p. en bleu/***etc* to paint blue/*etc*.
**peine (à)** *adv* hardly.
**peine** *f* (*châtiment*) **la p. de mort** the death penalty; **p. de prison** prison sentence. ▪ (*chagrin*) sorrow; **avoir de la p.** to be upset; **faire de la p. à** to upset. ▪ (*effort, difficulté*) trouble; **se donner de la p.** to go to a lot of trouble (**pour faire** to do); **avec p.** with difficulty; **ça vaut la p. d'attendre/***etc* it's worth (while) waiting/*etc*; **ce n'est pas** *ou* **ça ne vaut pas la p.** it's not worth it.
**peintre** *m* painter; **p. (en bâtiment)** (house) painter.
**peinture** *f* (*tableau, activité*) painting; (*matière*) paint; **'p. fraîche'** 'wet paint'.
**pelage** *m* (*d'animal*) coat, fur.
**peler 1** *vt* (*fruit*) to peel. **2** *vi* (*peau bronzée*) to peel.
**pelle** *f* shovel; (*d'enfant*) spade; **p. à poussière** dustpan.
**pelleteuse** *f* steam shovel.
**pellicule** *f* (*pour photos*) film; (*couche*) layer; **pellicules** (*dans les cheveux*) dandruff.
**pelote** *f* (*de laine*) ball.
**peloton** *m* (*cyclistes*) pack.
**pelotonner (se)** *vpr* to curl up (into a ball).
**pelouse** *f* lawn.
**peluche** *f* **peluches** (*flocons*) fluff; **jouet en p.** = stuffed animal; **chien en p.** (*jouet*) stuffed dog; **ours en p.** teddy bear.
**penalty** *m Football* penalty.
**penché, -ée** *a* leaning.
**pencher 1** *vt* (*objet*) to tilt; (*tête*) to lean. **2** *vi* (*arbre etc*) to lean (over).
**pencher (se)** *vpr* to lean (over *ou* forward); **se p. par** (*fenêtre*) to lean out of.
**pendant** *prép* during; **p. la nuit** during the night; **p. deux mois** for two months; **p. que** while.
**penderie** *f* closet.
**pendre** *vti* to hang (**à** from); **p. qn** to hang s.o. (**pour** for); **se p.** (*se suspendre*) to hang (**à** from).
**pendu, -ue** *a* (*objet*) hanging (**à** from).
**pendule** *f* clock.
**pénétrer** *vi* **p. dans** to enter; (*profondément*) to penetrate (into).
**pénible** *a* difficult; (*douloureux*) painful.
**péniblement** *adv* with difficulty.
**péniche** *f* barge.
**pénicilline** *f* penicillin.
**pensée** *f* (*idée*) thought.
**penser 1** *vi* to think (**à** of, about); **p. à qch/à faire qch** (*ne pas oublier*) to remember sth/to do sth. **2** *vt* to think (**que** that); **je pensais rester** I was thinking of staying; **je pense réussir** I hope to succeed; **que pensez-vous de?** what do you think of *ou* about?
**pension**[1] *f* boarding school; (*somme à payer*) board; **être en p.** to board (**chez** with); **p. complète** full board.
**pension**[2] *f* (*de retraite etc*) pension.
**pensionnaire** *mf* (*élève*) boarder; (*d'hôtel*) resident; (*de famille*) lodger.
**pensionnat** *m* boarding school.
**pente** *f* slope; **en p.** sloping.
**Pentecôte** *f* Pentecost.
**pépin** *m* (*de fruit*) seed, pit.
**perçant, -ante** *a* (*cri, froid*) piercing; (*yeux*) sharp.
**percepteur** *m* tax collector.
**percer 1** *vt* to pierce; (*avec une perceuse*) to drill (a hole in); (*ouver-*

*ture*) to make. **2** *vi* (*avec un outil*) to drill.
**perceuse** *f* (*outil*) drill.
**perche** *f* (*bâton*) pole.
**percher (se)** *vpr* (*oiseau*) to perch.
**perchoir** *m* perch.
**percuter** *vt* (*véhicule*) to crash into.
**perdant, -ante** *mf* loser.
**perdre 1** *vt* to lose; (*gaspiller*) to waste; **p. de vue** to lose sight of. **2** *vi* to lose.
**perdre (se)** *vpr* (*s'égarer*) to get lost; **je m'y perds** I'm lost *ou* confused.
**perdrix** *f* partridge.
**perdu, -ue** *a* lost; (*gaspillé*) wasted; **c'est du temps p.** it's a waste of time.
**père** *m* father.
**perfection** *f* perfection; **à la p.** perfectly.
**perfectionné, -ée** *a* (*machine*) advanced.
**perfectionner** *vt* to improve; **se p. en anglais**/*etc* to improve one's English/*etc*.
**perforeuse** *f* (paper) punch.
**performance** *f* (*d'athlète etc*) performance.
**péril** *m* danger, peril.
**périlleux, -euse** *a* dangerous.
**périmé, -ée** *a* (*billet*) expired.
**période** *f* period.
**périphérique** *a* & *m* **(boulevard) p.** beltway.
**perle** *f* (*bijou*) pearl; (*de bois, verre*) bead.
**permanence** *f* (*salle d'étude*) study hall; **être de p.** to be on duty; **en p.** permanently.
**permanent, -ente 1** *a* permanent; (*spectacle*) continuous. **2** *f* (*coiffure*) perm.
**permettre*** *vt* to allow; **p. à qn de faire** to allow s.o. to do; **vous permettez?** may I?; **je ne peux pas me p. d'acheter** I can't afford to buy.
**permis, -ise 1** *a* allowed. **2** *m* license; **p. de conduire** driver's license; **passer son p. de conduire** to take one's driving test.
**permission** *f* permission; (*congé de soldat*) leave; **demander la p.** to ask permission (**de faire** to do).
**perpendiculaire** *a* perpendicular (**à** to).
**perpétuel, -elle** *a* (*incessant*) continual, non-stop.
**perron** *m* (front) steps.
**perroquet** *m* parrot.
**perruche** *f* parakeet.
**perruque** *f* wig.
**persécuter** *vt* to persecute.
**persécution** *f* persecution.
**persévérance** *f* perseverance.
**persévérer** *vi* to persevere (**dans** in).
**persil** *m* parsley.
**persister** *vi* to persist (**à faire** in doing, **dans qch** in sth).
**personnage** *m* (important) person; (*de livre, film*) character.
**personnalité** *f* personality.
**personne 1** *f* person; **personnes** people; **grande p.** grown-up; **en p.** in person. **2** *pron* (*négatif*) nobody; **je ne vois p.** I don't see anybody; **mieux que p.** better than anybody.
**personnel, -elle 1** *a* personal. **2** *m* staff.
**personnellement** *adv* personally.
**perspective** *f* (*idée, possibilité*) prospect (**de** of).
**persuader** *vt* to persuade (**qn de faire** s.o. to do); **être persuadé que** to be convinced that.
**persuasion** *f* persuasion.
**perte** *f* loss; (*gaspillage*) waste (**de temps/d'argent** of time/money).
**perturbation** *f* disruption.
**perturber** *vt* (*trafic etc*) to disrupt; (*personne*) to disturb.
**pesant, -ante** *a* heavy.
**pesanteur** *f* (*force*) gravity.
**pèse-personne** *m* (bathroom) scales.
**peser** *vti* to weigh; **p. lourd** to be heavy.

**pessimiste** *a* pessimistic.

**peste** *f* (*maladie*) plague.

**pétale** *m* petal.

**pétanque** *f* (French) bowling game.

**pétard** *m* firecracker.

**pétillant, -ante** *a* fizzy; (*vin, yeux*) sparkling.

**pétiller** *vi* (*champagne*) to fizz; (*yeux*) to sparkle.

**petit, -ite 1** *a* small, little; (*de taille*) short; (*bruit, coup*) slight; (*jeune*) little; **tout p.** tiny; **un p. Français** a (little) French boy. **2** *mf* (little) boy *ou* girl; (*personne*) small person; **petits** (*d'animal*) young. **3** *adv* **p. à p.** little by little.

**petite-fille** *f* (*pl* **petites-filles**) granddaughter.

**petit-fils** *m* (*pl* **petits-fils**) grandson.

**petits-enfants** *mpl* grandchildren.

**petit-suisse** *m* soft cheese (*for dessert*).

**pétrole** *m* oil.

**pétrolier** *m* (*navire*) (oil) tanker.

**peu** *adv* (*manger etc*) not much, little; **un p.** a little, a bit; **p. de sel/de temps/***etc* not much salt/time/*etc*; **un p. de fromage/***etc* a little cheese/*etc*; **p. de gens/***etc* few people/*etc*; **un (tout) petit p.** a (tiny) little bit; **p. intéressant/***etc* not very interesting/*etc*; **p. de chose** not much; **p. à p.** little by little; **à p. près** more or less; **p. après** shortly after.

**peuple** *m* people.

**peuplé, -ée** *a* **très/peu/***etc* **p.** highly/sparsely/*etc* populated; **p. de** populated by.

**peur** *f* fear; **avoir p.** to be afraid *ou* frightened (**de qch/qn** of sth/s.o.; **de faire** to do, of doing); **faire p. à** to frighten; **de p. que** (+ *subjonctif*) for fear that.

**peureux, -euse** *a* easily frightened.

**peut, peuvent, peux** *voir* **pouvoir.**

**peut-être** *adv* perhaps, maybe; **p.-être qu'il viendra** perhaps *ou* maybe he'll come.

**phare** *m* (*pour bateaux*) lighthouse; (*de véhicule*) headlight; **faire un appel de phares** to flash one's lights.

**pharmacie** *f* drugstore, pharmacy; (*armoire*) medicine cabinet.

**pharmacien, -ienne** *mf* pharmacist.

**philatélie** *f* stamp collecting.

**philatéliste** *mf* stamp collector.

**philosophe 1** *mf* philosopher. **2** *a* (*résigné*) philosophical.

**philosophie** *f* philosophy.

**phonétique** *a* phonetic.

**phoque** *m* (*animal*) seal.

**photo** *f* photo; (*art*) photography; **prendre une p. de** to take a photo of; **se faire prendre en p.** to have one's photo taken.

**photocopie** *f* photocopy.

**photocopier** *vt* to photocopy.

**photocopieuse** *f* (*machine*) photocopier.

**photographe** *mf* photographer.

**photographier** *vt* to photograph.

**photographique** *a* photographic.

**photomaton®** *m* photo booth.

**phrase** *f* sentence.

**physique 1** *a* physical. **2** *m* (*corps, aspect*) physique; (*science*) physics.

**physiquement** *adv* physically.

**pianiste** *mf* pianist.

**piano** *m* piano.

**pic** *m* (*cime*) peak.

**pic (à)** *adv* **couler à p.** to sink to the bottom.

**pichet** *m* jug.

**pickpocket** *m* pickpocket.

**picorer** *vti* to peck.

**picoter** *vt* (*yeux*) to make sting; **les yeux me picotent** my eyes are stinging.

**pièce** *f* (*de maison etc*) room; (*de pantalon*) patch; **p. (de monnaie)** coin; **p. (de théâtre)** play; **p. d'identité** identity card; **pièces déta-**

**chées** (*de véhicule etc*) spare parts; **cinq dollars p.** five dollars each.
**pied** *m* foot (*pl* feet); (*de meuble*) leg; (*de verre, lampe*) base; **à p.** on foot; **au p. de** at the foot of; **coup de p.** kick; **donner un coup de p.** to kick (**à qn** s.o.).
**piège** *m* trap.
**piéger** *vt* (*animal*) to trap; (*voiture*) to booby-trap.
**pierre** *f* stone; (*précieuse*) gem; **p. (à briquet)** flint.
**piétiner 1** *vt* to trample (on). **2** *vi* to stamp (one's feet).
**piéton** *m* pedestrian.
**piétonne** *a* **rue p.** pedestrian street.
**pieu, -x** *m* post, stake.
**pieuvre** *f* octopus.
**pigeon** *m* pigeon.
**pile 1** *f* (*électrique*) battery; (*tas*) pile; **radio à piles** battery radio; **en p.** in a pile; **p. (ou face)?** heads (or tails)? **2** *adv* **s'arrêter p.** to stop short; **à deux heures p.** at two o'clock sharp *ou* on the dot.
**pilier** *m* pillar.
**pillage** *m* looting.
**piller** *vti* to loot.
**pilotage** *m* **poste de p.** cockpit.
**pilote** *m* (*d'avion*) pilot; (*de voiture*) driver.
**piloter** *vt* (*avion*) to fly; (*voiture*) to drive.
**pilule** *f* pill; **prendre la p.** to be on the pill.
**piment** *m* pepper.
**pimenté, -ée** *a* spicy.
**pin** *m* (*arbre*) pine; **pomme de p.** pine cone.
**pince** *f* (*outil*) pliers; (*de cycliste*) clip; (*de crabe*) pincer; **p. (à linge)** (clothes) pin; **p. (à épiler)** tweezers; **p. (à sucre)** (sugar) tongs; **p. à cheveux** bobby pin.
**pinceau, -x** *m* (paint)brush.
**pincée** *f* (*de sel etc*) pinch (**de** of).
**pincer** *vt* to pinch; **se p. le doigt** to get one's finger caught (**dans** in).
**pingouin** *m* penguin.
**ping-pong** *m* table tennis.
**pin's** *m inv* button, lapel pin.
**pioche** *f* pick(axe).
**piocher** *vti* to dig (with a pick).
**pion** *m* (*au jeu de dames*) piece; *Échecs* pawn.
**pipe** *f* pipe; **fumer la p.** to smoke a pipe.
**pipi** *m* **faire p.** *Fam* to take a pee.
**piquant, -ante** *a* (*plante, barbe*) prickly.
**pique** *m* (*couleur*) *Cartes* spades.
**pique-nique** *m* picnic.
**pique-niquer** *vi* to picnic.
**piquer 1** *vt* (*percer*) to prick; (*langue, yeux*) to sting; (*coudre*) to (machine-)stitch; **p. qn** (*abeille*) to sting s.o.; **p. qch dans** (*enfoncer*) to stick sth into; **p. une colère** to fly into a rage. **2** *vi* (*avion*) to dive; (*moutarde etc*) to be hot.
**piquet** *m* (*pieu*) stake; (*de tente*) peg.
**piqûre** *f* (*d'abeille*) sting; (*avec une seringue*) injection, shot.
**pirate** *m* pirate; **p. de l'air** hijacker; **p. informatique** (computer) hacker.
**pire 1** *a* worse (**que** than); **le p. moment**/*etc* the worst moment/*etc*. **2** *mf* **le** *ou* **la p.** the worst.
**piscine** *f* swimming pool.
**pissenlit** *m* dandelion.
**pistache** *f* pistachio.
**piste** *f* (*traces*) trail; (*de course*) racetrack; (*de cirque*) ring; (*de patinage*) rink; **p. (d'envol)** runway; **p. cyclable** bicycle path; **p. de danse** dance floor; **p. de ski** ski run *ou* slope.
**pistolet** *m* gun; **p. à eau** water pistol.
**pitié** *f* pity; **j'ai p. de lui** I feel sorry for him.
**pittoresque** *a* picturesque.
**pivoter** *vi* (*personne*) to swing round; (*fauteuil*) to swivel.
**pizza** *f* pizza.
**pizzeria** *f* pizzeria.
**placard** *m* (*dans la cuisine*) cupboard, cabinet; (*pour linge, vêtements etc*) closet.

**place** *f* (*endroit, rang*) place; (*espace*) room; (*lieu public*) square; (*siège*) seat, place; (*emploi*) job; **p. de parking** parking place *ou* space; **à la p. (de)** instead (of); **à votre p.** in your place; **sur p.** on the spot; **en p.** in place; **mettre en p.** (*installer*) to set up; **changer de p.** to change places; **changer qch de p.** to move sth.

**placement** *m* (*d'argent*) investment.

**placer** *vt* to place; (*invité, spectateur*) to seat; (*argent*) to invest (**dans** in).

**placer (se)** *vpr* (*debout*) to (go and) stand; (*s'asseoir*) to (go and) sit; **se p. troisième**/*etc* (*en sport*) to come third/*etc*.

**plafond** *m* ceiling.

**plage** *f* beach; **p. arrière** (*de voiture*) (back) window shelf.

**plaie** *f* wound; (*coupure*) cut.

**plaindre*** *vt* to feel sorry for.

**plaindre (se)** *vpr* to complain (**de** about, **que** that); **se p. de** (*douleur*) to complain of.

**plaine** *f* plain.

**plainte** *f* complaint; (*cri*) moan.

**plaire*** *vi* **p. à qn** to please s.o.; **elle lui plaît** he likes her; **ça me plaît** I like it; **s'il vous** *ou* **te plaît** please.

**plaire (se)** *vpr* (*à Paris etc*) to like *ou* enjoy it.

**plaisanter** *vi* to joke (**sur** about).

**plaisanterie** *f* joke; **par p.** as a joke.

**plaisir** *m* pleasure; **faire p. à** to please; **pour le p.** for fun.

**plan** *m* (*projet, dessin*) plan; (*de ville*) map; **au premier p.** in the foreground.

**planche** *f* board; **p. à repasser** ironing board; **p. (à roulettes)** skateboard; **p. (à voile)** sailboard; **faire de la p. (à voile)** to go windsurfing.

**plancher** *m* floor.

**planer** *vi* (*oiseau, avion*) to glide.

**planète** *f* planet.

**plante**[1] *f* plant; **p. verte** house plant.

**plante**[2] *f* **p. des pieds** sole (of the foot).

**planter** *vt* (*fleur etc*) to plant; (*clou, couteau*) to drive in; **se p. devant** to come *ou* go and stand in front of, plant oneself in front of.

**plaque** *f* plate; (*de verre, métal, verglas*) sheet; (*de chocolat*) bar; **p. chauffante** hotplate; **p. d'immatriculation** license plate.

**plaqué, -ée** *a* **p. or** gold-plated.

**plaquer** *vt Sport* to tackle; (*aplatir*) to flatten (**contre** against).

**plastique** *a* & *m* **(matière) p.** plastic; **en p.** (*bouteille etc*) plastic.

**plat, plate 1** *a* flat; **à p. ventre** flat on one's face; **à p.** (*pneu, batterie*) flat; **poser à p.** to put down flat; **assiette plate** dinner plate; **eau plate** still water. **2** *m* (*récipient, nourriture*) dish; (*partie du repas*) course; **'p. du jour'** 'today's special'.

**platane** *m* plane tree.

**plateau, -x** *m* (*pour servir*) tray; **p. à fromages** cheeseboard.

**plate-forme** *f* (*pl* **plates-formes**) platform; **p.-forme pétrolière** oil rig.

**plâtre** *m* (*matière*) plaster; **un p.** a (plaster) cast; **dans le p.** in plaster.

**plâtrer** *vt* (*bras, jambe*) to put a cast on.

**plein, pleine 1** *a* full (**de** of); **en pleine mer** out at sea; **en pleine figure** right in the face. **2** *prép* & *adv* **des billes p. les poches** pockets full of marbles; **du chocolat p. la figure** chocolate all over one's face; **p. de lettres/d'argent**/*etc Fam* lots of letters/money/*etc*. **3** *m* **faire le p. (d'essence)** to fill up (the tank).

**pleurer** *vi* to cry.

**pleuvoir*** *vi* to rain; **il pleut** it's raining.

**pli** *m* (*de papier*) fold; (*de jupe*) pleat; (*de pantalon*) crease; **(faux) p.** crease; **mise en plis** (*coiffure*) set.

**pliant, -ante** *a* (*chaise etc*) folding.

**plier 1** *vt* to fold; (*courber*) to bend. **2** *vi* (*branche*) to bend.
**plier (se)** *vpr* (*lit, chaise etc*) to fold (up).
**plissé, -ée** *a* (*tissu, jupe*) pleated.
**plisser** *vt* (*front*) to wrinkle; to crease, fold; **p. les yeux** to squint.
**plomb** *m* (*métal*) lead; (*fusible*) fuse; **plombs** (*de chasse*) lead shot.
**plombage** *m* (*de dent*) filling.
**plomber** *vt* (*dent*) to fill.
**plomberie** *f* plumbing.
**plombier** *m* plumber.
**plongée** *f* (*sport*) diving.
**plongeoir** *m* diving board.
**plongeon** *m* dive.
**plonger 1** *vi* (*personne*) to dive. **2** *vt* (*mettre*) to plunge (**dans** into).
**plongeur, -euse** *mf* diver.
**plu** *voir* **plaire, pleuvoir.**
**pluie** *f* rain; **sous la p.** in the rain.
**plume** *f* (*d'oiseau*) feather; (*de stylo*) (pen) nib; **stylo à p.** (fountain) pen.
**plumer** *vt* (*volaille*) to pluck.
**plupart (la)** *f* most; **la p. des cas** most cases; **la p. du temps** most of the time; **la p. d'entre eux** most of them; **pour la p.** mostly.
**pluriel, -ielle** *a* & *m* plural; **au p.** in the plural.
**plus**[1] **1** *adv comparatif* (*travailler etc*) more (**que** than); **p. d'une livre/de dix** more than a pound/ten; **p. de thé** more tea; **p. beau** more beautiful (**que** than); **p. tard** later; **p. petit** smaller; **de p. en p.** more and more; **p. ou moins** more or less; **en p.** in addition (**de** to); **de p.** more (**que** than); (*en outre*) moreover; **(âgé) de p. de dix ans** over ten; **j'ai dix ans de p. qu'elle** I'm ten years older than she is; **il est p. de cinq heures** it's after five. **2** *adv superlatif* **le p.** (*travailler etc*) (the) most; **le p. beau** the most beautiful (**de** in); **le p. grand** the biggest (**de** in); **j'ai le p. de livres** I have (the) most books.
**plus**[2] *adv de négation* **p. de** (*pain, argent*) no more; **il n'a p. de pain** he has no more bread, he doesn't have any more bread; **tu n'es p. jeune** you're not young any more; **je ne la reverrai p.** I won't see her again.
**plus**[3] *prép* plus; **deux p. deux** two plus two; **il fait p. deux (degrés)** it's two degrees above freezing.
**plusieurs** *a* & *pron* several.
**plutôt** *adv* rather (**que** than).
**pluvieux, -euse** *a* rainy.
**pneu** *m* (*pl* **-s**) tire.
**pneumatique** *a* **matelas p.** air mattress; **canot p.** rubber dinghy.
**poche** *f* pocket; (*de kangourou*) pouch.
**pocher** *vt* (*œufs*) to poach; **p. l'œil à qn** to give s.o. a black eye.
**pochette** *f* (*sac*) bag; (*d'allumettes*) book; (*de disque*) sleeve; (*sac à main*) (clutch) bag.
**poêle 1** *m* stove. **2** *f* **p. (à frire)** frying pan.
**poème** *m* poem.
**poésie** *f* (*art*) poetry; (*poème*) poem.
**poète** *m* poet.
**poétique** *a* poetic.
**poids** *m* weight; **au p.** by weight.
**poids lourd** *m* (heavy) truck.
**poignard** *m* dagger.
**poignarder** *vt* to stab.
**poignée** *f* (*quantité*) handful (**de** of); (*de porte etc*) handle; **p. de main** handshake; **donner une p. de main à** to shake hands with.
**poignet** *m* wrist; (*de chemise*) cuff.
**poil** *m* hair; (*pelage*) fur.
**poilu, -ue** *a* hairy.
**poinçonner** *vt* (*billet*) to punch.
**poing** *m* fist; **coup de p.** punch.
**point** *m* (*lieu, score etc*) point; (*sur i, à l'horizon*) dot; (*tache*) spot; (*de couture*) stitch; **sur le p. de faire** about to do; **p. (final)** period; **p. d'exclamation** exclamation point; **p. d'interrogation** question mark; **points de suspension** ellipsis; **p. de vue** (*opinion*) point of view; **à p.**

(*steak*) medium rare; **au p. mort** (*véhicule*) in neutral; **p. de côté** (*douleur*) stitch (in one's side).
**pointe** *f* (*extrémité*) tip; (*clou*) nail; **sur la p. des pieds** on tiptoe; **en p.** pointed.
**pointer 1** *vt* (*cocher*) to check (off); (*braquer*) to point (**sur** at). **2** *vi* **p. vers** to point (upwards) towards.
**pointillé** *m* dotted line.
**pointu, -ue** *a* (*en pointe*) pointed.
**pointure** *f* (*de chaussure, gant*) size.
**point-virgule** *m* (*pl* **points-virgules**) semicolon.
**poire** *f* pear.
**poireau, -x** *m* leek.
**poirier** *m* pear tree.
**pois** *m* pea; **petits p.** peas; **p. chiche** chickpea.
**poison** *m* poison.
**poisseux, -euse** *a* sticky.
**poisson** *m* fish; **p. rouge** goldfish.
**poissonnerie** *f* fish market.
**poissonnier, -ière** *mf* fish merchant.
**poitrine** *f* chest; (*de femme*) bust.
**poivre** *m* pepper.
**poivré, -ée** *a* (*piquant*) peppery.
**poivrer** *vt* to pepper.
**poivrière** *f* peppershaker.
**poivron** *m* (*légume*) pepper.
**pôle** *m* **p. Nord/Sud** North/South Pole.
**poli, -ie** *a* (*courtois*) polite (**avec** to, with); (*lisse*) polished.
**police**[1] *f* police; **p. secours** police emergency services.
**police**[2] *f* **p. (d'assurance)** (insurance) policy.
**policier, -ière 1** *a* **enquête**/*etc* **policière** police investigation/*etc*; **roman p.** mystery novel. **2** *m* policeman, detective.
**poliment** *adv* politely.
**polio 1** *f* (*maladie*) polio. **2** *mf* (*personne*) polio victim.
**polir** *vt* to polish.
**politesse** *f* politeness.
**politique 1** *a* political; **homme p.** politician. **2** *f* (*activité*) politics; **une p.** a policy.
**pollen** *m* pollen.
**polluer** *vt* to pollute.
**pollution** *f* pollution.
**polo** *m* (*chemise*) polo shirt.
**polochon** *m* bolster.
**polonais, -aise 1** *a* Polish. **2** *mf* Pole. **3** *m* (*langue*) Polish.
**polycopié** *m* duplicated course notes.
**polyester** *m* polyester; **chemise**/*etc* **en p.** polyester shirt/*etc*.
**pommade** *f* ointment.
**pomme** *f* apple; **p. de terre** potato; **pommes frites** french fries; **pommes chips** potato chips.
**pommier** *m* apple tree.
**pompe** *f* pump; **p. à essence** gas station; **pompes funèbres** undertaker's; **entrepreneur de pompes funèbres** undertaker.
**pomper** *vt* (*eau*) to pump out (**de** of).
**pompier** *m* fireman; **voiture des pompiers** fire engine.
**pompiste** *mf* gas station attendant.
**pompon** *m* pompon.
**poncer** *vt* to rub down, sand.
**ponctuation** *f* punctuation.
**ponctuel, -elle** *a* (*à l'heure*) punctual.
**pondre 1** *vt* (*œuf*) to lay. **2** *vi* (*poule*) to lay (eggs *ou* an egg).
**poney** *m* pony.
**pont** *m* bridge; (*de bateau*) deck.
**pop** *m* & *a inv* (*musique*) pop.
**populaire** *a* (*qui plaît*) popular; (*quartier*) working-class; (*expression*) colloquial.
**population** *f* population.
**porc** *m* pig; (*viande*) pork.
**porcelaine** *f* china.
**porche** *m* porch.
**porcherie** *f* (pig)sty.
**port** *m* port, harbor.
**portable** *a* (*portatif*) portable.
**portail** *m* (*de jardin*) gate(way).
**portant, -ante** *a* **bien p.** in good health.

**portatif, -ive** *a* portable.
**porte** *f* door; (*de jardin*) gate; (*de ville*) entrance; **p. (d'embarquement)** (*d'aéroport*) (departure) gate; **p. d'entrée** front door; **p. coulissante** sliding door; **mettre à la p.** to throw out.
**porte-avions** *m inv* aircraft carrier.
**porte-bagages** *m inv* luggage rack.
**porte-bonheur** *m inv* (lucky) charm.
**porte-clefs** *m inv* key ring.
**porte-documents** *m inv* briefcase.
**portée** *f* (*de fusil etc*) range; (*animaux*) litter; **à p. de la main** within (easy) reach; **à p. de voix** within earshot; **hors de p.** out of reach.
**porte-fenêtre** *f* (*pl* **portes-fenêtres**) French door *ou* window.
**portefeuille** *m* wallet.
**portemanteau, -x** *m* coatrack; (*crochet*) coat hook.
**porte-monnaie** *m inv* purse.
**porte-parole** *m inv* spokesman; (*femme*) spokeswoman.
**porter 1** *vt* to carry; (*vêtement, lunettes, barbe etc*) to wear; **p. qch à** (*apporter*) to take sth to; **p. bonheur/malheur** to bring good/bad luck. **2** *vi* (*voix*) to carry.
**porter (se)** *vpr* (*vêtement*) to be worn; **se p. bien/mal** to be well/ill; **comment te portes-tu?** how are you?
**porte-revues** *m inv* newspaper rack.
**porte-savon** *m* soapdish.
**porte-serviettes** *m inv* towel rack.
**porteur** *m* (*à la gare*) porter.
**porte-voix** *m inv* loudspeaker, megaphone.
**portier** *m* doorman.
**portière** *f* (*de véhicule, train*) door.
**portion** *f* (*partie*) portion; (*de nourriture*) helping.
**portique** *m* (*de balançoire etc*) crossbar.
**portrait** *m* portrait.
**portugais, -aise 1** *a* Portuguese. **2** *mf* Portuguese man *ou* woman, Portuguese *inv*; **les P.** the Portuguese. **3** *m* (*langue*) Portuguese.
**pose** *f* (*installation*) putting up; putting in; laying; (*attitude de modèle*) pose.
**poser 1** *vt* to put (down); (*papier peint, rideaux*) to put up; (*sonnette, chauffage*) to put in; (*moquette*) to lay; (*question*) to ask (**à qn** s.o.). **2** *vi* (*modèle*) to pose (**pour** for).
**poser (se)** *vpr* (*oiseau, avion*) to land.
**positif, -ive** *a* positive.
**position** *f* position.
**posséder** *vt* to possess; (*maison etc*) to own.
**possessif, -ive** *a* & *m Grammaire* possessive.
**possibilité** *f* possibility.
**possible 1** *a* possible (**à faire** to do); **il (nous) est p. de le faire** it is possible (for us) to do it; **il est p. que** (+ *subjonctif*) it is possible that; **si p.** if possible; **le plus tôt p.** as soon as possible; **autant que p.** as far as possible; **le plus p.** as much *ou* as many as possible. **2** *m* **faire son p.** to do one's best (**pour faire** to do).
**postal, -e, -aux** *a* postal; **boîte postale (BP)** PO Box; **code p.** zip code.
**poste 1** *f* (*service*) post; **(bureau de) p.** post office; **la P.** the Post Office; **par la p.** by post; **p. aérienne** airmail. **2** *m* (*lieu, emploi*) post; (*radio, télévision*) set; **p. de secours** first aid station; **p. de police** police station.
**poster** *vt* (*lettre*) to mail.
**postier, -ière** *mf* postal worker.
**pot** *m* pot; (*à confiture*) jar; (*à lait*) jug; (*à bière*) mug; (*de crème, yaourt*) carton; (*de bébé*) potty; **p. de fleurs** flower pot.
**potable** *a* drinkable; **'eau p.'** 'drinking water'.
**potage** *m* soup.

**potager** *a* & *m* **(jardin) p.** vegetable garden.

**pot-au-feu** *m inv* beef stew.

**pot-de-vin** *m* (*pl* **pots-de-vin**) bribe.

**poteau, -x** *m* post; **p. indicateur** signpost; **p. d'arrivée** winning post; **p. télégraphique** telegraph pole.

**poterie** *f* (*art*) pottery; **une p.** a piece of pottery; **des poteries** (*objets*) pottery.

**potier** *m* potter.

**potiron** *m* pumpkin.

**pou, -x** *m* louse; **poux** lice.

**poubelle** *f* garbage can.

**pouce** *m* thumb; (*mesure*) inch.

**poudre** *f* powder; (*explosif*) gunpowder; **en p.** (*lait*) powdered; **chocolat en p.** cocoa powder.

**poudrer (se)** *vpr* (*femme*) to powder one's face.

**poudrier** *m* (powder) compact.

**pouf** *m* (*siège*) (cushioned) ottoman *ou* footstool.

**poulailler** *m* henhouse.

**poulain** *m* (*cheval*) foal.

**poule** *f* hen.

**poulet** *m* chicken.

**poulie** *f* pulley.

**pouls** *m* pulse.

**poumon** *m* lung; **à pleins poumons** (*respirer*) deeply; (*crier*) loudly.

**poupée** *f* doll.

**pour 1** *prép* for; **p. toi**/*etc* for you/*etc*; **partir p.** (*Paris, cinq ans*) to leave for; **elle est p.** she's in favor; **p. faire** (in order) to do; **p. que tu saches** so (that) you know; **p. quoi faire?** what for?; **trop petit**/*etc* **p. faire** too small/*etc* to do; **assez grand**/*etc* **p. faire** big/*etc* enough to do. **2** *m* **le p. et le contre** the pros and cons.

**pourboire** *m* (*argent*) tip.

**pourcentage** *m* percentage.

**pourquoi** *adv* & *conj* why; **p. pas?** why not?

**pourra, pourrai(t)** *etc voir* **pouvoir.**

**pourri, -ie** *a* (*fruit, temps etc*) rotten.

**pourrir** *vi* to rot.

**poursuite** *f* chase; **se mettre à la p. de** to go after, chase (after).

**poursuivant, -ante** *mf* pursuer.

**poursuivre*** *vt* to chase, go after; (*lecture, voyage etc*) to continue (with).

**poursuivre (se)** *vpr* to continue, go on.

**pourtant** *adv* yet.

**pourvu que** *conj* (*condition*) provided *ou* providing (that); (*souhait*) **p. qu'elle soit là!** I only hope (that) she's there!

**pousser 1** *vt* to push; (*cri*) to utter; (*soupir*) to heave; **p. qn à faire** to urge s.o. to do. **2** *vi* (*croître*) to grow; **faire p.** (*plante etc*) to grow.

**poussette** *f* stroller.

**poussière** *f* dust.

**poussiéreux, -euse** *a* dusty.

**poussin** *m* (*poulet*) chick.

**poutre** *f* (*en bois*) beam; (*en acier*) girder.

**pouvoir* 1** *v aux* (*capacité*) can, be able to; (*permission, éventualité*) may, can; **je peux deviner** I can guess; **tu peux entrer** you may *ou* can come in; **il peut être sorti** he may *ou* might be out; **elle pourrait/pouvait venir** she might/could come; **j'ai pu l'obtenir** I managed to get it; **j'aurais pu l'obtenir** I could have gotten it; **je n'en peux plus** I'm utterly exhausted. **2** *m* (*capacité, autorité*) power; **les pouvoirs publics** the authorities; **au p.** in power.

**pouvoir (se)** *vpr* **il se peut qu'elle parte** (it's possible that) she might leave.

**prairie** *f* meadow.

**pratique 1** *a* practical. **2** *f* (*exercice, procédé*) practice; **la p. de la natation/du golf** swimming/golfing.

**pratiquement** *adv* (*presque*) practically.

**pratiquer** *vt* (*sport, art etc*) to practice.

**pré** *m* meadow.
**préau, -x** *m* (*d'école*) covered playground.
**précaution** *f* precaution (**de faire** of doing); (*prudence*) caution.
**précédent, -ente 1** *a* previous. **2** *mf* previous one.
**précéder** *vti* to precede.
**précieux, -euse** *a* precious.
**précipice** *m* chasm, precipice.
**précipitamment** *adv* hastily.
**précipitation** *f* haste.
**précipiter** *vt* (*hâter*) to rush.
**précipiter (se)** *vpr* to throw oneself; (*foncer*) to rush (**à, sur** on to); (*s'accélérer*) to speed up.
**précis, -ise** *a* precise; **à deux heures précises** at two o'clock sharp.
**préciser** *vt* to specify (**que** that).
**préciser (se)** *vpr* to become clear(er).
**précision** *f* precision; (*explication*) explanation.
**précoce** *a* (*fruit etc*) early; (*enfant*) precocious.
**prédécesseur** *m* predecessor.
**prédiction** *f* prediction.
**prédire*** *vt* to predict (**que** that).
**préfabriqué, -ée** *a* prefabricated.
**préface** *f* preface.
**préféré, -ée** *a* & *mf* favorite.
**préférence** *f* preference (**pour** for); **de p.** preferably.
**préférer** *vt* to prefer (**à** to); **p. faire** to prefer to do.
**préfet** *m* prefect (*chief administrator in a department*).
**préfixe** *m* prefix.
**préhistorique** *a* prehistoric.
**préjugé** *m* prejudice; **être plein de préjugés** to be full of prejudice.
**premier, -ière 1** *a* first; **nombre p.** prime number; **le p. rang** the front row; **P. ministre** Prime Minister. **2** *mf* first (one); **arriver le p.** to arrive first; **être le p. de la classe** to be (at the) head of the class. **3** *m* (*date*) first; (*étage*) second floor; **le p. de l'an** New Year's Day. **4** *f* (*wagon, billet*) first class; (*au lycée*) = junior year; (*de véhicule*) first (gear).
**premièrement** *adv* firstly.
**prendre*** **1** *vt* to take (**à qn** from s.o.); (*attraper*) to catch; (*voyager par*) to take (*train etc*); (*douche, bain*) to take, have; (*repas*) to have; (*photo*) to take; (*temps*) to take (up); **p. qn pour** (*un autre*) to mistake s.o. for; (*considérer*) to take s.o. for; **p. feu** to catch fire; **p. de la place** to take up room; **p. du poids** to put on weight. **2** *vi* (*feu*) to catch; (*ciment*) to set; (*vaccin*) to take.
**prendre (se)** *vpr* (*objet*) to be taken; (*s'accrocher*) to get caught; **se p. pour un génie** to think one is a genius; **s'y p.** to go about it; **s'en p. à** to attack; (*accuser*) to blame.
**prénom** *m* first name.
**préoccupation** *f* worry.
**préoccupé, -ée** *a* worried.
**préoccuper** *vt* (*inquiéter*) to worry; **se p. de** to be worried about.
**préparatifs** *mpl* preparations (**de** for).
**préparation** *f* preparation.
**préparer** *vt* to prepare (**qch pour** sth for, **qn à** s.o. for); (*examen*) to prepare for; **se p.** to get (oneself) ready (**à** *ou* **pour qch** for sth); **se p. à faire** to prepare to do.
**préposition** *f Grammaire* preposition.
**près** *adv* **p. de** (*qn, qch*) near (to); **p. de deux ans**/*etc* nearly two years/*etc*; **tout p.** nearby (**de qn/qch** s.o./sth); **de p.** (*lire, suivre*) closely.
**prescrire*** *vt* (*médicament*) to prescribe.
**présence** *f* presence; (*à l'école etc*) attendance (**à** at); **feuille de p.** attendance sheet; **en p. de** in the presence of.
**présent, -ente 1** *a* (*non absent*) present (**à** at, **dans** in); (*actuel*) present. **2** *m Grammaire* present (tense); **à p.** at present.

**présentateur, -trice** *mf* announcer.
**présentation** *f* presentation; (*d'une personne à une autre*) introduction.
**présenter** *vt* to present; **p. qn à qn** to introduce s.o. to s.o.
**présenter (se)** *vpr* to introduce oneself (**à** to); **se p. à** (*examen*) to take; (*élections*) to run in.
**préservatif** *m* condom.
**préserver** *vt* to protect (**de, contre** from).
**présidence** *f* (*de nation*) presidency; (*de firme*) chairmanship.
**président, -ente** *mf* (*de nation*) president; (*de réunion, firme*) chairman, chairwoman; **p. directeur général** chief executive officer.
**présidentiel, -ielle** *a* presidential.
**presque** *adv* almost.
**presqu'île** *f* peninsula.
**presse** *f* (*journaux, appareil*) press; **conférence**/*etc* **de p.** press conference/*etc*.
**presse-citron** *m inv* lemon juicer.
**pressé, -ée** *a* (*personne*) in a hurry; (*travail*) urgent.
**pressentir*** *vt* to sense (**que** that).
**presser 1** *vt* (*serrer*) to squeeze; (*bouton*) to press; (*fruit*) to squeeze, juice. **2** *vi* (*temps*) to press; **rien ne presse** there's no hurry.
**presser (se)** *vpr* (*se serrer*) to squeeze (together); (*se hâter*) to hurry (**de faire** to do).
**pressing** *m* (*magasin*) dry cleaner's.
**pression** *f* pressure.
**prestidigitateur, -trice** *mf* magician.
**prestidigitation** *f* **tour de p.** magic trick.
**prêt** *m* (*emprunt*) loan.
**prêt, prête** *a* (*préparé*) ready (**à faire** to do, **à qch** for sth).
**prêt-à-porter** *m inv* ready-to-wear clothes.
**prétendre** *vt* to claim (**que** that, **être** to be); **elle se prétend riche** she claims to be rich.
**prétendu, -ue** *a* so-called.
**prétentieux, -euse** *a* & *mf* conceited (person).
**prêter** *vt* (*argent, objet*) to lend (**à** to); **p. attention** to pay attention (**à** to).
**prétexte** *m* excuse; **sous p. de/que** on the pretext of/that.
**prêtre** *m* priest.
**preuve** *f* **preuve(s)** proof, evidence; **faire p. de** to show.
**prévenir*** *vt* (*avertir*) to warn (**que** that); (*aviser*) to inform (**que** that).
**prévention** *f* prevention; **p. routière** road safety.
**prévision** *f* forecast.
**prévoir*** *vt* (*anticiper*) to foresee (**que** that); (*prédire*) to forecast (**que** that); (*temps*) to forecast; (*organiser*) to plan; (*préparer*) to provide, make provision for.
**prévu, -ue** *a* **un repas est p.** a meal is provided; **au moment p.** at the appointed time; **comme p.** as expected; **p. pour** (*véhicule, appareil*) designed for.
**prier 1** *vti* to pray (**pour** for). **2** *vt* **p. qn de faire** to ask s.o. to do; **je vous en prie** (*faites donc*) please; (*en réponse à 'merci'*) don't mention it, you're welcome.
**prière** *f* prayer; **p. de répondre**/*etc* please answer/*etc*.
**primaire** *a* primary.
**prime** *f* (*d'employé*) bonus; **en p.** (*cadeau*) as a free gift; **p. (d'assurance)** (insurance) premium.
**primevère** *f* primrose.
**primitif, -ive** *a* (*société etc*) primitive.
**prince** *m* prince.
**princesse** *f* princess.
**principal, -e, -aux 1** *a* main. **2** *m* (*de collège*) principal, headmaster; **le p.** (*essentiel*) the main thing.
**principe** *m* principle; **en p.** theoretically; (*normalement*) as a rule.
**printemps** *m* (*saison*) spring.

**prioritaire** *a* **être p.** to have priority; (*en voiture*) to have the right of way.

**priorité** *f* priority (**sur** over); **la p.** (*sur la route*) the right of way; **la p. à droite** right of way to traffic coming from the right; **'cédez la p.'** 'yield'.

**pris, prise** (*pp of* **prendre**) *a* (*place*) taken; (*crème, ciment*) set; (*nez*) congested; **être (très) p.** to be (very) busy; **p. de** (*peur, panique*) stricken with.

**prise** *f* (*de judo etc*) hold; (*objet saisi*) catch; **p. (de courant)** (*mâle*) plug; (*femelle*) outlet, socket; **p. multiple** (*électrique*) adaptor; **p. de sang** blood test.

**prison** *f* prison, jail; **en p.** in prison *ou* jail.

**prisonnier, -ière** *mf* prisoner; **faire qn p.** to take s.o. prisoner.

**privé, -ée** *a* private.

**priver** *vt* to deprive (**de** of); **se p. de** to do without.

**prix**[1] *m* (*d'un objet etc*) price; **à tout p.** at all costs; **à aucun p.** on no account.

**prix**[2] *m* (*récompense*) prize.

**probable** *a* likely, probable (**que** that); **peu p.** unlikely.

**probablement** *adv* probably.

**problème** *m* problem.

**procédé** *m* process.

**procès** *m* (*criminel*) trial; (*civil*) lawsuit; **faire un p. à** to take to court.

**procès-verbal, -aux** *m* (*contravention*) (traffic) ticket.

**prochain, -aine** *a* next.

**prochainement** *adv* shortly.

**proche** *a* (*espace*) near, close; (*temps*) close (at hand); (*parent, ami*) close; **p. de** near (to), close to.

**procurer** *vt* **p. qch à qn** (*personne*) to obtain sth for s.o.; **se p. qch** to obtain sth.

**prodigieux, -euse** *a* extraordinary.

**producteur, -trice 1** *mf* producer. **2** *a* **pays p. de pétrole** oil-producing country.

**production** *f* production.

**produire*** *vt* (*fabriquer, causer etc*) to produce.

**produire (se)** *vpr* (*événement etc*) to happen.

**produit** *m* (*article etc*) product; (*pour la vaisselle*) liquid; **produits** (*de la terre*) produce; **p. (chimique)** chemical; **p. de beauté** cosmetic.

**prof** *mf Fam* = **professeur.**

**professeur** *m* teacher; (*à l'université*) professor.

**profession** *f* occupation; (*de médecin etc*) profession; (*manuelle*) trade.

**professionnel, -elle 1** *a* professional; (*école*) vocational. **2** *mf* professional.

**profil** *m* **de p.** (viewed) from the side, in profile.

**profit** *m* profit; **tirer p. de** to benefit from *ou* by.

**profitable** *a* (*utile*) beneficial (**à** to).

**profiter** *vi* **p. de** to take advantage of; **p. à qn** to profit s.o.

**profond, -onde 1** *a* deep; **p. de deux mètres** seven feet deep. **2** *adv* (*pénétrer etc*) deep.

**profondément** *adv* deeply; (*dormir*) soundly.

**profondeur** *f* depth; **à six mètres de p.** at a depth of 20 feet.

**progiciel** *m* (software) package.

**programmateur** *m* (*de four etc*) timer.

**programme** *m* program; (*scolaire*) syllabus; (*d'ordinateur*) program.

**programmer** *vt* (*ordinateur*) to program.

**progrès** *m* & *mpl* progress; **faire des p.** to make progress.

**progresser** *vi* to progress.

**progressif, -ive** *a* gradual.

**progressivement** *adv* gradually.

**proie** *f* prey.

**projecteur** *m* (*de monument*) floodlight; (*de film etc*) projector.

**projectile** *m* missile.

**projection** *f* (*de film*) projection; (*séance*) showing.

**projet** *m* plan.
**projeter** *vt* (*lancer*) to hurl; (*film*) to project; (*voyage, fête etc*) to plan; **p. de faire** to plan to do.
**prolonger** *vt* to extend.
**prolonger (se)** *vpr* (*séance, rue*) to continue.
**promenade** *f* (*à pied*) walk; (*en voiture*) drive; (*en vélo, à cheval*) ride; **faire une p. = se promener.**
**promener** *vt* to take for a walk *ou* ride.
**promener (se)** *vpr* to (go for a) walk; (*en voiture*) to (go for a) drive.
**promeneur, -euse** *mf* stroller.
**promesse** *f* promise.
**promettre*** *vt* to promise (**qch à qn** s.o. sth, **que** that); **p. de faire** to promise to do; **c'est promis** it's a promise.
**promotion** *f* **en p.** (*produit*) on (special) offer.
**pronom** *m* pronoun.
**prononcer** *vt* (*articuler*) to pronounce; (*dire*) to utter; (*discours*) to deliver.
**prononcer (se)** *vpr* (*mot*) to be pronounced.
**prononciation** *f* pronunciation.
**propager** *vt*, **se propager** *vpr* to spread.
**proportion** *f* proportion; (*rapport*) ratio.
**propos 1** *mpl* (*paroles*) remarks. **2** *prép* **à p. de** about. **3** *adv* **à p.!** by the way!
**proposer** *vt* to suggest, propose (**qch à qn** sth to s.o., **que** (+ *subjonctif*) that); (*offrir*) to offer (**qch à qn** s.o. sth, **de faire** to do); **je te propose de rester** I suggest you stay; **se p. pour faire** to offer to do.
**proposition** *f* suggestion; *Grammaire* clause.
**propre[1] 1** *a* clean; (*soigné*) neat. **2** *m* **mettre qch au p.** to make a clean copy of sth.
**propre[2]** *a* own; **mon p. argent** my own money.
**proprement** *adv* cleanly; (*avec netteté*) neatly.
**propreté** *f* cleanliness; (*netteté*) neatness.
**propriétaire** *mf* owner; (*qui loue*) landlord, landlady.
**propriété** *f* (*bien, maison*) property.
**prose** *f* prose.
**prospectus** *m* leaflet.
**prospère** *a* thriving.
**protecteur, -trice 1** *mf* protector. **2** *a* (*geste etc*) protective.
**protection** *f* protection; **de p.** (*écran etc*) protective.
**protège-cahier** *m* note book cover.
**protéger** *vt* to protect (**de** from, **contre** against).
**protestant, -ante** *a* & *mf* Protestant.
**protestation** *f* protest (**contre** against).
**protester** *vi* to protest (**contre** against).
**prouver** *vt* to prove (**que** that).
**provenir*** *vi* **p. de** to come from.
**proverbe** *m* proverb.
**province** *f* province; **la p.** the provinces; **en p.** in the provinces; **de p.** (*ville etc*) provincial.
**provincial, -e, -aux** *a* & *mf* provincial.
**proviseur** *m* (*de lycée*) principal.
**provision** *f* supply; **provisions** (*achats*) shopping; (*nourriture*) food; **sac à provisions** shopping bag; **chèque sans p.** bad *ou* bounced check.
**provisoire** *a* temporary.
**provisoirement** *adv* temporarily.
**provoquer** *vt* (*causer*) to bring (*sth*) about; (*défier*) to provoke (*s.o.*).
**proximité** *f* closeness; **à p.** close by; **à p. de** close to.
**prudemment** *adv* cautiously, carefully.
**prudence** *f* caution, care.
**prudent, -ente** *a* cautious, careful.

**prune** *f* (*fruit*) plum.
**pruneau, -x** *m* prune.
**prunier** *m* plum tree.
**psychiatre** *mf* psychiatrist.
**psychologique** *a* psychological.
**psychologue** *mf* psychologist.
**PTT** *abrév fpl* (*Postes, Télégraphes, Téléphones*) Post Office.
**pu** *voir* **pouvoir**.
**puanteur** *f* stink.
**public, -ique 1** *a* public. **2** *m* public; (*de spectacle*) audience; **en p.** in public.
**publication** *f* publication.
**publicité** *f* advertising, publicity; (*annonce*) advertisement; (*filmée*) commercial.
**publier** *vt* to publish.
**puce** *f* flea; (*d'ordinateur*) chip; **marché aux puces** flea market.
**puer 1** *vi* to stink. **2** *vt* to stink of.
**puéricultrice** *f* pediatric nurse.
**puis** *adv* then.
**puiser** *vt* to draw (**dans** from).
**puisque** *conj* since, as.
**puissance** *f* (*force, nation*) power.
**puissant, -ante** *a* powerful.
**puisse(s), puissent** *etc voir* **pouvoir**.
**puits** *m* well; (*de mine*) shaft.
**pull(-over)** *m* sweater.
**pulvérisateur** *m* spray.
**pulvériser** *vt* (*liquide*) to spray.
**punaise** *f* (*insecte*) bug; (*clou*) thumbtack.
**punir** *vt* to punish (**de qch** for sth, **pour avoir fait** for doing).
**punition** *f* punishment.
**pupille** *f* (*de l'œil*) pupil.
**pur, -e** *a* pure.
**purée** *f* purée; **p. (de pommes de terre)** mashed potatoes.
**pureté** *f* purity.
**puzzle** *m* (jigsaw) puzzle.
**p.-v.** *m inv* (*procès-verbal*) (traffic) ticket.
**pyjama** *m* pajamas; **un p.** a pair of pajamas.
**pylône** *m* pylon.
**pyramide** *f* pyramid.

# Q

**QI** *m inv abrév* (*quotient intellectuel*) IQ.
**quadrillé, -ée** *a* (*papier*) squared.
**quai** *m* (*de port*) (*pour passagers*) quay; (*pour marchandises*) wharf; (*de fleuve*) embankment; (*de gare*) platform.
**qualifié, -ée** *a* (*équipe etc*) that has qualified; (*ouvrier*) skilled.
**qualifier (se)** *vpr* (*en sport*) to qualify (**pour** for).
**qualité** *f* quality.
**quand** *conj* & *adv* when; **q. je viendrai** when I come; **q. même** all the same.
**quant à** *prép* as for.
**quantité** *f* quantity; **une q.** (*beaucoup*) a lot (**de** of).
**quarantaine** *f* **une q. (de)** about forty.
**quarante** *a* & *m* forty.
**quarantième** *a* & *mf* fortieth.
**quart** *m* quarter; **q. (de litre)** quarter liter (= one cup); **q. d'heure** quarter of an hour; **une heure et q.** an hour and a quarter; **il est une heure et q.** it's a quarter past *ou* after one; **une heure moins le q.** quarter to one.
**quartier**[1] *m* (*de ville*) neighborhood, district; (*chinois etc*) quarter; **de q.** (*cinéma etc*) local.
**quartier**[2] *m* (*de pomme*) quarter; (*d'orange*) segment.
**quartz** *m* **montre**/*etc* **à q.** quartz watch/*etc*.
**quatorze** *a* & *m* fourteen.
**quatre** *a* & *m* four; **q. heures** (*goûter*) afternoon snack.
**quatre-vingt(s)** *a* & *m* eighty; **q.-vingts ans** eighty years; **q.-vingt-un** eighty-one; **page quatre-vingt** page eighty.
**quatre-vingt-dix** *a* & *m* ninety.
**quatrième** *a* & *mf* fourth.
**que** (**qu'** *before a vowel or mute h*) **1** *conj* that; **je pense qu'elle restera** I think (that) she'll stay; **qu'elle**

vienne ou non** whether she comes or not; **qu'il s'en aille!** let him leave! ▪ **(ne) . . . q.** only; **tu n'as qu'un franc** you only have one franc. ▪ (*comparaison*) than; (*avec aussi, même, tel, autant*) as; **plus âgé q.** older than; **aussi sage q.** as wise as; **le même q.** the same as. **2** *adv* **(ce) qu'il est bête!** how silly he is! **3** *pron rel* (*chose*) that, which; (*personne*) that; (*temps*) when; **le livre q. j'ai** the book (that *ou* which) I have; **l'ami q. j'ai** the friend (that) I have; **un jour q.** one day when. **4** *pron interrogatif* what; **q. fait-il?, qu'est-ce qu'il fait?** what is he doing?; **qu'est-ce qui est dans ta poche?** what's in your pocket?

**quel, quelle 1** *a interrogatif* what, which; (*qui*) who; **q. livre/acteur?** what *ou* which book/actor?; **je sais q. est ton but** I know what your aim is. **2** *pron interrogatif* which (one); **q. est le meilleur?** which (one) is the best? **3** *a exclamatif* **q. idiot!** what a fool!

**quelconque** *a* any (whatever); **une raison q.** any reason (whatever).

**quelque 1** *a* **quelques femmes/livres/***etc* some *ou* a few women/books/*etc*; **les quelques amies qu'elle a** the few friends she has. **2** *pron* **q. chose** something; (*interrogation*) anything, something; **il a q. chose** (*un problème*) there's something the matter with him; **q. chose d'autre/de grand/***etc* something else/big/*etc*. **3** *adv* **q. part** somewhere; (*interrogation*) anywhere, somewhere.

**quelquefois** *adv* sometimes.

**quelques-uns, -unes** *pron pl* some.

**quelqu'un** *pron* someone; (*interrogation*) anyone, someone; **q. d'intelligent/***etc* someone smart/*etc*.

**question** *f* question; (*problème*) matter; **il est q. de** there's some talk about (**faire** doing); **il a été q. de vous** we *ou* they talked about you; **il n'en est pas q.** it's out of the question.

**questionner** *vt* to question (**sur** about).

**quête** *f* (*collecte*) collection; **faire la q.** = **quêter.**

**quêter** *vi* to collect money.

**queue[1]** *f* (*d'animal etc*) tail; (*de fleur*) stem; (*de fruit*) stalk; (*de poêle*) handle; (*de train*) rear; **q. de cheval** (*coiffure*) ponytail; **à la q. leu leu** in single file.

**queue[2]** *f* (*file*) line; **faire la q.** to line up.

**qui** *pron* (*personne*) who, that; (*interrogatif*) who; (*chose*) which, that; **l'homme q.** the man who *ou* that; **la maison q.** the house which *ou* that; **q. est là?** who's there?; **q. désirez-vous voir?, q. est-ce que vous désirez voir?** who do you want to see?; **la femme de q. je parle** the woman I'm talking about; **l'ami sur l'aide de q. je compte** the friend on whose help I rely; **à q. est ce livre?** whose book is this?

**quiche** *f* quiche.

**quille** *f* (*de jeu*) (bowling) pin; **jouer aux quilles** to bowl.

**quincaillerie** hardware store.

**quincaillier, -ière** *mf* hardware store owner.

**quinzaine** *f* **une q. (de)** about fifteen; **q. (de jours)** two weeks.

**quinze** *a & m* fifteen; **q. jours** two weeks.

**quinzième** *a & mf* fifteenth.

**quitte** *a* even (**envers** with).

**quitter 1** *vt* to leave; **q. qn des yeux** to take one's eyes off s.o. **2** *vi* **ne quittez pas!** (*au téléphone*) hold on!

**quitter (se)** *vpr* (*se séparer*) to part, say goodbye.

**quoi** *pron* what; (*après prép*) which; **à q. penses-tu?** what are you thinking about?; **de q. manger** something to eat; **de q. couper/**

**écrire** something to cut/write with; **il n'y a pas de q.!** (*en réponse à 'merci'*) don't mention it!

**quotidien, -ienne 1** *a* daily. **2** *m* daily (paper).

# R

**rabattre*** *vt* to pull down; (*refermer*) to close (down).

**rabattre (se)** *vpr* (*barrière*) to come down; (*après avoir doublé un véhicule*) to cut in.

**rabbin** *m* rabbi.

**rabot** *m* (*outil*) plane.

**raboter** *vt* to plane.

**raccommodage** *m* mending; darning.

**raccommoder** *vt* to mend; (*chaussette*) to darn.

**raccompagner** *vt* to see *ou* accompany back (home); **r. à la porte** to see to the door.

**raccord** *m* (*dispositif*) connection, connector; (*de papier peint*) seam.

**raccourci** *m* (*chemin*) short cut.

**raccourcir 1** *vt* to shorten. **2** *vi* to get shorter.

**raccrocher 1** *vt* (*objet tombé*) to hang back up; (*téléphone*) to put down. **2** *vi* (*au téléphone*) to hang up.

**race** *f* (*groupe ethnique*) race; (*animale*) breed.

**racheter** *vt* **r. un manteau/une voiture/***etc* to buy another coat/car/*etc*; **r. des chaussettes/du pain/***etc* to buy some more socks/bread/*etc*.

**racial, -e, -aux** *a* racial.

**racine** *f* root; **prendre r.** (*plante*) to take root.

**racisme** *m* racism.

**raciste** *a* & *mf* racist.

**racler** *vt* to scrape; (*enlever*) to scrape off; **se r. la gorge** to clear one's throat.

**raconter** *vt* (*histoire*) to tell; **r. qch à qn** (*vacances etc*) to tell s.o. about sth; **r. à qn que** to tell s.o. that.

**radar** *m* radar.

**radeau, -x** *m* raft.

**radiateur** *m* heater; (*de chauffage central, voiture*) radiator.

**radieux, -euse** *a* (*personne, visage*) beaming; (*soleil*) brilliant; (*temps*) glorious.

**radio[1]** *f* radio; (*poste*) radio (set); **à la r.** on the radio.

**radio[2]** *f* (*examen, photo*) X-ray; **passer une r.** to have an X-ray.

**radioactif, -ive** *a* radioactive.

**radiodiffuser** *vt* to broadcast (on the radio).

**radiographier** *vt* to X-ray.

**radis** *m* radish.

**radoucir (se)** *vpr* (*temps*) to become milder.

**radoucissement** *m* **r. (du temps)** milder weather.

**rafale** *f* (*vent*) gust.

**raffoler** *vi* **r. de** (*aimer*) to be crazy about.

**rafistoler** *vt Fam* to patch up.

**rafraîchir** *vt* to cool (down).

**rafraîchir (se)** *vpr* (*boire*) to refresh oneself; (*temps*) to get cooler.

**rafraîchissant, -ante** *a* refreshing.

**rafraîchissement** *m* (*de température*) cooling; (*boisson*) cold drink; **rafraîchissements** (*glaces etc*) refreshments.

**rage** *f* (*colère*) rage; (*maladie*) rabies; **r. de dents** violent toothache.

**ragoût** *m* stew.

**raid** *m* raid.

**raide** *a* (*rigide*) stiff; (*côte*) steep; (*cheveux*) straight; (*corde*) tight.

**raidir** *vt*, **se raidir** *vpr* to stiffen; (*corde*) to tighten.

**raie** *f* (*trait*) line; (*de tissu, zèbre*) stripe; (*de cheveux*) part.

**rail** *m* (*barre*) rail (*for train*).

**rainure** *f* groove.

**raisin** *m* **(grain de) r.** grape; **du r., des raisins** grapes; **r. sec** raisin.

**raison** *f* reason; **la r. de/pour laquelle . . .** the reason for/why . . . ; **en r. de** on account of; **avoir r.** to be right (**de faire** to do).

**raisonnable** *a* reasonable.
**raisonnement** *m* reasoning.
**raisonner 1** *vi* (*penser*) to reason. **2** *vt* **r. qn** to reason with s.o.
**rajeunir** *vt* to make (*s.o.*) (feel *ou* look) younger.
**ralenti** *m* **au r.** (*filmer*) in slow motion; **tourner au r.** (*moteur*) to turn over.
**ralentir** *vti* to slow down.
**rallonge** *f* (*de table*) extension; (*électrique*) extension cord.
**rallonger** *vti* to lengthen.
**rallumer** *vt* (*feu, pipe*) to light again; (*lampe*) to switch on again.
**rallye** *m* (*automobile*) rally.
**ramassage** *m* picking up; collection; gathering; **r. scolaire** school bus service.
**ramasser** *vt* (*prendre par terre, réunir*) to pick up; (*ordures, copies*) to collect; (*fruits, coquillages*) to gather.
**rame** *f* (*aviron*) oar; (*de métro*) train.
**ramener** *vt* to bring *ou* take (*s.o.*) back.
**ramer** *vi* to row.
**ramollir** *vt,* **se ramollir** *vpr* to soften.
**ramoner** *vt* (*cheminée*) to sweep.
**rampe** *f* (*d'escalier*) banister(s); **r. (d'accès)** ramp; **r. de lancement** (*de fusées*) launching pad.
**ramper** *vi* to crawl.
**ranch** *m* ranch.
**rançon** *f* (*argent*) ransom.
**rancune** *f* grudge; **garder r. à qn** to bear s.o. a grudge.
**rancunier, -ière** *a* spiteful.
**randonnée** *f* (*à pied*) hike; (*en voiture*) drive; (*en vélo*) ride.
**rang** *m* (*rangée*) row, line; (*classement*) rank; **se mettre en rang(s)** to line up (**par trois**/*etc* in threes/*etc*).
**rangé, -ée** *a* (*chambre etc*) tidy.
**rangée** *f* row, line.
**rangements** *mpl* (*placards*) storage space.
**ranger** *vt* (*papiers etc*) to put away; (*chambre etc*) to tidy (up); (*chiffres, mots*) to arrange; (*voiture*) to park.
**ranger (se)** *vpr* (*élèves etc*) to line up; (*s'écarter*) to stand aside; (*voiture*) to pull over.
**ranimer** *vt* (*réanimer*) to revive (*s.o.*); (*feu*) to poke, stir.
**rapace** *m* bird of prey.
**râpe** *f* (*à fromage etc*) grater.
**râper** *vt* (*fromage, carottes*) to grate.
**rapetisser** *vi* to get smaller.
**rapide 1** *a* fast, quick. **2** *m* (*train*) express (train).
**rapidement** *adv* fast, quickly.
**rapidité** *f* speed.
**rapiécer** *vt* to patch (up).
**rappeler** *vt* to call back; (*souvenir*) to recall; **r. qch à qn** to remind s.o. of sth.
**rappeler (se)** *vpr* to remember (**que** that).
**rapport** *m* (*lien*) connection; (*récit*) report; **rapports** (*entre personnes*) relations; **par r. à** compared to; **ça n'a aucun r.!** it has nothing to do with it!
**rapporter 1** *vt* to bring *ou* take back; (*profit*) to bring in; **se r. à** to relate to. **2** *vi* (*dénoncer*) *Fam* to tell tales; (*investissement*) to bring in a good return.
**rapporteur, -euse 1** *mf* telltale. **2** *m* (*en géométrie*) protractor.
**rapprocher** *vt* to bring closer (**de** to); (*chaise*) to pull up (**de** to).
**rapprocher (se)** *vpr* to come *ou* get closer (**de** to).
**raquette** *f* (*de tennis*) racket; (*de ping-pong*) paddle.
**rare** *a* rare; **il est r. que** (+ *subjonctif*) it's seldom that.
**rarement** *adv* rarely, seldom.
**ras, rase** *a* (*cheveux*) close-cropped; (*herbe, poil*) short; **en rase campagne** in the open country; **à r. bord** (*remplir*) to the brim.
**rasé, -ée** *a* **être bien r.** to have shaved; **mal r.** unshaven.
**raser** *vt* (*menton, personne*) to shave; (*barbe, moustache*) to

shave off; (*démolir*) to knock down; (*frôler*) to skim.
**raser (se)** *vpr* to (have a) shave.
**rasoir** *m* razor; (*électrique*) shaver.
**rassemblement** *m* gathering.
**rassembler** *vt* (*gens, objets*) to gather (together).
**rassembler (se)** *vpr* to gather.
**rassis,** *f* **rassie** *a* (*pain etc*) stale.
**rassurant, -ante** *a* reassuring.
**rassurer** *vt* to reassure; **rassure-toi** don't worry.
**rat** *m* rat.
**râteau, -x** *m* (*outil*) rake.
**rater** *vt* (*bus, cible etc*) to miss; (*travail, gâteau etc*) to ruin; (*examen*) to fail.
**ration** *f* ration.
**rationnement** *m* rationing.
**rationner** *vt* to ration.
**ratisser** *vt* (*allée etc*) to rake; (*feuilles etc*) to rake up.
**rattacher** *vt* (*lacets etc*) to tie up again.
**rattrapage** *m* **cours de r.** remedial class.
**rattraper** *vt* to catch; (*prisonnier*) to recapture; (*temps perdu*) to make up for; **r. qn** (*rejoindre*) to catch up with s.o.
**rature** *f* crossing out.
**raturer** *vt* to cross out.
**ravager** *vt* to devastate.
**ravages** *mpl* havoc; **faire des r.** to cause havoc *ou* widespread damage.
**ravaler** *vt* (*façade etc*) to clean (and restore).
**ravi, -ie** *a* delighted (**de** with, **de faire** to do).
**ravin** *m* ravine.
**ravioli** *mpl* ravioli.
**ravir** *vt* (*plaire*) to delight.
**ravissant, -ante** *a* beautiful.
**ravisseur, -euse** *mf* kidnapper.
**ravitaillement** *m* supplying; (*denrées*) supplies.
**ravitailler** *vt* to supply (**en** with).
**ravitailler (se)** *vpr* to stock up (with supplies).
**rayé, -ée** *a* scratched; (*tissu*) striped.
**rayer** *vt* (*érafler*) to scratch; (*mot etc*) to cross out.
**rayon** *m* (*de lumière, soleil*) ray; (*de cercle*) radius; (*de roue*) spoke; (*planche*) shelf; (*de magasin*) department.
**rayonnant, -ante** *a* (*visage etc*) beaming (**de** with).
**rayure** *f* scratch; (*bande*) stripe; **à rayures** striped.
**raz-de-marée** *m inv* tidal wave.
**re-, ré-** *préfixe* re-.
**réacteur** *m* (*d'avion*) jet engine; (*nucléaire*) reactor.
**réaction** *f* reaction; **avion à r.** jet (aircraft).
**réagir** *vi* to react (**contre** against, **à** to).
**réalisateur, -trice** *mf* (*de film*) director.
**réaliser** *vt* (*projet etc*) to carry out; (*rêve*) to fulfill; (*fabriquer*) to make; (*film*) to direct.
**réaliser (se)** *vpr* (*vœu*) to come true; (*projet*) to materialize.
**réaliste** *a* realistic.
**réalité** *f* reality; **en r.** in fact.
**réanimation** *f* **en r.** in intensive care.
**réanimer** *vt* to revive, resuscitate.
**rebond** *m* bounce.
**rebondir** *vi* to bounce.
**rebord** *m* **r. de (la) fenêtre** windowsill.
**reboucher** *vt* (*flacon*) to put the top back on; (*trou*) to fill in again.
**rébus** *m inv* rebus (*word guessing game*).
**récemment** *adv* recently.
**récent, -ente** *a* recent.
**réception** *f* (*réunion, de radio etc*) reception; (*d'hôtel*) reception (desk); **dès r. de** on receipt of.
**recette** *f* (*de cuisine*) recipe (**de** for); (*argent, bénéfice*) takings.
**recevoir* 1** *vt* to receive; (*accueillir*) to welcome; **être reçu (à)**

(*examen*) to pass. **2** *vi* to have guests.

**rechange (de)** *a* (*outil etc*) spare; **vêtements de r.** a change of clothes.

**recharge** *f* (*de stylo*) refill.

**recharger** *vt* (*fusil, appareil photo*) to reload; (*briquet, stylo*) to refill; (*batterie*) to recharge.

**réchaud** *m* (portable) stove.

**réchauffement** *m* (*de température*) rise (**de** in).

**réchauffer** *vt* to warm up; **se r.** to warm oneself up; (*temps*) to get warmer.

**recherche** *f* **la r., des recherches** (*scientifique etc*) research (**sur** on, into); **faire des recherches** to (do) research; (*enquêter*) to investigate.

**recherché, -ée** *a* **r. pour meurtre** wanted for murder.

**rechercher** *vt* (*personne, objet*) to search for.

**récif** *m* reef.

**récipient** *m* container.

**réciproque** *a* mutual.

**récit** *m* (*histoire*) story.

**récitation** *f* (*poème*) poem (learned by heart and recited aloud).

**réciter** *vt* to recite.

**réclamation** *f* complaint.

**réclame** *f* advertising; (*annonce*) advertisement; **en r.** on (special) offer.

**réclamer 1** *vt* (*demander*) to ask for (*sth*) back. **2** *vi* to complain.

**recoin** *m* nook.

**recoller** *vt* (*objet cassé*) to stick back together; (*enveloppe*) to reseal.

**récolte** *f* (*action*) harvest; (*produits*) crop.

**récolter** *vt* to harvest.

**recommandation** *f* recommendation.

**recommander** *vt* to recommend (**à** to, **pour** for); **r. à qn de faire** to recommend to s.o. to do; **lettre recommandée** certified letter; **en recommandé** (*envoyer*) by certi. mail.

**recommencer** *vti* to start again.

**récompense** *f* reward (**pour** for).

**récompenser** *vt* to reward (**de, pour** for).

**réconciliation** *f* reconciliation.

**réconcilier (se)** *vpr* to settle one's differences, make it up (**avec** with).

**reconduire*** *vt* **r. qn** to see s.o. back.

**réconfortant, -ante** *a* comforting.

**réconforter** *vt* to comfort.

**reconnaissance** *f* (*gratitude*) gratitude.

**reconnaissant, -ante** *a* grateful (**à qn de qch** to s.o. for sth).

**reconnaître*** *vt* to recognize (**à qch** by sth); (*admettre*) to admit (**que** that); **reconnu coupable** found guilty.

**reconstruire*** *vt* (*ville*) to rebuild.

**recopier** *vt* to copy out.

**record** *m* & *a inv* (*en sport etc*) record.

**recoudre*** *vt* (*bouton*) to sew (back) on; (*vêtement*) to stitch (up).

**recourbé, -ée** *a* (*clou etc*) bent; (*nez*) hooked.

**recouvrir*** *vt* (*livre, meuble etc*) to cover.

**récréation** *f* (*à l'école*) recess.

**recroquevillé, -ée** *a* (*personne, papier etc*) curled up.

**recrue** *f* recruit.

**rectangle** *m* rectangle.

**rectangulaire** *a* rectangular.

**rectification** *f* correction.

**rectifier** *vt* to correct.

**recto** *m* front (of the page).

**reçu, reçue 1** *pp of* **recevoir**. **2** *m* (*écrit*) receipt.

**recueil** *m* anthology, collection (**de** of).

**recueillir*** *vt* to collect; (*prendre chez soi*) to take (*s.o.*) in.

**reculer 1** *vi* to move back; (*véhicule*) to reverse. **2** *vt* to push back.

**reculons (à)** *adv* backwards.
**récupérer 1** *vt* (*objet prêté*) to get back. **2** *vi* to get one's strength back.
**récurer** *vt* (*casserole etc*) to scrub.
**recycler** *vt* (*matériaux*) to recycle.
**rédacteur, -trice** *mf* (*de journal*) editor; **r. en chef** editor(-in-chief).
**rédaction** *f* (*devoir de français*) essay, composition.
**redescendre 1** *vi* (*aux* **être**) to come *ou* go back down. **2** *vt* (*aux* **avoir**) to bring *ou* take back down.
**rediffusion** *f* (*de film etc*) repeat, rerun.
**rédiger** *vt* to write.
**redire*** *vt* to repeat.
**redonner** *vt* (*donner plus*) to give more (*bread etc*); **r. un franc**/*etc* to give another franc/*etc.*
**redoublant, -ante** *mf* student repeating a grade.
**redoublement** *m* repeating a grade.
**redoubler** *vti* **r. (une classe)** to repeat a grade.
**redoutable** *a* formidable.
**redouter** *vt* to dread (**de faire** doing).
**redresser** *vt* (*objet tordu etc*) to straighten (out).
**redresser (se)** *vpr* to sit up; (*debout*) to stand up.
**réduction** *f* reduction (**de** in); (*prix réduit*) discount; **en r.** (*copie, modèle*) small-scale.
**réduire*** *vt* to reduce (**à** to, **de** by); **r. en cendres** to reduce to ashes.
**réduit, -uite** *a* (*prix, vitesse*) reduced; (*modèle*) small-scale.
**réel, -elle** *a* real.
**réellement** *adv* really.
**réexpédier** *vt* (*faire suivre*) to forward (*letter*).
**refaire*** *vt* (*exercice, travail*) to do again, redo; (*chambre etc*) to redecorate.
**réfectoire** *m* refectory.
**référence** *f* reference.
**refermer** *vt,* **se refermer** *vpr* to close (again).
**réfléchir 1** *vt* (*image*) to reflect; **se r.** to be reflected; **verbe réfléchi** reflexive verb. **2** *vi* (*penser*) to think (**à** about).
**reflet** *m* (*image*) reflection; **reflets** (*couleurs*) highlights.
**refléter** *vt* (*image etc*) to reflect; **se r.** to be reflected.
**réflexe** *m* reflex.
**réflexion** *f* (*méditation*) thought; (*remarque*) remark.
**réforme** *f* (*changement*) reform.
**refrain** *m* (*de chanson*) chorus.
**réfrigérateur** *m* refrigerator.
**refroidir** *vti* to cool (down).
**refroidir (se)** *vpr* (*prendre froid*) to catch cold; (*temps*) to get cold.
**refroidissement** *m* (*rhume*) chill; **r. de la température** fall in the temperature.
**refuge** *m* refuge; (*pour piétons*) median; (*de montagne*) (mountain) hut.
**réfugié, -ée** *mf* refugee.
**réfugier (se)** *vpr* to take refuge.
**refus** *m* refusal.
**refuser 1** *vt* to refuse (**qch à qn** s.o. sth, **de faire** to do); (*candidat*) to fail. **2** *vi* to refuse.
**regagner** *vt* to regain, get back; (*revenir à*) to get back to.
**régaler (se)** *vpr* to have a feast.
**regard** *m* look; (*fixe*) stare; **jeter un r. sur** to glance at.
**regarder[1] 1** *vt* to look at; (*fixement*) to stare at; (*observer*) to watch; **r. qn faire** to watch s.o. do. **2** *vi* to look; to stare; to watch.
**regarder[2]** *vt* (*concerner*) to concern; **ça ne te regarde pas!** it's none of your business!
**régime[1]** *m* (*politique*) (form of) government; (*alimentaire*) diet; **se mettre au r.** to go on a diet; **suivre un r.** to be on a diet.
**régime[2]** *m* (*de bananes, dattes*) bunch.
**régiment** *m* (*soldats*) regiment.
**région** *f* region, area.
**régional, -e, -aux** *a* regional.

**registre** *m* register.
**réglable** *a* (*siège*) adjustable.
**réglage** *m* adjustment; (*de moteur*) tuning.
**règle** *f* rule; (*instrument*) ruler; **en r. générale** as a rule; **règles** (*de femme*) (monthly) period.
**règlement** *m* (*règles*) regulations; (*paiement*) payment; **contraire au r.** against the rules.
**régler 1** *vt* (*problème etc*) to settle; (*mécanisme*) to adjust; (*moteur*) to tune. **2** *vti* (*payer*) to pay; **r. qn** to settle up with s.o.
**réglisse** *f* licorice.
**règne** *m* (*de roi*) reign.
**régner** *vi* (*roi, silence*) to reign (**sur** over).
**regret** *m* regret; **à r.** with regret.
**regrettable** *a* unfortunate, regrettable.
**regretter** *vt* to regret; **r. qn** to miss s.o.; **r. que** (+ *subjonctif*) to be sorry that; **je (le) regrette** I'm sorry.
**regrouper** *vt*, **se regrouper** *vpr* to gather together.
**régularité** *f* regularity; steadiness.
**régulier, -ière** *a* regular; (*progrès, vitesse*) steady.
**régulièrement** *adv* regularly.
**rein** *m* kidney; **les reins** (*dos*) the (small of the) back.
**reine** *f* queen.
**rejeter** *vt* to throw back; (*refuser*) to reject.
**rejoindre*** *vt* (*famille, lieu etc*) to get back to; **r. qn** (*se joindre à*) to join s.o.; (*rattraper*) to catch up with s.o.
**rejoindre (se)** *vpr* (*personnes, routes*) to meet.
**réjouir (se)** *vpr* to be delighted (**de** at, about; **de faire** to do).
**réjouissances** *fpl* festivities.
**relâcher** *vt* (*corde etc*) to slacken; **r. qn** to release s.o.
**relais** *m* **prendre le r.** to take over (**de** from).
**relatif, -ive** *a* relative.
**relation** *f* relation(ship); (*ami*) acquaintance; **entrer en relations avec** to come into contact with.
**relativement** *adv* (*assez*) relatively.
**relayer** *vt* to take over from (*s.o.*).
**relayer (se)** *vpr* to take (it in) turns (**pour faire** to do).
**relevé** *m* (*de compteur*) reading; **r. de compte** (bank) statement.
**relever** *vt* to raise; (*personne tombée*) to help up; (*col*) to turn up; (*manches*) to roll up; (*compteur*) to read.
**relever (se)** *vpr* (*personne tombée*) to get up.
**relief** *m* (*forme*) relief; **en r.** (*cinéma*) three-D.
**relier** *vt* to connect (**à** to); (*livre*) to bind.
**religieux, -euse 1** *a* religious. **2** *f* nun.
**religion** *f* religion.
**relire*** *vt* to read again, reread.
**reliure** *f* (*de livre*) binding.
**reluire*** *vi* to shine.
**remarquable** *a* remarkable (**par** for).
**remarquablement** *adv* remarkably.
**remarque** *f* remark; (*écrite*) note.
**remarquer** *vt* to notice (**que** that); **faire r.** to point out (**à** to, **que** that); **se faire r.** to attract attention; **remarque!** mind you!, you know!
**rembobiner** *vt*, **se rembobiner** *vpr* (*bande*) to rewind.
**rembourré, -ée** *a* (*fauteuil etc*) padded.
**remboursement** *m* repayment; refund.
**rembourser** *vt* to pay back, repay; (*billet*) to refund.
**remède** *m* cure; (*médicament*) medicine.
**remerciements** *mpl* thanks.
**remercier** *vt* to thank (**de qch, pour qch** for sth); **je vous remercie d'être venu** thank you for coming.
**remettre*** *vt* to put back; (*vêtement*) to put back on; (*donner*) to hand over (**à** to); (*démission,

*devoir*) to hand in; (*différer*) to postpone (**à** until); **r. en question** to call into question; **r. en état** to repair; **se r. à** (*activité*) to go back to; **se r. à faire** to start to do again; **se r. de** (*chagrin, maladie*) to get over.

**remise** *f* (*rabais*) discount.

**remonte-pente** *m* ski lift.

**remonter 1** *vi* (*aux* **être**) to come *ou* go back up; **r. dans** (*voiture*) to get back in(to); (*bus, train*) to get back on(to); **r. sur** (*cheval, vélo*) to get back on(to). **2** *vt* (*aux* **avoir**) (*escalier, pente*) to come *ou* go back up; (*porter*) to bring *ou* take back up; (*montre*) to wind; (*relever*) to raise; (*col*) to turn up; (*objet démonté*) to put back together.

**remords** *m* & *mpl* remorse; **avoir des r.** to feel remorse.

**remorque** *f* (*de voiture etc*) trailer; **prendre en r.** to tow; **en r.** in tow.

**remorquer** *vt* to tow.

**remorqueur** *m* tug(boat).

**remplaçant, -ante** *mf* (*personne*) replacement; (*enseignant*) substitute teacher; (*en sport*) reserve.

**remplacement** *m* replacement; **assurer le r. de qn** to stand in for s.o.

**remplacer** *vt* to replace (**par** with, by); (*succéder à*) to take over from.

**rempli, -ie** *a* full (**de** of).

**remplir** *vt* to fill (up) (**de** with); (*fiche etc*) to fill in *ou* out.

**remplir (se)** *vpr* to fill (up).

**remporter** *vt* (*objet*) to take back; (*prix, victoire*) to win.

**remuant, -ante** *a* (*enfant*) restless.

**remuer 1** *vt* to move; (*café etc*) to stir; (*salade*) to toss. **2** *vi* to move; (*gigoter*) to fidget.

**renard** *m* fox.

**rencontre** *f* meeting; (*en sport*) match, game; **aller à la r. de qn** to go to meet s.o.

**rencontrer** *vt* to meet; (*équipe*) to play.

**rencontrer (se)** *vpr* to meet.

**rendez-vous** *m inv* appointment; (*d'amoureux*) date; (*lieu*) meeting place; **donner r.-vous à qn** to make an appointment with s.o.

**rendormir* (se)** *vpr* to go back to sleep.

**rendre 1** *vt* to give back; (*monnaie*) to give; (*vomir*) to bring up; **r. célèbre/plus grand/***etc* to make famous/bigger/*etc*. **2** *vti* (*vomir*) to throw up.

**rendre (se)** *vpr* to surrender (**à qn** to s.o.); (*aller*) to go (**à** to); **se r. utile/***etc* to make oneself useful/*etc*.

**rênes** *fpl* reins.

**renfermé** *m* **sentir le r.** (*chambre etc*) to smell stuffy.

**renfermer** *vt* to contain.

**renflement** *m* bulge.

**renforcer** *vt* to strengthen.

**renforts** *mpl* (*troupes*) reinforcements.

**renifler** *vti* to sniff.

**renne** *m* reindeer.

**renommé, -ée** *a* famous (**pour** for).

**renommée** *f* fame.

**renoncer** *vi* **r. à qch/à faire** to give up sth/doing.

**renouveler** *vt* to renew; (*erreur, question*) to repeat.

**renouveler (se)** *vpr* (*incident*) to happen again.

**renseignement** *m* (piece of) information; **des renseignements** information; **les renseignements** (*au téléphone*) directory assistance, information.

**renseigner** *vt* to inform, give some information to (**sur** about).

**renseigner (se)** *vpr* to find out, inquire (**sur** about).

**rentrée** *f* return; **r. (des classes)** beginning of the school year.

**rentrer 1** *vi* (*aux* **être**) to go *ou* come back; (*chez soi*) to go *ou* come (back) home; (*entrer de nouveau*) to go *ou* come back in; (*élèves*) to go back to school; **r. dans** to go *ou* come back into; (*pays*) to return to; (*heurter*) to crash into; (*s'emboîter* *dans*) to fit into. **2** *vt* (*aux* **avoir**) to bring *ou* take in; (*voiture*) to put away; (*chemise*) to tuck in; (*griffes*) to draw in.

**renverse (à la)** *adv* (*tomber*) backwards.

**renverser** *vt* (*mettre à l'envers*) to turn upside down; (*faire tomber*) to knock over; (*piéton*) to knock down; (*liquide*) to spill.

**renverser (se)** *vpr* (*vase etc*) to fall over; (*liquide*) to spill.

**renvoi** *m* (*d'un employé*) dismissal; (*rot*) burp.

**renvoyer*** *vt* to send back; (*employé*) to dismiss; (*élève*) to expel; (*balle etc*) to throw back.

**réorganiser** *vt* to reorganize.

**repaire** *m* den.

**répandre** *vt* (*liquide*) to spill; (*nouvelle*) to spread; (*odeur*) to give off; (*lumière, larmes*) to shed; (*gravillons etc*) to scatter.

**répandre (se)** *vpr* (*nouvelle*) to spread; (*liquide*) to spill; **se r. dans** (*fumée, odeur*) to spread through.

**répandu, -ue** *a* (*opinion etc*) widespread.

**reparaître** *vi* to reappear.

**réparateur, -trice** *mf* repairer.

**réparation** *f* repair; **en r.** under repair.

**réparer** *vt* to repair, mend; (*erreur*) to correct.

**repartir*** *vi* (*aux* **être**) to set off again; (*s'en retourner*) to go back.

**répartir** *vt* (*partager*) to share (out).

**repas** *m* meal; **prendre un r.** to have a meal.

**repassage** *m* ironing.

**repasser 1** *vi* to come *ou* go back. **2** *vt* (*traverser*) to go back over; (*leçon*) to go over; (*film*) to show again; (*linge*) to iron.

**repêcher** *vt* (*objet*) to fish out.

**repentir* (se)** *vpr* to be sorry (**de** for).

**repère** *m* (guide) mark; **point de r.** (*espace, temps*) landmark.

**repérer** *vt* to locate.

**repérer (se)** *vpr* to get one's bearings.

**répertoire** *m* **r. d'adresses** address book.

**répéter** *vti* to repeat; (*pièce de théâtre*) to rehearse.

**répéter (se)** *vpr* (*événement*) to happen again.

**répétitif, -ive** *a* repetitive.

**répétition** *f* repetition; (*au théâtre*) rehearsal.

**replacer** *vt* to put back.

**repli** *m* fold.

**replier** *vt* to fold (up); (*couverture*) to fold back; (*ailes, jambes*) to tuck in.

**replier (se)** *vpr* (*siège*) to fold up; (*couverture*) to fold back.

**réplique** *f* (sharp) reply; (*au théâtre*) lines.

**répliquer 1** *vt* to reply (sharply) (**que** that). **2** *vi* to answer back.

**répondeur** *m* (*téléphonique*) answering machine.

**répondre 1** *vi* to answer; (*être impertinent*) to answer back; (*réagir*) to respond (**à** to); **r. à qn** to answer s.o.; (*avec impertinence*) to answer s.o. back; **r. à** (*lettre, question*) to answer. **2** *vt* **r. que** to answer that.

**réponse** *f* answer.

**reportage** *m* (news) report; (*en direct*) (live) commentary.

**reporter**[1] *vt* to take back; (*différer*) to put off (**à** until).

**reporter**[2] *m* reporter.

**repos** *m* rest; (*tranquillité*) peace (and quiet); **jour de r.** day off.

**reposant, -ante** *a* restful.

**reposer** *vt* (*objet*) to put back down; (*délasser*) to relax.

**reposer (se)** *vpr* to rest.

**repousser 1** *vt* to push back; (*écarter*) to push away; (*différer*) to put off. **2** *vi* (*cheveux, feuilles*) to grow again.

**reprendre* 1** *vt* (*objet*) to take back; (*évadé*) to recapture; (*souffle, forces*) to get back; (*activité*) to take up again; (*refrain*) to take up; **r. de la viande/un œuf/***etc* to take (some) more meat/another egg/*etc*. **2** *vi* (*recommencer*) to start (up) (again); (*affaires*) to pick up; (*dire*) to go on.

**reprendre (se)** *vpr* to correct oneself; **s'y r. à deux fois** to give it another try.

**représentant, -ante** *mf* representative; **r. de commerce** (traveling) salesman *ou* saleswoman.

**représentation** *f* (*au théâtre*) performance.

**représenter** *vt* to represent; (*pièce de théâtre*) to perform.

**reprise** *f* (*d'émission de télévision*) rerun, repeat; (*de tissu*) mend; *Boxe* round; (*économique*) recovery; (*pour nouvel achat*) trade-in; **à plusieurs reprises** on several occasions.

**repriser** *vt* (*chaussette etc*) to mend.

**reproche** *m* criticism; **faire des reproches à qn** to criticize s.o.

**reprocher** *vt* **r. qch à qn** to criticize s.o. for sth.

**reproduction** *f* breeding; (*copie*) copy.

**reproduire*** *vt* (*modèle etc*) to copy.

**reproduire (se)** *vpr* (*animaux*) to breed; (*incident etc*) to happen again.

**reptile** *m* reptile.

**républicain, -aine** *a* & *mf* republican.

**république** *f* republic.

**réputation** *f* reputation; **avoir la r. d'être** to have a reputation for being.

**requin** *m* (*poisson*) shark.

**rescapé, -ée** *mf* survivor.

**réseau, -x** *m* network.

**réservation** *f* reservation, booking.

**réserve** *f* (*provision*) stock, reserve; (*entrepôt*) storeroom; **en r.** in reserve; **r. naturelle** nature reve.

**vé, -ée** *a* (*personne, place*) d.

**réserver** *vt* (*garder*) to save, reserve (**à** for); (*place, table*) to book, reserve; **se r. pour** to save oneself for.

**réservoir** *m* (*citerne*) tank; **r. d'essence** gas tank.

**résidence** *f* residence; **r. secondaire** second home.

**résidentiel, -ielle** *a* (*quartier*) residential.

**résider** *vi* to be resident (**à, en, dans** in).

**résigner (se)** *vpr* to resign oneself (**à qch** to sth, **à faire** to doing).

**résistance** *f* resistance (**à** to); (*électrique*) (heating) element; **plat de r.** main dish.

**résistant, -ante** *a* tough; **r. à la chaleur** heat-resistant; **r. au choc** shockproof.

**résister** *vi* **r. à** to resist; (*chaleur, fatigue*) to withstand.

**résolu, -ue** *a* determined (**à faire** to do).

**résolution** *f* (*décision*) decision.

**résonner** *vi* (*cris etc*) to ring out; (*salle*) to echo (**de** with).

**résoudre*** *vt* (*problème*) to solve; (*difficulté*) to clear up.

**respect** *m* respect (**pour, de** for).

**respecter** *vt* to respect.

**respectueux, -euse** *a* respectful (**envers** to).

**respiration** *f* breathing; (*haleine*) breath.

**respirer 1** *vi* to breathe; (*reprendre haleine*) to get one's breath back. **2** *vt* to breathe (in).

**resplendissant, -ante** *a* (*visage*) glowing (**de** with).

**responsabilité** *f* responsibility.

**responsable 1** *a* responsible (**de qch** for sth, **devant qn** to s.o.). **2** *mf* (*chef*) person in charge; (*coupable*) person responsible (**de** for).

**ressemblance** *f* likeness (**avec** to).

**ressembler** *vi* **r. à** to look *ou* be like.

**ressembler (se)** *vpr* to look *ou* be alike.

**ressentir*** *vt* to feel.

**resserrer** *vt*, **se resserrer** *vpr* (*nœud etc*) to tighten.

**resservir*** *vi* (*outil etc*) to come in useful (again); **se r. de** (*plat*) to have another helping of.

**ressort** *m* (*objet*) spring.

**ressortir*** *vi* (*aux* **être**) to go *ou* come back out; (*se voir*) to stand out.

**ressources** *fpl* (*moyens, argent*) resources.

**restaurant** *m* restaurant.

**restaurer** *vt* (*réparer*) to restore.

**reste** *m* rest (**de** of); **restes** (*de repas*) leftovers; **un r. de fromage**/*etc* some left-over cheese/*etc*.

**rester** *vi* (*aux* **être**) to stay; (*calme, jeune etc*) to keep, stay; (*subsister*) to be left; **il reste du pain**/*etc* there's some bread/*etc* left (over); **il me reste une minute** I have one minute left; **l'argent qui lui reste** the money he *ou* she has left.

**restreindre*** *vt* to limit (**à** to).

**résultat** *m* (*score, d'examen etc*) results; (*conséquence*) outcome, result.

**résumé** *m* summary.

**résumer** *vt* to summarize; (*situation*) to sum up.

**rétablir** *vt* to restore.

**rétablir (se)** *vpr* (*malade*) to recover.

**rétablissement** *m* (*de malade*) recovery.

**retard** *m* (*sur un programme etc*) delay; **en r.** late; **en r. dans qch** behind in sth; **en r. sur qn/qch** behind s.o./sth; **rattraper son r.** to catch up; **avoir du r.** to be late; (*sur un programme*) to be behind; (*montre*) to be slow; **avoir une heure de r.** to be an hour late.

**retardataire** *mf* latecomer.

**retarder 1** *vt* to delay; (*date, montre*) to put back; **r. qn** (*dans une activité*) to put s.o. behind. **2** *vi* (*montre*) to be slow; **r. de cinq minutes** to be five minutes slow.

**retenir*** *vt* (*empêcher d'agir*) to hold back; (*souffle*) to hold; (*réserver*) to book; (*se souvenir de*) to remember; (*fixer*) to hold (in place); (*chiffre*) to carry; (*chaleur, odeur*) to retain; **r. qn prisonnier** to keep s.o. prisoner.

**retenir (se)** *vpr* (*se contenir*) to restrain oneself; **se r. de faire** to stop oneself (from) doing; **se r. à** to cling to.

**retentir** *vi* to ring (out) (**de** with).

**retenue** *f* (*punition*) detention.

**retirer** *vt* (*sortir*) to take out; (*ôter*) to take off; (*éloigner*) to take away; **r. qch à qn** (*permis etc*) to take sth away from s.o.

**retomber** *vi* to fall (again); (*pendre*) to hang (down); (*après un saut etc*) to land.

**retouche** *f* (*de vêtement*) alteration.

**retoucher** *vt* (*vêtement*) to alter.

**retour** *m* return; **être de r.** to be back (**de** from); **à mon retour** when I get *ou* got back.

**retourner 1** *vt* (*aux* **avoir**) (*matelas, steak etc*) to turn over; (*terre etc*) to turn; (*vêtement, sac etc*) to turn inside out. **2** *vi* (*aux* **être**) to go back, return.

**retourner (se)** *vpr* to turn around, look around; (*sur le dos*) to turn over; (*voiture*) to overturn.

**retraite** *f* (*d'employé*) retirement; (*pension*) (retirement) pension; **prendre sa r.** to retire; **à la r.** retired.

**retraité, -ée 1** *a* retired. **2** *mf* senior citizen, pensioner.

**retransmettre** *vt* to broadcast.

**retransmission** *f* broadcast.

**rétrécir** *vi* (*au lavage*) to shrink.

**rétrécir (se)** *vpr* (*rue etc*) to narrow.

**rétro** *a inv* (*personne, idée etc*) old-fashioned.

**retrousser** *vt* (*manches*) to roll up.

**retrouver** *vt* to find (again); (*rejoindre*) to meet (again); (*forces, santé*) to get back; (*se rappeler*) to recall.

**retrouver (se)** *vpr* to find oneself

(back); (*se rencontrer*) to meet (again); **s'y r.** to find one's way.
**rétroviseur** *m* (*de véhicule*) rear-view mirror.
**réunion** *f* (*séance*) meeting.
**réunir** *vt* (*objets*) to gather; (*convoquer*) to call together.
**réunir (se)** *vpr* to meet, get together.
**réussi, -ie** *a* successful.
**réussir 1** *vi* to succeed (**à faire** in doing); **r. à** (*examen*) to pass; **r. à qn** (*aliment*, *climat*) to agree with s.o. **2** *vt* to make a success of.
**réussite** *f* success.
**revanche** *f* (*en sport*) rematch; **en r.** on the other hand.
**rêve** *m* dream; **faire un r.** to have a dream (**de** about); **maison/***etc* **de r.** dream house/*etc*.
**réveil** *m* (*pendule*) alarm (clock); **à son r.** when he wakes (up) *ou* woke (up).
**réveillé, -ée** *a* awake.
**réveiller** *vt*, **se réveiller** *vpr* to wake (up).
**réveillon** *m* midnight supper (*on Christmas Eve or New Year's Eve*).
**révéler** *vt* to reveal (**que** that).
**revenant** *m* ghost.
**revendication** *f* claim; demand.
**revendiquer** *vt* to claim; (*exiger*) to demand.
**revenir*** *vi* (*aux* **être**) to come back; (*coûter*) to cost (**à qn** s.o.); **r. à** (*activité*, *sujet*) to go back to; **r. à qn** (*forces*, *mémoire*) to come back to s.o.; **r. à soi** to come to; **r. de** (*surprise*) to get over; **r. sur** (*décision*, *promesse*) to go back on.
**revenu** *m* income (**de** from).
**rêver 1** *vi* to dream (**de** of, **de faire** of doing). **2** *vt* to dream (**que** that).
**revers** *m* (*de veste*) lapel; (*de pantalon*) cuff.
**revêtement** *m* (*de route etc*) surface.
**rêveur, -euse** *mf* dreamer.
**revient** *m* **prix de r.** (production) cost.
**réviser** *vt* (*leçon*) to revise; (*machine*, *voiture*) to service.
**révision** *f* revision; service.
**revoir*** *vt* to see (again); (*texte*, *leçon*) to revise; **au r.** goodbye.
**révoltant, -ante** *a* revolting.
**révolte** *f* rebellion, revolt.
**révolté, -ée** *mf* rebel.
**révolter** *vt* to sicken.
**révolter (se)** *vpr* to rebel (**contre** against).
**révolution** *f* revolution.
**révolutionnaire** *a* & *mf* revolutionary.
**revolver** *m* gun.
**revue** *f* (*magazine*) magazine.
**rez-de-chaussée** *m inv* ground floor, first floor.
**rhabiller (se)** *vpr* to get dressed again.
**rhinocéros** *m* rhinoceros.
**rhubarbe** *f* rhubarb.
**rhum** *m* rum.
**rhumatisme** *m* rheumatism; **avoir des rhumatismes** to have rheumatism.
**rhume** *m* cold; **r. des foins** hay fever.
**ri, riant** *pp* & *pres p of* **rire**.
**ricaner** *vi* to snicker.
**riche 1** *a* rich. **2** *mf* rich person; **les riches** the rich.
**richesse** *f* wealth; **richesses** (*trésor*) riches.
**ricocher** *vi* to ricochet.
**ricochet** *m* (*de pierre*) ricochet.
**ride** *f* wrinkle.
**ridé, -ée** *a* wrinkled.
**rideau, -x** *m* curtain; (*de magasin*) shutter.
**ridicule** *a* ridiculous.
**ridiculiser (se)** *vpr* to make a fool of oneself.
**rien 1** *pron* nothing; **il ne sait r.** he knows nothing, he doesn't know anything; **r. du tout** nothing at all; **r. d'autre/de bon/***etc* nothing else/good/*etc*; **de r.!** (*je vous en prie*) don't mention it!; **ça ne fait r.** it doesn't matter; **r. que** just. **2** *m* (mere) nothing.

**rigide** *a* rigid; (*carton, muscle*) stiff.
**rigoler** *vi Fam* to laugh; (*s'amuser*) to have fun.
**rigolo, -ote** *a Fam* funny.
**rime** *f* rhyme.
**rimer** *vi* to rhyme (**avec** with).
**rinçage** *m* rinsing.
**rincer** *vt* to rinse; (*verre*) to rinse (out).
**ring** *m* (boxing) ring.
**rire*** **1** *vi* to laugh (**de** at); (*s'amuser*) to have a good time; (*plaisanter*) to joke; **pour r.** as a joke. **2** *m* laugh; **rires** laughter; **le fou r.** the giggles.
**risque** *m* risk (**de faire** of doing, **à faire** in doing); **assurance tous risques** comprehensive insurance.
**risqué, -ée** *a* risky.
**risquer** *vt* to risk; **r. de faire** to stand a good chance of doing.
**rivage** *m* shore.
**rival, -e, -aux** *a* & *mf* rival.
**rivaliser** *vi* to compete (**avec** with, **de** in).
**rive** *f* (*de fleuve*) bank; (*de lac*) shore.
**rivière** *f* river.
**riz** *m* rice; **r. au lait** rice pudding.
**RN** *abrév* = **route nationale.**
**robe** *f* (*de femme*) dress; **r. du soir/de mariée** evening/wedding dress; **r. de chambre** bathrobe.
**robinet** *m* tap, faucet; **eau du r.** tap water.
**robot** *m* robot.
**robuste** *a* sturdy.
**roche** *f*, **rocher** *m* rock.
**rocheux, -euse** *a* rocky.
**rock** *m* (*musique*) rock.
**roder** *vt* (*moteur, voiture*) to break in.
**rôder** *vi* to prowl (about).
**rôdeur, -euse** *mf* prowler.
**rognon** *m* (*d'animal*) kidney.
**roi** *m* king.
**rôle** *m* (*au théâtre*) role, part; (*d'un père etc*) job; **à tour de r.** in turn.
**romain, -aine** *a* & *mf* Roman.
**roman** *m* novel; **r. d'aventures** adventure story.
**romancier, -ière** *mf* novelist.
**romantique** *a* romantic.
**rompre* (se)** *vpr* (*corde etc*) to break; (*digue*) to burst.
**ronces** *fpl* brambles.
**ronchonner** *vi Fam* to grumble.
**rond, ronde 1** *a* round; **dix francs tout r.** ten francs exactly. **2** *m* (*cercle*) circle, ring; **en r.** (*s'asseoir etc*) in a ring *ou* circle; **tourner en r.** to go round and round.
**ronde** *f* (*de soldat*) round; (*de policier*) beat, round.
**rondelle** *f* (*tranche*) slice.
**rondin** *m* log.
**rond-point** *m* (*pl* **ronds-points**) traffic circle.
**ronflement** *m* snore; **ronflements** snoring.
**ronfler** *vi* to snore.
**ronger** *vt* to gnaw (at); (*ver, mer, rouille*) to eat into (*sth*); **se r. les ongles** to bite one's nails.
**ronronnement** *m* purr(ing).
**ronronner** *vi* to purr.
**rosbif** *m* **du r.** roast beef; (*à rôtir*) (beef) roast; **un r.** (beef) roast.
**rose 1** *f* (*fleur*) rose. **2** *a* & *m* (*couleur*) pink.
**rosé** *a* & *m* (*vin*) rosé.
**roseau, -x** *m* (*plante*) reed.
**rosée** *f* dew.
**rosier** *m* rose bush.
**rossignol** *m* nightingale.
**rot** *m Fam* burp.
**roter** *vi Fam* to burp.
**rôti** *m* **du r.** roast; (*cuit*) roast/meat roast; **un r.** a roast; **r. de porc** pork roast.
**rotin** *m* cane.
**rôtir** *vti*, **se rôtir** *vpr* to roast; **faire r.** to roast.
**roue** *f* wheel.
**rouge 1** *a* red; (*fer*) red-hot. **2** *m* (*couleur*) red; **r. (à lèvres)** lipstick; **le feu est au r.** the (traffic) light is red.
**rouge-gorge** *m* (*pl* **rouges-gorges**) robin.

**rougeole** *f* measles.
**rougir** *vi* (*de honte*) to blush; (*de colère*) to flush (**de** with).
**rouille** *f* rust.
**rouillé, -ée** *a* rusty.
**rouiller** *vi*, **se rouiller** *vpr* to rust.
**roulant, -ante** *a* (*escalier*) moving; (*meuble*) on wheels.
**rouleau, -x** *m* (*outil*) roller; (*de papier etc*) roll; **r. à pâtisserie** rolling pin; **r. compresseur** steamroller.
**rouler 1** *vt* to roll; (*brouette*) to push; (*crêpe, ficelle etc*) to roll up. **2** *vi* to roll; (*train, voiture*) to go; (*conducteur*) to drive.
**rouler (se)** *vpr* to roll; **se r. dans** (*couverture etc*) to roll oneself (up) in.
**roulette** *f* (*de meuble*) castor; (*de dentiste*) drill.
**roulotte** *f* (*de gitan*) caravan.
**round** *m Boxe* round.
**rouspéter** *vi Fam* to complain.
**rousse** *voir* **roux.**
**rousseur** *f* **tache de r.** freckle.
**roussir** *vt* (*brûler*) to scorch.
**route** *f* road (**de** to); (*itinéraire*) way; **r. nationale/départementale** main/secondary road; **en r.!** let's go!; **par la r.** by road; **mettre en r.** (*voiture etc*) to start (up); **se mettre en r.** to set out (**pour** for); **une heure de r.** an hour's drive; **bonne r.!** have a good trip!
**routier, -ière 1** *a* **carte/sécurité routière** road map/safety. **2** *m* (long-distance) truck driver.
**roux, rousse 1** *a* (*cheveux*) red; (*personne*) red-haired. **2** *mf* redhead.
**royal, -e, -aux** *a* (*famille, palais*) royal.
**royaume** *m* kingdom.
**ruban** *m* ribbon; **r. adhésif** (adhesive) tape.
**rubéole** *f* German measles.
**rubis** *m* ruby; (*montre*) jewel.
**ruche** *f* (bee)hive.
**rude** *a* (*pénible*) tough; (*hiver, voix*) harsh; (*grossier*) crude; (*rêche*) rough.
**rudement** *adv* (*parler, traiter*) harshly; (*très*) *Fam* awfully.
**rue** *f* street; **à la r.** (*sans domicile*) on the streets.
**ruelle** *f* alley(way).
**ruer** *vi* (*cheval*) to kick (out).
**ruer (se)** *vpr* to rush (**sur** at).
**rugby** *m* rugby.
**rugbyman,** *pl* **-men** *m* rugby player.
**rugir** *vi* to roar.
**rugissement** *m* roar.
**rugueux, -euse** *a* rough.
**ruine** *f* ruin; **en r.** in ruins; **tomber en r.** (*bâtiment*) to become a ruin, crumble; (*mur*) to crumble.
**ruiner** *vt* (*personne, santé etc*) to ruin; **se r.** to be(come) ruined, ruin oneself.
**ruisseau, -x** *m* stream.
**ruisseler** *vi* to stream (**de** with).
**rural, -e, -aux** *a* **vie/école/***etc* **rurale** country life/school/*etc*.
**ruse** *f* (*subterfuge*) trick; **la r.** (*habileté*) cunning.
**rusé, -ée** *a* & *mf* cunning (person).
**russe 1** *a* & *mf* Russian. **2** *m* (*langue*) Russian.
**rythme** *m* rhythm; (*de travail*) rate; **au r. de trois par jour** at a rate of three a day.
**rythmé, -ée** *a* rhythmical.

# S

**sa** *voir* **son.**
**sable** *m* sand.
**sabler** *vt* (*rue*) to sand.
**sablier** *m* (*de cuisine*) egg timer.
**sablonneux, -euse** *a* sandy.
**sabot** *m* (*de cheval etc*) hoof; (*chaussure*) clog; **s. (de Denver)** (Denver) boot.
**sac** *m* bag; (*grand et en toile*) sack, tote; **s. (à main)** handbag; **s. à dos** rucksack, backpack.
**saccadé, -ée** *a* jerky.
**saccager** *vt* (*détruire*) to wreck.

**sachant, sache(s), sachent** *etc voir* **savoir**.
**sachet** *m* (small) bag; **s. de thé** teabag.
**sacoche** *f* bag; (*de vélo*) saddlebag.
**sacré, -ée** *a* (*saint*) sacred; **un s. menteur/***etc Fam* a damned liar/*etc.*
**sacrifice** *m* sacrifice.
**sacrifier** *vt* to sacrifice (**à** to, **pour** for); **se s.** to sacrifice oneself.
**sage** *a* wise; (*enfant*) good.
**sage-femme** *f* (*pl* **sages-femmes**) midwife.
**sagement** *adv* wisely; (*avec calme*) quietly.
**saignant, -ante** *a* (*viande*) rare.
**saignement** *m* bleeding; **s. de nez** nosebleed.
**saigner** *vti* to bleed.
**sain, saine** *a* healthy; **s. et sauf** safe and sound.
**saint, sainte 1** *a* holy; **s. Jean** Saint John; **la Sainte Vierge** the Blessed Virgin. **2** *mf* saint.
**Saint-Sylvestre** *f* New Year's Eve.
**sais, sait** *voir* **savoir.**
**saisir** *vt* to grab (hold of); (*occasion*) to jump at; (*comprendre*) to understand; **se s. de** to grab (hold of).
**saison** *f* season.
**salade** *f* (*laitue*) lettuce; **s. (verte)** (green) salad; **s. de fruits/***etc* fruit/*etc* salad.
**saladier** *m* salad bowl.
**salaire** *m* wage(s).
**salarié, -ée** *mf* wage earner.
**sale** *a* dirty; (*dégoûtant*) filthy.
**salé, -ée** *a* (*goût, plat*) salty; (*aliment*) salted.
**saler** *vt* to salt.
**saleté** *f* dirtiness; filthiness; (*crasse*) dirt, filth; **saletés** (*détritus*) garbage.
**salière** *f* saltshaker.
**salir** *vt* to (make) dirty.
**salir (se)** *vpr* to get dirty.
**salissant, -ante** *a* dirty; (*étoffe*) that shows the dirt.
**salive** *f* saliva.
**salle** *f* room; (*très grande*) hall; (*de théâtre*) theater, auditorium; (*de cinéma*) cinema; (*d'hôpital*) ward; **s. à manger** dining room; **s. de bain(s)** bathroom; **s. d'opération** operating room.
**salon** *m* sitting room, lounge; (*exposition*) show.
**salopette** *f* (*d'enfant, d'ouvrier*) overalls.
**saluer** *vt* to greet; (*de la main*) to wave to; (*de la tête*) to nod to.
**salut 1** *m* greeting; wave; nod. **2** *int* hello!, hi!; (*au revoir*) bye!
**samedi** *m* Saturday.
**sandale** *f* sandal.
**sandwich** *m* sandwich; **s. au fromage/***etc* cheese/*etc* sandwich.
**sandwicherie** *f* sandwich shop.
**sang** *m* blood.
**sang-froid** *m* self-control; **garder son s.-froid** to keep calm; **avec s.-froid** calmly.
**sanglant, -ante** *a* bloody.
**sanglier** *m* wild boar.
**sanglot** *m* sob.
**sangloter** *vi* to sob.
**sanguin** *a* **groupe s.** blood group.
**sans** *prép* without; **s. faire** without doing; **s. qu'il le sache** without him *ou* his knowing; **s. cela** otherwise; **s. importance** unimportant.
**sans-abri** *mf inv* homeless person.
**santé** *f* health; **(à votre) s.!** your (good) health!, cheers!
**sapin** *m* (*arbre, bois*) fir; **s. de Noël** Christmas tree.
**sardine** *f* sardine.
**satellite** *m* satellite.
**satin** *m* satin.
**satisfaction** *f* satisfaction.
**satisfaire*** *vt* to satisfy (*s.o.*); **satisfait (de)** satisfied (with).
**satisfaisant, -ante** *a* satisfactory.
**sauce** *f* sauce; (*jus de viande*) gravy; **s. tomate** tomato sauce.
**saucisse** *f* sausage.
**saucisson** *m* (cold) sausage.
**sauf** *prép* except (**que** that).
**saule** *m* willow.
**saumon** *m* salmon.

**sauna** *m* sauna.
**saupoudrer** *vt* to sprinkle (**de** with).
**saura, saurai(t)** *etc voir* **savoir**.
**saut** *m* jump, leap; **faire un s.** to jump, leap; **faire un s. chez qn** to drop in on s.o., pop over to see s.o.
**sauter 1** *vi* to jump, leap; **faire s.** (*détruire*) to blow up; **s. à la corde** jump rope; **ça saute aux yeux** it's obvious. **2** *vt* to jump (over); (*mot, repas*) to skip.
**sauterelle** *f* grasshopper.
**sauvage** *a* (*animal, plante*) wild; (*tribu, homme*) primitive.
**sauver** *vt* to save; (*d'un danger*) to rescue (**de** from); **s. la vie à qn** to save s.o.'s life.
**sauver (se)** *vpr* to run away *ou* off.
**sauvetage** *m* rescue.
**sauveteur** *m* rescuer.
**sauveur** *m* savior.
**savant** *m* scientist.
**savate** *f* old slipper.
**saveur** *f* flavor.
**savoir*** *vt* to know; **s. lire/nager/***etc* to know how to read/swim/*etc*; **faire s. à qn que** to inform s.o. that; **je n'en sais rien** I have no idea.
**savon** *m* soap; (*morceau*) (bar of) soap.
**savonner** *vt* to wash with soap.
**savonnette** *f* bar of soap.
**savonneux, -euse** *a* soapy.
**savourer** *vt* to enjoy.
**savoureux, -euse** *a* tasty.
**saxophone** *m* saxophone.
**scandale** *m* scandal; **faire un s.** to make a scene.
**scandaleux, -euse** *a* shocking.
**scandaliser** *vt* to shock.
**scandinave** *a* & *mf* Scandinavian.
**scanner** *m* (*appareil*) scanner.
**scarlatine** *f* scarlet fever.
**scénario** *m* (*dialogues etc*) movie

*plateau*) stage; (*décors,*
*pièce, dispute*) scene;
**s.** to direct.
diagram.

**scie** *f* saw.
**science** *f* science; **étudier les sciences** to study science.
**science-fiction** *f* science fiction.
**scientifique 1** *a* scientific. **2** *mf* scientist.
**scier** *vt* to saw.
**scintiller** *vi* to sparkle; (*étoiles*) to twinkle.
**scolaire** *a* **année/***etc* **s.** school year/*etc*.
**score** *m* (*de match*) score.
**scotch®** *m* (*ruban*) scotch tape®.
**scrutin** *m* voting, ballot.
**sculpter** *vt* to carve, sculpture.
**sculpteur** *m* sculptor.
**sculpture** *f* (*art, œuvre*) sculpture.
**se** (**s'** *before vowel or mute h*) *pron* (*complément direct*) himself; (*féminin*) herself; (*non humain*) itself; (*indéfini*) oneself; *pl* themselves. ▪ (*indirect*) to himself; to herself; to itself; to oneself. ▪ (*réciproque*) each other, one another; (*indirect*) to each other, to one another. ▪ (*possessif*) **il se lave les mains** he washes his hands.
**séance** *f* (*au cinéma*) show(ing).
**seau, -x** *m* bucket.
**sec, sèche 1** *a* dry; (*légumes*) dried; (*ton*) harsh; **coup s.** (sharp) knock, bang; **frapper un coup s.** to knock (sharply), bang; **bruit s.** (*rupture*) snap. **2** *m* **à s.** (*rivière*) dried up; **au s.** in a dry place.
**sécateur** *m* pruning shears.
**sèche-cheveux** *m inv* hair dryer.
**sèche-linge** *m inv* tumble dryer.
**sécher 1** *vti* to dry. **2** *vt* (*cours*) to skip.
**sécheresse** *f* (*période*) drought.
**séchoir** *m* **s. à linge** drying rack.
**second, -onde 1** *a* & *mf* second. **2** *m* (*étage*) third floor. **3** *f* (*de lycée*) = sophomore year; (*vitesse*) second (gear).
**secondaire** *a* secondary.
**seconde** *f* (*instant*) second.
**secouer** *vt* to shake.
**secourir** *vt* to assist.
**secouriste** *mf* first-aid worker.

**secours** *m* assistance, help; **(premiers) s.** first aid; **au s.!** help!; **sortie de s.** emergency exit; **roue de s.** spare tire.

**secousse** *f* jolt.

**secret, -ète 1** *a* secret. **2** *m* secret; **en s.** in secret.

**secrétaire 1** *mf* secretary; (*de médecin etc*) receptionist. **2** *m* (*meuble*) writing desk.

**secrétariat** *m* (*bureau*) secretary's office.

**secteur** *m* (*électricité*) mains.

**sécurité** *f* safety; **en s.** safe; **S. sociale** = social services *ou* Social security.

**séduisant, -ante** *a* attractive.

**segment** *m* segment.

**seigneur** *m* lord.

**sein** *m* breast.

**seize** *a* & *m* sixteen.

**seizième** *a* & *mf* sixteenth.

**séjour** *m* stay; **(salle de) s.** living room.

**séjourner** *vi* to stay.

**sel** *m* salt; **sels de bain** bath salts.

**sélection** *f* selection.

**sélectionner** *vt* to select.

**self(-service)** *m* self-service restaurant *ou* shop.

**selle** *f* saddle.

**selon** *prép* according to (**que** whether).

**semaine** *f* week; **en s.** during the week.

**semblable** *a* similar (**à** to).

**semblant** *m* **faire s.** to pretend (**de faire** to do).

**sembler** *vi* to seem (**à** to); **il (me) semble vieux** he seems *ou* looks old (to me); **il me semble que** (+ *indicatif*) I think that, it seems to me that.

**semelle** *f* (*de chaussure*) sole.

**semer** *vt* (*graines*) to sow.

**semestre** *m* half (year); (*scolaire*) semester.

**semi-remorque** *m* semi(trailer).

**semoule** *f* semolina.

**sénat** *m* senate.

**sens**[1] *m* (*signification*) meaning, sense; **avoir du bon s.** to have sense, be sensible; **avoir un s.** to make sense; **ça n'a pas de s.** that doesn't make sense.

**sens**[2] *m* (*direction*) direction; **s. giratoire** traffic circle; **s. interdit** *ou* **unique** (*rue*) one-way street; **'s. interdit'** 'no entry'; **s. dessus dessous** upside down; **dans le s./le s. inverse des aiguilles d'une montre** clockwise/counterclockwise.

**sensation** *f* feeling.

**sensationnel, -elle** *a* sensational.

**sensible** *a* sensitive (**à** to); (*douloureux*) tender; (*progrès etc*) noticeable.

**sentier** *m* path.

**sentiment** *m* feeling.

**sentir*** *vt* to feel; (*odeur*) to smell; (*goût*) to taste; **s. le parfum/***etc* to smell of perfume/*etc*; **s. le poisson/***etc* (*avoir le goût de*) to taste of fish/*etc*; *Fam* **je ne peux pas le s.** (*supporter*) I can't stand him; **se s. fatigué/***etc* to feel tired/*etc*.

**séparément** *adv* separately.

**séparer** *vt* to separate (**de** from).

**séparer (se)** *vpr* (*se quitter*) to part; (*couple*) to separate; **se s. de** (*chien etc*) to part with.

**sept** *a* & *m* seven.

**septante** *a* (*en Belgique, Suisse*) seventy.

**septembre** *m* September.

**septième** *a* & *mf* seventh.

**sera, serai(t)** *etc voir* **être.**

**série** *f* series; (*ensemble*) set.

**sérieusement** *adv* seriously; (*travailler*) conscientiously.

**sérieux, -euse 1** *a* serious. **2** *m* **prendre au s.** to take seriously; **garder son s.** to keep a straight face.

**seringue** *f* syringe.

**serment** *m* oath; **faire le s. de faire** to promise to do.

**serpent** *m* snake.

**serpillière** *f* floor cloth.

**serre** *f* greenhouse; **effect de s.** greenhouse effect.

**serré, -ée** *a* (*nœud etc*) tight; (*gens*) packed (together).
**serrer 1** *vt* (*tenir*) to grip; (*presser*) to squeeze; (*nœud, vis*) to tighten; (*poing*) to clench; (*frein*) to apply; **s. la main à qn** to shake hands with s.o.; **s. qn** (*embrasser*) to hug s.o. **2** *vi* **s. à droite** to keep (to the) right.
**serrer (se)** *vpr* to squeeze up *ou* together; **se s. contre** to squeeze up against.
**serrure** *f* lock.
**serveur, -euse** *mf* waiter, waitress; (*au bar*) bartender, barmaid.
**serviable** *a* helpful.
**service** *m* service; (*pourboire*) service (charge); (*dans une entreprise*) department; **un s.** (*aide*) a favor; **rendre s.** to be of service (**à qn** to s.o.); **s. (non) compris** service (not) included; **s. après-vente** aftersales service; **être de s.** to be on duty.
**serviette** *f* towel; (*sac*) briefcase; **s. hygiénique** sanitary napkin; **s. (de table)** napkin, serviette.
**servir* 1** *vt* to serve (**qch à qn** s.o. with sth, sth to s.o.). **2** *vi* (*être utile*) to be useful; **s. à qch/à faire** (*objet*) to be used for sth/to do; **ça ne sert à rien** it's useless (**de faire** doing); **ça me sert à faire/de qch** I use it to do/as sth.
**servir (se)** *vpr* (*à table*) to help oneself (**de** to); **se s. de** (*utiliser*) to use.
**ses** *voir* **son.**
**set** *m Tennis* set; **s. (de table)** place mat.
**seuil** *m* doorstep.
**seul[1], -e 1** *a* alone; **tout s.** by oneself, on one's own; **se sentir s.** to feel lonely. **2** *adv* **(tout) s.** (*rentrer, vivre etc*) by oneself, on one's own, alone; (*parler*) to oneself.
**seul[2], -e 1** *a* (*unique*) only; **la seule femme/***etc* the only woman/*etc*; **un s. chat/***etc* only one cat/*etc*; **pas un s. livre/***etc* not a single book/*etc*. **2** *mf* **le s., la seule** the only one; **un s., une seule** only one; **pas un s.** not (a single) one.
**seulement** *adv* only.
**sévère** *a* severe; (*parents etc*) strict.
**sévérité** *f* (*de parents etc*) strictness.
**sexe** *m* sex.
**sexuel, -elle** *a* sexual; **éducation/vie sexuelle** sex education/life.
**shampooing** *m* shampoo; **faire un s. à qn** to shampoo s.o.'s hair.
**short** *m* (pair of) shorts.
**si[1] 1** (= **s'** *before* **il, ils**) *conj* if; **je me demande si** I wonder whether *ou* if; **si on restait?** what if we stayed? **2** *adv* (*tellement*) so; **pas si riche que toi** not as rich as you; **un si bon dîner** such a good dinner; **si bien que** (+ *indicatif*) with the result that.
**si[2]** *adv* (*après négative*) yes; **tu ne viens pas? — si!** you're not coming? —yes (I am)!
**SIDA** *m* AIDS.
**siècle** *m* century; (*époque*) age.
**siège** *m* seat; (*de parti etc*) headquarters; **s. (social)** head office.
**sien, sienne** *pron poss* **le s., la sienne, les sien(ne)s** his; (*de femme*) hers; (*de chose*) its; **les deux siens** his *ou* her two.
**sieste** *f* **faire la s.** to take a nap.
**sifflement** *m* whistling; hiss(ing).
**siffler 1** *vi* to whistle; (*avec un sifflet*) to blow one's whistle; (*gaz, serpent*) to hiss. **2** *vt* (*chanson*) to whistle; (*chien*) to whistle to; (*acteur*) to boo.
**sifflet** *m* whistle; **(coup de) s.** (*son*) whistle; **sifflets** (*des spectateurs*) boos.
**signal, -aux** *m* signal; **s. d'alarme** (*de train*) alarm.
**signaler** *vt* to point out (**à qn** to s.o., **que** that); (*à la police etc*) to report (**à** to).
**signature** *f* signature.
**signe** *m* sign; **faire s. à qn** (*geste*) to motion (to) s.o. (**de faire** to do).
**signer** *vt* to sign.

**signification** *f* meaning.
**signifier** *vt* to mean (**que** that).
**silence** *m* silence; **en s.** in silence; **garder le s.** to keep silent (**sur** about).
**silencieusement** *adv* silently.
**silencieux, -euse** *a* silent.
**silhouette** *f* outline; (*ligne du corps*) figure.
**simple** *a* simple.
**simplement** *adv* simply.
**simplifier** *vt* to simplify.
**simultané, -ée** *a* simultaneous.
**simultanément** *adv* simultaneously.
**sincère** *a* sincere.
**sincèrement** *adv* sincerely.
**sincérité** *f* sincerity.
**singe** *m* monkey, ape.
**singeries** *fpl* antics.
**singulier, -ière** *a* & *m* (*non pluriel*) singular; **au s.** in the singular.
**sinistre 1** *a* sinister. **2** *m* disaster.
**sinon** *conj* (*autrement*) otherwise, or else.
**sirène** *f* (*d'usine etc*) siren.
**sirop** *m* syrup; **s. contre la toux** cough medicine *ou* syrup.
**situation** *f* situation.
**situé, -ée** *a* situated, located.
**situer (se)** *vpr* to be situated, located.
**six** *a* & *m* six.
**sixième** *a* & *mf* sixth.
**sketch** *m* (*pl* **sketches**) (*de théâtre*) sketch.
**ski** *m* ski; (*sport*) skiing; **faire du s.** to ski; **s. nautique** water skiing.
**skier** *vi* to ski.
**skieur, -euse** *mf* skier.
**slip** *m* (*d'homme*) briefs, underwear; (*de femme*) panties, underwear; **s. de bain** (swimming) trunks.
**slogan** *m* slogan.
**SNCF** *f abrév* (*Société nationale des chemins de fer français*) French railroad system.
**social, -e, -aux** *a* social.
**socialiste** *a* & *mf* socialist.
**société** *f* society; (*compagnie*) company.
**socquette** *f* anklet.
**sœur** *f* sister.
**soi** *pron* oneself; **cela va de soi** it's evident (**que** that).
**soie** *f* silk.
**soient** *voir* **être**.
**soif** *f* thirst; **avoir s.** to be thirsty; **donner s. à qn** to make s.o. thirsty.
**soigné, -ée** *a* (*vêtement*) neat; (*travail*) careful.
**soigner** *vt* to look after, take care of; (*maladie*) to treat; **se faire s.** to get (medical) treatment, be treated.
**soigneusement** *adv* carefully.
**soigneux, -euse** *a* careful (**de** with); (*propre*) neat.
**soi-même** *pron* oneself.
**soin** *m* care; **soins** (*à un malade*) treatment, care; **avec s.** carefully; **prendre s. de qch** to take care of sth; **les premiers soins** first aid.
**soir** *m* evening; **le s.** (*chaque soir*) in the evening; **à neuf heures du s.** at nine in the evening.
**soirée** *f* evening; (*réunion*) party.
**sois, soit** *voir* **être**.
**soit** *conj* **s. . . . s. . . .** either . . . or . . . .
**soixantaine** *f* **une s. (de)** about sixty.
**soixante** *a* & *m* sixty.
**soixante-dix** *a* & *m* seventy.
**soixante-dixième** *a* & *mf* seventieth.
**soixantième** *a* & *mf* sixtieth.
**sol** *m* ground; (*plancher*) floor.
**solaire** *a* solar; **crème/huile s.** sun(tan) lotion/oil.
**soldat** *m* soldier.
**solde** *m* (*de compte*) balance; **en s.** (*acheter*) on sale; **soldes** (*marchandises*) sale goods; (*vente*) (clearance) sale(s).
**soldé, -ée** *a* (*article etc*) reduced.
**solder** *vt* (*articles*) to put on sale.
**sole** *f* (*poisson*) sole.
**soleil** *m* sun; (*chaleur, lumière*) sunshine; **au s.** in the sun; **il fait**

… sunny; **coup de s.**

…**l, -elle** *a* solemn.

…**ité** *f* (*de personnes*) solidarity.

**solide** *a* & *m* solid.

**solidement** *adv* solidly.

**solitaire** *a* (*tout seul*) all alone.

**solitude** *f* **aimer la s.** to like being alone.

**sombre** *a* dark; **il fait s.** it's dark.

**somme 1** *f* sum; **faire la s. de** to add up. **2** *m* (*sommeil*) nap; **faire un s.** to take a nap.

**sommeil** *m* sleep; **avoir s.** to be *ou* feel sleepy.

**sommes** *voir* **être.**

**sommet** *m* top.

**somnifère** *m* sleeping pill.

**son** *m* (*bruit*) sound.

**son, sa,** *pl* **ses** (**sa** *becomes* **son** *before a vowel or mute h*) *a poss* his; (*de femme*) her; (*de chose*) its; (*indéfini*) one's; **son père/sa mère** his *ou* her *ou* one's father/mother; **son ami(e)** his *ou* her *ou* one's friend; **sa durée** its duration.

**sondage** *m* **s. (d'opinion)** opinion poll.

**songer** *vi* **s. à qch/à faire** to think of sth/of doing.

**sonner** *vi* to ring; **on a sonné** (*à la porte*) someone has rung the (door)bell.

**sonnerie** *f* (*son*) ring(ing); (*appareil*) bell; (*au téléphone*) ring; **s. 'occupé'** busy signal.

**sonnette** *f* bell; **coup de s.** ring.

**sonore** *a* (*rire*) loud; (*salle*) resonant.

**sont** *voir* **être.**

**sorcière** *f* witch.

**sort** *m* (*destin, hasard*) fate; (*condition*) lot.

**sorte** *f* sort, kind (**de** of); **toutes sortes de** all sorts *ou* kinds of; **de (telle) s. que** (+ *subjonctif*) so that; **faire en s. que** (+ *subjonctif*) to see to it that.

**sortie** *f* (*promenade à pied*) walk; (*en voiture*) drive; (*excursion*) outing; (*porte*) exit, way out; (*de disque, film*) release; **à la s. de l'école** when the children get out of school.

**sortir* 1** *vi* (*aux* **être**) to go out, leave; (*venir*) to come out; (*pour s'amuser, danser etc*) to go out; (*film etc*) to come out; **s. de table** to leave the table; **s'en s.** to pull *ou* come through. **2** *vt* (*aux* **avoir**) to take out (**de** of).

**sottise** *f* (*action, parole*) foolish thing; **faire des sottises** (*enfant*) to misbehave.

**sou** *m* **sous** (*argent*) money; **elle n'a pas un s.** she doesn't have a penny; **appareil** *ou* **machine à sous** slot machine.

**souche** *f* (*d'arbre*) stump.

**souci** *m* worry; (*préoccupation*) concern (**de** for); **se faire du s.** to worry; **ça lui donne du s.** it worries him *ou* her.

**soucier (se)** *vpr* **se s. de** to be worried about.

**soucieux, -euse** *a* worried (**de qch** about sth).

**soucoupe** *f* saucer; **s. volante** flying saucer.

**soudain** *adv* suddenly.

**souder** *vt* to weld.

**souffle** *m* puff; (*haleine*) breath; (*respiration*) breathing; (*de bombe etc*) blast.

**souffler 1** *vi* to blow. **2** *vt* (*bougie*) to blow out; (*chuchoter*) to whisper.

**souffrance(s)** *f*(*pl*) suffering.

**souffrant, -ante** *a* unwell.

**souffrir*** *vi* to suffer (**de** from); **faire s. qn** to hurt s.o.

**souhait** *m* wish; **à vos souhaits!** (*après un éternuement*) bless you!, gesundheit!

**souhaitable** *a* desirable.

**souhaiter** *vt* to wish for; **s. qch à qn** to wish s.o. sth; **s. faire** to hope to do; **s. que** (+ *subjonctif*) to hope that.

**soulagement** *m* relief.

**soulager** *vt* to relieve (**de** of).

**soulever** *vt* to lift (up); (*poussière, question*) to raise.

**soulier** *m* shoe.

**souligner** *vt* to underline; (*faire remarquer*) to emphasize.
**soupçon** *m* suspicion.
**soupçonner** *vt* to suspect (**de** of, **d'avoir fait** of doing, **que** that).
**soupe** *f* soup.
**souper 1** *m* supper. **2** *vi* to have supper.
**soupir** *m* sigh.
**soupirer** *vi* to sigh.
**souple** *a* supple; (*tolérant*) flexible.
**souplesse** *f* suppleness; flexibility.
**source** *f* (*point d'eau*) spring; (*origine*) source; **eau de s.** spring water.
**sourcil** *m* eyebrow.
**sourd, sourde 1** *a* deaf; (*douleur*) dull; **bruit s.** thump. **2** *mf* deaf person.
**sourd-muet** (*pl* **sourds-muets**), **sourde-muette** (*pl* **sourdes-muettes**) *a* & *mf* deaf and dumb (person), deaf-mute.
**sourire* 1** *vi* to smile (**à qn** at s.o.). **2** *m* smile; **faire un s. à qn** to give s.o. a smile.
**souris** *f* mouse (*pl* mice).
**sous** *prép* (*position*) under (-neath), beneath; **s. la pluie** in the rain; **s. Charles X** under Charles X; **s. peu** (*bientôt*) shortly.
**sous-entendre** *vt* to imply.
**sous-marin** *m* submarine.
**sous-sol** *m* (*d'immeuble*) basement.
**sous-titre** *m* subtitle.
**soustraction** *f* subtraction.
**soustraire*** *vt* (*nombre*) to take away, subtract (**de** from).
**sous-vêtements** *mpl* underwear.
**soutenir*** *vt* to support; **s. que** to maintain that.
**soutenir (se)** *vpr* (*blessé etc*) to hold oneself up straight.
**souterrain, -aine 1** *a* underground. **2** *m* underground passage.
**soutien** *m* support; (*personne*) supporter.
**soutien-gorge** *m* (*pl* **soutiens-gorge**) bra.
**souvenir** *m* memory; (*objet*) memento; (*cadeau*) keepsake; (*pour touristes*) souvenir.
**souvenir* (se)** *vpr* **se s. de** to remember; **se s. que** to remember that.
**souvent** *adv* often; **peu s.** seldom; **le plus s.** usually.
**soyez, soyons** *voir* **être.**
**spacieux, -euse** *a* spacious.
**spaghetti(s)** *mpl* spaghetti.
**sparadrap** *m* Band-Aid®.
**speaker** *m*, **speakerine** *f* (*à la radio etc*) announcer.
**spécial, -e, -aux** *a* special.
**spécialement** *adv* specially.
**spécialiste** *mf* specialist.
**spécialité** *f* specialty.
**spécimen** *m* specimen.
**spectacle** *m* (*vue*) sight; (*représentation*) show.
**spectaculaire** *a* spectacular.
**spectateur, -trice** *mf* spectator; (*témoin*) onlooker; **les spectateurs** (*le public*) the audience.
**sphère** *f* sphere.
**spirale** *f* spiral.
**spirituel, -elle** *a* (*amusant*) witty.
**splendide** *a* splendid.
**spontané, -ée** *a* spontaneous.
**sport** *m* sport; **faire du s.** to play sports; **voiture/veste/terrain de s.** sports car/jacket/ground.
**sportif, -ive 1** *a* (*personne*) fond of sports. **2** *mf* sportsman, sportswoman, athlete.
**spot** *m* (*lampe*) spotlight; **s. (publicitaire)** commercial.
**squash** *m* (*jeu*) squash.
**squelette** *m* skeleton.
**stable** *a* stable.
**stade** *m* stadium.
**stage** *m* (*cours*) (training) course; (*en entreprise*) internship.
**stand** *m* (*d'exposition etc*) stand.
**standard 1** *m* (*téléphonique*) switchboard. **2** *a inv* (*modèle etc*) standard.
**station** *f* station; (*de ski etc*) resort; (*d'autobus*) stop; **s. de taxis** taxi stand.
**stationnement** *m* parking.

**stationner** *vi* (*se garer*) to park; (*être garé*) to be parked.
**station-service** *f* (*pl* **stations-service**) service station, gas station.
**statistique** *f* (*donnée*) statistic.
**statue** *f* statue.
**steak** *m* steak.
**stéréo** *a inv* stereo.
**stériliser** *vt* to sterilize.
**stock** *m* stock, supply (**de** of); **en s.** in stock.
**stocker** *vt* (*provisions etc*) to store.
**stop 1** *int* stop. **2** *m* (*panneau*) stop sign; (*feu arrière*) brake light; **faire du s.** to hitchhike.
**stopper** *vti* to stop.
**store** *m* (window) shade.
**stress** *m inv* stress.
**stressé, -ée** *a* under stress.
**strict, -e** *a* strict.
**strictement** *adv* strictly.
**structure** *f* structure.
**studio** *m* studio; (*logement*) studio apartment.
**stupéfaction** *f* amazement.
**stupéfait, -faite** *a* amazed (**de** at, by).
**stupide** *a* stupid.
**stupidité** *f* stupidity; (*action, parole*) stupid thing.
**style** *m* style.
**stylo** *m* pen; **s. à bille** ballpoint (pen); **s.-plume** fountain pen.
**su, sue** *pp of* **savoir.**
**subir** *vt* to undergo; (*conséquences, défaite*) to suffer; (*influence*) to be under.
**subit, -ite** *a* sudden.
**subitement** *adv* suddenly.
**subjonctif** *m Grammaire* subjunctive.
**submergé, -ée** *a* flooded (**de** with); **s. de travail** overwhelmed with work.
**substance** *f* substance.
**subtil, -e** *a* subtle.
**succéder** *vi* **s. à qch** to follow sth; **se s.** to follow one another.
**succès** *m* success; **avoir du s.** to be successful.
**successif, -ive** *a* successive.
**succession** *f* (*série*) sequence (**de** of).
**sucer** *vt* to suck.
**sucette** *f* lollipop; (*tétine*) pacifier.
**sucre** *m* sugar; (*morceau*) sugar lump; **s. cristallisé** granulated sugar; **s. en morceaux** lump sugar; **s. en poudre, s. semoule** fine sugar.
**sucré, -ée** *a* sweet.
**sucrer** *vt* to sugar.
**sucrier** *m* sugar bowl.
**sud** *m* south; **au s. de** south of; **du s.** (*vent*) southerly; (*ville*) southern.
**sud-est** *m* & *a inv* southeast.
**sud-ouest** *m* & *a inv* southwest.
**suédois, -oise 1** *a* Swedish. **2** *mf* Swede. **3** *m* (*langue*) Swedish.
**suer** *vi* to sweat; **faire s. qn** *Fam* to get on s.o.'s nerves.
**sueur** *f* sweat; **en s.** sweating.
**suffire*** *vi* to be enough (**à** for); **ça suffit!** that's enough!; **il suffit d'une goutte/***etc* **pour faire** a drop/*etc* is enough to do.
**suffisamment** *adv* sufficiently; **s. de** enough.
**suffisant, -ante** *a* sufficient.
**suffocant, -ante** *a* stifling.
**suggérer** *vt* to suggest (**à** to, **de faire** doing, **que** (+ *subjonctif*) that).
**suggestion** *f* suggestion.
**suicide** *m* suicide.
**suicider (se)** *vpr* to commit suicide.
**suis** *voir* **être, suivre.**
**suisse 1** *a* Swiss. **2** *mf* Swiss *inv*; **les Suisses** the Swiss.
**Suissesse** *f* Swiss woman *ou* girl, Swiss *inv*.
**suite** *f* (*reste*) rest; (*de film, roman*) sequel; (*série*) series; **faire s. (à)** to follow; **par la s.** afterwards; **à la s.** one after another; **à la s. de** (*événement etc*) as a result of; **de s.** (*deux jours etc*) in a row.
**suivant, -ante 1** *a* next, following. **2** *mf* next (one); **au s.!** next!
**suivre* 1** *vt* to follow; (*accompa-*

*gner*) to go with; (*classe*) to attend, go to; **s. (des yeux** *ou* **du regard)** to watch; **se s.** to follow each other. **2** *vi* to follow; **faire s.** (*courrier*) to forward; **'à s.'** 'to be continued'.

**sujet** *m* (*question*) & *Grammaire* subject; (*d'examen*) question; **au s. de** about; **à quel s.?** about what?

**super 1** *a inv* (*bon*) great. **2** *m* (*essence*) premium gas.

**superbe** *a* superb.

**superficie** *f* surface.

**superficiel, -ielle** *a* superficial.

**supérieur, -e** *a* upper; (*qualité etc*) superior (**à** to); (*études*) higher; **l'étage s.** the floor above.

**supériorité** *f* superiority.

**supermarché** *m* supermarket.

**superposer** *vt* (*objets*) to put on top of each other.

**superstitieux, -euse** *a* superstitious.

**superstition** *f* superstition.

**supplément** *m* (*argent*) extra charge; **en s.** extra.

**supplémentaire** *a* extra.

**supplier** *vt* **s. qn de faire** to beg s.o. to do.

**support** *m* support; (*d'instrument etc*) stand.

**supporter**[1] *vt* to bear; (*résister à*) to withstand; (*soutenir*) to support.

**supporter**[2] *m* supporter.

**supposer** *vti* to suppose (**que** that).

**supposition** *f* assumption.

**suppositoire** *m* suppository.

**suppression** *f* removal; (*de train*) cancellation.

**supprimer** *vt* to get rid of; (*mot*) to cut out; (*train*) to cancel.

**sur** *prép* on, upon; (*par-dessus*) over; (*au sujet de*) on, about; **six s. dix** six out of ten; **un jour s. deux** every other day; **six mètres s. dix** 20 by 33 feet.

**sûr, sûre** *a* sure, certain (**de** of, **que** that); (*digne de confiance*) reliable; (*lieu*) safe; **c'est s. que** (+ *indicatif*) it's certain that; **s. de soi** self-assured; **bien s.!** of course!

**sûrement** *adv* certainly.

**sûreté** *f* safety; **être en s.** to be safe; **mettre en s.** to put in a safe place.

**surexcité, -ée** *a* overexcited.

**surf** *m* surfing; **faire du s.** to go surfing.

**surface** *f* surface; (*dimensions*) (surface) area; **(magasin à) grande s.** hypermarket.

**surgelé, -ée** *a* (*viande etc*) frozen.

**surgelés** *mpl* frozen foods.

**surgir** *vi* to appear suddenly (**de** from); (*problème*) to arise.

**sur-le-champ** *adv* immediately.

**surlendemain** *m* **le s.** two days later; **le s. de** two days after.

**surmener (se)** *vpr* to overwork.

**surmonter** *vt* (*obstacle etc*) to get over.

**surnom** *m* nickname.

**surnommer** *vt* to nickname.

**surpasser (se)** *vpr* to surpass oneself.

**surprenant, -ante** *a* surprising.

**surprendre*** *vt* (*étonner*) to surprise; (*prendre sur le fait*) to catch; (*conversation*) to overhear.

**surpris, -ise** *a* surprised (**de** at, **que** (+ *subjonctif*) that); **je suis surpris de te voir** I'm surprised to see you.

**surprise** *f* surprise.

**sursauter** *vi* to jump, start.

**surtout** *adv* especially; (*avant tout*) above all; **s. pas** certainly not; **s. que** especially since.

**surveillant, -ante** *mf* (*lycée*) monitor; (*prison*) (prison) guard.

**surveiller** *vt* to watch; (*contrôler*) to supervise.

**survêtement** *m* tracksuit.

**survivant, -ante** *mf* survivor.

**survivre*** *vi* to survive (**à qch** sth).

**survoler** *vt* to fly over.

**susceptible** *a* touchy.

**suspect, -ecte 1** *a* suspicious. **2** *mf* suspect.

**suspendre** *vt* (*accrocher*) to hang (up) (**à** on); **se s. à** to hang from.

**…uspendu, -ue** *a* **s. à** hanging from.
**suspense** *m* suspense.
**suspension** *f* (*de véhicule*) suspension.
**suture** *f* **point de s.** stitch (*in wound*).
**SVP** *abrév* (*s'il vous plaît*) please.
**syllabe** *f* syllable.
**symbole** *m* symbol.
**symbolique** *a* symbolic.
**sympa** *a inv Fam* = **sympathique.**
**sympathie** *f* liking; **avoir de la s. pour qn** to be fond of s.o.
**sympathique** *a* nice, pleasant.
**symphonie** *f* symphony.
**symptôme** *m* symptom.
**synagogue** *f* synagogue.
**syndicat** *m* (*d'ouvriers*) (labor) union; **s. d'initiative** tourist (information) office.
**syndiqué, -ée** *mf* union member.
**synonyme 1** *a* synonymous (**de** with). **2** *m* synonym.
**système** *m* system.

# T

**ta** *voir* **ton**.
**tabac** *m* tobacco; (*magasin*) tobacco store.
**table** *f* table; (*d'école*) desk; **t. de nuit** bedside table; **t. basse** coffee table; **t. à repasser** ironing board; **t. roulante** (serving) cart; **t. des matières** table (of contents); **à t.** sitting at the table; **à t.!** (food's) ready!
**tableau, -x** *m* (*image*) picture; (*panneau*) board; (*liste*) list; (*graphique*) chart; **t. (noir)** (black) board; **t. d'affichage** bulletin board; **t. de bord** dashboard.
**tablette** *f* (*de chocolat*) bar; (*de lavabo etc*) shelf.
**tablier** *m* apron; (*d'écolier*) smock.
**tabouret** *m* stool.
**tache** *f* spot; (*salissure*) stain.
**tacher** *vti*, **se tacher** *vpr* to stain.
**tâcher** *vi* **t. de faire** to try to do.
**tact** *m* tact; **avoir du t.** to be tactful.
**tactique** *f* **la t.** tactics; **une t.** a tactic.
**tag** *m* spray-painted graffiti.
**taie d'oreiller** *f* pillowcase.
**taille** *f* (*hauteur*) height; (*dimension, mesure*) size; (*ceinture*) waist; **tour de t.** waist measurement.
**taille-crayon(s)** *m inv* pencil sharpener.
**tailler** *vt* to cut; (*haie, barbe*) to trim; (*arbre*) to prune; (*crayon*) to sharpen.
**tailleur** *m* (*personne*) tailor; (*vêtement*) suit.
**taire* (se)** *vpr* (*ne rien dire*) to keep quiet (**sur qch** about sth); (*cesser de parler*) to stop talking; **tais-toi!** be quiet!
**talent** *m* talent; **avoir du t. pour** to have a talent for.
**talon** *m* heel; (*de chèque, carnet*) stub.
**talus** *m* slope, embankment.
**tambour** *m* drum; (*personne*) drummer.
**tambourin** *m* tambourine.
**tamis** *m* sieve.
**tamiser** *vt* (*farine*) to sift.
**tampon** *m* (*marque, instrument*) stamp; (*de coton*) wad; **t. hygiénique** tampon; **t. à récurer** scrubbing pad.
**tandis que** *conj* while.
**tant** *adv* (*travailler etc*) so much (**que** that); **t. de** (*temps etc*) so much (**que** that); (*gens etc*) so many (**que** that); **t. que** (*aussi longtemps que*) as long as; **t. mieux!** good!; **t. pis!** too bad!
**tante** *f* aunt.
**tantôt** *adv* **t. . . . t.** sometimes . . . sometimes.
**tapage** *m* din, uproar.
**tape** *f* slap.
**taper[1] 1** *vt* (*enfant, cuisse*) to slap; (*table*) to bang. **2** *vi* **t. sur qch** to bang on sth; **t. du pied** to stamp one's foot.
**taper[2]** *vti* **t. (à la machine)** to type.

**tapis** *m* carpet; **t. roulant** (*pour marchandises*) conveyor belt.
**tapisser** *vt* (*mur*) to (wall)paper.
**tapisserie** *f* (*papier peint*) wallpaper; (*broderie*) tapestry.
**tapoter** *vt* to tap; (*joue*) to pat.
**taquiner** *vt* to tease.
**tard** *adv* late; **plus t.** later (on); **au plus t.** at the latest.
**tarder** *vi* **t. à faire** to take one's time doing; **elle ne va pas t.** she won't be long; **sans t.** without delay.
**tarif** *m* (*prix*) rate; (*de train*) fare; (*tableau*) price list.
**tarte** *f* (open) pie, tart.
**tartine** *f* slice of bread; **t. (de beurre/de confiture)** slice of bread and butter/jam.
**tartiner** *vt* (*beurre etc*) to spread.
**tas** *m* pile, heap; **un** *ou* **des t. de** (*beaucoup*) *Fam* lots of; **mettre en t.** to pile *ou* heap up.
**tasse** *f* cup; **t. à café** coffee cup; **t. à thé** teacup.
**tasser** *vt* to pack, squeeze (*sth*, *s.o.*) (**dans** into).
**tasser (se)** *vpr* (*se serrer*) to squeeze together.
**tâter** *vt* to feel.
**tâtonner** *vi* to grope around.
**tâtons (à)** *adv* **avancer à t.** to feel one's way (along); **chercher à t.** to grope for.
**tatouage** *m* (*dessin*) tattoo.
**tatouer** *vt* to tattoo.
**taudis** *m* slum.
**taupe** *f* mole.
**taureau, -x** *m* bull.
**taux** *m* rate; **t. d'alcool**/*etc* alcohol/*etc* level.
**taxe** *f* (*impôt*) tax; (*de douane*) duty; **t. à la valeur ajoutée** value-added tax.
**taxé, -ée** *a* taxed.
**taxi** *m* taxi.
**te** (**t'** *before vowel or mute h*) *pron* (*complément direct*) you; (*indirect*) (to) you; (*réfléchi*) yourself.
**technicien, -ienne** *mf* technician.
**technique 1** *a* technical. **2** *f* technique.
**technologie** *f* technology.
**tee-shirt** *m* tee-shirt.
**teindre*** *vt* to dye; **t. en rouge** to dye red.
**teindre (se)** *vpr* to dye one's hair.
**teint** *m* complexion.
**teinte** *f* shade.
**teinture** *f* (*produit*) dye.
**teinturerie** *f* (*boutique*) (dry) cleaner's.
**teinturier, -ière** *mf* (dry) cleaner.
**tel, telle** *a* such; **un t. livre**/*etc* such a book/*etc*; **un t. intérêt**/*etc* such interest/*etc*; **de tels mots**/*etc* such words/*etc*; **rien de t. que** (there's) nothing like.
**télé** *f* TV; **à la t.** on TV.
**télécommande** *f* remote control.
**télécopie** *f* fax.
**télécopieur** *m* fax (machine).
**téléfilm** *m* TV film.
**télégramme** *m* telegram.
**téléphérique** *m* cable car.
**téléphone** *m* (tele)phone; **coup de t.** (phone) call; **passer un coup de t. à qn** to give s.o. a call; **au t.** on the (tele)phone.
**téléphoner 1** *vt* (*nouvelle etc*) to (tele)phone (**à** to). **2** *vi* to (tele)phone; **t. à qn** to (tele)phone s.o.
**téléphonique** *a* **appel**/*etc* **t.** (tele)phone call/*etc*.
**télescope** *m* telescope.
**télésiège** *m* chair lift.
**téléspectateur, -trice** *mf* (television) viewer.
**télévisé** *a* **journal t.** television news.
**téléviseur** *m* television (set).
**télévision** *f* television; **à la t.** on (the) television.
**telle** *voir* **tel**.
**tellement** *adv* (*si*) so; (*tant*) so much; **t. de** (*travail etc*) so much; (*soucis etc*) so many; **pas t.!** not much!
**témoignage** *m* evidence; (*récit*) account.
**témoigner** *vi* to give evidence (**contre** against).
**témoin** *m* witness; **être t. de** to witness.

**température** *f* temperature; **avoir de la t.** to have a temperature.
**tempête** *f* storm; **t. de neige** snowstorm.
**temple** *m* (*romain, grec*) temple.
**temporaire** *a* temporary.
**temps**[1] *m* time; (*de verbe*) tense; **il est t. (de faire)** it's time (to do); **ces derniers t.** lately; **de t. en t.** from time to time; **à t.** (*arriver*) in time; **à plein t.** (*travailler*) full-time; **à t. partiel** (*travailler*) part-time; **dans le t.** (*autrefois*) once.
**temps**[2] *m* (*climat*) weather; **quel t. fait-il?** what's the weather like?
**tenailles** *fpl* (*outil*) pincers.
**tendance** *f* tendency; **avoir t. à faire** to tend to do.
**tendeur** *m* (*à bagages*) bungee/ (cord).
**tendre**[1] *vt* to stretch; (*main*) to hold out (**à qn** to s.o.); (*bras, jambe*) to stretch out; (*piège*) to set, lay; **t. qch à qn** to hold out sth to s.o.; **t. l'oreille** to prick up one's ears.
**tendre**[2] *a* (*viande etc*) tender; (*personne*) affectionate (**avec** to).
**tendrement** *adv* tenderly.
**tendresse** *f* affection.
**tendu, -ue** *a* (*corde*) tight; (*personne, situation, muscle*) tense; (*main*) held out.
**tenir*** **1** *vt* to hold; (*promesse, comptes, hôtel*) to keep; (*rôle*) to play; **t. sa droite** (*conducteur*) to keep to the right. **2** *vi* to hold; (*résister*) to hold out; **t. à** (*personne, jouet etc*) to be attached to; **t. à faire** to be anxious to do; **t. dans qch** (*être contenu*) to fit into sth; **tenez!** (*prenez*) here (you are)!; **tiens!** (*surprise*) well!
**tenir (se)** *vpr* (*avoir lieu*) to be held; **se t. (debout)** to stand (up); **se t. droit** to stand up *ou* sit up straight; **se t. par la main** to hold hands; **se t. bien** to behave oneself.
**tennis** *m* tennis; (*terrain*) (tennis) court; (*chaussure*) sneaker; **t. de table** table tennis.
**tension** *f* tension; **t. (artérielle)** blood pressure; **avoir de la t.** to have high blood pressure.
**tentant, -ante** *a* tempting.
**tentation** *f* temptation.
**tentative** *f* attempt.
**tente** *f* tent.
**tenter**[1] *vt* to try (**de faire** to do).
**tenter**[2] *vt* (*faire envie à*) to tempt.
**tenue** *f* (*vêtements*) clothes; (*conduite*) (good) behavior; **t. de soirée** evening dress.
**tergal**® *m* Dacron®.
**terme** *m* (*mot*) term; (*fin*) end; **mettre un t. à** to put an end to; **à court/long t.** (*conséquences*) short-/long-term; **en bons/mauvais termes**on good/bad terms (**avec** with).
**terminaison** *f* (*de mot*) ending.
**terminal, -e, -aux 1** *a* & *f* **(classe) terminale** senior year. **2** *m* **t. (d'ordinateur)** (computer) terminal.
**terminer** *vt* to end.
**terminer (se)** *vpr* to end (**par** with, **en** in).
**terne** *a* dull.
**terrain** *m* ground; (*étendue*) land; (*à bâtir*) plot; *Football etc* field; **un t.** a piece of land; **t. de camping** campsite; **t. de jeux** (*pour enfants*) playground; (*stade*) playing field; **t. vague** vacant lot.
**terrasse** *f* terrace; (*de café*) sidewalk area.
**terre** *f* (*matière, monde*) earth; (*sol*) ground; (*opposé à mer*) land; **par t.** (*poser, tomber*) to the ground; (*assis, couché*) on the ground; **sous t.** underground.
**terrestre** *a* **la surface t.** the earth's surface; **globe t.** globe (*model*).
**terreur** *f* terror.
**terrible** *a* awful, terrible; (*formidable*) *Fam* terrific.
**terrifiant, -ante** *a* terrifying.
**terrifier** *vt* to terrify.
**territoire** *m* territory.
**terroriser** *vt* to terrorize.
**terroriste** *a* & *mf* terrorist.
**tes** *voir* **ton.**
**test** *m* test.
**testament** *m* (*en droit*) will.

**tester** *vt* to test.
**tête** *f* head; (*visage*) face; (*d'arbre*) top; **tenir t. à** to stand up to; **faire la t.** to sulk; **à la t. de** (*entreprise*) at the head of; (*classe*) at the top *ou* head of; **en t.** (*sportif*) in the lead.
**tête-à-tête** *adv* **(en) t.-à-tête** alone together.
**téter 1** *vt* to suck. **2** *vi* **le bébé tète** the baby is feeding; **donner à t. à** to feed.
**tétine** *f* (*de biberon*) nipple; (*sucette*) pacifier.
**têtu, -ue** *a* stubborn.
**texte** *m* text.
**textile** *a* & *m* textile.
**TGV** *abrév m* = **train à grande vitesse.**
**thé** *m* tea.
**théâtre** *m* theater; (*œuvres*) drama; **faire du t.** to act.
**théière** *f* teapot.
**théorie** *f* theory; **en t.** in theory.
**thermomètre** *m* thermometer.
**thermos**® *m ou f* Thermos®.
**thermostat** *m* thermostat.
**thon** *m* tuna (fish).
**tibia** *m* shin (bone).
**ticket** *m* ticket.
**tiède** *a* (luke)warm.
**tien, tienne** *pron poss* **le t., la tienne, les tien(ne)s** yours; **les deux tiens** your two.
**tiens, tient** *voir* **tenir.**
**tiercé** *m* **jouer/gagner au t.** = to bet/win on the horses.
**tiers** *m* (*fraction*) third.
**tige** *f* (*de plante*) stem; (*barre*) rod.
**tigre** *m* tiger.
**timbre** *m* stamp.
**timbre-poste** *m* (*pl* **timbres-poste**) (postage) stamp.
**timbrer** *vt* (*lettre*) to stamp.
**timide** *a* shy.
**timidement** *adv* shyly.
**timidité** *f* shyness.
**tinter** *vi* (*cloche*) to ring; (*clefs*) to jingle.
**tir** *m* shooting; *Sport* shot; **t. à l'arc** archery.
**tirage** *m* (*de journal*) circulation; (*de loterie*) draw; **t. au sort** drawing of lots.
**tire-bouchon** *m* corkscrew.
**tirelire** *f* coin bank.
**tirer 1** *vt* to pull; (*langue*) to stick out; (*trait, rideaux*) to draw; (*balle, canon*) to shoot; **t. de** (*sortir*) to pull *ou* draw out of; (*obtenir*) to get from: **t. qn de** (*danger, lit*) to get s.o. out of; **se t. de** (*travail*) to cope with; (*situation*) to get out of; **se t. d'affaire** to get out of trouble. **2** *vi* to pull (**sur** on, at); (*faire feu*) to shoot (**sur** at); *Sport* to shoot; **t. au sort** to draw lots; **t. à sa fin** to draw to a close.
**tiret** *m* (*trait*) dash.
**tireur** *m* (*au fusil*) gunman.
**tiroir** *m* drawer.
**tisonnier** *m* poker.
**tisser** *vt* to weave.
**tissu** *m* material, cloth; **du t.-éponge** toweling.
**titre** *m* title; **(gros) t.** (*de journal*) headline; **à t. d'exemple** as an example; **à juste t.** rightly.
**toast** *m* (*pain grillé*) piece *ou* slice of toast.
**toboggan** *m* slide; (*pour voitures*) overpass.
**toc** *int* **t. t.!** knock knock!
**toi** *pron* (*complément, sujet*) you; (*réfléchi*) **assieds-t.** sit (yourself) down; **dépêche-t.** hurry up.
**toile** *f* cloth; (*à voile, sac etc*) canvas; (*tableau*) painting; **t. d'araignée** spider's web.
**toilette** *f* (*action*) wash(ing); (*vêtements*) clothes; **eau de t.** toilet water; **faire sa t.** to wash (and dress); **les toilettes** the toilet(s), the men's *ou* ladies' room; **aller aux toilettes** to go to the toilet *ou* to the men's *ou* ladies' room.
**toi-même** *pron* yourself.
**toit** *m* roof; **t. ouvrant** (*de voiture*) sunroof.
**tôle** *f* **une t.** a piece of sheet metal; **t. ondulée** corrugated iron.
**tolérant, -ante** *a* tolerant (**à l'égard de** of).
**tolérer** *vt* to tolerate.

**tomate** *f* tomato.
**tombe** *f* grave.
**tombeau, -x** *m* tomb.
**tombée** *f* **t. de la nuit** nightfall.
**tomber** *vi* (*aux* **être**) to fall; **t. malade** to fall ill; **t. (par terre)** to fall (down); **faire t.** (*personne*) to knock over; **laisser t.** to drop; **tu tombes bien/mal** you've come at the right/wrong time; **t. sur** (*trouver*) to come across.
**tombola** *f* raffle.
**ton, ta,** *pl* **tes** (**ta** *becomes* **ton** *before a vowel or mute h*) *a poss* your; **t. père** your father; **ta mère** your mother; **ton ami(e)** your friend.
**ton** *m* (*de voix etc*) tone.
**tonalité** *f* (*téléphonique*) dial tone.
**tondeuse** *f* **t. (à gazon)** (lawn)-mower.
**tondre** *vt* (*gazon*) to mow.
**tonne** *f* metric ton; **des tonnes de** (*beaucoup*) *Fam* tons of.
**tonneau, -x** *m* barrel.
**tonner** *vi* **il tonne** it's thundering.
**tonnerre** *m* thunder; **coup de t.** burst of thunder.
**tonton** *m Fam* uncle.
**torche** *f* (*flamme*) torch; **t. électrique** flashlight.
**torchon** *m* (*à vaisselle*) dish towel; (*de ménage*) dust cloth.
**tordre** *vt* to twist; (*linge*) to wring (out); (*barre*) to bend; **se t. la cheville** to twist *ou* sprain one's ankle.
**tordre (se)** *vpr* to twist; (*barre*) to bend; **se t. de douleur** to be doubled up with pain; **se t. (de rire)** to split one's sides (laughing).
**torrent** *m* (mountain) stream; **il pleut à torrents** it's pouring (down).
**torse** *m* chest; **t. nu** stripped to the waist.
**tort** *m* **avoir t.** to be wrong (**de faire** to do, in doing); **être dans son t.** to be in the wrong; **donner t. à qn** (*accuser*) to blame s.o.; **à t.** wrongly; **parler à t. et à travers** to talk nonsense.
**torticolis** *m* **avoir le t.** to have a stiff neck.
**tortiller** *vt* to twist, twirl.
**tortue** *f* turtle.
**torture** *f* torture.
**torturer** *vt* to torture.
**tôt** *adv* early; **le plus t. possible** as soon as possible; **t. ou tard** sooner or later; **je n'étais pas plus t. sorti que** no sooner had I gone out than.
**total, -e, -aux** *a* & *m* total.
**totalement** *adv* totally.
**totalité** *f* **en t.** (*détruit etc*) entirely; (*payé*) fully.
**touchant, -ante** *a* moving, touching.
**touche** *f* (*de clavier*) key; (*de téléphone*) (push-)button; **téléphone à touches** touch-tone phone.
**toucher 1** *vt* to touch; (*paie*) to draw; (*chèque*) to cash; (*cible*) to hit; (*émouvoir*) to touch, move. **2** *vi* **t. à** to touch. **3** *m* (*sens*) touch.
**toucher (se)** *vpr* (*lignes, mains etc*) to touch.
**touffe** *f* (*de cheveux, d'herbe*) tuft.
**toujours** *adv* always; (*encore*) still; **pour t.** for ever.
**tour**[1] *f* tower; (*immeuble*) high-rise; *Échecs* castle, rook.
**tour**[2] *m* turn; (*de magie etc*) trick; **t. de poitrine**/*etc* chest/*etc* measurement **faire le t. de** to go around; **faire un t.** to go for a walk; (*en voiture*) to go for a drive; (*voyage*) to go on a trip; **jouer un t. à qn** to play a trick on s.o.; **c'est mon t.** it's my turn; **à t. de rôle** in turn.
**tourisme** *m* tourism; **faire du t.** to go sightseeing.
**touriste** *mf* tourist.
**touristique** *a* **guide**/*etc* **t.** tourist guide/*etc*.
**tournage** *m* (*de film*) shooting.
**tournant** *m* (*de route*) bend.
**tourne-disque** *m* record player.
**tournée** *f* (*de livreur, boissons*) round; (*de spectacle*) tour.
**tourner 1** *vt* to turn; (*film*) to shoot. **2** *vi* to turn; (*tête*) to spin; (*moteur*) to run; (*lait*) to go off; **t. autour de** (*objet*) to go around.
**tourner (se)** *vpr* to turn (**vers** to).
**tournevis** *m* screwdriver.

**tournoi** *m* tournament.
**Toussaint** *f* All Saints' Day.
**tousser** *vi* to cough.
**tout, toute,** *pl* **tous, toutes 1** *a* all; **tous les livres** all the books; **t. l'argent/le temps** all the money/time; **t. le village** the whole village; **toute la nuit** all night; **tous (les) deux** both; **tous (les) trois** all three. ▪ (*chaque*) every; **tous les ans** every *ou* each year; **tous les cinq mois/mètres** every five months/16 feet. **2** *pron pl* all; **ils sont tous là** they're all there. **3** *pron m sing* **tout** everything; **t. ce que** everything that, all that; **en t.** (*au total*) in all. **4** *adv* (*tout à fait*) quite, very; **t. simplement** quite simply; **t. petit** very small; **t. neuf** brand new; **t. seul** all alone; **t. autour** all around; **t. en chantant**/*etc* while singing/*etc*; **t. à coup** suddenly; **t. à fait** completely; **t. de même** all the same; **t. de suite** at once. **5** *m* **le t.** everything, the lot; **pas du t.** not at all; **rien du t.** nothing at all.
**toux** *f* cough.
**toxique** *a* poisonous.
**trac** *m* **avoir le t.** to be *ou* become nervous.
**tracasser** *vt*, **se tracasser** *vpr* to worry.
**trace** *f* trace (**de** of); (*marque*) mark; **traces** (*de bête, pneus*) tracks; **traces de pas** footprints.
**tracer** *vt* (*dessiner*) to draw.
**tracteur** *m* tractor.
**tradition** *f* tradition.
**traditionnel, -elle** *a* traditional.
**traducteur, -trice** *mf* translator.
**traduction** *f* translation.
**traduire*** *vt* to translate (**de** from, **en** into).
**trafic** *m* traffic.
**tragédie** *f* tragedy.
**tragique** *a* tragic.
**trahir** *vt* to betray.
**trahir (se)** *vpr* to give oneself away.
**trahison** *f* betrayal.
**train[1]** *m* train; **t. à grande vitesse** high-speed train; **t. couchettes** sleeper.
**train[2]** *m* **être en t. de faire** to be (busy) doing.
**traîneau, -x** *m* sled.
**traînée** *f* (*de peinture etc*) streak.
**traîner 1** *vt* to drag. **2** *vi* (*jouets etc*) to lie around; (*s'attarder*) to lag behind; **t. (par terre)** (*robe etc*) to trail (on the ground).
**traîner (se)** *vpr* (*par terre*) to crawl.
**train-train** *m* routine.
**traire*** *vt* to milk.
**trait** *m* line; (*en dessinant*) stroke; (*caractéristique*) feature; **t. d'union** hyphen.
**traitement** *m* treatment; (*salaire*) salary; **t. de texte** word processing; **machine de t. de texte** word processor.
**traiter** *vt* **1** to treat; (*problème*) to deal with; **t. qn de lâche**/*etc* to call s.o. a coward/*etc*. **2** *vi* **t. de** (*sujet*) to deal with.
**traiteur** *m* **chez le t.** at the delicatessen.
**traître** *m* traitor.
**trajectoire** *f* path.
**trajet** *m* trip; (*distance*) distance; (*itinéraire*) route.
**tramway** *m* streetcar, trolley.
**tranchant, -ante** *a* (*couteau, voix*) sharp.
**tranche** *f* (*morceau*) slice.
**tranchée** *f* trench.
**trancher** *vt* to cut.
**tranquille** *a* quiet; (*mer*) calm; (*conscience*) clear; **laisser t.** to leave alone.
**tranquillement** *adv* calmly.
**tranquillisant** *m* tranquilizer.
**tranquilliser** *vt* to reassure.
**tranquillité** *f* (peace and) quiet.
**transférer** *vt* to transfer (**à** to).
**transfert** *m* transfer.
**transformation** *f* change.
**transformer** *vt* to change; (*maison*) to remodel; **t. en** to turn into.
**transfusion** *f* **t. (sanguine)** (blood) transfusion.
**transistor** *m* transistor (radio).
**transitif, -ive** *a Grammaire* transitive.

**transmettre*** *vt* (*message etc*) to pass on (**à** to).
**transparent, -ente** *a* clear, transparent.
**transpercer** *vt* to pierce.
**transpirer** *vi* to sweat.
**transport** *m* transportation (**de** of); **moyen de t.** means of transportation; **les transports en commun** public transportation.
**transporter** *vt* to transport; (*à la main*) to carry; **t. d'urgence à l'hôpital** to rush to the hospital.
**trappe** *f* trap door.
**travail, -aux** *m* (*activité, lieu*) work; (*à effectuer*) job, task; (*emploi*) job; **travaux** (*dans la rue*) roadwork, construction; (*aménagement*) alterations; **travaux pratiques** (*à l'école etc*) practical work.
**travailler** *vi* to work (**à qch** at *ou* on sth).
**travailleur, -euse 1** *a* hard-working. **2** *mf* worker.
**travers 1** *prép & adv* **à t.** through; **en t. (de)** across. **2** *adv* **de t.** (*chapeau etc*) crooked; (*comprendre*) badly; **j'ai avalé de t.** it went down the wrong way.
**traversée** *f* crossing.
**traverser** *vt* to cross, go across; (*foule, période*) to go through.
**traversin** *m* bolster.
**trébucher** *vi* to stumble (**sur** over); **faire t. qn** to trip s.o. (up).
**trèfle** *m* (*couleur*) *Cartes* clubs.
**treize** *a & m inv* thirteen.
**treizième** *a & mf* thirteenth.
**tremblement** *m* shaking, trembling; **t. de terre** earthquake.
**trembler** *vi* to shake, tremble (**de** with).
**tremper 1** *vt* to soak; (*plonger*) to dip (**dans** in). **2** *vi* to soak; **faire t. qch** to soak sth.
**tremplin** *m* springboard.
**trentaine** *f* **une t. (de)** about thirty.
**trente** *a & m* thirty; **un t.-trois tours** an LP.
**trentième** *a & mf* thirtieth.
**très** *adv* very; **t. aimé**/*etc* (*with past participle*) much *ou* greatly liked/*etc*.
**trésor** *m* treasure.
**tresse** *f* (*cheveux*) braid.
**tresser** *vt* braid.
**triangle** *m* triangle.
**triangulaire** *a* triangular.
**tribu** *f* tribe.
**tribunal, -aux** *m* court.
**tribune** *f* (*de stade*) (grand)stand.
**tricher** *vi* to cheat.
**tricheur, -euse** *mf* cheater.
**tricolore** *a* red, white and blue; **feu t.** traffic light.
**tricot** *m* (*activité*) knitting; (*chandail*) sweater.
**tricoter** *vti* to knit.
**tricycle** *m* tricycle.
**trier** *vt* to sort (out).
**trimestre** *m* (*période*) quarter; (*scolaire*) term.
**trimestriel, -ielle** *a* (*revue*) quarterly; **bulletin t.** (quarter) report card.
**tringle** *f* rail, rod.
**triomphe** *m* triumph (**sur** over).
**triompher** *vi* to triumph (**de** over).
**triple** *m* **le t.** three times as much (**de** as).
**tripler** *vti* to treble, triple.
**tripoter** *vt* to fiddle around with.
**triste** *a* sad; (*couleur, temps*) gloomy.
**tristement** *adv* sadly.
**tristesse** *f* sadness; (*du temps*) gloom(iness).
**trognon** *m* (*de fruit*) core.
**trois** *a & m* three.
**troisième** *a & mf* third.
**troisièmement** *adv* thirdly.
**trombone** *m* trombone; (*agrafe*) paper clip.
**trompe** *f* (*d'éléphant*) trunk.
**tromper** *vt* to deceive; (*être infidèle à*) to be unfaithful to.
**tromper (se)** *vpr* to be mistaken; **se t. de route**/*etc* to take the wrong road/*etc*; **se t. de date**/*etc* to get the date/*etc* wrong.
**trompette** *f* trumpet.
**tronc** *m* trunk.
**tronçonneuse** *f* chain saw.

**trône** *m* throne.

**trop** *adv* too; too much; **t. dur**/*etc* too hard/*etc*; **t. fatigué pour jouer** too tired to play; **boire**/*etc* **t.** to drink/*etc* too much; **t. de sel**/*etc* (*quantité*) too much salt/*etc*; **t. de gens**/*etc* (*nombre*) too many people/*etc*; **un franc**/*etc* **de t.** *ou* **en t.** one franc/*etc* too many.

**tropical, -e, -aux** *a* tropical.

**trot** *m* trot; **aller au t.** to trot.

**trotter** *vi* (*cheval*) to trot.

**trottinette** *f* (*jouet*) scooter.

**trottoir** *m* sidewalk.

**trou** *m* hole; **t. de (la) serrure** keyhole; **t. (de mémoire)** lapse (of memory).

**trouble** *a* (*liquide*) cloudy; (*image*) blurred; **voir t.** to see things blurred.

**troubler** *vt* to disturb; (*vue*) to blur.

**troubles** *mpl* (*de santé*) trouble; (*désordres*) disturbances.

**trouer** *vt* to make a hole *ou* holes in.

**troupe** *f* (*groupe*) group; (*de théâtre*) company; **troupes** (*armée*) troops.

**troupeau, -x** *m* (*vaches*) herd; (*moutons, oies*) flock.

**trousse** *f* (*étui*) case, kit; (*d'écolier*) pencil case; **t. à outils** toolkit; **t. à pharmacie** first-aid kit; **t. de toilette** (*de femme*) cosmetic case, (*d'homme*) shaving kit.

**trousseau, -x** *m* (*de clefs*) bunch.

**trouver** *vt* to find; **aller/venir t. qn** to go/come and see s.o.; **je trouve que** I think that.

**trouver (se)** *vpr* to be; (*être situé*) to be located; (*se sentir*) to feel; (*dans une situation*) to find oneself.

**truc** *m* (*astuce*) trick; (*moyen*) way; (*chose*) *Fam* thing.

**truite** *f* trout.

**TTC** *abrév* (*toutes taxes comprises*) inclusive of tax.

**tu** *pron* you (*familiar form of address*).

**tu, tue** *voir* **taire.**

**tube** *m* tube; (*chanson*) *Fam* hit.

**tuberculose** *f* TB.

**tue-tête (à)** *adv* at the top of one's voice.

**tuer** *vti* to kill; **se t.** to kill oneself; (*dans un accident*) to be killed.

**tuile** *f* tile.

**tulipe** *f* tulip.

**tunisien, -ienne** *a* & *mf* Tunisian.

**tunnel** *m* tunnel.

**turbulent, -ente** *a* (*enfant*) disruptive.

**tutoyer** *vt* **t. qn** to use the familiar *tu* form with s.o.

**tutu** *m* ballet skirt.

**tuyau, -x** *m* pipe; **t. d'arrosage** hose(pipe); **t. d'échappement** exhaust (pipe).

**TVA** *f abrév* (*taxe à la valeur ajoutée*) VAT.

**type** *m* type; (*individu*) fellow, guy.

**typique** *a* typical (**de** of).

# U

**UE** *f abrév* (*Union Européenne*) EU.

**ulcère** *m* ulcer.

**ultramoderne** *a* ultramodern.

**ultra-secret, -ète** *a* top-secret.

**un, une 1** *art indéf* a, (*devant voyelle*) an; **une page** a page; **un ange** an angel. **2** *a* one; **la page un** page one; **un mètre** one yard. **3** *pron* & *mf* one; **l'un** one; **les uns** some; **j'en ai un** I have one; **l'un d'eux, l'une d'elles** one of them; **la une** (*de journal*) the front page.

**unanime** *a* unanimous.

**unanimité** *f* **à l'u.** unanimously.

**uni, -ie** *a* united; (*famille*) close; (*surface*) smooth; (*couleur*) plain.

**unième** *a* (*after a number*) (-)first; **trente et u.** thirty-first; **cent u.** hundred and first.

**uniforme** *m* uniform.

**union** *f* union.

**Union Européenne** *f* European Union.

**unique** *a* (*fille, espoir etc*) only;

(*prix, marché*) single; (*exceptionnel*) unique.
**uniquement** *adv* only.
**unir** *vt* (*efforts, forces*) to combine; (*deux pays etc*) to unite, join together; **u. deux personnes** (*amitié*) to unite two people.
**unir (s')** *vpr* (*étudiants etc*) to unite.
**unité** *f* (*mesure, élément*) unit.
**univers** *m* universe.
**universel, -elle** *a* universal.
**universitaire** *a* **ville**/*etc* **u.** university town/*etc*.
**université** *f* university; **à l'u.** at college, at school.
**urgence** *f* (*cas*) emergency; (*de décision etc*) urgency; **faire qch d'u.** to do sth urgently; **(service des) urgences** (*d'hôpital*) emergency room.
**urgent, -ente** *a* urgent.
**urne** *f* ballot box; **aller aux urnes** to go to the polls, vote.
**usage** *m* use; (*habitude*) custom; **faire u. de** to make use of; **hors d'u.** not in service.
**usagé, -ée** *a* worn.
**usager** *m* user.
**usé, -ée** *a* (*tissu etc*) worn (out).
**user** *vt*, **s'user** *vpr* (*vêtement*) to wear out.
**usine** *f* factory.
**ustensile** *m* utensil.
**usure** *f* wear (and tear).
**utile** *a* useful (**à** to).
**utilisateur, -trice** *mf* user.
**utilisation** *f* use.
**utiliser** *vt* to use.
**utilité** *f* use(fulness); **d'une grande u.** very useful.

# V

**va** *voir* **aller**[1].
**vacances** *fpl* vacation; **en v.** on vacation; **les grandes v.** the summer vacation.
**vacancier, -ière** *mf* vacationer.
**vacarme** *m* din, uproar.
**vaccin** *m* vaccine; **faire un v. à** to vaccinate.
**vaccination** *f* vaccination.
**vacciner** *vt* to vaccinate.
**vache 1** *f* cow. **2** *a* (*méchant*) *Fam* mean.
**vachement** *adv Fam* (*très*) damned; (*beaucoup*) a hell of a lot.
**vagabond, -onde** *mf* tramp, hobo.
**vague 1** *a* vague; (*regard*) vacant. **2** *f* wave; **v. de chaleur** heat wave; **v. de froid** cold spell.
**vaguement** *adv* vaguely.
**vain (en)** *adv* in vain.
**vaincre*** *vt* to beat.
**vaincu, -ue** *mf* (*sportif*) loser.
**vainqueur** *m* (*sportif*) winner.
**vais** *voir* **aller**[1].
**vaisselle** *f* dishes; (*à laver*) dirty dishes; **faire la v.** to wash the dishes.
**valable** *a* (*billet etc*) valid.
**valet** *m Cartes* jack.
**valeur** *f* value; **avoir de la v.** to be valuable; **objets de v.** valuables.
**valise** *f* (suit)case; **faire ses valises** to pack (one's bags).
**vallée** *f* valley.
**valoir*** *vi* to be worth; **v. cher** to be worth a lot; **un vélo vaut bien une auto** a bicycle is just as good as a car; **il vaut mieux rester** it's better to stay; **il vaut mieux que j'attende** I'd better wait; **ça ne vaut rien** it's no good; **ça vaut le coup** it's worth it (**de faire** to do).
**valoir (se)** *vpr* to be as good as each other; **ça se vaut** it's all the same.
**valse** *f* waltz.
**vandale** *mf* vandal.
**vanille** *f* vanilla; **glace à la v.** vanilla ice cream.
**vaniteux, -euse** *a* conceited.
**vantard, -arde** *mf* braggart.
**vanter (se)** *vpr* to boast (**de** about, of).
**vapeur** *f* **v. (d'eau)** steam.
**variable** *a* (*humeur, temps*) changeable.
**varicelle** *f* chicken pox.
**varié, -ée** *a* varied; (*divers*) various.
**varier** *vti* to vary.

**variété** *f* variety; **spectacle de variétés** variety show.
**vas** *voir* **aller**[1].
**vase** *m* vase.
**vaste** *a* vast, huge.
**vaut** *voir* **valoir.**
**veau, -x** *m* calf; (*viande*) veal; (*cuir*) calfskin, (calf) leather.
**vécu, -ue** (*pp of* **vivre**) *a* (*histoire etc*) true.
**vedette** *f* (*de cinéma etc*) star.
**végétarien, -ienne** *a* & *mf* vegetarian.
**végétation** *f* vegetation.
**véhicule** *m* vehicle; **v. tout terrain** all-terrain *ou* four-wheel drive vehicle.
**veille** *f* **la v. (de)** the day before; **la v. de Noël** Christmas Eve.
**veiller** *vi* to stay up; (*sentinelle*) to keep watch; **v. à qch** to see to sth; **v. sur qn** to watch over s.o.
**veilleur** *m* **v. de nuit** night watchman.
**veilleuse** *f* (*de voiture*) parking light; (*de cuisinière*) pilot light; (*lampe allumée la nuit*) night-light.
**veine** *f* vein; (*chance*) *Fam* luck.
**vélo** *m* bike, bicycle; (*activité*) cycling; **faire du v.** to cycle; **v. tout terrain** mountain bike.
**vélomoteur** *m* motorcycle.
**velours** *m* velvet; **v. côtelé** corduroy.
**vendeur, -euse** *mf* sales clerk; (*de voitures etc*) salesman, saleswoman.
**vendre** *vt* to sell (**qch à qn** s.o. sth, sth to s.o.); **à v.** for sale.
**vendre (se)** *vpr* to sell; **ça se vend bien** it sells well.
**vendredi** *m* Friday; **V. saint** Good Friday.
**vénéneux, -euse** *a* poisonous.
**vengeance** *f* revenge.
**venger (se)** *vpr* to get one's revenge, get one's own back (**de qn** on s.o., **de qch** for sth).
**venimeux, -euse** *a* poisonous.
**venin** *m* poison.
**venir*** *vi* (*aux* **être**) to come (**de** from); **v. faire** to come to do; **viens me voir** come and see me; **je viens/venais d'arriver** I've/I'd just arrived; **où veux-tu en v.?** what are you getting at?; **faire v.** to send for, get.
**vent** *m* wind; **il y a du v.** it's windy; **coup de v.** gust of wind.
**vente** *f* sale; **v. (aux enchères)** auction; **en v.** on sale; **prix de v.** selling price.
**ventilateur** *m* fan.
**ventre** *m* stomach; **avoir mal au v.** to have a stomachache.
**venu, -ue** *mf* **nouveau v., nouvelle venue** newcomer; **le premier v.** anyone.
**ver** *m* worm; (*de fruits etc*) maggot; **v. de terre** (earth)worm.
**véranda** *f* (*en verre*) sunroom (*attached to house*).
**verbe** *m* verb.
**verdict** *m* verdict.
**verger** *m* orchard.
**verglas** *m* (black) ice.
**vérification** *f* check(ing).
**vérifier** *vt* to check.
**véritable** *a* true, real; (*non imité*) real.
**véritablement** *adv* really.
**vérité** *f* truth.
**vernir** *vt* to varnish.
**vernis** *m* varnish; **v. à ongles** nail polish.
**verra, verrai(t)** *etc voir* **voir.**
**verre** *m* glass; **boire** *ou* **prendre un v.** to have a drink; **v. de bière** glass of beer; **v. à bière** beer glass.
**verrou** *m* bolt; **fermer au v.** to bolt.
**verrue** *f* wart.
**vers**[1] *prép* (*direction*) toward(s).
**vers**[2] *m* (*de poème*) line.
**verse (à)** *adv* **pleuvoir à v.** to pour (down).
**verser** *vt* to pour; (*larmes*) to shed; (*argent*) to pay.
**version** *f* (*de film, d'incident etc*) version.
**verso** *m* **'voir au v.'** 'see over'.
**vert, verte 1** *a* green; (*pas mûr*) unripe. **2** *m* green.
**vertical, -e, -aux** *a* vertical.

**vertige** *m* **avoir le v.** to be *ou* feel dizzy; **donner le v. à qn** to make s.o. (feel) dizzy.
**veste** *f* jacket.
**vestiaire** *m* locker room.
**veston** *m* (suit) jacket.
**vêtement** *m* garment; **vêtements** clothes; **vêtements de sport** sportswear.
**vétérinaire** *mf* vet.
**veuf, veuve 1** *a* widowed. **2** *m* widower. **3** *f* widow.
**veuille(s), veuillent** *etc voir* **vouloir.**
**veulent, veut, veux** *voir* **vouloir.**
**vexant, -ante** *a* upsetting.
**vexer** *vt* to upset.
**viande** *f* meat.
**vibration** *f* vibration.
**vibrer** *vi* to vibrate.
**vice** *m* vice.
**victime** *f* victim; (*d'un accident*) casualty; **être v. de** to be the victim of.
**victoire** *f* victory; (*en sports*) win.
**victorieux, -euse** *a* victorious; (*équipe*) winning.
**vidange** *f* (*de véhicule*) oil change.
**vide 1** *a* empty. **2** *m* emptiness; (*trou*) gap.
**vidéo** *a inv* video.
**vidéocassette** *f* video cassette.
**vide-ordures** *m inv* garbage chute.
**vide-poches** *m inv* glove compartment.
**vider** *vt*. **se vider** *vpr* to empty.
**vie** *f* life; (*durée*) lifetime; **le coût de la v.** the cost of living; **gagner sa v.** to earn one's living; **en v.** living.
**vieil** *voir* **vieux.**
**vieillard** *m* old man.
**vieille** *voir* **vieux.**
**vieillesse** *f* old age.
**vieillir 1** *vi* to get old; (*changer*) to age. **2** *vt* **v. qn** (*vêtement etc*) to make s.o. look old(er).
**vieux** (*or* **vieil** *before vowel or mute h*), **vieille,** *pl* **vieux, vieilles 1** *a* old. **2** *m* old man; **les vieux** old people; **mon v.!** (*mon ami*) buddy!, pal! **3** *f* old woman; **ma vieille!** (*ma chère*) dear!
**vif, vive** *a* (*enfant*) lively; (*couleur, lumière*) bright; (*froid*) biting; **brûlé v.** burned alive.
**vignette** *f* (*de véhicule*) road tax sticker.
**vignoble** *m* vineyard.
**vilain, -aine** *a* (*laid*) ugly; (*enfant*) bad; (*impoli*) rude.
**villa** *f* (detached) house.
**village** *m* village.
**villageois, -oise** *mf* villager.
**ville** *f* town; (*grande*) city; **aller/être en v.** to go (in)to/be in town.
**vin** *m* wine.
**vinaigre** *m* vinegar.
**vinaigrette** *f* oil-and-vinegar dressing, vinaigrette.
**vingt** *a* & *m* twenty; **v. et un** twenty-one.
**vingtaine** *f* **une v. (de)** about twenty.
**vingtième** *a* & *mf* twentieth.
**viol** *m* rape.
**violemment** *adv* violently.
**violence** *f* violence.
**violent, -ente** *a* violent.
**violer** *vt* to rape.
**violet, -ette** *a* & *m* purple.
**violeur** *m* rapist.
**violon** *m* violin.
**vipère** *f* adder.
**virage** *m* (*de route*) bend; (*de véhicule*) turn.
**virgule** *f* comma; (*de nombre*) (decimal) point; **2 v. 5** 2 point 5.
**virus** *m* virus.
**vis**[1] *voir* **vivre, voir.**
**vis**[2] *f* screw.
**visa** *m* (*de passeport*) visa.
**visage** *m* face.
**viser 1** *vi* to aim (**à** at). **2** *vt* (*cible*) to aim at.
**visible** *a* visible.
**visite** *f* visit; **rendre v. à** to visit; **v. (médicale)** medical examination; **v. guidée** guided tour.

**visiter** *vt* to visit.
**visiteur, -euse** *mf* visitor.
**visser** *vt* to screw on.
**vit** *voir* **vivre, voir.**
**vitamine** *f* vitamin.
**vite** *adv* quickly.
**vitesse** *f* speed; (*sur un véhicule*) gear; **boîte de vitesses** transmission; **à toute v.** at full speed.
**vitrail, -aux** *m* stained-glass window.
**vitre** *f* (window)pane; (*de véhicule, train*) window.
**vitrine** *f* (shop) window; (*meuble*) display cabinet.
**vivant, -ante** *a* living; (*récit, rue*) lively.
**vive** *int* **v. le roi**/*etc*! long live the king/*etc*!; **v. les vacances!** hurray for vacation!
**vivre*** **1** *vi* to live; **v. vieux** to live to be old; **v. de** (*fruits etc*) to live on; (*travail etc*) to live by. **2** *vt* (*vie*) to live; (*aventure*) to live through.
**vocabulaire** *m* vocabulary.
**vodka** *f* vodka.
**vœu, -x** *m* wish.
**voici** *prép* here is, this is; *pl* here are, these are; **me v.** here I am; **v. dix ans que** it's ten years since.
**voie** *f* road; (*rails*) track; (*partie de route*) lane; (*chemin*) way; (*de gare*) platform; **v. sans issue** dead end; **sur la bonne v.** on the right track.
**voilà** *prép* there is, that is; *pl* there are, those are; **les v.** there they are; **v., j'arrive!** all right, I'm coming!; **v. dix ans que** it's ten years since.
**voile¹** *m* (*tissu*) veil.
**voile²** *f* (*de bateau*) sail; (*sport*) sailing; **faire de la v.** to sail.
**voilier** *m* (*de plaisance*) sailboat.
**voir*** *vti* to see; **faire v. qch** to show sth; **fais v.** let me see; **v. qn faire** to see s.o. do *ou* doing; **je ne peux pas la v.** *Fam* I can't stand (the sight of) her; **ça n'a rien à v. avec** that's got nothing to do with.
**voir (se)** *vpr* (*se fréquenter*) to see each other; **ça se voit** that's obvious.
**voisin, -ine 1** *a* neighboring; (*maison, pièce*) next (**de** to). **2** *mf* neighbor.
**voisinage** *m* neighborhood.
**voiture** *f* car.
**voix** *f* voice; (*d'électeur*) vote; **à v. basse** in a whisper.
**vol¹** *m* (*d'avion, d'oiseau*) flight.
**vol²** *m* (*délit*) theft; (*hold-up*) robbery.
**volaille** *f* **une v.** a fowl.
**volant** *m* (steering) wheel.
**volcan** *m* volcano.
**voler¹** *vi* (*oiseau, avion etc*) to fly.
**voler²** *vti* (*prendre*) to steal (**à** from).
**volet** *m* (*de fenêtre*) shutter.
**voleur, -euse** *mf* thief; **au v.!** stop thief!
**volontaire 1** *a* (*voulu*) (*geste etc*) deliberate. **2** *mf* volunteer.
**volontairement** *adv* (*exprès*) deliberately.
**volonté** *f* will; **bonne v.** goodwill; **mauvaise v.** ill will.
**volontiers** *adv* gladly.
**volume** *m* (*de boîte, de son, livre*) volume.
**volumineux, -euse** *a* bulky.
**vomir 1** *vt* bring up. **2** *vi* to be sick, to vomit.
**vont** *voir* **aller¹**.
**vos** *voir* **votre.**
**vote** *m* vote; (*de loi*) passing; **bureau de v.** polling place.
**voter 1** *vi* to vote. **2** *vt* (*loi*) to pass.
**votre,** *pl* **vos** *a poss* your.
**vôtre** *pron poss* **le** *ou* **la v., les vôtres** yours; **à la v.!** (your) good health, bottoms up!
**voudra, voudrai(t)** *etc voir* **vouloir.**
**vouloir*** *vt* to want (**faire** to do); **je veux qu'il parte** I want him to go; **v. dire** to mean (**que** that); **je voudrais rester** I'd like to stay; **je voudrais un pain** I'd like a loaf of bread; **voulez-vous me**

**suivre** will you follow me; **si tu veux** if you like *ou* wish; **en v. à qn d'avoir fait qch** to be angry with s.o. for doing sth; **je veux bien (attendre)** I don't mind (waiting); **sans le v.** unintentionally.

**vous** *pron* (*sujet, complément direct*) you; (*complément indirect*) (to) you; (*réfléchi*) yourself, *pl* yourselves; (*réciproque*) each other.

**vous-même** *pron* yourself.

**vous-mêmes** *pron pl* yourselves.

**vouvoyer** *vt* **v. qn** to use the formal *vous* form with s.o.

**voyage** *m* trip, journey; **aimer les voyages** to like traveling; **faire un v., partir en v.** to go on a trip; **bon v.!** have a pleasant trip!; **v. organisé** (package) tour; **agent/agence de voyages** travel agent/agency.

**voyager** *vi* to travel.

**voyageur, -euse** *mf* traveler; (*passager*) passenger.

**voyelle** *f* vowel.

**voyou** *m* hooligan.

**vrac (en)** *adv* (*en désordre*) in a muddle, haphazardly.

**vrai, -e** *a* true; (*réel*) real; (*authentique*) genuine.

**vraiment** *adv* really.

**vraisemblable** *a* (*probable*) likely.

**VTT** *abrév m inv*(*vélo tout terrain*) mountain bike.

**vu, vue** *pp of* **voir.**

**vue** *f* (*spectacle*) sight; (*sens*) (eye)-sight; (*panorama, photo*) view; **en v.** (*proche*) in sight; **de v.** (*connaître*) by sight.

**vulgaire** *a* vulgar.

## W

**wagon** *m* (*de voyageurs*) car; (*de marchandises*) freight car.

**wagon-lit** *m* (*pl* **wagons-lits**) sleeping car.

**wagon-restaurant** *m* (*pl* **wagons-restaurants**) dining car.

**waters** *mpl* toilet, men's *ou* ladies' room.

**w-c** *mpl* toilet, men's *ou* ladies' room.

**week-end** *m* weekend.

**western** *m* (*film*) western.

**whisky,** *pl* **-ies** *m* whiskey.

## Y

**y 1** *adv* there; **allons-y** let's go; **j'y suis!** now I get it!; **je n'y suis pour rien** I have nothing to do with it. **2** *pron* (= *à cela*) **j'y pense** I think of it; **je m'y attendais** I was expecting it; **ça y est!** that's it!

**yacht** *m* yacht.

**yaourt** *m* yogurt.

**yeux** *voir* **œil.**

## Z

**zèbre** *m* zebra.

**zéro** *m* zero; **deux buts à z.** two nothing.

**zigzag** *m* zigzag; **en z.** (*route etc*) zigzag(ging).

**zigzaguer** *vi* to zigzag.

**zone** *f* zone, area; **z. bleue** restricted parking area; **z. industrielle** industrial park.

**zoo** *m* zoo.

**zut!** *int* oh dear!

# WEBSTER'S NEW WORLD

## Put the World in Your Pocket

Get the information you need in the handy, go-anywhere format you want.

**Pocket Dictionary**
Over 33,000 concise entries
0-02-861887-4
$4.95

**Pocket Thesaurus**
Thousands of synonyms & antonyms
0-02-861886-6
$4.95

**Pocket Style Guide**
Grammar, punctuation, and usage basics
0-02-862157-3
$5.95

**Pocket Desk Set**
Dictionary, Thesaurus, & Style Guide in a handy slip case
0-02-862379-7
$14.95

**Pocket Spanish Dictionary**
More than 25,000 entries
0-02-862383-5
$5.95

**Pocket French Dictionary**
More than 25,000 entries
0-02-862384-3
$5.95

**Pocket Internet Directory & Dictionary**
Most popular Web site addresses
0-02-861889-0
$5.95

**Pocket Book of Facts**
Thousands of useful facts at your fingertips
0-02-862750-4
$6.95 October